"Invaluable to both students and scholars, M(Law is smart, concise and highly readable. It introduces some of the most intractable debates within the field with ease, leaving the reader with a superb grasp of the fundamental issues at stake."

Stephen Bogle, *University of Glasgow, UK*

"Debates in tort law are as numerous as they are difficult to navigate. From contested theories of justice to the formulation of specific torts, disagreement is pervasive. This is an ideal companion for the intellectual tort law journey, guiding the reader through the most significant of these debates without dogmatism."

Sarah Green, *Law Commission, UK*

"In this excellent volume, Dr Morgan carves clear and helpful pathways through the densest, most prominent and hotly contested theories of tort law. For newcomers, it is an essential roadmap to what would otherwise probably be a daunting and trackless morass, with warnings of all the major hazards carefully highlighted."

John Murphy, *Lancaster University, UK*

"This sophisticated and wide-ranging guide to current debates in tort law and scholarship will enable students to rapidly develop a deep understanding of this dynamic and challenging subject. *Great Debates in Tort Law* brilliantly weaves together a plethora of writings on tort law and makes fascinating connections between different parts of the syllabus. As a supplement to the core textbooks it is without equal."

Donal Nolan, *University of Oxford, UK*

"*Great Debates in Tort Law* is a gem of a book. The reader is taken on an engaging and insightful tour of the most significant controversies in tort law by a wise and even-handed guide. This is tort theory at its practical best."

Andrew Robertson, *University of Melbourne, Australia*

'Tort law is deceptively difficult. Legal doctrine, theory, and public policy all jostle for attention. Jonathan Morgan is a sure-footed guide to the subject, alive to the flaws and limitations within these traditions. His work is incisive, and sometimes contentious – but never dull.'

Warren Swain, *University of Auckland, New Zealand*

Great Debates in Law

Series Editor
Jonathan Herring, Professor of Law, University of Oxford

Commercial and Corporate Law
Andrew Johnston & Lorrain Talbot (eds)

Company Law
Lorraine Talbot

Contract Law
Jonathan Morgan

Criminal Law
Jonathan Herring

Employment Law
Simon Honeyball

Equity and Trusts
Alastair Hudson

EU Law
Jeremias Adams-Prassl and Sanja Sanja Bogojevic

European Convention of Human Rights
Fiona de Londras & Kanstantsin Dzehtsiarou

Family Law
Jonathan Herring, Rebecca Probert & Stephen Gilmore

Gender and Law
Rosemary Auchmuty (ed)

Jurisprudence
Nicholas J McBride & Sandy Steel

Land Law
David Cowan, Lorna Fox O'Mahony & Neil Cobb

Medical Law and Ethics
Imogen Goold & Jonathan Herring

Tort Law
Jonathan Morgan

Great Debates in Tort Law

Jonathan Morgan
University of Cambridge

·HART·
OXFORD · LONDON · NEW YORK · NEW DELHI · SYDNEY

HART

Bloomsbury Publishing Plc

50 Bedford Square, London, WC1B 3DP, UK

1385 Broadway, New York, NY 10018, USA

29 Earlsfort Terrace, Dublin 2, Ireland

BLOOMSBURY, BLOOMSBURY ACADEMIC and the Diana logo
are trademarks of Bloomsbury Publishing Plc

First published in Great Britain 2022

Copyright © Jonathan Morgan, 2022

Jonathan Morgan has asserted his right under the Copyright, Designs and
Patents Act, 1988, to be identified as Author of this work.

For legal purposes the Acknowledgements on p. xv constitute an extension of this copyright page.

Cover design: Jade Barnett

All rights reserved. No part of this publication may be reproduced or transmitted in any form or by any
means, electronic or mechanical, including photocopying, recording, or any information storage
or retrieval system, without prior permission in writing from the publishers.

Bloomsbury Publishing Plc does not have any control over, or responsibility for, any third-party
websites referred to or in this book. All internet addresses given in this book were correct
at the time of going to press. The author and publisher regret any inconvenience caused
if addresses have changed or sites have ceased to exist, but can accept
no responsibility for any such changes.

A catalogue record for this book is available from the British Library.

A catalogue record for this book is available from the Library of Congress.

Library of Congress Control Number: 2022946137

ISBN: HB: 978-1-50996-136-8
PB: 978-1-50996-135-1
ePDF: 978-1-50996-138-2
ePub: 978-1-50996-137-5

Series: Great Debates in Law

Typeset by Compuscript Ltd, Shannon
Printed and bound in Great Britain by CPI Group (UK) Ltd, Croydon CR0 4YY

To find out more about our authors and books visit www.bloomsbury.com
and sign up for our newsletters.

For Lottie and Ludo

Contents

Long Contents	ix
Acknowledgements	xv
Table of Cases	xvii
Table of Legislation	xxvii

1. Introduction — 1

PART I
TRESPASS

2. Trespass: Tort and the Vindication of Rights — 9

PART II
NEGLIGENCE

3. Negligence: Introduction — 45
4. Causation and Corrective Justice — 53
5. Concepts of Causation: But-For and Remoteness — 95
6. What Is the Function of the Duty of Care? — 133
7. Defining the Duty of Care — 153
8. 'Physical Injury' in Negligence — 191
9. Psychiatric Illness, Emotional Harm and 'Shock' — 219

PART III
NUISANCE

10.	Private Nuisance and Property Rights	263
11.	Economic Analysis of Nuisance	303
12.	Nuisance and the Environment: Tort, Regulation and Pollution	321

Index   355

LONG CONTENTS

Contents | vii
Acknowledgements | xv
Table of Cases | xvii
Table of Legislation | xxvii

1. Introduction | 1
   Not an Introduction | 1
   What Makes a Good Theory? | 3

PART I
TRESPASS

2. Trespass: Tort and the Vindication of Rights | 9
   Introduction | 9
   Debate 1: Justifying Strict Liability and Actionability Per Se | 12
   Strict Liability and Defences | 12
   Actionability Per Se and Vindication | 17
   Debate 2: Remedies and Vindication of Rights | 19
   The Lumba *Debate* | 22
   Nominal Damages | 24
   Vindication by Declaration? | 27
   Rights and Loss | 30
   Debate 3: Trespass and 'Constitutional Rights' | 31
   Debate 4: 'Informed Medical Consent' – Which Tort? | 36
   Conclusion: Negligence and Trespass Distinguished | 39

PART II
NEGLIGENCE

3. **Negligence: Introduction** — 45
   Negligence and Rights — 45
   Tort as an Instrument of Social Policy — 47
   The Structure of Negligence — 49
   Negligence: Further Issues — 51
   Breach of Duty — 51
   Defences — 51
   Pure Economic Loss — 51
   Omissions and Public Authority Liability — 52
   Assumption of Responsibility — 52

4. **Causation and Corrective Justice** — 53
   Debate 1: Causation and Compensation — 54
   Accident Compensation Schemes — 55
   Compensation and Tort Doctrine — 55
   Fairchild *Enclave: 'Single Causal Agent'* — 57
   Fairchild *Enclave: 'Scientific Uncertainty'* — 60
   Fairchild *Enclave: A Special Rule for Mesothelioma?* — 62
   Debate 2: Causation and Deterrence — 66
   Punishment and Justice: Tort and Crime — 66
   Deterrence, Economic Analysis and Causation — 69
   Causation, the Burden of Proof and the 'Empty Duty' Argument — 72
   Exceptional Cases? Fairchild *and* Chester — 75
   Conclusion — 76
   Debate 3: Questioning Corrective Justice – Moral and Doctrinal Critique — 77
   'Two Hunters' (or 'the Indeterminate Defendant') — 77
   The 'Matching' Problem: Sindell v Abbot Laboratories — 82
   Aggregation and Corrective Justice — 84
   Moral Critique of Corrective Justice — 88
   Conclusion — 92

5. **Concepts of Causation: But-For and Remoteness** — 95
   Introduction: Causation, Proof, 'Damage' and Consequential Loss — 95
   Debate 1: The But-For Test — 100
   The Problem of Multiple Causes: But-For 'Disapplied' — 102
   Multiple Sufficient Factors: Each Causal? — 103
   The 'No Better Off' Principle — 107

	Does It Make Any Difference?	109
	Conclusion: 'Involvement' or 'Necessity'?	112
	Debate 2: Remoteness, Causation and 'Common Sense'	**113**
	'Foreseeable Kind of Harm'	115
	Interventions	120
	Coincidences: Chester v Afshar	123
	'The Scope of Duty' Limitation	126
	Conclusion: 'Common Sense Causation' and the Scope of Responsibility	127
6.	What Is the Function of the Duty of Care?	133
	Debate 1: Is the Duty of Care an Essential Component of the Tort of Negligence?	**135**
	Foreseeability: The Unity of Duty, Breach and Damage?	139
	The Triviality of Foreseeability?	140
	The Redundancy of Foreseeability?	142
	Debate 2: Does the Duty of Care Serve a Useful Function?	**145**
	Duty of Care: Then and Now	146
	Abolishing the Duty of Care?	148
	Conclusion	151
7.	Defining the Duty of Care	153
	Debate 1: The Caparo 'Test' – Decline and Fall?	**154**
	A Defence of the Three-Stage Test	157
	Duty: Division between Justice and the Public Interest?	159
	Debate 2: Policy and the Duty of Care	**160**
	Common Law Rights, Public Interest Legislation?	164
	Policy and Legal Certainty	166
	Policy, Evidence and Judicial Capacity	169
	The Politics of Corrective Justice	173
	Policy: Conclusions	175
	Debate 3: 'Incrementalism'	**177**
	Fashion and Incrementalism	177
	Incrementalism: Critique	182
	Incrementalism: Conclusions	187
8.	'Physical Injury' in Negligence	191
	Personal Injury: So Obvious That It Goes Without Saying?	191
	Clarification: 'Gist Damage' and 'Consequential Loss'	195

**Debate 1: What is 'Personal Injury'? The Boundaries
of 'Bodily Harm'**   **196**
   Minor Injuries: A 'Hook' for Consequential Loss?   197
   'Actionable Damage' and Limitation Periods   199
   The Outer Limits of 'Personal Injury'?   200
Debate 2: 'Preventive' Damages   **202**
   Caught in the Crossfire: Preventive Damages and Anns   206
Debate 3: 'Wrongful Birth' and Physical Injury   **207**
   'Wrongful Life'   208
   'Wrongful Birth' and the Sanctity of Life   209
   'Wrongful Race'?   211
   Categorisation: Duty and Damage   212
   Gendered Reasoning About 'Actionable Damage'?   213
   'Loss of Autonomy' as Actionable Damage?   216
   Conclusion   218

9. **Psychiatric Illness, Emotional Harm and 'Shock'**   **219**
   **Debate 1: Physical Injuries, Shock, Distress and 'Recognisable
Psychiatric Illness' – What Interest Should Tort Law Protect?**   **219**
     A Preference for the Physical?   219
     'Psychiatric Illness' or 'Nervous Shock'?   220
     'Recognisable Psychiatric Illness'   223
     'Mere Distress'   225
   Debate 2: Justifying the Restrictive Rules on Psychiatric Illness   **228**
     The Alcock *Rules on 'Secondary Victims'*   228
     Alcock *Rules: Rights-Based Critique*   231
     Alcock *Rules: Policy Critique*   232
     'Floodgates'   235
     'Primary Victims': Zone of Danger or 'Involvement'?   236
     Stress at Work   240
   **Debate 3: How Should the Law on Psychiatric Illness
be Reformed?**   **244**
     A Foreseeability-Based Approach?   245
     Outright Abolition?   249
     The Law Commission and 'Muddling Through'?   251
     Retention: 'Recognisable Psychiatric Illness'   251
     Abolition: 'Sudden Shocking Event'   252
     Abolition: Proximity in Time and Space; Own Unaided Senses   254
     Reform: Ties of Love and Affection   255
     Another Compromise: Quid Pro Quo?   256
     Conclusion   257

PART III
NUISANCE

10. Private Nuisance and Property Rights — 263
Debate 1: Is Nuisance a Tort for Protecting Property Rights? — 263
Property Rights: Standing to Bring a Claim — 264
Property Rights: Compensation — 266
Nuisance and Human Rights — 268
The Boundaries of Nuisance: The Absence of Rights — 271
Debate 2: Justifying the Rights-Based Approach — 276
Protecting the 'More Fundamental' Use of Land: Beever's Theory of Nuisance — 278
Beever's Theory: Appraisal and Criticism — 280
Defining Property Rights: The Role of the Public Interest — 284
Purity and Transparency — 288
Debate 3: Balancing or Strict Liability? Property Damage, Nuisance and Trespass — 289
Strict Liability for Property Damage and Trespass — 290
Balancing Rights: 'Live and Let Live' — 293
Balancing Rights: Locality and 'Ordinary Human Existence' — 295
Conclusion — 300

11. Economic Analysis of Nuisance — 303
Coase's Analysis — 303
Critique of Coase: Misdescription of Nuisance Doctrine — 308
Critique of Coase: Judicial Capacity to Identify 'Highest Value Use of Land' — 310
Information Theory in Nuisance and Trespass: Clear Rules and 'Coasian Bargaining' — 313

12. Nuisance and the Environment: Tort, Regulation and Pollution — 321
Debate 1: Nuisance and Environmental Protection – Potential and Limits — 322
Private Property and the Environment — 322
Private Enforcement — 325
Debate 2: The Interaction of Tort and Regulation – Nuisance and Planning Permission — 327
The Defence of Statutory Authority — 328
Planning Permission: No Defence — 329

xiv LONG CONTENTS

Regulation and the Scope of Nuisance	333
Remedies and Planning Permission	334
Tort and Regulation: Analysis	338
Conclusion	343
Debate 3: Pollution and the Industrial Revolution – Nuisance in the Nineteenth (and the Twenty-First) Century	**344**
The Received Historical Account	345
Nuisance and Pollution Control: Underrated?	348
Conclusion: Climate Change and Nuisance in the Twenty-First Century	350
Index	**355**

Acknowledgements

> I returned, and saw under the sun, that the race is not to the swift, nor the battle to the strong, neither yet bread to the wise, nor yet riches to men of understanding, nor yet favour to men of skill; but time and chance happeneth to them all. (Ecclesiastes 9:11)

I have incurred many debts of gratitude while writing this book. The Faculty of Law and Corpus Christi College granted me two terms' sabbatical leave in 2019–20. The burden falls less on the institutions, however, and more on those assuming additional obligations in one's absence. I am accordingly grateful to my colleagues Janet O'Sullivan, Stelios Tofaris, Louise Gullifer and Jodi Gardner for shouldering the lecturing load. As for my college duties, I am indebted to Andrew Sanger, Julian Ghosh and Emily Gordon.

I would also like to thank my editor, Ursula Gavin, for her support and great patience in awaiting the significantly if unavoidably delayed manuscript. I am also extremely grateful to Devon Airey for her assistance with the proofs, index and tables, and to Cambridge University's Yorke Fund, for financial assistance.

I have been sustained by information, advice, friendship and encouragement from many other colleagues too, including Colm McGrath, Sandy Steel, Sarah Worthington, Donal Nolan, Nick McBride, Neil Andrews, John McLeod, Steve Hedley and Andrew Robertson. I wish to single out two people. Jane Stapleton, whose tuition at Balliol began my fascination with tort law, and David Ibbetson, whose legal history tutorials so enlarged my understanding of it. With Jane and David both about to retire from the pinnacle of academia (as Master of Christ's; as Regius Professor and sometime President of Clare Hall), I reflect on the immense good fortune of counting these world-leading scholars as my undergraduate teachers – and then such supportive colleagues.

Half of this book had been written when in March 2020, Covid-19 changed everything. My children's nursery and primary school abruptly closed. Family life was enriched by the legally mandated home confinement – endless time

to dig a vegetable garden, learn chess, play cricket or learn to ride a bike. But progress on *Great Debates in Tort Law* became very difficult. Returning to academic duties in 2020–21, time available for writing became even more constrained. The impossible situation in Lent Term 2021 – the winter lockdown and home-schooling combined with full university teaching loads (including self-recorded lectures) – was the nadir. Everyone will have their own memories of those strange and difficult years.

It is paradoxical to scramble frantically throughout a long period of time. For two years following the coronavirus outbreak, however, this sums up the authorial process. Theories and debates about tort law spooled away endlessly like *The Key to All Mythologies* and I despaired of ever completing the book. That I did finish at last, being spared (so far) the Rev Casaubon's fate, would not have been possible without Sophie: my own Dorothea, headmistress of the home-school, and (in her spare time) scholar of five centuries of English literature. Yet, being uncertain I will ever write another one, I dedicate this book to our children. Perhaps one day they too will acquire the taste for tort law. For now, I know they will be rather disappointed by the lack of heroes, dragons and any plot whatsoever. They may at least be amused that after Hart's (ultimately Bloomsbury Publishing's) acquisition of the Great Debates series, daddy's Torts have magically become very distant stable-mates of the boy wizard and other fantastic beasts.

The book should be complete up to 1 May 2022 (though it has been possible to make some further changes during production).

Jonathan Morgan
Cambridge, Lammas Day 2022

TABLE OF CASES

ALL JURISDICTIONS

A v A Health & Social Services Trust
[2010] NIQB 108 .... 164, 211
ACB v Thomson Medical [2017]
SGCA 20 .... 211, 217
Adams v Ursell [1913]
1 Ch 269 298
*Alcock v Chief Constable of
South Yorkshire* [1992]
1 AC 310 .... 64, 228, 230–239,
246, 249, 250–252,
255, 258
Aldred's Case (1610) 9 Co
Rep 57b 271
Allen v Bloomsbury Health Authority
[1993] 1 All ER 651 209
Allen v Gulf Oil Refining Ltd
[1981] AC 1001 .... 328, 330, 337
Alphacell Ltd v Woodward
[1972] AC 824 104
Andrae v Selfridge Ltd [1938]
Ch 1 .... 267, 295, 309
*Annetts v Australian Stations Pty
Ltd* [2002] HCA 35 .... 240, 241,
253
Anns v Merton LBC [1978]
AC 728 .... 160, 179, 180,
187, 188, 206, 207
Anslow v Norton Aluminium
[2012] EWHC 2610 (QB) 326

Armory v Delamirie (1721)
1 Str 505 97
Arneil v Paterson [1931]
AC 560 243
Ashby v White (1703) 2 Ld
Raym 938; 1 Sm LC
(13th edn) 253 .... 34, 235
*Ashley v Chief Constable of
Sussex* [2007] 1 WLR 398 14
*Ashley v Chief Constable of
Sussex* [2008] 1 AC 962 14,
28, 29
Athey v Leonati [1996]
3 SCR 458 .... 98, 103,
107
Attia v British Gas [1988]
QB 304 221
Attorney-General v Birmingham
(1858) 4 K & J 528 .... 326, 349
Attorney-General v Doughty
(1752) 2 Ves Sen 453 274
*Attorney-General of Trinidad
and Tobago v Ramanoop*
[2005] UKPC 15 25
Austin v MPC [2009] 1 AC 564 15
*BAE Systems (Operations) Ltd
v Konczak* [2018] ICR 1 243
Bailey v Ministry of Defence
[2009] 1 WLR 1052 .... 108, 109,
111
Baker v Bolton (1808) 1 Camp 493 ... 265

xvii

Baker v TE Hopkins & Son Ltd [1959] 1 WLR 966 238
Baker v Willoughby [1970] AC 467 .... 60, 80, 82, 111, 112
Bamford v Turnley (1860) 3 B & S 62 .... 282, 289, 291, 294, 304, 312
Barker v Corus [2006] 2 AC 572 .... 59, 60, 64, 95, 96, 98, 244
Barr v Biffa Waste Services [2011] 4 All ER 1065 328
Barr v Biffa Waste Services [2013] QB 455 .... 285, 328, 329, 332, 343
Barratt Homes Ltd v DWR Cymru Cyfyngedig (No 2) [2013] 1 WLR 3486 275
Barrett v Enfield LBC [2001] 2 AC 550 147
Bass v Gregory (1890) 25 QBD 481 306
BCCI v Price Waterhouse (No 2) [1998] PNLR 564 156
Begum v Maran (UK) Ltd [2021] EWCA Civ 326 59
Lord Bernstein v Skyviews [1978] QB 479 .... 315, 316
Berry v Sugar Notch Borough, 191 Pa 345, 43 A 240 (1899) 114
Blue Circle Industries v Ministry of Defence [1999] Ch 289 .... 197, 325
Bocardo SA v Star Energy UK Onshore Ltd [2011] 1 AC 380 315
Bolton v Stone [1951] AC 850 135
Boomer v Atlantic Cement Co, 26 NY 2d 219 (1970) 352
Bourhill v Young [1943] AC 92 .... 220, 229
Boyd v Ineos Upstream Ltd [2019] EWCA Civ 515 135
Bradford Corporation v Pickles [1895] AC 587 271
Brand v Hammersmith Railway Co (1867) LR 2 QB 223 .... 276, 290
Bridlington Relay v Yorkshire Electricity Board [1965] Ch 436 287
Brooks v MPC [2005] 1 WLR 1495 172
Broome v Cassell & Co [1972] AC 1027 .... 27, 68
Brown v North British Steel Foundry Ltd (1968) SC 51 200
Browning v War Office [1963] 1 QB 750 .... 53, 74
Bryan v Maloney (1995) 128 ALR 163 188
Bryant v Lefever (1878) 4 CPD 172 .... 306, 308, 309
Bugg v DPP [1993] QB 473 15
C & G Homes Ltd v Secretary of State for Health [1991] Ch 365 273
Caltex Refineries (Qld) Pty Ltd v Stavar [2009] NSWCA 258 167
Calvert v William Hill Credit [2008] EWHC 454 (Ch) 123
Cambridge Water Co v Eastern Counties Leather [1994] 2 AC 264 .... 116, 141, 143, 267, 285, 286, 291, 292, 323–325, 333
Campbelltown CC v Mackay (1989) 15 NSWLR 501 253
Canadian National Railway v Norsk Pacific Steamship Co [1992] AC 669 183
Caparo Industries v Dickman [1989] QB 653 .... 155, 157
Caparo Industries v Dickman [1990] 2 AC 605 .... 46, 153–159, 168, 169, 179, 180–182, 188, 189, 246
Capital & Counties v Hampshire CC [1997] QB 1004 170
Cartledge v Jopling [1963] AC 758 .... 199, 200
Catternach v Melchior {2003} 215 CLR 1 210
CES v Superclinics (1995) 38 NSWLR 47 210

Chadwick v British Railways
    Board [1967] 1 WLR 912 238
Chalmers v Diageo Scotland
    Ltd [2019] CSOH 63 268
Chapman v Hearse (1961)
    106 CLR 112 141
Chastey v Ackland [1895]
    2 Ch 389 271
Chatterton v Gerson [1981]
    QB 432 36
Chester v Afshar [2005]
    1 AC 134 .... 38, 71, 75–76,
                                        95, 121,
                                  123–126, 218
Chic Fashions (West Wales)
    Ltd v Jones [1968] 2 QB 299 14
Childs v Desormeaux [2006]
    1 SCR 643 .... 185, 187
Christie v Davey [1893]
    1 Ch 316 .... 279, 282
CJD Litigation; Group B Plaintiffs
    v UK MRC [2000] Lloyd's
    Rep Med 161. 224
Clay v TUI UK Ltd [2018]
    4 All ER 672 .... 114, 121
Clements v Clements [2012]
    2 SCR 181 .... 61, 87
Coates v Government Insurance
    Office (1995) 36 NSWLR 1 254,
                                         255
Collins v Wilcock [1984] 1 WLR
    1172 .... 16, 18
Colls v Home & Colonial Store
    Ltd [1904] AC 179 334
Connor v Chief Constable of Merseyside
    [2006] EWCA Civ 1549 2
Constantine v Imperial Hotels
    Ltd [1944] KB 693 19
Cook v Lewis [1951] SCR 830 78
Cooper v Hobart [2001] 3 SCR
    537 159
Re Corby Group Litigation [2009]
    QB 335 318
Corr v IBC Vehicles [2008]
    AC 884 49
Coventry v Lawrence (No 1)
    [2014] AC 822 .... 268, 300,
                                   329–343

Cox v Ministry of Justice
    [2016] AC 660 56
Crimmins v Stevedoring Industry
    Finance Committee [1999]
    HCA 59 168,
                                     184, 189
Customs & Excise Commissioners
    v Barclays Bank [2007]
    1 AC 181 .... 52, 156,
                                 180–181, 188
Cutler v Vauxhall Motors Ltd
    [1971] 1 QB 418 98
Cutler v Wandsworth Stadium
    [1949] AC 398 342
D&F Estates v Church Commissioners
    [1989] AC 177 182
Dalton v Angus (1881) 6 App
    Cas 740 274
Darby v National Trust [2001]
    EWCA Civ 189 114
Darnley v Croydon NHS Trust
    [2019] A.C. 831 .... 157, 182,
                                         184
Davies v Taylor [1974] AC 207 96
Degg v Midland Railways Co
    (1857) 1 H&N 773 140
Deloitte & Touche v Livent Inc
    [2017] 2 SCR 855 186
Dennis v Ministry of Defence
    [2003] EWHC (QB) 793 334
Dickins v O2 plc [2009]
    IRLR 58 243
Dillon v Legg 68 Cal.2d 728
    (1968) 247, 248, 250
Dobson v Thames Water [2009]
    3 All ER 319 266
Donoghue v Stevenson [1932]
    AC 562 .... 32, 45, 133, 139,
                                     147, 161,
                                 177–179, 187
Dooley v Cammell Laird & Co
    [1951] 1 Lloyd's Rep 271 239
Dorset Yacht Co Ltd v Home Office
    [1969] 2 QB 412 (CA) 149
Dorset Yacht Co Ltd v Home Office
    [1970] AC 1004 .... 56, 122, 134,
                                 149, 151, 171,
                                     178, 179

Doughty v Turner Bros [1964]
1 QB 518 119
Doyle v Olby (Ironmongers) Ltd
[1969] 2 QB 158 116
Dryden v Johnson Matthey [2019]
AC 403 .... 201, 202, 207
Dulieu v White [1901]
2 KB 669 .... 221, 228
Dutton v Bognor Regis UDC
[1972] 1 QB 373 160
Equitable Life Assurance Society
v Ernst & Young [2003]
Lloyd's Rep PN 88 128
Emeh v Kensington and Chelsea
HA [1985] QB 1012 209
Entick v Carrington (1765)
19 St Tr 1029 .... 17, 32
Environment Agency v Empress
Car Co (Abertillery) Ltd
[1999] 2 AC 22 .... 105, 123
Euclid v Ambler Realty Co
272 US 365 (1926) 298
In Re F [1990] 2 AC 1 .... 16–18, 36
Fairchild v Glenhaven Funeral
Services [2003] 1 AC 32 .... 54, 57–65, 75–77, 84, 87, 92, 95, 96, 128
Fairfax Media Publications Pty
Ltd v Voller [2021] HCA 27 13
Farnworth v Manchester
Corporation [1930] AC 171 349
Farr v Butter Bros [1932]
KB 606 139
Fearn v Tate Gallery [2020]
Ch 621 .... 263, 269–275, 333
Financial Conduct Authority v
Arch Insurance (UK) Ltd
[2021] AC 649 .... 106, 107
Fitzgerald v Lane [1987]
QB 781 58
Fontainebleau Hotel v Forty-Five
Twenty-Five, Inc 114 So.2d
357 (1959) 279
Frost v Chief Constable of South
Yorkshire [1998] QB 254 .... 229, 253

Gammell v Wilson [1982] AC 27 64
GE v Commissioner of an Garda
Síochána [2021] IECA 113 ..... 19, 21, 23, 24, 31
Gillingham BC v Medway
(Chatham) Dock Co Ltd
[1993] QB 343 332
GN v Poole BC [2020] AC 780 .... 157, 182, 186
Goldberg v City of Newark
(1962) 186 A 2d 291 155
Gorringe v Calderdale MBC
[2004] 1 WLR 1057 .... 148, 151
Gorris v Scott (1874) LR 9
Ex 125 126
Gouriet v Union of Post Office
Workers [1978] AC 435 66
Greenway v Johnson Matthey
[2016] 1 WLR 4487 201
Gregg v Scott [2005]
2 AC 176 .... 46, 96–97, 198, 199
Gulati v MGN Ltd [2016] FSR 12 31
Gwilliam v West Hertfordshire
NHS Trust [2003] QB 443 183
JS Hall & Co v Simons [2002]
AC 615 172
Halliday v Nevill (1984)
57 ALR 331 17
Halsey v Esso Ltd [1961]
1 WLR 683 .... 267, 326, 350
Hambrook v Stokes Bros
[1925] 1 KB 141 .... 221, 227, 250
Hammersmith & City Railway
v Brand (1869) LR 4 HL 171 338
Hatton v Sutherland [2002]
ICR 613 .... 51, 240–243
Harwood v Wyken Colliery Co
[1913] 2 KB 158 98
Hedley Byrne & Co v Heller &
Partners [1964] AC 465 .... 134, 178, 180
Henderson v Merrett Syndicates
[1995] 2 AC 145 .... 52, 180
Heneghan v Manchester Dry Docks
[2014] EWHC 4190 (QB) 63

Heneghan v Manchester Dry Docks
  [2016] EWCA Civ 86 63
Herrington v British Rail [1972]
  AC 877 178
Heskell v Continental Express
  [1950] 1 All ER 1033 97
Hicks v Chief Constable of South
  Yorkshire [1992] 2 All ER 65 225
Hill v Chief Constable of West
  Yorkshire [1989] AC 53 172
Hinz v Berry [1970] 2 QB 40 .... 223, 252
Hochester v de la Tour (1853)
  2 E & B 678 205
Hole v Barlow (1858) 4
  CBNS 334. 291
Hollywood Silver Fox Farm Ltd v
  Emmett [1936] 2 KB 468 .... 279, 282, 309
Holmes v Mather (1875)
  LR 10 Ex 261 13
Holtby v Brigham & Cowan
  [2000] ICR 1086............................. 75
Homans v Boston Elevated Railway
  62 NE 737 (1902) 223
Hotson v East Berkshire HA [1987]
  AC 750 97
Huckle v Money (1763) 2 Wils
  KB 205 20
Hughes v Lord Advocate [1963]
  AC 837 118
Hughes v Turning Point Scotland
  [2019] CSOH 42........................... 115
Hunter v Canary Wharf [1997]
  AC 655 .... 263, 264, 265, 266, 267, 268, 269, 272, 275, 279, 285, 287, 288, 291, 323, 326, 332, 333, 342
Hussain v Lancaster CC
  [2000] QB 1 270
Imperial Gas Light & Coke
  Co v Broadbent (1859)
  7 HLC 600 337
Iqbal v Prison Officers' Association
  [2010] QB 732 20
Jacque v Steenberg Homes Inc
  209 Wis. 2d 605 (1997).......... 26, 314

Jaensch v Coffey (1984) 155
  CLR 549.. 253
Jain v Trent SHA [2009]
  1 AC 853 .... 149, 151
JD v East Berkshire NHS Trust
  [2005] 2 AC 373 .... 46, 135, 149, 195
JD v Mather [2012] EWHC
  3063 (QB).................................... 199
JJ v Rankin's Garage [2018]
  1 SCR 587 .... 49, 140, 141, 142, 187
Jobling v Associated Dairies
  [1982] AC 794 98
Jolley v Sutton LBC [2000]
  1 WLR 1082 .... 118, 119, 143
Jones v Kaney [2011] 2 AC 398 183
Jones v Livox Quarries [1952]
  2 QB 608 113
Jordan House Hotel v Menow
  [1974] SCR 239 184
Junior Books v Veichi [1983]
  1 AC 520 180
Kaiser Aetna v United States,
  444 US 164 (1979)....................... 314
Keefe v Isle of Man Steam Packet Co
  [2010] EWCA Civ 683 79
Kennaway v Thompson [1981]
  QB 88.. 334
Khatun and 180 others v
  United Kingdom (1998)
  26 EHRR CD212 .... 285, 300, 326
Khorasandjian v Bush [1993]
  QB 727 .... 263, 265, 266
Kimathi v Foreign & Commonwealth
  Office [2018] EWHC 1305
  (QB).. 202
King v Philips [1953] 1 QB 429 228
Knightley v Johns [1982]
  1 WLR 349 114
Koehler v Cerebos (Australia) Ltd
  [2005] HCA 15 249
Kozarov v Victoria [2022]
  HCA 12 249
Kuchenmeister v Home Office
  [1958] 1 QB 496 22

Kuddas v Chief Constable of
  Leicestershire [2002]
  2 AC 122 .... 67, 68
Kuwait Airways v Iraqi Airways
  (Nos 4 and 5) [2002]
  2 AC 883 .... 103, 116
Lam v Torbay BC [1998]
  PLCR 30 331
Lamb v Camden LBC [1981]
  QB 625 .... 114, 149
Lamb v Cotogno (1987) 164
  CLR 1 68
Lancashire CC v Municipal Mutual
  Insurance [1997] QB 897 68
Laws v Florinplace Ltd [1981]
  1 All ER 659 .... 273, 318
Le Lievre v Gould [1893]
  1 QB 491 134
Leakey v National Trust [1980]
  QB 485 45
Lewis v Australian Capital
  Territory [2020] HCA 26 .... 20, 21,
                                         22, 23, 27,
                                          195, 196
Leyland Shipping v Norwich
  Union Fire Insurance [1918]
  AC 350 .... 120, 131
Lim Poh Choo v Camden AHA
  [1980] AC 174 203
Liversidge v Anderson [1942]
  AC 206 71
Lloyd v Google [2021] 3 WLR
  1268 31
Lumba v Home Secretary [2012]
  1 AC 245 .... 20, 22, 23, 24,
                                      25, 28, 31,
                                         39, 336
Malcolm v Broadhurst [1970]
  3 All ER 508 .... 219, 242
Mallett v McMonagle [1970]
  AC 166 97
Malone v Metropolitan Police
  Commissioner [1979]
  Ch 344 .... 32, 33
Manchester Building Society
  v Grant Thornton UK LLP
  [2022] AC 783 .... 126, 128
Manchester Corporation v
  Farnworth [1930] AC 171 350

Marc Rich v Bishop Rock Marine
  (The Nicholas H) [1996]
  AC 211 185
March v Stramare (1991)
  171 CLR 506 .... 101, 103
Marcic v Thames Water [2002]
  QB 929 270
Marcic v Thames Water [2004]
  2 AC 42 342–344
Marsh v Baxter [2015] WASCA
  169 288
Martin v Reynolds Metals Co
  221 (1959) 315
Mayfair Ltd v Pears [1987]
  2 NZLR 459 18 116
McFarlane v Tayside Health
  Board [2000] 2 AC 59 .... 156, 164,
                                        208, 209, 210,
                                         212, 213,
                                          214, 215
McGhee v National Coal
  Board [1973] 1 WLR 1 .... 58, 59, 60
McKay v Essex AHA [1982]
  QB 1166 .... 208, 209,
                                          210, 211
McKennitt v Ash [2008] QB 73 271
McLoughlin v O'Brian [1983]
  1 AC 410 .... 165, 222,
                                        228–233, 247
Meadows v Khan [2019] EWCA
  Civ 152 127
Meadows v Khan [2022]
  AC 852 .... 46, 50, 114, 115,
                                      126–127, 149,
                                          210, 212, 213
Merest v Harvey (1814) 5
  Taunton 442 26
Merlin v British Nuclear Fuels Plc
  [1990] 2 QB 557 325
Michael v Chief Constable of
  South Wales [2015]
  AC 1732 .... 52, 56, 157,
                                          164, 169, 172
Milieudefensie v Royal Dutch
  Shell plc (unreported 2021) 353
Miller v Jackson [1977] QB 966 279,
                                          286, 334
MK v Oldham NHS Trust
  [2003] Lloyd's Rep Med 1 227

Modbury Triangle Shopping Centre Pty Ltd v Anzil (2000) 205 CLR 254 141
Mohammed v Home Office [2011] 1 WLR 2862 15
Montgomery v Lanarkshire Health Board [2015] AC 1430 36
Moore v Liszewski 838 F 3d 877 (2016) 26
Morris v Murray [1991] 2 QB 6 49
Mount Isa Mines v Pusey (1970) 125 CLR 383 168
Moy v Stoop (1909) 25 TLR 262 309
Mulcahy v Ministry of Defence [1996] QB 732 150
Mullin v Richards [1998] 1 WLR 1304 18
Murphy v Brentwood DC [1991] 1 AC 398 .... 180, 182, 183, 206, 207
Murray v Ministry of Defence [1988] 1 WLR 692 19
Mustapha v Culligan of Canada Ltd [2008] SCR 114 220
Network Rail v Williams [2019] QB 601 .... 272, 273, 275
O'Rourke v Camden LBC [1998] AC 188 151
OBG Ltd v Allan [2008] 1 AC 1 352
Ogwo v Taylor [1988] AC 431 238
Omychund v Barker (1744) 1 Atk 21 92
One Step (Support) Ltd v Morris-Garner [2019] AC 649 .... 21, 97, 268
Osman v United Kingdom (2000) 29 EHRR 245 147
Owens v Liverpool Corporation [1939] 1 KB 394 222
P Perl (Exporters) Ltd v Camden LBC [1984] QB 342 122
Page v Smith [1996] 1 AC 155 .... 119, 220, 221, 242
Palsgraf v Long Island Railroad 248 NY 339 (1928) 130, 140, 143, 144
Parker v Chief Constable of Essex [2018] EWCA Civ 2788 24
Parkinson v St James and Seacroft University Hospital NHS Trust [2002] QB 266 .... 156, 208, 210, 212, 214, 215
Parry v Cleaver [1970] AC 1 .... 212, 233
Patel v Home Secretary [2014] EWHC 501 (Admin) 19
Paul v Cooke [2012] NSWSC 840 .... 125, 256
Paul v Royal Wolverhampton NHS Trust [2022] 2 WLR 917 219
Percy v Hall [1997] QB 924 15
Performance Cars Ltd v Abraham [1962] 1 QB 33 109
Perre v Apand Pty Ltd (1999) 198 CLR 180 183
Plenty v Dillon (1991) 98 ALR 353 25
Re Polemis [1921] 3 KB 560 .... 115, 120, 143, 144
Polsue & Alfieri Ltd v Rushmer [1907] AC 121 296
Prah v Maretti (1982) 321 NW 2d 182 282
Pride & Partners v Institute for Animal Health [2009] EWHC 685 (QB) 197
Pride of Derby Angling Association v British Celanese [1953] Ch 149 112
Rahman v Arearose [2001] QB 351 .... 102, 242, 243
Rahman v ARY Network [2016] EWHC 3570 (QB) 30
Raymond v Young [2015] EWCA Civ 456 268
Read v J Lyons & Co Ltd [1947] AC 156 324
Rees v Darlington NHS Trust [2004] 1 AC 309 .... 15, 39, 167, 168, 208, 210, 212, 215, 216
Reeves v Metropolitan Police Commissioner [2000] 1 AC 360 122–123
Regan v Paul Properties [2007] Ch 135 334
Regina v Governor of Blundeston Prison, ex p Gaffney [1986] 1 WLR 696 13

Regina v Governor of Brockhill
  Prison, ex p Evans (No 1)
  [1997] QB 443 13
Regina v Governor of Brockhill
  Prison, ex p Evans (No 2)
  [1999] QB 1043 20
Regina v Governor of Brockhill
  Prison, ex p Evans (No 2) [2001]
  2 AC 19 13
Regina (Friends of the Earth) v
  Heathrow Airport Ltd [2020]
  UKSC 52 351
Regina (Gujra) v Crown Prosecution
  Service [2013] AC 484 67
Regina (Jollah) v Home Secretary
  [2019] 1 WLR 394 24
Regina (Jalloh) v Home Secretary
  [2021] AC 262 13
Regina (Rusbridger) v Attorney-
  General [2004] 1 AC 357 29
Rhodes v OPO [2016] AC 219 219
Robinson v Chief Constable of West
  Yorkshire [2018] AC 736 .... 32, 52,
      156, 172,
      181–189, 353
Robinson v Kilvert (1889)
  41 Ch D 88 296
Robinson v PE Jones (Contractors)
  Ltd [2012] QB 44 182
Rogers v Elliot 146 Mass 349
  (1888) 296
Ronayne v Liverpool Women's
  Hospital [2015] EWCA
  Civ 588 .... 254, 256
Rookes v Barnard [1964] AC
  1129 27, ... 136
Rothwell v Chemical & Insulating
  Co [2008] 1 AC 281 .... 197, 198,
      199, 200, 201,
      202, 203, 221
Royal Bank of Scotland v
  JP SPC 4 [2022] 3 WLR 261 189
Rushbond Plc v JS Design Partnership
  LLP [2021] EWCA Civ 1889 122
Ryan v New York 35 NY 210
  (1866) 130
Rylands v Fletcher (1868)
  LR 3 HL 330 .... 143, 291, 293,
      323, 324, 333

S v France (1990) 65 DR 250 270
Sanderson v Hull [2008]
  EWCA Civ 1211 .... 61, 62
Salvin v Brancepath Coal
  (1874) 9 Ch App 705 288
Schloendorff v Society of
  New York Hospital (1914)
  105 NE 92 .... 36, 38
Sedleigh-Denfield v O'Callaghan
  [1940] AC 880 276
Sharma v Minister for the
  Environment [2021] FCA 560 353
Sharma v Minister for the
  Environment [2022] FCAFC
  35 .... 188, 353
Shaw v Kovac [2017] EWCA
  Civ 1028 18
Shelfer v City of London Electric
  Lighting Co [1895] 1 Ch 287 334
Sidaway v Bethlem Royal Hospital
  [1985] AC 871 37
Sienkiewicz v Greif [2011]
  2 AC 229 .... 60, 62, 64, 87
Simaan v Pilkington Glass [1988]
  QB 758 206
Sindell v Abbott Laboratories
  26 Cal 3d 588 57,
      82–86, 92
Sion v Hampstead HA (1994)
  5 Med LR 170 230
Smith v Attorney-General
  [2022] NZHC 1693 ..... 170, 188, 353
Smith v Charles Baker & Sons
  [1891] AC 32 57
Smith v Chief Constable of Sussex
  [2009] AC 225 172
Smith v Eric S Bush [1990]
  1 AC 831 .... 180, 182
Smith v Fonterra Co-operative
  Group Ltd [2021] NZCA 552 178,
      188, 353
Smith v Lancashire Teaching
  Hospitals [2018] QB 804 256
Smith v Leech Brain & Co [1962]
  2 QB 405 .... 99, 118
Smith v Littlewoods Organisation
  [1987] AC 241 .... 118, 134,
      135, 149,
      150, 162, 187

TABLE OF CASES   xxv

Smith v Ministry of Defence [2014]
    AC 52 150
Smith New Court Securities v
    Citibank [1997] AC 254 126
South Australian Asset Management
    Corporation v York Montague
    Ltd [1997] AC 191 114,
                                    126–127, 143
Southwark LBC v Mills [2001]
    1 AC 1 .... 286, 290
Spartan Steel & Alloys Ltd
    v Martin & Co (Contractors)
    Ltd [1973] QB 27 .... 144, 279
Spring v Guardian Assurance
    [1995] 2 AC 296 45
St George v Home Office [2009]
    1 WLR 1670 115
St Helen's Smelting Co v Tipping
    (1865) 11 HLC 642 278,
                                    279, 290–292,
                                    297, 322, 329,
                                    339, 345–348
St Helen's Smelting Co v Tipping
    (1865) LR 1 Ch App 66 322
Stacey v Autosleeper Group Ltd
    [2014] EWCA Civ 1551 121
Stansbie v Troman [1948] 2 KB 48 ... 122
Stovin v Wise [1996] AC 923 148
Stubbings v Webb [1993] AC 498 138
Sturges v Bridgeman (1879)
    11 Ch D 852 .... 279, 299,
                                    300, 303
Summers v Tice 33 Cal 2d 80
    (1948) 78
Sutherland Shire Council v
    Heyman (1985) 60 ALR 1 179
Takitota v Attorney-General
    of the Bahamas [2009]
    UKPC 11 25
Tame v New South Wales (2002)
    211 CLR 317 .... 220, 245,
                                    247, 248, 252,
                                    253, 255
Tampling v James (1865)
    11 HLC 290 274
Tapp v Australian Bushmen's
    Rodeo [2022] HCA 11 128
Taylor v A Novo (UK) Ltd [2014]
    QB 150 .... 240, 254, 256

Tetley v Chitty [1986]
    1 All ER 663 .... 326, 341
Thake v Maurice [1986] QB 644 209
The Achilleas [2009] 1 AC 61 123
The Hua Lien [1991] 1 Lloyd's
    Rep 309 191
The Mediana [1900] AC 113 19
The Orjula [1995] 2 Lloyd's
    Rep 395 180
The Oropesa [1943] P 32 121
The Wagon Mound (No 1)
    [1961] AC 388 .... 50, 115–118,
                                    120, 144
Thing v La Chusa 48 Cal.3d
    644 (1989) 247, 250
Thomas v Taylor Wimpey [2019]
    EWHC 1134 (TCC) 207
Thompson-Schwab v Costaki
    [1956] 1 WLR 335 .... 273, 275
Thompson v Smiths Shiprepairers
    (North Shields) Ltd [1984]
    QB 405 .... 60, 98, 243
Tindall v Chief Constable of
    Thames Valley [2022] EWCA
    Civ 25 52
Tomlinson v Congleton BC [2004]
    1 AC 46 .... 49, 165
Transco v Stockport MBC [2004]
    2 AC 1 .... 276, 293,
                                    324, 333
Tremain v Pike [1969] 1 WLR
    1556 119
United States v Carroll Towing Co,
    159 F.2d 169 (1947) 69, 117
University College Cork v Electricity
    Supply Board [2020] IESC 38 186
Van Soerst v Residential Health
    Management [2000]
    1 NZLR 179 255
Vanderpant v Mayfair Hotel Co
    [1930] 1 Ch 138 287
Vasquez v Alameda 49 Cal.2d 674
    (1958) 81
Vaughan v Taff Vale Railway
    (1860) 5 Hurl & N 679 347
Vellino v Chief Constable of
    Manchester [2002] 1 WLR 218 114
Victorian Railways Commissioners v
    Coultas (1888) 13 App Cas 222 222

W v Essex CC [2001] 2 AC 592 239
Wainwright v Home Office
 [2002] QB 1334 .... 32, 271
Wainwright v Home Office
 [2004] 2 AC 406 33
Wainwright v United Kingdom
 (2007) 44 EHRR 40 33
Walker v Northumberland CC
 [1995] ICR 702 240
Wallace v Shoreham Hotel
 49 A.2d 81 (1946) 226
Walter v Selfe (1851) 4 De G &
 Sm 315 296
Walters v Glamorgan NHS Trust
 [2002] EWCA Civ 1792 .... 248, 254
Ward v James [1966] 1 QB 273 147
Ward v McMaster [1988] IR 337 183
Watkins v Home Secretary
 [2005] QB 883 33
Watkins v Home Secretary
 [2006] 2 AC 395 .... 33, 34
Watson v Croft Promo-Sport
 [2009] 3 All ER 249 .... 334, 340, 341
Watson, Laidlaw & Co v Pott Cassels
 & Williamson (1914) SC 18 97
Watt v Jamieson (1954) SC 56 290
Weller v Associated Newspapers
 [2014] EWHC 1163 (QB) 30, 31
Wernke v Halas 600 N.E.2d
 117 (1992) 294
West Bromwich Albion Football
 Club Ltd v El-Safty [2006]
 EWCA Civ 1299 265

Westdeutsche Landesbank
 Girozentrale v Islington LBC
 [1996] AC 669 183
Wheeler v JJ Saunders Ltd
 [1996] Ch 19 .... 298, 330, 331, 336, 341
White v Chief Constable of
 South Yorkshire [1999]
 2 AC 455 .... 64, 220–230, 233–240, 249, 250, 258
White v Jones [1995] 2 AC 207 4
Wildtree Hotels v Harrow LBC
 [2001] 2 AC 1 338
Wilkes v Deputy International
 [2018] QB 627 344
Wilsher v Essex AHA [1988]
 AC 1074 .... 58, 59
Wilson v Pringle [1987] QB 237 12
Wood v DPP [2008] EWHC
 1056 (Admin) 22, 23
Woodland v Essex CC [2014]
 1 AC 537 52, ... 174
Wright v Cambridge Medical Group
 [2010] EWCA Civ 683 .... 79, 80
Wright v McCormack [2022]
 EWHC 2068 (QB) 25, 97
Yeo v Times Newspapers [2015]
 1 WLR 971 29
Young v Charles Church (Southern)
 Ltd (1997) 39 BMLR 146 237
Z v United Kingdom (2002)
 34 EHRR 3 147
Zurich Insurance v International
 Energy Group [2016] AC 509 .... 63, 65

Table of Legislation

UK

Alkali Act 1863 347
Alkali Act 1881, s 28 346
Civil Aviation Act 1982
   s 76(1) 315
   s 76(2) 315
Civil Liability (Contribution)
   Act 1978 99
Climate Change Act 2008 351
Compensation Act 2006 .... 62, 63
   s 3 .... 63, 96
Consumer Protection Act 1987 ..... 51, 83
   s 4(1)(a) 344
   s 5(2) 207
Defamation Act 2013, s 11 29
Environmental Protection Act 1990
   s 80(7) 348
   Part III 3, 326
Fatal Accidents Act 1976 .... 4, 265
   s 1A 217, 233, 256
Human Fertilisation and
   Embryology Act 1990, s 44 209
Human Rights Act 1998 .... 32, 268
Law Reform (Contributory Negligence)
   Act 1945 99
Law Reform (Personal Injuries)
   Act 1948, s 2 233

Limitation Act 1980 .... 138, 200
Marine Insurance Act 1906,
   s 55(1) 120
Nuclear Installations Act 1965 3
   s 12 325
Offences against the Person
   Act 1861, s 18 37
Planning Act 2008 .... 330, 332
Prosecution of Offences Act 1985,
   s 6 67
Protection From Harassment
   Act 1997 266
Public Health Act 1875 348
Senior Courts Act 1981, s 32A 203
Sentencing Act 2020, ss 133–46 67
Water Industry Act 1991 .... 342, 343

Australia

Civil Liability Act 1936 258

New Zealand

Accident Compensation Act 1972 55

Introduction

Welcome to *Great Debates in Tort Law*! This chapter explains the book's aims and intended audience (including some other recommended books). It also introduces a metric for appraising the success of theories of tort (or any other legal institution).

NOT AN INTRODUCTION

This book is not intended for complete beginners. It presupposes some familiarity with the rules and 'black letter' doctrine of the relevant areas of law. It looks, instead, at wider issues and theoretical debates. It contains material that, as a lecturer, I often wish I could cover, but find there is no time once tort law's doctrinal rules have been 'straightforwardly' covered. Some issues (the relationship between different torts; the interaction between concepts within a tort) are better considered at the end of a course once the foundations have been studied. It is, in that sense, an advanced textbook.

It is 'advanced' in another sense too. As we will discover, there is deep disagreement about how tort law should be understood. There are theorists of different schools who argue that a true understanding of tort flows from one perspective that makes the subject a coherent unified whole. Examples include corrective justice and rights theories, and their instrumental rivals including 'accident compensation' (and 'loss spreading') and 'efficient incentives' (encouraging economically optimal behaviour). It is tempting to dismiss all such theories out of hand. Mainstream doctrinal lawyers, let alone practising tort lawyers, are atheoretical in approach (consciously or otherwise). They focus on the legal rules without feeling the need for any overarching theory. The dominant approach is practical rather than theoretical. If we had to label this mainstream attitude it could be dignified as 'pragmatic', 'pluralist' or 'eclectic'.

Pragmatism has an appealing sound – robust, down-to-earth common sense. But it could be a delusion. Keynes famously wrote (albeit not about tort law):

> The ideas of economists and political philosophers ... are more powerful than is commonly understood. Indeed the world is ruled by little else. Practical men,

who believe themselves to be quite exempt from any intellectual influence, are usually the slaves of some defunct economist. Madmen in authority, who hear voices in the air, are distilling their frenzy from some academic scribbler of a few years back.[1]

The claim readily translates to law ('some defunct tort theorist'). Even simple factual disputes presuppose background theoretical concepts, and how to classify a 'fact' for legal purposes may lead directly to difficult theoretical disputes.[2] Tort law is not untheorised. It is *already* theorised, whether we acknowledge it or not. For reasons of intellectual honesty, it is better if we do.

Moreover, insights from the various theoretical schools are used in development of the law. Courts frequently justify 'exceptional' liabilities (or extensions of liability) as directing compensation to claimants who need it, or having a salutary effect on defendants' behaviour. A renewed emphasis on the vindication of rights influences doctrinal developments, both liability (who can claim and in respect of what – see private nuisance) and remedies ('vindicatory' damages;[3] 'conventional' awards for intangible harms).[4] Undergraduate courses study 'tort law' not tort *theory*. But when theories have been influencing legal development – either overtly or (more contentious) without explicit acknowledgement – they should be appraised if we are to understand not just the law as it is, but its direction of travel. A core aim of this book is to help students in that deeper understanding by introducing theoretical debates about tort.

There are so many 'full' tort textbooks that it would be quite invidious to recommend any. (My advice is that students should try several and find the most congenial style and level of detail.) Genuine introductory textbooks are a rarer breed. For someone who has not yet studied tort, I suggest Tony Weir's *Introduction to Tort Law*,[5] or Peter Cane's *Tort Law* in Hart's 'Key Ideas in Law' series.[6] A different approach would start with the tort chapters of David Ibbetson's *Historical Introduction to the Law of Obligations*,[7] or PS Atiyah's polemic *The Damages Lottery*.[8] Books like the present volume, designed to complement 'basic' doctrinal texts, are rarer still. Although none is precisely designed as such, several could be read profitably after studying the doctrinal foundations. These include *Atiyah's Accidents, Compensation and the Law*,[9] and Anthony Ogus's *Costs and*

---

[1] JM Keynes, *The General Theory of Employment, Interest and Money* (Cambridge, Palgrave Macmillan, 1936) 383.
[2] R Dworkin, *Justice in Robes* (Harvard 2006) 69; ch 7, 'Incrementalism: Critique'.
[3] *Lumba v Home Secretary* [2012] 1 AC 245; ch 2, 'The Lumba Debate'.
[4] *Rees v Darlington NHS Trust* [2004] 1 AC 309; ch 8, 'Physical Injury'.
[5] 2nd edn (Oxford, Clarendon, 2006).
[6] (Oxford, Hart, 2017).
[7] (Oxford, Oxford University Press, 1999).
[8] (Oxford, Hart, 1997).
[9] P Cane and J Goudkamp (eds), 9th edn (Cambridge, Cambridge University Press, 2018).

Cautionary Tales.¹⁰ Both take an 'instrumental' approach. Determinedly otherwise, and equally recommended, is Robert Stevens's *Torts and Rights*.¹¹

What Makes a Good Theory?

We need a method to evaluate theories of tort law. A theory-of-theories might sound impossibly abstract or pretentious ('meta-theory'). Yet it is indispensable when assessing the merits of an account of the law. In fact lawyers do this all the time, so it is more a matter of bringing to the surface what happens implicitly without much conscious thought. An excellent account is given by Stephen Smith.¹² Although considering theories of contract law, Smith's exploration of the criteria for a theory's success are applicable across private law. Very broadly, Smith argues that a successful 'interpretation' of a legal institution must both 'fit' the legal rules that are to be explained, and 'justify' them by placing them in a good light.¹³ The theory should also be internally coherent (eg not self-contradictory). All these elements need a little more explanation.

A successful theory must fit the relevant legal rules and provide a 'transparent' explanation, that is, one that accords with the way that lawyers understand the rules in question.¹⁴ That the theory must fit the rules seems obvious. How could it otherwise be a theory *of* that branch of law? More difficult is just how much 'fit' a successful theory must display. It is unlikely that any account could explain all the rules of tort law. A 'theory' that did so would simply be a 'redescription' of all the rules, adding little to existing textbook accounts.¹⁵ Selectivity is inevitably required.

As Smith warns however, a theory fails the fit criterion if it cannot explain ('rejects as misclassified or exceptional') so much of the legal institution 'that those familiar with the law would not recognize what remains as "[tort]" law'.¹⁶ This clearly requires judgement. There is no authoritative or universally agreed definition of what is tort's 'core' and what is peripheral, anomalous or '*sui generis*' (in a special category of its own). A theory of nuisance, for example, would surely need to explain the tort of private nuisance. Must it also explain *public* nuisance, *statutory* nuisance,¹⁷ specific liability regimes such as the Nuclear Installations Act 1965, 'the rule in *Rylands v Fletcher*' and even planning law? As John Murphy notes, rights theories of tort struggle to explain public nuisance and *Rylands v Fletcher* because they do not involve

---

¹⁰ (Oxford, Hart, 2006) (esp chs 6–7).
¹¹ (Oxford, Oxford University Press, 2007).
¹² SA Smith, *Contract Theory* (Oxford, Oxford University Press, 2004) 7–37.
¹³ Cf R Dworkin, *Law's Empire* (Cambridge MA, Belknapp Press, 1986).
¹⁴ Smith (n 12) 24–32.
¹⁵ W Lucy, 'Method and Fit: Two Problems for Contemporary Philosophies of Tort Law' (2007) 52 *McGill LJ* 605.
¹⁶ Smith (n 12) 10.
¹⁷ Environmental Protection Act 1990, Part III.

the defendant's breach of a duty to the claimant (correlative to a claim-right against the defendant).[18] (Stevens also dismisses as anomalous/'non-tortious' other actions including misfeasance in public office, dependency claims under the Fatal Accidents Act, *White v Jones*[19] and various intentional economic torts.) It is therefore problematic for such theories to claim that they explain tort law 'as it is' rather than being a programme for law reform.

A theory should be made to fit the law rather than the other way round. The 'backwards' approach is typically compared to the legendary innkeeper Procrustes who cut guests down to size to fit his beds. Or as Weir recalled Groucho Marx doing on film, shearing off bits of clothing sticking out of a badly packed suitcase.[20] Allan Beever, himself a prominent rights theorist, cautions against a subtler violation. It is unconvincing merely to 'posit[ ] a right delineated so that it fits the contours of the action'.[21] As Murphy says, if theorists could simply declare what rights tort law recognises 'their theories could never be falsified. Wherever one were needed, a right could simply be formulated or modified in order to make the cases fit the theory'.[22] The stronger a commentator's theoretical 'pre-commitments', the more likely the Procrustean approach becomes.[23]

A 'transparent' theory accounts for tort lawyers' understanding of the law. Transparency seems a challenging requirement for any 'unitary' theory of law. Lawyers and judges do not reason from one 'master theory'. Given that the common law is the product of many judges over centuries, there is inevitably great diversity in reasoning. (Still less would we expect homogeneity among tort *statutes*.)[24] Transparency is a notorious problem for economic analysis of law. The great pioneer of Law and Economics, Richard Posner, alleges that the common law is actually driven by economic efficiency, but to appreciate this we must 'dig beneath the rhetorical surface' of judgments which often 'conceal' the 'true grounds of legal decision'.[25] This is the exact opposite of Stapleton's approach to tort.[26] It is extraordinary to accuse judges either of deliberately misleading reasoning or suffering some kind of false consciousness. The blatant failure to 'take the judges seriously' is a major reason why lawyers dismiss economic analysis as counter-intuitive.[27] Arguably corrective

---

[18] J Murphy, 'The Heterogeneity of Tort Law' (2019) 39 *OJLS* 455.
[19] [1995] 2 AC 207.
[20] T Weir, 'Reviewed Works: *Tort Law* by Ernest J. Weinrib; *Contract Law* by Larry Alexander' (1992) 51(2) *CLJ* 388; J Stapleton, *Three Essays on Torts* (Oxford, Oxford University Press, 2021) 24–25; Stevens (n 11) 348.
[21] A Beever, *A Theory of Tort Liability* (Oxford, Hart, 2016) 113.
[22] Murphy (n 18) 466.
[23] Lucy (n 15) 649.
[24] See TT Arvind and J Steele (eds), *Tort Law and the Legislature* (Oxford, Hart, 2013).
[25] RA Posner, *Economic Analysis of Law* 6th edn (New York, Aspen, 2003) 25.
[26] Stapleton (n 20) ch 1 ('Taking the Judges Seriously v Grand Theories').
[27] Lucy (n 15) 628.

justice-based theories suffer the same drawback. Courts do not reason directly from that theoretical stance either. Corrective justice theorists claim instead that the approach is implicit (or 'immanent') within tort law. As Lucy notes, this is an 'embarrassment' since it effectively dismisses the courts' actual reasoning as 'surface froth', just like law and economics.[28] It is problematic for any 'grand theory' that courts are required to 'show their working' but do not cite the theories as we would expect, were they truly tort law's foundation. Even though judges 'sometimes grasp for principles they can't quite articulate … for the most part, they are pretty good at saying what they mean, and the reasons they marshal in their opinions are in fact the grounds for their decisions'.[29]

Of course a grand unified theory would score very highly for 'coherence'. By definition every aspect of the theory would be perfectly consistent with all the other parts. But (as seen) the law is just not like that. Smith suggests a less demanding criterion of success. A successful theory shows the law as *intelligible* – that is, comprehensible and not self-contradictory. A good theory would not present tort as 'a hodge-podge of entirely unconnected rules'.[30] As Smith notes however, legal institutions often act for a *plurality* of reasons. It seems that the greater the emphasis on coherence, inevitably the lesser the degree of fit with the legal materials that the theory purports to explain. 'Grand Theorists' seem to assume that tort law is in need of a good 'dose of philosophical rigour' to straighten it out and keep complexity ('the forces of entropy') at bay.[31] The likely result is a 'slide to normativity' – emphasising 'what tort law should be about'.[32] Nor does Stapleton think this unintentional since a Grand Theorist's audience is 'other academics' whose main concern is 'evaluating the elegance of a reductive theory'.[33] Stapleton herself stresses 'the manifest heterogeneity' of judicial reasoning about tort, inevitable given that tort liability must take account of numerous collective, public interest, concerns in addition to the immediate parties' rights and obligations.[34]

A theory 'justifies' the law by presenting an attractive picture of it. For law to maintain *justified* authority, there must be good moral (or other) reasons for following its 'commands'. As Smith notes, most theorists contend that their approach would provide such a moral justification, and indeed a superior one to rival theories.[35] (To adjudicate such disputes involves longstanding philosophical debates between utilitarians, deontologists and others.) Again however the

---

[28] ibid.
[29] S Hershovitz, 'The Search for a Grand Unified Theory of Tort Law' (2017) 130 *Harv LR* 942, 969.
[30] Smith (n 12) 12.
[31] Lucy (n 15) 649.
[32] Stapleton (n 20) 25.
[33] ibid 33.
[34] ibid 11–12 (and xvii – tort not homogenous 'like carrot puree').
[35] Smith (n 12) 18.

danger is that emphasis on 'justification' shifts away from an account of what the law *is*, towards what it *should* be.

The perfect theory would score the best on all of these metrics. But evaluation is rarely so simple. As indicated, the criteria are often in tension. Poetry translated from one language into another may be faithful to the original or beautiful, but not both. Equally a choice arises between justification and fit. A detailed description of the whole of tort law defies any unified explanation. Conversely, an elegant model with clear moral force may not fit the law well at all. In attempting to make it fit, the theorist may have to reject so much that it would no longer constitute a theory 'of tort'. 'Justification' and 'fit' are often inversely related: emphasising one diminishes the other. Ought we to choose an account that fits the law better (despite weakness in 'justification') or a more attractive theory with serious problems of fit? Each is desirable but the comparison is extremely difficult. The criteria are *incommensurable*. As Finnis once complained about the original 'interpretive' approach to jurisprudence, it is as 'senseless' as trying to decide which novel is the '"shortest and most romantic" (or "funniest and best", or "most English and most profound")'.[36]

We have outlined the criteria of a good theory of tort and suggested why it is difficult for theories to satisfy them all. Given how 'messy' tort is, we shouldn't expect 'tidy theories' – Grand Theories 'nearly never succeed' given these descriptive difficulties.[37] On the other hand, a normative theory might provide strong reasons to change existing rules, practices and understanding. If, as some leading accounts contend,[38] the received picture of tort law is seriously confused, expecting (as it does) undemocratic and ill-informed policy-making beyond the competence of the judiciary, a radical change of direction would be justified – indeed required. (Guido Calabresi, both senior US judge and first rank tort scholar,[39] conceives the scholar's role as courageously writing the truth even when it is 'at war with past experience' – but the scholar's lot is also to be 'ignored' by judges who can adopt 'wonderful, new, and seemingly correct theories' only 'slowly, step by step, and with infinite caution'. The judge's duty is to produce 'rulings that work' and novel theories must be carefully tested before implementation.)[40]

These theoretical debates are a thread running through the book. They are particularly prominent in the first chapter on causation (Chapter 4), the debate about policy's role in the duty of care (in Chapter 7), and the first two chapters on nuisance (Chapters 10–11).

---

[36] J Finnis, 'On Reason and Authority in *Law's Empire*' (1987) 6 *Law & Phil* 357, 372–73.
[37] Hershovitz (n 29) 961–62, 969.
[38] A Beever, *Rediscovering the Law of Negligence* (Oxford, Hart, 2007); Stevens (n 11).
[39] See G Calabresi, *The Costs of Accidents* (New Haven, CT, Yale University Press, 1970).
[40] G Calabresi, 'Reflections of a Torts Teacher on the Bench' (2018) 11 *J Tort L* 161, 170–72.

PART I

Trespass

2

Trespass: Tort and the Vindication of Rights

INTRODUCTION

'Oranges are not the only fruit'. And negligence is not the only tort.

A road accident is probably the average tort lawyer's paradigm. It is the commonest kind of tort litigation. Road accidents, and tort's role in compensating their victims, are prominent in the legal and public consciousness. Drivers know they are legally required to insure against harm they cause to other road-users. Law students spend much of their tort courses studying various aspects of the tort of negligence. Yet this gives an incomplete picture of tort law and its function. Rival paradigms would be a slap in the face, a police search without warrant, or an arrest without due process. Here there is no 'accident' nor even any obvious 'loss'. A slap is quite deliberate, as are police searches and arrests. They may cause no loss in the sense central to negligence, which connotes physical injury to person or property. Slaps hurt yet in negligence, in the absence of bodily injury like cuts or broken bones, 'mere distress' is not actionable. Sometimes police officers may seize or break the claimant's things (or the claimant themselves) during a search or arrest. But typically no physical damage results. Approached through negligence, there seems to be no concrete loss and no claim since 'damage is the gist of the action'.

These scenarios engage *other* torts. Trespass protects against direct physical invasion of a protected right: the claimant's person, liberty, land or goods. Such an invasion is of itself a legal wrong. There is no need to show any other 'loss' ('gist damage'): the trespass torts are complete without it, 'actionable per se'. Defendants may be able to justify the invasion: e.g. reasonable force used in self-defence, police holding a valid arrest warrant or a prison governor jailing persons sentenced by the courts. But the onus of justification lies on the defendant. It is 'heavy' and their conduct 'closely scrutinised by the courts'.[1] Rightly so when every direct invasion of this kind is prima facie wrongful – as assault, battery, false imprisonment, trespass to land or goods.

---

[1] *Connor v Chief Constable of Merseyside* [2006] EWCA Civ 1549 [65] (Hallett LJ).

Tony Weir emphasised the trespassory torts' importance and distinctiveness.[2] Tort does not exist solely to compensate accidental harms. It also 'vindicate[s] constitutional rights'. The question is simply whether the rights have been infringed, not whether the infringer can be *blamed*. Hence strict liability, strictly construed defences and actionability per se ('Not every infraction of a right causes damage'). Weir lamented that negligence had obscured the vital role of trespass. Although relatively modern, negligence had 'thrived so mightily and grown so lusty' that like a 'cuckoo in the nest' it threatened to supplant the older torts. Negligence's dominant role – 'for no better reason than that a great many people are mangled on the highway' – means lawyers view trespass as 'antiquated', a 'vestigial exception' to the negligence principle. The 'classic form' of trespass is, after all, 'completely at odds' with the structure of negligence liability.[3] But Weir warned that downgrading trespass would be socially harmful, undermining the rights of the citizen, particularly (although not only) in claims against state officials.

However not all commentators agree. Dan Priel thinks trespass's traditional nature is problematic.[4] In modern mechanised societies, negligence forms part of a de facto public system for addressing mass accidental injuries. Whereas trespass has been unaffected by these socio-political currents, and remains 'uniquely "private"'. The trespass torts seem 'relics from a very different past, a shrinking and little loved island of private law in constant danger of being completely submerged under the rising seas of the more openly public negligence law'.[5] Priel suggests it is significant that new social problems that would fall 'naturally' into the orbit of trespass have been dealt with through negligence, citing the question of patients' 'informed consent' to medical procedures (examined in this chapter's final debate). Varuhas agrees that negligence has 'never been organised around protection of primary rights, but continued to serve wider public goals'.[6] But trespass has traditionally been 'resilient' to such 'socialisation', remaining 'squarely focused on protecting private rights'. Varuhas apprehends what Priel and Beurmann welcome – the 'fundamental recalibration of these ancient actions in favour of affording greater protection to public interests and accommodating "ordinary" social norms' – involving an erosion of the courts' 'insistence upon the inviolability of basic rights'.[7]

Similar disagreement characterises current debates about US tort law's fragmented protection of human dignity. The trespass torts play a prominent role here, although by no means exhaust the field (since invasions of dignity

---

[2] T Weir, *A Casebook on Tort* 10th edn (London, Sweet & Maxwell, 2004) 321–27.

[3] T Weir, 'The Staggering March of Negligence' in P Cane and J Stapleton (eds), *The Law of Obligations: Essays in Celebration of John Fleming* (Oxford, Oxford University Press, 1998) 108.

[4] D Priel, 'A Public Role for the International Torts' (2011) 22 *King's LJ* 183.

[5] ibid 187.

[6] JNE Varuhas, 'The Socialisation of Private Law: Balancing Private Right and Public Good' (2021) 137 *LQR* 141, 142.

[7] ibid 144.

might also engage defamation, negligence, nuisance, misuse of private information …). Traditionally minded scholars reason that an overarching, unified 'dignitary tort' is impossible.[8] The common law has evolved self-contained causes of action. This structure resists 'even partial conceptual unification or cross-pollination'. Others strongly disagree.[9] There should be a unified tort. The inconsistent rules in different torts cannot be justified, having developed from the common law's 'silo' mentality. A generic tort would protect indignities all kinds, dispensing with the fact-based distinctions central to trespassory torts (eg was there physical touching or not?). Crucially, the generic tort would be founded on *negligence* – a suitably broad approach to address all unreasonable affronts to dignity. Sugarman and Boucher argue that limiting liability to *intentional* dignitary invasions (as in trespass) 'does not capture all wrongful behavior'.[10]

The distinctiveness of trespass is the subject of this chapter. According to Weir, the trespass torts' structure and function cohere around their *rights-protecting* role. Negligence has a different logic – the compensation of unreasonably-inflicted *loss*. Negligence should not expand unthinkingly into the territory of trespass (and other, older nominate torts) – which it always threatens to do since negligence is not confined to the protection of particular interests (eg land, reputation, liberty).[11] Weir feared negligence had colonised the other torts as Britain was said to acquire its Empire, 'in a fit of absence of mind'.[12] For others though, the imperial progress is positively welcome. Negligence's expansionary potential enables it to address new kinds of harm beyond the reach of old established torts like trespass. Trespass protects rights strongly, but within a strictly limited scope (direct physical invasion). Negligence has begun to recognise intangible harms as 'gist damage' – that is, to protect rights of autonomy in addition to its familiar protection against personal injury or property damage.[13] Given such trends, does Weir exaggerates the danger of the trespass torts' encroachment by the 'rising seas' of negligence?

This chapter examines the trespassory torts' rights-protecting role. This protection flows from, and justifies, the torts' characteristic strictness of liability and actionability per se (Debate 1). A more difficult legal question is how best to vindicate invasions of rights through damages (Debate 2). We also examine two distinctive contributions of these torts: their constitutional function and their surprisingly limited role in protecting patient's rights to informed consent to medical treatment (Debates 3 and 4). The focus will be trespass to the person – battery and false imprisonment.

---

[8] KS Abraham and GE White, 'The Puzzle of the Dignitary Torts' (2019) 104 *Cornell LR* 317.
[9] SD Sugarman and C Boucher, 'Re-imagining the Dignitary Torts' (2021) 14 *Jo Tort Law* 101.
[10] ibid 189.
[11] Weir (n 3).
[12] JR Seeley, *The Expansion of England* (London, Macmillan, 1883) Lecture 1.
[13] D Nolan, 'New Forms of Damage in Negligence' (2007) 70 *MLR* 59.

Interference with bodily interests other than by direct physical contact will not be trespass, but may be actionable in negligence. (Negligence law's prioritisation of *physical* injury over intangible or 'emotional' harms is assessed in later chapters.) Similarly, interference with land except by direct boundary intrusions will not be trespass, but may amount to nuisance. (The contrast between the torts – and the necessity for a balancing of interests in nuisance – is again considered below.)[14] Tort law contains an historic division between the rights-based trespass torts and loss-based torts like negligence. The structure is long-standing and deeply entrenched.[15] But pressure to erode the distinction comes from two directions. First – Weir's bête noire – trespass being 'infected' with negligence-type thinking. Conversely, some scholars seek to restate the entire law of torts around the protection of rights – including negligence. Direct physical intrusion upon important rights clearly warrants legal protection. But intangible interests are ever-more important, and non-physical intrusion ever-more common, in the twenty-first century's 'information age'. Is trespass ultimately an historical artefact, of decreasing importance to modern problems?

Debate 1
Justifying Strict Liability and Actionability Per Se

Strict Liability and Defences

Trespass liability is classically strict. But this is increasingly challenged by reasonableness-/fault-based defences. We examine the doctrinal controversies to assess these developments.

The trespass torts are sometimes described as 'strict liability' but also as 'intentional'. An ambiguity in their structure therefore needs to be clarified. Trespass involves intentional conduct, but only in a trivial sense. The *conduct* constituting the tort has to be voluntary: imprisoning the claimant, or touching them/their property (eg walking on the claimant's land). Provided this is satisfied, as it virtually always will be, 'D will be liable even if D was ignorant of the facts which rendered the acts trespassory, and even if D acted in perfect innocence and good faith'.[16] This means trespass is *not* 'intentional' in the more natural sense requiring intention to produce a harmful result (ie knowingly invading the claimant's right). *Wilson v Pringle* held there is no need to show intention to *harm*: all that must be intentional is 'the application of force', or 'the act of touching'.[17] The necessity that the acts constituting

---

[14] See ch 10, 'Strict Liability for Property Damage and Trespass'.
[15] DJ Ibbeston, *A Historical Introduction to the Law of Obligations* (Oxford, Oxford University Press, 1999).
[16] P Cane, *Tort Law and Economic Interests* 2nd edn (Oxford, Oxford University Press, 1996) 29.
[17] [1987] QB 237, 247–48.

trespass were 'voluntary' requires little more than the defendant being conscious when acting.[18]

Fundamentally then, these torts do not involve fault.[19] (Compare negligence where it is clearly insufficient that a defendant was *voluntarily driving* the vehicle that struck the claimant: the question is whether the driver was careless about the *consequences* of their conduct.)[20] If I walk on land which I quite reasonably believe is mine, I am liable in trespass if in fact it belongs to you (not a far-fetched example in a boundary dispute). If I tap you on the shoulder to attract attention, jostle you in horseplay or kiss your cheek, I have intentionally applied direct physical force to your person which is (prima facie) battery – absenting a valid defence (such as consent). It is irrelevant that I reasonably think you would not resent – or might positively welcome – the touch.

A vivid example of strict liability is *R v Governor of Brockhill Prison, ex p Evans (No 2)*. Here the defendant prison governor had used High Court jurisprudence to calculate the claimant's release date. But the High Court got the law wrong and the case which the governor had loyally applied was overruled.[21] Although he reasonably relied on the High Court's guidance (indeed he had surely had no choice – 'what more could he have done?'), the governor had, objectively, imprisoned the claimant past the correct legal release date. He had had no legal authority for that continued detention. The governor was therefore liable for the tort of false imprisonment – even though quite 'blameless'.[22] (Indeed, the House of Lords expressed sympathised with his position.)

Evans illustrates the trespassory torts' double strictness. First, it is usually straightforward to show that the defendant intentionally touched or imprisoned the claimant.[23] That is all the claimant need prove. It is irrelevant that the defendant reasonably believed they had the legal power to do so. Which leads to the second point: defences are strictly construed. It is not enough to *believe*, quite genuinely and reasonably, that one has the power (indeed duty) to keep a prisoner locked up. The defendant must actually *have* the power. There is no general defence of having acted reasonably. As Weir pointed out, 'those who invade our rights generally do so on reasonable grounds, that is, for our own good or for someone else's good or for the public good'.[24] Hence

---

[18] D Howarth, 'Is There a Future for the Intentional Torts?' in PBH Birks (ed), *The Classification of Obligations* (Oxford, Clarendon, 1997).

[19] See also *Fairfax Media Publications Pty Ltd v Voller* [2021] HCA 27 [115] (Edelman J) (defamation) citing R Stevens, *Torts and Rights* (Oxford, Oxford University Press, 2007) 101.

[20] *Holmes v Mather* (1875) LR 10 Ex 261.

[21] *R v Governor of Blundeston Prison, ex p Gaffney* [1986] 1 WLR 696 (overruled by *ex parte Evans (No 1)* [1997] QB 443).

[22] [2001] 2 AC 19.

[23] Cf *Regina (Jalloh) v Home Secretary* [2021] AC 262 (meaning of 'imprisonment').

[24] Weir (n 2) 323.

why the defendant must prove that they actually had legal authority (not the 'insidious' plea that they reasonably thought they had it): 'the most important, as well as the oldest, rule in the book'.[25]

From tort's usual fault-based perspective, this seems harsh on blameless defendants. But the fault principle is of dubious relevance in the protection of rights. It is wrongful, in itself, to cross the boundary (physical and metaphysical) which protects a right, 'regardless of whether it causes any harm to the right-holder and regardless of whether the boundary-crossing was negligent, reckless or intentional'.[26] The logic is that certain core rights 'deserve protection in their own right regardless of any fault'; this places them 'at the top of the hierarchy of legally protected interests'.[27] 'To require the right-holder to prove fault on the [defendant's] part ... or to allow the [defendant] to plead contributory fault on the part of the right-holder, would be inconsistent with full protection of rights'.[28] Cane makes these points in relation to property interests. The points apply *a fortiori* to battery and false imprisonment. Strict liability is arguably here 'morally demanded'.[29]

But this strict liability has been questioned. Diplock LJ argued that although trespass to goods 'historically did not necessarily involve blameworthiness', recent developments indicated 'protecting those who act reasonably in intended performance of what rightminded men would deem a duty to their fellow men'.[30] This signals the intrusion of 'negligence thinking'. There are many other examples. In *Ashley v Chief Constable of Sussex* the Court of Appeal held that self-defence will succeed in a battery claim if the defendant *reasonably thought* their use of force justified (although, in fact, there was no threat).[31] Clarke MR rejected textbook statements that mistaken beliefs, even reasonably mistaken ones, were never a defence in trespass.[32] A defence based on *reasonably* mistaken beliefs fairly 'held the balance' between the parties, since 'a defendant may fear for his life and have only a split second to decide what to do'.[33] Arden LJ agreed, despite her observation that 'Any claim to commit a trespass ... out of self-defence must be jealously regarded by the law because it amounts to the creation of an exception to the rule of law'.[34] This approach clearly departs from the model of strict protection of rights given above. (On appeal, three law lords left the question open.)[35]

---

[25] ibid 322.
[26] P Cane, 'Mens Rea in Tort Law' (2000) 20 *OJLS* 533, 552.
[27] Cane (n 16) 29.
[28] P Cane, 'Causing Conversion' (2002) 118 *LQR* 544.
[29] A Beever, 'The Form of Liability in the Torts of Trespass' (2011) 40 *Common Law World Rev* 378, 392.
[30] *Chic Fashions (West Wales) Ltd v Jones* [1968] 2 QB 299, 315.
[31] [2006] EWCA Civ 1085; [2007] 1 WLR 398.
[32] ibid [64]–[65].
[33] ibid [78].
[34] ibid [192].
[35] [2008] UKHL 25; [2008] 1 AC 962 [20] (Lord Scott).

Percy v Hall is another departure. The defendant policemen arrested the plaintiff for breaching a bye-law prohibiting access to military premises. It was later held that the bye-law was void (because *ultra vires*).[36] Nobody realised that at the time of the arrest. A claim for false imprisonment failed.[37] Simon Brown LJ reasoned that the 'innocent constables' had acted precisely as they should have done: the public interest required enforcement of the apparently valid bye-law. Its retrospective invalidation ('surely') could not transform the police officers' conduct into an actionable tort and deprive them of the defence of lawful justification.[38] *Percy v Hall* prioritised (perceived) fairness to the police defendants over protection of the plaintiff's right not to be arrested. The court suggested the real culprit was the Secretary of State who promulgated the invalid bye-law. Morally that may be correct. It was of no help to the plaintiff. As Simon Brown LJ accepted, no damages action exists for unlawful administrative action.[39] But the absence of a claim against the minister was 'no basis for creating a cause of action instead against those, here the defendant constables, who are not responsible for the invalidity'.

Weir attacks these developments. *Percy v Hall* exemplifies tort law's infiltration by the negligence principle.[40] The court's reluctance to hold liable police officers who had acted reasonably undermined tort's previously strict protection of fundamental rights (the right of liberty in *Percy*). This cannot be reconciled with the strict approach to the prison governor's liability in *Evans*. The fault principle, alien to trespass, has undermined its structure and in consequence, its constitutional function.[41]

Conversely, Priel suggests that trespass focuses unduly on the claimant's rights. Trespass traditionally ignores the curtailment of *defendants*' autonomy by imposing strict liability for 'innocuous trifles that cause no harm'.[42] Priel accordingly welcomes the rise of reasonableness-based defences (arguing this should go further in assault and battery, torts that any individual might commit, than in false imprisonment which usually involves government defendants).[43] Donal Nolan questions the transformation of negligence into a rights-protecting tort (a doctrinal possibility following the acceptance of invasion of autonomy as 'gist damage').[44] Nolan observes that the requirement of direct physical invasion keeps trespass within 'very particular' limits. Whereas holding every *negligent* invasion of rights actionable per se would

---

[36] *Bugg v DPP* [1993] QB 473.
[37] *Percy v Hall* [1997] QB 924.
[38] ibid 947–48.
[39] See further *Mohammed v Home Office* [2011] 1 WLR 2862 [24] (Sedley LJ).
[40] Weir (n 3); Weir (n 2) 354 (*Percy v Hall* 'disgraceful').
[41] See further Varuhas (n 6) 148: *Austin v MPC* [2009] 1 AC 564 reverses burden of proof of lawful authority defence with 'no real explanation'.
[42] Priel (n 4) 197.
[43] ibid 193 (noting the particular strictness of *Evans* (false imprisonment)).
[44] Nolan (n 13) (discussing *Rees v Darlington NHS Trust* [2004] 1 AC 309).

'unduly ... restrict people's freedom of action' since negligence 'encompasses a limitless variety of actions or omissions'. Unlike Priel, Nolan thinks the stringency of trespass liability is tolerable *given its narrow scope* (direct physical violation).

Christine Beuermann argues that negligence should supersede trespass.[45] At its heart, negligence balances the parties' interests. It assesses 'reasonableness' using the risks posed, social context and all other relevant circumstances. In Beuermann's view, this open balancing process is more effective and transparent than the ('anachronistic') trespass torts, where balancing (she argues) plays a similar but concealed role. Beuermann cites the fault-influenced adaptation of trespass defences described above, and also the rule that 'everyday' touching is not actionable in trespass. This requires brief explanation.

There is no liability in battery for 'physical contact which is generally acceptable in the ordinary conduct of daily life'.[46] Hence: 'nobody can complain of the jostling which is inevitable from his presence in, for example, a supermarket, an underground station or a busy street; nor can a person who attends a party complain if his hand is seized in friendship'. Some have suggested that by going out into the world, we all *consent* to inevitable or innocuous touching. Lord Goff rejected that 'consent' rationale. It was 'artificial' – 'in particular, it is difficult to impute consent to those who, by reason of their youth or mental disorder, are unable to give their consent'.[47] Therefore some freestanding exception 'to allow for the exigencies of everyday life' seems inevitable.[48]

Beuermann argues that the 'socially acceptable touching' defence implicitly involves negligence-style balancing of claimants' and defendants' interests. Should this not be carried out openly in the tort of negligence, rather than obliquely through 'social acceptability' in trespass? David Howarth argues that tort law should avoid unnecessary duplication of actions (numerous torts covering essentially the same ground). Not through (aesthetic) concerns about jurisprudential elegance but because law will achieve its social goals better by avoiding inexplicably complex distinctions and categories.[49] Do these arguments this undermine Weir's campaign to preserve trespass against negligence-based thinking? Not necessarily.

First, the trespassory torts have a different social goal, the protection of rights (reflected not only in strict liability, but as discussed below its remedies and constitutional function). Second, the 'everyday life' exception is narrower than Beuermann's argument suggests.[50] A clear example is *Re F*,

---

[45] C Beuermann, 'Are the Torts of Trespass to the Person Obsolete? Part II: Continued Evolution' (2018) 26 *Tort LR* 6.
[46] *Collins v Wilcock* [1984] 1 WLR 1172, 1177 (Robert Goff LJ).
[47] *In Re F* [1990] 2 AC 1, 72.
[48] ibid.
[49] Howarth (n 18).
[50] Although cf Varuhas (n 6) 146–47 ('creeping' expansion).

where the House of Lords ruled that surgery could be performed on adults lacking mental capacity in the patient's best interests.[51] Significantly, the suggestion that such medical treatment could fall within the 'everyday conduct' exception was unanimously rejected. There was good reason to confine the exception strictly: it could be oppressive to extend it from physical contact unavoidable in daily life to other supposedly 'desirable' invasions of rights.

As Beever asks: 'Why should one have to put up with being intentionally touched just because that form of touching is ordinary or thought reasonable by a judge?'[52] He argues that 'acceptable' trespass encompasses only the parties' *joint* interests. For example, their common interest in circulating in crowded places, or a householder's interest in people (eg postmen) walking up their garden path to communicate with them.[53] Importantly, this rules out 'socially acceptable' exceptions derived from the general public interest – as in the questionable Australian decision that police officers enjoyed a householder's 'implied permission' to enter his land to arrest him![54] Brennan J, dissenting, had correctly argued that the 'consent' was a fiction and, moreover, reversed *Entick v Carrington* (the great constitutional case requiring officials to show legal authority for entry, seizure or arrest).[55]

A general balancing approach weakens the protection of rights. Whether invoking 'general acceptability', 'implied permission', or the defendant's lack of fault, wide defences undermine rights. A 'reasonableness' inquiry departs from the tradition of specific defined defences in trespass. The traditional structure is complex and detailed. But those who invade (not just imperil) others' rights should face stricter limitations. Although the categories of justification are not formally closed, they should only expand 'with the greatest caution, for every extension … constitutes the erosion of a right'.[56]

Actionability Per Se and Vindication

Actionability per se equally reflects trespass's role in protecting rights. Trespass is actionable in tort whether or not it causes material loss – that is, irrespective of whether it leaves the claimant 'factually worse off … as a result of the wrong'.[57] All that has to be shown is a direct physical invasion of the right. In battery:

> The fundamental principle, plain and incontestable, is that every person's body is inviolate. It has long been established that any touching of another person,

---

[51] [1990] 2 AC 1.
[52] (n 29) 392.
[53] A Beever, *A Theory of Tort Liability* (Oxford, Hart, 2016) ch 6.
[54] *Halliday v Nevill* (1984) 57 ALR 331.
[55] ibid 343; *Entick v Carrington* (1765) 19 St Tr 1029.
[56] Weir (n 2) 324. Cf Varuhas (n 6) 148: *Austin v MPC* [2009] 1 AC 564 another 'significant expansion of police powers' (false imprisonment).
[57] Stevens (n 19) 61.

however slight, may amount to a battery ... The effect is that everybody is protected not only against physical injury but against any form of physical molestation.⁵⁸

Tort law takes these rights seriously by granting an action 'to mark even miniscule interferences'.⁵⁹ Here trespass contrasts with torts, especially negligence, where 'damage is the gist of the action'. Only when actual loss ('actionable damage') occurs can the claimant claim in negligence. It is therefore difficult to conceive negligence as having the same rights-protective function.⁶⁰

A number of debateable points arise. First, is it accurate to assume that negligence is *not* concerned with the protection of rights? Courts have recognised certain abstract interests as 'actionable gist damage' in negligence – including liberty and 'reproductive autonomy'.⁶¹ A wider conception of 'damage' erodes the distinction between negligence (actionable only when damage present) and trespass (actionable per se).

Second, what if material loss (like a broken leg) *does* result from intentional touching? In principle, victims can claim in trespass or negligence at their option. However there is uneasiness about extending strict liability in trespass from infringement of rights to the resulting *injuries*. In *Wilson v Pringle* the defendant schoolboy playfully jumped on his classmate who landed awkwardly, injuring his leg. As seen, the court confirmed that only the intention to *touch* the plaintiff had to be shown for an action in battery (clear on the facts); there did not have to be intention to *injure*. But from the negligence perspective, liability here seems anomalous. A schoolboy might intentionally touch another *without being negligent* about the *injuries* caused by that physical contact. The risk of injury might be unforeseeable, or at least not to a teenager.⁶² (The Court of Appeal in *Wilson v Pringle*, sensing harshness, added the dubious requirement that touching had to be 'hostile'. The 'hostility' limitation has since been authoritatively disapproved.)⁶³

Even Weir accepted that in cases involving actual personal injury, negligence has to be proven.⁶⁴ Weir thought this concession made it easier to resist the negligence principle where it is *not* relevant, that is, 'where the plaintiff is seeking, not compensation for harm, but rather vindication of the rights

---

⁵⁸ *Collins v Wilcock* [1984] 1 WLR 1172, 1177 (Robert Goff LJ).

⁵⁹ JNE Varuhas, 'The Concept of "Vindication" in the Law of Torts: Rights, Interests and Damages' (2014) 34 OJLS 253, 290.

⁶⁰ NB *Shaw v Kovac* [2017] EWCA Civ 1028 [56]–[57] (nominal damages not available in negligence).

⁶¹ Nolan (n 13).

⁶² *Mullin v Richards* [1998] 1 WLR 1304.

⁶³ *In Re F* [1990] 2 AC 1, 73 (Lord Goff).

⁶⁴ Weir (n 3) 109–10; T Weir, *An Introduction to Tort Law* 2nd edn (Oxford, Clarendon, 2006) 134–35. See eg *Mayfair Ltd v Pears* [1987] 2 NZLR 459 (trespass to land causing property damage; no liability unless negligent).

by whose infringement he is aggrieved'.[65] The law should therefore allocate 'harm' cases exclusively to negligence and 'invasion of rights' cases exclusively to trespass. Such a clear demarcation of function justifies a separate tort of trespass – whereas the present law appears 'schizophrenic in having two torts with fundamentally ingredients' co-existing on identical facts.[66]

The final question is how best to *remedy* an invasion of rights, actionable per se, which causes no loss. This is considered in the next debate. But note, even to suggest that remedies in the absence of loss might be problematic adopts the loss-focused mindset of negligence. This cannot simply be assumed as the starting point. The 'relentless' insistence on proof of concrete loss stands in the way of a 'meaningful remedy', and may even 'defeat the object of the cause of action', for torts which 'afford protection to basic rights recognised by the common law'.[67]

Debate 2
Remedies and Vindication of Rights

How should the law remedy invasions of rights? When actual loss results, it is universally accepted that this may be compensated (eg property damage, personal injury or – especially here – distress). Serious, knowing invasions may also attract aggravated damages and (against government defendants) exemplary damages.[68] But what if there is no intentional wrongdoing and *no loss* results? There will clearly be *liability*, given that trespass is actionable per se. But should *substantial* damages be awarded for 'the infringement itself'? Is it sufficient vindication to award 'nominal damages' (the traditional remedy) and/or a declaration?

Nominal damages are the orthodox approach.[69] In *Murray v MOD* Lord Griffiths considered false imprisonment of persons unaware of their confinement. Such a claimant would 'normally … recover no more than nominal damages' having suffered no harm. Yet *liability* was not in doubt: 'The law attaches supreme importance to the liberty of the individual and if he suffers a wrongful interference with that liberty it should remain actionable even without proof of [actual] damage'.[70] Similarly, in *Lumba v Home Secretary* the Supreme Court reasoned that the absence of loss caused by the claimant's detention under an unlawful government policy (when he would anyway have

---

[65] Weir (n 3) 110.
[66] ibid 109.
[67] *GE v Commissioner of an Garda Síochána* [2021] IECA 113 [103] (Murray J).
[68] Eg *Patel v Home Secretary* [2014] EWHC 501 (Admin) (£110,000 general and aggravated damages, plus £15,000 exemplary damages, for 'monstrous series of miscarriages of justice'). But such awards are rare: J Goudkamp and E Katsampouka, 'An Empirical Study of Punitive Damages' (2018) 38 *OJLS* 90.
[69] *The Mediana* [1900] AC 113, 116; *Constantine v Imperial Hotels Ltd* [1944] KB 693.
[70] [1988] 1 WLR 692, 703.

been detained under the correct, *lawful* policy) did not prevent liability in a tort actionable per se.[71] But (by a majority) the court awarded only nominal damages on the particular facts. Note, however, there are authorities supporting substantial damages for imprisonment 'itself'.[72] (As discussed in the following section, the *Lumba* decision is especially controversial.)

Jason Varuhas welcomes the cases awarding substantial damage: compensation for loss of liberty should be assessed objectively.[73] The claimant's lack of distress (or even awareness) does not diminish the fact of imprisonment. Varuhas cites *Huckle v Money* where the plaintiff recovered substantial damages despite being treated very well by his gaolers and fed beef-steaks and beer.[74] Other prisoners might be unusually phlegmatic, or defiant. Nevertheless, substantial damages should be awarded. Varuhas conceives this as a special form of 'compensation'.[75] It does *not* compensate loss in the usual sense (loss 'which correspond[s] with real-world effects' harming the claimant). The loss involved in infringement of a right exists 'exists solely on the legal plane'; the law 'constructs' a loss which Varuhas calls 'normative damages'.[76] Their function is not compensation but *vindication*: 'attesting to, affirming and reinforcing the fundamental nature of the interest and its inherent value'.[77]

As Eric Descheemaeker puts it, under this 'alternative model, increasingly influential in an age saturated with the language of rights', the law is no longer concerned with 'a concrete loss that flows from the violation of a right, rather we are talking about an abstract loss or harm defined as the injury to the right itself'.[78] Long visible in damages for loss of liberty 'itself', such remedies have become more prominent. As common with new concepts, a terminological battle has erupted. The most common label in current use is probably 'vindicatory damages' (also 'substitutive' or 'normative' damages). All are used to mean *substantial damages for the invasion of a right* (awarded in addition to any compensation for concrete loss). *Nominal* damages are 'unintelligible' on the rights model according to which every 'right-violation is a genuine loss which deserves genuine, hence more than nominal, damages'.[79]

However, *Lumba* controversially reaffirms the place of nominal damages. The Supreme Court's rejection of 'vindicatory damages' has been followed in Australia: *Lewis v Australian Capital Territory*.[80] The novel remedy

---

[71] [2012] 1 AC 245 [62]–[66] (Lord Dyson) (*Lumba*).
[72] *Evans* [1999] QB 1043, 1059 (Lord Woolf MR) (approved [2001] 2 AC 19, 39); *Iqbal v Prison Officers' Association* [2010] QB 732, [46]–[49] (Lord Neuberger MR).
[73] Varuhas (n 59).
[74] (1763) 2 Wils KB 205.
[75] Varuhas (n 59) 268.
[76] See Stevens (n 19) 78 ('Instead of referring to factual losses we could say the loss is legal or normative whenever a right is infringed').
[77] Varuhas (n 59) 254.
[78] E Descheemaeker, 'Unravelling Harms in Tort Law' (2016) 132 *LQR* 595, 595, 599.
[79] ibid 616.
[80] [2020] HCA 26 (*Lewis*).

was both unprecedented and unnecessary.⁸¹ Edelman J rejected a 'radical reinterpretation' that would alter our entire understanding of the law of damages.⁸² His Honour found it impossible to quantify the remedy if 'the extent and manner of the deprivation [of liberty] would not be relevant', seeming baffled by the claimant's submission that 'vindicatory damages' 'should be the same whether he was imprisoned in conditions of luxurious comfort or appalling depravity'.⁸³

Edelman J accepted that while in 'the vast majority' of cases damages compensate loss flowing from a wrong, there are also remedies that focus on rectifying the wrong itself.⁸⁴ Injunctions can prevent or reverse wrongs. Moreover, 'user damages' aim 'to rectify the wrongful act by requiring payment of an amount that would have made the use lawful'.⁸⁵ Such 'user damages' are awarded where property (or analogous rights) are taken without the owner's permission.⁸⁶ The defendant has to pay a reasonable licence fee for that tortious usage. But Edelman J held that this remedy was *not* available for false imprisonment (the tort in both *Lewis* and *Lumba*). It would be 'nonsensical' to reason that in such a case, the claimant could ratify their unlawful detention.⁸⁷ There could be no lawful negotiation about such matters (by contrast with permitting others to use one's property). User damages would be 'incoherent' since the claimant imprisonment's by the government 'could never have been a matter the subject of a monetary payment for [his] permission'.⁸⁸

This reasoning has been questioned in an important Irish case rejecting the Australian and English approach.⁸⁹ Murray J queried whether the law should give weaker protection to liberty than to interests that can be traded ('commodified and reduced to rational economic formula').⁹⁰ It should not and did not. In Murray J's view, tort 'unsurprisingly' recognises substantial damages for imprisonment which does not cause conventional material loss. He thought user damages' 'real point' was that tort law can where appropriate give 'the concept of loss or damage a wider meaning'.⁹¹ In particular, so that it can protect important interests by awarding more than nominal damages. It is now time to scrutinise the reasoning in *Lumba*.

---

⁸¹ ibid [104]–[109] (Gordon J).
⁸² ibid [153].
⁸³ ibid [157].
⁸⁴ ibid [150].
⁸⁵ ibid [145].
⁸⁶ *One Step (Support) Ltd v Morris-Garner* [2019] AC 649.
⁸⁷ *Lewis* (n 80) [149].
⁸⁸ ibid [155].
⁸⁹ *GE v Commissioner of an Garda Síochána and Governor of Cloverhill Prison* [2021] IECA 113 (*GE*).
⁹⁰ ibid [111].
⁹¹ ibid [109].

The Lumba *Debate*

A loss-based model of damages lies the heart of *Lumba* (and *Lewis v ACT*). Unless the claimant in a false imprisonment action can show that the tort made them worse off, they cannot claim substantial damages. From a negligence perspective this sounds unobjectionable. Yet to reach this conclusion, the courts have to draw a sharp line between liability and remedy. Whether the distinction can be maintained is the central controversy. Critics of *Lumba* argue that allowing 'what would have happened' to determine the question of loss and remedy undermines the tort's supposedly strict protection of rights to liberty.

The fact that someone *could* have been lawfully detained (but was not) is certainly irrelevant in deciding *liability*. As once observed, 'It is no answer, when a man says "I have been unlawfully arrested without a warrant" [for the police] to say "Well, had [we] taken the trouble to go and ask for a warrant, [we] would undoubtedly have got it"'.[92] As Lord Dyson said in *Lumba*, 'the law of false imprisonment does not permit history to be rewritten in this way'.[93] Lord Kerr agreed: 'Detention cannot be justified on some putative basis, unrelated to the actual reasons for it, on which the detention might retrospectively be said to be warranted'.[94] Clearly this is correct throughout the law of trespass: 'where a police officer restrains a person, but does not at that time intend or purport to arrest him, then he is committing an assault, even if an arrest would have been justified'.[95] Similarly, sexual contact with sleeping persons must be unlawful as they are incapable of consenting. The defendant is not permitted to argue that 'they surely would have consented' to sex when in fact they did not (and could not). It is vitally important that the conditions of lawful arrest/detention are respected, or consent actually obtained. Lord Kerr thought this 'elementary', 'self evident' and 'fundamental'.[96]

The High Court of Australia agrees. In deciding *liability* 'there is no role for a counterfactual analysis'.[97] As Gaegler J explained, even criminals vulnerable to imprisonment retain the protection of tort's insistence that correct legal authority must be obtained before detaining them: a criminal is 'not an outlaw'.[98]

But quite a different approach was taken to *remedies*.[99] Damages compensate *loss*. To ascertain the claimant's loss, the court *necessarily* compares their actual position with the hypothetical (or 'counterfactual') position if there had been no tort. (Again, this is trite in the loss-based model of negligence.) If but

---

[92] *Kuchenmeister v Home Office* [1958] 1 QB 496, 512 (Barry J).
[93] *Lumba* (n 71) [62].
[94] ibid [242].
[95] *Wood v DPP* [2008] EWHC 1056 (Admin) [7] (Latham LJ).
[96] *Lumba* (n 71) [239], [242].
[97] *Lewis* (n 80) [45] (Gordon J).
[98] ibid [25].
[99] See especially ibid [50]–[74] (Gordon J).

for the *illegal* detention the claimant would clearly have been detained *lawfully*, as on the facts of *Lumba* and *Lewis*, false imprisonment is established but it has caused no loss – and there cannot be substantial damages. Liability and remedy were 'not to be elided'.[100] Lord Dyson put the *Lumba* approach in a nutshell:

> If the power [of detention] could and would have been lawfully exercised, that is a powerful reason for concluding that the detainee has suffered no loss and is entitled to no more than nominal damages. But that is not a reason for holding that the tort has not been committed.[101]

Critics, however, complain that refusing to award substantial damages contradicts the finding of liability – undermining tort's protection of liberty. Varuhas fears a 'disconnect between judicial *rhetoric* of rights protection, and watering down *practical* protection' (noting that in *Lumba*, someone held to be imprisoned wrongfully for two years received only nominal damages).[102] The connexion between remedy and right had been stressed by the dissenting judges in *Lumba* itself. Lord Brown thought consistency required the approach to loss to apply to the prior question of liability too. The majority's correct recognition that there was no loss meant the claimant 'was in truth rightly in detention' – a finding that was 'the very negation of the tort'.[103] To award *nominal* damages because someone would have been detained anyway would 'seriously devalue the whole concept of false imprisonment'.[104] Rather than 'risk bringing the law into disrepute' by 'speak[ing] with two voices' about remedy and liability, Lord Brown held there had been no tort at all. For him, the majority decision about *remedy* entailed that the claimant had not actually been falsely imprisoned.

Others agree that right and remedy are linked, rejecting the other half of the equation. The Irish Court of Appeal agrees that it would 'negate' liability to refuse substantial damages. In Murray J's view however, the approach to *loss* was therefore mistaken. Although the English and Australian courts believed they were applying an orthodox loss-based analysis this was questionable.[105] The defendants had been found to have imprisoned the claimants unlawfully. But when the courts assessed damages, they shifted to assuming that the defendant would have acted *lawfully*. This 'new normative hypothesis' had no analogue anywhere else in tort law – rather a 'contradiction' when the 'professed object ... is to *align*' the approaches.[106] The approach was not

---

[100] ibid [43] (Gordon J).
[101] *Lumba* (n 71) [71].
[102] Varuhas (n 6) 157, 169 (emphasis added).
[103] *Lumba* (h 71) [344].
[104] ibid [343].
[105] *GE* (n 89) [48].
[106] ibid [92].

merely novel (unprecedented prior to *Lumba*).¹⁰⁷ It was for Murray J dangerously incorrect. To assume that if the government had not acted unlawfully it would have complied with the law was a 'fiction' ignoring the illegality at the tort's core.¹⁰⁸ ('False' imprisonment connotes *illegal* imprisonment, not 'mendacity'.)¹⁰⁹ The right protected is freedom from *unlawful* detention. Requiring the court 'to ignore the illegality in its assessment of damages' cannot be 'reconciled with the essential objective of the cause of action'.¹¹⁰ For Varuhas, the way *Lumba* has been applied¹¹¹ 'turns the tort on its head: the starting presumption in favour of liberty, is supplanted by an irrebuttable presumption of legality in favour of government' when the court turns to the assessment of damages.¹¹²

The Irish court upheld the tort's traditional strictness and took a broader view of compensation.¹¹³ Although the 'loss principle' had 'sound logic' behind it, it was a mistake to apply it with 'unyielding rigidity': tort law has evolved rather untidily, providing different actions for 'particular exigencies'. The correct question is whether a remedy would meaningfully advance the object of a particular cause of action – 'excessive focus upon abstract theory' could 'obscure [that] reality'. False imprisonment required substantial – not nominal – damages.¹¹⁴

Nominal Damages

The *Lumba* debate reveals deep disagreement whether nominal damages afford sufficient vindication of the right to liberty in false imprisonment. Among the minority, favouring the award of substantial damages, Baroness Hale asserted that 'a modest conventional sum' was necessary 'to mark the law's recognition that a wrong has been done' and that an important right has been invaded, even in the absence of loss.¹¹⁵ The award would also 'encourage all concerned to avoid anything like it happening again' (although Lady Hale also stated that it was not 'exemplary' damages and did not purport to punish). Lord Hope emphasised that the defendant officials' behaviour in *Lumba* had been 'deplorable', 'a serious abuse of power'; 'It is not enough merely to declare that this was so'.¹¹⁶ Lord Hope also insisted, however, that the award was not

---

¹⁰⁷ ibid [86].
¹⁰⁸ ibid [84].
¹⁰⁹ *R (Jollah) v Home Secretary* [2019] 1 WLR 394 [43]–[44].
¹¹⁰ *GE* (n 89) [71].
¹¹¹ *Parker v Chief Constable of Essex* [2018] EWCA Civ 2788 (criticised: *Lewis* (n 80) [182]).
¹¹² Varuhas (n 6) 251.
¹¹³ *GE* (n 89) [102]–[103].
¹¹⁴ ibid [152].
¹¹⁵ *Lumba* (n 71) [212]–[217].
¹¹⁶ ibid [176].

exemplary damages. It 'should do no more than afford some recognition of the wrong done, without being nominal or derisory'.[117] Noting the equivocation, and pre-*Lumba* authorities holding it duplicative to award *both* 'vindicatory' *and* exemplary damages,[118] Vanessa Wilcox concludes that they are in fact one and the same – 'monozygotic [or "identical"] twins'.[119] At least any difference is a matter of emphasis rather than real substance. But it would be better to 'call a spade a spade' and recognise, with Lord Collins in *Lumba*, that 'In truth … vindicatory damages are akin to punitive or exemplary damages'.[120]

For Varuhas however, the routine award of substantial compensation for 'normative damage', even in the absence of actual loss, is the 'golden thread' running through the trespassory torts – showing their engrained concern with *vindication*.[121] For example, in *Plenty v Dillon* police officers entered private land without lawful authority. The High Court of Australia scorned the idea that the trespass was 'trifling' or that absenting physical damage to the land, damages must be nominal.[122] Substantial damages were needed to vindicate the claimant's property rights. 'Social disorder' (even 'anarchy') would result unless 'effective remedies' protected unlawful invasion of rights (especially by government officials). Law would become 'meaningless rhetoric' if it lacked 'effective sanctions'.[123]

A common theme equates nominal with 'derisory' damages. But is this correct? First, we could try to distinguish nominal damages, awarded to symbolise a wrong done, from the award of

> such a conspicuously trifling sum that [the judge] thereby expresses contempt for the plaintiff who was such a stickler for his rights that he insisted on upholding them expensively and painfully in court even when the defendant's violation of them caused him no loss.[124]

But can the distinction between awarding £1 and one penny (the smallest coin of the realm) bear such weight? If a penny 'expresses contempt' then does one pound really express ringing confidence in the claimant's rights?[125] Sadie Blanchard suggests that it might.[126] A court decision making objective findings

---

[117] ibid [180].
[118] *Attorney General of Trinidad and Tobago v Ramanoop* [2005] UKPC 15 [19]; *Takitota v Attorney General (Bahamas)* [2009] UKPC 11 [13].
[119] V Wilcox, 'Vindicatory Damages: The Farewell?' (2012) 3 *JETL* 390.
[120] *Lumba* (n 71) [233].
[121] Varuhas (n 59).
[122] (1991) 98 ALR 353.
[123] ibid 367 (Gaudron and McHugh JJ).
[124] J Gardner, 'Torts and Other Wrongs' (2011) 39 *Florida State Univ LR* 43, 57.
[125] Cf *Wright v McCormack* [2022] EWHC 2068 (QB) (award of £1 'nominal damages' when it would be 'unconscionable' to award substantial damages for the (proven) significant harm to libel claimant's reputation *because he had advanced a deliberately false case* to the court).
[126] S Blanchard, 'Nominal Damages as Vindication' (2022) 29 *George Mason LR* (forthcoming).

of fact, assessing the parties' conduct against the relevant legal norms and ruling in the claimant's favour, has a potent effect on the parties' public reputation, irrespective of whether substantial damages are awarded. Blanchard cites the argument that explicitly judgemental company law 'sermons' have a powerful effect on shaping conduct of company directors and others, despite the frequent absence of any tangible personal sanction imposed by the court on such actors (given the prevalence of comprehensive liability insurance).[127] It may be too simplistic to assert that only through the award of *substantial* damages can the law perform its 'expressive' and 'behaviour-guiding' functions.

However, the concern remains that nominal damages will fail to deter persons inclined to commit torts. They might even see nominal damages as a price worth paying for unlawful conduct. Edelman recounts the story of Lucius Veratius who walked around Rome slapping people, then paying them the (by then trivial) sums laid down for assault in Roman law's ancient Twelve Tables![128] While Lucius certainly discharged a secondary legal obligation to remedy his delicts, nobody could find his behaviour satisfactory. Rather his legend shows a legal system being exposed to derision, impotent to protect citizens' rights not to be assaulted. In one old English case, Gibbs CJ accordingly upheld a trespass damages award challenged as 'excessive'. He refused to limit damages to the plaintiff's 'absolute pecuniary damage'.[129] Gibbs CJ gave an example reminiscent of Lucius Veratius:

> Suppose a gentleman has a paved walk in his paddock, before his window, and that a man intrudes and walks up and down before the window of his house, and looks in while the owner is at dinner, is the trespasser to be permitted to say, "here is a halfpenny for you, which is the full extent of all the mischief I have done?"

A modern US case cites *Merest v Harvey* with approval. 'Society has an interest in preserving the integrity of the legal system' which extends to deterrence of trespasses involving 'utter disregard' for the claimant's rights, even when they cause no material loss.[130] Sadie Blanchard, as seen, disagrees with Judge Richard Posner's view that nominal damages are 'mysterious', of 'negligible value' and potentially open claimants up to ridicule.[131] Even Blanchard, however, accepts that sometimes a nominal award is not enough. When a defendant like Steenberg Homes Inc appears insensitive to the reputational effects of a judgment for nominal damages, it may be necessary to award

---

[127] EB Rock, 'Saints and Sinners: How Does Delaware Corporate Law Work?' (1997) 44 *UCLA LR* 1009.

[128] J Edelman, 'Vindicatory Damages' in K Barker et al (eds), *Private Law in the 21st Century* (Oxford, Hart, 2017).

[129] *Merest v Harvey* (1814) 5 Taunton 442.

[130] *Jacque v Steenberg Homes Inc* 209 Wis. 2d 605 (1997). See ch 11, 'Information Theory in Nuisance and Trespass: Clear Rules and "Coasian" Bargaining'.

[131] *Moore v Liszewski* 838 F 3d 877 (2016).

exemplary damages to rectify their open defiance of social norms. 'Punitives are for the shameless'.[132] Scott Hershovitz argues that like tort law as a whole, exemplary damages have a primarily 'expressive' function – declaring what rights claimants have, and the wrongfulness of the defendant violating them.[133] In particular, exemplary damages are not assessed in line with economic theories of 'optimal deterrence' – for example, they are not multiplied to correct for 'under-enforcement' in situations where tort claims are unlikely to be made in practice. Rather, exemplary damages are imposed to mark judicial condemnation of egregiously wrongful conduct.

Even assuming that 'ordinary' compensation for a light, painless slap from a modern-day Lucius Veratius would be nominal, other remedies might certainly be available too. Lucius' behaviour epitomises the high-handed arrogance that would attract an additional award of aggravated damages for the affront of deliberate wrongdoing.[134] It might satisfy English law's solitary category of exemplary damages against *private* defendants: calculating that a tort will be profitable after paying compensation. The law surcharges exemplary damages precisely to teach the defendant that 'tort does not pay'.[135] While Lucius probably derived sadistic pleasure rather than cash profits from his slapping-and-paying, such a 'gain' arguably qualifies. (In *Merest v Harvey*, decided when exemplary damages were more freely available, Heath J even justified their award 'to prevent the practice of duelling'.) Note that exceptionally, exemplary damages remain *generally* available against *government* defendants where their conduct deserves the court's condemnation. As seen, some argue that the minority support for 'vindicatory damages' in *Lumba* 'depended on considerations that were very closely associated with exemplary damages'.[136]

The court could also award the claimant's full legal costs against the defendant on the punitive 'indemnity' basis, ensuring that 'vindication of a right comes at no cost to the [claimant]'.[137] Finally, a determined repeated tortfeasor could be restrained by injunction.

Vindication by Declaration?

Should *damages* be the focus? Kit Barker argues that private law does not require a novel category of substantial 'vindicatory' damages.[138] Reasons for vindication include the educational and symbolic mission of 'norm projection

---

[132] Blanchard (n 126).

[133] S Hershovitz, 'Treating Wrongs as Wrongs: An Expressive Argument for Tort Law' (2017) 10 *Jo Tort L* 405.

[134] *Rookes v Barnard* [1964] AC 1129.

[135] *Broome v Cassell & Co* [1972] AC 1027, 1073 (Lord Hailsham LC).

[136] *Lewis* (n 80) [175] (Edelman J).

[137] ibid [120] (Gordon J).

[138] K Barker, 'Public and Private: The Mixed Conception of Vindication in Torts and Private Law' in SGA Pitel et al (eds), *Tort Law: Challenging Orthodoxy* (Oxford, Hart, 2013).

and reinforcement' and the deterrence of wrongdoing. More fundamentally, any functioning system for protecting legal rights requires a process of institutional announcements about their infringement. Barker argues that a *reasoned declaratory judgment* is the better vehicle. Using money as a 'symbol' is problematic. The level of damages is an ambiguous signal, apt to be misinterpreted. As seen, some attempt to distinguish a separate category of 'contemptuous damages' but the distinction with a 'nominal' £1 is not easy to draw or to understand.

Barker also queries the difference between the nominal £1 awarded in *Lumba* and the minority judges' preferred 'modest' substantial damages (variously £1,000, £500 or even less). Given such ambiguities, Barker argues that nominal damages should no longer be awarded as a vindicatory remedy. Instead courts should issue reasoned declarations that a tort has been committed (right invaded). These will be more informative – and do a better job of vindicating rights – than the bare award of damages: 'Money is a powerful incentive, but an inarticulate mode of expression'.[139] By contrast, we would not expect the courts to mince their words when identifying and condemning serious invasions of rights. Let those words speak, not money.

There is much to be said for this. In *Lumba* Lord Kerr observed that the court's finding of liability, 'the unambiguous recognition and declaration by the law that an individual has been falsely imprisoned', was itself vindicatory (irrespective of whether compensation was also awarded).[140] False imprisonment was therefore not (in his view) 'devalued' by the award of nominal damages. Moreover, *pace* Lady Hale, the wrong was sufficiently 'marked' and 'emphatic recognition of the seriousness of the defendant's default' made without awarding substantial damages. 'The defendant's failures have been thoroughly examined and exposed.'[141]

A similar notion of vindication through hearing and judgment underlies *Ashley v Chief Constable*. The House of Lords permitted a battery claim to go to trial despite the defendant's full admission of liability for the claimant's death *in negligence*.[142] That admission entitled the claimants to full compensation. Thus the defendant objected – what purpose would a trial of the battery claim serve? The claimants could recover no greater sum (the chief constable having conceded liability for compensatory *and* aggravated damages). But as Lord Scott asked: 'How is the deceased Mr Ashley's right not to be subjected to a violent and deadly attack to be vindicated if the claim for assault and battery, a claim that the chief constable has steadfastly and consistently disputed, is not allowed to proceed?'[143] He thought the claimants were entitled to

---

[139] ibid 84. Cf Hershovitz (n 133) 431 ('money is not just a medium of exchange; it is also a medium for sending messages').
[140] *Lumba* (n 71) [252].
[141] ibid [256].
[142] [2008] 1 AC 962.
[143] ibid [22].

seek 'a public admission or finding that the deceased Mr Ashley was unlawfully killed'.¹⁴⁴ Lord Scott noted how 'the chief constable has gone to considerable lengths to try to avoid the possibility of an adverse finding' in the battery claim (namely the sweeping admission of liability in negligence).¹⁴⁵

Priel has accordingly suggested a specifically 'public role' for the trespassory torts. They facilitate judicial scrutiny of alleged government unlawfulness – its public trial should not be defeated by admission of liability on other grounds.¹⁴⁶ Priel notes that in such intentional torts claims, the courts make an exception to their usual hostility towards hypothetical litigation.¹⁴⁷ The *Ashley* majority rejected the suggestion that the battery claim was merely 'academic'.¹⁴⁸ Lord Neuberger, although dissenting, accepted tort's 'ombudsman' role: 'the publicity resulting from an action … may do most to protect rights'.¹⁴⁹ Lord Carswell, however, disagreed:

> the civil courts exist to award compensation, not to conduct public inquiries. Nor is it their function to provide explanations … On the contrary, the existence of a sanction by way of damages is the essential mark of a tort.¹⁵⁰

In defamation, damages have long been awarded to vindicate and restore the claimant's reputation. Very substantial awards are routinely made even when a libel has not caused any material (ie economic) loss. Again however, the emphasis on vindicatory *damages* has been questioned. Arguably it reflects the historical position whereby libel cases were decided by juries – a process that continued much longer than in other torts (eg negligence), ceasing only after the Defamation Act 2013.¹⁵¹ Juries decided liability and assessed damages but did not give *reasoned judgments* – only a bare unreasoned 'verdict'. (As is familiar from criminal law – the jury announces 'guilty or not guilty?', but does not explain *why*.) In such a system the quantum of damages has to do all the talking – there was literally nothing else the libel jury could say. This has now changed. As elsewhere in tort, judges decide defamation cases and give full reasons. Indeed, the court can now order the defendant to publish a summary of its judgment as an additional remedy.¹⁵² But the practice of reasoned judgments has not superseded 'vindicatory damages' here altogether. In the first

---

¹⁴⁴ ibid [23] (and cf [33] 'unimportant' whether 'vindication should be marked by an award of vindicatory damages or simply a declaration of liability').
¹⁴⁵ ibid. Lord Carswell at [78] noted 'the Government has declined to order a public inquiry'.
¹⁴⁶ Priel (n 4).
¹⁴⁷ Compare eg *R (Rusbridger) v Attorney General* [2004] 1 AC 357.
¹⁴⁸ Eg *Ashley* (n 142) [68]–[71] Lord Rodger.
¹⁴⁹ ibid [115] citing *Clerk & Lindsell on Torts*, 19th edn (London, Sweet & Maxwell, 2006), paras 1–10.
¹⁵⁰ *Ashley* (n 142) [81].
¹⁵¹ *Yeo v Times Newspapers* [2015] 1 WLR 971.
¹⁵² Defamation Act 2013, s 11.

case ordering publication of a judgment, the court also awarded £185,000 'to convince any fair-minded bystander of the baselessness of the [libel]'.[153] While accepting that publication of a vindicatory statement could reduce damages, Sir David Eady reasoned that casual readers of the original libel, if they took any interest in the subsequent litigation, would still ask the question 'how much did the claimant get in damages?' Defamation law does not accept Barker's argument that a reasoned decision is always, of itself, sufficient vindication for the invasion of the right to reputation.[154]

Rights and Loss

Finally we discuss another challenge to the proposed new head of substantial 'vindicatory' (or 'normative') tort damages. Descheemaeker argues that a binary choice must be made: the law can either 'intrinsically' remedy the invasion of rights, or it can compensate losses caused by such an invasion, but *not both*. These are (Descheemaeker claims) logically incompatible. To award both means 'double counting' (remedying the wrong twice, risking overcompensation). There is, he suggests, 'absurdity' in awarding damages for (eg) 'distress, pecuniary loss *and* loss of privacy'.[155] Yet the courts have done precisely that.

When the privacy of three minors was invaded, two were infants (under a year old) and recovered £2,500 each while the third (aged 16) recovered £5,000: *Weller v Associated Newspapers*. The difference, apparently, was that the babies had suffered 'no embarrassment' (obviously such young children could not be aware of the publication) whereas the teenage claimant had.[156] In Descheemaeker's view, the award to the blissfully ignorant infants must have remedied their invaded privacy per se; for the teenaged claimant, damages were for her mental distress. Thus both 'logics' were used in the same case. Descheemaeker accepts that given the 'arbitrary amounts' awarded *both* for mental distress and for invasion of rights it is difficult to assess whether 'double counting' has taken place. In some situations the choice of approach is vital. Certain claimants cannot be distressed by a tort but can still have their rights invaded: the very young, comatose persons, or corporations. However, Descheemaeker complains that English law 'meanders' between the fundamentally distinct approaches. Although compensation of loss is the dominant paradigm, sympathetic courts frequently switch to 'abstract definition of wrong-as-loss in order to grant substantial damages to the claimant' who has

---

[153] *Rahman v ARY Network* [2016] EWHC 3570 (QB).
[154] See further Wilcox (n 119) 395–96 (earlier debates about vindication by judge-only trial, and reasoned judgments, when juries unavailable during World War II).
[155] Descheemaeker (n 78) 608 (fn 49).
[156] [2014] EWHC 1163 (QB), [189]–[197].

not suffered any material loss. The result is an 'unstable equilibrium between two incompatible logics'.[157]

Descheemaeker identifies an important issue. *Every* tort involves an 'invasion of right' in some sense. The law would be destabilised if every violation justified the award of substantial damages *in addition* to any compensation for actual, concrete loss. Lord Dyson rejected 'vindicatory damages' in *Lumba* for this reason.[158] Even the *Weller* court noted the risk of 'double counting'.[159] The risk is diminished if 'vindicatory damages' are available only in certain torts. There is clear authority that in claims for misuse of private information, compensation 'can be given for the commission of the wrong itself' and 'to reflect infringements of the right itself'.[160] Lord Leggatt comments:

> The privacy tort, like other torts for which damages may be awarded without proof of material damage or distress, is a tort involving strict liability for deliberate acts, not a tort based on a want of care.[161]

Thus while substantial vindicatory damages have a place in torts such as trespass (deliberate infringements of rights), the remedy cannot be read across into torts involving negligent infliction of loss. This variegated picture chimes with Murray J's view that tort law 'has not always developed in straight lines towards neatly defined and symmetrically proportioned categories', and different actions may require different approaches.[162] Rights and loss have often been run together in English law. But a renewed emphasis on vindication, including the controversy around *Lumba* which undermines that function in false imprisonment, means such debates will flourish in coming years.

Debate 3
Trespass and 'Constitutional Rights'

Trespass plays an important constitutional role. Its strength, but also its limits, are illustrated by the distinction with other parts of tort law. The rights covered by trespass are deep-rooted, well-protected, and apply against all who infringe them – that is, against public officials as much as private individuals. Hence Weir's insistence that the trespassory torts protect the foundations of individual liberty in English law. Stevens argues that tort enforces our true 'human rights' – those that every individual has by virtue simply of being human, protected against all comers. By contrast modern 'human rights' (which Stevens suggests should be called state or civil rights) involve

---

[157] Descheemaeker (n 78) 608, 610.
[158] *Lumba* (n 71) [101].
[159] *Weller* (n 156) [191].
[160] *Gulati v MGN Ltd* [2016] FSR 12 [111], [114] (Mann J) (affirmed [2017] QB 149).
[161] *Lloyd v Google* [2021] 3 WLR 1268 [133].
[162] *GE* (n 89) [102].

claims against the state to a range of goods 'as many and varied as the wit of human imagination permits', coined by legislatures using arguments of public policy.[163] The extent of ECHR rights' 'horizontal effect' (against other individuals) remains an important controversy about the Human Rights Act 1998 (HRA). By contrast tort is applicable equally to public and private defendants in the 'Diceyan' tradition.[164] Weir praised the trespassory torts' ability to 'trip up' 'the officious citizen' – as well as 'the zealous bureaucrat [and] the eager policeman'.[165]

But trespass has drawbacks too. The strong and deep protection is limited in scope. Tort law as a whole is flexible – of *negligence*, Lord Macmillan famously remarked that 'the categories ... are never closed' (given the 'manifold' nature of 'human errancy').[166] By contrast the categories of torts actionable per se *are* closed, or certainly much less fluid. This will be seen in *Watkins v Home Office*, discussed below. Why should trespass be limited to its historic concern with direct physical invasions of rights? Buxton LJ reasoned that the advantages enjoyed by a trespass claimant[167] provided 'strong policy reasons why the tort of trespass to the person should be limited to its proper sphere'.[168]

The boundaries of trespass show the limits of the common law tradition, in which tort law plays the leading role in protection of rights against government interference. Not everything that the government may wish to do to its citizens involves a tort. Much does, and in such cases trespass can vindicate liberty effectively. Significantly, most of what the police force do to unwilling members of the public will prima facie be tortious, for example touching (battery) in the course of arrest, or confinement (false imprisonment) or physical intrusion on land and goods when carrying out searches. As seen, the onus is strictly on the police to show legal authority for what they do, or some other defence. There is no general defence to be found in the elastic (and oppressive) concept of 'state necessity' as the great case of *Entick v Carrington* established (trespass to land and goods).[169] But all this heroic protection fades away in the absence of a recognised cause of action in tort. Thus, in the pre-HRA era, the police were not liable when tapping private telephone conversations without legal authority: their conduct was not tortious and there was no need to show any authority.[170] In *Wainwright v Home Office*, again in the absence of

---

[163] R Stevens, 'The Conflict of Rights' in A Robertson and TH Wu (eds), *The Goals of Private Law* (Oxford, Hart, 2009) 145, 163.

[164] *Robinson v Chief Constable* [2018] AC 736 [33] (Lord Reed).

[165] Weir (n 2) at 322.

[166] *Donoghue v Stevenson* [1932] AC 562, 619.

[167] Viz actionability per se; no need to establish 'fair, just and reasonable' duty of care; and more generous 'remoteness' rules.

[168] *Wainwright v Home Office* [2002] QB 1334, [69]–[71].

[169] n 55.

[170] *Malone v Metropolitan Police Commissioner* [1979] Ch 344.

a common law tort of privacy invasion, there was nothing tortious about a strip search in the absence of physical contact (battery).[171] It was therefore irrelevant that the prison officers, by not following correct procedures, had exceeded their authority under the Prison Rules. The European Court of Human Rights held in each case that English law was deficient in its protection of fundamental rights of privacy, because of the gaps in the law of torts.[172]

Even when a tort exists, it may not provide the full protection afforded by trespass. The tort of misfeasance in public office has a significant potential role in sanctioning deliberately unlawful behaviour (it is a double exception to the principles that tort law applies to public and private defendants alike, and that bad motive cannot of itself generate liability). Yet unlike trespass, the misfeasance tort is not actionable per se. This limits its usefulness, as the leading case shows. In *Watkins v Home Secretary* prison officers had read correspondence between the claimant and his solicitors, in knowing breach of the Prison Rules. This behaviour caused the claimant no tangible loss (economic, physical or otherwise). The claimant submitted that this was irrelevant because an important right had been infringed. The Court of Appeal agreed.[173] Confidential communication with legal advisers, an aspect of the right of access to the courts, was a fundamental right. Knowingly to intercept such correspondence should be actionable even if no harm resulted. Laws LJ reasoned that constitutional rights were the 'paradigm' of '[the] kind which the law protects without proof of any loss'.[174] Yet the House of Lords disagreed.[175] A clear line of authority held that actual loss had to be shown as the 'gist of an action' for misfeasance in public office. In the absence of tangible loss, the claim therefore failed (and Mr Watkins' claim for exemplary damages failed with it: there was no liability on which to hang an exemplary award).

Watkins v Home Secretary contains notably open discussion about actionability per se – the hallmark of the trespassory torts. Lord Carswell thought it 'theoretically possible' to abolish the requirement of damage altogether: 'It might not unreasonably be said that any civil wrong should carry damages'. However, such a bold step of making all torts actionable per se should be for the Law Commission to consider.[176] Lord Walker (who concurred reluctantly) noted the greater potential for *intentional* torts (including misfeasance in public office) to be actionable per se.[177] The law lords' hesitancy reflects Stevens' observation that 'it is difficult to find a single principle with identifies those wrongs which require proof of loss before they are actionable', even though the

---

[171] [2004] 2 AC 406.
[172] *Malone v UK* (1985) 7 EHRR 14; *Wainwright v UK* (2007) 44 EHRR 40.
[173] [2005] QB 883.
[174] ibid [67].
[175] [2006] 2 AC 395.
[176] ibid [80]–[82].
[177] ibid [72].

classification of torts actionable per se 'should reflect a choice between those rights which are, and are not, as a question of social fact sufficiently important to be deserving of protection irrespective of the consequences of violation'.[178] On *Watkins* itself, Stevens approves the House of Lords' decision. Misfeasance does not relate to particular genuine rights, the 'constitutional rights' relied on by the Court of Appeal being 'too uncertain to be an appropriate guide'.[179]

In *Watkins* Lord Bingham declared 'the primary role of the law of tort is to provide compensation for those who have suffered material damage rather than to vindicate the rights of those who have not'.[180] (As Varuhas points out, this 'explicitly conflated negligence's principal function with that of all torts'.)[181] Lord Bingham thought that adequate alternative mechanisms existed to hold public officials accountable if they violated rights without inflicting 'material damage'. These included disciplinary sanctions, judicial review and criminal prosecution.[182] Moreover he reasoned that Parliament envisaged that violations of constitutional rights should be remedied using the HRA 1998, 'not by development of parallel remedies' in domestic tort law.[183] Lord Rodger thought the whole category of common law 'constitutional rights' had been superseded by the HRA. Previously, courts had made 'heroic efforts' to discover such rights in domestic law: but such 'means of incorporation [of the ECHR into English law] *avant la lettre*' were no longer necessary following enactment of the HRA.[184]

Lord Walker appeared sympathetic to generalising the trespassory torts' vindicatory function. Mr Watkins had suffered a 'deliberate affront' by having his correspondence read in knowing breach of the rules. Yet 'whereas even the most trifling and transient physical assault would undoubtedly have given [him] a cause of action in private law for trespass to the person', he had no tort remedy here.[185] (As Lord Walker noted, 'a far cry from the stirring language of Holt CJ in *Ashby v White*'.)[186] However the rest of the House of Lords in *Watkins* distinguished trespass sharply. Other mechanisms, most prominently the HRA, were now preferable to control public authorities and vindicate rights. Which view is correct?

Bills of Rights, such as the ECHR, clearly list individuals' rights and freedoms. They have declaratory power. They are a prominent explicit political

---

[178] Stevens (n 19) 89.
[179] ibid 90.
[180] [2006] 2 AC 395, [9].
[181] Varuhas (n 6) 165.
[182] Cf Lord Walker, *Watkins* (n 175) at [69] ('rather sceptical' about these alternative remedies' effectiveness).
[183] ibid [26].
[184] ibid [64]. Compare generally M Elliott and K Hughes (eds), *Common Law Constitutional Rights* (Oxford, Hart, 2020).
[185] (n 175) [68].
[186] (1703) 1 Sm LC (13th edn) 253.

statement of the most vital human interests according to contemporary perceptions. Despite Stevens' jibes, these typically comprise the interests central to classic tort law (eg life, liberty, possessions) as well as many others that tort does not protect straightforwardly or at all (privacy; freedom of speech, religion and association; non-discrimination). Naturally such declarations evolve with time and may be amended. Rights to 'peaceful enjoyment of possessions', education and free elections were added in the ECHR's First Protocol (1952): none of these seems a whimsical flight of imagination. Contrast the relatively static nature of tort law. It also acts more quietly. The trespassory torts powerfully protect intrinsic human goods. While this might be obvious to tort scholars, tort law does not proclaim its rights with the same fanfare as the ECHR. It scarcely has the same status in public and political discourse. As Priel notes, the common law was never in the business of going around declaring abstract rights of any kind.[187] The courts historically placed remedies and actions first: and working back from that concrete protection, the rights may be said to have emerged indirectly. Sprinkled with the intellectual stardust of Latin: *ubi remedium, ibi ius*.

Some would defend the wisdom of the common law. The problem with abstract declarations is that they often promise more than they deliver. Appearances can deceive. The 1977 USSR Constitution contained one of the most impressive lists of individual civil and political rights in the world. But these were essentially meaningless – in practice unenforceable because no mechanisms (such as independent courts) existed for individuals to exercise them. That sounds like an extreme case.[188] But recall that although Britain was the first state to sign the ECHR in 1950, only 50 years later was the ECHR enforceable *in domestic UK courts* (when the HRA 1998 came into force). At time of writing (2022) the Government is contemplating significant reforms to the 1998 system.[189] Better, perhaps, to guarantee protection by real remedies arising from the long history of the common law – which it would be very difficult for a hostile government to suspend or repeal. Dicey claimed 'nothing less than a revolution' would be required to destroy rights 'inherent in the ordinary law of the land'.[190] There could yet be value in tort law's traditional constitutional role.

---

[187] Priel (n 4) 194.

[188] NB AV Dicey, *Introduction to the Study of the Law of the Constitution* 8th edn (London, Macmillan, 1915) 117 thought that 'foreign constitutionalists' generally had placed too much emphasis on abstract rights and 'insufficient attention on the absolute necessity for the provision of adequate remedies' to enforce them.

[189] Ministry of Justice, *A Modern Bill of Rights: A consultation to reform the Human Rights Act 1998* (CP 588, 2021).

[190] Dicey (n 188) 120.

Debate 4
'Informed Medical Consent' – Which Tort?

The trespassory torts have a curiously limited role concerning consent to medical procedures. Doctors have a *duty of care* to inform patients about the risks of contemplated/recommended medical procedures. The landmark decision in *Montgomery v Lanarkshire Health Board* established that it is for the court to decide whether sufficient information was given for an informed choice to be made by the patient.[191] Baroness Hale said the restated law protects patients' 'autonomy, their freedom to decide what shall and shall not be done with their body'.[192] For as Lord Donaldson MR previously observed:

> Prima facie, in the absence of consent all, or almost all, medical treatment and all surgical treatment of an adult is unlawful, however beneficial such treatment might be. This is incontestable.[193]

The curiosity is that these rights are protected within the framework of *negligence*. It might seem more natural for a patients who did not give full (informed) consent to a procedure to claim in *battery*. Cardozo J once stated:

> Every human being of adult years and sound mind has a right to determine what shall be done with his own body; and a surgeon who performs an operation without his patient's consent commits an assault.[194]

As Lord Goff accepted, 'we have to bear well in mind [Cardozo J's] libertarian principle of self-determination'.[195] Why then does English law deal with the issue of informed consent within negligence? Should we rely instead upon trespass to protect 'patient autonomy'? Are there practical implications or is this simply an abstract question about classification?

That negligence is the appropriate claim is well established in English law:

> once the patient is informed in broad terms of the nature of the procedure which is intended, and gives her consent, that consent is real, and the cause of the action on which to base a claim for failure to go into risks and implications is negligence, not trespass.[196]

Lord Diplock traced the rule back at least to 1767 (when a trespass claim for surgical injuries was dismissed 'with scant sympathy'): in his view, all aspects of

---

[191] [2015] AC 1430.
[192] ibid [108].
[193] *In Re F (Mental Patient: Sterilisation)* [1990] 2 AC 1, 12.
[194] *Schloendorff v Society of New York Hospital* (1914) 105 NE 92, 93.
[195] *In Re F* (n 193) 73.
[196] *Chatterton v Gerson* [1981] QB 432, 443.

doctors' duties to patients fall within negligence.[197] Lord Scarman thought 'it would be deplorable to base the law in medical cases of this kind on the torts of assault and battery'.[198]

No *reason* apart from precedent appears from these unequivocal statements. Could one unstated concern be *criminal* not tortious liability? Imagine that a doctor surgically removes a diseased organ. Imagine further that the patient was given insufficiently detailed information about the risks of the operation. Does that mean that the patient did not (and could not) validly consent? If not, it seems that the doctor would be guilty of exceptionally serious crimes: wounding with intent to do grievous bodily harm.[199] For the only thing that legally distinguishes a surgical incision from a pub-brawl stabbing is the patient's *consent* to being cut open. In the criminal context, recognising patient consent when risks were explained 'in broad terms' makes obvious good sense. A doctor's failure to be insufficiently detailed might disrespect patients' autonomy and dignity, but that is far removed from an offence with a sentencing range of three to 16 years' custody (Sentencing Council guidelines for section 18). If this is the reason for the 'negligence' classification, then could it be addressed by formally separating tort and crime at this point,[200] or at least using different labels? Beever argues that traditional tort terminology's 'connection with the criminal law' involves 'connotations that do not readily apply to surgeons acting in what they consider to be the best interests of their patients'.[201]

Nevertheless, Beever maintains that trespass to the person should be the proper action: battery vindicates patients' rights to autonomy over their bodies in a way that negligence does not and cannot.[202] Damage is the gist of the action in negligence. That confines its use to situations where a doctor 'carelessly' omits to provide sufficient information *and* that failure causes the patient to sustain an injury – for example where, had she been informed, the patient would not have proceeded with treatment which has caused side-effects or complications. (*Montgomery* is a clear example.) But what if the patient would have gone ahead anyway? Or what if they would have refused, but the operation has actually been entirely successful? In neither case is there any *loss* necessary as the basis for a negligence claim.

The problem that Beever identifies has been faced by the courts but given rather an awkward solution. *Chester v Afshar* imposed negligence liability even though the claimant would still have had the operation, had she been warned of the risk of paralysis (which then, unfortunately, occurred). This was acknowledged as an exception to the normal rules on causation (since the

---

[197] *Sidaway v Bethlem Royal Hospital* [1985] AC 871, 892, 894.
[198] ibid 883.
[199] Offences against the Person Act 1861, s 18.
[200] Eg Tan Keng Feng, 'Failure of Medical Advice: Trespass or Negligence?' (1987) 7 *Legal Studies* 149 (defining consent differently in tort and crime).
[201] Beever (n 53)) 244.
[202] ibid ch 15.

failure to inform had not increased the risk of the side-effect occurring). The House of Lords majority thought such an exceptional approach necessary to 'vindicate' the 'autonomy and dignity' of a patient who had not given her 'informed consent to the surgery in the full legal sense'.[203] But this seems odd. Surely (as Beever says) the violation of that autonomy occurred as soon as the surgeon operated without the patient's full consent – and not at the later point when the 'gist damage' manifested itself as paralysis. A strong objection to *Chester v Afshar* is that it made the doctor liable for physical injuries that he did not cause in order to vindicate a different right – not a right to be protected against physical injury, but the right to choose.

Lord Hoffmann dissented. The majority's reasons did not justify their decision. A different wrong was at stake: 'Even though the failure to warn did not cause the patient any damage, it was an affront to her personality and leaves her feeling aggrieved'.[204] He wondered whether a '*solatium*' should be awarded (ie damages to soothe the affront), but concluded that 'the cost of litigation [makes] the law of torts an unsuitable vehicle for distributing the modest compensation'.[205] But that seems questionable. Lord Hoffmann surely cannot intend to doubt the actionability per se of trespass which causes no concrete harm. His reference to the 'ordinary principles of tort'[206] really means the ordinary principles of *negligence* law, where concrete loss is the gist of the action. If 'flawed consent' cases were viewed as battery rather than negligence claims, the remedy for invasion of rights that Lord Hoffmann dismissed as an expensive novelty would be available on ordinary principles.

Chester v Afshar did violence to the rules on causation of damage to ensure a damages remedy for the patient who suffered side-effects that the operation had not caused. What if the procedure is a total success? In negligence, no claim could be made. There would be no injury. It has been held 'contrary to principle' to award damages where an operation has turned out successfully, even if the patient did not give fully informed consent.[207] (Nor was the court willing to recognise a new, free-standing head of damages for 'invasion of autonomy'.)[208] Yet the violation of dignity and autonomy (when the doctor embarks on the procedure) is independent of the ultimate consequences. Tort law purports to protect patient autonomy to reject medical intervention 'however beneficial'. As Beever says, it fails to live up to its own pronouncements.

---

[203] [2005] 1 AC 134 [24] (Lord Steyn); see further [85] (Lord Hope).
[204] ibid [33].
[205] ibid [34].
[206] ibid [32].
[207] *Shaw v Kovac* [2017] 1 WLR 4773 [71] (Davis LJ).
[208] Discussed by C Purshouse, 'Autonomy, Affinity, and Assessment of Damages' (2017) 26 *Medical LR* 675 (concluding that autonomy is too 'nebulous', 'slippery' and 'over-inclusive' to constitute actionable damage in negligence – while criticising *Shaw v Kovac*'s 'scant' reasoning).

Negligence could generalise from *Rees v Darlington*, and treat 'invasion of autonomy' as compensable harm (ie as 'gist damage').[209] All informed consent cases could then be dealt with under the tort of negligence. But this approach was directly rejected in *Shaw v Kovac* (and implicitly by Lord Hoffmann in *Chester v Afshar*). The paradigm requiring concrete physical harm in negligence is hard to shift; examples to the contrary, like *Rees*, are deemed anomalous. Negligence focuses on protecting *welfare*, not *choices*. No wonder that tort did a poor job of protecting the patient's right to choose in *Chester*.[210] By contrast, trespass focuses on the invasion of rights. Non-consensual medical treatment would *in itself* attract substantial damages.[211] There is a strong argument for reviewing *Chatterton v Gerson* and reclassifying 'informed consent' cases as trespass to the person.[212] The emphasis would be vindication of patients' rights to make informed choices.

CONCLUSION: NEGLIGENCE AND TRESPASS DISTINGUISHED

Many accept the trespass torts' distinctive role in the vindication of certain rights. Their historical function still remains relevant. Arthur Ripstein defends the place of 'sovereignty torts'.[213] For Ripstein, tort law should address not just wrongful loss but also 'despotism' – whether of the state or other individuals. An example of 'private despotism' would be a dentist surreptitiously administering fluoride to a patient known to object to fluoridation. The dentist would usurp the patient's sovereign right to decide how their body is should be treated. More generally:

> Intentional touching is objectionable even if harmless or undetected, or the injury is small. Your person – your body – is yours to use for your own purposes, and if I take it upon myself to touch you without your permission I use it for a purpose you have not authorized. ... I violate your independence by using your powers for my purposes. ... Sovereignty can only be violated by the intentional deeds of others, because it is an interest in independence of those deeds.[214]

---

[209] *Rees v Darlington NHS Trust* [2004] 1 AC 309 (see ch 8, '"Loss of Autonomy" as Actionable Damage?').

[210] T Clark and D Nolan, 'A Critique of *Chester v Afshar*' (2014) 34 *OJLS* 659.

[211] *Lumba* (n 71) may enable a doctor to argue that the patient would (if informed) have given consent to reduce damages to nothing: see Debate 2.

[212] Cf Clark and Nolan (n 210) battery 'impractical and inappropriate' (not every case involves physical contact (eg prescribing drugs that patient self-administers); distinction between consent based on incomplete information and deceptive/wholly non-consensual medical treatment).

[213] A Ripstein, 'Beyond the Harm Principle' (2006) 34 *Philosophy & Public Affairs* 215.

[214] ibid 235, 239.

Ripstein thus justifies distinct tortious protection against intentional touching even in the absence of concrete loss. Stevens is also sensitive to the distinction:

> The division between wrongs actionable per se and those only actionable upon proof of consequential loss should reflect a choice between those rights which are, and are not, as a question of social fact sufficiently important to be deserving of protection irrespective of the consequences of violation.[215]

Further, as Keating says, when autonomy is at stake the defendant's fault in the invasion of the right is 'simply irrelevant' – 'the right itself would be fatally compromised by tolerating all reasonable (or justified)' invasions without the claimant's consent.[216]

Beever notes that identifying a right to 'bodily integrity' does not of itself explain tort law's complex pattern of protection.[217] That right is harmed by both a road accident and a punch in the face. It cannot explain tort law's sharp differences: the requirements of *carelessness* and *loss* in the road accident (negligence), requirements of *intended direct contact* for the punch (battery). Beever instead justifies the law's stricter protection against intentional touching because of its greater impact on the claimant's *freedom*. Someone who intentional invades the person (or property) of another asserts control over them. This is 'coercive' – a clear violation of the claimant's freedom.[218] Trespass epitomises 'torts of control' – unwanted kisses or kindly meant medical treatment are just as 'paradigmatic' here as conduct causing material harm. They violate the right to choose what happens to our bodies.[219] Doctrinally then, trespass's actionability per se is not anomalous but of vital importance. It protects against coercive behaviour, irrespective of actual loss. Beever finds trespass's requirement of a 'direct' physical invasion harder to justify, suggesting this malleable concept is applied to track 'control' of the claimant by the defendant.[220]

Negligence, he argues, is entirely different. Accidents do not involve *controlling* the claimant.[221] Rather, claimants are injured incidentally by defendants pursuing their own projects. In such situations, the freedom of claimants and the freedom of defendants must be balanced against each other. Broadly, by protecting claimants against loss which would deprive them of the means of pursuing their life projects.[222] It would be too restrictive of defendants' freedoms to impose strict liability for *all* accidental

---

[215] Stevens (n 19) 89.
[216] GC Keating, 'Is the Role of Tort to Repair Wrongful Losses?' in A Robertson and D Nolan (eds), *Rights and Private Law* (Oxford, Hart, 2012) 400.
[217] Beever (n 53) 2–3.
[218] ibid ch 2.
[219] ibid ch 4.
[220] ibid 61–67.
[221] ibid 54.
[222] ibid ch 2.

losses.[223] The common law's objective negligence standard balances claimants' and defendants' freedom.[224]

There are various ways to defend a distinct place for trespass. *Pace* Howarth's critique, affording greater protection for victims of intentional (or 'coercive' or 'controlling') behaviour may not merely be tort law's excuse for not making up its mind whether certain interests deserve legal protection or not.[225] (Howarth's thesis is that expansion of the interests protected against intentional violation follows from a restrictive law of negligence: pure economic loss being the central example, cf the intentional economic torts.) This chapter suggests the value of trespass protecting certain rights through strict liability and actionability per se. But the powerful negligence principle threatens to erode this function. In addition to the insidious 'genuine and reasonable belief' defences criticised by Weir, *Lumba* even allows defendants to argue 'if I hadn't have behaved unlawfully I'd have behaved lawfully' to bar a claim for substantial (rather than nominal) damages, even though the argument would be impermissible at the stage of *justifying* the trespass.

But in other areas, as debates above about consent to medical treatment suggest, trespass could be due for a renaissance – expanding from its traditional heartlands of physical restraint, search and seizure to protection of intangible interests of autonomy.

---

[223] ibid ch 1.
[224] ibid ch 3.
[225] D Howarth, 'Is There a Future for the Intentional Torts?' in PBH Birks (ed), *The Classification of Obligations* (Oxford, Clarendon, 1997).

PART II

Negligence

3

Negligence: Introduction

NEGLIGENCE AND RIGHTS

Negligence occupies the largest part of this work, as in most other books on tort. But it is deliberately not the book's first nor its only part – torts are more diverse in their doctrinal structure, aims and remedies. Negligence is here sandwiched between torts more overtly focused on rights: trespass and nuisance.

The previous chapter, on trespass, considered Weir's thesis that negligence has infiltrated those (and other) nominate torts.[1] The same could happen to nuisance, or at least parts of nuisance.[2] Or any other nominate tort.[3] An overlap is inevitable. Negligence is relatively formless – unified solely by the carelessness of the defendant's conduct. It is not limited to the protection of any particular interests. Famously, its categories are 'never closed'.[4] As Stevens comments, negligence is bound to cut across torts classified by the primary rights that they protect.[5] Indeed for Stevens, negligence's potential to respond to *any* carelessly-caused loss makes it incoherent: 'Because of the diverse rights which are actionable upon proof of the defendant's negligence, there is no "tort of negligence", anymore [sic] than there is a law of tort [singular]'. Negligence should be 'abandoned as an organizing idea'. It is a 'cuckoo in the nest'.[6]

As Stevens implies, however, the tort of negligence involves no more conceptual impossibility than 'the law of torts' itself. In his view, all 'torts' are invasions of primary rights (which makes tort law wholly 'parasitic' on those various rights, with 'little underlying unity').[7] The negligence tort could be defined in a similar way. Its 'unity' is, on examination, equally loose.

---

[1] T Weir, 'The Staggering March of Negligence' in P Cane and J Stapleton (eds), *The Law of Obligations: Essays in Celebration of John Fleming* (Oxford, Oxford University Press, 1998).
[2] eg *Leakey v National Trust* [1980] QB 485; C Gearty, 'The Place of Private Nuisance in a Modern Law of Tort' [1989] *CLJ* 214.
[3] eg *Spring v Guardian Assurance* [1995] 2 AC 296 (defamation).
[4] *Donoghue v Stevenson* [1932] AC 562, 619 (Lord Macmillan).
[5] R Stevens, *Torts and Rights* (Oxford, Oxford University Press, 2007) 296.
[6] ibid 296–303.
[7] ibid 299.

'Negligence' is merely an umbrella sheltering various legal rights not to have material loss carelessly caused us. (Reflecting the unifying conduct requirement (carelessness) and the need to prove causation of actionable damage – unlike trespass, negligence is not 'actionable per se'.) Stevens complains that structuring negligence around the defendant's culpable conduct 'takes the focus away from the underlying primary right'.[8] But law students soon learn that some types of severe, material loss are not actionable in negligence at all: 'the world is full of harm for which the law furnishes no remedy'.[9] This point has traditionally been given effect by defining the duty of care around particular interests (kinds of harm). Increasingly, 'actionable damage' is treated as a distinct issue.[10] Either way, the question of which rights negligence should protect is vital. It provides the running theme for this part of the book. We examine two pillars of negligence liability – causation and duty of care – and the most important kind of harm, personal injury.

Surprisingly often, causation forces to the surface questions about what interests tort law should protect. To circumvent difficulties in proving causation in the ordinary way, = claims are reformulated around an interest that the claimant *can* prove has been damaged. A clear example is the unsuccessful attempt to have 'loss of a chance' recognised as actionable damage.[11] We examine other theories of 'damage' invoked to explain or evade causal problems, including 'evidential damage', interrupting a claim against another defendant and 'market share' liability. As noted, duties of care are defined around particular kinds of damage (eg physical injury, psychiatric illness, pure economic loss):

> [duty] is inseparable from the damage which the plaintiff claims to have suffered from its breach. It is not a duty to take care in the abstract but a duty to avoid causing to the particular plaintiff damage of the particular kind which he has in fact sustained.[12]

Therefore the 'rights' question has always been implicit in the duty inquiry.

After the chapters on causation we turn to personal injury – tort's protection of a particularly precious interest. Negligence struggles with situations beyond 'classic' physical injuries (and the borders of those are less clear than might be assumed). Should it recognise claims in anticipation of future harm, to enable pre-emptive or prophylactic treatment? Negligence seems to find it particularly puzzling to classify claims about reproductive rights, emotional distress and mental illness. These fit awkwardly with the physical loss 'paradigm'.

---

[8] ibid 291–92.
[9] *JD v East Berkshire NHS Trust* [2005] 2 AC 373 [100] (Lord Rodger).
[10] *Meadows v Khan* [2022] AC 852 [31]–[32] (Lord Hodge and Lord Sales); cf [80] (Lord Burrows).
[11] *Gregg v Scott* [2005] 2 AC 176.
[12] *Caparo Industries v Dickman* [1990] 2 AC 605, 651 (Lord Oliver).

Given the innate conservatism of legal doctrine, this leads to systematic under-recognition of harms disproportionately suffered by women.

Greater attention on which rights (and whose rights) negligence should protect is needed. But having focused on the question, how do we decide whether there *should* be a right, and its appropriate scope? Rights theorists of tort (Stevens included) share a dislike of public interest concerns. We specifically examine the legitimacy of 'policy reasoning' in the duty of care. But the issue runs throughout the book. As gendered critiques of personal injury law emphasise,[13] the exclusive analysis of 'pure' doctrine conceals choices which affect victims of real-world injuries. Rights theorists would strenuously defend their theories' apolitical character. Their overriding concern is to exclude politically controversial questions from tort adjudication. The lesson of feminist critique is that superficially neutral doctrine can have effects that are anything but neutral – yet self-referential doctrinal reasoning seals itself off from such 'external' matters. Indeed, one critic of rights theories identifies a distinctly ideological scepticism of government.[14]

Whether rights theories are really 'right wing' (ie libertarian) is debatable.[15] But Priel is on to something when he criticises private law theorists for 'airily dismissing' the intense political debates about entitlements and duties, treating the answers as 'really self-evident and politically neutral'. On this view, rights theories do not remove politics from tort law but simply move questions about entitlements to a different stage of the inquiry.[16] At worst, they obscure the controversies inherent in questions about rights, duties and freedoms ('messengers who try to hide their message').

Tort as an Instrument of Social Policy

It is an equal and opposite error to eliminate rights from tort altogether. Negligence law seems prone to this. The tort awards compensation for material harm when the defendant acts unreasonably. It therefore offers potential to those seeking to remake tort: either as a system for *compensating* victims of accidents, or for *deterring* behaviour that causes accidents.[17] As discussed in chapter four on causation and corrective justice, this soon runs into irretrievable difficulties. Not only are the compensation and deterrence goals in tension with each other, the single-minded pursuit of either one of them directly contradicts tort's basic logic. Tort liability might have a compensatory or deterrent *effect* but that is incidental (albeit welcome), not the ultimate goal. 'Compensation'

---

[13] J Conaghan, 'Tort Law and Feminist Critique' [2003] *CLP* 175.
[14] D Priel, 'Torts, Rights, and Right-Wing Ideology' (2011) 19 *Torts LJ* 1 ('extreme, visceral, dislike for state institutions').
[15] See further ch 7, 'The Politics of Corrective Justice'.
[16] Cf Stevens (n 5) 350 ('serious objection' that rights-based approach is 'essentially empty').
[17] G Calabresi, *The Costs of Accidents* (New Haven, Yale University Press, 1970).

would destroy tort because it is incompatible with *any* limits on liability – all that matters is meeting the victim's needs by parties/institutions better able to bear the costs.[18] Deterrence would (conversely) dispense with the need for a *victim*, being concerned solely with the defendant's conduct. It also seems incompatible with liability insurance (prevalent in the tort system to make sure claimants actually receive the compensation awarded).

Since few torts scholars advocate the subject's abolition,[19] such proposals sound like an Aunt Sally. However, arguments from compensation or deterrence are commonly used *within* negligence law. In light of their incompatibility with tort's basic structure, this seems questionable. It has led to unstable doctrine, as the courts struggle to find principled limits for 'exceptional' liabilities. The 'bilateral, inter-personal' nature of litigation precludes coherent advancement of either the compensatory or the deterrence goals. Yet it can be queried whether identifying this 'essential structure' is more than a question-begging exercise – the assertion of a particular normative view of tort's function by corrective justice theorists, disguised as description of tort's true 'nature'.[20] Even from the perspective of morality, some question whether tort's basic 'inter-personal' structure can be reconciled with basic fairness, justice and desert.[21]

Moreover, not every instrumental concern is incompatible with tort's structure. Arguably an account of tort that incorporates social concerns is superior to one that does not.[22] Coherence is a valuable attribute of legal theories – but they must also fit the law, account transparently for how it is understood and present a moral justification.[23] Certainly, tort law itself is not purely an intellectual construct whose only goal is coherence. It is not a philosopher's toy. Tort has a real financial effect on real people. Liability can be life-changing for claimants and defendants. Tort sends moral messages. It has constitutional and political implications, quite apart from its economic impact. It holds wrongdoing to account and lays down rules of behaviour. Should tort lawyers really ignore these effects? Why accept that 'the sole purpose of private law is to be private law'?[24] Shouldn't its 'purpose' include the welfare of society? Many would think that must obviously be relevant to a branch of law with significant social *effects*. An account of tort including instrumental goals arguably scores

---

[18] Cf J Stapleton, 'In Restraint of Tort' in PBH Birks (ed), *The Frontiers of Liability, Volume 2* (Oxford, Oxford University Press, 1994) (to claim that tort is 'about compensation' is 'simply inadequate to convey what is the "meat" of negligence law, which is the analysis of the *boundaries* of the tort which explain why only *some* victims of negligence are allowed to recover compensation').

[19] Cf Lord Sumption, 'Abolishing Personal Injuries Law – A Project' (2018) 34 *Prof Neg* 113.

[20] D Priel, 'Structure, Function, and Tort Law' (2020) 13 *Jo Tort L* 31.

[21] J Waldron, 'Moments of Carelessness and Massive Loss' in DG Owen (ed), *Philosophical Foundations of Tort Law* (Oxford, Clarendon, 1995) (discussed in Ch4, Debate 3 under 'Moral Critique of Corrective Justice').

[22] G Turton, *Evidential Uncertainty in Causation in Negligence* (Oxford, Hart, 2016) ch1.

[23] SA Smith, *Contract Theory* (Oxford 2004) ch 1; (see ch 1, 'What Makes a Good Theory?').

[24] EJ Weinrib, *The Idea of Private Law* (Oxford, Oxford University Press, 2012) 8.

better for its moral attractiveness than a 'pure' theory that excludes them. Since the courts constantly consider such social concerns, a theory that includes them also fits the law much better, and most lawyers' understanding of it.

THE STRUCTURE OF NEGLIGENCE

The conventional structure of negligence liability requires: (1) duty of care; (2) its negligent breach; (3) causation of (4) actionable damage which is (5) not too remote; and (6) absence of defences. The claim must satisfy all these requirements. They therefore appear like a series of obstacles, a hurdle race where one failure precludes liability. That metaphor is potentially misleading. Unlike actual hurdles which are physically unconnected, the doctrines of negligence interrelate.[25]

As seen in two debates in the following chapters (remoteness; the function of duty), certain concerns trip several doctrinal switches simultaneously. For example, concerns about malicious third party interventions arise at both 'duty' and 'remoteness' stages. Where the claimant deliberately harms themselves, a case may raise problems of duty, causation, remoteness *and* defences. That does not mean that the elements of negligence can or should be merged, simply that while distinct they often react in similar ways, guided by common principles like the 'individualist values of the common law'.[26] The doctrinal route may be crucial. Denying duty or causation precludes a claim in its entirety, whereas the contributory negligence defence only reduces compensation.[27] The *volenti* defence may survive as a means for denying liability altogether, not merely reducing it, when the claimant acted with gross folly.[28] In the absence of an illegality defence, courts may resort to novel interpretations of duty of care to restrict liability.[29]

The choice may matter in subtler ways too. It is dangerous to use causation too freely as a limit on liability. According to *Markesinis and Deakin*, 'causal devices' can 'conceal policy-based value judgements', pretending that these follow 'almost effortlessly from the application of rules of natural science'.[30] We will see sharp disagreement about the nature of 'remoteness', critics fearing that courts succumb to the illusion that remoteness involves 'factual' real-world phenomena rather than normative choices. As discussed in chapter six on duty's functions, denial of liability by holding 'no duty of care' offers advantages flowing from duty's general categorical (rather than specific fact-based)

---

[25] J Stapleton, 'Conceptual Interplay Between Elements of the Tort of Negligence' in *Three Essays on Torts* (Oxford, Oxford University Press, 2021).
[26] *Tomlinson v Congleton BC* [2004] 1 AC 46 [47] (Lord Hoffmann).
[27] Consider *Corr v IBC Vehicles* [2008] AC 884.
[28] Consider *Morris v Murray* [1991] 2 QB 6.
[29] *JJ v Rankin's Garage* [2018] 1 SCR 587 (see ch 6, 'The Triviality of Foreseeability').
[30] S Deakin and Z Adams, *Markesinis & Deakin's Tort Law* 8th edn (Oxford, Oxford University Press, 2019) 94.

nature. But some object that the instrumental use of duty as a convenient 'control device' mistakes its true nature and risks undermining the binding nature of tort obligations. Yet others question whether the distinctive duty of care should survive at all, suggesting that its multiple doctrinal functions could be divided up among other concepts in negligence.

This leads to a wider jurisprudential reflection. Are concepts 'real', constraining judicial decisions? Or are they simply convenient matters of exposition? Most tort lawyers pragmatically adopt the second attitude. The recent elaborate restatement of the 'structure of negligence' by Lord Hodge and Lord Sales was questioned by their colleagues in the Supreme Court.[31] Nolan and Plunkett plead for 'simplicity' in the analysis of negligence, warning against the danger of conflating distinct elements.[32] They accordingly criticise the 'scope of duty' concept for confusing the straightforward rule generally limiting liability to 'harm that results from the materialisation of the risks that made the defendant's conduct negligent in the first place'.[33] Others doubt the value of such classificatory efforts. 'Attachment to concepts as such, to the exclusion of the socio-economic pressures that guide the way in which they are used', should be avoided.[34] The arch-sceptic Leon Green declared:

> The search never ends for some neat formula by which the adjudication of a controversy can be made easy and simple. Every tort lawyer is familiar with the formulas ... These and similar terms have had their day when their very mention was supposed to unlock the mysteries of some complex case and produce an incontrovertible result.[35]

(Needless to say Green thought the 'all purpose' *Wagon Mound* foreseeability formula[36] particularly unsuccessful: 'An attempt to rest liability in negligence cases wholly on the gossamer of foreseeability seems so far removed from the practical world of affairs as to suggest the Wizard of Oz'.)[37] For decades Green urged courts not to be distracted from open discussion of the extent of legal responsibility by undue emphasis on 'smooth phrases' ('word-serfdom').[38] A more moderate scepticism accepts that doctrine matters as a way of framing questions and presenting the answers. Yet conceptual

---

[31] *Meadows v Khan* (n 10) [28]; cf [78] (Lord Burrows), [96] (Lord Leggatt) ('undesirable as well as unnecessary').

[32] D Nolan and L Plunkett, 'Keeping Negligence Simple' (2022) 138 *LQR* 175.

[33] ibid 176 (suggesting at 179–81 that the 'scope' or 'nexus' question is relevant *only* in 'relationship' cases where the defendant exercises control over the extent of duty owed 'by making clear the purpose for which some advice or service is being given').

[34] Markesinis and Deakin (n 30) 26.

[35] L Green, 'Foreseeability in Negligence Law' (1961) 61 *Columbia LR* 1401, 1402–03.

[36] *The Wagon Mound (No 1)* [1961] AC 388.

[37] Green (n 35) 1412.

[38] L Green, 'Are There Dependable Rules of Causation?' (1929) 77 *Univ Penn LR* 601.

precision does not necessarily mean clearer limits on liability and 'the present preoccupation with formal subdivisions of the duty concept' may obscure more than it illuminates.³⁹

Negligence: Further Issues

It is impossible to analyse every doctrine in negligence in depth within the compass of this book. Causation, duty and personal injury have been chosen to illustrate a number of wider themes. Rights theories and their rivals; the relevance of policy and instrumental concerns; the distributive choices that courts make in elaborating 'purely doctrinal' law. Naturally, similar questions arise across the law of negligence, both about its general concepts and in particular areas of liability. Here are a few further examples, which do not (of course) exhaust the enormous number of controversial questions found in negligence law today.

Breach of Duty

The core of negligence, its objective standard of reasonable care, can be debated from many angles. It could be viewed as a fair compromise between defendants' freedom of action and claimants' freedom from injury. But is an impersonal, *objective* standard of fault morally unfair to defendants incapable of meeting it? Should 'reasonable care' instead be understood as a standard requiring *economically efficient investment* in accident prevention? Such questions are thrown into relief by stricter liabilities, for example, for defective products (Consumer Protection Act 1987). When is strict liability preferable to negligence from (1) moral/rights-based or (2) economic perspectives?

Defences

Contributory negligence involves a broad apportionment of harm according to the respective responsibility of claimant and defendant. Does this justify a more general divisibility of harm, requiring reconsideration of the 'all or nothing' approach to causation (whereby defendants are liable *in full* for contributing to the claimant's 'indivisible' injury)?⁴⁰

Pure Economic Loss

Just as negligence strongly protects personal injury but struggles with non-tangible emotional, mental and bodily harms, it readily compensates physical

---

³⁹ Markesinis and Deakin (n 30) 94.
⁴⁰ Cf *Hatton v Sutherland* [2002] ICR 613 (see ch 9, 'Stress at Work'); T Weir, 'All or Nothing' (2004) 78 *Tulane LR* 511; K Barker and R Grantham (eds), *Apportionment in Private Law* (Oxford, Hart, 2019).

property damage but not economic loss. Should this exclusionary rule be conceived in terms of rights,⁴¹ or is it justified by policy?⁴²

Omissions and Public Authority Liability

Is the absence of liability for omissions a matter of fundamental moral principle?⁴³ Should it apply equally to public authorities as to private defendants?⁴⁴ Does it provide an adequate, policy-free solution to the long-running debate about the negligence liability of the police and other public authorities?⁴⁵ Can the distinction with 'positive obligations' under the ECHR be justified?⁴⁶ Should the law in this area be reformed?⁴⁷

Assumption of Responsibility

Voluntary undertakings may create rights that would otherwise not exist.⁴⁸ They are (therefore) important exceptions to the last two rules. Assumption of responsibility may exceptionally create (eg) liability for pure economic loss,⁴⁹ positive obligations to protect others from harm⁵⁰ or duties to ensure that care is taken by third parties.⁵¹ Is it applied consistently with its purported basis (willingly undertaken extraordinary liabilities)?⁵² Or is 'assumption of responsibility' dependent upon (unarticulated?) policy concerns?⁵³

---

⁴¹ P Benson, 'The Basis for Excluding Liability for Economic Loss' in DG Owen (ed), *Philosophical Foundations of Tort Law* (Oxford, Clarendon, 1995); A Beever, *Rediscovering the Law of Negligence* (Oxford, Hart, 2007) ch 7.

⁴² J Stapleton, 'Duty of Care and Economic Loss: A Wider Agenda' (1991) 107 *LQR* 249; J Stapleton, *Three Essays on Torts* (Oxford, Oxford University Press, 2021) ch 2.

⁴³ T Honoré, 'Are Omissions Less Culpable?' in P Cane and J Stapleton (eds), *Essays for Patrick Atiyah* (Oxford, Oxford University Press, 1991); Beever (n 41) ch 6.

⁴⁴ Beever (n 41) ch 9; cf S Tofaris and S Steel, 'Negligence Liability for Omissions and the Police' [2016] *CLJ* 128; T Cornford, 'The Negligence Liability of Public Authorities for Omissions' [2019] *CLJ* 545.

⁴⁵ *Michael v Chief Constable of South Wales* [2015] AC 1732; *Robinson v Chief Constable of West Yorkshire* [2018] AC 736.

⁴⁶ D Nolan, 'Negligence and Human Rights Law: The Case for Separate Development' (2013) 76 *MLR* 286.

⁴⁷ Law Commission CP187, 'Administrative Redress: Public Bodies and the Citizen' (2008).

⁴⁸ Stevens (n 5) 9–14.

⁴⁹ *Henderson v Merrett Syndicates* [1995] 2 AC 145.

⁵⁰ *Tindall v Chief Constable of Thames Valley* [2022] EWCA Civ 25.

⁵¹ *Woodland v Essex CC* [2014] 1 AC 537.

⁵² D Nolan, 'Assumption of Responsibility: Four Questions' [2019] *CLP* 123.

⁵³ *Customs & Excise v Barclays Bank* [2007] 1 AC 181; K Barker, 'Unreliable Assumptions in the Modern Law of Negligence' (1993) 109 *LQR* 461.

4

Causation and Corrective Justice

INTRODUCTION

For a proper understanding of tort law, some engagement with theoretical debates is unavoidable. This is certainly true of the topic of causation, notoriously one of the most difficult. Why so? Because *theoretical* disagreements underlie causation's most heated controversies. Many attempts to expand liability by reformulating the rules on causation are alleged to be incoherent with tort's basic model of justice. In particular, a common justification for relaxation of causal doctrine (or modifying rules requiring claimants to *prove* causation) is the concern to compensate injured claimants, or to sanction defendants' wrongful behaviour. Yet arguably such concerns are inconsistent with tort law's basic hard-wired structure. Tort liability is *personalised*. A tort claim lies only *against* the person(s) who have wronged the claimant. A defendant is only liable *to* the person(s) they have wronged. Tort liability links particular individuals. This two-sided structure is often called 'corrective' or 'inter-personal' justice.

The practical lawyer, wary of theory, might think this sounds like another example of academic theorists inventing fancy-sounding labels for entirely obvious things. Corrective justice might sound rather banal. Does anyone doubt that tort claims can be made only against parties responsible for the claimant's injury? Or could it be doubted that only wrongful conduct *which harms another* constitutes a tort? 'A person who acts without reasonable care does no wrong in law; he commits no tort. He only does wrong, he only commits a tort, if his lack of care causes damage to the plaintiff'.[1]

But corrective justice theory is not entirely banal. The characteristic interpersonal or 'bipolar' connection between tort parties fits very awkwardly with certain rival approaches. In particular, tort's basic structure seems inconsistent with purely compensation-based or punishment-based rationales. Compensation is concerned solely with the claimant's need. Punishment is concerned solely with the defendant's culpability. Each ignores the other side of the equation (ie the other party's role). If either of these goals (compensation or

---

[1] *Browning v War Office* [1963] 1 QB 750, 765 (Diplock LJ).

punishment) were followed through to their logical conclusion, they would destroy tort law rather than merely 'reform' it. In practice, they are allowed a much more limited role. But when there is no logical stopping point, limits can only be imposed arbitrarily. And arbitrary limits are by definition unprincipled, which creates injustice. Whether clear-cut arbitrary limits can be imposed successfully through common law (by contrast with legislation) is doubtful. These points will be illustrated by considering the most important (and controversial) exceptional rule on proof of causation, *Fairchild v Glenhaven Funeral Services*.[2]

However not all theorists accept the corrective justice approach. It may well underlie the present structure of tort law. But perhaps that structure should be questioned, if we wish to have a comprehensive system of accident compensation or to deter risky behaviour effectively. Indeed not all critics accept that any deviation from narrowly defined 'bilateral corrective justice' violates tort law as we know it. Arguably, tort can accommodate some aggregation of claimants and/or defendants to solve problems in proving *whose* wrongful conduct has injured *which* claimant (a problem which is not as unreal as it sounds). A degree of collectivisation may be consistent with our moral obligations to persons that we injure – it could even offer morally superior solutions.

Causation is therefore a key battleground in tort theory, whether we adopt the radical, revisionist perspective of compensation or punishment, or a more traditional moral responsibility approach. By uncovering these theoretical disagreements, we see it is hardly surprising that causation, and many other questions arising on the frontiers of tort liability, are often so controversial. Disagreements about doctrinal rules flow from semi-concealed disagreements about the very nature of tort law.

Debate 1
Causation and Compensation

Securing compensation for injured claimants is a common justification for tort liability. It is always a ready argument for the expansion of tort doctrines – recommending more generous rules on causation, fault and much else. Yet in pure form, the compensation argument fails because it has no stopping point. It would eliminate *all* barriers to tort claims. It entails the complete replacement, not just the expansion, of tort law. Despite this, the compensatory imperative is often used to justify the enlargement of liability. This seems questionable. Because compensating the claimant is *always* an argument in favour of liability, it is little use in deciding where to set tort's *limits*. The extreme difficulty of marking out a compensation-based 'exceptional' rule of causation is painfully illustrated by the *Fairchild* saga. Before turning to that, we examine

---

[2] [2003] 1 AC 32 (*Fairchild*).

the campaign to replace tort with a universal compensation scheme, and the dubious history of 'compensation' arguments in tort doctrine.

Accident Compensation Schemes

A significant reform movement has advocated tort's replacement by a comprehensive scheme for the compensation of injuries. The central moral claim is that everyone with the same injury has an equal need for compensation. Yet tort cannot award compensation based *only* on need – tort damages only compensate (fully and generously) the victims of torts. Those with equally serious injuries which were not the result of another's wrongdoing are (obviously) unable to bring a claim. This is the inevitable logic of tort liability. But to discriminate between people with identical injuries (and identical needs) according to the degree of fault by which others caused those injuries makes no sense whatsoever from a purely compensatory perspective. On this view, need would be the *sole* criterion.

These radical reform movements are out of political fashion. Historically they have had successes – most notably (in the common law world) in New Zealand, where the Accident Compensation Act 1972 abolished tort liability for accidental injuries in favour of a government-administered compensation scheme. Such replacements follow an *insurance* model, either state-run or privately operated. The cost of injuries is born neither by an injured person alone, nor by the person (if any) who injured them – rather, *shared* by a wide class of people (taxpayers funding a government scheme, or premium-payers in private insurance). By design, this discards the bilateral, interpersonal model of corrective justice, which determines whether an individual defendant should have the individual claimant's loss transferred to them. The essence of a universal compensation scheme is to bear the costs of injuries *collectively*, rather than individuals bearing the cost of the injuries they tortiously cause.

It therefore seems difficult to incorporate the compensatory rationale *within* tort law. Tort claims are brought *by individuals against other individuals*: a claim cannot issue against the world as a whole, against the public in general, or against nobody in particular. Tort cannot be the vehicle for a comprehensive needs-based scheme. It simply cannot reach those who are injured but not by the fault of another. However, the compensatory imperative arguably explains important developments within tort law too – although the extent of its influence heavily contested.

Compensation and Tort Doctrine

Claimants (and their legal advisers) do not necessarily accept the boundaries of liability as they are. The unceasing 'search for the deep pocket' often creates expansionary pressure. For example, vicarious liability claims for intentional wrongdoing that would traditionally be outside the 'scope of employment', and in contexts beyond the traditional employment relationship. Similarly, claims against solvent if peripheral parties are tactically preferable to suing impecunious primary wrongdoers. The Dorset Yacht Company understandably sued the government employer of prison guards, not the prisoners who smashed up the company's yachts when the guards negligently allowed them to escape.[3]

Such expansionary arguments have had a chequered career. Vicarious liability has been transformed since 2000. Its twin pillars, the employment relationship and the 'course of employment', have broadened dramatically. The transformation's basis is contestable. The Supreme Court has, however, expressly rejected the cogency of 'compensating claimants' as the justification.[4] Simultaneous with the growth of vicarious liability the courts have firmly *restricted* public authorities' liability for failing to prevent one individual from harming another.[5] In practice this means the victim will often recover no compensation – since the principal wrongdoer is typically impecunious. As it seems unlikely that the courts would adopt the compensatory approach so inconsistently, it is doubtful that it ever provides a satisfactory rationale.

It cannot coherently explain *any* expansion of liability. If we wished to ensure compensation of injured claimants, the imperative would not merely justify wider vicarious liability, or positive duties on public authorities to protect third parties.[6] The compensation imperative would eliminate *all* restrictions on liability. It is inconsistent with the nature of *tortious* liability, which transfers a loss to the defendant when and only when they are responsible to the claimant. As Stapleton (for example) observes, it misses the point to say that tort is 'about compensation': the core problem is 'analysis of the *boundaries* of the tort which explain why only *some* victims of negligence are allowed to recover compensation'.[7] The basic objection applies similarly against expansive tests of causation and relaxed standards of proof.

Yet is it not simply *fairer* to expand liability? It obviously seems appealing to transfer a loss from an innocent injured claimant (whose need for compensation would otherwise go unmet) to someone insured against that liability, or an organisation such as an employer or public authority. In colloquial terms such defendants have deep pockets or broad shoulders – they can bear the risk, or spread it widely among insurance premium-payers, shareholders, or taxpayers. It minimises the economic dislocation of accidents if costs are allocated to bodies best able to absorb and/or distribute them (ie rather than leaving them to crush individual victims). Again, however, if that is to be the guiding principle, why stop short of collectivising *all* costs across the broadest cross-section of

---

[3] [1970] AC 1004.

[4] *Cox v Ministry of Justice* [2016] UKSC 10, [2016] AC 660 [20] (Lord Reed).

[5] eg *Michael v Chief Constable of South Wales* [2015] UKSC 2.

[6] Or (eg) a strict approach to breach of duty: J Morgan, 'Tort, Insurance and Incoherence' (2004) 67 *MLR* 384.

[7] J Stapleton, 'In Restraint of Tort' in PBH Birks (ed), *The Frontiers of Liability, Volume 2* (Oxford, Oxford University Press, 1994) 101.

society, through some New Zealand style state-run scheme? The half-hearted loss-spreading of wider tort liability would not go nearly far enough.[8]

But it is questionable in its own terms. Having accepted the 'understandable popular appeal' of the 'deep pocket' argument, the dissent in a leading Californian causation case reasoned that 'wealth is an unreliable indicator of fault' and was simply not 'pertinent':

> A system priding itself on 'equal justice under law' does not flower when [liability] is determined by a defendant's wealth. The inevitable consequence of such a result is to create and perpetuate two rules of law – one applicable to wealthy defendants, and another standard pertaining to defendants who are poor or who have modest means.[9]

Such developments could be seen as progressive or egalitarian. But most lawyers would view radical changes to doctrine designed to redistribute wealth across society as a decidedly political choice – outside the courts' competence. Expansionary decisions may be praised as generous. But that presumes the claimant's greater merits against the defendant even though both are entitled to just treatment. It is too easy for judges to be generous with other people's money – by increasing their liabilities. As Lord Bramwell once complained (in dissent) 'Let us hold to the law. If we want to be charitable, gratify ourselves out of our own pockets'.[10]

The illogicality of 'compensation' arguments was well summarised by Gary Schwartz. The imperative of spreading losses through compensation

> as a rationale for any tort law rule, seems inherently unstable, since it is in a basic sense promiscuous. If loss spreading is deemed the law's fundamental purpose, a compensation right should accordingly be extended to the victim of every serious accident ... Yet tort law as we know it is 'tort law' instead of a compensation program exactly because it is selective – that is, because the liability rules it fashions exclude recovery for some accident victims while permitting recovery for others. If the loss-spreading rhetoric is taken with sufficient seriousness, it ultimately augers not the reform of tort law but rather (for better or worse) the supersession of tort law by some general compensation program.[11]

Fairchild *Enclave: 'Single Causal Agent'*

Fairchild v Glenhaven Funeral Services is surely the most significant and controversial causation case of the age.[12] It created an exceptional 'enclave' where

---

[8] S Hedley, 'Making Sense of Negligence' (2016) 36 *Legal Stud* 491.
[9] *Sindell v Abbott Laboratories* 26 Cal 3d 588 (Richardson J).
[10] *Smith v Charles Baker & Sons* [1891] AC 325, 346.
[11] GT Schwartz, 'The Supreme Court of California 1977–1978 Term Foreword: Understanding Products Liability' (1979) 67 *Calif LR* 435, 445.
[12] *Fairchild* (n 2).

claimants succeed despite the *absence of proof* that the defendant was historically involved as a cause of their harm. A grave problem with *Fairchild* is confining this 'exception'. It requires arbitrary boundaries to be drawn. But these make no normative sense, which discredits the law.

Artificial limits are made necessary by the width of *Fairchild*'s rationale: the perceived unfairness of denying compensation to those unable to prove causation because the limits of scientific knowledge create a 'rock of uncertainty'.[13] We can understand the judicial determination to compensate victims of such a horrible disease as mesothelioma (an untreatable, rapidly fatal lung cancer). Yet exactly the same compensatory imperative arises in *every* case where the claimant is unable to prove whether a breach of duty caused their injury. If *Fairchild* were applied by analogy to other situations within its compensatory rationale, it would in no way be 'exceptional' – *Fairchild* would replace entirely the requirement for claimants to prove causation (and indeed all other elements of the cause of action). Again, compensation's justificatory 'promiscuity' removes any clear stopping point. Hence the arbitrary requirement of a 'single causal agent' for the special *Fairchild* rule to apply.

The general rule on proof of causation is illustrated by *Wilsher v Essex*.[14] The claimant, a premature baby, had damaged eyesight. The defendant doctor had negligently permitted excess oxygen in the claimant's blood, a known risk factor for blindness. But there were four additional 'background' risk factors present, attributable solely to the claimant's premature birth (ie not caused by the defendant's negligence). It was impossible to say which of these five potential risk factors had caused his injury, thus impossible to say that the negligence was more likely than not a cause. The House of Lords therefore dismissed the claim (overruling the Court of Appeal whose short-lived decision had been a 'benevolent principle [that] smiles on these factual uncertainties and melts them all away').[15]

In *Fairchild*, the House of Lords approved *Wilsher* for exemplifying the general rule, while also rehabilitating the earlier decision in *McGhee v National Coal Board*.[16] Four of the law lords reconciled the authorities by limiting *McGhee* to situations involving a 'single noxious agent'. In *McGhee* it was known that the dermatitis was caused *by brick dust* (but unknowable whether the cause was the ineradicable dust inside the brick kiln, or the dust that remained on the pursuer's skin as he travelled home because the employers, in breach of duty, had not provided washing facilities). In *Fairchild* similarly, it was known that mesothelioma was caused *by asbestos* (but unknowable *which* defendant's breach had supplied the single 'fatal fibre' that triggered the disease). Lord Hoffmann alone stated that this was 'not a principled difference', suggesting *Fairchild* should be decided identically if one employer exposed the claimant

---

[13] ibid [7] (Lord Bingham).
[14] [1988] AC 1074.
[15] *Fitzgerald v Lane* [1987] QB 781, 800 (Nourse LJ) commenting on *Wilsher* [1987] QB 730.
[16] [1973] 1 WLR 1.

to asbestos while another employer exposed them to some different causal agent.[17] (In *Barker v Corus* Lord Hoffmann subsequently declared his minority opinion incorrect, ultimately also accepting the 'single causal mechanism' criterion for *Fairchild* liability.)[18]

The 'single causal mechanism' concept is vital for confining *Fairchild* (and preserving the authority of *Wilsher*). Yet many commentators have criticised its normative irrelevance. To adapt Lord Hoffmann's initial scepticism, why should *Fairchild* not apply when D1 exposes the claimant to asbestos, D2 emits a carcinogenic chemical and D3 is responsible for radioactive contamination (which is also a risk factor for the claimant's cancer)? The 'single mechanism' rule simply seems an ad hoc way of drawing a line *somewhere* (in particular, to reconcile the apparently inconsistent decisions in *McGhee*, *Wilsher* and then *Fairchild*).

Notably, one commentator defends a narrower version of 'single causal agency' as a principled basis for *McGhee*.[19] In Ernest Weinrib's view, it is significant that the employer/defender in *McGhee* caused the presence of *both* the dust in the kiln (albeit non-tortiously) *and* the 'tortious' dust which should have been removed by workplace showers. Weinrib argues that the law should not 'segregate the innocence of creating the risk from the culpability of not alleviating it'. For, he notes, 'the very creation of [a] risk obligates the risk creator to follow through with appropriate precautions'. So when the defendant (non-tortiously) creates a risk but then fails in its duty to alleviate that risk, they are 'unlike the rest of the world, ... at no point a stranger to the normative implications of [their] own activity'. Weinrib thus concludes:

> Given the defendant's responsibility for creating the risk to begin with, the plaintiff should not have to prove that the injury was not caused by the innocent segment of the defendant's activity. The innocent segment is not truly innocent unless the defendant follows through by taking the precautions that make it so.

Weinrib's novel rationalisation seems questionable, however. First, it is not clear that it explains claims brought against employers (as in *McGhee*). It is quite true that one exceptional situation where the law recognises positive duties to protect others from dangers is where the defendant is responsible for creating that danger.[20] Indeed one way to analyse this is to combine the initial creation of danger with the later failure to address it into one episode of positive conduct, therefore not a true exception to the absence liability for 'omissions'.[21] Yet that is not the basis for an *employer's* positive duty to ensure

---

[17] *Fairchild* (n 2) [72].
[18] [2006] 2 AC 572 [23]–[24].
[19] EJ Weinrib, 'Causal Uncertainty' (2016) 36 *OJLS* 135.
[20] eg *Begum v Maran (UK) Ltd* [2021] EWCA Civ 326, [51]–[66].
[21] S Steel, 'Rationalising Omissions Liability in Negligence' (2019) 135 *LQR* 484.

a reasonably safe working environment. The duty does not depend on the employer's having initially created the danger in question. The employer is clearly required to provide employees with reasonable protection against risks that are (for example) inherent or naturally occurring (such as sunburn or frostbite in extreme weather conditions), fully as much as against risks that the employer creates themselves. In a situation like *McGhee*, employers are required to provide washing facilities irrespective of whether they introduced the dirt to be washed off. A further problem is that Weinrib's thesis fits awkwardly with decisions holding employers liable only for harms caused in breach of duty, and not for injuries suffered prior to the date at which exposure became negligent.[22] Would Weinrib permit claimants to recover in full by 'repudiating the artificial segmentation' between periods of tortious and non-tortious exposure?

If we accept Weinrib's argument despite these doubts about its fit, it justifies a narrower *McGhee* doctrine. It would be insufficient to show a 'single causal mechanism'; the claimant would also have to show that all instances of the 'mechanism' were attributable to the defendant (whether in breach of duty or otherwise). That would not succeed in *Fairchild* itself (where some exposure was attributable to other defendants), nor *Barker v Corus* (exposure attributable to the claimant, during self-employment).

Another possible explanation would limit *Fairchild's* application to situations where *all* possible causes were tortious (eg in negligence all exposures would be in breach of duty). That attractively justifies the outcome in *Fairchild* where *somebody's* tort had certainly caused the claimant's mesothelioma, but impossible to identify whose. Such liability would be consistent with other causal rules.[23] But again, it does not fit the present state of the law. *Fairchild* currently applies to *any* significant exposure to asbestos, even if non-tortious sources also made a significant contribution (eg background exposure through the atmosphere) – for example *Barker*, *Sienkiewicz*[24] and *McGhee*. In those cases it is not possible to say that the disease definitely occurred tortiously. A narrowed *Fairchild* rule justified on such grounds would be possible, but it would require *Barker* and *Sienkiewicz* to be overruled – and *McGhee* explained on other grounds as Weinrib has suggested. Short of such radical revision, the *Fairchild* enclave as it stands seems difficult to defend on principled grounds.

Fairchild *Enclave: 'Scientific Uncertainty'*

Another limit to its application is the requirement that proof is impossible because of *scientific* uncertainty. This apparently requires some fundamental gap in medical/scientific knowledge. *Fairchild* has for this reason been

---

[22] *Thompson v Smiths Shiprepairers* [1984] QB 405.
[23] *Baker v Willoughby* [1970] AC 467.
[24] [2011] 2 AC 229.

held inapplicable in a case where although it was not possible for the claimant to prove causation on the evidence before the court, it was not 'inherently impossible ... because of the current state of scientific knowledge'.[25] This case involved the difficult hypothetical question of whether, had the claimant turkey-plucker been provided with protective gloves by her employer, she would have been protected against food poisoning bacteria, or whether she would still have been infected by touching her face while wearing gloves. Again, we can understand the need to interpret narrowly the *Fairchild* exception and its 'rock of uncertainty'. If *Fairchild* allowed the burden of proof to be relaxed whenever it was difficult to prove causation, this would abolish the rule entirely.

Nevertheless, it is not clear why the law should be more sympathetic where impossibility of proof is 'inherent' or 'scientific' rather than arising from an everyday lack of evidence. If an accident renders a claimant unconscious and there are no eye-witnesses, it may be impossible to say who or what caused their injuries. The frontiers of scientific knowledge have nothing to do with it. But the 'rock of uncertainty' would be just as impossible to surmount as was the limited knowledge about mesothelioma in *Fairchild*. So why the difference? Because of its uncertain boundaries, '"scientific" impossibility' has been rejected as the criterion for relaxing proof of causation in Canada.[26] It would be difficult to distinguish 'true' or 'conceptual' impossibility, but unless a clear line can be drawn between this and ordinary failures to prove causation on the facts, the requirement of proof would effectively cease to apply. That would 'fundamentally change the law of negligence and sever it from its anchor in corrective justice'.

We could note an alternative proposal on 'scientific' uncertainty. Where the limits of scientific or medical knowledge make proof of causation impossible, defendants who create 'unknowable' risks could be legally required to fund the relevant research – 'to pay for the production of knowledge about the harm [they are] alleged to have caused'.[27] Such gaps in knowledge are inevitable given the finite public budget for scientific research and it would be prohibitively expensive for *claimants* to undertake it. The production of further knowledge would be a 'public good' and the defendant's creation of the relevant risk would justify charging the cost to them. The aim would be to commission sufficient research to allow a confident scientific determination of the causal question. This avoids the need to dismiss claims (or as in *Fairchild*, create a dubious exception in favour of claimants) when the science is unclear.

As Alexandra Lahav notes, a major drawback for claimants would be the delay in resolving their claims while research took place. That is still a better

---

[25] *Sanderson v Hull* [2008] EWCA Civ 1211 [53] (Smith LJ).
[26] *Clements v Clements* [2012] 2 SCR 181, [36]–[38].
[27] AD Lahav, 'The Knowledge Remedy' (2020) 98 *Texas LR* 1361.

outcome than simply dismissing their claims altogether, as ordinary principle dictates. Of course in English law, claimants currently recover full compensation for their injuries notwithstanding the 'rock of uncertainty' – but would the 'knowledge remedy' be a more proportionate response to the problem of uncertainty than full liability under *Fairchild*? It would arguably be a satisfactory solution to proof problems arising from the limits of scientific knowledge. (However it could do nothing to solve evidential problems such as in *Sanderson v Hull* or the 'unconscious accident victim' – for missing case-specific evidence cannot be supplied retrospectively by scientific study.)

We have examined the two major limits on the *Fairchild* enclave: the need for a 'single causal mechanism' and 'inherent scientific uncertainty'. Each can reasonably be accused of arbitrariness. Sandy Steel finds 'The state of the current law [on the exceptional rule in *Fairchild*] cannot be justified'.[28] Neither of the limits is rationally connected to the three rationales advanced to justify the *Fairchild* exception. Whether our concern is the claimant's need for compensation, the defendants' 'hollow duties',[29] or the disadvantage of several careless defendants' simultaneous presence, such concerns apply no less forcefully when there are *multiple* 'causal agents' or '*non-scientific*' uncertainty. Yet as Steel notes the law is 'caught in a dilemma'. If it removed the artificial restrictions there would be 'an annihilation of the general burden of proof on causation'; but if they are maintained 'the law faces the charge of incoherence'.[30]

Fairchild *Enclave: A Special Rule for Mesothelioma?*

One further judicial attempt to confine *Fairchild* has notably failed. In *Sienkiewicz* Lord Brown argued that following section 3 of the Compensation Act 2006, the breadth of liability within the *Fairchild* enclave's 'quixotic' evolution[31] had become so 'unsatisfactory' that it should be confined to mesothelioma cases *only*.[32] Although doubting whether there was anything sufficiently exceptional about that particular disease to justify such special treatment, Lord Brown reasoned that strict confinement of *Fairchild* would stop the law of causation being turned upside down and prevent 'yet further anomalies in an area of law which benefits perhaps above all from clarity, consistency and certainty in its application'.[33] However, Lord Brown's redefinition has been rejected. Applying *Fairchild* subsequently in a lung cancer case, Lord Dyson MR

---

[28] S Steel, *Proof of Causation in Tort Law* (Cambridge, Cambridge University Press, 2015) 237.
[29] See below, 'Empty Duty'.
[30] Steel (n 28) 239 (proposing a narrower rule applicable only when *every* possible cause is tortious – the 'which defendant?' problem).
[31] *Sienkiewicz v Greif* [2011] 2 AC 229 [174] (*Sienkiewicz*).
[32] ibid [186]–[187].
[33] ibid [187].

reasoned that the law would be 'inconsistent and incoherent' unless it applied to other, 'truly analogous' diseases apart from mesothelioma.[34]

Therefore the courts seem willing to tolerate some arbitrary boundaries but not others. Some limits (like Lord Brown's proposed confinement) are thought unacceptably artificial, rejected to preserve coherence and consistency. (A rather inconsistent consistency.) Application of rules by analogy is of course the usual common law method. The anomaly is *Fairchild*'s remaining artificial boundaries, as discussed in the previous two sections. By contrast, *statutory* rules can be clear-cut and arbitrary: they either apply or they do not. There is no question of their extension by analogy. Notably indeed, Parliament *did* limit section 3 of the Compensation Act (which restored joint and several liability in the *Fairchild* enclave) to 'mesothelioma'. Hence in *Heneghan*, when *Fairchild* was applied to cancers other than mesothelioma, the common law 'proportionate liability' rule applied but section 3 did not.[35]

The law seems irredeemably confused and illogical. As Jay J stated at first instance in *Heneghan*:

> Had the common law adhered to strict logic and principle, all the difficulties which bedevil cases such as these would not have arisen, and would not continue to arise. The disadvantage of strict adherence to logic and principle is that frank injustice may arise in certain types of case, and therefore the common law constantly strains at the leash of the intellectually pure approach.[36]

This echoes Lord Nicholls' frank remarks in *Fairchild* itself. His Lordship had 'no hesitation' in permitting the claimants to recover:

> Any other outcome would be deeply offensive to instinctive notions of what justice requires and fairness demands. The real difficulty lies is elucidating in sufficiently specific terms the principle being applied in reaching this conclusion. To be acceptable the law must be coherent. It must be principled. The basis on which one case, or one type of case, is distinguished from another should be transparent and capable of identification. When a decision departs from principles normally applied, the basis for doing so must be rational and justifiable if the decision is to avoid the reproach that hard cases make bad law.[37]

Yet Lord Hoffmann (another party to the decision in *Fairchild*) later accepted that 'in retrospect', the House of Lords failed 'quite badly' the test that Lord Nicholls had set.[38]

---

[34] *Heneghan v Manchester Dry Docks* [2016] EWCA Civ 86; [2016] 1 WLR 2036 [48].

[35] Similarly for *Fairchild* cases in Guernsey, a jurisdiction where the 2006 Act does not apply: *Zurich Insurance v International Energy Group* [2016] AC 509 (*Zurich*).

[36] [2014] EWHC 4190 (QB), [50].

[37] *Fairchild* (n 2) [36].

[38] Lord Hoffmann, '*Fairchild* and After' in A Burrows et al (eds), *Judge and Jurist: Essays in Memory of Lord Rodger of Earlsferry* (Oxford, Oxford University Press, 2013).

The evolution in Lord Hoffmann's thinking is fascinating. We have seen his criticism of the 'single causal mechanism' theory in *Fairchild* before ultimately accepting it in *Barker v Corus*. In his extrajudicial essay, Lord Hoffmann reverted back to his original scepticism, now describing the distinction between single and multiple causal agents as 'absurd'. He proposed that the courts should overrule *Fairchild* and allow Parliament to replace it with a statutory mesothelioma compensation scheme, if it wishes. The problem with *Fairchild* was:

> We could not simply enact a rule with arbitrary limitations. Parliament can do that, but judges are not in the business of laying down arbitrary rules based on general considerations of fairness and public policy. They are supposed to declare the principles of the common law.[39]

Fairchild had been a mistake, 'creating confusion … by trying to legislate for special cases' but using judge-made law. By overruling it 'the common law would be rid of an arbitrary rule masquerading as a principled decision'.[40] The policy question would then fall to Parliament, which has better tools (sharp-edged legislative rules) to answer it.

Sarah Green thinks Lord Hoffmann's repudiation of *Fairchild* rather like Dr Frankenstein disowning the monster he'd created![41] Judicial pleas for the legislature to 'extricate' the common law of torts from a 'morass' of its own creation are not unique.[42] Pertinently, they have been made in the context of psychiatric injury (nervous shock) claims. In the leading case, Lord Oliver commented: 'Policy considerations such as this could, I cannot help feeling, be much better accommodated if the rights of persons injured in this way were to be enshrined in and limited by legislation'.[43] Despite a chorus of criticism, Parliament has declined to intervene. The 'striking anomalies' of the common law on psychiatric injury remain in place.[44]

The same remains true for *Fairchild*. The Supreme Court has not seriously entertained Lord Hoffmann's call to reverse *Fairchild*. Lord Brown noted that only by overruling it could the courts avoid imposing 'Draconian' liabilities in *Sienkiewicz*.[45] But overruling would be 'a remarkable thing' after Parliament had legislated on the basis of the *Fairchild* exception in the 2006 Act.[46] Baroness Hale, sympathetic to Lord Brown's critique, thought (a little despairingly) that 'Even if we thought it right to [reverse *Fairchild*], Parliament would

---

[39] ibid 65.
[40] ibid 69.
[41] S Green, *Causation in Negligence* (Oxford, Hart, 2015) 141.
[42] *Gammell v Wilson* [1982] AC 27, 62 (Lord Diplock).
[43] *Alcock v Chief Constable* [1992] 1 AC 310, 419.
[44] *White v Chief Constable* [1999] 2 AC 455, 506 (Lord Hoffmann) (see further ch 9 below).
[45] *Sienkiewicz* (n 31) [184].
[46] ibid [183].

soon reverse us' (given how 'dreadful' mesothelioma is, and employers' widespread failure to appreciate the dangers of asbestos).[47] (Lord Neuberger and Lord Reed later suggested that 'on one view', the likelihood of Parliament's responding to *Fairchild*'s overruling 'might have been regarded as the best of reasons' for the court doing just that).[48]

Despite further criticism of *Fairchild*, Lords Neuberger and Reed also shrank from overruling it in *Zurich Insurance*. The 'ad hoc' *Fairchild* exception's basic flaw was that:

> unlike legislation, the common law cannot confine itself to a particular situation and deal with it in isolation from the remainder of the law; nor can it resolve problems on a purely pragmatic basis. It is a complex and extensive network of interconnected principles applicable to all situations falling within their scope.[49]

> ... the courts need to recognise that, unlike Parliament, they cannot legislate in the public interest for special cases, and they risk sowing confusion in the common law if they attempt to do so.[50]

Hence the difficulty of confining the *Fairchild* rule: 'Enclaves are ... notoriously difficult to police'.[51] *Fairchild* had unleashed 'a sort of juridical version of chaos theory',[52] because applying an exception created 'pragmatically but without any clear basis in principle' had constantly created 'a new set of problems requiring resolution at the highest level'.[53]

Notwithstanding this broadside, Lords Neuberger and Reed accepted the outcome of *Fairchild* was 'not only humane, but obviously right'. To have dismissed the claims would have been 'hard-headed (and, many people would say, hard-hearted)'.[54] While it 'may very well have been a better solution' if the courts had stuck to principle and let Parliament intervene to provide a remedy, 'that observation is made with the wisdom of hindsight'.[55]

Given that comparable difficulties of proof hamper many claimants with diseases or injuries as serious as mesothelioma, the 'exception' was always bound to come under irresistible pressure to expand. As noted, the compensatory imperative is so indiscriminate that it bursts through any principled limits on tort liability. It can be kept under control only by arbitrary, artificial rules. *Fairchild* demonstrates the incoherence of pursuing 'compensation' through tort only too clearly.

---

[47] ibid [167].
[48] *Zurich* (n 35) [197].
[49] ibid [192].
[50] ibid [209].
[51] ibid [207].
[52] ibid [191].
[53] ibid [210].
[54] ibid [191].
[55] ibid [211].

Debate 2
Causation and Deterrence

Punishment and Justice: Tort and Crime

The mirror-image problem arises if the law attempts to use tort law as a mechanism for punishment of wrongdoers, or the deterrence of wrongdoing. A purely defendant-sided rationale fits awkwardly with tort's structure. A tortfeasor is liable *only* if their conduct wrongs another individual, and liable only *to* that specific wronged individual. By contrast with tort, the legal system as a whole is concerned to deter behaviour that *risks* harm to others, including situations where it has not yet harmed anyone. It is legitimate to punish such behaviour given the public interest in discouraging careless (etc) risks to other people's safety. The enforcement of laws against such 'abstract' (or 'inchoate') wrongs is allocated to some representative of the public interest, such as a prosecutor or attorney-general.

From this perspective of punishment and deterrence, tort's basic structure makes no sense. A tort can only be committed against a particular individual, and legal action to redress a tort is vested exclusively in that individual. Tort remedies redress the wrong suffered by the individual claimant. But this is not a valid criticism of tort. It operates according to different logic, from a different starting point. It is, however, a criticism of punitive or deterrent theories *of tort*. They invoke tort law for a purpose for which it is not designed and cannot coherently pursue.

Criminal law and tort sometimes overlap (in particular in the territory of intentional torts). But they remain distinct. The contrast between them shows how tort is a poor vehicle for deterrence. First, there are many crimes that are punishable without any individual having been injured (eg inchoate offences, attempts, the offence of 'careless driving'). The rationale for punishing such crimes is obvious. Yet there can be no *tort* in the absence of any claimant injured by the defendant's conduct.

Second, although many crimes *are* defined as interference with other individuals' interests (eg offences against the person; many property offences), criminal procedure is quite distinct. It is unusual for the affected individual to enforce the criminal law. In practice most prosecutions are brought by a government agency, the Crown Prosecution Service. Individuals are entitled to bring criminal prosecutions in the name of the Crown, 'a valuable constitutional safeguard against inertia or partiality on the part of authority',[56] but note this right is not confined to the victims of an offence. In theory *anyone* can bring a private prosecution. Although statute preserves the citizen's right to do so, the CPS has a wide discretion to take over private proceedings either

---

[56] *Gouriet v Union of Post Office Workers* [1978] AC 435, 477 (Lord Wilberforce).

to prosecute or to discontinue them, in the public interest.⁵⁷ The CPS's power reflects the advantages of an objective public prosecutor over those 'inexperienced in the criminal justice system, and (often …) involved, frequently as a victim, and therefore far from dispassionate'.⁵⁸ In short, enforcement of the criminal law is very largely a government activity undertaken in the public interest. Enforcement by victims is potentially suspect. In complete contrast, initiating tort proceedings is *purely* a private matter for the claimant (ie the victim of the tort).

Yet another sharp distinction is at the 'remedy' stage. The criminal court passes a sentence designed (among other things) to visit retribution upon the defendant and to deter similar offending in future. The sentence is proportionate to such goals; the degree of harm (if any) to any victim of the crime is a relevant factor, but cannot determine the penalty imposed. Tort remedies, by contrast, are directly concerned with restoring the claimant's position. Compensation is quantified by the harm caused to the claimant, no more and no less. And obviously, this may depart from what would be required by punitive notions of just deserts: tort 'requires compensation from persons that exactly equals the amount of harm they have caused; and this requirement will frequently cause suffering either more than or less than retributively deserved, either absolutely or comparatively'.⁵⁹ Moreover, tort damages are (by definition) awarded to the claimant, whereas criminal fines are usually paid to the state. The systems have fundamentally separate goals.

The contrast is not diminished by such remedies as, in criminal prosecutions, 'compensation orders' (for loss resulting from an offence),⁶⁰ and in tort, the power to award exemplary (or 'punitive') damages. The latter are often criticised as anomalous. Allan Beever rejects the argument that exemplary damages in tort have a valid role of supplementing the criminal law.⁶¹ Beever's objections are both practical and theoretical. Where is the empirical evidence that exemplary damages in fact deter tortfeasors? As Street said, exemplary damages' 'practical usefulness', a debate 'to which no amount of theorising can provide an answer', requires study of the law in action. But this has not been carried out by the Law Commission or anyone else.⁶² Lord Wilberforce

---

⁵⁷ Prosecution of Offences Act 1985, s 6; *Regina (Gujra) v CPS* [2012] UKSC 52; [2013] AC 484 (Lord Wilson noting at [33] regular private prosecutions by Transport for London (evasion of fares), the RSPCA (animal welfare offences), and large retailers (shoplifting) – and a 'residue of prosecutions brought by individual citizens').

⁵⁸ *Gujra* ibid [69] (Lord Neuberger).

⁵⁹ Larry A Alexander, 'Causation and Corrective Justice: Does Tort Law Make Sense?' (1987) 6 *Law & Phil* 1, 4.

⁶⁰ Sentencing Act 2020, ss 133–46.

⁶¹ A Beever, 'The Structure of Aggravated and Exemplary Damages' (2003) 23 *OJLS* 87.

⁶² See *Kuddus v Chief Constable of Leicestershire* [2001] UKHL 29; [2002] 2 AC 122 [37] (Lord Mackay of Clashfern). Cf J Goudkamp and E Katsampouka, 'An Empirical Study of Punitive Damages' (2018) 38 *OJLS* 90.

suggested the common law 'may have been wiser than it knew' in refusing to commit to a sharp distinction between compensation (in tort) and punishment) in crime ('logic has never been the vice of English law').[63] But Beever rejects such traditional arguments as intellectually unsatisfactory.

Reasons to doubt exemplary damages' deterrent effect include their award against vicariously liable employers rather than wrongdoers personally,[64] and that exemplary damages are usually paid by liability insurers. (The fact that the defendant is known to be insured does not preclude an award of exemplary damages, so as to mark the court's disapproval.)[65] The courts have refused to extend the rule of public policy that one cannot insure against *criminal* liability to preclude insurance against exemplary damages. Simon Brown LJ accepted that insurance 'must undoubtedly reduce the deterrent and punitive effect of the order', but against that would 'greatly improve the plaintiff's prospects of recovering the sum awarded'.[66] Beever however argues that these are serious misunderstandings stemming from the confused idea that exemplary damages are designed somehow to *compensate* the claimant.[67]

For Beever, the decisive objection is that exemplary damages are inconsistent with tort law's bilateral inter-personal structure. Even if we accept that the criminal law is under-enforced and tort could thus usefully supplement it (when the tort in question is also a crime), why limit such supplementary claims to the *victims* of torts? Wouldn't a free-for-all by *any* willing private enforcer do a better job in correcting under-enforcement? Yet that would be impossible to reconcile with the logic of tort, under which only the *claimant* has standing to enforce the claimant's rights. But that is Beever's point: the 'supplementation' rationale leads away from private law's basic structure altogether. Why should it matter whether *anyone* has been injured before permitting 'enforcement through tort'?

Beever endorses Lord Scott's critique: 'Victims of tortious conduct should receive due compensation for their injuries, not windfalls'.[68] As Beever accepts, there is a danger of reasoning in a circle, assuming what needs to be proved, in ‛simply asserting dogmatically that 'tort is about compensation'. The point is a deeper one. As seen, the basic logic of corrective justice is that a claim lies by *this* claimant, against *this* defendant, in respect of the *specific* injury wrongfully sustained by the former at the latter's hands. That the action relates to the claimant's rights shows why they, and only they, can bring it. No similar connexion exists in respect of a payment designed to punish or deter the defendant. The claimant has no particular entitlement to recover such a windfall from the defendant. Supporters of exemplary damages sometimes support them as

---

[63] *Broome v Cassell & Co* [1972] AC 1027, 1114.
[64] Eg *Kuddus* (n 62) [125]–[138] (Lord Scott) (but compare Lord Hutton at [79]).
[65] *Lamb v Cotogno* (1987) 164 CLR 1.
[66] *Lancashire CC v Municipal Mutual Insurance* [1997] QB 897, 909.
[67] (n 61) 96.
[68] *Kuddus* (n 62) [121].

a 'bounty', an incentive for the claim to be brought. Beever responds that on that reasoning, and unlike true tort remedies, such bounties ought to be available to anyone who enforces the rule in question. There is no sensible reason to limit their payment to the victims of wrongs only.

Beever concludes that the structural differences between tort and crime mean that exemplary damages should be abolished. Their rationale is to deter (and to encourage proceedings against) wrongs of *any* kind, at the suit of *any* capable enforcer. This is incompatible with the corrective justice logic of tort, where only the claimant has standing to recover redress for the wrongful harm done to their interests. Indeed even those who accept the place of exemplary damages note how far the courts' practice diverges from theories of optimal deterrence.[69] Hershovitz argues that rather than calibrating their level to provide efficient incentives against wrongdoing, courts award exemplary damages to send a message about the wrongfulness of the defendant's conduct and the importance of the claimant's interest.[70] On this view even exemplary damages are more 'expressive' than deterrent. Tort law's punitive role remains dubious and controversial, even with a remedy as overtly concerned with punishment as exemplary damages.

Deterrence, Economic Analysis and Causation

The debate ranges far beyond the curious hybrid of exemplary damages. The Law and Economics movement analyses law as a system to guide behaviour. More specifically, that rules should be designed to give incentives for economically efficient decisions. But this runs into serious objections as a model of *tort* law.

A basic mismatch arises because *incentives* affect how law's subjects choose to behave at the time when they are engaging in the behaviour. Whether the behaviour actually causes harm to anyone subsequently, and in what amount, is strictly irrelevant to the 'ex ante' perspective, examining the time at which the relevant decisions are made. According to the most famous equation in economic analysis of tort, a defendant is negligent when they fail to take cost-justified precautions. The court must compare, in Judge Learned Hand's formula, the cost of taking precautions against the harm foreseeably avoided by those precautions.[71] The 'expected harm' at the time of the relevant decision (whether to take precautions or not) must mean the extent of the expected harm multiplied by the probability of its occurrence. The timing point is crucial. In the Learned Hand formula as in the standard law of negligence,

---

[69] AM Polinsky and S Shavell, 'Punitive Damages: An Economic Analysis' (1998) 111 *Harv LR* 869.

[70] S Hershovitz, 'Treating Wrongs as Wrongs: An Expressive Argument for Tort Law' (2017) 10 *Jo Tort L* 405.

[71] *United States v Carroll Towing Co*, 159 F.2d 169 (1947).

the court does not use hindsight. It does not use hindsight to conclude that the accident that has actually happened was always definitely going to happen (which would mean a 100 per cent chance of the actual injuries sustained, to compare with the cost of taking precautions against this). Obviously, to give useful incentives to the defendant at the time of their decision the court must scrutinise the decision taken on information available *at that time*. As Richard Wright puts it, 'ex post information regarding how things actually turned out, which is relevant for determination of factual causation ... is not relevant for determination of whether the actor's conduct was negligent' in the Learned Hand formula.[72]

The corollary is that causation of loss is irrelevant in economic analysis of tort law. Its leading figures have admitted as much. Guido Calabresi argued that when identifying 'risky' behaviour as the subject for legal regulation (whether through tort law or otherwise), what matters is how it affects the recurrent *chance* of injuries happening – not whether in fact it has caused particular injuries.[73] At best, Calabresi suggested, tort liability for harm caused could help make the price of an economic activity reflect the cost of the social harm that it inflicts. But Calabresi ultimately rejected this 'cost deterrence' function for causation too. Some form of 'fine or tax based on random sampling of past injuries associated with the activity' would carry lower administrative costs ('a far less expensive alternative') compared to tort litigation. Since only a fraction of tortious injuries result in successful claims, fines would be a better approximation of total costs.

Calabresi's retreat from the role of causation has been questioned. Mark Geistfeld queries whether the information to calculate the 'average costs of accidents' is likely to be present in practice.[74] If not, it will be difficult to set the 'fine or tax' at the right level, producing considerable dangers of over- or under-deterrence. Thus in Geistfeld's view, it is cost-effective to focus on the loss the defendant's activity has inflicted on a particular claimant, a more limited and therefore manageable factual inquiry. The point, he insists, is not that tort (including its traditional focus on losses caused) produces the economically *optimal* level of deterrence. But it might be the most feasible approximation to that ideal system.

In Wright's view however, Calabresi's arguments demonstrate the failure of economic analysis of tort law.[75] Law and Economics can accommodate only

---

[72] RW Wright, 'The New Old Efficiency Theories of Causation and Liability' (2014) 7 *Jo Tort Law* 65.

[73] G Calabresi, 'Concerning Cause and the Law of Torts: An Essay for Harry Kalven, Jr' (1975) 43 *G Chicago LR* 69.

[74] M Geistfeld, 'Economics, Moral Philosophy, and the Positive Analysis of Tort Law' in GJ Postema (ed), *Philosophy and the Law of Torts* (Cambridge, Cambridge University Press, 2001).

[75] RW Wright, 'Actual Causation vs. Probabilistic Linkage: The Bane of Economic Analysis' (1985) 14 *JLS* 435.

awkwardly, if at all, the requirement that the defendant caused injury to the claimant. Yet that causal connexion is at the centre of tort law:'The linchpin of corrective justice is "but for" causation'.[76] It is not some contingent feature serving an instrumental purpose, as in Calabresi's and Geistfeld's accounts. The linkage between claimant to defendant, the basic logic and moral structure of tort law, derives from a particular defendant having *caused* this particular claimant's injury. In the absence of that connexion, there can be no tort liability 'no matter how unreasonable, dangerous, or inefficient' the defendant's conduct.[77] If Law and Economics cannot explain causation, 'the most enduring and pervasive element of tort liability', its theories have been falsified as accounts of tort law. Gregory Keating also contrasts corrective justice accounts of tort, which readily explain the central and intrinsic role of causation, with economic accounts like Calabresi's. Those have to 'work hard to explain why plaintiffs always have rights against and only against those who have wronged them', resorting to strained and implausible arguments such as causation of loss as 'evidentiary markers that do a respectable job of identifying cheapest cost-avoiders'.[78] In short, the irrelevance of causation to economic accounts of tort as 'efficient incentives' are a major and perhaps fatal embarrassment.

One possible response comes from leading economic theorists, William Landes and Richard Posner.[79] They argue that theorists can choose what they mean by 'causation'. A chemist may identify the presence of oxygen as the cause of a fire; a safety inspector would choose non-compliance with fire regulations as the cause of the same event. So far, Landes and Posner's argument is familiar. Many would accept that defining what counts as 'causation' in law, both at an abstract level and in selecting 'the causes' of a particular event, there are normative choices.[80] Landes and Posner's next move is more controversial. For an economist whose concern is in supplying incentives for efficient decisions, they claim 'a defendant's conduct will be deemed the cause of an injury when making him liable for the consequences of the injury would promote an efficient allocation of resources to safety and care'. But such 'deeming' seems reminiscent of Humpty Dumpty's notorious claim (in *Through the Looking-Glass*) that words meant only what he personally defined them as meaning.[81] For as Landes and Posner admit, 'From here it is but a short step to the conclusion that the idea of causation can very largely be dispensed with in an

---

[76] Alexander (n 59) 12.
[77] Wright (n 75) 437.
[78] Gregory C Keating, 'Corrective Justice: Sovereign or Subordinate?' in Andrew S Gold et al, *The Oxford Handbook of the New Private Law* (Oxford, Oxford University Press, 2020).
[79] WM Landes and RA Posner, 'Causation in Tort Law: An Economic Approach' (1983) 12 *J Legal Stud* 109.
[80] See ch 5, 'Multiple Sufficient Factors: Each Causal?'.
[81] *Liversidge v Anderson* [1942] AC 206, 245 (Lord Atkin, dissenting).

economic analysis of torts'. No wonder, when the key questions are the ex ante probability of the accident happening and the cost of administering the resulting test of liability. As Landes and Posner accept, 'In so analyzing the causation cases we are admittedly far from the language and concepts in which the courts analyze these cases'.[82]

This seems a classic example of trying to win a debate by defining its terms to suit the answer. Landes and Posner's extraordinary argument seems to highlight the divergence between tort lawyers' and economic analysts' understanding of causation. Nor are they the only theorists to attempt such a stipulative definition of 'causation'. In Wright's view it is a *general* failing of economic analysis to elide ex ante risk with the historical question of whether X *caused* Y by using the confusing label of 'probalistic causation'.

In conclusion, Law and Economics is much the most developed and sophisticated account of tort law as a system of incentives. For this very reason, it misdescribes tort. In particular, economic analysis cannot explain the central importance of causation in tort claims. It is of the essence that the defendant's faulty conduct *harms this particular claimant* before a tort claim exists. A deterrence-oriented account focuses *solely* on the defendant's conduct. Tort law cannot adopt such a purely defendant-sided view, consistent with its basic structure.

Causation, the Burden of Proof and the 'Empty Duty' Argument

Law and Economics is a minority pursuit in English law. Yet deterrence-oriented accounts are not altogether absent. An argument prominent in several leading cases justifies unorthodox findings of causation to prevent the defendant's duty being 'emptied of content'. This is surely a deterrence-based argument, albeit less sophisticated than the models and equations used in Law and Economics. But it is ultimately incoherent, for similar reasons.

The 'empty duty' argument features prominently in two leading causation cases – *Fairchild v Glenhaven* and *Chester v Afshar*.[83] In each it was impossible to establish causation in the ordinary way. In *Fairchild*, it was impossible to prove *which* defendant was responsible for the 'fatal' triggering asbestos fibre. In *Chester v Afshar*, failing to disclose the risk of paralysis meant the claimant had the operation earlier than she would otherwise have done. But since the day of the week did not (of course) affect her chance of suffering the complication, the delay appeared an irrelevant 'coincidence'. But in each case the House of Lords was unwilling to accept that, logically, the claimants' inability to establish causation meant they must fail. The defendants were found to have *breached* their respective duties (employers' to protect employees' health; the surgeon's duty to disclose risks of side-effects). In both cases, the court

---

[82] Landes and Posner (n 79) 110, 134.
[83] For *Chester v Afshar*, see ch 2, 'Debate 4: "Informed Medical Consent" – Which Tort?'.

'exceptionally' imposed liability notwithstanding the absence of proven causation (in the ordinary sense). The concern was that if defendants found to have breached their duties escaped liability because of the impossibility of proving causation, this the relevant duties would be 'emptied of content'.

This 'exceptional' reasoning is superficially attractive. It is much less persuasive on examination. The burden of proof of causation (and other elements of the claim) lies on the claimant. There are numerous justifications for the general principle of claimants bearing the onus of proving their claims ('he who asserts must prove'). It is found in all legal systems. It seems questionable to reverse that burden of proof, assuming causation in the claimant's favour, as soon as a breach of duty can be shown.

Coons notes the 'healthy conservatism' of the legal process, which does not intervene 'until impelled by sufficient proof to move to the aid of a litigant seeking its intervention'.[84] Coons thought this did not justify 'universal judicial inertia' – because the virtuous 'preference for doing nothing' could be outweighed by claims of justice. Nevertheless, his argument suggests that 'inertia' (the absence of liability) should be the starting point, albeit not necessarily the end point. Law (which ultimately involves coercion by the state) should not swing into action without good reason. Weir argues that law correctly begins with non-intervention since it is 'better to leave a possible injustice uncured than to cause one' (ie by intervening incorrectly in the absence of sufficient factual proof). That outcomes may turn on the 'litigational posture' of the parties is not arbitrary: 'one must remember that the defendant, as a result simply of his posture as such, starts with a moral advantage'.[85]

Steel also identifies a principle of 'civility'.[86] The law begins with the courteous presumption that the defendant is *not* a tortfeasor, unless the claimant proves otherwise. Given the opprobrium of being held a wrongdoer, the law's refusal to reach such decisions without proof is understandable. There are also pragmatic arguments for inertia. Given the costly nature of litigation (including the public cost of court time), the starting point of non-intervention minimises those costs. Cumulatively, these arguments present a cogent albeit not overwhelming case for placing the onus of proof on the claimant. The argument's modesty reflects the relatively light burden on the claimant, who must only prove their case is more likely than not – by contrast with the criminal prosecutor's onus of proof beyond reasonable doubt.[87]

It follows from this 'presumption of non-intervention' that unless the claimant proves all elements of their case, the claim should fail. In particular, in the absence of proof of causation the defendant (even where culpable) cannot

---

[84] JE Coons, 'Approaches to Court Imposed Compromise-The Uses of Doubt and Reason' (1964) 58 *Nw Univ LR* 750, 756.

[85] T Weir, 'Shields and Swords' (1983) 7 *Trent LJ* 1.

[86] Steel (n 28) 124–25.

[87] Cf higher onus of 'convincing proof' in *civil* cases in German law: Steel (n 28) 53–55.

properly be described as a *tortfeasor*.⁸⁸ When breach of duty alone is proven, the defendant is a 'wrongdoer' only in that limited sense. Are we justified in modifying (or waiving) the claimant's onus to prove causation because the defendant is a wrongdoer? Arguably not. Even those found in breach of duty are entitled to the presumption of inertia (and 'civility'). In the criminal law, the prosecution is not relieved from proving causation once they have established mens rea (the mental element of the offence). Even when *culpability* has been established beyond reasonable doubt, the defendant does not lose the protection of the burden of proof. Steel questions whether a culpable tort defendant 'forfeits his right to our solicitude over whether we correctly assign liability'. He concludes it is 'simply unjust that the worse one behaves the less a case needs to be proven against one'.⁸⁹

There is no sensible reason to believe that a 'guilty' possible cause is more likely to be causal than an innocent possible cause, simply because of its 'guilt'. Imagine someone at the foot of a crumbling cliff is struck by a falling stone. Numerous stones fall naturally (through erosion) but a defendant climber's negligence has dislodged other stones. In the (artificial) situation of having no evidence whether the claimant was injured by one of the 'natural' or 'negligent' stones, their claim would fail. Fault does not increase the 'causal potency' of the defendant's possible contribution. Moore suggests that to claim otherwise is like believing that moral wickedness could cause earthquakes or train crashes. Hence Moore objects to the idea that culpability could have an 'aphrodisiac' effect on causation, the wrongfulness of the defendant's behaviour supplying a causal link that would otherwise be absent.⁹⁰ It is a mistake to allow 'fervor' on one issue (culpability) to 'cloud our judgment' on another (causation) – this would 'double-count our culpability judgments'.⁹¹ (Note the view that Moore's critique misses the mark: nobody claims that culpability can cause anything in and of itself, but when we selecting between a number of historically involved factors, we do attribute particular causal potency to culpable actions.)⁹²

It would violate the basic principle that claimants bear the burden of proof to reverse it on the issue of causation whenever the defendant were proven to be at fault. But *Fairchild* and *Chester* were presented as more limited exceptions. Can those authorities be confined?

---

⁸⁸ *Browning v War Office* [1963] 1 QB 750, 765.
⁸⁹ Steel (n 28) 287.
⁹⁰ MS Moore, *Causation and Responsibility: An Essay in Law, Morals, and Metaphysics* (Oxford, Oxford University Press, 2009) 135.
⁹¹ ibid 137.
⁹² J Knobe and S Shapiro, 'Proximate Cause Explained: An Essay in Experimental Jurisprudence' (2021) 88 *Univ Chicago LR* 165, 206 (and see ch 5, 'Conclusion: "Common Sense Causation" and the Scope of Responsibility').

Exceptional Cases? Fairchild *and* Chester

A particular problem of 'under-deterrence' emerges in situations where it will *regularly and repeatedly* be impossible to prove causation. The duty of care in a whole category of cases could then be breached with impunity, as causation could never be established. It is not clear, however, that this concern fits perfectly with either *Fairchild* or *Chester*. The problems of proof in the former case do not arise in *every* scenario where employees are negligently exposed to asbestos. For example, where the defendant employer is the only source of asbestos. Even where there are several sources, some asbestos-related diseases develop and worsen 'cumulatively' – that is, each employer's exposure to asbestos contributes to the overall disease.[93] Even if the law rejected the exceptional *Fairchild* rule then, there would still be many situations where the employer's duty would *not* be 'hollow' because proof of causation would be quite feasible. Only a very well-informed, calculating and devious employer would be able, first, to identify employees who would find their claims obstructed by the *Fairchild* 'rock of uncertainty' and then, second, expose *only those employees* to asbestos. That scenario seems absurdly unlikely.

As for *Chester v Afshar*, the 'special rule' addresses the 'hollowing' of the duty to disclose risks only very incompletely.[94] In one common situation, where the patient would still have gone ahead with the operation had they been warned, then causation would still not be established under the *Chester* approach. Thus doctors would still have a 'hollow duty' in that situation (which may well be the commonest situation – since many patients have no real choice but to proceed with life-saving or medically significant treatment, despite the risk of side-effects). Conversely, to repeat the argument in the previous paragraph, even if the *Chester* rule were abolished some patients would still be able to show causation in the ordinary way: that is, those who would *not* have proceeded with the treatment had the risks been disclosed to them as the duty required.

Steel suggests that we rarely have the information needed to craft an exceptional rule on causation using the 'hollow duty' justification. There would need to be reliable empirical evidence of a recurrent problem of causal uncertainty, and that the impossibility (or difficulty) of proving causation was leading defendants to behave less carefully. But such evidence does not exist. At best we find 'reasoned conjectures' (for example the standard claim in economic analysis that difficulties of causal proof lead to underdeterrence). But there is good reason to question such assumptions. As Steel notes, defendants (including employers and doctors) have many reasons to perform their duties, quite apart from potential tort liability – for example 'moral emotions', market pressures,

---

[93] *Holtby v Brigham & Cowan* [2000] ICR 1086 (asbestosis).
[94] T Clark and D Nolan, 'A Critique of *Chester v Afshar*' (2014) 34 *OJLS* 659 (a 'colossal failure' to sanction all failures to warn).

and other species of legal regulation. Steel concludes that it is not justified to alter the burden of proof on this ground, 'given the conjectural state of the empirical case'. Even if convincing evidence could be collected, he points out that it is likely to be highly specific (eg limited to particular kinds of illness). Recognition of such case-specific exceptions to rules of proof would make tort law 'highly dappled'. This would not merely violate abstract concerns for legal coherence. It could lead to a 'sense of injustice' if some, but only some, claimants succeeded 'simply because of the impoverished state of knowledge about the causes of their injury'.[95]

Again, the law faces a dilemma. If it were generalised, the 'hollow duty' argument would reverse the burden of proof in *every* case. The law would always presume that a proven breach had caused the claimant's injury (to give content to the duty breached), unless the defendant could prove otherwise. But given the sensible reasons for placing the burden of proof on claimants, an across-the-board change seems questionable. But it is difficult to justify a more limited 'hollow duty' exception to proof of causation and the factual basis for doing so is absent. Note that whereas in *Fairchild* Lord Hoffmann scorned the idea that *doctors*' duties to their patients 'would be virtually drained of content' without a reformulated test of causation (by implicit contrast with the employer-defendants in *Fairchild* itself),[96] the self-same argument was later used in *Chester v Afshar* to extend liability in the medical context (failures to warn).

Conclusion

Both compensation and deterrence are goals that range far beyond than the necessarily limited, *discriminating* law of torts. Tort awards compensation only to those who have been wronged, and only from the individual that wronged them. The causal link between the defendant's wrong and the claimant's loss is central. It is not surprising that arguments derived from compensation or deterrence are often used to justify relaxation of tort law's normal causal requirements – given that ultimately, neither argument has need for causal requirements of any kind. In Donal Nolan's words there is 'an irreconcilable tension between these two goals and the fundamental nature of the mechanism [ie tort] through which they are sought to be achieved'. The inevitable result is incoherence. Because the goals have 'no obvious stopping point' short of a no-fault compensation scheme or criminal regulation – that is, no stopping point logically compatible with the basic idea of tort – 'the courts have had to resort to illogical ones instead'.[97]

---

[95] Steel (n 28) 269–75.
[96] *Fairchild* (n 2) [69].
[97] D Nolan, 'Causation and the Goals of Tort Law' in A Robertson and TH Wu (eds), *The Goals of Private Law* (Oxford, Hart, 2009) 189.

Debate 3
Questioning Corrective Justice – Moral and Doctrinal Critique

The preceding debates suggest that tort law cannot serve external goals such as 'compensating the injured' or 'deterring wrongdoing', without descending into utter incoherence. The 'bilateral' essence of tort precludes such approaches. They threaten to unravel tort law's structure altogether. This can only be resisted by place arbitrary limitations on them. The '*Fairchild* enclave' is an infamous example. Neither the 'intuitive fairness' of compensating mesothelioma victims nor preserving 'meaningful duties' on employers can justify its arbitrary limits.

However, many commentators suggest that at least some exceptional approaches to causation can be reconciled with corrective justice. We will consider one example here, that could and does arise in 'mass torts' situations: where a number of proven tortfeasors have injured a number of known victims, but it is impossible to say *which* particular defendant caused *which* particular claimant's injury. Once we explain the scenario (and its plausibility), we will see that there appears to be a strong corrective justice argument favouring liability. However some writers in the corrective justice tradition (eg Weinrib) resist the conclusion that there should be liability, arguing that it would involve impermissible 'aggregation' of unconnected parties. We examine this debate, before turning to critique of 'corrective justice' itself. For some critics, it is a poor fit with tort law – the institution that it sets out to describe. Others question whether corrective justice is morally justifiable.

The clearest point to emerge from this debate is that corrective justice cannot be taken as a given. Considerable disagreement remains about tort law's structure and content, even between those who accept that it should be understood through the lens of justice, and reject such instrumental goals as compensation and deterrence.

'Two Hunters' (or 'the Indeterminate Defendant')

We begin with a famous problem in the law on proof of causation. Let us imagine two sportsmen independently hunting rabbits (and unaware of the other's existence). By coincidence they both carelessly fire in the direction of the (unsuspected) claimant. The claimant's eye is injured by *one* piece of lead shot. It is impossible to say from which hunter's gun it came. We know that each hunter (defendant) breached their duty of care. We also know that only one defendant's breach caused the claimant's injury. The chance it was D1 is precisely 50 per cent, as for D2. Neither can be shown more likely than not, on the balance of probabilities, to have shot the claimant (worse where there are three or more negligent hunters). Therefore on orthodox grounds the claimant would fail *both* in their claim against D1 *and* against D2.[98]

---
[98] R Stevens, *Torts and Rights* (Oxford, Oxford University Press, 2007) 149.

Indeed, French courts once thought it *'une inqiuité flagrante'* to hold a non-causative defendant liable (which seems unavoidable in any solution that awards damages against both).[99] Nevertheless, celebrated decision have upheld (literal) 'two hunter' claims, including *Summers v Tice* (California)[100] and *Cook v Lewis* (Canada).[101]

The intuitive fairness of liability in 'two rabbit hunters' seems strong. But it is not easy to explain. Liability cannot be rationalised by holding the hunters engaged in a joint enterprise (so that they must either be the primary wrong-doer who caused the injury, or an accomplice with accessory liability for the other's tort). Where the hunters were acting *independently*, it is a fiction to postulate *joint* action.[102]

A second possibility is that although only one hunter shot the claimant, the other hunter has destroyed their possibility of bringing a claim. They have created insoluble causal uncertainty by shooting at the same time as the hunter who did actually shoot the claimant. This disruption of the claimant's 'remedial right' to damages from the defendant who shot them could make the non-shooting hunter liable too. The theory can be traced to Rand J's concurring judgment in *Cook v Lewis*. One hunter shot the claimant; the other

> violated not only the victim's substantive right of security, but he has also culpably impaired the latter's remedial right of establishing liability. By confusing his act with environmental conditions, he has, in effect, destroyed the victim's power of proof.[103]

However as Steel points out, this faces a number of problems. First, doesn't obstructing someone's right to claim damages involve pure economic loss – something for which a duty of care arises only exceptionally in English law? Second, it involves a mismatch with why we deem culpable the 'claim obstructing' defendant's conduct. Both defendants' breach of duty consists in carelessly risking *physical harm* to the claimant. The non-shooting defendant has not been negligent with respect to the claimant's ability to bring a successful claim for damages, but rather (just as with the shooting defendant) with respect to their physical safety.

As Steel accepts, in exceptional situations defendants are liable for creating evidential harm.[104] But such cases involve duties of care designed to create or preserve the relevant evidence. For example in *Keefe v Isle of Man Steam Packet Co* the defendant breached its duty to monitor noise levels on board ship. The claimant suffered hearing loss; although he could not prove that he had been

---

[99] Steel (n 28) 154.
[100] 33 Cal 2d 80 (1948).
[101] [1951] SCR 830.
[102] Steel (n 28) 155–60 (decline of French *faute collective* theory).
[103] [1951] SCR 830, 832.
[104] Steel (n 28) 249–51.

exposed to excessive noise, his claim succeeded since 'any difficulty of proof for the claimant has been caused by the defendant's breach of duty in failing to take any measurements'.[105] By contrast, in the 'Two Hunters' scenario, the defendants' duty is to avoid physical harm rather than evidential damage.

However Ernest Weinrib supports Rand J's 'brilliant' solution.[106] Weinrib accepts the thrust of the critique just mentioned: it would be 'fantasy' and 'artificial' to say that the second hunter is liable for negligence towards a *remedial* right, since 'the only negligence in play' is towards the claimant's ('substantive') right not to be physically injured. Weinrib also accepts the 'implausibility' of freestanding actions for evidential damage against someone innocent of the 'substantive' negligence (eg a nurse who fails to keep proper notes of a hospital operation would not be liable to a patient who, as a result, cannot prove whether there was medical malpractice). Robert Stevens agrees, reasoning that we have no general right, good against the world, to have evidence preserved or collected.[107] However Weinrib argues that the 'substantive' negligence in the 'Two Hunters' case – carelessly risking personal injury to the claimant – encompasses both physical injury *and* the right to claim damages for it. 'The shot that actually wounded the plaintiff damaged the plaintiff's right [to bodily integrity] in its substantive aspect. The other shot interfered with that right in its remedial aspect'.[108] Thus a defendant guilty of such 'substantive' negligence (ie the hunter, but not the record-keeping nurse) is liable *either* for the injury itself *or* the loss of the claim for damages to that injury.

As Weinrib notes, there is authority supporting his view. Obiter dicta in *Wright v Cambridge Medical Group* suggest that if a GP negligently failed to refer a sick patient to hospital, but it emerges that the hospital would anyway have administered unsatisfactory treatment, the GP could be liable either for the patient's lost opportunity to be treated by the hospital *or* to recover damages for the hospital's unsatisfactory treatment.[109] Lord Neuberger MR specifically rejected counsel's objection that 'it is not within the scope of a doctor's duty to protect his patient from financial or economic loss'. While true in the ordinary run of cases, Lord Neuberger reasoned

> an award of damages for clinical negligence is, in a sense, the legal equivalent of proper clinical treatment: it is the nearest the law can get to putting the patient into the position that she should have been in if the doctor had not been negligent.[110]

---

[105] [2010] EWCA Civ 683, [29] (Longmore LJ).
[106] Weinrib (n 19).
[107] Stevens (n 98) 150.
[108] Weinrib (n 19) 146.
[109] [2011] EWCA Civ 669; [2013] QB 312 [61] (Lord Neuberger MR), [98] (Elias LJ).
[110] ibid [60].

But McBride and Steel object that while a damages award might be 'the nearest thing', it is not the *same* thing as the 'proper clinical treatment': 'A substitute for the real thing does not amount, even in part, to the real thing'.[111] While damages are, of course, designed to restore the claimant's position, to stress the 'normative continuity' between right and remedy (as Weinrib does) conflates two separate things.[112]

McBride and Steel note that as a matter of authority, *Wright* revived the 'corpse of an idea that would have been better left undisturbed'.[113] It was a solution consciously not adopted by the House of Lords in *Baker v Willoughby* (where the Court of Appeal had suggested, to stop the claim falling between two stools, that the *second* tortfeasor in the sequence would be liable both for the physical injuries inflicted *and for depriving the plaintiff of his claim in damages against the first tortfeasor*).[114] McBride and Steel argue the law lords were correct not to rely on 'loss of the right to sue'. If the second tortfeasor were responsible for causing such a loss, then equally the *first* tortfeasor would be liable for interfering with a parallel claim against the second. This 'infinite regress'[115] would lead the law into 'logical paralysis'.[116] (Stevens similarly identifies a 'circularity problem').[117] McBride and Steel also suggest that consequential 'loss of the right to sue' would be too remote: while it is readily foreseeable that the defendants' conduct in *Baker v Willoughby* (or 'Two Hunters') could cause *physical* injury, it is considerably less foreseeable that it could obstruct a damages claim against some third party.[118]

A further problem arises when one of the defendants (hunters etc) is impecunious (eg insolvent and uninsured). This is a common and important situation. In practice, claimants sue only defendants with enough money to satisfy judgment (eg claiming only against the *insured* negligent driver (D1), not the uninsured (!) armed robbers (D2), in *Baker v Willoughby*). In 'Two Hunters', the claim might be brought against the one solvent hunter who can be identified. If the other hunter could not be sued successfully (eg unidentified, untraceable, insolvent or uninsured), the notional claim against him would be worthless. Thus liability premised on *interrupting* a claim against the second hunter ought to be valued at zero since the claim was valueless in any event.[119] The first hunter has merely 'culpably impaired the [claimant's] remedial right'

---

[111] NJ McBride and S Steel, 'Suing for the Loss of a Right to Sue: Why *Wright* is Wrong' (2012) 28 *Prof Neg* 27, 34.

[112] Compare Steel (n 28) 181 ('nonetheless true that there is a significant normative continuity', citing in support *Wright v Cambridge*!).

[113] McBride and Steel (n 111) 39.

[114] eg [1970] AC 467, 483 (Harman LJ) (CA).

[115] Steel (n 28) 179 (and 182–83).

[116] McBride and Steel (n 111) 37.

[117] Stevens (n 98) 150.

[118] McBride and Steel (n 111) 33 (similarly Stevens (n 98) 150).

[119] Steel (n 28) 178.

against someone who was not worth suing. Thus Steel concludes that the 'prevented claim theory' is only fully convincing when all defendants are solvent and traceable.[120] That condition will frequently not be satisfied.

A final problem, noted by Stevens, is that just as it cannot be shown more likely than not which defendant in isolation caused physical harm, similarly it cannot be shown more likely than not which caused the loss of a claim.[121] This seems another aspect of the 'paradox objection' to the interrupted claim theory.

Could 'Two Hunters' be justified on another basis? The great Californian judge Traynor J held that *Summers v Tice*

> is based on the policy that it is preferable to hold liable a negligent defendant who did not in fact cause the injury than to deny an innocent plaintiff any remedy when it cannot be determined which of the defendants is responsible for the harm but it appears that one of them was.[122]

A similar justification was suggested by Glanville Williams: 'To deny a remedy means that justice is certainly not done; to give a remedy would mean a fifty per cent possibility that justice is done'.[123] However as Steel points out, from the perspective of the defendant who did not actually cause any harm, 'there is a 100 per cent chance of injustice'.[124] The fact that the claimant is *identifiable* as the victim of injustice if the claim fails (whereas we do not know *which* defendant is unjustly held liable) seems irrelevant. Stevens similarly rejects the idea that the exceptional rule substitutes the single injustice of making a non-causal party liable for the '(double) injustice of allowing both the party whose bullet did strike off and leaving the party struck with no claim': this is double counting, because the choice is between allowing 'one claim which ought to fail to succeed, instead of one claim which ought to succeed, if it could be proved, to fail'.[125]

However Steel accepts the probable correctness of our intuition that justice exceptionally requires liability in 'Two Hunters'.[126] Given that all the possible sources of injury were wrongs (and would be torts if causation could be shown), we *know* that the claimant was injured tortiously – just not by whom. As damage is the gist of the action, the non-causative hunter is not a tortfeasor. But it is not inaccurate to label them a *wrongdoer*, for breaching their duty of care. When all defendants have wrongfully *risked* harm to the claimant (even though not all have actually *caused* harm), we can draw an analogy with the

---

[120] ibid 182–83, 197.
[121] Stevens (n 98) 150.
[122] *Vasquez v Alameda* 49 Cal.2d 674, 682 (1958).
[123] Glanville Williams, 'Comment on *Cook v Lewis*' (1953) *Can Bar Rev* 315, 317.
[124] Steel (n 28) 186.
[125] Stevens (n 98) 151.
[126] Steel (n 28) 188–92.

situations where causation is 'overdetermined' by multiple wrongs. Namely where both D1 and D2 are known to do things that would each be sufficient to cause the claimant's harm, neither is permitted to raise the other's wrong. This would allow each to hide behind the other, and produce the answer that neither was a cause.[127] Although the problem here is a different one (inability of proof rather than the conceptual difficulties of the but-for test),[128] 'the law is generally averse to allowing the mere multiplicity of wrongful actors to [deprive compensation from] a person whose injury would not have occurred had no one behaved wrongfully'.[129]

The 'Matching' Problem: Sindell v Abbot Laboratories

There is a strong case for liability when many defendants injure many claimants but nobody can tell precisely who was injured by whom. This sounds an unlikely situation, but is by no means implausible – as with side-effects from mass-market generic drugs.

To take another stylised example. This time, five hunters are independently hunting deer with identical rifles. The hunters negligently shoot simultaneously into a forest where unsuspected ramblers are walking. Five ramblers are shot, once each, by five different bullets. Compare this with the 'two rabbit hunters'. In the second, deer hunting example, we again know that every claimant has been the victim of a wrong. But unlike 'two hunters' we also *know that each defendant is a tortfeasor.* Each has negligently *caused* harm. The problem is matching the claimants and defendants.

Each claimant can sue one of the defendants, but which? Each defendant is liable to one of the claimants – but who? If we apply the ordinary rules on proof, it seems that each claim will fail. If C1 sues D1, it is only 20 per cent likely that D1 shot C1 (and 80 per cent likely that it was one of D2, D3, D4, D5). The same is true if C1 sues D2, and so on. And the same problem faces the other four claimants.

Yet can this be right? As Ken Oliphant notes, there seems an even stronger case for liability here than in the previous 'two hunters' situation.[130] We are certain that each claimant was the victim of a tort, and each defendant acted tortiously. This situation is superior in the hierarchy of justice, compared to 'two hunters' cases, when we examine the justifiability of exceptions to the orthodox rules on proof of causation. It is therefore surprising that (as we will see) some interpretations of corrective justice rule out liability for the 'deer hunters'.

---

[127] *Baker v Willoughby* [1970] AC 467.
[128] See ch 5, 'Debate 1: The But-For Test'.
[129] Steel (n 28) 191–92.
[130] K Oliphant, 'Causation in Cases of Evidential Uncertainty: Juridical Techniques and Fundamental Issues' (2016) 91 *Chi-Kent LR* 587.

The deer hunting situation looks absurdly unlikely, yet it has occurred in real life. Take numerous pharmaceutical companies producing a widely prescribed generic drug (ie one outside patent protection that can be manufactured by anyone, like aspirin and paracetamol). Let us imagine that one particular generic drug causes serious injuries to a significant number of people, years after taking it. Given the lapse of time it may be impossible for victims to prove which manufacturer produced the drug that they took (especially if it was administered in hospital and the patient never saw the branded packaging). This is in all essentials the 'deer hunters' problem. We can be sure that any supplier of significant quantities of the drug must have caused *some* of the injuries. We know that every victim has been wronged by *one* of the manufacturers.[131] We merely do not know which company caused which injuries.

Faced with this situation, *Sindell v Abbott Laboratories* imposed liability based on each defendant's share of the relevant market.[132] The majority noted that it was likely to be a 'recurring' problem: 'In our contemporary complex industrialized society, advances in science and technology create fungible goods which may harm consumers and which cannot be traced to any specific producer'.[133] In *Sindell*, the generic drug had been supplied by about 200 different manufacturers. Unless all 200 were before the court as defendants (which was not true in *Sindell* itself), the 'two hunters' logic was unavailable: it could not be said that *one* of the defendants *must* have injured the claimant. The court side-stepped that problem by holding each defendant liable not for the full value of a claimant's injury, but only for a *proportion* of each claimant's injuries, reflecting the percentage of the total supply of drugs that each company had produced. While accepting the practical difficulties of this approach ('It is probably impossible, with the passage of time, to determine market share with mathematical exactitude'), the majority reasoned: 'Under this approach, each manufacturer's liability would approximate its responsibility for the injuries caused by its own products'.[134] If we imagine that every person injured by those generic drugs brings an action against every manufacturer that would, on aggregate, be the end result.

Is such aggregation acceptable? The following section considers objections from corrective justice. In *Sindell v Abbott Laboratories* itself Richardson J dissented, complaining that the majority had turned the pharmaceutical industry into the collective insurer 'of all injuries attributable to defective drugs of uncertain or unprovable origin'.[135] That development had such wide-ranging implications it was properly a matter for the legislature to consider. Turning to each defendant individually, the objections were stronger still. In principle,

---

[131] Consumer Protection Act 1987.
[132] 26 Cal. 3d 588 (1980).
[133] ibid 610.
[134] ibid 612–13.
[135] ibid 621 (an 'unreasonable overreaction for the purpose of achieving what is perceived to be a socially satisfying result').

defendants are not liable because there is a possibility that they caused harm – it must be shown more likely than not. But under the new *Sindell* doctrine, 'a defendant is fair game if it happens to be engaged in a similar business and causation is *possible*, even though remote'.[136] Richardson J rejected the plaintiff's 'striking' submission ('that while one manufacturer's product may not have injured a particular plaintiff, we can assume that it injured a different plaintiff and all we are talking about is a mere matching of plaintiffs and defendants').[137] The requirement to match parties was no 'mere' matter – it was 'absolutely essential' for liability.

Aggregation and Corrective Justice

Corrective justice requires proof of a link *between these particular parties* to justify the imposition of tort liability. The requirement of identification works in both directions. To quote Allan Beever, it is irrelevant (for corrective justice) that an injured claimant deserves compensation from just *somebody*: the question is whether they are 'deserving of recovery *from some particular person*' (the defendant in their action).[138] By similar logic, a defendant is liable only *to* the particular person they have wronged: it is insufficient that they must have wronged somebody, if we cannot identify who that somebody was. As Gemma Turton explains, we cannot look at the claimant and defendant separately: corrective justice is concerned 'with both of them in their interaction'.[139]

On this view corrective justice precludes an answer to the 'two hunters' problem proceeding from the insight that we know that *one* of the careless hunters must have shot the claimant. As between claimant and *defendants* (plural), justice seems to favour liability. But Nolan argues the intuition is flawed because 'it refers not to each defendant as an individual but to the defendants as a collective entity'.[140] It is proper to 'collectivise' liability only when defendants join together in concerted action, which is not true in 'two hunters' cases – or *Fairchild*. These situations involve independent wrongdoers. From the perspective of each defendant individually, it is irrelevant whether the other possible cause was another person's negligence or some naturally occurring event.[141]

The same corrective justice theory opposes *Sindell v Abbott Laboratories*. Weinrib declares that 'Injustice in private law is relational, connecting a particular defendant's conduct to a particular plaintiff's injury'.[142] This could not be done in *Sindell*. The doctrine's disavowal of corrective justice, according

---

[136] ibid 617.
[137] ibid 616.
[138] Beever (n 61) 457–58.
[139] G Turton, *Evidential Uncertainty in Causation in Negligence* (Oxford, Hart, 2016) 205.
[140] Nolan (n 97) 174.
[141] ibid 175.
[142] (n 19) 150.

to Weinrib, lies in its 'effacement of the significance of the causal connection between the manufacturers and particular plaintiffs'.[143] Yet other theorists in the tradition disagree. Analysing 'Corrective Justice in an Age of Mass Torts', Ripstein and Zipursky defend *Sindell* despite their common ground with Weinrib.[144] They accept the inter-personal nature of tort liability. They also agree that in general it is impermissible to aggregate defendants absenting concerted wrongdoing. Even in 'mass tort' cases (such as *Sindell*), exceptions cannot be too freely made or they will swallow the whole of tort law. But crucially, Ripstein and Zipursky suggest that 'sensitive pragmatism' may justify suitably narrow exceptions. *Sindell* is such a case.

Given the large number of injured claimants and each defendant's significant supply of the harmful drugs in *Sindell*, we know that *all* defendants *did* injure others. (We have already seen Oliphant's observation that this makes it a stronger case for liability than in classic 'two hunters' cases where all defendants are in *breach*, but only one has *caused* any harm.) Claimants cannot discharge the 'burden of identification' on a strict view of the law. But Ripstein and Zipursky think it justified to relax that burden. *Sindell* prevents defendants arguing, unacceptably, in answer to each claimant, that they are unable to show that *they* injured them, while admitting causing identical injuries to other unidentifiable members of the pool of plaintiffs. Without the *Sindell* rule this could be asserted 'serially' by each defendant against each claimant, producing a 'merry go round of defences'.[145]

Beever is unpersuaded. The proposition that the defendants are known to be wrongdoers, and the claimants victims of wrong, holds only if the claimants and defendants are grouped together. 'But if they are taken individually, then it is clearly not true'. Beever thus thinks Ripstein and Zipursky's account is 'in tension with one of the main functions of the causal enquiry: to link particular acts of wrongdoing to particular injuries, to link particular defendants to particular claimants'. It is unacceptable to treat claimants (or defendants) together as a single entity or unit. The fundamental objection, on this view, is precisely that in a mass tort situation *Sindell* focuses not on the relationship between individual tortfeasor and victim, 'but between groups of persons'.[146]

If corrective justice requires that no claimant can recover damages in the 'deer hunters' example, we might wonder whether corrective justice in its sternest form is a principle that tort law should wish to retain. Weinrib himself anticipates such criticisms. Corrective justice is not without resources to address these difficult cases, he claims. Weinrib advances the theory (discussed above under 'two hunters') of the 'normative continuity' between inflicting

---

[143] ibid 152.
[144] In GJ Postema (ed), *Philosophy and the Law of Torts* (Cambridge, Cambridge University Press, 2001).
[145] ibid 234.
[146] Beever (n 61) 455–57 (the source for the quotations in this paragraph).

harm and precluding the legal remedy for harm. As seen however, this solution involves difficulties.

Weinrib's is simply one example of attempts to redefine *damage* (or the relevant *rights*) – as in the famous argument that one who cannot prove it more likely than not that the defendant harmed then can nevertheless show that the defendant *reduced their chances* of avoiding the harm. (This engages the debate – is a 'lost chance' actionable damage; or do we have a right not to be exposed to *risks*, as opposed to injuries.) As Ripstein and Zipursky note, such arguments indirectly show the *centrality* of causation. The aim is to redefine actionable damage – rather than suggest that causation could be dispensed with altogether.

If Weinrib's 'normative continuity' thesis fails, does corrective justice deny a remedy in 'deer hunters' and *Sindell*? Not necessarily. Returning to the identification problem, Steel asks:

> Given that each defendant cannot identify the individual to whom it owes [the duty to pay compensation], what should it do? Surely, the answer is not nothing. The mere fact that the victim cannot be identified does not release the defendant from its obligation.[147]

The 'reasonable course of action' would be for every defendant in this situation to authorise other defendants to settle claims brought against them on each other's behalf. In practice that means each would contribute to a collective compensation fund, in proportion to each defendant's share of the harm. After working this arrangement through, 'each defendant can be assured of actually compensating its own victim'. In the absence of an actual agreement of this kind, the court should award proportionate compensation in this way (ie the *Sindell* approach). Effectively this 'serves the same pooling function as the authorisation agreement which should have occurred between the Ds'. Note that Steel denies that this is 'aggregate or collective corrective justice'. Rather, contribution towards a shared fund is the best way for each defendant, individually, to comply with its duty to pay compensation to the particular victim of its wrong ('individualised or relational corrective justice').[148]

Steel postulates a hypothetical agreement between individual defendants to aggregate the mechanism for discharging their independent liabilities. This ingenious suggestion blurs the line between collective and individual solutions. Each defendant would be required, by their individual obligation to compensate their victim, to join an *aggregate* process which dispenses with individualised matching between particular claimants and defendants. Steel argues that his proposals are 'conservative' because defendants are liable only when proven to have caused injury – although he accepts: 'Proof of causation is preserved, even if proof of *individual* causation is not'.[149]

---

[147] S Steel, 'Justifying Exceptions to Proof of Causation in Tort Law' (2015) 78 *MLR* 729, 734.
[148] ibid 736.
[149] ibid 757 (emphasis added).

Does this type of argument elide a distinction that corrective justice theory holds to be vitally important? A similar blurring is found in *Clements v Clements*.[150] McLachlin CJ held that in Canadian law, the exceptional English '*Fairchild* enclave' should be confined to situations where all possible causes were wrongful breaches of duty.[151] The exception applied where 'the plaintiff would not have contracted the disease, "but for" the negligence of the defendants as a group'.[152] Such a plaintiff can show that their injury has been caused tortiously, when 'viewed globally'; 'It is only when it is applied separately to each defendant that the "but for" test breaks down because it cannot be shown which of several negligent defendants actually launched the event that led to the injury'.[153] It would *violate* corrective justice 'to allow the defendants to each escape liability by pointing the finger at one another'.[154]

> [The] deficit in the relationship between the plaintiff and the *defendants viewed as a group* that would exist if the plaintiff were denied recovery is corrected. The plaintiff has shown that she is in a correlative relationship of doer and sufferer of the same harm with the group of defendants as a whole, *if not necessarily with each individual defendant*.[155]

Turton rejects McLachlin CJ's reasoning, stating that 'corrective justice does not allow for defendants to be aggregated in this way'.[156] Compare, again, Steel's more nuanced view. Beever rejects the 'relative injustice' solution to the 'two hunters' case, on the grounds that it works only if we aggregate both defendants' fault. For Steel 'this objection is confused'. Parties are entitled, under corrective justice, that courts consider their rights and obligations owed as individuals to other individuals. 'It is another [thing] to say that each individual has a legal entitlement to have their case considered by a judge in isolation from its consequences upon other cases'. If both hunters are before the court, the court knows there will be a 100 per cent injustice (erroneous dismissal) to victim if the claim is dismissed, but only a 50 per cent injustice (erroneous liability) to each hunter if liability is imposed. Steel claims: 'This does not involve treating the defendants as if they were a collective, each responsible for the actions of the other. It simply involves the judge taking into account the consequences of a finding of liability upon the parties'.[157]

---

[150] [2012] 2 SCR 181.
[151] cf *Sienkiewicz* (n 31) (cause of mesothelioma was probably non-tortious, yet *Fairchild* applied).
[152] [2012] 2 SCR 181, [32].
[153] ibid [40].
[154] ibid [32].
[155] ibid [41] (emphasis added).
[156] Turton (n 139) 205.
[157] Steel (n 28) 186–87.

Moral Critique of Corrective Justice

Should we accept corrective justice at all? The last section outlined attempts to reconcile a degree of 'aggregation' with corrective justice. Others, however, reject the premise. There are morally based critiques of corrective justice, and the causation-based tort law that embodies it. Critics taking this view, for example Jeremy Waldron and Christopher Schroeder, argue that a collectivised approach would be superior on grounds of *justice*. (This seems surprising insofar as most calls for collectivised compensation or accident-deterrence are instrumental in focus, deeming justice an obstacle to collectivised approaches rather than a supportive argument.)[158]

Both Waldron and Schroeder criticise tort liability's divergence from moral desert. They emphasise different aspects of this problem. Waldron takes issue with fundamental tenets of tort liability.[159] He questions whether tort law is morally justified in visiting 'massive loss' on a defendant whose momentary inattention leads to (eg) a fatal traffic accident. Crushing liability seems disproportionate to the defendant's modest fault. Can it be right to ruin defendants financially because of careless mistakes? (Waldron recommends that we ignore liability insurance – merely an attempt to make a fundamentally unjust system just, thereby blurring our consideration of the defendant's moral predicament.) Waldron accepts that tort is not solely about desert. It is not a pure system of retribution, concerned only with administering 'just deserts' punishment. But nor is desert irrelevant. The basic fairness of a legal institution is always a legitimate concern, even when the institution claims to be the legal embodiment of a distinctive form of justice ('corrective justice'). It would be troubling if there were 'systematic and sustained dissonance' between tort liability and our moral intuitions about desert. Which, in Waldron's view, there is. Tort's outcomes seem 'manifestly at odds with what [individuals] may plausibly be said to deserve'.[160]

A tort lawyer's standard response to Waldron runs as follows. Where an innocent person is injured by a tortfeasor, we must compare the justice of leaving the innocent claimant bearing the loss compared with transferring it to the defendant. From that perspective, it is obviously more just to transfer the loss by holding the tortfeasor liable, even though it might be disproportionate to the tortfeasor's culpability. Tort liability is not quantified in proportion to culpability. It transfers all loss to the defendant's account when as a matter of corrective justice, the defendant should bear it rather than the claimant.

Waldron, however, queries the starting point for this argument. He accepts that if the law's only options are leaving 'massive loss' on the claimant, or

---

[158] G Calabresi, *The Costs of Accidents* (New Haven, CT, Yale University Press, 1970) Part V.

[159] J Waldron, 'Moments of Carelessness and Massive Loss' in DG Owen (ed), *Philosophical Foundations of Tort Law* (Oxford, Clarendon, 1995).

[160] ibid 391.

transferring it to the tortfeasor, the second option seems less unjust. Yet if *either* outcome seems deeply unfair, 'why not abandon the framework that confines our attention to the two [parties]'? Is tort's exclusive focus on the individual parties 'non-arbitrary from a moral point of view'?[161] Waldron thinks not. He claims that 'manifestly disproportionate' liability is 'arbitrarily' imposed. Several drivers may be equally careless, but those who happen to cause no harm escape tort liability entirely (even if their negligence is much greater than another driver's, which does inflict harm). Tort liability turns, then, on the essential fortuity of causation. Waldron accepts, of course, that causation is at the heart of tort law. He quotes Weinrib's description of the bilateral relationship between the parties, connected by a 'single unbroken process' of doing and suffering harm. But, he comments, that is entirely the problem. Tort law premises its ruin of defendants (through crushing liabilities) upon the *chance* fact of their conduct causing loss.

But is the fact that the defendant's conduct *causes harm* an irrelevance, a mere coincidence or fortuity? Against Waldron's view, other philosophers contend that we should be held responsible for the *outcomes* of what we do. For what actually happens, for what we *cause*. Honoré claims '[our] community allocates responsibility according to outcomes' – whether or not those outcomes are intended, or foreseeable, or could have been prevented.[162] Honoré thinks we are correct to do so. This allocation of responsibility is fair because people view the positive results of our actions favourably (as well as – tort's focus – censuring the negative results). 'Human action invites assessment, and the credit we receive from what turns out well balances the discredit we incur for what turns out badly'.[163] Honoré claims that such responsibility 'makes for a better society because it encourages us to do well and to enjoy the credit that comes from doing well'.[164] At a deeper level, responsibility for what we do and its outcomes 'is central to the identity and character of the agent', indeed 'inseparable from our status as persons'.[165] If we could not ascribe actions and outcomes to our bodily movements and mental processes 'we could have no continuing history or character', and we could hardly be said to *decide* things and *do* things at all. Whereas we correctly hold such 'processes' to be our actions and our decisions – by ascribing to us the *outcomes* of those actions and decisions.[166] For Honoré then, there is a significant moral difference between conduct that does and does not cause harm (even if the conduct is otherwise identical).

---

[161] ibid 397.
[162] T Honoré, 'Responsibility and Luck: The Moral Basis of Strict Liability' (1988) 104 *LQR* 530.
[163] T Honoré, *Responsibility and Fault* (Oxford, Hart, 1999) 9.
[164] ibid 10.
[165] ibid.
[166] Honoré (n 162).

Schroeder accepts that there is a moral obligation to take *some* responsibility for harm that we cause.[167] But it does not determine what level of response is required. An appropriate response could be public acknowledgement of our responsibility, or offering an apology to the person injured. Such 'owning up' arguably discharges the moral debt. It falls dramatically short of legal liability to make full repair of the harm caused. 'Outcome responsibility' does not of itself justify *legal* liability to bear all the costs of negative outcomes. Indeed, Honoré too rejects the idea that causing harm *always* justifies legal liability irrespective of fault, noting that some 'extra element' (like conduct creating a special risk of harm) is needed to justify legal imposition of strict liability. Honoré clarifies the distinction between outcome responsibility and legal liability with an example. If you run out into the road without warning and I run you over when I simply could not avoid the accident (so I am entirely blameless), nevertheless 'just because I have hurt you, I am responsible, and by virtue of that responsibility bound to take certain steps'.[168] But those 'certain steps' are giving assistance and calling an ambulance – Honoré stresses: 'My responsibility is not as great as if I had been at fault'.[169] There may not be *legal* liability in such a case.

Schroeder argues that when two defendants are equally *culpable*, but one causes harm and the other does not, holding only the first defendant liable fails to treat similar cases alike. We judge culpability according to what was intended or foreseen when choosing how to act. That is what we can control. Causation of harm, by contrast, is out of our hands. That one careless driver causes harm but another, equally careless, does not cannot be correlated with different degrees of culpability. The sheer misfortune of causation in the former case is too slender a reed to support tort law's sharp difference in treatment. Why should we exonerate equally blameworthy people whose conduct does no harm?

Like Waldron, Schroeder accepts that given the basic structure of tort claims, pitting an innocent claimant against a culpable tortfeasor, liability seems just. But again like Waldron, Schroeder questions the first step. Why constitute the claim between the particular claimant and particular defendant *only*? A preferable alternative, in Schroeder's view, would compare the claims of all equally deserving victims against all equally deficient defendants.

Schroeder accepts that such a collectivisation of claimants and defendants violates accounts of corrective justice.[170] He praises Weinrib's theory for explaining 'why tort law and causation are essentially, not merely instrumentally and

---

[167] CH Schroeder, 'Causation, Compensation, and Moral Responsibility' in DG Owen (ed), *Philosophical Foundations of Tort Law* (Oxford, Clarendon, 1995).

[168] Honoré (n 162) 544 ('Indeed, unless I am wholly insensitive, I shall feel and express regret for the harm I have done').

[169] ibid.

[170] CH Schroeder, 'Corrective Justice and Liability for Increasing Risks' (1990) 37 *UCLA LR* 439.

contingently, connected'; Weinrib 'makes admirably plain what others simply assume'. While admiring Weinrib's candour, Schroeder nevertheless attacks his theory of corrective justice. It merely 'stipulates' or 'assumes' bipolar linkage between particular individuals. Weinrib's tort theory is 'precommitted to such a highly constrained structure'.[171]

In Schroeder's view, a better interpretation of corrective justice requires everyone who is *at* fault to pay into a fund that compensates everyone injured *by* fault. The fund would 'sanction defendants in accordance with their moral responsibility and compensate plaintiffs to the degree they have been wrongfully injured'.[172] It would eliminate the random element that only those whose faulty conduct *causes* harm should pay. Schroeder argues that his approach would be morally superior to the insistence on bilateral linkage between particular individuals – liability only of the one who causes harm and only to the one whose harm they cause. Making *all* who are at fault share the cost of compensation would 'eliminate the normative significance of uncertainty, contingency, or "luck"'.[173] Tort, by contrast, singles out those whose fault turns out to cause harm. But such liability depends on 'facts that could not have been known to the actor prior to her taking the relevant action'.[174] For liability to turn on things that the actor could neither control nor predict is 'anomalous'. Such liability is a 'lottery', turning not on the degree of fault but the chance occurrence of harm.[175] Schroeder cites Holmes' criticism that tort's rules

> cannot enable [a person] to predict with certainty whether a given act under given circumstances will make him liable, because an act will rarely have that effect unless followed by damage, and for the most part, if not always, the consequences of an act are not known, but only guessed at as more or less probable.[176]

Schroeder argues that both claimants and defendants would benefit from an aggregated approach. Compensation would be more secure because the fund would eliminate the problem of the defendant who injured the claimant's being impecunious or unidentifiable. Since defendants would collectively pay into the scheme, the burden of the 'missing defendant' would be spread across all whose conduct is wrongful, rather than falling heavily on one uncompensated claimant. Schroeder emphasises that only those injured *by others' wrongs* would be entitled to compensation. His proposal retains the essential moral structure of corrective justice: only those who are *wronged* are compensated

---

[171] ibid 445, 447, 449.
[172] ibid 450.
[173] ibid 452.
[174] Ibid 455.
[175] Ibid 464.
[176] OW Holmes, *The Common Law* (1881) 78.

(by those who wronged them). The scheme does not collapse (as other purely compensation-based theories do) into a needs-based entitlement to compensation for *all* victims of injuries.

Defendants, too, would prefer to *share* the aggregate costs of their wrongdoing. This would smooth the financial burden. It compares favourably to tort's 'roulette game', where negligence might lead to enormous liability or none whatever, depending on what harm happens to result. Most people are 'risk averse'. They prefer the certainty of paying a lower sum to a small chance of ruinous liabilities. Evidence comes from the widespread practice of insuring against tort liability. (Sometimes legally compulsory, but many defendants also insure voluntarily.)

Schroeder admits that his fund linking all wrongdoers with all victims of wrongs would require a profound change of approach. The main obstacle is, indeed, the bipolar form of tort claims. But since on his argument, the bipolar link of causing and suffering harm is morally arbitrary, he suggests we should not let bipolar form override moral substance. (Similarly, he denies that his proposal is a 'public' or 'administrative' compensation scheme – such dismissive labelling would 'commit the same mistake of eliding form and substance'.) Schroeder accepts the weight of history behind tort's approach. But law can discard inherited institutions when 'working itself pure'.[177] In the past, tort claims by private initiative were the only game in town. Now it is increasingly feasible to identify and levy charges on *all* wrongdoers, not merely the subset who cause harm. (Technical innovations since Schroeder's 1990 article support that point.) Should we accept the radical view that *Sindell v Abbott Laboratories* represents a new start for tort law – by aggregating what wrongdoers pay and what victims of wrongs receive?

Conclusion

This chapter has considered the constraints imposed by corrective or inter-personal justice. Tort's basic structure links a wrongdoer with the person that they have injured. Causation of the claimant's injury by the defendant is central to that inter-personal link. Arguably, tort would be exceeding its logical limits if it subscribed to the goals of compensation or deterrence.

The compensation goal ultimately dispenses with the need for a defendant altogether. It is concerned exclusively with the victim's injuries and needs. The compensation's precise source is immaterial or guided by capacity to bear/spread loss, considerations quite alien to tort's foundation in responsibility and fault. The idea of 'compensating the injured' is powerfully appealing. It is frequently invoked by claimants, commentators and judges – despite Weir's acidic

---

[177] *Omychund v Barker* (1744) 1 Atk 21, 33.

suggestion that its pull is really 'emotional', 'encouraging us to be generous with other people's money'.[178] But it is dangerous – because 'promiscuous', boundless and illimitable. If the logic of compensation is followed through, there is no stopping place short of meeting the full needs of every victim of every misfortune. This would be a direct contradiction of tort, which identifies when one person is obliged to bear another's loss – against the background of 'the loss lying where it falls' (viz borne, by default, by the person who suffers it). The first Debate considers examples from the law on causation, above all the '*Fairchild* enclave'. Its labyrinthine development justifies Nolan's criticism that in the absence of logical limits on a principle like 'compensation of harm', the law has to use illogical limits instead.

A pure goal of deterrence is equally incoherent – for the converse reasons. It would dispense with the need for a *claimant*. The sole concern is the defendant's conduct. The second Debate reviewed culpability's 'aphrodisiac' effect on causation – leaping evidentiary gaps using the 'empty duty' argument. Again, there seems no logical stopping point short of abolishing the need to prove a causal link whenever the defendant is shown to have acted wrongfully. That would ignore the law's sensible reasons for assigning claimants the burden of proof in the first place.

Should we even start from the perspective of corrective justice? While many accept that it explains tort's intrinsic structure, even that has been questioned. As Hedley forcefully objects, corrective justice theories forget that most tort compensation is paid by insurers, not by tortfeasors personally: supposedly 'bilateral' tort law would be unviable without the financial underpinning of the *collective* insurance system.[179] Even accepting the bilateral structure's descriptive fit, how strictly does it require an individual linkage between particular claimants and particular defendants? Does corrective justice preclude *any* aggregation of claimants and/or defendants? The third Debate explored those questions in the problematic situations of 'two hunters' and 'many victims of many hunters'. In such situations, as Steel notes, most legal systems make an exception to the normal rules on proof, both common law (eg England, USA) and civil law (eg France, Germany).[180] This convergence of outcomes shows lawyers' widely shared sense that liability is justified notwithstanding the inability to show a specific, individual causal link. The controversy is precisely *how* to justify that outcome. On that, legal systems and commentators are divided. Some support aggregation, either by rejecting bilateral

---

[178] T Weir, 'The Staggering March of Negligence' in P Cane and J Stapleton (eds), *The Law of Obligations* (Oxford, Clarendon, 1998) 137–38.
[179] S Hedley, 'Making Sense of Negligence' (2016) 36 *Legal Stud* 491. See also D Rosenberg, 'Individual Justice and Collectivizing Risk-Based Claims in Mass-Exposure Cases' (1996) 71 *NYULR* 210, 232 (criticising Weinrib's 'selective regard for the facts, including the myriad collective (non-bipolar) features of the tort system').
[180] Steel (n 28) ch 4.

corrective justice altogether, or attempting to reconcile the two. Another school (eg Weinrib and Beever) insist strictly on the need for an individual causal link. They suggest solutions to the 'hunter problems' with difficulties of their own. Given these philosophical controversies and their 'vast and sophisticated academic literature', it is hardly surprising that proof of causation has become 'the most troublesome general issue in the law of negligence', vexing courts and producing tangled and arcane doctrine.[181]

---

[181] Weinrib (n 19) 136.

5

Concepts of Causation: But-For and Remoteness

The two main debates in this chapter assess two fundamental causal concepts: the but-for test of causal connexion, and the doctrine of remoteness of damage. The conceptual problems in those areas arise when all facts are known and provable. As seen in the previous chapter, many other controversies about causation involve difficulties of proof. We draw out some further themes in an introduction before examining but-for and remoteness.

Introduction: Causation, Proof, 'Damage' and Consequential Loss

The way we define 'actionable damage' – in contrast to 'consequential loss' – is crucial to understanding the law on causation. Claimants commonly lack evidence to prove whether the tort caused their injury. A common strategy is to invite the court to recognise a new interest, new 'actionable damage' which the claimant *is* able to prove on the balance of probabilities. Examples in the previous chapter include: a right to have defendants fund research into unknown risks that they have created;[1] compensation for creating uncertainty that prevents a claim against another defendant. Many other reconceptualisations of protected interest have been suggested. While it was troublesome to establish that the 'failure to warn' caused the patient's paralysis in *Chester v Afshar*, it clearly did breach her right to make informed choices. An alternative solution to *Chester* would remedy what the surgeon's failure *did* cause (violation of autonomy).[2] Following *Barker v Corus* it was for a brief period arguable that liability under *Fairchild* was for *creating risks* (rather than *causing injury*).[3] A right to be protected against the *risk* of harm would have significant implications across the law. But that view of

---

[1] AD Lahav, 'The Knowledge Remedy' (2020) 98 *Texas LR* 1361.
[2] [2005] 1 AC 134 [33]–[34] (Lord Hoffmann); see ch 2, 'Debate 4: "Informed Medical Consent" – Which Tort?'.
[3] [2006] 2 AC 57.

Barker has not survived its legislative reversal (Compensation Act 2006, section 3) following which *Fairchild* has since been treated as orthodox liability for 'causing mesothelioma'.[4] Certainly, a direct invitation to recognise 'loss of a chance' as actionable damage was declined in *Gregg v Scott*.[5]

A sharp distinction was drawn in *Gregg* between actionable 'gist damage' and consequential loss. Compensation is routinely awarded when a personal injury causes (eg) pain and suffering, or a lost chance of being promoted at work. The law compensates those losses to reverse the harmful consequences of the tort. It does *not* follow that economic loss (wages), or chances (of promotion), or pain and suffering, must constitute 'actionable damage'. The law defines a narrower category of rights that are in themselves the basis for a claim. Unless the three losses mentioned here are consequent on harm to a protected right they will be uncompensated: on its own pure economic loss, a lost chance or mental distress is categorised as loss without invasion of a legal right (*'damnum absque injuria'*).

Also, importantly, there are different approaches to *proof* of 'gist' and consequences. The claimant must prove it more likely than not that the defendant's breach of duty caused the actionable damage on which their claim is based. There is good reason for that assignment of the evidential burden.[6] But it is not necessary to show that *consequential* loss, for example the lost promotion at work, was more likely than not. If a significant chance has been lost owing to personal injury, the court assesses damages accordingly (ie in proportion to the strength of that chance – if there were four other candidates competing with the claimant for one promotion, she might recover 20 per cent of the increased salary in proportion to her one-in-five chance of success). Equally, medical estimates of a 10 per cent risk of arthritis developing in future from a fracture would receive proportionate recognition in damages.

These everyday examples show that consequential loss is apportioned: proved and quantified according to its likelihood. Why? Courts sometimes rely on the distinction between past facts which can be proven on a binary basis (either it happened or it didn't), and future/hypothetical events where the law is 'not so foolish' as to suppose they can be proven either way; 'All that you can do is to evaluate the chance'.[7] But this is not wholly satisfactory. In cases like *Gregg v Scott*, there is no problem proving what factually happened (failure to diagnose cancer led to the claimant's disease progressing). The difficulty is the hypothetical question of what *would have happened* – would earlier diagnosis have led to successful treatment?

---

[4] S Steel, *Proof of Causation in Tort Law* (Cambridge, Cambridge University Press, 2015) 228–37.
[5] [2005] 2 AC 176.
[6] See ch 4, 'Causation, the Burden of Proof and the "Empty Duty" Argument'.
[7] *Davies v Taylor* [1974] A.C. 207, 213 (Lord Reid).

A more convincing reason for relaxed proof standards for consequential loss is precisely that it is *consequential* upon a proven wrong.[8] It is familiar across the law that once the claimant proves they've been wronged by the defendant, courts endeavour to solve over evidential difficulties. They strive to award appropriate compensation for the proven wrong.[9] Where measurement of loss is inherently impossible the law does not require the claimant to prove the impossible.[10] The court may need 'sound imagination and the practice of the broad axe'.[11] The chance-based assessment of consequential loss is one familiar example. Fairness justifies more generosity to the claimant once liability has been established.

Conversely, why does the law require that 'gist damage' must be proved more likely than not? Mr Gregg's claim failed because he could not show it was more likely than not that had he been promptly diagnosed, treatment would have cured his cancer. He *could* show that there was a non-negligible chance of recovery which the delay had reduced, but that was not enough to show a causal link between misdiagnosis and cancer. The House of Lords, affirming the orthodox approach, feared that abandoning it would unsettle the law with massive consequences for NHS liabilities. Lord Nicholls in dissent thought the orthodox approach was crude. One response was from Baroness Hale. In the long run it suits both claimants and defendants (as a class) to have the 'all or nothing' approach. To depart from it, her Ladyship noted, 'cuts both ways'.[12] Currently claimants recover in full once they discharge the burden of proof. If a claimant proves that causation is more likely than not, the court does not reduce his damages 'by the extent to which he has failed to prove his case with 100 per cent certainty'.[13] 'Anything that is more probable than not [the law] treats as certain'.[14] (It prefers binary outcomes, win or lose, 'with a win on points counting as a knock-out'.)[15]

There are other rules of causation which favour claimants in this way. They only need prove that the tort was *a* cause of their injury, not *the sole cause*. The tortfeasor 'cannot excuse himself by pointing to another cause'.[16] If the law were otherwise, claimants 'would rarely receive full compensation': 'Since

---

[8] Steel (n 4) 322–25.

[9] Eg *Armory v Delamirie* (1721) 1 Str 505 (stolen jewel – court estimating its value by size of gap in ring where it had been set). In *Wright v McCormack* [2022] EWHC 2068 (QB) [128]–[130], Chamberlain J distinguishes the general principle that courts will not let difficulties in quantification deprive the claimant of a remedy from the '*separate and stronger*' *Armory* presumption, applied when '*morally culpable conduct* on the part of the defendant … contributes to the absence of evidence'.

[10] *One Step (Support) Ltd v Morris-Garner* [2018] UKSC 20 [37].

[11] *Watson, Laidlaw & Co v Pott Cassels & Williamson* 1914 SC (HL) 18, 29–30.

[12] *Gregg v Scott* (n 5) [225].

[13] *Hotson v East Berkshire HA* [1987] AC 750, 793.

[14] *Mallett v McMonagle* [1970] AC 166, 176.

[15] T Weir, 'All or Nothing' (2004) 78 *Tulane LR* 511.

[16] *Heskell v Continental Express* [1950] 1 All ER 1033, 1047.

most events are the result of a complex set of causes, there will frequently be non-tortious causes contributing to the injury'.[17] Where several wrongdoers independently contribute to a single harm, each is liable *in full*.

When *these* rules are challenged it is by defendants. (As per Lady Hale's point, claimants wish to depart from the orthodox 'all or nothing' approach when it entails there would be *no* liability; defendants challenge its imposition of *full* liability.) Defendants have a number of possible strategies. First they may argue that the claimant's injury is not truly single and 'indivisible'. If different tortfeasors have caused different aspects of the claimant's harm they should only be liable for their own 'part' – equally if tortious and non-tortious factors cause distinct injuries. In principle this is correct. It is uncontroversial when applied to obviously separate injuries (D1 breaks C's leg, D2 breaks her arm) or a measurable portion of a progressively worsening disease.[18] But it has been extended to injuries that appear indivisible. We examine this in the section on stress at work.[19] The objection is not only conceptual.[20] Where some among multiple tortfeasors are insolvent, holding the injury 'divisible' places the risk of insolvency on *claimants* (whereas if each tortfeasor is liable in full subject to a subsequent contribution claim, the defendants bear the risk of fellow tortfeasors' impecuniosity in the contribution proceedings). The most notorious case to implement 'divisibility' was *Barker v Corus*, which Parliament hastily reversed fearing precisely such difficulties for mesothelioma victims seeking to recover full damages for their illness.

Defendants may also seek to reduce damages if the claimant would (or might) have suffered the same injury in any event, for reasons outside the defendant's responsibility. For example where an accident required the claimant to have surgery that he would anyway have needed two to three years later for an underlying health condition, the court held that the acceleration of the inevitable caused him no harm.[21] This is merely an extreme example of the courts' invariable practice of discounting damages to reflect misfortunes that the claimant might have suffered apart from the tort (eg ill health, losing their job). Even in the absence of specific evidence, the courts knock a little off the total damages awarded to represent the general 'vicissitudes of life'. This is necessary to ensure that the claimant 'should not make a profit out of the wrong done to him' – damages should 'place him in as good a position as he was in before the wrong, *but not in any wise in a better one*'.[22] This 'no better off' principle is sometimes said to be about causation.[23] As we will see in the first

---

[17] *Athey v Leonati* [1996] 3 SCR 458 [20].

[18] *Thompson v Smiths Shiprepairers* [1984] QB 405.

[19] See ch 9, 'Stress at Work'.

[20] Weir (n 15) 524 ('to conceal the revolutionary nature of this development, the courts are pretending that the harm in question is not indivisible, when it plainly is').

[21] *Cutler v Vauxhall Motors Ltd* [1971] 1 QB 418.

[22] *Harwood v Wyken Colliery Co* [1913] 2 KB 158, 169–70 (emphasis added).

[23] eg *Jobling v Associated Dairies* [1982] AC 794.

debate in this chapter, commentators argue that it actually involves the law's choice how to value what has been lost.

Note that this 'no better off' principle offsets tort's apparent generosity to vulnerable claimants. Most famously the 'eggshell skull' rule compensating consequential personal injuries even if they were entirely unforeseeable. In the leading case a small burn unforeseeably triggered cancer from which the claimant died.[24] The defendant was liable for the unexpected cancer. But the claimant's extraordinary (unknown) susceptibility meant he had always been likely to succumb to cancer following any minor injury (eg a scratch). His damages were therefore reduced under the 'no better off' principle. In aphoristic terms, people with thin skulls would suffer a lot of cranial injuries even in a world where nobody was ever negligent, and the damages awarded when a tort *is* the cause must take that likelihood into account.

These are important examples of loss being quantified on a proportionate basis. Should this be read back to 'actionable harm' itself? Is it right that courts insist that the 'gist of the action' be proved on an all-or-nothing basis, with liability in full or not at all? Arguably the law has to insist that *rights* have this all-or-nothing character: there would be something absurd in giving someone 'half a judgment' (or awarding partial damages *because there were dissenting judgments*).[25] Such compromises would diminish the authority of the law. Some interests cannot sensibly be divided.[26] As Jaconelli and Weir both accept however, *money* (damages) certainly can be apportioned.

As noted, damages are apportioned between tortfeasors (Civil Liability (Contribution) Act 1978) and also, of course, between claimant and defendant in post-1945 contributory negligence. The law seems to require express statutory authority to do this. But Weir suggests it is part of a wider trend towards division and compromise. (He speculates that it is simply making explicit a power of apportionment that civil juries routinely carried out implicitly, concealed beneath their inscrutable verdicts on damages.[27]) So should the apportionment trend replace the all-or-nothing definition of actionable damage? Steele and Barker argue that the 'drift to proportionate liability' should be resisted.[28] The analogy with contributory negligence is 'superficial, formal and technical'. The Law Reform (Contributory Negligence) Act 1945 was a specific response to the great unfairness of *totally* defeating claims by the common law contributory negligence defence. The 1945 Act does not state some general ethical principle of sharing loss. It is a rough-and-ready compromise, based on the 'fiction' that courts can compare the incommensurable: the defendant negligently harming another and the claimant's failure to take care of their own

---

[24] *Smith v Leech Brain & Co* [1962] 2 QB 405.
[25] J Jaconelli, 'Solomonic Justice and the Common Law' (1992) 12 *OJLS* 480.
[26] eg the disputed child in *1 Kings* 3 vv16–28.
[27] Weir (n 15).
[28] K Barker and J Steele, 'Drifting Towards Proportionate Liability: Ethics and Pragmatics' [2015] *CLJ* 49.

safety. (Although as Glanville Williams said, lawyers often have to undertake impossible valuations: 'We have to act more or less arbitrarily because the alternative is not to act at all'.)[29]

Repealing multiple defendants' full 'joint and several' liability for the same indivisible harm also has few advocates. It would complicate the law and create 'glaring unfairness' for claimants.[30] It is sometimes suggested that the law has become reluctant to impose positive protective duties on defendants such as the police because courts know they will be liable in full, even though primary responsibility rests with the criminals they have failed to apprehend.[31] In other words, joint and several liability is so harsh for 'peripheral parties' that the law chooses to absolve them from liability altogether. Thus it has been suggested that a reasonable quid pro quo for expansion of public authority liability might be to reduce their liability to a proportionate share of responsibility in place of holding them (jointly with the primary wrongdoers) liable in full.[32] Steele and Barker comment that this would have such important distributive consequences it is a 'primarily political choice' for Parliament. Moreover they suggest, if particular activities are disproportionately burdened it is preferable to deny liability or legislate for a statutory cap on damages. Better, in their view, to make the policy choice openly and not 'mask' it with a pseudo-ethical preference for 'loss sharing'.

Both claimants and defendants will continue to invite courts to redefine 'actionable damage' in ways that advance their cases. (Such litigant-led creativity has been the engine of common law development for centuries.) Although the issues appear abstract and technical, they are of great practical importance. Questions of cause, proof and 'damage' are intimately related. The law is complex, reflecting a compromise of sorts between claimants' and defendants' interests.

Debate 1
The But-For Test

The 'but-for' test appears to be the fixed centre of causation. It states that something caused the claimant's injury only if, but for that event, the injury would not have happened. In other words the question is – was the tort a *necessary condition*? The but-for test does not recognise causation when the injury would have been sustained anyway, that is, if the claimant would still

---

[29] G Williams, *Joint Torts and Contributory Negligence* (London, Stevens, 1951) 158.

[30] A Burrows, 'Should One Reform Joint and Several Liability?' in NJ Mullany and AM Linden (eds), *Torts Tomorrow: A Tribute to John Fleming* (Sydney, LBC, 1998).

[31] J Stapleton, 'Duty of Care: Peripheral Parties and Alternative Opportunities for Deterrence' (1995) 111 *LQR* 301.

[32] Law Commission CP187, *Administrative Redress: Public Bodies and the Citizen* (2008) 4.65–4.68.

have been injured even if the tort had never happened. Yet like everything else in the law of causation,[33] the but-for test is controversial. It is widely acknowledged to be both over-inclusive and under-inclusive – in different situations. The main debate is whether but-for test should be discarded altogether or supplemented with exceptions.

The Australian case *March v Stramare* contains strong criticisms of the but-for test.[34] Deane J said that to use it as 'a comprehensive definitive test … would lead to the absurd and unjust position that there was no "cause" of an injury in any case where there were present two independent and sufficient causes of the accident'.[35] The but-for test was therefore too restrictive. Yet in other respects it would not be restrictive enough. Something that 'constitutes an essential condition (in the "but for" sense) of an occurrence [is not necessarily], for the purposes of ascribing responsibility or fault, … properly to be seen as a "cause" of that occurrence as a matter of either ordinary language or common sense'.[36] Deane J gave this vivid example:

> it could not, as a matter of ordinary language, be said that the fact that a person had a head was a 'cause' of his being decapitated by a negligently wielded sword notwithstanding that possession of a head is an essential precondition of decapitation.[37]

Mason CJ similarly reasoned that it was mistaken to elevate the but-for test as the 'exclusive criterion' of causation. This would lead to 'unacceptable' results. The cases revealed that it was 'either inadequate or troublesome in various situations in which there are multiple acts or events leading to the plaintiff's injury'. Thus exceptions had been made to the test. Causation was not a pure question of fact but ultimately a matter of 'common sense'. The but-for test 'must be tempered by the making of value judgments and the infusion of policy considerations'.[38]

This illustrates the orthodox approach to causation. The but-for test is certainly the starting point. But it is disapplied to avoid absurdity in cases of multiple 'independent and sufficient causes'. Equally, but-for can also deem too many factors to be 'causes'. That problem is dealt with by distinguishing between 'mere conditions' and 'operative causes' (or *causa sine qua non* and *causa causans*). However as Laws LJ noted, 'the law has dug no deeper in the philosophical thickets of causation' than that, and the categories are

---

[33] R Pound, 'Causation' (1957) 67 *Yale LJ* 1, 1 ('one who essays a systematic exposition of causation [undertakes] unscrewing the inscrutable').
[34] (1991) 171 CLR 506.
[35] ibid 523.
[36] ibid.
[37] ibid.
[38] ibid.

virtually meaningless: 'The latter [*causa causans*] is an empty tautology. The former [*causa sine qua non*] proves everything, and therefore nothing'.³⁹ In Laws LJ's view, judges should keep 'the metaphysics of causation' in their place and ensure just results even if the reasoning is 'heavily pragmatic'. The law's ultimate causal inquiry considers for what defendants should 'justly be held responsible'.⁴⁰

What Laws LJ calls 'pragmatism' others might criticise as judicial manipulation of causal concepts to produce intuitively just results. In *March v Stramare* McHugh J criticised his fellow judges. Applying the but-for test in a 'practical commonsense way' would confer an 'unfettered discretion to ignore a condition or relation which was in fact a precondition of the occurrence of the damage'. Judges would be imposing 'idiosyncratic values' under 'the guise of commonsense'. The majority's approach invited courts to use 'subjective, unexpressed and undefined extra-legal values'.⁴¹

Can 'absurdity' be avoided without resorting to ad hoc, intuitive discretion? Many academics advocate a looser or wider test of 'causation'. Instead of the but-for test (which equates causation with strict *necessity*), the court should ask whether the tort was *involved* in the injury (as explored below). Its adherents claim that this approach would avoid the absurd conclusion that when there is more than one sufficient causal factor, *none* is a (necessary or but-for) cause. Yet one obvious danger is that in solving this under-inclusiveness problem, the looser causal test will exacerbate the converse problem of *over*-inclusiveness. The debate examines these problems – although fuller consideration of legal limitations on caused harm follows in the debate about 'remoteness of damage'.

The Problem of Multiple Causes: But-For 'Disapplied'

Sometimes coincidences happen. When two independent factors coincide and each of them would (on its own) have produced the damaging outcome, neither can be a 'but-for cause'. When each factor in turn is hypothetically 'removed' from the situation, the outcome still would have happened – that is, because of the presence of the other factor sufficient to bring it about. If we define causation using the but-for test, this seems to entail that *neither* is a cause – so the event must somehow be 'uncaused'. This so self-evidently absurd that (on orthodox accounts) the law is obliged exceptionally to disapply the but-for test. As Lord Nicholls once explained:

> The classic example is where two persons independently search for the source of a gas leak with the aid of lighted candles. According to the simple 'but for' test, neither would be liable for damage caused by the resultant explosion.

---

³⁹ *Rahman v Arearose* [2001] QB 351, [32].
⁴⁰ ibid.
⁴¹ *March* (n 34) 532–33.

In this type of case, involving multiple wrongdoers, the court may treat wrongful conduct as having sufficient causal connection with the loss for the purpose of attracting responsibility even though the simple 'but for' test is not satisfied. In so deciding the court is primarily making a value judgment on responsibility. In making this judgment the court will have regard to the purpose sought to be achieved by the relevant tort, as applied to the particular circumstances.[42]

Hence 'mechanically' applying the but-for test did not provide 'infallible' answers to questions of causation in the 'infinite' variety of tort cases.[43] In the same case Lord Hoffmann said:

There is therefore no uniform causal requirement for liability in tort. Instead, there are varying causal requirements, depending upon the basis and purpose of liability. One cannot separate questions of liability from questions of causation. They are inextricably connected.[44]

Yet if the but-for test can be displaced by judgements about responsibility, is it even the right test? Some argue for its replacement by causation defined as 'involvement'. When numerous independent factors coincide where each would suffice to bring the harm about, their sufficiency means that *each* is a cause.

Multiple Sufficient Factors: Each Causal?

On the rival account of causation, *both* candle flames in Lord Nicholls' example cause the gas explosion. Each suffices to bring it about. (Strictly speaking, neither candle is sufficient on its own as the explosion requires various other factors – the presence of the leaking gas; and oxygen in the air, etc. No occurrence is ever produced by just one cause – and naturally the law does not require claimants to show the tort was the *sole* cause of their injury.[45] Strictly, the question is whether each flame was a necessary part of a set of conditions collectively sufficient to trigger the explosion. This is often described as the 'NESS' test ('necessary element of a sufficient set'). The technical and non-intuitive label, compared with the simplicity of the 'but for' test, is one reason for lawyers' resistance to it.)

Questions of causation have troubled philosophers for centuries. Honoré offers an accessible explanation for the 'sufficiency' approach.[46] He suggests

---

[42] *Kuwait Airways v Iraqi Airways (Nos 4 and 5)* [2002] 2 AC 883, [74].

[43] ibid [73].

[44] ibid [128]. See further [129] (and Lord Nicholls at [82]–[83]) (why 'but-for' causation is inapplicable/does not diminish defendants' liability when successive conversion of claimant's goods by different parties).

[45] *Athey v Leonati* [1996] 3 SCR 458.

[46] T Honoré, 'Necessary and Sufficient Conditions in Tort Law' in DG Owen (ed), *Philosophical Foundations of Tort Law* (Oxford, Clarendon, 1995).

that through human history causal explanations have been used to show how to achieve a given outcome. If we want X to happen, what conditions have to be in place to bring X about? What actions are *sufficient* to produce the desired outcome? Honoré argues that this notion of 'sufficient cause' is therefore not some fictitious 'deemed' species of causation, invented by lawyers specifically to circumvent the multi-factor problem. The wider notion of causation as a as a 'recipe' for outcomes arose outside law. (Although Honoré also thinks sufficiency solves legal disputes about multiple causes better than undefined 'pragmatism', whereby judges make 'exceptions' without addressing the nature of causation.)

Most judges would reply that theoretical problems in the philosophy of causation are not their concern. Lord Salmon typified this attitude, remarking that causal questions 'can best be answered by ordinary common sense rather than by abstract metaphysical theory'.[47] Perhaps this simply proves Honoré's point about the evasiveness of undefined pragmatism. At worst it epitomises English law's characteristic 'manly disregard for vulgar logic'.[48]

However, postponing until the next debate the meaning here of 'ordinary common sense', Lord Salmon's attitude may well be defensible. The judiciary not only exhibit a philistine pride in untheoretical reasoning. They are obliged to answer questions that arise before them and cannot postpone decisions because they are contentious – 'pragmatism' may be necessary to reach 'concrete decisions [without] waiting for philosophical accord'.[49] Moreover, courts use causation for purposes fundamentally different from philosophers. For Lord Wright, the *judicial* inquiry was 'the quest of justice, the search for the responsible person'. Decisions about responsibility require value-judgements, unlike the philosophical search for abstract truth ('eternal verity') – a search that could lead judges onto 'a shifting sand'.[50]

Lord Hoffmann, as seen, acknowledges the normative quality of causal inquiries in law. He suggests it would avoid confusing debates about 'causation's' supposed true meaning if judges and lawyers instead referred to a given legal rule's 'causal requirements'. It would indicate that these causal requirements are 'creatures of the law and nothing more'.[51] (In this he echoes Bertrand Russell's complaint that 'the word "cause" is so inextricably bound up with misleading associations as to make its complete extrusion from the philosophical vocabulary desirable'.)[52] Lord Hoffmann stresses that causal requirements are 'fashioned so as best to suit the purpose of the rules which

---

[47] *Alphacell v Woodward* [1972] AC 824, 847.
[48] JR Spencer, 'Motor-Cars and the Rule in *Rylands v. Fletcher*' [1983] *CLJ* 65, 70.
[49] G Turton, *Evidential Uncertainty in Causation in Negligence* (Oxford, Hart, 2016) 37.
[50] Lord Wright, 'Notes on Causation and Responsibility in English Law' [1955] *CLJ* 163.
[51] Lord Hoffmann, 'Causation' in R Goldberg (ed), *Perspectives on Causation* (Oxford, Hart, 2011) 9.
[52] B Russell, 'Notion of Cause' in *Mysticism and Logic* (London, Longmans Green & Co, 1918) 180.

impose liability'.[53] There is nothing mysterious about causation. It has no 'God-given' definition that logically determines the law's causal requirements. As Glanville Williams remarked, 'when the lawyer uses the concept of causation, he is not bound to use it in the same way as a philosopher, or a scientist, or an ordinary man'.[54]

Jane Stapleton builds on this traditional approach. Lawyers should define causation in a way that serves *the law's* functions – 'like any specialist discourse, the law can choose what a term will mean for its own purposes'.[55] Stapleton advocates the sufficiency-based test (the 'NESS' test rather than strict necessity in the traditional but-for test).[56] The wider test captures all the ways that a factor might be involved. This 'provides the width of coverage that is needed to accommodate smoothly all the many diverse enquiries the Law makes'. Stapleton emphasises that sufficiency is not, as some claim, inherently superior or self-evident. It is not 'itself the meaning of causation', its 'essence' or 'fundamental identity'.[57] Rather, the law should consciously *choose* 'involvement' in preference to accounts of causation based on (eg) blame or explanation. Defining causal relationships using 'sufficient' connection is 'an extremely effective algorithm for identifying all the relationships of involvement (between a specified factor and the existence of a particular phenomenon) with which the Law must deal'.[58]

Take, for example, a person taking a pleasant stroll in the woods who is shot by a negligent hunter. We would intuitively think that firing the gun caused the walker's injuries. Can it really be suggested that the victim's presence in the woods was equally 'a cause' of the accident? To elevate into causal status what seems to be a mere background condition (the victim's presence) seems as absurd as Deane J's example that a decapitated person's possession of a head is a cause of its being cut off. It seems offensive as well as absurd – verging on victim-blaming. Yet the broad test of 'involvement' would include the victim's presence as a cause, and Stapleton defends this. Legislators may wish to formulate regulations to prevent shooting injuries. The law might do so by prohibiting people strolling in certain woods during the shooting season. From *that* perspective (ie preventive regulation) it is important to have 'all the relationships of [causal] involvement' as potential factors to be regulated. Law might deliberately choose an all-encompassing definition of causal relationships, for good reason. There are several important examples.

In *Environment Agency v Empress Car Co (Abertillery) Ltd* a company was convicted of the criminal offence of causing polluting matter to enter

---

[53] Lord Hoffmann, 'Causation' (2005) 121 *LQR* 592.
[54] G Williams, 'Causation in the Law' [1961] *CLJ* 62, 75–76.
[55] J Stapleton, 'Unnecessary Causes' (2013) 129 *LQR* 39.
[56] J Stapleton, 'Choosing What We Mean by Causation in the Law' (2008) 73 *Missouri LR* 433.
[57] *Pace* RW Wright, 'Causation in Tort Law' (1985) 73 *California LR* 1735 (cited Stapleton, ibid at 472, 477).
[58] Stapleton, ibid 474.

controlled waters, when an unknown malicious person turned on the tap of a diesel storage tank on its premises. Lord Hoffmann reasoned in familiar terms:

> one cannot give a common sense answer to a question of causation for the purpose of attributing responsibility under some rule without knowing the purpose and scope of the rule. Does the rule impose a duty which requires one to guard against, or makes one responsible for, the deliberate acts of third persons? If so, it will be correct to say, when loss is caused by the act of such a third person, that it was caused by the breach of duty.[59]

The House of Lords held that legislative policy had created a strict liability offence which extended to the defendant company's contribution, that is, its providing the background conditions of pollution that were triggered by vandalism. Commentators have criticised the decision as aberrant, perverse, confused and 'profoundly unsatisfactory'. But Lord Hoffmann remains unmoved by the 'distress' of what he called 'fundamentalists who believe that the deliberate acts of third parties should *always* relieve the original actor from liability under any rule of criminal law, irrespective of the purpose or policy of the rule'.[60] How could it be said that the presence of oil in the defendant's tank was not *a* cause of the ultimate pollution of the river?

The Supreme Court recently declined to apply the but-for test in a test case about business interruption insurance.[61] The policies covered legal restrictions on trading resulting from outbreaks of a notifiable disease (eg Covid-19) within a specified geographical distance of the insured business. Accepting that there had been Covid-19 infections within the relevant areas, the insurers argued that they were not but-for causes of the national coronavirus lockdowns. Localised infections had not determined the national government decisions: the lockdowns would still have been imposed even if there had been no Covid-19 outbreaks in a particular geographical area. The court rejected this argument. Properly interpreted, the insurance policies did not exclude public health measures adopted in response to notifiable diseases occurring *both* inside *and* outside the policies' limited territorial scope. Particularly not when diseases 'can spread rapidly, widely and unpredictably. It is obvious that an outbreak of an infectious disease may not be confined to a specific locality or to a circular area delineated by a radius of 25 miles around a policyholder's premises'.[62] Crucially, the court was not constrained to adopt an interpretation 'clearly contrary to the spirit and intent of the relevant [insurance] policies', rendering the insurance 'illusory' against nationwide pandemic restrictions,[63] by the supposedly inexorable logic of the but-for test.

---

[59] [1999] 2 AC 22, 31.
[60] Hoffmann (n 51) (critics quoted at fn 12).
[61] *Financial Conduct Authority v Arch Insurance (UK) Ltd* [2021] UKSC 1; [2021] AC 649.
[62] ibid [194] (Lord Leggatt and Lord Hamblen).
[63] ibid [316] (Lord Briggs).

The wide notion of causal 'involvement' is also at the heart of a famously controversial theory of liability.[64] Ronald Coase, the intellectual godfather of the Law and Economics movement, maintained that if a railway engine emits sparks that burn crops in adjacent fields, *the farmer's use of the land to grow crops is just as surely a cause of the crop damage* as the railway's activities.[65] This is counter-intuitive. Rejecting Coase's theory, Epstein maintains that the railway has obviously caused harm to the farmer and ought to be liable accordingly.[66] However, for Coase's purpose (deciding the higher value of inconsistent uses of land) Epstein's one-sided notion of 'causing harm' is unsatisfactory. It would prejudice the very question that Coase sets out to investigate. A 'reciprocal' notion of causation (ie that *both* parties, or land-uses, are causally involved) is presupposed when comparing their value. Undoubtedly, Epstein's causal intuitions seems more obvious and appealing. They fit with ordinary legal notions of responsibility. Perhaps, however, that is only because of deep-seated psychological attachment to notions of 'physical intervention' by which, as very young children, we learn about the world around us![67] While there are many valid objections to the economic prism on tort law, it is questionable to assert that the essential nature of causation is a conceptual barrier to Coase's approach.

The 'No Better Off' Principle

Law (and scholarship about law) undoubtedly has a diverse range of concerns. But does the reasoning above necessarily apply to *tort*?[68] A criticism of 'sufficient involvement' causation is that it seems to lead to over-broad liability. Tort compensation restores the claimant to their starting position. But it should not make them better off than they were to start with. The state to which the claimant is restored must reflect 'all of its attendant risks and shortcomings, and not a better position'.[69] An example mentioned in the introduction to this chapter is the court's customary discount for 'the vicissitudes of life' – a recognition that 'full' compensation would be *over*-compensation since some other misfortunate might have befallen the claimant, even had it not been the defendant's tort. When we *know* that quite apart from the defendant's tort, there was another factor which would have been sufficient to produce the same injuries, should the claimant be entitled to compensation? They would have

---

[64] See further ch 11, 'Coase's Analysis' and 'Critique of Coase'.
[65] RH Coase, 'The Problem of Social Cost' (1960) 3 *JL&E* 1.
[66] Richard A Epstein, 'Nuisance Law: Corrective Justice and Its Utilitarian Constraints' (1979) 8 *JLS* 49.
[67] DH Gjerdingen, 'The Coase Theorem and the Psychology of Common-Law Thought' (1983) 56 *S Calif LR* 711.
[68] Cf *Arch Insurance* at [320]: interpretation of insurance policies 'a quite distinct process from, for example, applying the law about causation and remoteness of loss for the purpose of identifying the harm liable to be made good by tortfeasors to their victims' (Lord Briggs).
[69] *Athey v Leonati* [1996] 3 SCR 458, [35] (Major J).

suffered the loss in any case. To compensate them would make them better off than they'd have been anyway. This would surely be wrong as a matter of elementary tort principle. Does this not show that, after all, the but-for test of causation which insists on the causal *necessity* of the defendant's actions is inherent in tort law's causal requirements?

Jane Stapleton argues not. She accepts, of course, that the 'no better off principle' is central to tort's definition of compensation: 'In most cases, in fairness to defendants the law requires that D's tort make C worse off before it recognises that C has suffered "damage"'.[70] She even accepts that, traditionally, the 'no better off' principle is implemented by the but-for test of causation.[71] Nevertheless, Stapleton insists, valuing the claimant's loss should be kept strictly separate from the question of cause. She argues that failing to maintain that separation has led to muddled reasoning and questionable decisions. A central example is the controversial case of *Bailey v Ministry of Defence*.[72] The claimant, a hospital patient, suffered brain damage after suffocating because of her physically weakened state. That physical weakness resulted from two factors in combination: the illness that had initially hospitalised the patient (which was not the defendant's fault), and negligent treatment for which the hospital *was* responsible. It could not be said whether the background illness would anyway have weakened the patient severely enough for her suffocation (ie even without the contribution of the medical negligence). It therefore could not be shown that the negligence was a but-for cause, on the evidence. Yet the Court of Appeal made an 'exception' to the but-for test, holding the hospital liable in full for the claimant's brain damage.

Stapleton argues that the reasoning process was flawed. The court felt hamstrung by the but-for 'rule' and obliged to make an obscurely reasoned 'exception' to it. In doing so, the court overlooked the 'no worse off' principle for valuing the loss. Stapleton argues that *Bailey* ought to have been decided like this: the but-for test should *never* be applied, but instead the court must decide whether the negligence was historically involved in the claimant's injury. Clearly it was in *Bailey*: when she suffocated the patient was as physically weak as she was because of the medical negligence. On Stapleton's preferred causal approach (ie 'involvement' not 'but-for'), the claimant should have succeeded on the question of causation. But that was not the end of the matter. To recover substantial damages the claimant must also show that she suffered a loss valued by the law as greater than zero. But *that* was impossible on the evidence in *Bailey*. Since the claimant could not prove that the negligence had made her worse off, her claim for damages should have failed. Stapleton criticises *Bailey*'s far-reaching, 'explosive' precedent for medical negligence.[73]

---

[70] J Stapleton, 'Cause in Fact and the Scope of Liability for Consequences' (2003) 119 *LQR* 388, 413.
[71] ibid.
[72] [2008] EWCA Civ 883; [2009] 1 WLR 1052.
[73] Stapleton (n 55) 58.

Because most patients are (by definition) already ill when they receive negligent medical treatment, the *Bailey* problem is a common one. It is frequently hard to disentangle (in order to value) the impact of medical negligence from the patient's pre-existing illness. Thus *Bailey* 'would expose medical providers to a radically expanded realm of liability'.[74] Yet the *Bailey* expansion did not happen through a clear-sighted decision to reverse the onus on the claimant to prove the value of their claim. In Stapleton's view, the 'radical' decision was the product of the confusion which follows from rolling together the separate questions of causal involvement and valuation of loss.

As seen, Stapleton states that the claimant must show the defendant made them worse off 'in most cases'. But not all. In particular, when a number of independent torts overlap, the law does *not* require a comparison between each individual tort and the claimant's hypothetical position in that tort's absence (ie just as badly off because the *other* tort(s) would still have produced the loss). Instead it compares the claimant's position with where they'd have been 'but for all the tortious contributions'.[75] Because this has been obscured by the confusion with 'causation', courts have 'not often squarely confronted the normative choice that tort law has'.[76] Stapleton comments: 'any concern for fairness to defendants is outweighed by a concern that the law would be embarrassed if it was seen to treat the victim of multiple torts worse than the victim of one'.[77] (As Stapleton notes however, citing the leading case *Performance Cars Ltd v Abraham*,[78] curiously 'the law's degree of embarrassment seems less the greater the length of time that transpired between [sequential] torts'.)[79] Stevens, although agreeing that we do not wish the victim of multiple torts 'to fall between two (or more) stools' suggests that it is not however a 'sufficient solution' since 'It fails to identify whether the first tortfeasor, the second, or both should be liable'.[80]

Does It Make Any Difference?

One objection to Stapleton's approach is that it simply restates the law in less familiar terms. If this is true, and it does little more than putting old wine (law) in new conceptual bottles, what is the point? (Stevens says we are 'entitled to feel slightly let down, as [the "no worse off" principle] is just the "but for" test reintroduced under another name'.)[81] Could Stapleton's restatement even

---

[74] ibid.
[75] ibid 58–61.
[76] ibid 60.
[77] Stapleton (n 70) 413.
[78] [1962] 1 QB 33.
[79] Stapleton (n 70) 388 fn 122. (But compare *Baker v Willoughby* [1970] AC 467.)
[80] R Stevens, *Torts and Rights* (Oxford, Oxford University Press, 2007) 139.
[81] ibid 144.

do more harm than good, over-complicating the law because of one specialised problem of 'over-determined' causation? The but-for approach is at least 'attractive' as 'a mechanical test, which is simple to apply, is of general application, and accords with our shared perception of the physical world'.[82]

Sarah Green is a prominent critic of the wide 'factual contribution' (or involvement, sufficiency or 'NESS') test.[83] Green's general critique of causation scholarship is that it has *over*-analysed the problem and produced theories of great complexity.[84] Such sophisticated accounts have, not surprisingly, failed to help judges and practising lawyers solve difficult causal problems. Green searches instead for a 'pragmatic' solution. To do so she defends *necessary connection*, as encoded in the traditional but-for test. To define causation more widely produces results too 'promiscuous' for the negligence inquiry.[85] If the defendant's breach is purely incidental because the claimant was fated to suffer the same loss in any case (given 'normal vicissitudes'), they rightly recover no tort damages. How, as a matter of corrective justice, does such a claimant 'suffer an injury as a result of the defendant's wrongdoing'?[86] There is 'a necessity-shaped hole' in broader accounts of causation.[87] It is better to frame the inquiry 'self-consciously to recognise as causes only those factors which *alter* a claimant's normal course of events'.[88]

As we have seen, Stapleton avoids this problem through the separate inquiry into whether the defendant's breach (or *breaches* (collectively)) made the claimant worse off, when valuing their claim. Green is critical of this too:

> There is something intuitively unwieldy about insisting that the law recognise as causal a factor which, whilst contributing in physical terms to an outcome, does so where that outcome is of no concern to the tort of negligence ... only to reinstate legal criteria at the subsequent state of evaluating 'damage'.[89]

What is to be achieved by 'merely postpone[ing] the inevitable question', having asked a causal question to which 'the answers may well turn out to be unnecessary'? Green argues that the law should resist Stapleton's separation and continue to incorporate necessity into the causal inquiry itself. This 'streamlines the process sooner rather than later, so that resources are not consumer by causal investigations which turn out ultimately to have no legal relevance' – a wasteful approach.[90]

---

[82] ibid 131.
[83] S Green, *Causation in Negligence* (Oxford, Hart, 2015).
[84] ibid, 1.
[85] ibid 28.
[86] ibid 29 (quoting A Beever, *Rediscovering the Law of Negligence* (Oxford, Hart, 2007) 414).
[87] ibid 31.
[88] ibid 15 (original emphasis).
[89] ibid 21.
[90] ibid 16.

Instead, Green proposes, the court should ask: Did *one or more* defendants' breaches of duty change the course of events, inflicting harm on the claimant that would not otherwise have occurred? (The 'necessary breach analysis' – was *a* breach necessary for the harm to occur?) Thus when there are multiple independent breaches, we examine where the claimant would have been had none of the breaches occurred. The justification for aggregating the breaches in this way is that the claimant should not lose out from, nor the defendants benefit from, the fortuitous presence of a second independent wrong.[91] This seems to produce the same outcomes as Stapleton's approach, by a shorter route. The first defendant remains liable in *Baker v Willoughby* because we compare the claimant's (perfectly healthy) leg had *neither* of the defendants' torts occurred.[92] Green also thinks *Bailey v MOD* incorrectly decided, simply because it was impossible to show whether the hospital's negligence was necessary for the ultimate injury.

Gemma Turton, however, defends the Stapletonian separation between causation and valuation. The former is a pure question of fact – whether the defendant's conduct was involved in the injury. Whereas deciding whether to compensate an injury which would anyway have been caused by another defendant's wrong concerns 'the appropriate extent of liability' – 'a normative question best addressed within a doctrine that is openly evaluative in nature'.[93] Sandy Steel makes a similar point. Sequences cases like *Baker v Willoughby* (with its different outcome from *Jobling v Associated Dairies* – tort followed by disabling natural illness)[94] cannot be explained by reasoning about *causation*. 'It is difficult to believe that the (factual) status of a tort in respect of some loss can vary depending upon the legal quality of some act in the future. It follows that these rules cannot be based solely upon causal considerations'.[95] *Baker v Willoughby* and *Jobling* are 'causally identical' cases. The difference between them depends rather on the scope of liability for the consequences of the (first) defendant's tort.

These arguments seem recondite. But they may have practical implications. As seen, Green claims that her rolled-up approach would avoid unnecessary (and expensive) causal investigations of questions which ultimately turn out to be irrelevant. But as Turton suggests in reply, it would be possible to address *quantification* as a preliminary issue if it appeared that the claimant would have suffered the same loss through non-negligent causes.[96] It is not clear that the conceptual structure should necessarily determine the order in which the questions are considered. The court's case-management powers would surely override doctrinal 'logic'.

---

[91] ibid 72.
[92] [1970] AC 467.
[93] Turton (n 49) 29.
[94] [1982] AC 794.
[95] S Steel, *Proof of Causation in Tort Law* (Cambridge, Cambridge University Press, 2015) 43.
[96] Turton (n 49) 29.

Conclusion: 'Involvement' or 'Necessity'?

Perhaps less separates the positions outlined above than first appears. All seem to agree that 'necessity' plays a vital role over tort's remedy for a given injury. Is it something that would have happened anyway, or was the defendant's wrong necessary to produce it? The disagreement is whether necessity should be built into the *causal* inquiry, as traditionally it is through the 'but-for' test (subject to a justice-based exception when there are several torts). Would it be clearer to use a broader concept of causal 'involvement', allocating the issue of 'necessary connection' (and exceptions such as *Baker v Willoughby*) to an overtly evaluative stage of the tort inquiry? Stapleton argues that the second approach makes reasoning about these questions more transparent.[97] The danger in using causation to do too much 'work', in her view, is that 'causation has a factual ring' for many lawyers. Posing as factual what are in truth *normative* questions risks courts 'being tempted by the camouflage of vacuous causal assertions' – instead of giving fully reasoned answers.

Robust, old-school, atheoretical common lawyers might wonder whether it really matters. Is this what comes from philosophers (or philosophically inclined legal scholars) caring too much about abstract concepts and too little about practical results? The President of the NSW Court of Appeal argues in reply that Stapleton's approach to causation would make little difference to the outcomes of cases.[98] However Stapleton (whose approach to tort law focuses on the practicalities of judicial decision-making)[99] replies that transparency matters. She also suggests that employing different concepts of 'causation' in different areas of law produces great uncertainty – a practical difficulty for those drafting (eg) contracts or legislation who will find it hard to predict how a court will interpret causal requirements.

Green suggests it is unnecessary to discard the but-for test to accommodate 'over-determined' causal situations because this 'rare' situation is more a 'theoretical glitch' than a practical problem.[100] But Stapleton argues that such situations are neither uncommon nor insignificant. What of a board of directors unanimously voting for an illegal resolution (which could be carried by a simple majority): would we say that none is responsible because none is a necessary cause (but for each individual director's vote, the resolution would still have been carried)? What about a severely polluted river into which a number of factories each discharge significant toxic waste (each breaching the limit of what is tolerable in nuisance)?[101] The law would hardly wish to encourage a

---

[97] J Stapleton, 'Reflections on Common Sense Causation in Australia' in S Degeling et al, *Torts in Commercial Law* (Pyrmont, NSW, Lawbook Co, 2011).

[98] J Allsop, 'Causation in Commercial Law' in S Degeling et al (ibid).

[99] J Stapleton, *Three Essays on Torts* (Oxford, Oxford University Press, 2021) ch 1 (but cf ibid 78 – such 'reflexive' scholarship cannot reconcile incoherent, inconsistent judicial reasoning about 'causation').

[100] Green (n 83) 9.

[101] *Pride of Derby Angling Association v British Celanese* [1953] Ch 149.

'tort fest' – that is, encourage the participation of multiple wrongdoers since this would thwart the finding of (but-for) causation. These 'oversubscribed threshold' situations are not unusual. Neither are cases about a factor's impact on another person's decision-making (eg whether to have an operation or to make a certain investment decision). This is another situation in which ad hoc 'exceptions' to the but-for test are often made. The improbability of Lord Nicholls' 'two negligent candles' scenario should not mislead us about the scale of the problem.

Perhaps it is time to give up the seductive simplicity of the but-for test, if it has to be disapplied to cater for such a significant category of 'exceptions'. Stapleton's goal is to ensure that such questions are approached as genuine normative choices, not through ad hoc, 'common sense' exceptions, or obscured through pseudo-factual assertions.

Debate 2
Remoteness, Causation and 'Common Sense'

Tort law often has to decide, in various contexts, whether there is a sufficiently close legal connection between wrongful conduct and the injury which is the basis for the claim. We are in this debate considering situations in which the minimum threshold of causation has been met – whether on the traditional 'but-for' test or the rival test of 'historical involvement'. It is a truism that either test leads to results that are much too wide. For example, in *every* accident the tortfeasor's parents must clearly be a *cause*. Without their act of procreation the tortfeasor would not exist and the accident could not have happened. Of course, nobody would suggest they had legal responsibility. The main reason for that is the absence of any relevant legal duty or culpable breach of it on the parents' part. (For the law, the problem of overinclusion that vexes philosophers of causation is considerably reduced because the court only considers liability-generating conduct.)[102] Many lawyers would add that the parents' causal contribution is a mere background condition for, and not a substantial or operative cause of, the tort. Thus even a wrongful act will be ignored if it is only a 'circumstance' for the injury, merely 'part of the history'.[103] While using causal concepts to limit liability in this way is widespread, its cogency has been challenged. Critics argue that the causal approach obfuscates the true reasons for limiting liability. The *normative* basis for the limits should be articulated openly, not disguised by intuitive speculation about the injury's 'true cause'.

The most prominent doctrine addressing this problem is 'remoteness of damage'. Strictly, 'remoteness' concerns a tortious injury (for which the defendant is liable) that generates further consequential injuries or losses. (It is another truism that just as chains of causation stretch infinitely far back,

---

[102] Stapleton (n 70) 392 (this 'focus[es] the cause-in-fact inquiry only on the few factors of legal concern').

[103] *Jones v Livox Quarries* [1952] 2 QB 608, 616 (Denning LJ).

chains of consequences project infinitely into the future.) A driver negligently crashes; a traffic policeman attending the scene is then injured in trying to warn other motorists of the hazard.[104] A negligently damaged water-main floods a house; while uninhabited for repairs, squatters move into it and do further damage.[105] For which consequences should the defendant be liable? Rules that are employed include the foreseeability of the type of damage, the 'scope of the duty', and the '*novus actus interveniens*'. (Lord Burrows suggests that while these doctrines are 'generally regarded as different from each other' they are 'closely related [because] they are all concerned with limitations on the recovery of factually caused loss' – and 'the order in which one considers them may be largely a matter of convenience'.)[106]

In Lord Hoffmann's famous 'mountaineer' example, the question is whether the negligent doctor has any liability for the only harm that occurs (ie the weak-kneed mountaineer's death in an avalanche).[107] If a speeding driver is hit by a falling tree, is he liable?[108] (In each case, there is certainly historical involvement or but-for causation: had the doctor correctly diagnosed the knee problem the patient would not have gone mountain-climbing; had the driver not exceeded the speed limit, the car would not have been under the tree at the moment it fell.) If an occupier negligently fails to warn would-be bathers that a lake is contaminated with Weil's disease, is it liable to a swimmer who drowns in the lake (when there was *no* duty to warn against the (obvious) risk of drowning)?[109] These questions are not about consequential loss flowing from a tort, but whether there is sufficient connection between the defendant's wrongdoing and the *only* actionable injury.

Similar problems can arise about the claimant's contribution to their own injuries. Was it so great that they must be treated as the sole author of their misfortune, eclipsing the defendant's negligence and barring a claim altogether (rather than reducing damages through the contributory negligence doctrine)?[110] Conversely, when a drug-addicted prisoner fell out of a high bunk which had negligently been assigned to him, his irresponsibility in having initially become addicted to drugs was 'not a potent cause of his injury' – so the defence of contributory negligence was not engaged and he recovered full compensation. '[The addiction] was too remote in time, place and circumstance and was not sufficiently connected with the negligence of

---

[104] *Knightley v Johns* [1982] 1 WLR 349.
[105] *Lamb v Camden LBC* [1981] QB 625.
[106] *Meadows v Khan* [2022] AC 852 [80].
[107] *South Australian Asset Management Corporation v York Montague Ltd* [1997] AC 191, 213.
[108] *Berry v Sugar Notch Borough*, 191 Pa 345, 43 A 240 (1899).
[109] *Darby v National Trust* [2001] EWCA Civ 189.
[110] eg *Vellino v Chief Constable of Manchester* [2002] 1 WLR 218 (criminal jumped from window to escape arrest); *Clay v TUI UK Ltd* [2018] EWCA Civ 1177; [2018] 4 All ER 672 (guest trapped on hotel balcony slipped while climbing to neighbouring room).

the prison staff'.[111] Problems resembling 'remoteness' crop up in various guises.

The 'causal' flavour of the courts' reasoning is obvious. As noted, commentators are divided about this approach. Hart and Honoré's influential treatise on causation is its most prominent defender. Hart and Honoré discern certain concepts about the limits of causal responsibility with 'very deep roots in all our thinking', that guide both judicial decisions and 'the plain man's notions of causation'.[112] Accepting that it is no simple matter to define these limits clearly, Hart and Honoré caution against the 'blinding error' of assuming the concepts therefore have 'no meaning worth bothering about at all, but are used as a mere disguise for arbitrary decision or judicial policy'.[113] They maintain that the use of common-sense causal concepts to determine legal responsibility is *not* an 'illusion', 'a deception and a cheat', 'superstition' or 'a ghost to be exorcised'. Other commentators such as Jane Stapleton remain unconvinced. In Stapleton's view, causation is concerned *only* with the question of 'factual involvement'. Once this is established, the causal issue is spent. To decide the *limits of responsibility* for caused harm requires an *evaluative* judgement. It should be made squarely and openly, without the distraction of 'causal' rules that are misleading at best, a mask for intuitive decisions at worst.

This debate considers these rules on remoteness – the '"legal filters" ... developed to reflect the court's judgment of the extent of a defendant's liability for [their] wrongdoing'.[114] How well do the rules perform the filtering role? We scrutinise, in particular, the proper role of causation. We conclude by examining a renaissance in the ideas of Hart and Honoré, following empirical research into the psychology of everyday causal judgements.

'Foreseeable Kind of Harm'

Lawyers tend to think of foreseeability as the core remoteness rule in negligence. In *The Wagon Mound (No 1)* the Privy Council declared the normative superiority of this test compared to the earlier regime of liability for all 'direct' consequences, even when unforeseeable.[115] The court also deemed foreseeability analytically superior because it avoided difficult questions about causation. Let us examine these claims.

In delivering the landmark judgment in *The Wagon Mound*, Viscount Simonds declared that liability for direct-but-unforeseeable harm was a 'palpable injustice'. The criterion of reasonable foreseeability by contrast 'corresponds with the common conscience of mankind'.

---

[111] *St George v Home Office* [2008] EWCA Civ 1068; [2009] 1 WLR 1670 [46] Dyson LJ. Compare *Hughes v Turning Point Scotland* [2019] CSOH 42, [115].
[112] HLA Hart and AM Honoré, *Causation in the Law* (Oxford, Oxford University Press, 1959) 1.
[113] ibid 3.
[114] *Meadows* (n 106) [56] (Lord Hodge and Lord Sales).
[115] [1961] AC 388 (overruling *Re Polemis* [1921] 3 KB 560).

For it does not seem consonant with current ideas of justice or morality that for an act of negligence, however slight or venial, which results in some trivial foreseeable damage the actor should be liable for all consequences however unforeseeable and however grave, so long as they can be said to be 'direct'. It is a principle of civil liability, subject only to qualifications which have no present relevance, that a man must be considered to be responsible for the probable consequences of his act. To demand more of him is too harsh a rule, to demand less is to ignore that civilised order requires the observance of a minimum standard of behaviour.[116]

This is an overtly normative test. At first sight the reasoning appears unanswerable. Surely it is unfair to saddle a careless defendant with harm which they could not foresee and (therefore) could not avoid? This might impose liability quite out of proportion to the defendant's carelessness.

However, the reasoning may be questioned. Where the defendant has negligently injured the claimant, should unforeseeable *consequences* of that injury be borne uncompensated by the blameless claimant, rather than transferred to the negligent defendant? It is less obvious than Viscount Simonds claimed that such an extension of the defendant's liability would be 'palpably unjust'. As Prosser observed, even if it would be disproportionate to the defendant's culpability 'it can be no less out of proportion to the plaintiff's innocence'.[117]

Nor is there a necessary connexion between the defendant's culpability and the extent of liability for consequences, contrary to the *Wagon Mound* reasoning. The judgment presented the foreseeability test as the logical corollary of negligence, but it is not – as the remoteness rules in other torts demonstrates.[118] If the foreseeability rule were deduced from the nature of negligence liability – that is, failing to take reasonable care to prevent risks of foreseeable injury – we would expect a different (ie broader) rule to apply to strict liability torts. In fact the *Wagon Mound* approach has also been adopted in stricter torts such as *Rylands v Fletcher*.[119] In deceit (the tort of intentionally deceiving another), liability is *not* limited to losses that the defendant *intended* the claimant to sustain, as the *Wagon Mound* 'logic' might suggest. On the contrary, the courts have rejected even the foreseeability limit on remoteness. In deceit, liability extends to all 'direct' consequences of the fraud.[120] Prior to the Privy Council's decision, Hart and Honoré had noted that liability

---

[116] ibid, 422–23.

[117] W Prosser, *Selected Topics on the Law of Torts* (Ann Arbor, University of Michigan Press, 1953) 217.

[118] Stevens (n 80) 158–61 (*Wagon Mound*'s 'fallacious logic').

[119] *Cambridge Water Co v Eastern Counties Leather* [1994] 2 AC 264. (Consider also *Mayfair Ltd v Pears* [1987] 1 NZLR 459 (trespass to land);).

[120] *Doyle v Olby (Ironmongers) Ltd* [1969] 2 QB 158. See also *Kuwait Airways* (n 42) [100]–[104] (proposing different remoteness rules for innocent and dishonest conversion).

for intentional torts extends beyond intended consequences, disproving the 'consistency' rationale for a foreseeability limitation in negligence.[121]

A further 'consistency' claim fails because of foreseeability's 'ambiguous' use. Its 'apparent success in bringing culpability and compensation within a single formula' is spurious.[122] Hart and Honoré stressed that in the 'practical' inquiry into *careless breach* of duty, 'foreseeability' is a relative notion. Breach depends on many factors beside the mere degree of probability. Hart and Honoré cite Judge Learned Hand's equation balancing the severity and likelihood of harm, on the one hand, against the cost of eliminating it.[123] They put it in anecdotal terms too: 'A considerable risk is involved in crossing the streets of Oxford, but life would come to a standstill if we did not sometimes run such risks'.[124] Some risks can be overlooked without attracting liability in negligence – depending on the value of the conduct carried out while running the risk. By contrast in applying the remoteness test, 'the likelihood with which the relevant loss must be foreseen does not vary in this way'.[125]

The second strand of reasoning in *The Wagon Mound* was that the 'foreseeable kind of harm' criterion would simplify the law. This too may be doubted. Viscount Simonds hailed the replacement of:

> a test (the 'direct' consequence) ... which leads to no-where but the never-ending and insoluble problems of causation. 'The lawyer,' said Sir Frederick Pollock, 'cannot afford to adventure himself with philosophers in the logical and metaphysical controversies that beset the idea of cause'. Yet this is just what [the law] has most unfortunately done ... A conspicuous example occurs when the actor seeks to escape liability on the ground that the 'chain of causation' is broken by a '*nova causa*' or '*novus actus interveniens*'.[126]

It is often overlooked that *The Wagon Mound* sought to remove causal questions from the remoteness inquiry altogether, in line with Pollock's warning. It was unsuccessful. The *novus actus interveniens*, despite Lord Simonds' criticism, has not been replaced by the foreseeability question. A claim for damages must pass *both* filters. (For example, an intervention may 'break the chain of causation' despite being foreseeable – as many interventions are, to some degree.) This overtly causal 'survivor' is considered in the next section.

Another notorious problem with the *Wagon Mound* test is the slipperiness of the 'kind of harm' that has to be foreseen. The more precisely defined the 'kind of harm', the harder it is to foresee – for example, the requirement that 'property damage by fire' had to be foreseeable rather than 'property damage'

---

[121] Hart and Honoré (n 112) 235.
[122] ibid 238.
[123] *US v Carroll Towing* 159 F 2d 169 (1947).
[124] Hart and Honoré (n 112) 239.
[125] Stevens (n 80) 159.
[126] [1961] AC 388, 423.

generally or 'by oil-slick fouling', in the leading case itself. Allied to the element of evaluation inherent in deciding whether harm was *reasonably* foreseeable, there is a good degree of flexibility concealed within an apparently factual test. Speaking of the duty of care, Lord Goff warned judges to resist the 'very tempting' prospect of 'try[ing] to solve all problems of negligence by reference to an all-embracing criterion of foreseeability, thereby effectively reducing all decisions in this field to questions of fact'. The diversity of issues faced in the law of negligence meant 'this comfortable solution is, alas, not open to us'.[127] Or as Tony Weir remarked, 'Despite the categorical nature of Lord Simonds's ascerbities in *The Wagon Mound* foreseeability is not a universal solvent'.[128]

Decisions since *The Wagon Mound* have cast doubt on both its normative basis and its supposed 'simplicity'. In personal injury claims in particular, the test of what needs to be foreseen has been widened so far that it undermines the *Wagon Mound* philosophy of restricting liability out of fairness to defendants. Almost immediately after the Privy Council's decision, the Lord Chief Justice confirmed the survival of the 'thin skull' exception for claimants unforeseeably susceptible to physical injuries.[129] The House of Lords soon held that while the *kind* of injury had to be foreseeable, the precise *way* in which it had occurred did not.[130] This was confirmed by *Jolley v Sutton LBC*,[131] again overruling a narrower decision in the court below.[132] *Jolley*, like *Hughes v Lord Advocate*, concerned children injured while playing with a dangerous 'allurement' left negligently in their path. Lord Hoffmann commented that it would be rare to find such injuries unforeseeable, however unusual the circumstances, given that '[children's] ingenuity in finding unexpected ways of doing mischief to themselves and others should never be underestimated'.[133] Lord Steyn summarised the attenuated state of the *Wagon Mound* doctrine: 'Viscount Simonds was in no way suggesting that the precise *manner* of which the injury occurred nor its *extent* had to be foreseeable'.[134] As Steel notes, these qualifications always limited the potential for *Wagon Mound* to protect defendants against overly burdensome liabilities. From that perspective, the focus on the kind of harm is 'hard to understand' – crushing liability could result from the 'enormous' extent of a foreseeable type of harm.[135]

On that crucial question of how broadly or narrowly to define the 'kind of damage', Lord Hoffmann offered this guidance: 'what must have been foreseen

---

[127] *Smith v Littlewoods Organisation* [1987] AC 241, 280.
[128] T Weir, *A Casebook on Tort*, 10th edition (London, Sweet & Maxwell, 2004) 231.
[129] *Smith v Leech Brain & Co* [1962] 2 QB 405.
[130] *Hughes v Lord Advocate* [1963] AC 837.
[131] [2000] 1 WLR 1082 (*Jolley*).
[132] [1998] 1 WLR 1546.
[133] *Jolley* (n 131) 1093.
[134] ibid 1090 (original emphasis).
[135] S Steel, 'Culpability and Compensation' in J Goudkamp et al, *Taking Law Seriously: Essays in Honour of Peter Cane* (Oxford, Hart Publishing, 2021) 65.

is not the precise injury which occurred but injury of a given description. The foreseeability is not as to the particulars but the genus'.¹³⁶ This captures the idea at a high level of generality. The application of this abstraction has varied greatly. In some (earlier) cases the courts seem to have come close to require foresight of 'the precise injury which occurred', for example, transmission of the rare disease 'leptospirosis' specifically, rather than 'diseases' generally, in a rat-infested workplace;¹³⁷ scalding by an 'explosion' rather than a 'splash' when a cover fell into an industrial vat of chemicals.¹³⁸ At the other extreme is *Page v Smith*, which refused to distinguish physical and psychiatric injuries as different 'kinds of harm'.¹³⁹ In consequence, the 'eggshell skull' doctrine was controversially held to extend to 'eggshell personalities'. Reasons offered for this extension of liability included medical scepticism about any sharp dichotomy between 'physical' and 'psychiatric' causes for certain 'mental' illness. The House of Lords acknowledged the genuine normative choice before them. The court was not distracted from choosing by the pseudo-factual question of 'foreseeable kinds of harm'. As Lord Lloyd noted, 'Viscount Simonds did not attempt to define what he meant by "kind of damage", and the concept is apt to be elusive'.¹⁴⁰

Robert Stevens therefore criticises the *Wagon Mound* doctrine. In the form initially stated by Viscount Simonds it seemed to be a rough, intuitive but straightforward way of limiting consequential liability. But the courts have retreated from its liability-limiting policy, using fine and 'unattractive' distinctions such as the thin-skull rule. Stevens' central criticism is that 'there is no criterion by which [the type of damage] can be determined'. 'Distinctions of this kind, based on an unstable concept, with no demonstrably correct answer one way of the other, do no credit to our law'.¹⁴¹ Sarah Green defends *The Wagon Mound* against Stevens' critique.¹⁴² The 'foreseeable kind of harm' test is properly flexible and permits the 'intense focus on the circumstances of each case' that Lord Steyn correctly recommended.¹⁴³ In Green's view, it is better to be open about this flexibility. The outcomes of cases applying the flexible foreseeability rule have been 'largely uncontentious'. And what is the realistic alternative? A 'formulaic test might look conceptually elegant and intellectually neat, but would have a limited practical value'. 'There is nothing to be gained from pretending that questions of this nature are amenable to a mechanical analysis'.

---

¹³⁶ ibid 1091.
¹³⁷ *Tremain v Pike* [1969] 1 WLR 1556.
¹³⁸ *Doughty v Turner Bros* [1964] 1 QB 518.
¹³⁹ *Page v Smith* [1996] 1 AC 155.
¹⁴⁰ ibid 196.
¹⁴¹ Stevens (n 80) 155, 156.
¹⁴² Green (n 83) 54–56 (the source for quotations in this paragraph, excepting Lord Steyn's).
¹⁴³ *Jolley* (n 131) 1090.

Interventions

Liability is often – but not always – curtailed when the claimant's harm results from some unusual natural-world, or deliberate human, intervention. Similarly, where the claimant's harm seems wholly coincidental – for example, the coincidence of the defendant's driving at speed putting the claimant at the precise spot where a tree falls. Such results are often reached intuitively and commonly explained by causal reasoning. That the intervention curtailed the effect of the tort, 'breaking the chain of causation'. That because the harm was coincidental, the tort was merely a background condition for it or *condictio sine qua non*, not an 'effective cause' (*causa causans*). According to Hart and Honoré, the law here reflects and employs everyday common-sense notions of causation. Stapleton challenges this view. Appealing to 'common-sense' obscures rather than illuminates the reasons why liability is curtailed. These questions are not about causation at all. Rather they pose a normative question about the scope of liability. In Stapleton's view the causal language and concepts in this area should be eliminated.

Traditionally the law uses causal language, metaphors drawn from the physical world. Damage being too 'remote' (rather than 'proximate'). 'Chains' of causes being 'broken'. But are lawyers really misled by this? Discussing the phrase 'proximately caused',[144] Lord Shaw said it was 'out of the question' to suggest that the closest cause in time must always be the 'proximate' one.[145] In other words, the law did not take the word 'proximate' literally but gave it a looser meaning ('the real efficient cause'), derived from judgements about *responsibility*. 'Remoteness' is only a metaphor. It may be an inappropriate one. Take the notorious 'plank' case, *Re Polemis*, where a negligently dislodged plank unforeseeably caused a catastrophic fire. The case was overruled and the fire deemed too remote in *The Wagon Mound*. Yet given the physical proximity and immediacy of the connection between plank, spark and fire, in what sense was the fire *remote*? On the contrary, 'that consequence was temporally and spatially extremely close to the conduct constituting the breach'.[146] But even Stapleton seems to use the 'orthodox, albeit opaque, terminology "too remote"' as a convenient label for the inquiry.[147]

Lord Shaw also said: 'The chain of causation is a handy expression, but the figure is inadequate. Causation is not a chain, but a net'. Causes radiate out infinitely, not in a smooth sequence like 'beads in a row or links in a chain'.[148] Over a century ago then, nobody was deceived by the traditional metaphor. However Stapleton argues that the 'incoherent' and 'metaphysically mysterious' notion of the broken chain of causation should be eliminated. The causation threshold has (by definition) been crossed in such cases. There *was* a

---

[144] Marine Insurance Act 1906, s 55(1).
[145] *Leyland Shipping v Norwich Union Fire Insurance* [1918] AC 350, 369.
[146] Stapleton (n 99) 67.
[147] ibid 92.
[148] *Leyland Shipping* (n 145) 350, 369.

causal connexion: 'The sequence of what happened, happened. It was not interrupted'.[149] The real question, requiring judicial evaluation, is whether the intervention ends the defendant's responsibility. It would be clearer to pose such normative questions in 'completely non-causal terms'; 'If we must use mechanical imagery, let us have whether *and why* there has been a "break in the chain of legal *responsibility*" for the consequences of D's tort'.[150] In this at least, Hart and Honoré's position seems similar. Half a century earlier they regretted that 'metaphorical modes of expression … have clustered around the notion of cause'. These were artificial ('rarely appear in the vocabulary of the ordinary man'), unhelpful ('as baffling as the philosophical or psychological distinctions which they are designed to replace') and by inappropriately invoking physical forces have 'provoked needless puzzles for the law'.[151]

It is easy to say that the 'remoteness' inquiry is not literally about measuring the distance in time or space between tort and injury, then drawing a line. Nor is there literally any physical 'break' in a 'chain' of causes. Nobody seriously suggests the contrary. But it is harder to formulate a clear positive guide as to what these rules *do* require. On *novus actus interveniens*, the great judge Lord Wright said it was 'very difficult to formulate any precise and all-embracing rule'. He continued (a little despairingly):

> it must be shown that there is something which I will call ultroneous, something unwarrantable, a new cause which disturbs the sequence of events, something which can be described as either unreasonable or extraneous, or extrinsic. I doubt whether the law can be stated more precisely than that.[152]

Recent nutshell definitions hold that a *novus actus* 'obliterates the [defendant's] wrongdoing',[153] it becomes 'the sole effective cause of the loss … [so] that the wrongdoing, whilst it might still be a "but for" cause and therefore a cause in fact, has been eclipsed so that it is not an effective or contributory cause in law'.[154] The judges are open about determining the scope of responsibility. But they seem unable to devise any useful test to guide that choice. Obliteration and eclipse are merely colourful variations on the time-worn 'broken chain' metaphor.

Is it really impossible to state a useful test? Hart and Honoré concluded from a lengthy analysis of linguistic usage and decided cases that an event 'eclipses' wrongdoing's causative effect in broadly two situations: deliberate human interventions and unusual natural events. Liability would surely cease if the claimant, rendered unconscious at the roadside by the defendant's

---

[149] ibid 93.
[150] Stapleton (n 70) 422–23.
[151] HLA Hart and AM Honoré, 'Causation in the Law I – A Survey of Common-Sense Principles' (1956) 72 *LQR* 58, 61–62.
[152] *The Oropesa* [1943] P 32, 39.
[153] *Stacey v Autosleeper Group Ltd* [2014] EWCA Civ 1551, [14] (Floyd LJ).
[154] *Clay v TUI Ltd* [2018] EWCA Civ 1177, [27] (Hamblen LJ).

negligent driving, had their iPhone stolen by a passing thief, or were struck by lightning. Lord Hoffmann (whose tutor at Oxford had been Tony Honoré) accepted their thesis: 'the causal significance of acts of third parties or natural forces … gives rise to almost all the problems about the notion of "causing" and drives judges to take refuge in metaphor or Latin'.[155] This certainly corresponds with the *novus actus* case law. But Stapleton challenges Hart and Honoré's claims. She questions the methodology by which they reach their claims (a criticism examined below). Moreover, Stapleton argues that Hart and Honoré present as 'common-sense causation' matters which are actually evaluative and depend on the scope of responsibility imposed by law for the particular conduct (wrongdoing) in question.

It is true that a defendant is not usually responsible for a third party's deliberate criminal conduct. In a leading case illustrating the absence of such liability, Oliver LJ observed:

> the question of the existence of a duty and that of whether the damage brought about by the act of a third party is too remote are simply two facets of the same problem; for if there be a duty to take reasonable care to prevent damage being caused by a third party then I find it difficult to see how damage caused by the third party consequent upon the failure to take such care can be too remote a consequence of the breach of duty. Essentially the answer to both questions is to be found in answering the question, in what circumstances is a defendant to be held responsible at common law for the independent act of a third person.[156]

This is correct, and important. Exceptionally, the law does sometimes recognise duties to control 'independent acts of third persons'. For example based on a voluntary assumption of responsibility to the claimant,[157] or the defendant's high degree of control over prisoners being held in custody.[158] When such a duty *does* exist, its existence defeats any argument based on remoteness – that the 'true cause' of the loss was the third party whose criminality 'obliterates' the effect of the tort. Such an argument must necessarily fail, as Oliver LJ reasoned.

The point has also been recognised in cases involving failure to prevent claimants from harming themselves. Such duties are even more exceptional – given 'the individualist philosophy of the common law. People of full age and sound understanding must look after themselves'.[159] But they are not entirely unknown: for example custody officers' duties to prevent self-harm or suicide

---

[155] *Environment Agency v Empress Car Co (Abertillery) Ltd* [1999] 2 AC 22, 0000. See also Hoffmann (n 53) at 594–95.
[156] *P Perl (Exporters) Ltd v Camden LBC* [1984] QB 342, 353.
[157] *Stansbie v Troman* [1948] 2 KB 48; *Rushbond Plc v JS Design Partnership LLP* [2021] EWCA Civ 1889.
[158] *Dorset Yacht Co Ltd v Home Office* [1970] AC 1004.
[159] *Reeves v Metropolitan Police Commissioner* [2000] 1 AC 360, 368 (Lord Hoffmann).

of persons held in detention;[160] or a bookmaker which specifically undertook to bar a self-declared 'problem gambler' from betting with the firm.[161] Again, where such a duty exists it must defeat any 'causal' argument such as *novus actus interveniens*. The claimant might have injured themselves deliberately, but that cannot break the chain of causation since it was 'the very thing at which the duty was directed'.[162] As Lord Hoffmann put it, 'once it is admitted that this is the rare case in which such a duty is owed, it seems to me to be self contradictory to say that the breach could not have been a cause of the harm because the victim caused it himself'.[163]

Arguably there is no separate role for a *causal* doctrine to play. The judgement about 'intervention' is determined by the extent of the defendant's *obligations*. Ultimately they merge. Taking this view, Stapleton argues that trying to define the appropriate degree of 'causal connection' (in line with Hart and Honoré's approach):

> inserts an empty obfuscatory step in legal analysis. When courts try to deploy 'causal connection' as an analytical tool rather than as a conclusionary statement that liability is to be imposed, they face bewilderment … Moreover, it can obscure the factors which *do* influence a court in relation to which consequences of breach the defendant should be liable for.[164]

Coincidences: Chester v Afshar

A similar argument can be made about coincidences. What the law treats as 'coincidental' depends on how it defines the defendant's duty. A lightning strike is the classic example of a mere coincidence, 'a piece of abominable bad luck'.[165] Yet as Lord Walker has recognised, if the defendant is a manufacturer of lightning conductors and the claimant's house is burned down when struck by lightning because a conductor is defective, nobody would suggest that the damage was too remote, notwithstanding how rarely houses are thunder-struck.[166]

Stapleton accepts the 'soundness' of the evaluative judgement that 'burdening the [negligent] tortfeasor with liability for a coincidental consequence can do nothing to generate meaningful deterrence effects of such carelessness

---

[160] *Reeves* ibid.
[161] *Calvert v William Hill Credit* [2008] EWHC 454 (Ch) (compare assessment of damages: [2008] EWCA Civ 1427).
[162] *Reeves* (n 159) 374 (Lord Jauncey).
[163] ibid 368.
[164] J Stapleton, 'Occam's Razor Reveals an Orthodox Basis for *Chester v Afshar*' (2006) 122 LQR 426, 431, 432.
[165] *Chester* (n 2) [13] (Lord Steyn); and see Lord Walker at [94] ('fanciful scenario' of operating theatre struck by lightning).
[166] *The Achilleas* [2008] UKHL 48; [2009] 1 AC 61, [78] (discussing contract – but the same reasoning would apply to a duty imposed by tort).

in the future'.¹⁶⁷ She nevertheless supports the majority's decision *not* to dismiss the claim as 'coincidental' in *Chester v Afshar*. She contrasts the situation of a speeding car hit by a falling tree. There is (of course) a duty not to speed but it is not imposed because of *that* risk, which is entirely random and unaffected by the driver's speed. It would be silly to require drivers to warn passengers of the falling-tree risk, because it is no greater when driving at a particular speed than anywhere else. In *Chester v Afshar* however, since the operation did create a risk that the patient would not otherwise have faced, it was cogent to impose a duty to bring it to her attention.

What of the fact that in *Chester*, the patient would still have had the operation had she been warned, but on a different day? It was 99 per cent likely that she would not have been injured in the hypothetical postponed operation (had she been operated on 100 times she would probably have been injured only once). Thus, comparing the actual history with the hypothetical world in which the defendant discharged the duty to warn, the patient would not have been injured. There was historical involvement – a factual causal connection. The dissenting judges in *Chester v Afshar* thought this was pure coincidence. That the claimant had the operation on the day that she had not increased or affected her risk of injury.¹⁶⁸ As Lord Hoffmann has put it extrajudicially, when someone makes a fortune at a casino nobody would say 'they won *because it was Tuesday*' even though, had they gone on a different occasion, the odds were very much against them having made such large winnings.¹⁶⁹

Stapleton responds by suggesting that if we consider patients as a group, failing to warn of risks is not unconnected with the overall rate of injuries. Because some patients (albeit not the claimant in *Chester v Afshar*) *will* decline elective surgery when warned fully of the risks, the number of complications from surgery across the entire population of patients will decrease. By shifting the focus from the particular case to failures-to-warn generally, she queries the 'coincidence' objection to *Chester v Afshar*. Other commentators doubt the legitimacy or cogency of Stapleton's move. On the corrective justice approach to tort, what matters is the increase in risk for this particular claimant. That *other* patients might have declined to have the operation is simply irrelevant where (as in *Chester*) the failure to warn had not meaningfully increased the claimant's risk. Stapleton argues that it is sensible to adopt an approach which lowers the number of injuries (complications from elective surgery) across the population as a whole. She approves the *Chester* majority's view that liability prevents the duty to warn becoming 'empty'.¹⁷⁰

---

¹⁶⁷ Stapleton (n 150) 439.
¹⁶⁸ *Chester* (n 2) [8] Lord Bingham (dissenting) (timing of operation 'irrelevant').
¹⁶⁹ (n 53) 602.
¹⁷⁰ Cf ch 4, 'Causation, the Burden of Proof, and the "Empty Duty" Argument.

Such arguments fit poorly with the celebrated, elementary causation case of *Barnett v Chelsea Hospital*.[171] The doctor's negligent failure even to examine the patient did not cause his death because even had arsenic poisoning been diagnosed, no antidote was available. The defendant had failed to diagnose a lethal, untreatable condition – the plaintiff's death was inevitable. As Stevens points out,[172] criticising the reasoning in *Chester v Afshar*, *Barnett* involved clear breach of an important medical duty. The very reason why doctors are required to examine patients is because they might be suffering from a non-obvious complaint. Does that mean, on the authority of *Chester*, that damages should have been awarded against Chelsea Hospital so as not to 'empty the duty of content'? Of course not. *Barnett* is fairly unusual because most misdiagnosis cases involve health complaints that *could* (and should) have received medical treatment. The failure of the claim on the facts of *Barnett* does not therefore 'empty' the doctor's duty to carry out careful examination and diagnosis.[173]

Returning to *Chester v Afshar*, Clark and Nolan stress the inadequacy of the majority's deterrent or duty-reinforcing reasoning.[174] There would still be no compensation awarded against a doctor who fails to warn in numerous scenarios: when the patient (in ignorance) has the operation and does *not* suffer any of the undisclosed side-effect; or when a patient who does suffer the side-effects would still have had the identical operation, if the risks had been disclosed to them. In such situations the duty to warn remains 'empty'. Thus, Clark and Nolan comment, if the basic idea of *Chester* is to remedy every *breach* of the duty to inform patients of medical risks, it is a 'colossal failure'.[175] In their view, reasoning based on deterrence in inconsistent with tort. (Stevens comments, *pace* Stapleton, that if the purpose of the doctor's duty to warn were to reduce the overall number of injuries, they would presumably be permitted (or obliged?) to withhold off-putting information where patients (as a group) would be better off having the surgery (and running the risk), rather than declining it because of the risks disclosed.)[176]

Chester v Afshar is a particularly controversial decision. It was reasoned as a self-conscious exception to the normal rule which excludes liability for coincidental harm,[177] in order to vindicate the patient's right to be informed about risks.[178] It therefore confirms that basic rule – and illustrates that 'coincidences'

---

[171] [1969] 1 QB 428.
[172] Stevens (n 80) 165.
[173] Note *Paul v Cooke* [2012] NSWSC 840 (*Chester v Afshar* not followed when *misdiagnosis*, rather than failure to impart information, led to postponement of medical procedure in which (coincidentally) patient suffered injurious side-effects. Since the delay in diagnosis and treatment had not led to any deterioration of the claimant's latent and stable condition, no harm resulted from the doctor's negligence).
[174] T Clark and D Nolan, 'A Critique of *Chester v Afshar*' (2014) 34 *OJLS* 659.
[175] ibid 683.
[176] Stevens (n 80) 169.
[177] Compare *Paul v Cooke* (n 173).
[178] See ch 2, 'Debate 4: "Informed Medical Consent" – Which Tort?'.

(like a lightning strike) can only be defined by examining the scope of the defendant's duty and resulting responsibility.

'The Scope of Duty' Limitation

The 'scope of the duty' idea tends to be traced back to 'SAAMCO' and Lord Hoffmann's speech (with its famous 'mountaineer' example, cited above).[179] But duty's role in limiting liability for consequences is of general application and predates SAAMCO ('the question was not conjured up in that case').[180] When deciding whether a given loss fell within the scope of a *statutory* duty, the court makes a judgment about the harms Parliament intended protection against.[181] Nor is the doctrine limited to *negligence*. In the tort of deceit, a claimant recovered the coincidental fall in the market value of shares that the defendant had fraudulently induced it to buy.[182] That was in the same year as SAAMCO, where opposite conclusion was reached about a *negligent* property valuation. The different outcome on otherwise similar facts is explained by the wider scope of liability for *fraudulent* misstatements. The market fall in *Smith New Court Securities* was therefore not 'coincidental'. It remained within the scope of liability for deceit. Stapleton comments that Lord Steyn's 'normative reasons' were the true justification in *Smith New Court* (not his discussion of 'causal connection' which was 'empty of identifiable stable content').[183] Lord Steyn reasoned that wider liability was justified by moral condemnation of deliberate deception ('the very notion of deceit with its overtones of wickedness is drawn from the moral world'), as well as serving the beneficial purpose of deterring fraud.[184]

The Supreme Court recently applied SAAMCO in two important negligence cases.[185] Stapleton criticises the technique of inquiring whether the defendant 'assumed responsibility' for the accuracy of a particular kind of information. Often the court simply asserts the answer, unconvincingly presenting it as a *reason*. The 'judicial preference for responsibility for a consequence leads to an assertion that the defendant has assumed responsibility for the risk that it might eventuate'.[186] A more convincing argument excludes liability for risks that the claimant was happy to run, and would still have faced even if the information the defendant provided was correct. In the 'mountaineer' scenario,

---

[179] (n 107).

[180] *Meadows* (n 106) [33] (Lord Sales and Lord Hodge).

[181] *Gorris v Scott* (1874) LR 9 Ex 125 (duty to fence livestock in transit was to prevent spreading infections, not to protect them against being washed over side of ship).

[182] *Smith New Court Securities v Citibank* [1997] AC 254.

[183] Stapleton (n 150) 432.

[184] [1997] AC 254, 279–80.

[185] *Manchester Building Society v Grant Thornton UK LLP* [2022] AC 783; *Meadows v Khan* [2022] AC 852.

[186] Stapleton (n 99) 97.

the patient would willingly have run the risk of avalanches had the doctor correctly pronounced his knee fit for a climbing expedition. In *Meadows v Khan*, the claimant had been 'willing to accept the risk of having a child born with autism' if the doctor had advised correctly that she did not carry the gene for haemophilia.[187]

Stapleton suggests that this focus on the claimant's decision-making is more transparent than assertions about 'assumption of responsibility'. Yet surely the defendant's duty *also* matters? If someone was engaged to advise novice mountaineers about *all* the risks of such expeditions (including weak knees, avalanches and much else), injuries in avalanches *would* properly be attributable to them. Lord Burrows stressed the 'central importance' of the specific and limited purpose of the doctor's advice in *Meadows v Khan*: the defendant GP's sole responsibility was to advise about haemophilia specifically, making it unnecessary and even inappropriate to advise about risks of pregnancy more generally.[188] Therefore the hazard of an autistic baby was (like every mischance of pregnancy, other than haemophilia) 'allocated to the mother' who took *that* risk on herself.

While bare assertions about 'assumption of responsibility' could state a conclusion rather than a reason, it may have meaningful content. Lord Leggatt noted that SAAMCO cases (including *Meadows v Khan*) typically involve professional negligence. In that context it is certainly meaningful to ask precisely what the defendant was required to do. That will either have been expressly agreed or is 'implied from the role of a doctor or other professional person as that role is conventionally understood'.[189] Thus a property-valuer would not be expected to warn sophisticated investors about the risk that the property market might fall, when undertaking the valuation of an investment property. As Stapleton says, 'the professional investor is as aware as the adviser that markets can fall. These are just life risks for which, it might be thought, there is no reason to prefer the claimant to the defendant'.[190]

Conclusion: 'Common Sense Causation' and the Scope of Responsibility

Earlier in this debate we outlined Hart and Honoré's thesis that concepts of causation are infused with moral judgements. This is true of ordinary language and everyday reasoning – and equally true of the law. Jane Stapleton firmly rejects this approach. 'Causation', she argues, is solely a factual question about historical involvement. By contrast the truncation of liability for consequences requires an evaluative *choice*. Different cultures (and legal systems) make

---

[187] [2019] EWCA Civ 152 [26] (Nicola Davies LJ).
[188] *Meadows v Khan* [2022] AC 852, [77].
[189] ibid [96].
[190] Stapleton (n 150) 446.

that choice in different ways. Therefore it must not be framed as a 'causal' question at all:

> the scope of identification of consequences with a person's conduct is not based on any universal factual test nor can it be deduced by loose causal terminology because that has a range of meanings. It is an evaluative determination that is dependent on the context and purpose of the inquiry.[191]

Lord Leggatt has recently deplored 'common sense' causal reasoning when judges often disagree about what result it entails in a particular case.[192] In Australia too, 30 years after the debate in *March v Stramare*, the High Court has decisively rejected the 'common sense' approach: 'The task of adjudication requires transparent reasoning, not consideration of whether a judge's "sense" of a result might be common with that of others'.[193]

Lord Hoffmann's views are particularly telling in this respect. He accepted that the law's causal requirements are usually in conformity with 'common sense', but warned

> there is sometimes a tendency to appeal to common sense in order to avoid having to explain one's reasons. It suggests that causal requirements are a matter of incommunicable judicial instinct. I do not think that this is right.[194]

Lord Hoffmann stressed the 'essential point' that like rules of conduct, or rules limiting the scope of liability, 'the rules laying down causal requirements are not autonomous expressions of some form of logic or judicial instinct but creatures of the law, part of the conditions of liability'.[195]

This bears on one important objection to Hart and Honoré's project. Assuming that they accurately reported the causal judgements implicit in 'ordinary language', how good a guide is this to the *law*? In everyday life, people use causal concepts to explain how events have happened. They sometimes also use it to apportion blame. However, they are not using 'causation' to make detailed judgements about the extent of liability for different heads of loss that are the business of law. As Hart and Honoré accepted, 'There is no precise system of rewards, punishments or compensation to be administered by common sense' – by contrast with the legal process.[196] In other words, 'everyday causation' is being used for a different purpose – a somewhat looser

---

[191] Stapleton (n 70) 411.

[192] *Manchester Building Society v Grant Thornton UK LLP* (n 185) [117] ('or, as Langley J put it more bluntly in *Equitable Life Assurance Society v Ernst & Young* [2003] Lloyd's Rep PN 88, para 85: "One person's common sense may be another's nonsense"').

[193] *Tapp v Australian Bushmen's Rodeo* [2022] HCA 11 [101].

[194] *Fairchild* (n 2) [53].

[195] ibid [54].

[196] HLA Hart and AM Honoré, 'Causation in the Law I – A Survey of Common-Sense Principles' (1956) 72 *LQR* 58, 78.

one than the complex questions confronting a court. It could be appropriate, indeed necessary, to use a specifically *legal* causal approach, quite properly diverging from our 'instincts' in the social context. In trying to infer legal principles, judgements made for different purposes could be of 'limited value' or even misleading ('red herrings').[197]

Other objections to Hart and Honoré's thesis concern their methodology. First one could question the soundness of the 'everyday intuitions' reported by two philosophers *of law* (a mirror-image criticism to the one in the previous paragraph). Wouldn't the legally trained authors have viewed 'everyday causation' through a characteristically *legal* lens? Second and more broadly, their method was 'intuitive', reporting moral judgements implicit in ordinary language (as perceived by Hart and Honoré themselves). This is surely impressionistic. Reviewing Hart and Honoré's second edition, Stapleton objected that while their 'assertions' about everyday linguistic usage were 'easy to accept', 'the technique is deceptive'.[198] Hart and Honoré stated contestable normative judgements as if established facts about ordinary usage. Stapleton regretted the total neglect of empirical studies into how everyday judgements are made (including how those might be influenced by the law's assignment of responsibility). Instead Hart and Honoré offered 'bare assertions'.[199]

Belatedly, scholars are accepting Stapleton's challenge. Considerable research is now being done into the psychology of causal attribution, using experimental, scientific methods. It holds out the promise of rigorous, evidence-based models of how judgements about responsibility are made in everyday causal thought. Researchers present scenarios to volunteers raising problems of causation to uncover how they resolve them. By changing certain aspects of the scenario (eg to make interventions unusual, or wrongful) researchers can test the effect of particular variables, holding others constant as a control. With careful design, repeated experiments produce statistically robust evidence. This cognitive science lets jurisprudence advance beyond armchair theorising – replacing 'the methods of mid-century Oxford philosophy – intuition pumping and ordinary language analysis' (ie Hart and Honoré's approach) with 'experiments [to] see whether folk judgments line up with the law'.[200]

To date, this research broadly corroborates Hart and Honoré's findings.[201] Unusual occurrences are more likely to interrupt responsibility – they are perceived to take over as the dominant cause of a later event. That includes

---

[197] Sally Lloyd-Bostock, 'The Ordinary Man, and the Psychology of Attributing Causes and Responsibility' (1979) 42 *MLR* 143, 164.
[198] J Stapleton, 'Law, Causation and Common Sense' (1988) 8 *OJLS* 111, 123.
[199] ibid 124.
[200] J Knobe and S Shapiro, 'Proximate Cause Explained: An Essay in Experimental Jurisprudence' (2021) 88 *Univ Chicago LR* 165, 236.
[201] Knobe and Shaprio, ibid; A Summers, 'Common-Sense Causation in the Law' (2018) 38 *OJLS* 793.

both interventions that are descriptively unusual (ie happen uncommonly) and *normatively* unusual (ie things that *ought* not to happen – violations of norms and rules).

Andrew Summers concludes that Hart and Honoré have been vindicated. Their claims are now supported by scientific research into cognition – an improvement on Hart and Honoré's less rigorous methodology. The experimental findings are also an improvement on 'common sense'. Courts that appeal to 'common sense' are properly criticised for offering inadequate reasons – for it is notoriously difficult for people to explain and articulate their moral intuitions. The cognitive research *explains* the basis for common intuitions. As Hart and Honoré suggested all along, it is valid to frame remoteness questions in causal terms. Causal judgements are not purely factual in nature but incorporate moral judgements. Thus, Summers suggest, it is a 'false dichotomy' to contrast 'factual' causation and 'normative' questions about the scope of liability, insisting on a sharp separation between them.[202]

Hart and Honoré did not claim that 'ordinary notions of causation' were the *only* things that mattered in law. Such notions could not answer all questions of legal responsibility. Legal policy also matters. They gave as a clear example the following New York rule: one negligently starting a fire which spreads to neighbouring buildings is liable only for the *first* building destroyed, and not any subsequent ones.[203] Hart and Honoré accept the rule has 'nothing whatever to do with causation' but reflects 'what is expedient or just or both' under the policy of the particular legal system.[204] But Hart and Honoré denied that *every* decision limiting liability can be reduced to raw policy. They reject the (candid – or cynical) view that remoteness is 'all a question of expediency' – an 'arbitrary' truncation of responsibility derived solely from 'convenience' or 'rough justice', 'not logic [but] practical politics'.[205] For Hart and Honoré notions of causal responsibility have a role to play too – in law as in ordinary discourse.

There is clearly something attractive about incorporating widely-shared ideas about the limits of responsibility. Sally Lloyd-Bostock, writing in the infancy of scientific study of the psychology of cause, accepted that it was still 'somewhat hazardous' to discuss ordinary common-sense ideas. Yet she defended its desirability:

> At some level, standards and criteria of justice embodied in and enforced by law in a democratic society must presumably come from and respond to the wider norms of the society of which the legal system is a part, and on the whole appear just to its citizens.[206]

---

[202] Summers, ibid 819.
[203] *Ryan v New York* 35 NY 210 (1866).
[204] Hart and Honoré (n 112) 84 (cf *Ryan* ibid 217: wider liability 'would be the destruction of all civilized society').
[205] *Palsgraf v Long Island Railroad* 248 NY 339, 352–55 (1928) (Andrews J, dissenting).
[206] S Lloyd-Bostock, 'The Ordinary Man, and the Psychology of Attributing Causes and Responsibility' (1979) 42 *MLR* 143, 168.

With the growth of cognitive science described above, the project now seems feasible. It is desirable to promote legal *transparency*. If there are regular patterns of responsibility-assignment within ordinary causal judgements, courts promote the law's comprehensibility to wider society by incorporating those judgements.

Finally, so long as courts are open about the choice that they face in limiting responsibility, does the conceptual framework ultimately matter? Replying to Jane Stapleton's critique of 'common-sense' reasoning about causation, a senior Australian judge defended the traditional approach.[207] The 'linguistic and analytical simplicity' of common-sense made it easier for courts to explain, and for parties to understand, the outcomes of disputed cases.[208] There was a danger of losing touch with lay intuitions about responsibility by 'overcomplicating' the conceptual structure. Ultimately, substance matters more than structures. Even if the precise meaning of remoteness is 'diffuse', 'What intellectual process has been disguised?'[209]

This did not convince Stapleton, whose rejoinder warned judges not to be 'tempted by the camouflage of vacuous causal assertions'.[210] In her view, the greatest intellectual payoff of limiting causation to the factual question of historical involvement was open examination of the 'principles, policies and concerns [that] govern the scope issue', free of 'causal' distraction.[211] But if cognitive science can model attributive causal decision-making accurately in sufficient detail, the 'common-sense' causal tradition could be defended against such critiques. Courts unquestionably face a normative choice and should not conceal this behind doubtful causal 'logic'. Perhaps as Hart and Honoré explained, an amalgam of ordinary causal concepts (which encode judgements about responsibility) *and* specifically legal concerns is the true nature of remoteness, after all.

---

[207] Allsop (n 98).
[208] ibid 330 ('fundamentally important' that 'law must be understood by ordinary people').
[209] ibid 299 (commenting on *Leyland Shipping v Norwich Union Fire Insurance* n 145).
[210] Stapleton (n 97) 353.
[211] ibid 350.

What Is the Function of the Duty of Care?

The tort of negligence is conventionally divided into three elements: a *duty* to take reasonable care; its *breach* (by lack of such care); and actionable *damage caused* by that breach (which is not too remote). This formulation suggests that the duty of care logically comes first. After all, how can there be 'breach' without a duty?[1]

Some commentators argue that the duty of care plays a crucial role if the tort of negligence is to be seen as laying down binding rules of behaviour (ie to take care in particular situations) – and 'duty' should mean precisely what it says.[2] Others claim that if negligence is to be intelligible and principled, the duty of care must be coherent with the other elements of negligence – namely careless *breach* and the absence of liability for *unforeseeable consequences*.[3] That we owe duties to our 'neighbours' – those we can foresee may be harmed by what we do[4] – is not on this view a gratuitous flourish of Christian ethics nor a naïvely simple definition, hopelessly too broad. Rather, Weinrib claims that the 'Atkinian' duty of care is required by the 'normative unit' of careless fault. To act negligently with respect to some person or some kind of damage, it must have been foreseeable that they could suffer (and suffer such damage) from the conduct in question. One can only be *negligent* for failing to avoid that which one could have *foreseen*. Thus a duty can arise only where the damage was foreseeable. This underlines the 'relational' nature of negligence – an invasion of this particular claimant's rights by the defendant, not 'negligence in the air'.

Such arguments (considered further below) reject the dominant modern approach. The duty concept is more typically viewed as a 'control device' which the courts use to limit the scope of liability.[5] Such a 'device' is needed because the pull of the negligence principle ('pay for foreseeable harm you carelessly

---

[1] But cf J Plunkett, *The Duty of Care in Negligence* (Oxford, Hart, 2018) 96.

[2] NJ McBride, 'Duties of Care – Do they Really Exist?' (2004) 24 *OJLS* 417.

[3] EJ Weinrib, 'The Disintegration of Duty' in MS Madden (ed), *Exploring Tort Law* (Cambridge, Cambridge University Press, 2005).

[4] *Donoghue v Stevenson* [1932] AC 562, 580 (Lord Atkin).

[5] JG Fleming, 'Remoteness and Duty: The Control Devices in Liability for Negligence' (1953) 31 *Can Bar Rev* 471.

caused') is so strong.⁶ Sober tort lawyers desiring to keep their feet on the ground must somehow keep it within 'practical bounds'. They use the duty of care to do so. On this view, the duty of care is not logically 'anterior' to breach and loss. Rather, practically speaking, duty comes *afterwards*. That is, the court can (by finding that there is *no* duty of care) hold that there is no liability *even though* the defendant was careless and caused the claimant foreseeable harm.⁷ In the absence of a duty of care, 'A man is entitled to be as negligent as he pleases'.⁸ Which is preferable? Should duty of care be seen as essential to the normativity and inner logic of negligence liability? Or is it nothing more than a convenient device for limiting liability – a 'home' for countervailing factors that cannot be accommodated within the other facets of liability, that is, causation and carelessness?⁹

For over a half a century it has been the dominant judicial understanding that duty of care serves to *restrict* liability:

> [N]egligence has been deliberately limited in its range by the courts' insistence that there can be no actionable negligence *in vacuo* without the existence of some duty to the plaintiff. For it would be impracticable to grant relief to everybody who suffers damage through the carelessness of another ... How wide the sphere of the duty of care in negligence is to be laid depends ultimately upon the courts' assessment of the demands of society for protection from the carelessness of others.¹⁰

As Lord Goff significantly observed:

> It is very tempting to try to solve all problems of negligence by reference to an all-embracing criterion of foreseeability, thereby effectively reducing all decisions in this field to questions of fact. But this comfortable solution is, alas, not open to us.¹¹ The law has to accommodate all the untidy complexity of life; and there are circumstances where considerations of practical justice impel us to reject a general imposition of liability for foreseeable damage ... [The courts address problematic forms of liability] by means of the mechanism of the duty of care; though we have nowadays to appreciate that *the broad general principle of liability for foreseeable damage is so widely applicable that the function of the duty of care is not so much to identify cases where liability is imposed as to identify those where it is not.*¹²

---

⁶ T Weir, 'The Staggering March of Negligence' in P Cane and J Stapleton (eds), *The Law of Obligations: Essays in Celebration of John Fleming* (Oxford, Oxford University Press, 1998) 98–99, 137–38.
⁷ D Howarth, *A Textbook on Tort* (London, Butterworths, 1995) chs 2 and 5.
⁸ *Le Lievre v Gould* [1893] 1 QB 491, 497 (Lord Esher MR).
⁹ FH Lawson, 'Duty of Care in Negligence: A Comparative Study' (1947) 22 *Tulane LR* 111.
¹⁰ *Hedley Byrne & Co v Heller & Partners* [1964] AC 465, 534, 536 (Lord Pearce). Similarly: *Dorset Yacht v Home Office* [1969] 2 QB 412, 426 (Lord Denning MR).
¹¹ (See further L Green, 'Foreseeability in Negligence Law' (1961) 61 *Columbia LR* 1401 (discussed in ch 3, 'The Structure of Negligence'.)).
¹² *Smith v Littlewoods Organisation Ltd* [1987] AC 241, 280 (emphasis added).

If this 'control device' conception of the duty of care is accepted, questions arise about its usefulness and whether it should be retained at all. After all (as Lord Goff went on to note) other European legal systems manage to control liability without any notion of the duty of care.[13] Although not a conceptual necessity, does the duty of care at least draw the boundaries of liability in negligence in a satisfactory way? While few call for its abolition, at least some of duty's functions could be performed by other concepts. Lord Bingham thought that duty of care was 'a somewhat blunt instrument for dividing claims which ought reasonably to lead to recovery from claims which ought not'. A suitably calibrated test of fault (or 'breach') could perform the role better.[14] But his suggestion lacked majority support.[15]

We turn then to consider whether duty of care is indeed a conceptual necessity or merely a convenient device – and if the latter, whether it could be improved upon or even discarded.

Debate 1
Is the Duty of Care an Essential Component of the Tort of Negligence?

Nicholas J McBride has attacked the prevalent 'sceptical' view of duty of care as an ultimately dispensable device used to control liability.[16] McBride argues that this commits 'cynics' to the position that tort imposes no true 'ex ante' obligation to be careful. One is legally free to be careless – although liability to compensate those harmed by one's negligence may arise 'ex post'. The distinction sounds a fine one, but a number of consequences follow.

If there were no real duties of care, it would be impossible for the law to intervene unless and until actual compensable damage has been suffered. But sometimes it does. At least in principle, injunctions could be awarded to prevent threatened future negligent injury (*quia timet*, 'because he fears'). Imagine that someone daily walks past an unfenced golf-course where several times a week golf balls are mis-hit into the road, threatening pedestrians with serious injuries. Were the pedestrian struck she would have a negligence claim against the golf club for damages.[17] Arguably, even prior to that, the situation could meet the demanding test for a *quia timet* injunction to restrain the club's negligence – that is, 'a sufficiently real and imminent risk of a tort being committed'.[18] As McBride says, it would be strange to deny the conceptual possibility of such

---

[13] *Smith* ibid ('our brother lawyers in France find themselves able to dispense with any such concept …').
[14] *JD v East Berkshire NHS Trust* [2005] 2 AC 373 [49].
[15] *JD* ibid [92]–[94] (Lord Nicholls: 'not without attraction … [but] unlikely to clarify the law').
[16] McBride (n 2).
[17] *Bolton v Stone* [1951] AC 850.
[18] *Boyd v Ineos Upstream Ltd* [2019] EWCA Civ 515, [34] (not a negligence claim).

an injunction. Equally, courts have (very exceptionally) awarded 'preventive damages' against a negligent defendant in advance of damage actually occurring, when the compensation can be used to prevent their negligence ripening into loss (eg prophylactic medical treatment or underpinning a defective building).[19] This again seems inconsistent with the 'cynical' view.

Would the law tolerate defendants behaving as if they have no obligation to be careful (as the 'cynical' view holds)? For example, wanton refusal to take care or coldly calculating that the cost of doing so would not be worthwhile (because the expected costs of compensating those injured would be smaller than the costs of being careful)? According to legend an American car manufacturer made just such a calculation, consciously deciding not to install a safety feature but simply to compensate those injured in its consequently unsafe vehicles (which would, in total, cost less than making the safety improvement). The company was not merely held negligent but liable for exemplary damages, to punish its outrageous conduct.[20] While exemplary damages are less widely available in English law, McBride observes that such conduct could fall within one of the exceptional categories for such an award – that the tortfeasor has calculated that it would be more profitable to commit the tort than to comply with the law: 'Exemplary damages can properly be awarded whenever it is necessary to teach a wrongdoer that tort does not pay'.[21] Such condemnation presupposes, again, that there is a 'real duty' not to be negligent. Exemplary damages would reinforce that duty and its binding nature.

Does anyone actually hold the 'cynical' view? Surely most (even all?) lawyers fully accept that tort law imposes binding obligations not to act unreasonably. (Contract law might well be different. Here a plausible argument can be made, on both moral and economic grounds, that contractual obligations should indeed be construed 'disjunctively' to give a true option between their literal performance and payment of compensation instead.[22] While *pace* McBride it cannot simply be asserted that this view of contract has been 'widely rejected',[23] it is certainly contested.)[24] Whatever the better answer in the contract sphere, obligations in *tort* are different. Tort law reflects the moral duties we all owe to each other, irrespective of special arrangements agreed between particular parties. The law's universal scheme of inter-personal obligations is not optional, but compulsory.

---

[19] D Nolan, 'Preventive Damages' (2016) 132 *LQR* 68: discussed in ch 8, 'Debate 2: "Preventive" Damages'.

[20] GT Schwartz, 'The Myth of the Ford Pinto Case' (1991) 43 *Rutgers LR* 1013.

[21] *Rookes v Barnard* [1964] AC 1129, 1227 (Lord Devlin).

[22] S Shavell, 'Why Breach of Contract May Not Be Immoral Given the Incompleteness of Contracts' (2009) 107 *Michigan LR* 1569; D Markovits and A Schwartz, 'The Myth of Efficient Breach: New Defenses of the Expectation Interest' (2011) 97 *Virginia LR* 1939.

[23] McBride (n 2) 417.

[24] See eg SV Shiffrin, 'Could Breach of Contract Be Immoral?' (2009) 107 *Michigan LR* 1551; Shiffrin, 'Must I Mean What You Think I *Should* Have Said?' (2012) 98 *Virginia LR* 159; generally J Morgan, *Great Debates in Contract Law* 3rd edn (Oxford, Hart, 2020) 270–312.

Tort's binding nature would therefore be accepted by the many lawyers today who conceive the duty of care as a 'control device'. McBride argues that this involves them in contradiction. Negligence stripped of the duty of care would be 'Hamlet without the prince', removing its 'central organizing concept' removes its binding normative status.[25] So those who view the duty of care as simply a 'device' (that might be dispensable if better ways of limiting liability were proposed) are, for McBride, committed to the cynical view. In reply, David Howarth denies that there is any contradiction.[26] It is perfectly coherent to accept that there is a general legal duty not to act unreasonably. This is not contradicted by the court holding, in *particular* cases, that there was 'no duty of care' which excuses the defendant from the general duty and is thereby 'permitted to act unreasonably'.[27]

Howarth rejects the 'cynical' view as 'untenable' – but it is a 'straw man' (not a position actually held by anyone). Howarth argues that there is an overarching general (although defeasible) duty to be careful. He suggests this is 'ultra-idealistic' rather than cynical. Howarth explains using comparative law.[28]

French law famously imposes delictual liability on everyone who injures another person through their fault.[29] There is no concept of duty of care here. But that does not make the French system 'cynical', as McBride alleges.[30] French lawyers equally accept a legal *obligation* not to damage others culpably. The point seems to be this. One can accept in general terms the binding 'normativity' of delict/negligence without being committed to a particular version of 'the duty of care', or even to its existence. The true difference between French and English law, according to Howarth, is the way that they limit the scope of liability. The French system, in the absence of the duty of care, has 'no natural conceptual home for the negative creativity of English judges'.[31] French law still needs to confine the scope of liability, but its methods seem to the English lawyer 'obscure'. In particular the French have no easy way to say 'you are not liable even though you were negligent' (ie you acted unreasonably, but in circumstances which tort law does not censure). French courts say that defendants were not at fault when English courts would say there was no duty. This French 'conflation' 'mudd[ies] the idea of reasonable behaviour itself', thus making it *harder* to see what standard of care the law requires of its subjects. Howarth echoes a distinguished comparative lawyer's view that French and English law limit negligence liability in similar ways for

---

[25] McBride (n 2) 423.
[26] D Howarth, 'Many Duties of Care – Or A Duty of Care? Notes from the Underground' (2006) 26 *OJLS* 449.
[27] ibid 451.
[28] ibid 465–66.
[29] Code Civil art 1240 (formerly 1382).
[30] McBride (n 2) 439–40.
[31] Howarth (n 26) 465.

similar reasons, through different techniques: the French reasoning is 'amorphous' because it lacks the duty of care concept, an 'admirable instrument of cautious advance'.[32]

A different point is that other torts (of course) lack 'the duty of care' but are nevertheless understood, universally, as imposing binding obligations. For example, private nuisance imposes the obligation not to interfere with a neighbour's use and enjoyment of their land. Injunctions against future nuisance are usually seen as the standard remedy. Indeed, one of the main objections to granting 'damages in lieu' is that this amounts to permitting the defendant to continue their wrongful conduct (the nuisance-creating activity) on condition of payment. Yet nuisance has no separate concept of 'duty'. Nor does trespass. For Limitation Act purposes, battery does not fall within the provisions covering 'negligence, nuisance *and breach of duty*'.[33] While this turned partly on the legislative history of that phrase, Lord Griffiths also 'juxtaposed' breach of a duty of care against 'an obligation not to infringe any legal right of another person'. In illustration he suggested that while one clearly owes a visitor a duty to see that one's house is reasonably safe it would be odd to suggest there was 'a duty not to rape her'.[34] If we apply McBride's argument to this case we would be left with the grotesque implication that there is no tortious obligation to refrain from sexual assault – merely a liability to pay damages for doing so. In the absence of anyone arguing for such a strange conclusion, is McBride not fighting against a 'straw man' (as Howarth suggests)? The duty of care could be used in the way that Howarth recommends (as a useful 'control device' in the tort of negligence) without undermining the binding obligation to take reasonable care.

Another possible response is to accept McBride's charges but to deny that the resulting legal approach is 'cynical'. Dan Priel notes that only exceptionally are injunctions or exemplary damages available in negligence. But he proposes 'a less cynical view of [this] cynical view'![35] For example, there might be good reasons to be cautious about restraining conduct prior to any tort being committed – the law may prefer practicality to unobtainable idealism. More broadly, Priel notes that there are flourishing debates about the 'instrumental' use of injunctions or exemplary damages, particular from American law and economics scholars – and US law is much readier to grant those remedies than English negligence law. Priel suggests that it is healthy to address these questions about remedies directly. Weighing up questions of welfare, fairness, administrability and other public interest goals is part of deciding whether to award remedies more stringent than compensation. Such necessary debates are 'completely obscured by conceptual claims about what tort law really is'.

---

[32] Lawson (n 9) 130.
[33] *Stubbings v Webb* [1993] AC 498; Limitation Act 1980, s11(1) (emphasis added).
[34] ibid 508.
[35] D Priel, 'Tort Law for Cynics' (2014) 75 *MLR* 703.

Priel alleges that McBride's approach is symptomatic of those who claim an immutable conceptual 'truth' about how tort must be understood, 'as if tort law has some fixed nature, set in stone for eternity'.³⁶ Priel ridicules this idea: 'tort law does not descend on us from heaven to adopt it 'as is'; it is a practice that has been shaped and reshaped by changing societal needs, available technology, and political ideologies'.³⁷ Thus for Priel, the 'cynic's' approach is preferable – trying to identify the circumstances when certain types of protection will be appropriate, not answering questions about remedies using assertions 'masquerading as conceptual claims about what tort law "is"'.³⁸

Finally, Steve Hedley argues that it is not 'cynical' but merely a statement of fact to observe that negligence does a poor job of setting standards of behaviour.³⁹ Since few people deliberately set out to be careless, he wonders how realistic it is for tort law to tell them 'don't be negligent'. Moreover, the general imperative 'act like a reasonable person' is too vague to be of any real use. (Hedley queries whether negligence induces carefulness among doctors, for example, or simply 'panic' because they cannot predict what its ambiguous standard requires of them.) As Keating notes about the commonest situation of all, the common law is ill-suited to laying down 'comprehensive schemes' of carefulness. 'Tort turns to the traffic code to help determine the duties of care that people owe to one another … because it lacks the institutional competence to spell those duties out by itself'.⁴⁰

Foreseeability: The Unity of Duty, Breach and Damage?

In *Donoghue v Stevenson* Lord Atkin famously conceived the duty of care as owed to persons 'that I ought reasonably to have … in contemplation as [closely and directly] affected when I am directing my mind to the acts or omissions which are called in question'.⁴¹ In English law today such foreseeability is clearly *not* sufficient by itself for a duty to arise.⁴² But some revisionist scholars argue that Lord Atkin's 'neighbour principle' should still be taken seriously, not side-lined as a simplistic attempt to define the duty of care, long since superseded. The argument is that for duty of care to cohere with the other core elements of negligence – that is, *fault* and the kinds of *harm* which generate liability – the duty of care must be based squarely on *foreseeability*, in the same way as those other central concepts.⁴³

---

³⁶ ibid 730.
³⁷ ibid.
³⁸ ibid 706.
³⁹ S Hedley, 'Making Sense of Negligence' (2016) 36 *Legal Stud* 491, 496–99.
⁴⁰ GC Keating, 'Form and Substance in the "Private Law" of Torts' (2021) 14 *Jo Tort L* 45, 84.
⁴¹ [1932] AC 562, 580.
⁴² For early scepticism: *Farr v Butters Bros* [1932] KB 606, 614 (Scrutton LJ: Lord Atkin's 'neighbour' dictum 'wider than is necessary' and clearly 'needs qualification'). For the 'tests' ch 7 below.
⁴³ Weinrib (n 3).

The revisionist view stresses that negligence is 'relational'. A defendant must be careless *towards* the person injured and the type of injury suffered, rather than simply 'careless' in an abstract sense. There is no 'negligence in the air'.[44] In the leading American case, pivotal in the current debate, the defendant railway's employee carelessly dropped a passenger's ordinary-looking parcel. This clearly constituted negligence, if the owner claimed for damage to his property. But the claim was actually brought by somebody injured when the parcel (which unknown to the porter contained fireworks) exploded, causing weighing scales on the railway platform to topple onto her. Mrs Palsgraf's claim against the railway for the porter's negligence was dismissed (by a majority).[45] Neither this *kind* of harm (personal injury rather than damage to the parcel) nor injury to *this victim* (Mrs Palsgraf as opposed to the parcel's owner) had been reasonably foreseeable. Thus the railway porter had not been *negligent* in law: 'Relatively to her [the plaintiff] it was not negligence at all'.[46] 'What the plaintiff must show is "a wrong" to herself, i.e., a violation of her own right, and not merely a wrong to some one else'.[47] The fact that (relative to the parcel's owner) the porter was careless of the property was irrelevant to the *plaintiff's* claim.

As Bramwell B put it: 'There is no absolute or intrinsic negligence; it is always relative to some circumstances of time, place or person'.[48] Significantly perhaps, this was in one of the earliest judgments to insist that a duty of care was a necessary component of negligence.[49] The moral principle at stake is well summarised by Andrew Robertson: 'Foreseeability is a basic requirement of interpersonal justice' because it is unfair to require defendants to avoid harm that they could not foresee.[50] Hence the need for foreseeability before a duty of care arises has been described as 'self-evident'.[51] Foreseeability is the 'fundamental moral glue of tort'.[52]

The Triviality of Foreseeability?

However, objections can be made to the elevation of foreseeability into the major component – or even the sole governing factor – of duty of care. It could be thought trivial, so easily satisfied that insistence on foreseeability rarely makes any difference. And/or redundant because it duplicates what other

---

[44] Sir F Pollock, *The Law of Torts* 11th edn (London, Stevens, 1920) 455.
[45] *Palsgraf v Long Island Railroad Co* 248 NY 339 (1928).
[46] ibid 340 (Cardozo J).
[47] ibid 343–44.
[48] *Degg v Midland Railway Co* (1857) 1 H&N 773, 781–82.
[49] Plunkett (n 1) 16.
[50] A Robertson, 'Policy-Based Reasoning in Duty of Care Cases' (2013) 33 *Legal Stud* 119, 122.
[51] *JJ v Rankin's Garage* [2018] 1 SCR 587 [22].
[52] ibid quoting DG Owen, 'Figuring Foreseeability' (2009) 44 *Wake Forest LR* 1277, 1278.

components of the negligence inquiry anyway require (especially 'remoteness of damage' and 'breach of duty'). We examine the first point here.

Orthodoxy certainly requires that it was reasonably foreseeable that the claimant might suffer harm of the relevant kind before a duty of care to avoid it was owed to her – for example the first stage in the tripartite *Caparo* formulation. But this hurdle seems remarkably easy to cross (at least in English and Australian law). Dixon J once remarked 'I cannot understand why any event which does happen is not foreseeable by a person of sufficient imagination and intelligence'.[53] After quoting this, Hayne J stated: 'In almost every case in which a plaintiff suffers damage it is foreseeable that, if reasonable care is not taken, harm may follow. The conclusion that harm was foreseeable is well-nigh inevitable'.[54] Thus he concluded: 'Foresight of harm is not sufficient to show that a duty of care exists'. This Australian case raised the question whether a landowner who turned off the lights in a car park was liable to someone criminally assaulted there at night. The High Court held there was no duty of care even though such an assault had been *foreseeable*. 'Everyone can foresee the commission of crime virtually anywhere and at any time', notwithstanding its random and unpredictable incidence.[55]

It is unsurprising that most cases pass the test. It is quite hard to think of entirely unforeseeable outcomes.[56] Goudkamp and Plunkett think the foreseeability requirement is so undemanding in English law 'it is difficult to find clear examples of cases in which a duty has been denied on [that] basis'.[57] Foreseeability 'is in issue so rarely that it has enjoyed remarkably little by way of judicial elaboration'.[58] Against this, Robertson finds in a study of all English 'duty' decisions over a two-year period that foreseeability was a reason for denying a duty of care in 'a significant minority'.[59] Canadian law also seems to give foreseeability a more important role. In *JJ v Rankin's Garage* the defendant left a car unlocked with the keys in the glove box. It was stolen by a teenager too young to hold a driving licence. The thief crashed, injuring his accomplice, a passenger in the car. The Supreme Court of Canada held there was no duty of care because although the defendant garage could have foreseen theft in the circumstances, it had not been foreseeable that the vehicle would have been stolen *by a minor*, nor (then) that the theft would cause *personal injury*.[60]

---

[53] *Chapman v Hearse* (1961) 106 CLR 112, 115.
[54] *Modbury Triangle Shopping Centre Pty Ltd v Anzil* (2000) 205 CLR 254, [100].
[55] ibid [136] (Callinan J).
[56] Cf *Cambridge Water Co v Eastern Counties Leather plc* [1994] 2 AC 264.
[57] J Goudkamp and J Plunkett, 'The Foreseeability Element of the Duty of Care' (2019) 135 LQR 521, 524 (noting as an exception: *Smith v Littlewoods Organisation Ltd* [1987] AC 241, 250).
[58] Goudkamp and Plunkett, ibid.
[59] Robertson (n 50) 133–34.
[60] [2018] 1 SCR 587.

To an English lawyer, *JJ v Rankin's* looks odd. As Brown J said in dissent, there was 'a certain unreality' in the suggestion that teenagers were less likely to steal cars than anyone else ('a curious distinction').[61] Indeed not – vehicle theft is one of the most common criminal offences committed by adolescents. Goudkamp and Plunkett therefore suggest that *JJ*'s reasoning 'borders on being palpable wrong'.[62] (Moreover, the jury's decision at trial that Rankin's Garage had *breached* a duty is explicable only upon a factual finding that the plaintiff's injuries *had* been foreseeable.) A more general concern is that by manipulating what has to be foreseen the court can restrict liability – but such reasoning is concealed rather than open.[63] *JJ v Rankin's* diverges from the usual approach. Foreseeability had previously represented 'a low threshold' in Canadian law – usually, harm is 'plainly' foreseeable to all those within the area of danger and so it was hitherto 'rare' for courts to deny duty of care on that ground.[64]

By stipulating what the defendant had to foresee 'with considerable precision', the majority in *JJ v Rankin's Garage* gives new vitality to the foreseeability requirement ('essentially moribund' in other common law jurisdictions).[65] Goudkamp and Plunkett believe the absence of an illegality defence in Canadian tort law underlies this novel approach. In England or Australia, the *ex turpi causa* rule bars claims by one criminal against another for injuries during a criminal enterprise. In its absence the Canadian court reached the similar result by a different route. This illustrates how 'the way in which one part of the law of negligence is defined can profoundly influence the others'. The problem with the Canadian approach is that the court gave little 'meaningful guidance' on the appropriate degree of particularity with which to define what has to be foreseen. And its restrictive approach to foreseeability may bar many claims that would otherwise succeed even when there is no element of illegal conduct.

The Redundancy of Foreseeability?

The previous section suggests that the foreseeability requirement is either trivially easy to satisfy or, in its revitalised Canadian form, open to manipulation. But is foreseeability really a binary question – the harm is either foreseeable or not? The notion of *reasonable* foreseeability seems to require an evaluation rather than simply a yes-no answer on a question of fact. There is indeed considerable authority that 'reasonable foreseeability' requires a value judgement to be made. But does this simply duplicate the inquiry into breach and remoteness?

---

[61] ibid [83].
[62] Goudkamp and Plunkett (n 57) 524.
[63] See further ch 9, 'A Foreseeability-Based Approach'.
[64] [2018] 1 SCR 587 [78] (Brown J dissenting).
[65] Goudkamp and Plunkett (n 57) 525.

Lord Hoffmann explains that 'generation of a duty' depends on the *level* of foreseeability compared with other factors pertaining to the reasonableness of the defendant's conduct – foreseeability is not 'a fixed point on the scale of probability'.[66] On this view, it is not an isolated 'yes-no' question but needs weighing up, as a matter of degree. But what this resembles – indeed what it apparently reproduces – is the *breach* inquiry. Precisely such an exercise of weighing the foreseeable magnitude and chance of injury against its avoidability determines whether the defendant was negligent. In which case, is there any need to pre-empt the question whether the defendant was at fault by examining the same factors at the prior stage of duty of care? 'Was the defendant careless?' is itself a 'relational' question – did she fail to take care in respect of this class of claimant and this kind of harm?

Considering losses following from a negligent act, the primary test for recoverability is whether the 'kind of harm' was a reasonably foreseeable consequence. Again, the overlap between 'duty' and 'remoteness' is considerable. Lord Hoffmann remarked 'unless the injury is of a description which was reasonably foreseeable, it is *(according to taste)* "outside the scope of the duty" or "too remote"'.[67] It made no substantive difference whether the relevant factors were considered under 'duty' or 'remoteness'. Indeed in Lord Hoffmann's seminal formulation of the 'SAAMCO principle', whether the harm that eventuated was within the *scope of the defendant's duty* is a key limit on consequential loss.[68] This shows the links between the two concepts. They seem functionally interchangeable.

In some torts, such as *Rylands v Fletcher*, there is no concept of 'duty of care' by which to limit liability, and strictness precludes examination of whether the defendant's conduct was reasonable. Therefore 'remoteness' will be the appropriate framework.[69] In negligence the balance between duty and remoteness changed during the twentieth century. Negligence liability once included all 'direct' losses flowing from the defendant's negligence, even if unforeseeable: *Re Polemis*.[70] Therefore at the time when *Palsgraf* (the parcel case) was decided (1928), it was natural to limit liability using duty – because *remoteness* was then so generously defined. The limited, particularistic duties of care in pre-*Donoghue v Stevenson* negligence cohered with that generous remoteness rule.[71] However as negligence expanded steadily under the influence of Lord

---

[66] *Jolley v Sutton LBC* [2000] 1 WLR 1082, 1091–92.
[67] ibid 1091 (emphasis added).
[68] *South Australia Asset Management Corp v York Montague Ltd* [1997] AC 191. See further ch 5, '"The Scope of Duty" Limitation'.
[69] *Cambridge Water* (n 56).
[70] [1921] 3 KB 560.
[71] M Davies, 'The Road from Morocco: *Polemis* through *Donoghue* to No-Fault' (1982) 45 *MLR* 534, 541 ('A wide remoteness test was unexceptionable when duty was narrowly conceived. Extensive liability of defendants is not a problem when those defendants can only be liable to a limited class of plaintiffs, or even a single plaintiff only').

Atkin's 'general duty of care', the broad *Polemis* test of remoteness became intolerable.[72] It was no longer 'socially acceptable and legally appropriate' when combined with the relaxation of duty, but led to over-extensive liability.[73] Davies's argument is that the landmark *Wagon Mound* decision was not solely about ensuring consistency between the tests for 'duty', 'fault' and 'remoteness' (with foreseeability the controlling concept for each).[74] On the contrary, their historical development reveals an *inverse* relationship. As the duty of care expanded, the remoteness doctrine was narrowed in response.

At any rate, once foreseeability was held to underlie both duty and remoteness, a case like *Palsgraf* could just as easily today be decided on the basis that the plaintiff's injury was too remote from carelessly dropping an innocuous parcel. It is sometimes suggested that the two concepts relate to fundamentally different things: 'duty' to the existence of a *wrong to the claimant* in the first place, 'remoteness' to the kinds of harmful consequences that follow from the wrong. But since both are 'aspects of the same problem of limitation of responsibility',[75] James Plunkett dismisses such a distinction as 'entirely arbitrary', having 'little normative attraction'.[76] Fleming deems it merely 'fashion' whether a court limits liability using remoteness or duty.

Some praise the congruence of duty, breach and remoteness around the common idea of foreseeability. It demonstrates the unity of the tort of negligence. Others might ask why duty of care should be retained at all, if it merely reproduces other stages of the negligence inquiry. Duplication threatens conceptual untidiness. Lord Denning MR found it increasingly difficult to put cases into their 'proper pigeon-holes': 'Sometimes I say: "There was no duty". In others I say: "The damage was too remote"'.[77] We might well wonder about a conceptual structure that obliges courts to draw a distinction without a difference. Great judges like Lords Denning and Hoffmann thought the classification merely a 'matter of taste'. Intellectual disorder is not, perhaps, a convincing reason for radical reform. On the contrary, many would agree with Winfield's conservative warning against imposing 'too great a shock on ingrained habits of legal thought' by abandoning the duty of care.[78]

However Plunkett argues that 'foreseeability' should be abolished as a separate stage in the duty inquiry.[79] It is 'entirely unnecessary' since it will always be

---

[72] See especially *The Wagon Mound (No 1)* [1961] AC 388 (overruling *Re Polemis*).

[73] Davies (n 71) 542, 549 ('before [*Donoghue v Stevenson*], *Polemis* was never even criticised for giving rise to over-extensive liability').

[74] [1961] AC 388, 423 (foreseeability 'harmonised' all of negligence law 'with little difficulty').

[75] Fleming (n 5) 496.

[76] Plunkett (n 1) 98.

[77] *Spartan Steel & Alloys Ltd v Martin & Co (Contractors) Ltd* [1973] QB 27, 37. (The underlying unity was through 'public policy', not foreseeability (ibid).)

[78] PH Winfield, 'Duty in Tortious Negligence' (1934) 34 *Columbia LR* 41, 58.

[79] Plunkett (n 1) 107–09.

present when the other requirements of negligence are proven, and absent only when they are absent too. Foreseeability is superfluous – and 'actively harmful'. It clouds transparent reasoning about duty – judges can 'disguise' conclusions reached on other grounds by presenting them as 'factual' decisions about foreseeability. For those who argue that duty of care is determined *solely* by foreseeability, Plunkett's argument would mean the abolition of the duty of care in its entirety.

Plunkett himself recommends that duty should be retained (purged of the 'foreseeability' stage) as a way of handling the question – should this kind of situation/harm ever be actionable in negligence? As Jane Stapleton puts it, a ruling about duty 'allows courts to signal … relevant systemic factors going to the issue of liability'.[80] But such signals are muted when courts merely provide *fact-specific* conclusions about foreseeability to deny a duty of care. For Plunkett, duty should be confined to 'notional' questions about liability, with foreseeability confined to examining the culpability of the defendant's behaviour on the particular facts. A matter of fault (ie *breach*), not duty. It would be more coherent if each state of the negligence inquiry had a distinct function.

Debate 2
Does the Duty of Care Serve a Useful Function?

In a letter to John Fleming, WL Morison argued that 'duties of care' were not true ('Hohfeldian') duties at all. Rather, 'duty of care' is the heading under which the law of negligence 'abstracts certain issues for convenience' and considers them – that is, whether in the given situation 'the defendant may unreasonably create risks for the plaintiff with impunity'. Duty should be seen 'merely as a convenient repository into which we separate certain problems for the purpose of clarity of analysis'.[81] Fleming took a similar view.[82] He thought that the mechanisms by which the courts defined negligence liability were more or less interchangeable (eg 'remoteness, duty, negligence, standard of duty, foreseeability …'). The choice between them had little influence over the court's conclusion; 'in a sense, the selection of any particular formula is no more than "a matter of taste and finesse"'. However, Fleming accepted that 'the influence of deceptive connotations of the verbal formulas employed' could affect judicial reasoning. It potentially mattered which concept the court used, although 'Their respective suitability can be assessed only by reference to the degree to which they impair or assist forthright adversion to the real issue before the court'.

---

[80] J Stapleton, 'Duty of Care: Peripheral Parties and Alternative Opportunities for Deterrence' (1995) 111 *LQR* 301, 303.
[81] JG Fleming and WL Morison, 'Correspondence on Duty of Care and Standard of Care' (1953) 1 *Sydney LR* 69, 70–71.
[82] (n 5) 497–98.

Such views are inconsistent with the approaches considered in the previous Debate (that the duty of care is the foundation of obligations in negligence; that its definition using reasonable foreseeability ensures the 'relational' nature of the tort). If those positions are rejected, the duty of care no longer seems a conceptual necessity. The questions raised by Morison's and Fleming's comments remain. Even if not *necessary*, should duty be supported as a *useful* framing concept (or otherwise)? What functions does it serve, and how effectively?

Duty of Care: Then and Now

The duty of care's nineteenth-century development is explicable by procedural features of the time.[83] *Juries* decided questions of fact. Many questions in the negligence inquiry are essentially factual: whether the defendant was at fault, whether their faulty conduct caused the claimant's loss, etc. But the duty of care was consciously designed as a question of *law* for the court. The duty concept therefore allowed trial judges to control jury decisions. By ruling that no duty of care arose, judges could enter judgment for the defendant without leaving the case to the jury on the factual questions.

David Ibbetson explains how the duty concept derived from moral philosophers' attempts to state people's ethical duties. From such writing (especially the French author Pufendorf's), duty originally found its way into eighteenth-century English legal texts. Crucially however:

> Though the duty to take care was pivotal to [Pufendorf's] theoretical enterprise of deducing norms of human behaviour from basic facts of human nature, from a *legal* point of view it made no difference whether one said that liability stemmed from the breach of a duty of care or that liability stemmed from causing loss by careless conduct.[84]

Thus 'there is nothing in [the eighteenth-century English] writings to hint that any thought had been given to its playing an important role in legal analysis'.[85] That changed a century later when judges more actively intervened to control jury decisions. Nineteenth-century interventionism explains the 'tendency to load contentious questions about the scope of liability into the duty of care, where they could be decided by judges'.[86] Denial of duty was 'a constraint on

---

[83] DJ Ibbetson, *A Historical Introduction to the Law of Obligations* (Oxford, Oxford University Press, 1999) 170–74, 178–81, 188–95; DJ Ibbetson, 'How the Romans Did for Us: Ancient Roots of the Tort of Negligence' (2003) 26 *UNSWLJ* 475, 510–13.
[84] Ibbetson, 'How the Romans Did for Us' ibid 511 (emphasis added).
[85] ibid.
[86] ibid 512.

the potential expansiveness' of negligence.[87] The impulse for control affected not only the importance of duty but how it was defined. Judges (says Ibbetson) 'manipulated' the duty of care, realising that 'The more precisely this could be formulated, the more the judges could control the scope of liability'. Hence the 'highly particularistic approach to duty situations' in the pre-*Donoghue* era, a narrow conception of liability consistent with the prevailing 'individualist ideology'.[88]

This changed with *Donoghue v Stevenson*. But Ibbetson suggests that the decline of the civil jury in England explains the contemporaneous demise of the 'particularistic' duties of care, rather than Lord Atkin's 'neighbour principle' ('a more or less empty rule').[89] Yet the duty of care did not become obsolete with the negligence jury's disappearance.[90] Duty's survival is not solely attributable to doctrinal conservatism (albeit one 'well-known ailment of lawyers' is 'hardening of the categories').[91] It persists because it has continued to perform useful functions. It is framed as a relatively abstract categorical question of law: whether liability is possible in this kind of situation (assuming that loss has carelessly been inflicted). As Donal Nolan observes, duty's nature as a 'question of law' has proved as useful for modern procedural purposes as it was for curbing jury discretion.[92]

First, the duty question can be decided as a preliminary issue on the pleadings (as in *Donoghue* itself): assuming in the claimant's favour that she will be able to prove the defendant was negligent and caused the losses alleged, *does a duty of care arise*? Unlike questions of causation and breach, duty does not turn on the precise facts of the case. Hence it can be determined as a preliminary question – in advance of a trial to establish the facts. This gives the courts an effective way to decide cases earlier at considerably less expense. Pointless full-dress trials are avoided.

This function is valued by the courts. That emerges from the judicial dismay when it appeared (incorrectly) that striking cases out when no duty of care existed, without full findings of fact, might constitute a denial of the ECHR right to a fair hearing (article 6).[93] The courts also apprehend that duty's function would be undermined if duties depended on fact-dependent circumstances, for example a public authority's 'public-law irrational' failure to exercise its powers. That was once suggested as a possible exception to the

---

[87] ibid 513.
[88] ibid 478, 514.
[89] ibid 479.
[90] *Ward v James* [1966] 1 QB 273 (negligence juries obsolete).
[91] JP Dawson, 'Restitution or Damages' (1959) 20 *Ohio State LJ* 175, 187.
[92] D Nolan, 'Deconstructing the Duty of Care' (2013) 129 *LQR* 559.
[93] *Barrett v Enfield LBC* [2001] 2 AC 550, 559–60 (Lord Browne-Wilkinson: 'very unsatisfactory state of affairs'), commenting on *Osman v UK* (2000) 29 EHRR 245. Contrast *Z v UK* (2002) 34 EHRR 3.

rule that highway authorities are not liable for failing to use statutory road-improvement powers.⁹⁴ The suggestion's author came to regret it. Denying that duties of care can arise from 'broad public law duties', Lord Hoffmann deplored the extensive pre-trial investigation and six-day trial ('a hostile judicial inquiry into the council's administration') necessary to investigate the *Stovin* caveat.⁹⁵ Similar concerns have bearing on duty's 'foreseeability' component. This too threatens to turn duty into a fact-dependent question unsuitable for summary decision. As Nolan points out, if duty turns on whether this kind of risk to this kind of claimant was reasonably foreseeable the question 'cannot be answered until we know what the allegedly negligent conduct was'.⁹⁶

A second persisting advantage is that duty cases generate binding precedents. Decisions on questions of law do this in a way that fact-dependent decisions do not. (That D1 was careless cannot tell us whether D2 was careless in a later case. Hence Weir discouraged the search for breach cases as precedent 'on all fours', 'like a housewife seeking a matching thread in a haberdashery'!)⁹⁷ By contrast, 'through decisions on duty appellate courts can exercise effective control over the boundaries of negligence liability and provide prospective litigants, trial lawyers and lower court judges with clear guidance as to where those boundaries lie'.⁹⁸

Abolishing the Duty of Care?

Nolan, however, questions how effectively the duty of care polices the boundaries of negligence. Duty decisions certainly create 'categorical' liability rules. But 'duty questions can be framed at very different levels of generality' – 'there is nothing to say how broadly or narrowly [the duty] category is drawn'. This creates serious problems for courts attempting to decide duty cases 'by analogy'. The court can present almost any issue as one of duty of care, provided it is framed in 'categorical' terms. Duty is 'open-ended', drawing together questions that could be dealt with under other negligence doctrines because of its 'perceived procedural advantages and its apparent effectiveness as a mechanism of judicial control'. But those advantages are undermined precisely because too many disparate issues are lumped together under its rubric. In Nolan's view, these questions should be disaggregated – and reallocated to other parts of the negligence inquiry. He doubts what usefully remains of the 'deconstructed' duty of care.⁹⁹

---

⁹⁴ *Stovin v Wise* [1996] AC 923.
⁹⁵ *Gorringe v Calderdale MBC* [2004] 1 WLR 1057, [33].
⁹⁶ Nolan (n 92) 567.
⁹⁷ T Weir, *A Casebook on Tort* 10th edn (London, Sweet & Maxwell, 2004) 128.
⁹⁸ Nolan (n 92) 568.
⁹⁹ ibid.

At the 'core' of many controversial duty questions is what kind of interest should negligence law protect (eg pure economic loss, psychiatric harm or 'wrongful birth'). Does such loss involve violation of a right that the law protects against careless infringement? If not, it is irrecoverable. The claimant has suffered loss which is not legally recognised as harm: '*damnum absque injuria*'. These issues can be considered under the duty rubric, and often are. Indeed for Lord Nicholls, this was a powerful reason in favour of retaining the duty concept in negligence.[100] However, Nolan suggests that the 'actionable damage' question should be 'disaggregated'.[101] It can be obscured in the broader 'duty of care' inquiry. (An example is *Jain v Trent SHA* where the court focused on potential harm to vulnerable care-home residents,[102] 'at no point … advert[ing] to the fact' that the claimant's loss was purely economic – surprisingly not when this was dispositive in the defendant's favour in the absence of an assumption of responsibility.)[103] On the other hand, it would be incorrect to suggest that (eg) psychiatric injury can never constitute actionable damage. Such loss is recoverable in certain situations. The natural home for such nuanced constraints on liability seems to be the duty of care inquiry. It would be too crude to rely on the binary idea of 'actionable damage' outside clear-cut situations where the harm in question is *never* compensable.[104]

Nolan also criticises the overlap between 'duty' and 'causation' questions. Well-known cases such as *Dorset Yacht v Home Office*,[105] *Smith v Littlewoods*[106] and *Lamb v Camden LBC*[107] involve essentially the same question.[108] Is the defendant liable for deliberate wrongdoing by third parties which harms the claimant? In *Lamb* there was clearly a duty of care owed by the defendant to the claimant (insofar as they initially caused foreseeable physical damage to her house); thus the later damage by squatters had to be treated as a 'remoteness' question. But why should *Lamb* be put in a different 'pigeon hole' from *Dorset Yacht* or *Littlewoods* where the question was posed as one of *duty*? Nolan suggests that the latter cases could, and should, have been considered as remoteness cases too – meaning similar cases (like these three) would be considered alongside each other. (Lord Denning MR noted that 'too remote' and 'no duty' were the traditional, interchangeable, answers to such claims.)[109]

---

[100] *JD v East Berkshire NHS Trust* [2005] 2 AC 373 [94].
[101] See now *Meadows v Khan* [2022] AC 852[31]–[32] (Lords Hodge and Sales); cf [80] (Lord Burrows) ('conveniently treated as a sub-issue under the duty of care enquiry').
[102] [2009] 1 AC 853.
[103] Nolan (n 92) 579.
[104] eg *JD* (n 100) [100] (Lord Rodger: a spurned lover's mental anguish; loss through lawful trade competition).
[105] [1970] AC 1004.
[106] (n 12).
[107] [1981] QB 625.
[108] See ch 5, 'Interventions'.
[109] *Dorset Yacht* [1969] 2 QB 412, 424–25 (CA).

A possible objection is that 'remoteness' depends in part on factual questions (such as the likelihood or the outrageousness of the squatters' conduct in *Lamb*). That makes it difficult to lay down a general rule of law limiting liability as Lord Goff endeavoured to do in *Smith v Littlewoods*. Lord Goff's rule that there is no duty to control third parties is, however, subject to a large number of exceptions. Like remoteness, these exceptions require an assessment of the particular facts (eg how the initial danger was created; the extent of the defendant's power of control; whether the defendant assumed responsibility). The factual nature of the inquiry was yet more obvious in the other law lords' approach in *Littlewoods*. They thought that a high enough degree of knowledge about the third party vandals' activities would make the inactive occupier liable. As Nolan says, a considerable degree of factual inquiry is also built into the standard duty of care rules for 'secondary victims' of psychiatric injury (proximity in time and space, degree of personal relationship with the primary victim, etc).

Reflecting generally on the duty of care Nolan suggests its malleability diminishes its precedential force. It is misleading to refer to 'bright-line duty rules' (eg the 'omissions rule') when courts are so adept at finding exceptions. The result is a 'tangled web of overlapping rules pitched at differing levels of generality'. As a matter of *remoteness* the absence of liability for deliberate third party interventions can be formulated with as much, or rather as little, generality or precision. In cases involving self-harm by claimants (that the defendant failed to prevent) it has frequently been observed that whether we analyse the question using duty or causation, we arrive at the same result.[110] Nolan's preference is to decant these cases out of the duty inquiry so that they can be considered together.

Are there any true 'duty' issues (which cannot easily be handled by any other negligence doctrine)? Nolan accepts that negligence contains some true immunities – claims that fail despite proven fault causing actionable damage. For example, one soldier cannot sue another (nor the army, vicariously) for negligently injuring them during active combat.[111] Even though this is in all other respects a paradigmatic situation for negligence liability (direct infliction of personal injury), public policy reasons preclude such claims: the non-justiciability of conduct during the heat of battle.[112] The military immunity is expressed as the absence of a duty of care.

Nolan suggests that such immunities could instead be viewed as special policy-based *defences*. This would produce a more focused inquiry: are there community-welfare (policy) reasons to deny negligence liability that interpersonal justice would otherwise recognise? A separate stage would encourage clearer reasoning than simply weighing up a great 'melange' of justice

---

[110] See ch 5, 'Interventions'.
[111] *Mulcahy v Ministry of Defence* [1996] QB 732.
[112] cf *Smith v Ministry of Defence* [2014] AC 52.

and policy considerations under the heading of duty. Because the 'immunity defence' stage would follow after 'inter-personal justice' was considered, Nolan argues it would limit the occasions on which 'highly contested policy arguments' have to be considered. If liability were anyway precluded on causal grounds, or because the interest is not legally protected (compare Nolan's criticism of *Jain* above), there would be no need to consider countervailing policies.

Reverting to the questions posed above: Is duty of care the most 'convenient' home for categorical questions about liability? Does it impair or assist forthright consideration of the 'real issues'? Nolan makes a provocative case against. The duty of care as currently conceived obscures understanding – its 'disparate issues' would be better 'separated out and reclassified under the other components [of negligence]'.[113] Those other questions are (Nolan maintains) no less 'questions of law'. Perhaps that is correct: the clarity of the rules laid down in the form of duty of care might well be exaggerated. Ibbetson observes that modern negligence, an 'all-embracing but largely formless tort', falls 'far below an acceptable level' of predictability, though accepts an inevitable 'degree of messiness' as tort constantly adapts to new situations.[114]

There is also Weir's point that controlling liability by denying there was a duty to take care gives an 'unfortunate' impression. 'Of course' (he says) the prison officers in *Dorset Yacht* 'were under a duty to do their job – to say otherwise sends out quite the wrong signal – but it is quite another question whether the Home Office should have to pay'.[115] Weir's criticism may be answered by observing that the officers' duty *to their employers* (to do their jobs) is not enforceable at the suit of everyone in the world; just as a council's general public duties (eg to promote road safety or to house homeless persons) are enforceable through judicial review and not by tort claims for damages.[116] But is declaring 'no duty of care' the best way to express this conclusion?

Conclusion

Negligence lawyers understand that to say 'no duty' is (as Weir implies) simply a mechanism for denying liability to pay compensation. Its historical evolution as a tool for controlling jury decisions exemplifies this function. It remains useful in modern law too. A 'no duty' decision does *not* deny that there is a general moral and legal obligation to be careful. It is simply about placing limits on *liability*. But there is, at least, a presentational problem. Denial of duty hollows the obligatory force of tort law, in McBride's view. Some argue

---

[113] Nolan (n 92) 559.
[114] Ibbetson, 'How the Romans Did for Us' (n 83) 475, 479.
[115] Weir (n 6) 99 (deeming the decision in the plaintiffs' favour 'surely wrong' since it benefited the *insurers* of the damaged yachts).
[116] *Gorringe* (n 95); *O'Rourke v Camden LBC* [1998] AC 188.

the duty of care should be restated around Lord Atkin's 'neighbour principle' of foreseeability, consistent with the basic idea of reasonable care. But would this relegate the duty of care to duplicative redundancy? It would certainly prevent its pragmatic use as a categorial control on negligence liability (unless courts manipulate 'foreseeability', concealing value judgements behind a supposedly 'factual' façade). Yet many of duty's functions could be performed by other doctrines within the law of negligence. It could even be abolished and its separate dimensions disaggregated, as Nolan explores.

Ultimately, we may question whether fine points of doctrinal architecture determine the outcomes of disputes. Markesinis and Deakin warn: 'The fluidity and equivocation of the basic concepts of negligence make it important to avoid too rigid an insistence on finding the "correct" technical form in which to phrase an issue'.[117] Scepticism about legal concepts has a long history. Felix Cohen dismissed them as 'word charms' and 'supernatural entities' which 'hide from judicial eyes the ethical character of every judicial question, and thus serve to perpetuate ... uncritical moral assumptions which could not survive the sunlight of free ethical controversy'.[118] The duty of care, at least, does little to 'hide' the ethical controversies of tort law. They are only too apparent in a law of negligence 'brimming with antithetic decisions reflecting different philosophies'.[119] Perhaps, as Fleming said, the best we can hope for is a clear engagement with the relevant issues. Yet accepting an unavoidable 'degree of conceptual fluidity', we may legitimately voice concern if negligence 'lacks an adequate conceptual structure, a framework of principle within which the complex balancing of different factors can be placed'.[120] Should this 'inadequacy' be addressed by a tighter conceptual structure (eg an elevated role for foreseeability)? Or by embracing the fluidity of negligence, emphasising the central role of 'policy choices' whose outcome 'cannot be predicted in advance by the mechanical application of verbal formulae'?[121] Disagreements about the nature of legal reasoning are pervasive in tort law. We explore in the following chapter how such disagreements run through questions of how to define the duty of care, and the role of 'policy' within it.

---

[117] S Deakin and Z Adams, *Markesinis & Deakin's Tort Law* 8th edn (Oxford, Oxford University Press, 2019) 93.
[118] FS Cohen, 'Transcendental Nonsense and the Functional Approach' (1935) 35 *Columbia LR* 809.
[119] Markesinis and Deakin (n 117) 239.
[120] ibid 240.
[121] ibid 95.

7

Defining the Duty of Care

Negligence has an in-built expansionary tendency: it can, unlike nominate torts, potentially protect *any* interest against careless harm.[1] The colonisation of the entire law of torts by negligence has been resisted, above all, by wielding the duty concept. Denying a duty of care means the defendant is not liable *even though* they carelessly harmed the claimant.[2] That at least is the dominant view today, conceiving duty as the boundary stone of negligence – and by extension of tort law as a whole.

Given its vital function, we could expect the duty of care to be defined with precision. Yet it has been notoriously resistant to definition. Many courts have tried to explain when a duty of care should arise in novel cases. There have been famous attempts to summarise this in a simple formula. Yet the formulations have proved highly controversial. After heavy criticism from both academics and the judges themselves, the formulaic approach has been abandoned. Why these struggles?

This chapter examines, first, some of the much-maligned 'tests' for duty and examines why they have failed. As will be seen in the first debate, not every commentator accepts that the elements of a test like *Caparo* are as devoid of real meaning as critics have asserted. Can such a central concept as the duty of care really be indefinable? If the courts simply have to take all relevant considerations into account and weigh them up, does that not confer enormous discretionary power? No doubt it is naïve to think that a simple formula, let alone a mechanical test, could give easy answers to complex duty of care questions. But even if such a 'test' is unavailable, it might be possible to devise a structure to guide consideration of the underlying questions.

Some commentators would deny even that much. In their view, tort lawyers must accept with frank honesty that an open-ended weighing process cannot be avoided. Trenchant test-sceptics emphasise the role of 'public policy' in settling the limits of liability. That emphasis is controversial.

---

[1] T Weir, 'The Staggering March of Negligence' in P Cane and J Stapleton (eds), *The Law of Obligations: Essays in Celebration of John Fleming* (Oxford, Oxford University Press, 1998).

[2] D Howarth, *Textbook on Tort* (London, Butterworths, 1995) 161–62.

There are many good reasons for caution in the judicial development of policy. The courts' record is far from encouraging. Thus some argue that courts ought not to take policy into account in deciding the duty of care (or any other matter of tort law). This would require a significant shift in the courts' approach. Is that change justified? This second 'policy' debate involves deep jurisprudential controversy, reflecting wider disagreement about the nature and function of private law. As the duty question has provoked some of the sharpest disagreements, it is conveniently considered in this context.

The third debate examines the role of precedent. It seems banal to observe in a common-law subject like negligence, liability develops through case law. (How else could it?) Yet it has been elevated into a separate feature of the duty inquiry – inelegantly labelled 'incrementalism'. This suggests that precedent has a special role to play in the duty of care. Decided cases are given such emphasis as a reaction to more sweeping 'principled' approaches to the duty question, that have now fallen out of favour. An intellectual concern about the robustness of general 'tests' for duty, and pragmatic concerns about the wide and uncertain liability that such tests have produced, has historically been connected with 'incrementalism'. It has been given renewed prominence by the Supreme Court. The renaissance of precedent seems connected with contemporary scepticism about judicial policy-reasoning. We therefore inquire whether an emphasis on established liabilities is a useful stabilising force, or (as critics would suggest) ultimately just reactionary conservatism.

Debate 1
The *Caparo* 'Test' – Decline and Fall?

Students sometimes still read that the governing test for duty of care was laid down in *Caparo Industries plc v Dickman*.[3] When confronting a case not covered by existing authority the court must ask (1) whether this kind of injury was *foreseeable* to a class of persons including the claimant; (2) whether the claimant had a *proximate relationship* to the defendant; and (3) whether it would overall be *fair, just and reasonable* to recognise liability of this kind.

This is unfortunate. *Caparo* never purported to lay down a 'test' as such. First, the law lords emphasised that novel cases were *not* to be approached by making deductions from broad general principles. The starting place was always established authority. Would an *incremental* development from liability established in the decided cases extend to the new situation? The tripartite formulation was at best a general guide as to how a court should approach such 'incremental development'.

---

[3] [1990] 2 AC 605.

The formula was certainly no more than that. Immediately after his famous (and unwisely aphoristic) statement that 'proximity' and 'fair, just and reasonable' must be considered as well as foreseeability, Lord Bridge said:

> these additional ingredients are not susceptible of any such precise definition as would be necessary to give them utility as practical tests, but amount in effect to little more than convenient labels to attach to the features of different specific situations which, on a detailed examination of all the circumstances, the law recognises pragmatically as giving rise to a duty of care of a given scope.[4]

This was really a non-test. In similar vein, Lord Roskill said 'it has now to be accepted that there is no simple formula or touchstone to which recourse can be had in order to provide in every case … [whether to] impose liability for negligence'.[5] Lord Oliver thought that the three parts of the formula were not truly separate but 'at least in most cases, in fact merely facets of the same thing' (eg 'proximity' inferred from high degree of foreseeability, or excluded because liability would not be fair and reasonable). Lord Oliver warned that 'search[ing] for any single formula which will serve as a general test of liability is to pursue a will-o'-the wisp'.

Given the 'infinite variety of circumstances' where a duty might arise, a general principle 'serves not to clarify the law but merely to bedevil its development in a way which corresponds with practicality and common sense'.[6] In the Court of Appeal, Bingham LJ expressed a tripartite formula very similar to Lord Bridge's and opened his judgment by saying it was 'not possible to lay down hard-and-fast rules as to when a duty of care arises in [any] class of case'.[7] There was no 'single proposition' and no 'simple ready-made solution'.

Of the threefold formula, foreseeability's role has already been considered in the previous chapter. 'Proximity' was said by Lord Jauncey in *Caparo* to be 'somewhat elusive' once it was extended from 'mere physical proximity'. He thought it 'might be described as the circumstances in which the law considers it proper that a duty of care should be imposed on one person towards another'.[8] This is, of course, entirely circular.[9] As for the third 'fair, just and reasonable' element, Bingham LJ said it required the consideration of 'policy', an inquiry weighing 'the relationship of the parties, the nature of the risk, and the public interest in the proposed solution'.[10] Clearly, by its nature, such a broad exercise cannot be reduced to a tractable 'test'.

---

[4] ibid 617–18.
[5] ibid 628.
[6] ibid 633.
[7] [1989] QB 653, 678.
[8] [1990] 2 AC 605, 655.
[9] MC McHugh, 'Neighbourhood, Proximity and Reliance' in PD Finn (ed), *Essays on Torts* (Sydney, Law Book Co, 1989).
[10] [1989] QB 653, 680 (quoting *Goldberg v City of Newark* (1962) 186 A 2d 291, 293, per Weintraub CJ).

The *Caparo* 'test' has had rivals. Brooke LJ identified three further approaches to duty in a single House of Lords decision (assumption of responsibility, the purpose of the service provided by the defendant, and 'distributive justice') – and even these were not necessarily exhaustive.[11] We could dispute whether these are truly separate formulae or whether, for example, assumption of responsibility is a route to establishing 'proximity', or distributive concerns built into the 'fair, just and reasonable' stage. Brooke LJ was impatient with classificatory niceties: 'if the facts are properly analysed and the policy considerations are correctly evaluated the several approaches will yield the same result'.[12] This suggests that the various tests are alternative routes to the same conclusion. Yet the proliferation of ostensibly different approaches seems confusing. Should negligence pay attention to William of Ockham's philosophical maxim – cutting away needless complexity with his 'razor' ('Entities should not be multiplied without necessity')?

It is strange that so many have treated *Caparo* as a 'test' for duty of care when the judges stressed clearly that this was not their intention. Indeed they thought a test impossible, and attempting to formulate one downright harmful. In *Customs & Excise Commissioners v Barclays Bank* Lord Bingham made the point again. He concluded that notwithstanding the diversity of approaches the *outcomes* of leading negligence cases 'are in every or almost every instance sensible and just, *irrespective of the test applied* to achieve that outcome'.[13] Lord Walker thought it was 'progress of a sort' to recognise that 'the threefold [*Caparo*] test ... does not provide an easy answer to all our problems, but only a set of fairly blunt tools'.[14] Lord Mance said the various tests (including also 'incrementalism' and 'assumption of responsibility') all 'operate at a high level of abstraction' – what really mattered was 'how and by reference to what lower-level factors they are interpreted in practice'.[15] Lord Rodger said that while there was an 'obvious temptation' to search for a 'compact underlying rule' for duty of care, 'appellate judges should follow the philosopher's advice to "Seek simplicity, and distrust it"'.[16]

This criticism might have been expected to kill off further references to *Caparo* or any other 'test'.[17] Yet the Supreme Court has had to repeat the message, directly and forcefully. It is 'mistaken' to believe that *Caparo* created a test applicable to all cases – its whole point was to 'repudiate' a general test in favour of analogical development.[18] It was 'paradoxical' that 'Lord

---

[11] *Parkinson v St James and Seacroft University Hospital NHS Trust* [2001] EWCA Civ 530; [2002] QB 266 [26]–[27] (discussing *McFarlane v Tayside Health Board* [2000] 2 AC 59).

[12] *BCCI v Price Waterhouse (No 2)* [1998] PNLR 564, 586 (Sir B Neill) (cited Brooke LJ ibid).

[13] [2007] 1 AC 181, [6], [8] (emphasis added) (and Lord Walker [72]).

[14] ibid [71].

[15] ibid [83] (similarly Lord Hoffmann [36]).

[16] ibid [51] (apparently quoting Wittgenstein).

[17] J Morgan, 'The Rise and Fall of the General Duty of Care' (2006) 22 *Prof Neg* 206.

[18] *Robinson v Chief Constable of West Yorkshire* [2018] AC 736, [21] (Lord Reed).

Bridge's speech has sometimes come to be treated as a blueprint for deciding cases, despite the pains which the author took to make clear that it was not intended to be any such thing'.[19] *Caparo* has been 'widely misunderstood as establishing a general tripartite test'.[20] Lord Lloyd-Jones concludes: 'The common law in this jurisdiction has abandoned the search for a general principle capable of providing a practical test applicable in every situation in order to determine whether a duty of care is owed and, if so, what is its scope'.[21] That seems hard to deny. The most senior judges have spent over 30 years saying so.

Why has the idea of a general test died so hard? It is a deeply engrained habit of thought for lawyers to seek such a test.[22] Whether the Supreme Court's latest warnings are heeded remains to be seen. Lord Bridge's threefold test rolls so sweetly off the tongue that it will not easily be eradicated – even though (to heighten the irony further) Bingham LJ had presciently warned: 'It is only too easy to be mesmerised by expressions used in other cases which, however apt in those cases, provide no universally applicable yardstick. The language used in other cases guides but does not govern'.[23]

A Defence of the Three-Stage Test

This test-scepticism now seems to be generally accepted, and long overdue. George Christie argues that the 'illusion' that tort liability depend on a 'single principle' is

> as unwise as it is unachievable. To attempt to simplify the process by trying to reduce the choices involved in deciding a case to the application of a verbal formula ... may seem comforting to some but, in the end, as we have seen, leads to inconsistent decisions which only serve to reinforce the cynicism that the appeal to principle was designed to avert. It is not that the verbal formulas thus far chosen were inadequate; it is rather that the whole enterprise was doomed from the start. Social life is too rich in complicated details to permit decision-making by resort to these kinds of overriding abstractions. The best common-law judges have always known this, and their decisions reflect the exercise of seasoned judgment.[24]

Nevertheless, commentators such as Christian Witting argue that the tripartite test is not meaningless.[25] Witting accepts that in *Caparo* the House of

---

[19] *Michael v Chief Constable of South Wales* [2015] AC 1732, [106] (Lord Toulson).
[20] *GN v Poole BC* [2020] AC 780, [30] (Lord Reed).
[21] *Darnley v Croydon NHS Trust* [2019] A.C. 831, [15].
[22] L Green, 'Foreseeability in Negligence Law' (1961) 61 *Columbia LR* 1401.
[23] *Caparo* [1989] QB 653, 684.
[24] GC Christie, 'The Uneasy Place of Principle in Tort Law' in DG Owen (ed), *Philosophical Foundations of Tort Law* (Oxford, Clarendon, 1995) 128.
[25] C Witting, 'Duty of Care: An Analytical Approach' (2005) 25 *OJLS* 33.

Lords was 'ambivalent' about its own test. (An understatement.) Nevertheless, Witting insists, *Caparo*'s three stages have distinct content. Foreseeability is a necessary requirement because in its absence, the harm in question would be unavoidable – and a duty *of care* impossible. 'Proximity' is indeed about closeness. Not necessarily in time and space, or prior relationship. Proximity depends on the causal connection between the parties – whether there were 'significant causal pathways' by which the defendant's conduct might harm the claimant. Thus under these first two limbs

> courts must look for factors which indicate a minimum ability to avoid the causation of damage and for factors which identify particular persons as being appropriately placed to take care so as to avoid such damage. Foreseeability and proximity, respectively, serve these functions.[26]

By bracketing together the 'foreseeability' and 'proximity' requirements in this way, Witting's argument is vulnerable to the critique concerning foreseeability and the duty of care. Namely that it is fact-dependent and duplicative.[27] Similar objections can be made to Witting's 'distinctive' proximity criterion. It becomes impossible to lay down rules to define categorically the limits of negligence liability if we need to ask whether a given defendant's fault was 'a crucial element in the chain of causation leading to [the claimant's] damage'.[28] Such issues depend on the particular facts of each case – as Witting accepts.[29] This obstructs use of duty to set the boundaries of liability through abstract legal rulings. Moreover, Witting's conception of 'proximity' duplicates the causal inquiry that the court is anyway required to undertake. It is already a standard part of causation analysis ('remoteness') to ask whether the defendant's causal involvement was 'real and uncomplicated by any genuinely deliberative acts of intervention, or by the occurrence of other causally significant events'.[30]

Witting does not provide any convincing reason why the issue of close causal connexion should be duplicated by 'proximity' in the duty of care. He maintains that 'causal' proximity is duty's major determinant. It relates purely to the relationship of the parties and so provides an *unequivocal* factor in favour of liability.[31] He argues that proximity's relational and clear-cut nature is more tractable than the third *Caparo* stage ('fairness, justice and reasonableness'), which requires the court to balance policy factors. Although Witting does

---

[26] C Witting, 'The Three Stage Test Abandoned in Australia – Or Not?' (2002) 118 *LQR* 214, 221.
[27] See ch 6, 'The Redundancy of Foreseeability'.
[28] Witting (n 26) 219.
[29] Witting (n 25) 38 ('it is apparent that the foreseeability and proximity tests are grounded in an examination of factual states of affairs').
[30] Witting (n 26) 219.
[31] Witting (n 25) 40.

not suggest this is illegitimate, he asserts that the parties' (causal) interrelation should take priority over considerations of the wider public interest. Such policy reasoning is bound to be contestable, with cross-cutting factors. Since the third (policy) stage is likely to be equivocal, proximity should be the dominant factor in duty decisions.

Duty: Division between Justice and the Public Interest?

Andrew Robertson also divides the duty of care inquiry between 'interpersonal justice' and 'social welfare' factors.[32] This corresponds broadly to the second and third *Caparo* stages. Robertson deems proximity to be solely a matter of justice, while conceiving it in broader terms than Witting's causation-based definition. Robertson adopts McLachlin CJ's view of proximity: the courts 'evaluate the closeness of the relationship between the claimant and the defendant ... to determine whether it is just and fair having regard to that relationship to impose a duty of care'.[33] While turning primarily on how directly the defendant's conduct stands to affect the claimant, Robertson accepts wider considerations feature too. What was the nature of the risk (eg physical or economic harm)? Could the claimant be expected to protect themselves against it (or were they vulnerable)? Obviously such 'proximity' goes beyond mere physical closeness, or causal connexion. Robertson's approach balances the parties' respective autonomy and responsibility.

While such 'proximity' is central to 'justice between the parties', wider factors relate to interpersonal justice too. In Robertson's view, policy questions should not be incorporated into 'proximity' (or it will become incoherent). But some policy factors turn on the particular parties' relationship: for example whether negligence liability would be inconsistent with the contractual structure of dealings between them. Also, where it would impose a disproportionate burden: 'the lengths to which one person can expect another to go to prevent a particular type of harm is a fundamental issue of justice between those parties'.[34]

The *Caparo* division between proximity and 'fair just and reasonable' maps uneasily onto these aspects of interpersonal justice. Robertson does not defend the *Caparo* test per se. He notes that the 'ostensibly different' general duty approaches in England, Australia and Canada are similar in practical application and outcomes. Robertson's purpose is distinguish 'interpersonal justice' from a second stage, comprising all *other* factors relevant to the duty inquiry ('residual policy factors outside the relationship of the parties that may negative the imposition of a duty of care').[35] If interpersonal justice supports liability,

---

[32] A Robertson, 'Justice, Community Welfare and the Duty of Care' (2011) 127 *LQR* 370.
[33] *Cooper v Hobart* [2001] 3 SCR 537 [34].
[34] Robertson (n 32) 383.
[35] *Cooper* (n 33) [30].

a duty of care arises as a prima facie matter. Viz unless considerations of the wider public interest rebut liability. The latter involves such factors as non-justiciability and community welfare – for example, the effect on the wider legal system (cross-cutting duties or re-litigating decided issues), inefficient allocation of risks (eg double insurance against same loss), or undesirable effects on behaviour (eg 'overkill'). Such policy factors might sometimes favour liability (eg encouraging desirable behaviour, holding powerful defendants to account, or vindicating important interests). Thus the wider policy factors must be weighed against each other, and against interpersonal justice, in deciding whether to deny a prima facie liability on policy grounds. Robertson says that this separation makes clear that *justice* comes first. Liability is not imposed 'simply to advance community welfare', but only when it is just between the parties (considering matters relating only to their relationship). Wider public concerns come in only as a secondary matter, rebutting the claims of justice only when sufficiently convincing.

Robertson proposes a framework for analysis rather than a true 'test'. The framework indicates the two general groups of concerns that courts must consider: those relating to justice between the parties, and those bearing on the wider public interest. This gets us only so far. What is relevant to 'justice' or 'public policy', how much weight should the factors be given, and (therefore) how ultimately should they be balanced against each other? This is bound to be controversial. Indeed, some argue that 'policy factors outside the relationship of the parties' should not be considered at all. In the following debate we consider this challenge and the degree to which defenders of policy reasoning, pre-eminently Jane Stapleton, respond.

Debate 2
Policy and the Duty of Care

For at least 50 years English courts have explicitly taken policy considerations into account when drawing the boundaries of negligence.[36] Modern orthodoxy holds policy a significant component of the duty of care. But its central place has been challenged.[37] Critics argue that tort law should exclusively be concerned with the protection of rights. Further that such 'corrective' or 'interpersonal' justice is incompatible with the courts weighing up public policy. The objections have a number of dimensions, including justice, coherence, practical and constitutional concerns. These will be outlined before exploring possible responses.

---

[36] *Anns v Merton LBC* [1978] AC 728; *Dutton v Bognor Regis UDC* [1972] 1 QB 373, 397 (Lord Denning MR).

[37] A Beever, *Rediscovering the Law of Negligence* (Oxford, Hart, 2007) 20 (*Anns v Merton* 'a victory of ignorance from which we have not yet recovered').

An initial question is what we mean by 'policy'. This is surprisingly hard to pin down. Different commentators draw the line in different places. In 1928 Green identified the following 'factors' (accepting 'There are doubtless others'): administrative ('workability'); ethical/moral; economic; prophylactic (deterrence); and justice.[38] Perhaps the safest definition is a negative, open-ended one. 'Policy' means any factor in a decision other than the strictly legal-doctrinal. More generally, as seen in Andrew Robertson's duty of care framework, policy connotes matters of public interest (or 'community welfare') going beyond the dictates of justice between the immediate parties.

One central objection is that 'policy' is alien to the structure of tort law. Ernest Weinrib makes it forcefully. In Weinrib's view, tort is purely about correcting a wrong that the defendant has done to the claimant. To take 'external goals' into account 'effaces the coherence of the parties' relationship'.[39] In particular when policy is used to negative a prima facie duty that would otherwise arise as a matter of justice, Weinrib views this as 'confiscation of what was rightly due to the [claimant]'.[40] So policy intruding into negligence is not just incoherent but positively *unjust*. Similarly, Alan Beever warns that taking 'external' policy into account means that the interest of one or even both of the parties will be ignored – violating relational corrective justice. Why, he asks, should litigants bear the 'expense and indignity' of judges 'making social policy' under the 'pretence of dealing with their dispute'?[41]

Concerns about the *coherence* of the law also feature heavily in the critique of policy reasoning. Supporters of the rights-based, corrective justice approach praise its conceptual 'unity'.[42] Liability depends solely on what, as a matter of justice, the claimant is entitled to expect from the defendant. This informs causation, fault and duty alike. Such reasoning is principled, 'unified', 'more elegant, consistent with the law in general, and appropriate to judicial decision making' compared to policy reasoning.[43] For Beever, *Donoghue v Stevenson*'s 'neighbour principle' is not merely an ethically satisfying reference to Christian morality. It an intellectual necessity, 'connected to the very concept of negligence ... between two parties'.[44] Lord Atkin meant it when he said 'there must be, and is, some general conception of relations giving rise to a duty of care'.[45] And his conception was right.

The alternative, in Beever's view, is chaos. Before *Donoghue* duties were not derived from a general principle but imposed case by case 'in a more or less

---

[38] L Green, 'The Duty Problem in Negligence Cases' (1928) 28 *Columbia LR* 1014, 1034.
[39] EJ Weinrib, 'The Disintegration of Duty' in MS Madden (ed), *Exploring Tort Law* (Cambridge, Cambridge University Press, 2005), 184.
[40] ibid 166.
[41] Beever (n 37) 176.
[42] ibid 29.
[43] ibid 31.
[44] ibid 121.
[45] [1932] AC 562, 580.

arbitrary fashion', with 'unprincipled limitations … determined for convenience'. But that 'arbitrary' approach (which resembles the dominant view of negligence today) 'could not be a legal system in its proper sense'.⁴⁶ Policy reasoning makes it impossible to carry out fruitful intellectual analysis of tort law (ie giving a general account of it, not just listing heterogenous policy concerns).⁴⁷ Law even ceases to be a reputable academic discipline on the policy approach: it becomes merely the 'handmaid' of social-scientific analysis of those policies, with no distinct existence.⁴⁸

Weinrib agrees. Lord Atkin correctly identified the 'juridical necessity' of a general principle of duty, 'an implication of the internal coherence required by the law's systematic nature'.⁴⁹ But it has since 'fragmented'. The modern approach 'disintegrates' the duty of care into 'ad hoc [policy] compromises' – 'a chaotic miscellany of disparate and independent norms'.⁵⁰

Linked to accusations of incoherence are concerns about legal *certainty*. Grantham and Jensen praise the common law's 'slow but sure reflection of the deeply held values of the society', its stable development which provides a certain and predictable guide for behaviour. This tradition is said to be threatened by the 'short-term political or cultural fashions' and 'applied social science' that characterise policy reasoning.⁵¹ Policy's open-ended diversity complicates and destabilises judicial reasoning. Beever argues that considering an endless list of policies invites 'wide ranging debates on issues about which there is nothing even approaching a general consensus'. Since policy arguments can be adduced to support 'any conceivable position', controversy about negligence liability is unavoidable.⁵² The 'analytic smorgasbord' of policy guarantees a 'woefully invalid', unpredictable and incoherent tort law.⁵³ If there can be no principled test for the existence of duty, how can judges decide except through Lord Goff's 'educated reflex to facts'?⁵⁴ Beever dismisses that outright as 'extreme intuitionism'.⁵⁵

Another concern is that courts are not well placed to make judgments about policy. Robert Stevens argues that judges lack the *technical competence* to evaluate and weigh up such concerns.⁵⁶ Partly due to limited experience. Lawyers are expert in the application of legal doctrine, but not in policy analysis. There

---

⁴⁶ Beever (n 37) 121.
⁴⁷ A Beever, 'Policy in Private law: An Admission of Failure' (2006) 25 *Univ Queensland LJ* 287.
⁴⁸ A Beever and CEF Rickett, 'Interpretive Legal Theory and the Academic Lawyer' (2005) 68 *MLR* 320.
⁴⁹ Weinrib (n 39) 145, 148.
⁵⁰ ibid 144–45.
⁵¹ R Grantham and D Jensen, 'The Proper Role of Policy in Private Law Adjudication' (2018) 68 *Univ Toronto LJ* 187, 230.
⁵² Beever (n 37) 5.
⁵³ Beever (n 47) 287.
⁵⁴ *Smith v Littlewoods* [1987] AC 241, 280.
⁵⁵ Beever (n 37) 188.
⁵⁶ R Stevens, *Torts and Rights* (Oxford, Oxford University Press, 2007), ch 14.

are also inherent limits in the common law process. It develops (of course) through litigation, but court cases are poor occasions for the assessment of the public interest. The court hears only the parties to the claim and the arguments/evidence that they choose to advance. Much information, and many interested parties' perspectives (if we think of it as an occasion to rule on the interests of the community as a whole), will not be before the court – and consequently ignored.

Finally, do judges have *political legitimacy* to make such decisions? Policy reasoning is said to pose a threat to the rule of law.[57] First it renders law contestable and unstable. Second, judicial policy-making is neither transparent nor participative. It occurs in the closed world of litigation – excluding the general public. Third, it compromises judicial neutrality. Courts are drawn into a spiral of politicisation. For Stevens, the judiciary therefore lack constitutional authority to enter policy debates. Taking policy seriously requires a judiciary transformed – trained and experienced beyond technical legal analysis, and democratically accountable for their decisions. Beever thinks policy analysis an 'invitation for judges and commentators to pursue their personal visions of the good society ... [and] to abandon the rule of law for the rule of judges'.[58] On the policy approach, negligence 'cannot be other than deeply political ... a battleground on which various political views fight for supremacy'. But allowing the courts to join combat means 'judicial usurpation of democratic authority'.[59]

Other commentators defend the relevance – and importance – of the public interest against this powerful critique. While the critics identify serious problems with policy reasoning, might the problems be addressed by measures short of prohibiting it altogether? Finally, some of the claims in favour of the rival corrective justice approach could be questioned. In particular, its certainty and political neutrality. Perhaps the most potent argument in favour of policy reasoning is its openness and transparency. A concern is that if judges refuse to admit or articulate public policy reasons, policy may still influence the law in clandestine fashion. Legal development could then become even more unpredictable. The fear reflects a wider scepticism about conceptual-doctrinal reasoning. As Holmes said:

> The life of the law has not been logic: it has been experience. The felt necessities of the time, the prevalent moral and political theories, intuitions of public policy, avowed or unconscious, even the prejudices which judges share with their fellow-men, have had a good deal more to do than the syllogism in determining the rules by which men should be governed.[60]

We now assess the critique of policy reasoning with these points in mind.

---

[57] M Schwarzschild, 'Keeping it Private' (2006) 25 *Univ Queensland LJ* 215.
[58] Beever (n 37) 172.
[59] ibid 18–19.
[60] OW Holmes, *The Common Law* (Boston, Little, Brown, 1881) 1.

Common Law Rights, Public Interest Legislation?

Must tort law be understood solely as a matter of interpersonal justice, so that taking wider public concerns into account violates its structure? That claim is central to the critique of policy. Yet many would reject it. The corrective justice approach does not make hard questions go away. The law must define what rights we have against other individuals and (in correlation) our duties towards others. It is arguably necessary to look beyond the parties' relationship to each other and examine the wider public interest. Such an approach is inevitable in legislation – and arguably appropriate in developing the common law too.

Consider controversies in negligence. Whether the police owe a positive duty to protect vulnerable members of the public from violent crime.[61] Whether parents can recover the cost of raising a child when a sterilisation procedure is ineffectual.[62] Whether liability exists when, following a fertility clinic's mix-up, a child is racially different from its parents.[63] How are the rights and duties to be defined without examining ethical questions? Societal judgements about self-reliance balanced against (public) protection are unavoidable when deciding the extent to which people should protect themselves against certain kinds of harms. Such decisions have distributive implications – affecting the distribution of valuable goods (enforceable rights) and onerous burdens (corresponding liabilities) across society as a whole. As the 'wrongful birth' examples further suggest, other controversial moral questions (about eg the sanctity of life or racial identity) may be raised. Commentators like Keating argue that such questions cannot be considered as purely a private matter between the individual parties, ignoring the wider public interest.[64]

There is no pre-ordained catalogue of rights in tort law, no definitive list which the courts simply read and enforce. On the contrary, rights emerge *from* decisions in tort cases. Grantham and Jensen accept that judicial perceptions of society's 'fundamental values, philosophies, and ideologies' influences the development of private law.[65] Indeed, such 'deep values' are the ultimate foundation of all legal principles. Courts must therefore consider factors beyond interpersonal rights in the narrow sense. As seen, Grantham and Jensen nevertheless reject policy (its focus is 'not to do justice as between the parties to the immediate dispute [but] to further the interests and welfare of the community as a whole').[66] Grantham and Jensen distinguish controversial public welfare arguments ('policy') from the 'entrenched values' underlying the common law. But there seems a fine line between the impermissible 'short-term, political, and socio-economic [policy] considerations' and 'deeply held and deeply

---

[61] *Michael* (n 19).
[62] *McFarlane v Tayside Health Board* [2000] 2 AC 59.
[63] *A v A Health & Social Services Trust* [2010] NIQB 108; ch 8, 'Wrongful Race?'.
[64] GC Keating, 'Form and Substance in the "Private Law" of Torts' (2021) 14 *Jo Tort L* 45.
[65] Grantham and Jensen (n 51) 192.
[66] ibid 191.

seated societal values ... that constitute the relevant society' (the foundation of the common law).⁶⁷

Grantham and Jensen suggest that the latter are uncontroversial or at least less controversial, being deep-rooted in legal principle and long accepted. But such values have to be stated in very abstract terms. Consider 'liberalism and autonomy' that are said to underlie common law doctrine (eg a preference for private ordering over state-imposed obligations, and hostility towards positive duties to rescue). What 'liberalism and autonomy' actually mean or entail is surely controversial. Particularly when we descend (as the courts must) from the general theoretical level to apply such values to resolve concrete disputes. This involves choices between values. Value-laded choices cannot be apolitical. No doubt the courts are required to pay careful attention to values that have long been legally recognised. Stable legal development requires this. But values evolve and are frequently in tension with one another. If courts can be trusted with these kinds of value choices, why not others? A concern with Grantham and Jensen's approach is that they conceive the common law as incapable of adapting to changing social conditions. They praise the essential conservatism of the judicial role. But a static common law would be in danger of ever-decreasing relevance – and statutory replacement.

Indeed another difficulty with 'pure corrective justice' is its implication for tort *statutes*. Even if we accepted that tort *adjudication* must concern itself exclusively with the parties' rights and ignore wider public interests, Parliament surely cannot be subject to the same prohibition. Let us imagine a well-founded public concern that tort was producing certain socially undesirable effects. On the corrective justice view, such concerns would be entirely irrelevant. Even if convincingly demonstrated by empirical evidence, the court should ignore them. It would 'alien' to justice between the parties. (That is not the current approach.)⁶⁸ But if *courts* refused to entertain such arguments, heeding Lord Scarman's famous call,⁶⁹ *statutory* interventions in tort law would inevitably become more common. It cannot be constitutionally inappropriate for the legislature to consider general welfare, and legitimate public concern about tort liability. Indeed Lord Scarman's whole point was that such questions are better considered in the legislature rather than the courts. They would not be removed from tort law entirely, but enter via a different constitutional route: yet there is no sound reason to exclude statutory liabilities from our definitions of tort.⁷⁰

Statute has growing importance across the common law world. Grantham and Jensen accept that 'statutory private law' involves a wider impact of public policy.⁷¹ Beever blames this trend on *judicial* policy arguments. If negligence

---

⁶⁷ ibid 192.
⁶⁸ Eg *Tomlinson v Congleton BC* [2004] 1 AC 46 (negative effect on public amenity).
⁶⁹ *McLoughlin v O'Brian* [1983] 1 AC 410, 429–31 (see ch 9, 'Alcock Rules: Rights-Based Critique').
⁷⁰ J Murphy, 'The Heterogeneity of Tort Law' (2019) 39 *OJLS* 455, 467.
⁷¹ Grantham and Jensen (n 51) 187, fn14.

is shaped by policy concerns 'one could hardly blame the legislature for questioning the policies of the courts and substituting their own ... policy preferences [for those] of non-elected judges'.[72] Certainly, Parliament is entitled to take a different view. But does it really follow, as Beever seems to imply, that if the courts declined to take policy arguments into account the legislature would equally be disabled from taking a different, *policy-informed* view about the limits of liability? To suggest that corrective justice should be immune from legislative reform in the public interested is extraordinary – and untenable given parliamentary sovereignty. It contradicts Lord Scarman's view that policy should be avoided in *common law* adjudication – to leave it to the legislature.

To conclude, 'purified' common law would institute a sharp divide between judicially developed and statutory tort law – and contribute to the common law being superseded by policy-informed legislation. Stapleton queries whether the constitutional division of labour proposed by Lord Scarman and corrective justice theorists is really workable. Given the practical limits on parliamentary interventions about tort doctrine, the chance of unsatisfactory decisions would be high. When courts take wider public concerns into account it gives 'critical effectiveness' to the lawmaking partnership. Stapleton also argues that as the rules emerging from common law decisions effect everyone, not only the immediate parties to the litigation, courts are constitutionally required to take the wider public interest into account.[73]

Policy and Legal Certainty

Critiques of 'unsystematic' policy reasoning praise the clarity and unity of a justice-based 'principled' law of tort. Accepting that policy concerns introduce significant uncertainty, could it be tolerable and even desirable? Given the huge variability of negligence claims, how could it be otherwise? Tort law constantly faces new questions. Sometimes this is attributable to new ways of harming people, or new interests that might be 'harmed' – possibilities that open up with technological advances (such as the development of reliable contraceptive and reproductive-assisting techniques). Sometimes claims are brought when, for reasons of social convention or morality, it would in the past simply have been unthinkable to do so. Negligence 'needs to have the flexibility to respond to these [novel claims], and hence there is a degree of unavoidable uncertainty on its outer boundaries'.[74]

On this view, the supposed simple clarity of corrective justice stunts legal development and may anyway be an illusion. (We have already suggested that wider social/moral views are part of the determination of rights required by

---

[72] Beever (n 37) 8.

[73] J Stapleton, *Three Essays on Torts* (Oxford, Oxford University Press, 2021) 29–32.

[74] DJ Ibbetson, 'How the Romans Did for Us: Ancient Roots of the Tort of Negligence' (2003) 26 *UNSWLJ* 475, 475.

corrective justice accounts.) Legal certainty is obviously important. Yet (as Einstein apparently said) we should strive to make an explanation as simple as it can be – but no simpler. 'Pure' accounts risk over-simplification, attempting to answer a variety of complex questions using one formula such as 'reasonable foreseeability'. It would be nice if such a concept gave all the answers. But arguably it cannot. And even if it could, some (like Roderick Bagshaw) express 'a clear preference for a law of torts which can do good, ahead of a law of torts that can be straightforwardly explained'.[75] That is, Bagshaw doubts whether 'coherence' should be one of tort's primary goals, and questions whether 'preserving the explanatory power of a theory is a sufficient reasons for disregarding the consequences … for the welfare of human beings'.[76]

Defenders of policy argue that uncertainty can be managed, although not eliminated. The central recommendation is that courts must reason openly and consistently. Jane Stapleton's work exemplifies this approach. She urges courts to 'eschew the incantation of formulaic labels as devices for determining [duty of care]'.[77] Instead they must acknowledge all the substantive factors counting for and against liability, explaining why on balance they justify the court's decision. Stapleton 'unmasks' a (non-exhaustive!) list of 50 policy factors found in duty decisions – not all of them cogent on analysis. Australian law has followed this method (no under Professor Stapleton's influence). In 2009 the President of the NSW Court of Appeal listed 17 separate policy factors in a judgment on duty of care – 'a non-exhaustive universe of considerations'.[78]

For Beever, Stapleton's long and debateable 'menu' exemplifies the uncertainty of negligence law 'awash with policy considerations'.[79] However Stapleton attempts to build stability into her approach. Courts must display 'caution in relation to departing too radically from past judicial weightings of substantive policy factors'.[80] Of course courts acknowledge the need for such consistency. It would do the law no credit if later judges regularly rejected earlier decisions because they would have weighed the policy considerations differently.[81] In Lord Nicholls's opinion, while judges should not claim 'any special insight into what contemporary society regards as fair and reasonable, … their legal expertise enables them to promote a desirable degree of consistency from one

---

[75] R Bagshaw, 'Tort Law, Concepts and What Really Matters' in A Robertson and TH Wu (eds), *The Goals of Private Law* (Oxford, Hart, 2009) 259.
[76] ibid 256.
[77] J Stapleton, 'Duty of Care Factors: A Selection from the Judicial Menus' in P Cane and J Stapleton (eds), *The Law of Obligations: Essays in Celebration of John Fleming* (Oxford, Oxford University Press, 1998) 89.
[78] *Caltex Refineries (Qld) Pty Ltd v Stavar* [2009] NSWCA 258, [103]–[104] (Allsop P).
[79] Beever (n 37) 3–5.
[80] Stapleton (n 77) 90.
[81] Eg *Rees v Darlington NHS Trust* [2004] 1 AC 309 [7] (Lord Bingham), [33] (Lord Steyn).

case or type of case to the next'.[82] One judicial advocate of the Australian policy-weighing approach emphasised the importance of precedent as a counterweight. Reasoning from past cases 'imposes a necessary discipline upon the examination of policy factors'.[83]

The factors stabilising the common law generally extend to judicial policy reasoning in particular. Andrew Robertson emphasises these constraints.[84] Windeyer J denied that judges can impose their personal view of social interests: they act 'in company and not alone', guided by precedent and other 'authoritative pronouncements'.[85] Robertson agrees that these institutional features have a 'powerful stabilising influence' on policy reasoning.[86] As he notes, this moderate view has rather been overlooked in the polarised disputes about policy. On each side, theorists have tended to envisage unconstrained, free-ranging policy reasoning by the courts. But whether viewed (by 'instrumentalists') as beneficial or condemned (by corrective justice theorists) as illegitimate, each side exaggerates the true degree of judicial activism. This has overheated the policy debate.

Banning policy reasoning could prove counterproductive, unsettling judicial decision-making. Jenny Steele, considering leading 1990s' duty cases, argued that the courts' reluctance to debate policy openly made the law uncertain.[87] In Steele's view, the courts' unwillingness to acknowledge the influence of policy precluded public scrutiny of the court's reasons and impeded debate about the limits of negligence liability. It was left to the judges' 'untested assumptions'. Instead, judges advanced ostensibly principled reasons (such as 'lack of proximity') while simultaneously acknowledging that these labels were 'empty and meaningless'.[88] The courts' commitment to formal, doctrinal reasoning was 'strong enough to survive severe doubts about the possibility of the whole enterprise'. Steele characterised the resulting law of negligence as 'a partnership between exhausted principle and obscured pragmatism'.[89]

The point about transparency is of considerable constitutional importance. Also, as Llewellyn put it in a different context, 'Covert tools are never reliable tools'.[90] Certainty and constitutional concerns alike demand transparent judicial reasoning.

---

[82] ibid [14].

[83] *Crimmins v Stevedoring Industry Finance Committee* [1999] HCA 59, [77] (McHugh J).

[84] A Robertson, 'Constraints on Policy-Based Reasoning in Private Law' in A Robertson and TH Wu (eds), *The Goals of Private Law* (Oxford, Hart, 2009).

[85] *Mount Isa Mines v Pusey* (1970) 125 CLR 383, 396.

[86] Robertson (n 84) 270.

[87] J Steele, 'Scepticism and the Law of Negligence' [1993] *CLJ* 437.

[88] eg *Caparo*'s 'authoritative judicial statement that some of the principles which are applied in the law of negligence actually *have no content*' (Steele ibid 438, original emphasis).

[89] ibid 466.

[90] K Llewellyn, 'Book Review' (1939) 52 *Harvard LR* 700, 703.

Policy, Evidence and Judicial Capacity

Another aspect of the critique regards court process as ill-equipped to deal with policy. By contrast with legislative and government bodies, courts lack relevant information, cannot carry out public consultation and do not have the expertise to evaluate policy arguments. These are important points. They show the need for considerable caution before relying on policy arguments.

There are far too many examples of courts announcing unconvincing policies.[91] They frequently make essentially empirical claims (such as the prediction that liability would be 'uninsurable') without supporting evidence. The supposedly 'uninsurable' liability of the defendant auditor's was relied on to deny liability in *Caparo v Dickman*. The House of Lords' acceptance of the argument contrasts with the more properly sceptical approach below. Bingham and Taylor LJJ had dismissed the defendant's uninsurability argument because there was no evidence to support it.[92] Later courts have, from time to time, similarly refused to speculate about essentially empirical claims advanced in argument without firm proof.[93]

A sceptical stance towards poorly evidenced arguments is entirely appropriate. If the courts rigorously reject unevidenced ('speculative') arguments, it would encourage litigants to present robust data about, for example, insurance practice (to use the *Caparo* example) in support of their submissions. The courts could also permit interventions by a wider range of interested parties, and have started to do so. In *Michael v Chief Constable of South Wales*, the leading case on police duties to those at risk from violent crime, groups campaigning for victims of domestic violence intervened in the Supreme Court.[94] The interveners and claimant used government statistics to show the 'horrifying' levels of such crimes.[95]

The proper way to deal with speculative submissions is to insist on hard evidence to back them up. It would throw the baby out with the bathwater to exclude *all* policy concerns. That would mean the exclusion of well-evidenced or incontrovertible arguments which are cogent according to usual standards of proof in civil litigation. One straightforward way to improve the quality of judicial decision-making would be for court-appointed experts to assist the judge in explaining the known or likely effect of liability on a given organisation or activity.[96]

There is also a small but gradually increasing corpus of empirical studies of the impact of tort liability. These could inform evidence-based policy

---

[91] See Stapleton (n 77).
[92] [1989] QB 653, 689, 703.
[93] *Perret v Collins* [1998] 2 Lloyd's Rep 255.
[94] Refuge against Domestic Violence and Ferched Cymru (Welsh Women's Aid).
[95] [2015] AC 1732, 1738. Cf [118] (Lord Toulson).
[96] J Hartshorne et al, '*Caparo* Under Fire: A Study into the Effects upon the Fire Service of Liability in Negligence' (2000) *MLR* 502, 520.

reasoning. However, such studies tend to stress the difficulty of predicting the effects of liability. The prospect of tort litigation might cause different changes in practice (positive, negative or neutral) in different organisations, or at different levels (eg management or 'front line' workers).[97] Paula Case reaches the ('undoubtedly disappointing') conclusion that 50 years' research into doctors' reactions to tort liability has found no reliable evidence for a 'linear relationship between negligence liability and harmful defensive practice'.[98] She cautions against courts adopting the opposite 'instinctual reaction' (ie that liability *improves* standards of medical care). This equally lacks empirical evidence. Alysia Blackham argues persuasively that using empirical evidence in place of 'common sense' intuitions could improve decisions.[99] However, courts would need to give such evidence careful scrutiny to ensure its quality and objectivity. The current 'ad hoc, unprincipled, and unpredictable engagement with empirical evidence' needs significant improvement.[100]

Public law raises a further doubt about the policy critique. In tort cases, it is said, courts are unable to assess policy questions owing to judicial inexperience and lack of information. Yet in judicial review (especially Human Rights Act) claims, courts are frequently required to assess the cogency of government policy and the appropriateness ('proportionality') of its implementation, weighed against intrusive effects on individual rights and civil liberties.[101] There is no separate public law judiciary. The same judges sit in both the Administrative Court and the Queen's Bench Division. If they are constitutionally required to adjudicate on public policy in the administrative law jurisdiction, those judges cannot suddenly become incapable of such adjudication in tort claims. A New Zealand case holds accordingly that while courts should be cautious about recognising tort duties that involve 'polycentric' questions of 'competing social, economic, political and scientific considerations', this cannot not be *determinative* against a duty of care when courts often assess policy by considering expert evidence, 'particularly in relation to matters such as human rights'.[102]

Defenders of the policy approach must accept that many policy arguments are controversial. Take the efficient allocation of risks. Is it more efficient to place risks on owners of property (to take out first-party insurance against its loss) or those who may damage the property (ie third party/liability insurance)? Courts should tread warily here. As Clarke notes, the matter has been debated inconclusively for over a century between the key stakeholders in the

---

[97] ibid (fire brigades' reaction to *Capital & Counties v Hampshire CC* [1997] QB 1004).

[98] P Case, 'The Jaded Cliche of "Defensive Medical Practice": From Magically Convincing to Empirically (Un)convincing?' (2020) 36 *Prof Neg* 49.

[99] A Blackham, 'Legitimacy and Empirical Evidence in the UK Courts' (2016) 25 *Griffith LR* 414.

[100] ibid 435–36.

[101] Stapleton (n 73) 30.

[102] *Smith v Attorney-General* [2022] NZHC 1693 [136]–[146].

shipping industry (cargo-owners and shipowners).[103] Should such contested matters be left to expert government bodies, as policy sceptics suggest? Beever puts it forcefully: why do taxpayers pay significant sums to support government policy-making if judges are free to make such decisions without the benefit of such expert advice?[104]

There is again good sense behind Beever's objection. Courts do not have the researchers and advisers that characterise ministerial decision-making. But while courts cannot undertake their own policy research, they can require that parties present evidence to support policy-based arguments (as suggested above). Nor should we idealise government policy-making to reject 'inadequate' judicial decisions. The Law Commission, for example, rarely undertakes empirical research even when highly relevant to its inquiry.[105] Perhaps the Commission lacks the resources (staff numbers and skill-sets) to undertake social-scientific research into real-world costs and behavioural effects of existing laws and its proposed reforms. The fact remains that the government's own statutory advisor on law reform seems little better placed to assess policy arguments on the basis of rigorous empirical evidence than are the courts.

Whether in the Law Commission, in Whitehall or in judicial decisions, it is unrealistic to expect incontrovertible demonstration of the superiority of any given policy argument. Often they cut across each other, and deciding which prevails requires judgement. Some things are theoretically capable of empirical measurement (such as the effect of tort liability on insurance premiums or defendant behaviour). But studies into such complex economic or behavioural questions have inherent limits (real-world studies have too many independent variables; 'laboratory' studies are unrealistic simulations; and any study may generalise incorrectly from an atypical sample). Courts (and others) must not claim certainty where it does not exist. But more modest claims may be defensible.

In the well-known controversy about whether tort liability causes 'defensive administration', it is hard to make firm predictions about the effect on public authority (or other) defendants. The evidence is either entirely absent or, if it exists, equivocal. The argument has certainly had a chequered career, reflecting this absence of clear evidence. Lord Reid declared that even if American courts were concerned about 'defensive' reactions to liability, English judges should ignore it since (according to his experience) 'Her Majesty's servants are made of sterner stuff'.[106] But Lord Keith's intuition was precisely the opposite, fearing in a much-cited remark that police liability for failing

---

[103] M Clarke, *Policies and Perceptions of Insurance Law in the Twenty-First Century* (Oxford, Oxford University Press, 2005) 325–30.
[104] Beever (n 37) 174.
[105] cf Law Com CP 187, *Administrative Redress: Public Bodies and the Citizen* (2008), Appendix B (review of others' (patchy) empirical studies).
[106] *Dorset Yacht v Home Office* [1970] AC 1004, 1033.

to arrest dangerous criminals could produce 'a detrimentally defensive frame of mind'.[107]

Abolishing the immunity previously enjoyed by advocates, Lord Steyn dismissed the argument that this could compromise the advocate's paramount duty to the court. It had 'a most flimsy foundation, unsupported by empirical evidence'.[108] The Supreme Court has also found 'force' in criticisms made of 'defensive policing' as a prediction about behaviour lacking hard evidence ('the court has no way of judging the likely operational consequence').[109] However Lord Toulson seemed to accept that the prospect of negligence liability could affect police priorities for fighting crime, which would be damaging to the public interest. The one *certain* consequence was that liability would place greater pressure on constrained police budgets.[110] Departing from the majority view in *Robinson v Chief Constable*, Lord Hughes said that while the risk of defensive policing might 'technically' lack 'hard evidence', 'I for my part would regard that risk as inevitable. ... I do not see that it can seriously be doubted that the threat of litigation frequently influences [behaviour]'.[111]

A lesser but more defensible claim is that liability *threatens* to distort authorities' priorities. This might sound an insufficient reason for denying a claim. But a plausible threat of a severely negative impact might justify caution. A directly analogous idea is the 'precautionary principle' in environmental policy. A credible threat of irreparable environmental damage justifies action being taken to address it. In this most vital area of public policymaking the global community does not remain scrupulously neutral, pending conclusive demonstration of environmental catastrophe. Perhaps the future of the planet is a special case. But the 'precautionary principle' is one way to approach uncertain but potentially grave social harm. An analogous approach could be taken to negligence law.

Finally, we could challenge the argument that judges lack sufficient expertise to assess policy. As noted, they constantly do this in their public law role. Another point is that through the Law Commissions, many senior judges have direct personal experience of governmental law reform.[112] The potential limits of Law Commission procedure have been noted, but nobody denies that the Commissions rightly assess policy arguments when formulating proposals. More broadly, all trial judges are expert at deciding controversial issues of fact and it is not clear why the evidential difficulties that policy reasoning clearly involves should fall outside judicial experience.

---

[107] *Hill v Chief Constable of West Yorkshire* [1989] AC 53, 59. See also *Brooks v MPC* [2005] 1 WLR 1495 [30] (Lord Steyn); *Smith v Chief Constable of Sussex* [2009] AC 225 [108] (Lord Carswell).

[108] *JS Hall & Co v Simons* [2002] AC 615, 682.

[109] *Michael* (n 19) [121] (Lord Toulson).

[110] ibid [122].

[111] *Robinson* (n 18) [112] (see similarly *Smith* (n 102) [132] (Lord Brown: 'inevitable')).

[112] For example among the panel in *Michael v Chief Constable*, Baroness Hale, Lord Toulson and Lord Hodge had all previously served as (English or Scottish) Law Commissioners.

It has also been deemed *constitutionally improper* for unelected judges to decide public policy. Various responses are possible. First, judges do not have the power of government and legislature to rewrite the law at will, according to their personal vision of the public good.[113] We have noted that the usual common law constraints apply to judicial policy reasoning. The relevant 'policies' must be accepted collectively and applied consistently by judges, as the case-law develops. As HLA Hart observed, everyone holding 'responsible public office' is constrained to exercise discretion with regard to that office, not by 'indulg[ing] fancy or mere whim'.[114] Suggesting (as Beever does) that judges act on unconstrained personal intuitions exaggerates their discretion.

It is of course true that judges do not stand for election. But they are instead accountable through the duty to give reasons. A court which cannot satisfactorily explain its decision will rightly be criticised and vulnerable to overruling. This constraint again applies to policy reasoning. It may indeed apply with particular force given policy's contestable nature and potential to unsettle the law. Idiosyncratic or inconsistent policy reasoning will be especially scrutinised. It is true that this scrutiny occurs within the 'legal world'. The fine points of judicial reasoning are rarely debated by the general public. But the legal community, while unrepresentative, is expert. Lawyers are trained to expose weak arguments. This forms a major deterrent against courts 'going rogue' and transforming themselves into some kind of surrogate legislature. It is implausible to suggest that courts commonly exceed their constitutional function, notwithstanding the widespread acceptance of policy reasoning in tort law.

In conclusion, while there are clearly dangers in policy reasoning, these could be exaggerated. Rejecting the argument that when tort and regulation intersect tort law should *necessarily* defer to the 'expertise of regulators', Nolan argues that 'When it comes to institutional competence, ... an elite and well-resourced judiciary serviced by high-quality lawyers and experts [as witnesses] may be more than a match for a regulator'.[115] The court may be better placed to weight the policy concerns (undertaking 'a more thorough evaluation of the evidence than a regulator struggling to perform a multitude of tasks with limited resources'); courts are by definition objective and independent of 'sectoral interests'.[116]

The Politics of Corrective Justice

We could also question how uncontroversial (and constitutionally unproblematic) the rival corrective justice approach is. Corrective justice avoids contestable

---

[113] Cf B Cardozo, *The Nature of The Judicial Process* (New Haven CT, Yale University Press, 1921) 141 ('The judge is not the knight-errant, roaming at will in pursuit of his own ideal of beauty or of goodness').

[114] HLA Hart, 'Discretion' (2013) 127 *Harvard LR* 652, 657.

[115] D Nolan, 'Tort and Regulation' in J Goudkamp et al (eds), *Taking Law Seriously: Essays in Honour of Peter Cane* (Oxford, Hart, 2021) 202.

[116] ibid.

public welfare arguments – overtly at least. But the definition of rights has important distributive consequences.

For example, negligence law's tenderness towards physical property damage and unreceptiveness to 'pure economic loss'. This gives much greater protection to those with wealth in traditional forms such as land, and less to those dependent on (for example) investment funds or pensions. Not to mention less advantaged social groups whose entitlement to government support has been hailed as 'the new property' (ie a significant new form of wealth).[117] But this is not the traditional *physical* property that tort law protects so strongly. Also those who depend on public services rather than making their own private arrangements (consider: schooling, health care) are clearly disadvantaged by rules restricting claims in tort law which do not apply to (paying) customers suing in contract.[118] The differences between contract and tort can be justified in abstract doctrinal terms. But the effect may be socially regressive.

We have noted Grantham and Jensen's praise for the stability of the 'conservative' common law, developing slowly and in line with the 'deep ideology' of longstanding social values. For groups who feel historically marginalised and disadvantaged, this 'stability' could be criticised for perpetuating discriminatory effects of the law's foundational structure. This is explored further in the following two chapters: tort law's stuttering protection against fertility-related injuries, mental health and emotional distress has systematically disadvantaged women. It is a longstanding mistake of common lawyers to view its basis as neutral and apolitical[119] – by contrast with government regulation which is political on its face, or even partisan. Yet the common law 'baseline' of entitlements is not 'part of nature'.[120]

This point has been forcefully made against corrective justice theories. Beever calls his revisionist account 'a leap forward in our understanding of the law. Or, rather, a very welcome leap backwards'.[121] Critics allege this would not be politically neutral. Dan Priel argues that putting the clock back goes beyond Beever's admitted *legal* conservatism; 'the arguments invoked bear a clear and distinct mark of right-wing political ideology'.[122] Specifically, such arguments ignore the dramatic growth of state agencies and their vital social functions in the course of the twentieth century. To find private property rights 'self-evident' but to dismiss claims against the state takes the ideological position of Conservative philosophers like Hayek or Scruton. This is clearly both political and contestable. Priel accepts that those he criticises (Robert Stevens,

---

[117] CA Reich, 'The New Property' (1964) 73 *Yale LJ* 733.

[118] eg *Woodland v Swimming Teachers Association* [2014] AC 537 [25] (Lord Sumption), [31] (Baroness Hale).

[119] See further L Fox O'Mahony, 'Property Outsiders and the Hidden Politics of Doctrinalism' [2014] *CLP* 409 (see ch 10, 'Purity and Transparency').

[120] CR Sunstein, '*Lochner's* Legacy' (1987) 87 *Columbia LR* 873.

[121] Beever (n 37) 32.

[122] D Priel, 'Torts, Rights, and Right-Wing Ideology' (2011) 19 *Torts LJ* 1.

Nicholas McBride and Roderick Bagshaw) might be reporting accurately the 'individualistic' values of the common law. But 'they are messengers who try to hide their message, for what they should have told us is that the underlying structure of English tort law is not politically neutral, despite its attempts to present itself as such'. Priel's conclusion is that corrective justice theories present a deeply political thesis while attempting to preclude any discussion of it: the necessary debate 'cannot be properly conducted if one side insists it is not part of the debate and that its views can be shown to be true as a result of pure legal or conceptual analysis'.

Policy: Conclusions

Contemporary arguments against policy divide into two kinds. First, claims that would logically preclude policy reasoning altogether. It is said to be conceptually inconsistent with the basis of tort law. Secondly are diverse arguments suggesting that policy arguments are harmful to the judicial process. Policy is said to be unsettling, procedurally questionable, and constitutionally improper. These arguments do not necessarily entail that policy reasoning is incompatible with tort law. A less drastic solution, such as more rigorous and cautious assessment of policy by the courts, might be found.

As seen, the first argument claims that, at heart, tort is about corrective/inter-personal justice. Concerns about public welfare are extrinsic to the claimant's rights against the defendant, and the defendant's correlative duty to the claimant. Thus such 'alien' policy must be excluded from reasoning about tort. If it succeeds this argument proves that policy reasoning is *necessarily improper*. But decisions about rights and duties are arguably informed by the public interest. Even if enforcing rights is purely a matter of inter-personal justice, deciding what those rights should be in the first place has important distributional consequences. Should not society's view on what we owe to each other legitimately inform such decisions? Indeed how else could they be settled? Even if rights-based reasoning could take place in a vacuum, what if the outcome harms the public interest? While courts could be ordered to ignore public concerns as irrelevant to corrective justice, surely the public themselves (and their representative in Parliament) cannot be prohibited from raising such concerns. And in Parliament's case, legislating to give effect to the public interest. Arguably then, corrective justice can only be a project to purify *judicial* reasoning from the taint of policy. But if that took place, the common law would rapidly be subject to an ever-increasing raft of statutory reform. It would accelerate the process noted by Sir Jack Beatson whereby, as statutes correct its defects (through 'legislative microsurgery'), 'the core of pure common law doctrine continues to shrink'.[123]

---

[123] J Beatson, 'Has the Common Law a Future?' [1997] *CLJ* 291, 301.

176 GREAT DEBATES IN TORT LAW

The contrary view is that as tort law is ultimately a branch of state power whose rules affect the freedoms, entitlements and wealth of all members of society, it is entirely proper that public welfare concerns should be taken into account. In negligence, the duty of care is the primary, categorical boundary of liability. On this view, the duty inquiry rightly incorporates policy concerns.

Even if this is correct, other aspects of the policy critique indicate caution. Policy arguments are undeniably contentious, which threatens legal certainty. The judicial process is not the optimal forum for debating questions of public welfare. The ideal process would involve rigorous expert research into the potential economic and other social impact, following wide public consultation. But that is not so much ideal as Utopian. Parliament, the government and the Law Commission all fail to meet this high standard for policy-making too. Instead of attacking the judicial process for being suboptimal it would be more fruitful to improve its handling of policy concerns. Too frequently, English courts' policy reasoning has been slapdash. The volatile history of 'defensive administration' is a notorious example. In the absence of concrete evidence, courts have expressed different intuitions about its plausibility. Courts should only accept cogent, suitably-evidenced policy concerns.

A balanced conclusion could be: 'keep policy, but do it better'. Yet concerns about uncertainty remain. Weinrib raises an important challenge. He argues that the balancing public policy concerns against individual rights/justice is impossible. The two are *incommensurable*. Policy reasoning puts two different normative currencies into circulation with no rate of exchange between them.[124] Weinrib invokes the satirical attempt to judge a poetry competition by physically weighing the verses in a pair of scales![125] Beever agrees it is 'farcical' to expect judges to weigh justice against public welfare.[126]

Direct comparisons between policy and justice are difficult. They cannot simply be weighed up mechanically. But that is a familiar problem in law. Individual rights may also conflict. Here though, corrective justice theorists (like Stevens) accept that the proper resolution of such conflicts requires judgement from the courts.[127] Why should a similar judicial approach not mediate the conflict between rights and public policy? Such judgements have to be made continually by the legislature – and potentially by *courts* when reviewing legislation's compatibility with the ECHR, which requires balancing between individual and general-public interests on its face. Is the foundation of human rights and civil liberties across Europe also a farce, the butt of a satirical joke?

Corrective justice theorists identify a real problem (incommensurability) but exaggerate it – for it would not only rule out policy reasoning in tort, but

---

[124] Weinrib (n 39) 168.
[125] ibid fn 87 (Aristophanes' *Frogs*).
[126] Beever (n 37) 174.
[127] R Stevens, 'The Conflict of Rights' in A Robertson and HW Tang (eds), *The Goals of Private Law* (Oxford, Hart, 2009).

preclude human rights law and the core function of the legislature. Nevertheless policy's defenders cannot wish its difficulties away. Robertson's approach to duty questions, allocating interpersonal justice and public policy to different stages of the inquiry, provides a structure to approach the problem.[128] But there are genuine choices to be made. These have distributional effects and may be intensely controversial. Ultimately, such political choices are better made in the open than (as many fear) covertly under a supposedly 'policy free' approach. Should the courts make the wrong choices, the legislature can intervene to enlarge or restrict liability as representative of the public interest. This role fits naturally into the policy-inclusive view of tort law; for corrective justice, legislation is either dubiously legitimate or not properly part of 'tort law' at all.

Debate 3
'Incrementalism'

The law on duty of care develops by analogy with decided cases. Of course it does: in the same way as the rest of the common law. The observation seems thoroughly banal. Yet the courts think it meaningful. This apparently trivial point about incremental legal development receives considerable judicial emphasis. At times 'incrementalism' has been elevated into a distinct 'test' for duty for duty of care. The stress placed upon it has tended to come and go – greater prominence for incrementalism coinciding with judicial loss of confidence in rival approaches. As courts have grown wary of general tests for duty of care and (more recently) about policy reasoning, so they have emphasised the vital importance of analogical development.

However its usefulness has been questioned. One objection (as seen) is that 'incrementalism' is just a label for what courts are doing anyway, because reasoning by analogy is inherent in the common law process. A second objection is that strict adherence to precedent is too restrictive. If it rules out significant new duties of care, it stultifies negligence law's capacity to adapt to new situations (eg new technology). It also appears incompatible with some of the most celebrated leading cases which boldly established *new* kinds of liability. (Hence for their fame.) Conversely, a looser conception of precedent can provide little constraint on the courts and ultimately (it is claimed) no real structure for the duty of care. In this Debate we consider the extent to which incrementalism is a useful guide, test or approach for duty of care questions – assessing it against criticisms of banality, undue strictness, or obscuring the underlying questions of substance.

Fashion and Incrementalism

Over the last century incrementalism waxed and waned – popular in inverse proportion to wider sweeping approaches to the duty of care. Before *Donoghue*

---

[128] Robertson (n 32).

v Stevenson, negligence was broken down into a complex list of individual *duties* of care (emphasis on the plural). Ibbetson describes the late nineteenth century law of duties as 'overwhelmingly detailed'; in 1928, on the eve of *Donoghue*, the leading work in negligence still used 'nearly all' of its 1500 pages to describe the law on duties of care.[129] It was against this backdrop that Lord Atkin set out his famous 'general conception' of the duty of care, the neighbour principle. But, James Plunkett explains, the courts did not change their approach overnight.[130] Numerous stubborn areas of non-liability for foreseeable harm persisted after *Donoghue v Stevenson*, despite the 'neighbour principle' being satisfied.[131] Landon declared in 1941 that a duty of care should arise only where the wisdom of our ancestors had decreed it.[132] This is a flowery way of demanding strict adherence to precedent. Admittedly, Landon had unusually pronounced views. His dislike of *Donoghue v Stevenson* was so great that he dismissed its 'Celtic ideology' (an apparent reference to the two Scots and a Welshman who comprised the majority, respectively Lords Macmillan and Thankerton, and Lord Atkin himself)![133]

One by one the bastions of non-liability fell: for example, in the 1960s, *Hedley Byrne v Heller* (negligent statements)[134] and *Herrington v British Rail* (duties to trespassers).[135] The full significance of Lord Atkin's idea was belatedly accepted by the courts. Lord Reid's speech in *Dorset Yacht v Home Office* marks the turning point:

> About the beginning of [the 20th] century most eminent lawyers thought that there were a number of separate torts involving negligence, each with its own rules, and they were most unwilling to add more. They were of course aware from a number of leading cases that in the past the courts had from time to time recognised new duties and new grounds of action. But the heroic age was over; it was time to cultivate certainty and security in the law: the categories of negligence were virtually closed. The Attorney-General [counsel for the defendants] invited us to return to those halcyon days, but, attractive though it may be, I cannot accede to his invitation.

---

[129] DJ Ibbetson, '"The Law of Business Rome": Foundations of the Anglo-American Tort of Negligence' [1999] *CLP* 74 (citing T Beven, *Negligence in Law* 4th edn (London, Sweet & Maxwell, 1928)).

[130] J Plunkett, *The Duty of Care in Negligence* (Oxford, Hart, 2018) 36–43.

[131] Its limits still demand judicial attention: for example climate change is not one of the 'watershed moments in the development of the law such as *Donoghue v Stevenson* where courageous Judges were prepared to extend the existing law in order to address a significant problem'; 'radical change' in negligence liability would violate 'the common law tradition … of incremental development': *Smith v Fonterra Co-operative Group Ltd* [2021] NZCA 552 [14]–[15] (French J).

[132] (1941) 57 *LQR* 179, 183 (further declaring at 181: 'There is no universal test by which to decide whether the duty to take care exists; each set of facts must be brought within its appropriate category').

[133] PA Landon (1945) 61 *LQR* 203, 206.

[134] [1964] AC 465.

[135] [1972] AC 877.

In later years there has been a steady trend towards regarding the law of negligence as depending on principle so that, when a new point emerges, one should ask not whether it is covered by authority but whether recognised principles apply to it. *Donoghue v Stevenson* may be regarded as a milestone, and the well-known passage in Lord Atkin's speech should I think be regarded as a statement of principle. It is not to be treated as if it were a statutory definition. It will require qualification in new circumstances. But I think that the time has come when we can and should say that it ought to apply unless there is some justification or valid explanation for its exclusion.[136]

In *Anns v Merton London Borough Council* Lord Wilberforce based his influential approach on a 'trilogy' of leading cases (*Donoghue*, *Hedley Byrne* and *Dorset Yacht*). '[It] is not necessary to bring the facts ... within those of previous situations in which a duty of care has been held to exist'. The court first asked whether it was *foreseeable* that the defendant's conduct could harm the claimant. If so, secondly, 'whether there are any considerations which ought to negative, or to reduce or limit the scope of the [prima facie] duty or the class of person to whom it is owed or the damages to which a breach of it may give rise'.[137]

Anns was explosively controversial. It involved a local authority failing to exercise statutory its powers to prevent incompetent house-builders inflicting economic loss on the plaintiff. Treble caution is required given (1) the identity of the defendant (a public authority), (2) the kind of loss (purely economic), (3) inflicted by an omission (to supervise the negligent builders). A decade later *Caparo v Dickman* famously rejected Lord Wilberforce's general approach to duty of care. The 'three stage test' has been analysed in the first Debate. Lord Bridge also said that a better guide to the scope of duty of care came from 'the more traditional categorisation of distinct and recognisable situations'.[138] Lord Roskill emphatically agreed. If *Caparo* 'involves a return to the traditional categorisation of cases as pointing to the existence and scope of any duty of care ... I think this is infinitely preferable to recourse to somewhat wide generalisations which leave their practical application matters of difficulty and uncertainty'.[139] Their Lordships approvingly cited *Anns*' repudiation in the Australian case *Sutherland Shire Council v Heyman*:

> the law should develop novel categories of negligence incrementally and by analogy with established categories, rather than by a massive extension of a prima facie duty of care restrained only by indefinable 'considerations which ought to negative, or to reduce or limit the scope of the duty or the class of person to whom it is owed'.[140]

---

[136] [1970] AC 1004, 1026–27.
[137] *Anns v Merton* [1978] AC 728, 751–52.
[138] *Caparo v Dickman* [1990] 2 AC 605, 618.
[139] ibid 605, 628.
[140] (1985) 60 ALR 1, 43–44 (Brennan J).

In the 12 years between *Anns* and *Caparo*, courts were particularly concerned about the expansion of liability for economic loss. *Junior Books v Veichi* is the most notorious case in this respect.[141] (Although never formally overruled, Mance J quipped that *Junior Books* has fallen into 'the slumber of the uniquely distinguished [case]': it is most unlikely ever to be followed.)[142] *Caparo* itself was an unsuccessful economic loss claim. Shortly afterwards, *Murphy v Brentwood District Council* formally overruled *Anns v Merton* on the basis that the claimant suffered purely economic loss and not physical damage, and there was no special relationship of proximity between builders (or building inspectors) and the defective building's ultimate owner.[143] Jane Stapleton was scathing about this reasoning.[144] In its haste to confine liability for pure economic loss, all the highest court could do was assign a case to its correct 'pocket'. A particular absurdity was that while negligent *builders* fell into the *Murphy* and *D&F Estates* 'pocket' and thus owed no duty of care, a *surveyor* who failed to identify the defects in a negligently built house did owe a duty within the *Hedley Byrne* 'pocket' (which governed negligent *statements*).[145]

David Howarth similarly thought the strict precedent argument in *Murphy* and *Caparo* 'extraordinarily weak'. Every established category of negligence must once have been recognised for the first time. But as that crucial first precedent by definition lacks authority, 'The absurd consequence is that every case that declares that a duty of care exists is *ex hypothesi* liable to be overruled at any moment'.[146] The sheer conservatism of the approach appears particularly unfortunate if we accept Howarth's view of the purpose of negligence as a 'pioneer', that is, '[allowing] a relatively freewheeling examination of activities that have not yet been, or perhaps never will be, definitively declared to be beneficial or harmful' (along with 'the possibility of re-opening issues that need to be re-thought').[147] Strict 'incrementalism' would make such a role impossible.

In the decade after *Murphy* the law on economic loss was transformed again, being unified under the banner of the 'extended *Hedley Byrne* principle'. A defendant owes a duty whenever they assume a responsibility to avoid causing economic loss, irrespective of whether the context is a statement (what the defendant said) or a service (what the defendant did).[148] *Customs and Excise Commissioners v Barclays Bank* reviewed the economic loss jurisprudence, and the duty of care more generally. Lord Bingham accepted that duty was more likely to be recognised when the facts closely resembled a case of established liability. Nevertheless he thought the incremental approach 'of little value as a

---

[141] [1983] 1 AC 520.
[142] *The Orjula* [1995] 2 Lloyd's Rep 395.
[143] [1991] 1 AC 398.
[144] J Stapleton, 'Duty of Care and Economic Loss: A Wider Agenda' (1991) 107 *LQR* 249.
[145] *Smith v Eric S Bush* [1990] 1 AC 831.
[146] D Howarth, 'Negligence after *Murphy*: Time to Re-Think' [1991] *CLJ* 58, 70–71.
[147] ibid 93.
[148] *Henderson v Merrett Syndicates Ltd* [1995] 2 AC 145.

test in itself, ... only helpful when used in combination with a test or principle which identifies the legally significant features of a situation'.[149] Lord Mance said the statements in *Caparo* were concerned to reject 'generalised liability for negligently caused economic loss' in particular, rather than to preclude novel duties of care altogether (although accepting that 'caution and analogical reasoning are generally valuable accompaniments to judicial activity').[150] The *Caparo* three-stage approach and (in economic loss cases) assumption of responsibility were both relevant, albeit 'Incrementalism operates as an important cross-check on any other approach'.[151]

Once again, judicial fashions have now changed and incrementalism returned to prominence. According to Lord Reed's influential restatement in *Robinson v Chief Constable of West Yorkshire* precedent is not merely a 'cross-check' on other approaches to duty: to a large degree it precludes them. In Lord Reed's view, *Caparo's* 'whole point' was to re-establish 'an approach based, in the manner characteristic of the common law, on precedent'. Once case law clearly establishes a duty of care (or the absence of a duty) it is 'unnecessary and inappropriate' to consider the merits afresh in later cases. They have been weighed up by the court in establishing the precedent and it would be 'a recipe for inconsistency and uncertainty' to reopen the question in each case. Therefore in 'the ordinary run of cases' the court simply needs to follow the precedents. Lord Reed accepted that where a question is not covered by established authority, the court will need to 'weigh up the reasons for and against imposing liability' – yet even here the starting point is to 'consider the closest analogies in the existing law, with a view to maintaining the coherence of the law and the avoidance of inappropriate distinctions'.[152]

Lord Reed's important judgment reiterates the first principles of common law reasoning. It is not controversial to suggest that *Caparo* (the 'three-stage test') is in some situations irrelevant. It is established that drivers owe duties of care to fellow road-users. So well established as to be unarguably correct. There is no need to go through the three-stage *Caparo* reasoning to demonstrate this. A student who did so in an examination would lose marks for making heavy weather of an obvious point. A lawyer even attempting to argue that a motorist did *not* owe a duty of care would rapidly be stopped by the court, and a judge who questioned the axiom could expect harsh criticism from commentators and senior courts. It would be an elementary howler. Any tort lawyer knows this. So why did Lord Reed need to say it?

Robinson of course goes further.[153] Lord Reed rebuked the Court of Appeal in that case. They had incorrectly invoked *Caparo* to hold, on policy grounds,

---

[149] [2007] 1 AC 181, [7].
[150] ibid [84].
[151] ibid [93] (applied at [111] and [113]).
[152] [2018] AC 736, [21], [26]–[30].
[153] J Morgan, 'Nonfeasance and the End of Policy? Reflections on the Revolution in Public Authority Liability' (2019) 35 *Prof Neg* 32.

that police officers pursuing a suspect owed no duty of care to bystanders present at the scene of the attempted arrest.[154] The Supreme Court reversed this decision. But the majority (led by Lord Reed) did not hold that the Court of Appeal had weighed the policy factors incorrectly. Rather they were wrong to entertain them at all. Precedent showed a duty existed and that was, effectively, the end of the matter.

Lord Reed apparently thought the Court of Appeal had made an elementary blunder, the sort that (as suggested above) no competent tort lawyer would make. Again in *Darnley v Croydon NHS Trust* the Supreme Court held that a duty of care was so well established that the Court of Appeal had been wrong to consider policy reasons counting against liability.[155] It seems remarkable that two different benches of Lords Justices of Appeal should have committed such lapses of basic technique. But perhaps they did not. Plausibly, the Supreme Court had a wider view of 'established liability' in *Robinson* and *Darnley*. It was deployed to avoid the need for policy reasoning – making it seem not just unnecessary but improper. Lord Reed has explained that the 'widespread misunderstanding' of *Caparo* (before he clarified its scope in *Robinson*) meant courts too often considered whether liability would be fair, just and reasonable: but 'in practice [this] led to evaluations of public policy which the courts were not well equipped to conduct in a convincing fashion'.[156] The message seems clear: follow precedent instead of weighing up policy reasons, wherever possible. How realistic is this renewed faith in incrementalism?

Incrementalism: Critique

One common complaint is that strict adherence to precedent is too restrictive. Following the 'retreat from *Anns*' we have noted Stapleton's and Howarth's criticisms of the law. Recovery for pure economic loss depended on fact-based 'pockets' whose normative relevance was hard to understand. If anything one would expect the law to be warier about imposing liability for speech than for actions, but the contrasting results of *Smith v Bush* and *Murphy v Brentwood* stood that concern on its head. Although recovery for economic loss subsequently became more flexible through the 'extended *Hedley Byrne*' principle, *builders*' immunity remains intact. Thus at least one *Murphy*-era 'pocket' of non-liability survives.[157] Stanley Burnton LJ stated: 'it must now be regarded as settled law that the builder/vendor of a building does not by reason of his contract to construct or to complete the building assume any liability in the tort of negligence in relation to defects in the building giving rise to purely economic loss'.[158] More than a trace of the old philosophy.

---

[154] [2014] EWCA Civ 15.
[155] [2019] AC 831.
[156] *GN v Poole Borough Council* [2020] AC 780, [30].
[157] *Robinson v PE Jones (Contractors) Ltd* [2012] QB 44.
[158] ibid [92] citing *D&F Estates* [1989] AC 177, 206.

Such strict adherence to precedent has often been criticised. In an Australian economic loss case Gummow J declared: 'The emergence of a coherent body of precedents will be impeded, not assisted, by the imposition of a fixed system of categories'. Gummow J denied that the courts should seek the 'comfort' of reasoning by analogy from established liabilities.[159] He cited an Irish criticism: a precedent-bound approach 'suffers from a temporal defect – that rights should be determined by the accident of birth'.[160] When declining to recognise a new liability, Sedley LJ seemed troubled by his own conservatism: 'In my mind's ear is the sardonic voice of Professor Cornford who ... set out his celebrated argument for never doing anything for the first time' (in a satire on the (then) reactionary nature of Cambridge University politics).[161] Surely modern tort law should not embody such timidity. In a different context Lord Goff said he was 'startled' by the suggestion that law should be restricted to particular categories. When the jurisdiction is 'founded on a principle of justice' its extension to new categories cannot be foreclosed.[162] In a leading Canadian tort case, McLachlin J stated that acceptance of 'injustice merely for the sake of the doctrinal tidiness' was the 'motivating spirit' of the then-recent English case, *Murphy v Brentwood*. She rejected it for being inconsistent with 'the history of [negligence] which exhibits a sturdy refusal to be confined by arbitrary forms and rules where justice indicates otherwise'.[163]

Particular concerns may arise about the *absence* of duty. It could be perceived as an immunity favouring a particular class of defendants (eg the police, advocates or expert witnesses). Unless carefully justified, such immunities would undermine public confidence in the administration of justice: the constitutional principle that all are equal before the law. Hence Lord Dyson reasoned, when abolishing expert witnesses' negligence immunity, that denial of duty requires 'strict and cogent justification' which 'should be kept under review' by the courts.[164] Incrementalism also gives weight to established *immunities*. But Lord Reed in *Robinson* did not demand absolute adherence to precedent. The courts strike 'a balance between legal certainty and justice'. The established law on duty of care presumptively determines the case but not absolutely. Precedent is the starting point, but the court can decide to extend liability if it would be just and reasonable.[165]

Claimants have great incentives, nevertheless, to present their cases as falling within an established liability – and defendants, conversely, to demonstrate an established absence of duty. If they succeed, it will not be necessary to rebut

---

[159] *Perre v Apand Pty Ltd* (1999) 198 CLR 180, [199]–[200].
[160] *Ward v McMaster* [1988] IR 337, 347 (McCarthy J).
[161] *Gwilliam v West Hertfordshire NHS Trust* [2002] EWCA Civ 1041; [2003] QB 443 at [53]; F Cornford, *Microcosmographia Academica* (Cambridge, Cambridge University Press, 1908).
[162] *Westdeutsche Landesbank Girozentrale v Islington LBC* [1996] AC 669, 692.
[163] *Canadian National Railway v Norsk Pacific Steamship Co* [1992] 1 SCR 1021, 1146.
[164] *Jones v Kaney* [2011] UKSC 13, [2011] 2 AC 398 [113]–[114].
[165] *Robinson* [2018] AC 736, [29].

any policy arguments advanced by the other side, which (*Robinson* and *Darnley* both suggest) will simply be dismissed as irrelevant. Much therefore depends on what precisely counts as an 'established category'. This is harder to define, at the margins, than the Supreme Court assumes. Evidently the Court of Appeal in *Robinson* and *Darnley* disagreed that duty of care was so well established as to lie beyond argument, like the archetypal motorist's duty.

It is misleading to suppose that categories are neatly cut and dried. The inability of category-based reasoning to avoid underlying questions of substance is noted by various commentators and judges – including, significantly, Lord Mance and Lord Hughes in *Robinson*. Speaking about the common law generally, legal philosopher Ronald Dworkin attacked the idea that judges can avoid theoretical questions by concentrating 'in a more lawyer-like way' on reasoning by analogy:

> because ... analogy without theory is blind. An analogy is a way of stating a conclusion, not a way of reaching one, and theory must do the real work ... Is abortion more like infanticide or appendectomy? We cannot even begin to answer [such] questions without a deep expedition into theory.[166]

Many judges have acknowledged this too. McHugh J warned that the incremental approach to liability

> does not mean that duties in novel cases are determined by simply looking for factual similarities in decided cases or that neither principle nor policy has any part to play in the development of the law in this area. On the contrary, the precedent cases have to be examined to reveal their bases in principle and policy.[167]

Allan Beever similarly warns that 'incrementalism' cannot justify the shape of liability. Incremental arguments are rational only when we understand the principles underlying the rules from which analogies are to be drawn: yet such general principles '[are] precisely what the incremental approach attempts to do without'. This is the 'fundamental difficulty' with incrementalism.[168]

Duty of care cases are, of course, a source of guidance for future disputes. Duty's main function, according to the dominant explanation, is categorical policing of the outer boundaries of negligence liability. But as is familiar from across the common law process, a precedent's precise extent (its binding force and its 'penumbral' persuasive value) can often be controversial. Take the question of 'server's liability' when an intoxicated driver injures other road-users. If liability of publicans who sell alcohol to the driver is established,[169]

---

[166] R Dworkin, *Justice in Robes* (Cambridge MA, Harvard University Press, 2006) 69.
[167] *Crimmins v Stevedoring Industry Finance Committee* (1999) 200 CLR 1, [73].
[168] Beever (n 37) 193.
[169] *Jordan House Hotel v Menow* [1974] SCR 239.

does it extend to 'social hosts' serving wine to friends at home?[170] Plunkett argues there is no uniquely correct level of generality for the categories of duties of care: it requires a balance between conceiving them so widely that they require endless qualifications, or so narrowly that a case decides nothing except its own particular facts. The judicial guidance on this crucial question is 'vague-to-the-point-of-meaningless'.[171]

Here we return to *Robinson*. Although the case involved directly inflicted bodily injury – the paradigm negligence claim – Lord Mance did not think liability automatically followed. He noted that in *Marc Rich v Bishop Rock Marine* Lord Steyn was 'cautious to warn against absolute rules in that respect'.[172] Lord Steyn said: 'in most cases of the direct infliction of physical loss or injury through carelessness, it is self-evident that a civilised system of law should [recognise] a duty of care'.[173] But the crucial word was 'most': not 'all'. Lord Mance accepted that there would usually be liability yet was 'not persuaded that it is always a safe guide at the margins'. Disagreeing with Lord Reed, Lord Mance doubted whether direct physical damage constitutes 'axiomatically such a category [of established liability], whatever the precise circumstances'.[174]

Lord Mance placed considerably less emphasis on precedent and correspondingly more emphasis on policy. He agreed with Lord Reed's point that courts are not equipped to act as 'policy-making bodies in the sense in which that can be said of the Law Commission or government departments'.[175] But accepting that practical limitation, Lord Mance did not think policy could be ignored altogether. It is inherent in incremental development. *Policy choices* by previous generations of courts have created the liabilities established in today's law. Policy's crucial historical influence could only be denied by a 'fairy tale' in which 'the common law has not changed since the Saxon era, merely … revealed from time to time by an increasingly perceptive judiciary'. Rather, as Lord Mance said, 'in recognising the existence of any generalised duty in particular circumstances [courts] are making policy choices'.[176]

In Lord Mance's view, the historical shape of the law, the crux of 'incrementalism', is ultimately derived from previous courts' policy choices. He rejected any sharp distinction between 'a policy devised by a recent generation of judges' and 'a general and long-established principle':[177] in the end each derives from judicial choices, although the time-scale might differ. Unsurprisingly therefore, Lord Mance did not decide *Robinson* by simply identifying and applying a well-established category of liability He considered the policy arguments

---

[170] *Childs v Desormeaux* [2006] 1 SCR 643 (no liability).
[171] J Plunkett, *The Duty of Care in Negligence* (Oxford, Hart, 2018) 122.
[172] *Robinson* [2018] AC 736 [90].
[173] *Marc Rich* [1996] AC 211, 235.
[174] *Robinson* [2018] AC 736 [85].
[175] ibid [69](2) (Lord Reed).
[176] ibid [84].
[177] ibid [69](1) (Lord Reed).

raised by the police defendants. Lord Mance rejected those arguments, holding that concerns about 'defensive policing' were outweighed by the desirability of ensuring, where possible, the same tort liability for public officials and private individuals.[178] Thus Lord Mance agreed that there was liability. But the route to the decision matters. There is a significant difference between weighing up the policies differently from the court below (Lord Mance) and deciding that the lower court had been wrong even to take them into account (Lord Reed).

The merits of *Robinson* will continue to be debated. Lord Reed reaffirmed the approach in *GN v Poole*. Commenting on the *Poole* case, Christine Beurmann wonders how successful the approach is.[179] It is not 'straightforward' to identify the correct category for a case given 'the range of potentially competing available analogies'.[180] Counsel in *Poole* tried to manipulate the defendant authority's categorisation – acting either *qua* landlord or *qua* child protection agency (with different resulting duties). In Beurmann's view, the Supreme Court 'ultimately sidestepped the issue by drawing yet another analogy' – classifying *Poole* as an omission or 'failure to confer a benefit' case. This raised to prominence the concept of assumption of responsibility (as an exceptional way to generate liability for omissions). In Beurmann's view, this too was a doubtful move. The court was unable to define that slippery and debated concept with precision.[181] (Lord Hughes in *Robinson* held that decisions on 'assumption of responsibility' have also been shaped by policy concerns.)[182]

Interestingly, a parallel shift towards incrementalism is visible in a number of other common law jurisdictions. In *University College Cork v Electricity Supply Board*, the Irish Supreme Court emphasised a 'cautious' approach of incremental 'evolution by analogy', in preference to asking whether a duty of care would be 'just and equitable' (which simply 'begs the question').[183] However, critical commentators suggest that by seeking strictly to limit the role of policy, this 'incrementalism' merely obfuscates the true degree of judicial choice and law-making in duty of care cases.[184] Condon argues that 'openness and transparency' will suffer, for history teaches that 'it is simplifying frameworks that have been the real bane of the duty of care, and not policy analysis'.[185]

Canadian courts also now follow an approach similar to *Robinson*, but with greater awareness of its problems. *Deloitte & Touche v Livent Inc* was decided just weeks before *Robinson*.[186] Gascon and Brown JJ reasoned that when a case

---

[178] ibid [95]–[97].
[179] C Beuermann, 'The New Adventures of the Old Three-Stage Test: The Duty of Care Inquiry 30 Years after *Caparo*' (2019) 35 *Prof Neg* 247.
[180] ibid 250.
[181] Cf D Nolan, 'Assumption of Responsibility: Four Questions' [2019] *CLP* 123.
[182] *Robinson* [2018] AC 736 [115], [118].
[183] [2020] IESC 38, [7.3], [8.6]–[8.12].
[184] RR Condon, 'Closing the Sluice Gates: *UCC v ESB* and the Worrying Narrowing Duty of Care Analysis' (2022) 67 *Irish Jurist* 145.
[185] ibid 160.
[186] [2017] 2 SCR 855.

fits within 'a previously established category' of duty, engagement with policy reasoning will 'seldom' be necessary 'because any residual policy considerations will have already been taken into account when the proximate relationship was first identified'.[187] This closely resembles *Robinson*. However, Gascon and Brown JJ acknowledged the 'risk' that courts might reach decisions 'without any examination of pertinent second-stage residual policy considerations'. To guard against this omission of 'pertinent' factors, 'courts should avoid identifying established categories in an overly broad manner' and thereby consider whether the case is 'in fact, truly the same as or analogous'.[188]

The danger of short-circuited reasoning is a real one. In another recent Canadian case, *JJ v Rankin's Garage*, liability was denied partly because of an unusually restrictive approach to foreseeability (as discussed in the previous chapter).[189] The majority also defined the previously general duty category of 'physical injury' in a notably narrower way, which led Brown J (in dissent) to suggest that the court's 'misapplication' 'risks rendering meaningless a long established category of relationships ... and undermining the viability of the categorical approach altogether'.[190] As Brown J noted, the micro-division into manifold detailed duties of care 'is in tension with the great achievement of Lord Atkin in *Donoghue v Stevenson*, being his systematic integration of previously disparate, case-specific duties of care into a single conception'. The 'tension' is perhaps inevitable once, given 'the untidy complexity of life' the courts 'reject a general imposition of liability for foreseeable damage' (ie the neighbour principle).[191] But it is also unsatisfactory to reason in an abstract and formalistic way about 'categories', without considering the underlying reasons why those categories exist, their underlying justification, and thus their proper extent.

Incrementalism: Conclusions

There is something rather odd about making incremental development a special component of the duty of care inquiry. As McLachlin CJ says, 'The reference to categories simply captures the basic notion of precedent'.[192] Its elevation to prominence is clearly intended to serve some further function. This has happened twice in the tortured recent history of English negligence law. As the courts at the end of the 1980s struggled to control the expansion of liability under the *Anns* 'prima facie duty' test, incrementalism was seized on to restrict negligence liability. New duties were recognised cautiously, only if good reason

---

[187] ibid [26].
[188] ibid [28].
[189] [2018] 1 SCR 587: see ch 6, 'The Triviality of Foreseeability?'.
[190] ibid [75]–[76].
[191] *Smith v Littlewoods Organisation Ltd* [1987] AC 241, 280 (Lord Goff).
[192] *Childs v Desormeaux* [2006] 1 SCR 643, [15].

existed why the law *should* expand beyond established precedent (by comparison with the *Anns* question which was in effect 'why not?'). To the extent that this hardened into an absolute refusal to expand liability beyond established 'pockets', the *Caparo* retrenchment came at a high price. The duty of care was determined solely by the accidents of history. The courts appeared conservative, even reactionary.

Such an approach could not long survive its inherent arbitrariness and the scorn of (eg) Howarth and Stapleton. (The latter wrote in 1994 that incrementalism was a retreat to 'timid pragmatism', its concepts 'virtually empty', the method of selecting the relevant cases 'mysterious' and intuitive, and the assumption that this selection could be uncontroversial 'fallacious'; if this were not bad enough, Stapleton noted that the law on psychiatric injury/nervous shock was 'the best historical example of incremental development and yet also the area where the silliest rules now exist and where criticism is almost universal').[193] The following generations of judges, perhaps mindful of such critiques, were content to reason openly about policies for and against liability.[194]

But this openness has again fallen out of fashion. Above all in *Robinson*, the Supreme Court has placed renewed emphasis on precedent, apparently to curb the scope for policy reasoning. Yet if Lord Mance's concurring judgment is convincing, 'incrementalism' does not ultimately provide a satisfactory refuge. Established legal categories were themselves determined by policy. They are not self-defining and absolute. To decide whether a given case falls within them frequently involves a value judgement. Apart from the most obvious cases where duty of care truly is automatic (or axiomatic), such as driving a car, reasoning from established categories cannot avoid normative choices. Particularly if 'the very term "incremental" invites inquiry because what is incremental is to an extent in the eye of the beholder'.[195]

It is in the end a matter of emphasis. We cannot expect precedent (and analogical reasoning) to give uncontroversial answers to contested duty questions. It is moreover undesirable that the law should be absolutely fixed, incapable of developing beyond some arbitrarily fixed point in legal history. It would severely hamper the role of negligence confronting novel yet urgent social problems such as climate change.[196] This said, the duty of care should be stable enough to permit individuals to understand their potential legal liabilities. 'Policy' concerns (anything beyond a narrow concern with rights and doctrine) are influential in the development of liability, if only at the margins: as

---

[193] J Stapleton, 'In Restraint of Tort' in PBH Birks (ed), *The Frontiers of Liability, Volume 2* (Oxford, Oxford University Press, 1994) 85–86, 95 (for psychiatric injury see ch 9, this volume).
[194] *Customs v Barclays Bank* [2007] 1 AC 181.
[195] *Bryan v Maloney* (1995) 128 ALR 163, 197 (Toohey J).
[196] See *Sharma v Minister for the Environment* [2022] FCAFC 35 (Australia): *Smith v Fonterra* (n 131); *Smith v AG* (n 102): discussed in ch 12, 'Conclusion: Climate Change and Nuisance in the Twenty-First Century'.

the Supreme Court accepts in *Robinson*. But the endless balancing of an open-ended list of controversial factors could create considerable uncertainty. As far as possible policy should be weighed consistently from case to case. Which policies are relevant, and the degree of weight placed upon them, should be articulated openly and then applied consistently in later decisions. McHugh J feared that the 'general acknowledgment of the importance of frank discussion of policy factors' could degenerate into a discretionary approach with 'no predictability or certainty' or 'rigorous scrutiny'. McHugh J's proposed solution was:

> adherence to the incremental approach [which] imposes a necessary discipline upon the examination of policy factors with the result that the decisions in new cases can be more confidently predicted.[197]

The predictability of 'incrementalism' has been exaggerated by some. In order to draw analogies, courts use their 'underlying judgement as to what is fair, just and reasonable'; in that sense, incrementalism and *Caparo*-style weighing of factors are not rival tests but 'go together'.[198] Precedent is vital if policy-based reasoning is not to degenerate into ad hoc uncertainty. Stapleton now approves the 'humility' of the approach. While 'tentative' and 'unheroic', the judicial conversation with both their predecessors and successors gives the common law its 'power, adaptability, resilience' and stability.[199]

---

[197] *Crimmins v Stevedoring Industry Finance Committee* [1999] HCA 59, [77].
[198] *Royal Bank of Scotland v JP SPC 4* [2022] 3 WLR 261 [80] (Lord Hamblen and Lord Burrows).
[199] Stapleton (n 73) 13–14.

8

'Physical Injury' in Negligence

INTRODUCTION

This chapter considers the core of negligence. A duty of care is presumed to exist, without need for argument, when the defendant's careless conduct directly injures the claimant's person or property. Why? We should interrogate tort law's 'obvious' preference for protecting against physical injury. To argue from 'obviousness' not only ignores but also potentially *conceals* the foundation of liability. 'Physical injury' proves a less clear-cut concept than it seems. In the first debate, we examine cases at the margins. It is over-simplified to see them as raising purely factual questions. The second debate considers whether tort law can, and should, award compensation in advance of any physical injury occurring (ie 'preventive damages'). The third debate reviews the authorities on 'wrongful birth' – especially the interrelation between the sanctity of life and the classification of harm – as 'physical', 'purely economic' or a freestanding head of 'autonomy'. While wrongful birth cases notoriously raise difficult problems of law, morality and policy, a more radical critique suggests that *gendered* thinking has (unconsciously or not) influenced the contours of liability. Is tort law's hard-wired preference for physical injuries ultimately the product of masculine bias?

Personal Injury: So Obvious That It Goes Without Saying?

It is often difficult to find positive authority for elementary legal assumptions. Lord Brandon once held that in cases involving 'ordinary physical damage to property', liability usually 'does not give rise to any problem, because it is self-evident that such a duty exists and the contrary view is unarguable'.[1]

---

[1] *The Hua Lien* [1991] 1 Lloyd's Rep 309, 329.

With personal injuries the 'self-evidence' is even stronger. Martha Chamallas notes that tort law's 'deep structure' is usually unexamined:

> Although the standard texts do not always state so explicitly, there is little question that, in the contemporary law of torts, a higher value is placed on physical injury and property loss than on emotional and relational harm.[2]

The whole issue of 'actionable damage' is typically overlooked, Jane Stapleton notes that although 'crucial to an understanding of the limits of negligence, [issues about "damage"] are rarely addressed squarely by courts'.[3] As will be seen, difficulties emerge at the boundaries of 'physical damage'.

Deeper normative questions arise. *Why* does negligence place a higher value on physical damage? It is usually assumed rather than discussed. However there are dangers in purely *implicit* hierarchies of basic legal values. 'They have power to influence our thought, moreover, precisely because they are taken for granted and not often subjected to scrutiny by the courts or scholars'.[4] Yet tort's 'basic legal categories' depend on *human choice*.[5] They are not pre-ordained.

That might seem obvious. Tort law is not, like the laws of physics, derived by logic from the physical constants of the universe. Nor is it a matter of unchallengeable god-given wisdom, like a system of religious law. Tort liability must ultimately depend on society's decisions about which values deserve legal protection and which do not. In a common law system, those choices have been made by the judiciary over years and centuries. A principle as widely accepted and longstanding as negligence liability for physical harm reflects a stable legal consensus – a broadly shared value-judgement. The common law is heavily influenced by its inheritance from the past. Adaptation to new conditions – changing social attitudes, new technology – is incremental. The starting point is legal history, not a blank sheet of paper.

Physical harm has historically played a leading role in the law of negligence, and wider social attitudes. Medicine and health has traditionally focused on physical illness and injury, with emotional health and even mental illness facing comparative neglect. Physical property was the foundation of wealth (and social position) in pre-industrial England, in particular landowning. The frequency and importance of litigation about damage of this kind dominated the courts' diet during the evolution of tort liability.

Yet although the historical contingency of attitudes to health and wealth may explain tort law's focus on physical damage, it scarcely *justifies* it. (On one view, legal history is simply 'the first step toward an enlightened scepticism,

---

[2] M Chamallas, 'Architecture of Bias: Deep Structures in Tort Law' (1998) 146 *Univ Penn LR* 463, 490.

[3] J Stapleton, 'The Gist of Negligence: Part 1 Minimal Actionable Damage' (1988) 104 *LQR* 213, 213.

[4] Chamallas (n 2) 468.

[5] ibid 524.

that is, toward a deliberate reconsideration of the worth of [the current] rules'.)⁶ The focus on physical injury was never absolute. Some torts (eg defamation, deceit, conspiracy, passing-off) typically, or by definition, protect economic or wider interests (eg reputation). Nancy Levit explains how tort has evolved ('grudgingly') away from its historical concern with physical injury to protect 'ethereal' or 'ephemeral' interests: 'mental, psychic, relational, and probabilistic injuries'.⁷

Certainly today, negligence law's inherited focus on physical harm seems questionable. Mental illness is accepted to be no less serious than physical injuries – indeed a serious psychiatric disorder can surely do more catastrophic harm to an individual's life than (eg) a broken leg. Equally 'pure economic loss' might have much more serious effects on wealth than damage to physical property. The bulk of society's assets are now *intangible* in form. (Some have argued that our very notion of 'property' should expand to include new forms of wealth such as entitlements to government support.)⁸ An individual's life savings, or pension, is typically invested in assets (like shares or bonds) other than directly held physical property. Why should a pension fund rank lower in tort law's hierarchy of protection? If a pension is negligently depleted, the impact is no less ruinous than damage to a physical asset – and may now be more common. Notably, under the First Protocol to the ECHR the 'right to peaceful enjoyment of possessions' extends much wider than *physical* property, including also (eg) salaries, goodwill, state benefits.⁹

Given such concerns, how can we defend the heartland of negligence liability? Is it acceptable to privilege *physical* injuries to person (or property) over other harm with equally damaging effects? Two families of replies seem possible: rights-based and policy-based. The rights theorist highlights that we all have rights to be protected against physical damage to our bodies and tangible property. By contrast we do *not* have a right good against the world to enjoy our current level of wealth; nor a right not to suffer emotional distress;¹⁰ nor even perhaps a right not to suffer psychiatric illness.¹¹ But what do such arguments achieve, save to restate the current law in the formal language of rights? This restatement does little, by itself, to justify tort's historical focus on physical injury. At worst, it merely reproduces the historical legal position, with 'rights' as an intellectual garnish.

Alternatively, there are pragmatic 'policy' arguments. But here too we find scant discussion of positive justifications for favouring physical injuries.

---

⁶ OW Holmes, 'The Path of the Law' (1897) 10 *Harvard LR* 457, 469.

⁷ N Levit, 'Ethereal Torts' (1992) 61 *Geo Wash LR* 136.

⁸ CA Reich, 'The New Property' (1964) 73 *Yale LJ* 733.

⁹ Roderick Bagshaw, 'The Edges of Tort Law's Rights' in D Nolan and A Robertson (eds), *Rights and Private Law* (Oxford, Hart, 2012) 429.

¹⁰ R Stevens, *Torts and Rights* (Oxford, Oxford University Press, 1997) 52–56.

¹¹ A Beever, *Rediscovering the Law of Negligence* (Oxford, Hart, 2007) 404–11.

In Stapleton's view, physical harm is the 'most powerful of all [pro-liability] factors'.[12] Rather than being declared directly it 'can, in effect, merely be deduced from a remarkably consistent pattern of [case] outcomes'. But *why* should physical security 'clearly [be placed] on top of our menu of convincing pro-liability factors'? On this we find judicial 'silence', explicable partly because the pre-eminence of physical harm is 'so well-recognized and accepted' that it does not require explicit discussion, partly since 'the task of justification here would require the handling of delicate issues of moral philosophy'.[13]

The consensus is not quite universal. Richard Abel advocates abolishing tort liability for physical damage to *property*.[14] He accepts that personal injuries (physical and emotional) threaten 'the very core of selfhood'. But ownership of property is not integral to our personalities. Tort law should not symbolically 'proclaim that property interests are as important as physical [bodily] and emotional integrity, and (by extension) that property can and should be loved in the same way we love other people'.[15] Deciding whether to extend legal protection to property rights poses 'distributional' questions.[16] From an egalitarian perspective, tort liability for accidentally damaged property perpetuates and reinforces the current grossly unequal distribution of society's wealth. For example, drivers of very expensive new cars recover significantly more compensation when their vehicles are damaged by another's negligence, compared to drivers of older, modest vehicles – yet they pay the same liability insurance premiums. The rich take out more than they pay in. Driver's liability insurance (made compulsory by law) is 'a form of *regressive* quasi-public taxation'.[17] Moreover, the tort system in an expensive way of transferring losses from property-owners to those who damage their property. It would be more cost-effective to leave the risk of accidental loss on owners in all cases (*'res perit domino'*) 'as a concomitant of the broad dominion [they enjoy] over their property'.[18] The main effect of the reform, Abel concludes, would be to make the enjoyment of property more expensive. Owners would insure their own property without recourse against others who accidentally damage it.

While Abel's scepticism about property damage is exceptional, suspicion of *non-physical* harms runs deep. Levit describes the tenacity of tort's historical focus: 'Injuries – to be considered "real" – must be physical, visible, or discernible. ... [By contrast] the ethereal tort is treated as unreal, foundationless, and undeserving'.[19] This 'devaluation' is hard-wired into tort. Chamallas

---

[12] J Stapleton, 'Duty of Care Factors: A Selection from the Judicial Menus' in P Cane and J Stapleton (eds), *The Law of Obligations* (Oxford, Oxford University Press, 1998) 72.

[13] ibid 73.

[14] RL Abel, 'Should Tort Law Protect Property Against Accidental Loss?' in M Furmston (ed), *The Law of Tort* (London, Duckworth, 1986).

[15] ibid 165.

[16] ibid 157.

[17] ibid 163 (emphasis added).

[18] ibid 174.

[19] Levit (n 7) 174.

suggests this emphasis on 'bodily injury' excludes claims like 'wrongful birth' that are disproportionately brought by women. Moreover (as discussed in the next chapter), negligence takes a sceptical view of emotional or psychiatric harm. Such claims are 'problematic' by contrast with *physical* harm. The critics' central message is that we should openly debate tort's basic categories – their fairness and justifiability.

Clarification: 'Gist Damage' and 'Consequential Loss'

Tort law draws a fundamental distinction between actionable 'gist' damage and consequential loss. This is so important that it needs explanation. In negligence, 'damage is the gist of the action'. But 'damage' here does not simply mean 'loss', a factual deterioration. The claimant may be significantly worse off but unless their loss is *actionable*, it cannot form the basis for a claim. The loss falls outside the law's concern as '*damnum absque injuria*', harm in the absence of a legal injury: 'the world is full of harm for which the law furnishes no remedy'.[20] So 'gist' damage is that which is actionable in itself as the foundation of a negligence claim. Only damage to a legally recognised interest is sufficient. That leads on to the question of which interests are protected by negligence ('actionable') and why – the subject of these two chapters.

The law takes a wider approach to 'consequential loss'. There are various harms that are not themselves actionable as the basis for a negligence claim (eg 'mere distress'), or only exceptionally actionable (eg 'pure economic loss') – yet are *routinely* compensated when they result *from* 'actionable damage'. Nearly all personal injury compensation includes an element for 'pain and suffering' consequent on the physical injury. An action for physical damage to property will inevitably include the economic cost of replacement or repair ('consequential economic loss'). (In another important difference, a significant chance of future consequential losses is compensated proportionate to the chance that they will happen, rather than insisting on 'all or nothing' proof on the balance of probabilities as for the 'gist damage').[21] How can this sharp difference of approach be justified?

Rights-based theories equate kinds of damage held 'actionable' with the *rights* protected by the law of negligence. There is no general right 'not to be harmed' or not to suffer loss. Tort law protects *particular* rights, and only the invasion of a protected right is 'actionable'. Primarily, legal protection is through 'substitutive' remedies which aim to protect, or restore, the right itself. But not every violation can be prevented, undone or 'restored'.[22] Therefore to give rights full protection, loss *consequent* on a right's invasion must be compensated. This is 'the law's attempt to reach the "next best" position …

---

[20] *JD v East Berkshire NHS Trust* [2005] 2 AC 373 [100] (Lord Rodger).
[21] See ch 5, 'Introduction: Causation, Proof, 'Damage' and Consequential Loss'.
[22] *Lewis v Australian Capital Territory* [2020] HCA 26 [141], [149] (Edelman J).

[the] nearest approximation of the wrong not having occurred'.[23] This function dominates:

> In the vast majority of damages cases in the law of torts the focus of the compensatory principle, with its goal of putting the plaintiff in the position they would have been in if the wrongful act had not occurred, is upon rectifying the consequences of the wrong rather than rectifying the wrongful act itself.[24]

Harmful 'consequences' by definition go beyond the invasion of the right 'itself', and may well be different in kind. But, importantly, that does not establish a *freestanding* right to avoid such harms – some (like 'distress') are compensated only as an aspect of giving full protection to *other* rights (not to be subjected to bodily harm).

There are also pragmatic reasons to distinguish 'gist damage' from 'consequential loss.' Widespread, uncertain liability would result if everyone who was upset by another's carelessness had a claim in negligence. Hence why 'mere distress' is not actionable damage. But when distress is suffered as the consequence of an injury that *is* actionable (such as physical harm) – which presumably raises no insuperable 'indeterminacy' problems – the objection disappears. On this pragmatic approach, the 'actionable damage' concept draws the boundaries of liability examining (among other things) policy concerns. Once a claim falls within those boundaries, the concerns may be exhausted.

Note that on either view, consequential loss may be much more extensive, and quite different in kind, from the initial 'gist damage'. When the 'gist damage' is slight, it is sometimes described as the peg or hook on which a different (much more sizeable) claim hangs. Another (uncomplimentary) term is that consequential loss claims are 'parasitic' upon the gist damage. These labels can be used rhetorically to attack the distinction itself. In particular, to query why the 'peg' or 'hook' should be necessary at all. Or to suggest that there is something irrational about compensating some sorts of loss 'parasitically' only – the implication being that anything for which the law awards compensation should itself be recognised as 'gist damage'. Examples will be examined below.

Debate 1
What is 'Personal Injury'? The Boundaries of 'Bodily Harm'

The boundaries of 'personal injury' are fuzzy. Of itself this is unremarkable. Many (most, or all) legal distinctions are difficult in marginal cases. It is unsurprising that abstract categories (like 'bodily injury') sometimes prove controversial when applied to concrete facts. However, we should beware arguments

---

[23] Stevens (n 10) 59.
[24] *Lewis* (n 22) [150] (but cf Stevens (n 10) ch 4).

that negligence law's preferential treatment of physical harm is justified by ease of definition. Roderick Bagshaw inquires whether the distinction between physical *property* damage and pure economic loss is justified by the clearer boundaries around 'property damage'. He concludes not.[25] The 'edges' of physical damage to property are as hard to discern as the boundaries of economic loss.[26] (Bagshaw's examples include 'out of condition' pigs;[27] an antique vase whose value is diminished when its matching 'pair' is destroyed; a building 'contaminated' by poisonous spiders.)[28]

In Bagshaw's view, there are no demonstrably correct, factual answers. Decisions at the 'edges' necessarily involve *normative* assessments. But do courts fully acknowledge this in reasoning about 'physical harm to the person'? We examine the leading authorities with this concern in mind.

Minor Injuries: A 'Hook' for Consequential Loss?

One troublesome question is whether minor bodily changes are 'actionable damage'. Or, with a gradually worsening condition, at what point precisely do they become 'actionable'? Cases squarely considering the point tend to be rare: 'Because people do not often go to the trouble of bringing actions to recover damages for trivial injuries, the question of how trivial is [too trivial to justify a remedy] has seldom arisen directly'.[29] According to the leading case of *Rothwell*, there must be a physical change making the claimant worse off, for which compensation is an appropriate remedy.[30] Compensation is *not* appropriate in very minor cases:

> the policy of the law is not to entertain a claim for damages where the physical effects of the injury are no more than negligible. Otherwise the smallest cut, or the lightest bruise, might give rise to litigation the costs of which were out of all proportion to what was in issue.[31]

But as Lord Hope immediately accepted, 'The policy does not provide clear guidance as to where the line is to be drawn between effects which are and are not negligible'.

The claimants in *Rothwell* had developed plaques (growths) on their pleura (lung linings), a result they alleged of negligent exposure to asbestos by the defendants. These pleural plaques were held not to constitute actionable

---

[25] Bagshaw (n 9).
[26] See also in contract law *Farley v Skinner* [2002] 2 AC 732 [85] (Lord Scott) ('The distinction between the "physical" and the "non-physical" is not always clear and may depend on the context').
[27] *Pride & Partners v Institute for Animal Health* [2009] EWHC 685 (QB).
[28] *Blue Circle Industries v MOD* [1999] Ch 289 (radioactive contamination).
[29] *Rothwell v Chemical & Insulating Co* [2008] 1 AC 281 [8] (Lord Hoffmann).
[30] ibid [7].
[31] ibid [47] (Lord Hope).

damage. They were 'asymptomatic' (did not cause pain or discomfort, could not even be felt, and did not impair the claimants' lung function). The plaques were also 'benign' (rarely became more serious (eg thicker) over time, and never deteriorated into serious asbestos-related illness). The House of Lords accepted that the *effect* of the bodily changes was a crucial question. In the rare case when plaques caused significant discomfort, there would be actionable injury. Similarly for painless, benign lesions present on the body's surface, given scarring's 'disfiguring' effect.[32]

The plaques were not the claimants' only concern (nor the greatest of their concerns). Since they had been exposed to significant quantities of asbestos, they were anxious about developing serious/fatal conditions including lung cancers. Even if the plaques were not in themselves serious enough to be actionable damage, the claimants sought to 'aggregate' the plaques with the risk of *future* serious illness, and their current *anxiety* about that risk.

The 'aggregation theory' was rejected too. On the facts, it was clear that the plaques themselves did not *cause* the future risk (nor therefore the anxiety). Rather, another factor (inhalation of asbestos) was responsible *both* for the plaques, and the future risk. As the trial judge found, the plaques' significance was evidential only: their presence indicated significant inhaled asbestos in the lungs. But it was the presence of that asbestos rather than the plaques per se which occasioned anxiety.[33] It would be inappropriate to deem pleural plaques 'personal injury' to provide 'nothing more than a "hook" on which to hang a claim for damages for something which they did not cause'.[34]

Lord Hope had (alone among the law lords) proposed a similar reason for awarding 'orthodox' damages in the leading loss-of-chance case *Gregg v Scott*.[35] Again however, the 'hook' approach was rejected by the majority. In *Gregg*, negligent misdiagnosis of the claimant's cancer enabled a tumour to enlarge, which was painful. That enlarged tumour was clearly a physical injury caused by the delayed treatment. Thus, Lord Hope reasoned, Mr Gregg could show actionable damage and claim the reduced chance of recovery from the cancer *as consequential loss* (the crucial point being that claimants do not have to show that *consequences* would have been avoided on the balance of probabilities: proof of a significant chance is enough).[36]

The majority thought this inapplicable on the facts of *Gregg v Scott*.[37] As Baroness Hale observed, 'Consequential loss still has to be consequential upon, that is caused by, the injury'.[38] In a typical 'future loss' case, it may be unclear

---

[32] ibid [18]–[19].
[33] Quoted *Rothwell* ibid [11].
[34] ibid [91] (Lord Rodger).
[35] [2005] 2 AC 176 eg at [117].
[36] ibid [119]–[120].
[37] See also ibid [58] (Lord Nicholls, dissenting).
[38] ibid [200].

whether a claimant will suffer deteriorating health. But it *is* quite clear that the initial injury would be the cause of later deterioration (should it occur).[39] Not so in *Gregg v Scott*. If the claimant died of cancer, it would *not* be clear that the defendant's negligence caused his death. In the majority's view, Lord Hope was incorrect to reason that by classifying Mr Gregg's lost prospects of successful treatment as 'consequential loss' he could recover when that consequence *had probably not been caused by the negligence*. Mr Gregg would probably not have survived the cancer even if he had been promptly diagnosed and treated.[40]

Lord Phillips CJ stated in the Court of Appeal in *Rothwell*: 'The law attaches particular importance to physical damage as this is the gateway for recovery for secondary effects of negligence which give rise to no freestanding claims'.[41] The claimants argued that pleural plaques were a bodily change providing a readily demonstrable 'trigger'. Their presence could be used as a 'useful control mechanism' for anxiety-based claims, 'providing certainty as to when such a claim will lie'.[42] This argument was rejected too. Some who are exposed to similar quantities of asbestos do not develop pleural plaques. It would be illogical to discriminate between claimants with the same anxiety levels and same cancer risk, resulting from identical asbestos exposures, by examining 'the fortuity of whether or not the particular claimant has developed pleural plaques'.[43]

Illogical too was the 'aggregation' argument (described above). If the plaques were not actionable damage, nor was the claimants' anxiety, nor the future risk of illness, combining them could not magically produce a valid claim. 'Nought plus nought plus nought equals nought'.[44] But compare Smith LJ's dissent. Her Ladyship denied that the claimants' injuries were trivial and undeserving of damages. In Smith LJ's view, 'most people on the Clapham omnibus' would approve: the claimants had suffered 'real harm'.[45] Her dissent reveals that underneath the 'conceptual' surface, normative judgments determine what counts as actionable personal injury. It is not purely a question of fact.

'Actionable Damage' and Limitation Periods

By contrast with *Rothwell*, some 'minor injury' cases satisfy the 'actionability' threshold. In *Cartledge v Jopling* the claimants had long suffered (without realising) a gradually worsening lung disease.[46] But by the time they were diagnosed with the disease, they were too late to claim in negligence. They

---

[39] ibid [68]–[71] (Lord Hoffmann).

[40] NB a claim for consequential discomfort and 'reduction in median life expectancy' might have succeeded: *Gregg v Scott* [206]–[207] (Baroness Hale) (see *JD v Mather* [2012] EWHC 3063 (QB)).

[41] [2006] ICR 1458 [36].

[42] ibid [66].

[43] ibid [67] (cf [143] Smith LJ (dissenting)).

[44] *Rothwell* (n 29) [73] (Lord Scott) (compare [42] (Lord Hope)).

[45] [2006] ICR 1458 [144].

[46] [1963] AC 758.

had suffered actionable damage when their undiagnosed illnesses first became 'significant injury'. Their cause of action was complete at that moment and the limitation 'clock' started to run (under the then statutory rules). That had unfortunately occurred when the claimants still had 'no knowledge of the secret onset of [the disease] and suffer[ed] no present inconvenience from it'.[47] The injustice of this result is obvious, and the Limitation Act was amended so that time now begins to run at the point when the claimant ought reasonably to be aware of the injury – the period for claiming cannot now expire before the claimant even knows that they are injured.[48] (Following the amendments, there has been 'no need to focus on *when* the cause of action arose'.)[49]

While 'significant injury' might again seem a purely factual question, we should beware spurious logic. Courts apply concepts in marginal cases with an eye on the result. Stapleton suggests that the *Cartledge v Jopling* court attempted to ameliorate the decision's unfairness. They held that 'actionable damage' occurred at the point when the claimant's injury became 'real harm'.[50] Yet Stapleton argues it might be preferable if 'personal injury' occurred *as soon as the claimant is exposed* to the factor that ultimately makes them ill. The point of exposure must logically be when bodily changes first begin. The 'exposure' approach was not attractive on the facts of *Cartledge v Jopling* – but it might be preferable in other cases. In *Cartledge* exposure had occurred even earlier than the 'secret onset' of the disease, so to adopt the logic of that approach would have made it even harder to claim within the limitation period. As seen, amendments to the Limitation Act have now dealt with that problem. But Stapleton notes that *Cartledge* could cause problems of its own.

What about a claimant who *knows* that they have been exposed, and knows it will make them ill in future. Why make them wait for 'real and substantial' changes to their body (the *Cartledge v Jopling* test) before permitting a claim? It is often better to recover damages earlier (eg to provide medical treatment to prevent or slow the condition's progression). Defendants too could benefit if claims were litigated earlier, on fresher evidence. Yet such claims seem to be precluded by the well-meaning definition of 'actionable personal injury' in *Cartledge v Jopling*.[51] (Stapleton's points also support the recognition of 'preventive damages', considered in the next debate.)

The Outer Limits of 'Personal Injury'?

It is not easy to convince courts to recognise wholly new species of 'actionable damage', although exceptionally this does happen.[52] Claimants would much

---

[47] ibid 778 (Lord Pearce).
[48] Limitation Act 1980 ss 11(4) and 14.
[49] *Rothwell* [2006] ICR 1458 [128] (Smith LJ) (emphasis added).
[50] Stapleton (n 3).
[51] See *Brown v North British Steel Foundry Ltd* 1968 SC 51.
[52] D Nolan, 'New Forms of Damage in Negligence' (2007) 70 *MLR* 59.

rather present their claims within a well-established category of liability (or as a small analogical development). Given its pre-eminence in tort's hierarchy of protection, physical injury attracts claimants struggling to 'sell' the court an unusual or difficult claim. The strategy is understandable (although, frustratingly, involves parties and judges downplaying the novelty of what they are doing). The boundaries of 'physical harm' are not always clear. Sometimes (as in *Rothwell*, the pleural plaques test-case) the strategy fails. But in *Dryden v Johnson Matthey*, it succeeded.[53] The pair make an interesting contrast. Arguably the Supreme Court's reasoning in *Dryden* was inconsistent with *Rothwell*.

The *Dryden* claimants developed sensitivity to platinum salts (after alleged breach of safety rules in their employer's chemical factory). Clearly this was a bodily change – but could it satisfy the *Rothwell* test to count as 'injury'? While (like pleural plaques) the sensitisation was asymptomatic, the claimants successfully argued that sensitisation was *not* 'benign'. They had to avoid further exposure to platinum salts or they would develop full-blow platinum allergies. (Everyone accepted that *allergies*, given their unpleasant physical symptoms, would certainly be 'personal injury'.)

The defendant employer argued unsuccessfully that the allergies were notional and would never in fact develop. Outside the unusual environment of a platinum factory, people do not come into contact with platinum salts: the claimants had not suffered curtailment of their everyday lives (unlike someone sensitised to, and obliged to avoid, sunlight). When the defendants realised the claimants were sensitised, they had moved them to other jobs within the factory (at lower salaries), or in some cases dismissed them, to prevent further exposure to platinum salts. By this action, the allergies had been decisively avoided. The claimants would never develop platinum allergies given the employer's pre-emptive intervention. Nevertheless Lady Black held sensitisation 'undoubtedly' harmful, given the impact on the claimants' careers: their 'bodily capacity for work has been impaired and they [were] therefore significantly worse off'.[54]

The Supreme Court's reasoning resembles an argument rejected in *Rothwell*: combining slight bodily changes with other (non-actionable) forms of damage, to come up with actionable 'personal injury'. Lost wages would be pure economic loss unless they resulted from physical injury. The law recognises duties to avoid economic loss only exceptionally.[55] While the sensitisation placed certain restrictions on the claimants' freedom to carry on with their 'ordinary everyday lives' (which for *them* meant working with platinum salts),[56] no *freestanding* claim exists for interfering with another's 'everyday life', except by inflicting personal injuries. Perhaps adding three noughts can sometimes produce a sum greater than its parts?

---

[53] [2019] AC 403 (*Dryden*).

[54] ibid [40].

[55] The Court of Appeal held such a duty did not arise in *Dryden* (sub nom *Greenway v Johnson Matthey* [2016] 1 WLR 4487). (Not discussed in the Supreme Court.)

[56] *Dryden* (n 53) [39].

The courts below had rejected liability, for reasons that illuminate the Supreme Court decision. Sales LJ noted the potential 'mismatch' between actionable damage (physical injury) and consequential loss (diminished earnings).[57] But this mismatch could not justify expanding 'actionable damage' by reference to the (financial) consequences, 'in an effort to align more closely the wrong and the damages recoverable'. Sales LJ declined to award damages for pure economic loss whether directly or, on the claimants' alternative argument, 'by watering down the concept of physical injury so that it is taken to include mere physiological changes which happen to have financial consequences'.[58] 'The presence of [pure] economic loss does not convert a physiological change which does not in itself qualify as an actionable injury into such an injury'.

Sales LJ approved tort's emphasis on physical injury. It is a clear 'bright-line' concept to control liability in negligence. With respect, this may be doubted. However, the certainty of legal rules is a matter of degree, and Sales LJ argued that the degree of certainty should be maximised where possible. In particular, courts should beware blurring lines to award damages in sympathetic cases which 'would tend to undermine the virtue of having a bright line rule in the first place'.[59] It follows that a concern about the Supreme Court's more expansive decision is that it may have unsettled the boundaries of 'personal injury'. *Dryden* has been cited for the submission that negligently causing *fear* is actionable as personal injury. Fear produces physical effects ('albeit transitory'), including release of adrenaline, increased blood pressure and heart rate. That could be viewed as a non-negligible impairment of normal daily function.[60] Although this 'fear' claim was rejected, *Dryden* has been criticised as a source of 'speculative litigation', an authority used to 'circumvent' the normal categorisation of personal injury.[61] If the outer limits of 'personal injury' are acknowledged to be unclear, courts should give greater emphasis to the *reasons* for and against protecting such injuries by comparison with 'anxiety' or 'economic loss', instead of playing 'personal injury' as a trump card to settle the scope of negligence, supposedly by 'factual' means. The cases discussed in this debate indicate that a retreat into 'factual' characterisation can serve as a threadbare disguise for normative, value-laded choices.

Debate 2
'Preventive' Damages

People are sometimes negligently exposed to toxic substances which may make them seriously ill in future (eg a radioactive leak which creates a risk of cancer).

---

[57] ibid [54].
[58] ibid [53].
[59] ibid [30]–[31].
[60] *Kimathi v Foreign & Commonwealth Office* [2018] EWHC 1305 (QB).
[61] J Huang, 'The Boundaries of Actionable Damage' (2019) 82 *MLR* 737, 747.

Should the law give them a claim for damages immediately, or only when (and/ or if) the illness manifests itself? At present English law takes the second, later approach. *Rothwell* confirmed that it is impossible to claim in anticipation of a possible future disease. The doctrinal logic seems unanswerable: if you have not yet been harmed, no actionable damage has yet been suffered, and no claim can yet exist.

Yet the logic can be questioned. Why not redefine 'actionable damage' to include the prospect of future illness in addition to current physical injury? Perhaps because where the loss has not yet been sustained, and possibly never will be, it could be difficult or even speculative to value it. That seems a weak response: courts constantly assess future losses (eg lost earnings or medical costs) without undue 'speculation'.

The law currently says claimants must 'wait and see'. A claim arises only if and when the disease manifests itself. There is apparent good sense in this. Take an artificial example where four victims of toxic exposure each have a 25 per cent chance of becoming ill within a decade. Isn't it better to wait for ten years and award full compensation to the one who does fall ill, rather than grant *each* of them *one quarter* of that amount immediately? That would be open to an obvious objection (with hindsight):

> The passage of time is bound to demonstrate that the award was unjust. If the claimant contracts the disease, the award that he has received will be inadequate compensation. If he does not, it will become apparent that he has received a windfall.[62]

(Lord Phillips acknowledged that the risk is present in *every* routine damages award which 'takes into account the risk of subsequent disease'. Indeed, given the limits of prophecy, estimates about any kind future of future loss 'will almost surely be wrong. There is really only one certainty: the future will prove the award to be either too high or too low'.[63] The courts' statutory power to award provisional damages, an exception to 'once and for all' lump sums, helps mitigate the problem.)[64]

However, it is incorrect to assume that claimants can never be factually worse off, unless and until they fall ill. A victim of toxic exposure paying regular life-insurance premiums would find their premiums increasing *immediately*, that is, as soon as the exposure was known (and disclosed to the insurer). The premiums would rise in proportion to the increased risk of earlier death. It might also be prudent to undertake immediate medical examinations, or to prescribe prophylactic drugs, to guard against the possible future disease (or at least to monitor for signs of its occurrence). Fleming argued that such monitoring

---

[62] *Rothwell* [2006] ICR 1458 [62] (Lord Phillips CJ).
[63] *Lim Poh Choo v Camden AHA* [1980] AC 174, 183 (Lord Scarman).
[64] Senior Courts Act 1981 s 32A.

costs should be recoverable.⁶⁵ They are a present and quantifiable cost (by contrast with the 'imponderable' risk of possible future injury, or unquantifiable anxiety about it). Moreover, second, such damages could enable earlier detection and treatment of diseases. This is obviously beneficial for victims; it may also prove cheaper, in the long run, for defendants. Donal Nolan agrees.⁶⁶ He notes how in US 'mass tort' cases, defendants have been required to set up a fund to pay for medical monitoring of all those exposed to a toxic substance. This helps ensure that monitoring will actually take place, emphasising the disease-prevention function (ie compared with payment of risk-proportioned damages to each victim individually, which could be spent on anything the claimant wished).

Preventive awards have a strong intuitive appeal. The most powerful doctrinal argument is consistency with the rules on mitigation and contributory negligence. Mitigation requires that claimants should take reasonable steps to limit their losses following a tort. Losses that a claimant could have readily avoided by taking reasonable steps to protect their own health or property (eg seeking medical treatment; undertaking emergency repairs) will not be compensated. If the claimant spends their own money on reasonable steps of mitigation (eg shoring up a damaged building), that expenditure will be recoverable from the defendant. As Fleming and Nolan both argue, since the mitigation rules compensate expenditure to prevent *further* damage once the claimant *has* been injured, shouldn't the law equally compensate a claimant's efforts to avoid being injured in the first place? Significantly indeed, contributory negligence examines how a claimant could have protected their safety *prior to the accident/ injuries occurring*. For example (in standard road accident cases) the court examines whether the claimant looked properly before pulling out into traffic, wore a seat-belt, etc. Contributory negligence complements the mitigation policy which encourages (and reimburses) action to reduce loss *following* the accident.

Moreover these rules could when combined place the claimant in an invidious position, if 'preventive damages' were not available. Jane Stapleton points out that if a cause of action in negligence can only arise once physical damage has occurred to the claimant's body/property, they risk torpedoing their own claim if they take steps to prevent physical damage occurring (eg replacing a potentially defective medical device). But conversely, if the claimant consciously refrains from such actions, waiting until the physical damage occurs and then claiming, the defendant could plausibly argue that the claimant was contributorily negligent – or even (if the claimant deliberately took no action when faced with a severe threat of harm) were the sole cause of their own injuries.⁶⁷

---

⁶⁵ JG Fleming, 'Preventive Damages' in NJ Mullaney (ed), *Torts in the Nineties* (Sydney, Lawbook Co, 1997).
⁶⁶ D Nolan, 'Preventive Damages' (2016) 132 *LQR* 68.
⁶⁷ Stapleton (n 3) 226.

There are other doctrinal analogies, albeit more distant than mitigation and contributory negligence. First, trespass to the person includes the *apprehension* of physical touching (the tort of assault). Second, injunctions obviously have the purpose of preventing future harm/infringements of rights. Injunctions can exceptionally be ordered in advance of any tort having happened (the '*quia timet*' injunction, 'because [the wrong] is feared'). Given that courts have a power to award damages in lieu of an injunction, doing this with regard to a *quia timet* injunction would clearly involve 'preventive damages'.

Third, contract law recognises 'anticipatory breach'. When it is clear that a party cannot or will not perform a future contractual obligation, the innocent party can terminate the contract *immediately*. Yet no actual breach has happened at that point, since the time for performance has not yet arrived. While the analogy with tort seems weak here, anticipatory breach of contract shows that the common law can depart from 'logic'. A distinguished judge concluded that anticipatory breach could not be rationalised: it was 'a piece of positive law, firmly established but not anchored in or deducible from the ordinary course of the law of contract'.[68] Yet despite its fictitious basis, the doctrine is not viewed as anomalous. Anticipatory breach is 'firmly established' because it makes practical good sense. Notably it buttresses the mitigation principle (which applies in contract as in tort), because the innocent party need not wastefully prepare for performance which the other has indicated it will reject when the time comes. It is 'for the benefit of both parties' that the claimant is released from 'laying out money in preparations [for performance] which must be useless'.[69] The claimant avoids futile preparation, the defendant avoids paying for them. Shouldn't tort law recognise 'preventive damages', with the similar aim of forestalling the claimant's loss, thereby reducing the defendant's eventual liability?

Another possible argument is that when the claimant's preventive action relieves the defendant of (some) tortious liability, they are 'unjustly enriched' by the claimant's expenditure and should make restitution. Nolan doubts that this can justify a general doctrine of 'preventive damages'. First, English law does not include a general principle of reimbursement of those whose expenditure protects the property of another (unlike the civilian '*negotiorum gestio*' doctrine). Second, it is unsafe to assume that whenever the claimant 'rescues themselves', the defendant would have had a positive duty to rescue the claimant (which the claimant has performed on the defendant's behalf).

Society as a whole also benefits from the prevention of injuries. But is it tort law's function to provide incentives for economically efficient behaviour? Claimants already have powerful, self-interested motivation to protect themselves (and their property). As Atiyah says (commenting on contributory negligence and mitigation), 'if a person's instinct for self-preservation does not deter them from dangerous conduct, it is unlikely that a denial of monetary or other

---

[68] Lord Mustill, 'Some Reflections on *The Golden Victory*' (2008) 124 *LQR* 569.
[69] *Hochster v de la Tour* (1853) 2 E & B 678, 690.

assistance will do so'.[70] This undermines the most obvious policy justification. But equally for rights-based approaches, it is convincing to extend the law's concern to protect rights into a general action to *prevent* their infringement? Nolan suggests it is 'counter-intuitive' to treat every *threat* to a right as equivalent to its actual infringement, and the recognition of such 'extended' rights would create many difficulties beyond the preventive damages question.[71]

If the law were to allow such 'preventive damages', what should be the conditions for recovery? Nolan tentatively suggests that it would be better to avoid strict conditions that would cause disputes and uncertainty – for example, that the harm was 'imminent', or 'certain' to occur (that the claimant was 'doomed') etc. As Nolan points out, the rules in the current mitigation and contributory negligence doctrines simply ask whether the claimant took 'reasonable' steps to prevent or limit their injuries. A generalised reasonableness approach could similarly inform preventive damages, as in civilian legal systems (where preventive claims are well established).[72]

Caught in the Crossfire: Preventive Damages and Anns

It is unfortunate that the strongest English authority for recovery of preventive damages was *Anns v Merton LBC*,[73] subsequently overruled in *Murphy v Brentwood DC*.[74] *Anns* has been criticised on many grounds: for its general 'test' for duty of care; for erasing the distinction between acts and omissions; for its effect on local authority budgets; and for misclassifying pure economic loss as 'property damage'. The last is relevant here. The *Anns* court reasoned that if negligence made a building dangerously defective, the cost of repairs could be justified as *preventing* the 'material physical damage' of the building's collapse.

Anns clearly contained the germ of the preventive damages concept. But it was being used to circumvent concerns about pure economic loss. As Stapleton noted before *Anns* was overruled,[75] the courts seemed to think that by characterising defective building cases as ones involving *physical damage* (even *potential future* physical damage), concerns about economic loss did not arise. But this expedient led to questionable distinctions. Why distinguish between buildings which were *dangerous* and merely shoddily built?[76] Why distinguish defects that manifested themselves through physical changes (eg a fire-escape that became unsafe to use) and those that did not (a building designed without an adequate fire-escape in the first place)? Stapleton argued presciently that

---

[70] P Cane and J Goudkamp, *Atiyah's Accidents, Compensation and the Law* 9th edn (Cambridge, Cambridge University Press, 2018) 413.
[71] Nolan (n 66) 90–91.
[72] Principles of European Tort Law, art 2.104 (cited by Nolan).
[73] [1978] AC 728.
[74] [1991] 1 AC 398.
[75] Stapleton (n 3).
[76] See *Simaan v Pilkington Glass* [1988] QB 758 (glass wrong colour).

these questions would be addressed better through the duty of care to avoid economic loss rather than manipulating the concept of 'physical changes' to buildings.

In *Murphy* the House of Lords effectively agreed. None of these cases truly involved claims to avert physical damage. If a building was dangerous, it could simply be abandoned – left empty so that no persons or contents (other property) would be damaged by its collapse. Repairs were actually the cost of continuing to use the property (not the cost of preventing injury to others).[77] If the building collapsed injuring only 'itself', this was indeed pure economic loss. The court saw no relevant difference between (eg) a defective product which simply doesn't work, and one which blows up when plugged in ('injuring itself'). In each situation the loss is *economic* – that is, the product is worth less than the purchaser paid for it.[78]

Murphy was a turning point, restricting liability for pure economic loss. However, 'preventive damages' were arguably an undeserved casualty of the demise of *Anns*. Having criticised the 'sterile logic' of the *Murphy* reclassification, Fleming lamented: 'While motivated to slay the dragon of pure economic loss, their Lordships sacrificed its tradition protégé, the victim of physical risk'. For questions about preventive damages could just as easily arise in personal injury cases. Indeed, *Dryden v Johnson Matthey* raised the question whether the claimants' diminished earnings were compensable as the cost of preventing their platinum sensitisation deteriorating into a full-blown allergy. The argument was rejected by the Court of Appeal,[79] and not considered by the Supreme Court. Jarret Huang thinks this a 'thoroughly missed opportunity', regretting that Lady Black preferred 'dextrous gymnastics of reasoning' about physical injury to consideration of the preventive damages debate.[80] The temptation to conceptualise difficult cases as 'physical harm' characterised the controversial *Anns* jurisprudence and remains strong today. But there are strong arguments for the courts to revisit the preventive damages question.

Debate 3
'Wrongful Birth' and Physical Injury

'Wrongful birth' has posed difficult legal (and moral) problems. This debate focuses on the nature of the underlying harm. Is the sanctity of life undermined by holding a child's birth 'actionable damage'? Are such concerns avoided by repackaging liability as an infringement of parental 'autonomy'? Can these cases

---

[77] On this see Nolan (n 66) 76–78; *Thomas v Taylor Wimpey* [2019] EWHC 1134 (TCC).
[78] So a *contractual* remedy should be pursued against the person who supplied it. (NB manufacturers' statutory liability for defective products also excludes 'damage to the product itself': Consumer Protection Act 1987, s 5(2)).
[79] [2016] 1 WLR 4487 [32].
[80] Huang (n 61) 749.

instead be approached from the comforting perspective of 'physical injury'? To the extent that the 'physical injury' classification again proves troublesome, does this indicate that gendered (ie masculine) assumptions govern tort law's hierarchy of protection?

The common feature is a medical professional's reproductive (or *contra-ceptive*) negligence. The historical development has been complex. First, the court rejected a child's claim that they were 'wrongfully alive'. But *parents'* claims for the *cost* of raising an unplanned child were routinely accepted for 15 years, until *McFarlane v Tayside Health Board*.[81] However, damages were still awarded for pregnancy, childbirth and associated costs. The *additional* costs of raising a *disabled* child were also held recoverable.[82] *Rees v Darlington* confirmed the exclusionary rule in *McFarlane*, while awarding an additional 'conventional sum' for the parents' loss of autonomy.[83] These cases pose difficult moral questions. The judges' answers have been notably diverse. How should the law frame the 'gist damage' on which the claims are based? What are the protected rights or interests at stake?

'Wrongful Life'

The courts have rejected so-called 'wrongful life' claims. In *McKay v Essex AHA* the defendants failed to advise a pregnant woman about the consequences of contracting rubella ('German measles'); had she been properly advised she would have terminated the pregnancy; her child, the plaintiff, was born with disabilities caused by rubella.[84] The court dismissed the plaintiff child's claim for damages for the disabilities. She had to allege that the defendants negligently failed to prevent her being born. The claim was, in effect, that the plaintiff should not be alive at all. Ackner LJ declared that the common law could not recognise an obligation to terminate a foetus's existence, as 'wholly contrary to the concept of the sanctity of human life'.[85] Stephenson LJ agreed. This

> further inroad on the sanctity of human life ... would mean regarding the life of a handicapped child as not only less valuable than the life of a normal child, but so much less valuable that it was not worth preserving.[86]

Moreover, the court thought it would be impossible to quantify the 'loss' of being alive (compared to not existing at all). It 'would require a value judgment where a crucial factor [the consequences of death for the dead] lies

---

[81] [2000] 2 AC 59 (*McFarlane*).
[82] *Parkinson v St James NHS Trust* [2002] QB 266 (*Parkinson*).
[83] *Rees v Darlington NHS Trust* [2004] 1 AC 309 (*Rees*).
[84] [1982] QB 1166.
[85] ibid 1188.
[86] ibid 1180–81.

altogether outside the range of human knowledge'.[87] Ackner LJ asked, 'how can a court begin to evaluate non-existence, "the undiscovered country from whose bourn no traveller returns?"'[88] For Griffiths LJ, this 'intolerable and insoluble problem' of quantifying the loss was 'the most compelling reason' to reject the claim.[89]

(Note one exceptional statutory 'wrongful life' claim: fertility clinics are liable to the child for disabilities resulting from fertility treatment.[90] In jurisdictions lacking such legislation, common law claims are problematic. It has been suggested that the tort of public nuisance could offer a remedy for such mistakes on the basis that they harm the human gene pool, 'polluting' a public good.)[91]

'Wrongful Birth' and the Sanctity of Life

Following *McKay*, claims were made *by parents* for the costs of bringing up children whose birth was attributable to medical negligence. Such 'wrongful birth' claims soon succeeded.[92] Compensation could even include the cost of independent school fees, where the claimant's other children had been privately educated.[93] These decisions were overruled in *McFarlane v Tayside*. Parents could not recover the costs of bringing up a (healthy) child (on the facts their *fifth* child), although the mother recovered damages for pain, suffering and loss of amenity during pregnancy and childbirth, and consequent loss of earnings and expenses (eg medical care and maternity clothes).

What was the nature of the harm? Does reformulating the claim as one *by the parents* for *their financial loss* avoid the powerful 'sanctity of life' objection raised in *McKay*? Or is it obfuscation – a distinction without a difference?[94] Lord Millett thought so in *McFarlane*. He alone would have denied damages for pregnancy and childbirth altogether (agreeing with the majority that the costs of raising the child were also unrecoverable). Lord Millett simply declared that a child's birth could not be 'actionable damage': 'There is something distasteful, if not morally offensive, in treating the birth of a normal, healthy child as a matter for compensation'.[95] He rejected the argument that compensation was sought for 'economic injury to the parents ... rather than the birth

---

[87] ibid 1181–82 (Stephenson LJ).
[88] ibid 1189 (referring to Hamlet's 'To be or not to be' speech).
[89] ibid 1192.
[90] Human Fertilisation and Embryology Act 1990, s 44.
[91] BP Billauer, 'The Sperminator as a Public Nuisance: Redressing Wrongful Life and Birth Claims in New Ways (A.K.A. New Tricks for Old Torts)' (2019) 42 *UALR LR* 1.
[92] *Emeh v Kensington and Chelsea Health Authority* [1985] QB 1012 (disabled child), *Thake v Maurice* [1986] QB 644 (healthy child).
[93] *Allen v Bloomsbury Health Authority* [1993] 1 All ER 651, 662.
[94] PR Glazebrook, 'Unseemliness Compounded by Injustice' [1992] *CLJ* 226, 227 ('an affront to public decency ... deeply insulting to handicapped people').
[95] *McFarlane* (n 81) 111.

or existence of the child as such'.⁹⁶ The child's birth and its economic consequences were 'inseparable'.

Lord Millett's approach was uncompromising. Echoes are found in some of the other leading judgments. Lord Steyn cited *McKay v Essex*, reasoning that given the dismissal of the (child's own) 'wrongful life' claim, 'Coherence and rationality demand that the claim by the parents should also be rejected'.⁹⁷ Lord Steyn thought the parents' claim was 'equally repugnant to ideas of the sanctity and value of human life'.⁹⁸ In *Rees v Darlington*, Lord Nicholls refused to overrule *McFarlane* since this would (among other things) 'accord ill with the values society attaches to human life and to parenthood'.⁹⁹ Lord Scott said the essence of *McFarlane* was an exception to ordinary principles of tort recovery, justified by the uniqueness of every human life.¹⁰⁰

Stephenson LJ in *McKay* was concerned that the law should not imply that a disabled claimant's life was worth nothing – that they would be better off dead. But could *Parkinson* send a similarly offensive message? According to that post-*McFarlane* authority,¹⁰¹ parents can claim for the (additional) expense of raising a *disabled* child, although the costs of raising 'normal' children are unrecoverable. This appears to suggest that human lives have different values. Hale LJ in *Parkinson* denied this. In her Ladyship's view the award of damages 'treats a disabled child as having exactly the same worth as a non-disabled child. It affords him the same dignity and status. It simply acknowledges that he costs more'.¹⁰² Lord Hope said in *Rees*: 'love in the context of disability has to be backed by corresponding supportive resources'.¹⁰³ Nevertheless, the distinction has caused judicial unease.¹⁰⁴ Australian judges have made the fiercest criticisms. Kirby J found the premise for distinguishing disabled and healthy children 'offensive', reinforcing outdated attitudes towards disability.¹⁰⁵ (Note, however, that this was in the context of the outright rejection of *McFarlane* which Kirby J blamed for English law's 'unhappy differentiation' between healthy and disabled children.) Lord Millett later declared that whatever strict logic might require, he did not find the distinction drawn in *Parkinson* 'morally offensive', reflecting on the 'sorrow' and 'sympathy' society feels for parents of disabled children.¹⁰⁶ Might parents find this patronising, and Lord Millett's inconsistent commitment to the sanctity of life even a little disturbing?

---

⁹⁶ *CES v Superclinics* (1995) 38 NSWLR 47, 75 (Kirby ACJ).
⁹⁷ *McFarlane* (n 81) 83.
⁹⁸ Citing F Trindade and P Cane, *The Law of Torts in Australia* 3rd edn (Melbourne, Oxford University Press, 1999) 434.
⁹⁹ *Rees* (n 83) [16] (cf [51] per Lord Hope, on his own decision in *McFarlane*).
¹⁰⁰ ibid [138]–[140].
¹⁰¹ Approved in *Meadows v Khan* [2022] AC 852.
¹⁰² *Parkinson* (n 82) [90].
¹⁰³ *Rees* (n 83) [57].
¹⁰⁴ ibid [9] (Lord Bingham).
¹⁰⁵ *Cattanach v Melchior* (2003) 215 CLR 1 [164], [166].
¹⁰⁶ *Rees* (n 83) [112].

'Wrongful Race'?

A claim for negligent fertility treatment raised an even starker moral question. During IVF, eggs were mistakenly fertilised by donor sperm from a man of a different race from the couple being treated for infertility, after a label was misread. The resulting children had visibly different skin colours from their parents (and from each other). The children brought personal injury claims against the fertility service provider.[107] Gillen J expressed 'sympathy and concern' for the parents' 'understandable distress', but dismissed the children's claim. They had not suffered any harm (being 'normal', 'healthy' and 'well'). Their skin colour could not constitute actionable damage in 'a modern civilised society' – 'To hold otherwise would not only be adverse to the self-esteem of the children themselves but anathema to the contemporary views of right thinking people'.[108] It would violate 'the principles which underlie our multicultural society'. That the plaintiffs might suffer racial abuse from 'misguided and cruel' persons could not alter this. The 'crass behaviour of others' did not create actionable damage. The Northern Ireland Court of Appeal agreed.[109]

The decision seems obviously correct – inevitable in the light of *McKay* (it would be just as offensive to allow a claim for 'being alive with the wrong skin colour'). But there are problems.[110] First, a notable exception to rules preventing selective reproduction permits the choice of racially matching donor gametes. This helps preserve confidentiality around the use of fertility treatment. But how is the patient's legitimate expectation of racially-matched donor gametes to be enforced, if no claim lies for its negligent violation by the fertility clinic?[111] Second, the judge dismissed the relevance of skin colour (no more connoting 'damage' than a child's height or the colour of their eyes). This underplays the destructive effect on family life if a child is visibly of a different race from their father.[112] (A Singaporean court has since granted a remedy for 'loss of genetic affinity' when a fertility clinic negligently used a stranger's sperm instead of the patient's husband's.)[113] Gillen J's dismissal of the problem of racism in (99 per cent white) Northern Ireland shows how 'ideas of "race" are deployed in support of broader political projects: … Gillen J [being] at pains to describe a vision of a "modern", "civilised" "multicultural" Northern Ireland'.[114] Social attitudes affect the classification of 'damage'. As the judge himself said, 'Claims for personal injuries, loss or damage do not fit easily into situations which relate to human reproduction'.[115]

---

[107] *A v A Health & Social Services Trust* [2010] NIQB 108.
[108] ibid [18].
[109] [2011] NICA 28.
[110] S Sheldon, 'Only Skin Deep?' (2011) 19 *Med LR* 657.
[111] Cf [2010] NIQB 108 [33] (obiter suggestion that *parents* could receive 'conventional award').
[112] Sheldon (n 110) 665–66.
[113] *ACB v Thomson Medical* [2017] SGCA 20. (The donor was of a different racial group to the husband, but the court declared that fact irrelevant: [128].)
[114] Sheldon (n 110) 664.
[115] [2010] NIQB 108 [19].

Categorisation: Duty and Damage

McFarlane held pregnancy and childbirth to be actionable 'personal injury'. Yet the costs of bringing up the child were unrecoverable, classified as 'pure economic loss'. These characterisations seems questionable. The obligations (financial and legal) of parenthood are unavoidable *consequences* of conception, pregnancy and birth – as much as maternity clothes or labour pains. To characterise the costs of child-rearing as 'purely economic' seems dubious. On normal principles, these consequences of the defenders' breach of duty should have been recoverable.[116] The 'purely economic' label was attached in order to problematise the child-rearing costs.

As seen, Lord Millett alone refused to compensate pregnancy, childbirth and consequent discomfort and expense, in *McFarlane*. These were, in his view, as much 'the price of parenthood' as child-rearing costs: 'The only difference between the two heads of damage claimed is temporal' (ie occurring before or after the child's birth).[117] The reasons for the (unanimous) denial of damages for child-rearing costs applied just as strongly, in principle, to maternity expenses during and before birth. (Hale LJ later observed that we cannot 'draw a clean line at birth'; 'a woman never gets over' carrying and bearing a child.)[118] The logic of Lord Millett's approach is hard to dispute. The majority's award to Mrs McFarlane of damages for pregnancy and childbirth seems an awkward compromise. As Lord Bingham later suggested, after having (correctly) disallowed the cost of raising the child on policy grounds the court was reluctant to give no compensation at all – hence the award limited to pregnancy and childbirth.[119]

Lord Burrows argues 'it is hard to see that anything significant turns on that classification' (ie as 'pure' economic loss) in *McFarlane*.[120] Categorising child-raising costs as 'purely economic' was certainly not the sole reason for denying the claim. The *McFarlane* reasoning was rich and diverse – '[not] easy to assign to the traditional categories of duty, breach and damage'.[121] Looking back on *McFarlane*, Lord Steyn remarked that while some law lords had reasoned about duty of care and some by considering whether the relevant head of loss was recoverable damage, 'the difference in method [was] not of great importance', a mere matter of 'conceptualist thinking' or even 'professors' law'.[122] However, Lord Millett suggested that since a surgeon clearly owes

---

[116] *Parkinson* (n 82) [75]–[76] (Hale LJ). See further C Auckland and I Goold, 'Offsetting Damages in Wrongful Conception and Birth Cases: A Way Through the Post-*McFarlane* Mire' (2022) 138 *LQR* 407 ('doctrinally unsound' to offset the *financial* cost of raising children with the incalculable and *intangible* 'joys or parenthood' since these differ in 'intrinsic nature' (*Parry v Cleaver* [1970] AC 1, 15)).

[117] *McFarlane* (n 81) 114.

[118] *Parkinson* (n 82) [63], [73].

[119] *Rees* (n 83) [8].

[120] *Meadows v Khan* (n 101) [73].

[121] *Parkinson* (n 82) [79] (Hale LJ).

[122] *Rees* (n 83) [30].

a duty of care to their patient (eg regarding the vasectomy in *McFarlane*), it made for 'easier exposition to identify the issue by reference to the head of damage rather than the duty'.[123]

The Supreme Court has recently debated whether 'actionable damage' is a separate component of negligence liability, or better seen as a sub-issue in the duty of care inquiry.[124] Donal Nolan argues that 'the question of whether a given harm is *ever* actionable [should preferably be considered] under the heading of actionable damage' rather than subsumed under the duty of care. In this way, the question of actionable damage, which tends to be under-analysed or ignored altogether, is more likely to be 'addressed openly and comprehensively'.[125] Lord Steyn's dismissive attitude towards taxonomic niceties is understandable perhaps. The precise conceptual structure of negligence rarely determines the outcome of a case. But courts should aim for maximum transparency of reasoning. For Nolan, this justifies the disaggregation of the 'damage' question, to focus attention upon it. The structure of negligence may not be entirely academic (in Lord Steyn's pejorative sense).

Gendered Reasoning About 'Actionable Damage'?

Classification can be determinative. Yet it does not involve deduction from objective facts about the physical universe. A strong dose of morality drove the 'wrongful life' and 'wrong race' decisions. *McFarlane* too was arguably influenced by moral preconceptions – and gendered ones at that.

On what basis were damages awarded for pregnancy and childbirth (and their consequences)? Margaret Fordham identifies two possibilities, neither straightforward. *McFarlane* either 'regards pain and suffering as actionable without the need to attach them to recognisable damage, or, uniquely, it treats these natural and transient conditions [pregnancy and childbirth] as themselves constituting [personal injury]'.[126] *McFarlane* itself provides no clear answer (Fordham notes judges' strong tendency towards 'oblique' reasoning when addressing 'more expansive' forms of actionable damage). Surely though, Fordham's first option (compensating freestanding pain and suffering *not consequential on actionable (gist) damage*) is too radical to be *tacitly* ascribed to *McFarlane*. Thus under the second option, pregnancy and childbirth must have been treated as 'physical harm'. Fordham thinks that too is 'at best questionable'. Her doubts have been widely shared.

At first instance in *McFarlane*, Lord Gill held that pregnancy could not be 'personal injury'. Despite its discomfort, and the pain of labour and childbirth,

---

[123] ibid [108].
[124] Compare *Meadows v Khan* (n 101) [28] (Lord Hodge and Lord Sales) and [80] (Lord Burrows).
[125] Nolan (n 52) 61.
[126] M Fordham, 'The Protection of Personal Interests – Evolving Forms of Damage in Negligence' (2015) 27 *Singapore Ac LJ* 643.

these were all 'natural processes', the 'sequelae' of an event (conception) that 'can hardly be considered as a physical injury per se', and moreover 'leading to a happy outcome'.[127] The law lords disagreed. But even they did not seem to think pregnancy and childbirth were 'personal injuries' in the ordinary sense.

Christian Witting has sought to explain *McFarlane*.[128] Personal injury involves a negative physical change. Taking that view, there was *no damage* in *McFarlane* (as the trial judge had correctly held). Pregnancy and childbirth are 'entirely natural events' that women's constitutions are 'designed to induce and to accommodate' (and indeed 'Most women are only too glad to avail themselves of the opportunity to conceive' at some point in their lives). The changes inside a pregnant woman's body cannot therefore be seen as 'deleterious', compromising 'physiological integrity' or 'impairing their functioning'. Nevertheless Witting thinks the House of Lords' decision defensible. It transcended a strictly physical approach to 'harm'. *McFarlane* recognised pregnancy and childbirth as *socially constructed* personal injury. Although natural, those phenomena were justifiably deemed to be 'damage', given the cultural context of people legitimately seeking to limit the size of their families. To suggest there was no physical injury was

> correct as a matter of observable fact, but incorrect as a matter of jurisprudential logic. There was no actual deleterious change in the state of, or impairment to, the claimant's body in [*McFarlane*]. But the House of Lords recognised, nevertheless, a socially perceived form of physical injury.[129]

Nolan thinks it is not to the point that pregnancy is 'natural' (so, in its way, is the development of cancer), nor that many people might welcome being pregnant and giving birth to a child. What matters is the effect on a particular claimant, who did not wish to become pregnant. Nolan argues that despite this element of subjective perception,[130] pregnancy is no less a physical injury than a broken leg (emphasising the considerable curtailment of autonomy resulting from unwanted pregnancy).[131]

However, such arguments have proved controversial, especially Witting's insistence that pregnancy and childbirth are *not* 'physical injuries', only 'socially perceived' as such. The serious and lasting physical effects of pregnancy and labour were emphasised by Hale LJ in *Parkinson*.[132] This reinforced her point that an unwanted pregnancy is a serious invasion of a woman's autonomy.

---

[127] *McFarlane v Tayside* 1997 SLT 211.
[128] C Witting, 'Physical Damage in Negligence' [2002] *CLJ* 189.
[129] ibid 196.
[130] Compare *McFarlane* (n 81) 112 (Lord Millett): 'If the law regards an event as beneficial, plaintiffs cannot make it a matter for compensation merely by saying that it is an event they did not want to happen. In [tort] plaintiffs are not normally allowed, by a process of subjective devaluation, to make a detriment out of a benefit'.
[131] Nolan (n 52) 72–77.
[132] *Parkinson* (n 82) [63]–[68].

How could such significant bodily changes, usually accompanied by at least moderate pain and discomfort, not be thought 'injury'?

Joanne Conaghan refers sarcastically to Witting's 'truly remarkable conceptual feat' in presenting pregnancy and childbirth as 'non-physical' injuries.[133] In Conaghan's view such absurdities are characteristic of tort law's 'systematic, gender-based disadvantage' for women:

> the historical legacy of a predominantly male judiciary and legal academy has arguably conspired with the formal absence of gender from legal discourse to enshrine in law an ignorance of women's lives. [Tort law's] 'ragbag' of discrete and unconnected wrongs[134] begins to assume a more definite and recognizable form, one that is steeped in the biographies of men and an entrenched disregard of women.[135]

More specifically Conaghan notes that 'harm' in tort law is 'a deeply social concept and ... highly gendered'. Revealingly, 'judges seem perennially flummoxed by the injurious implications of pregnancy, leading them to classify miscarriage as a form of nervous shock, and involuntary motherhood as pure economic loss'.[136] (The illogicality of the last classification has been criticised above; Nolan also criticises this unfortunate example of 'shoehorn[ing] novel forms of harm into existing categories of actionable damage'.)[137] Labelling as 'pure economic loss' or (*pace* Witting) as a socially constructed, *deemed*-physical harm 'assert the dubiosity of wrongful conception as a physical harm of the first order and, thereby, to weaken claims as to its injurious nature'.[138]

Conaghan notes that *McFarlane* curtailed liability that lower courts had recognised for the previous 15 years. The reversal has affected female claimants disproportionately. Hale LJ evidently agrees. In *Parkinson* her Ladyship highlighted that *mothers* bear especially heavy financial (as well as physical and emotional) burdens of parenthood. She thought it was 'not surprising' that 'their Lordships [in *McFarlane*] did not go into detail about the invasion of bodily integrity caused by conception, pregnancy and childbirth' (unsurprising because this fell outside their personal experience?)[139] Perhaps the different perspectives of men and women was another reason why Lord Steyn's notorious moral arbiter, the hypothetical 'traveller on the [London] Underground',[140] might have given 'a less emphatic and less unanimous' answer than the House of Lords believed.[141]

---

[133] J Conaghan, 'Tort Law and Feminist Critique' [2003] *CLP* 175, 191.
[134] T Weir, *Tort Law* (Oxford, Oxford University Press, 2002) 1.
[135] Conaghan (n 133) 192.
[136] ibid.
[137] Nolan (n 52) 88.
[138] Conaghan (n 133) 191.
[139] *Parkinson* (n 82) [63].
[140] *McFarlane* (n 81) 82.
[141] *Parkinson* (n 82) [82].

Tort law is not overtly biased against female claimants. Historically there were explicitly gendered torts, now abolished as archaic. But in Conaghan's opinion, modern tort's apparent gender-neutrality conceals discriminatory *effects*. Tort's hierarchy of protection, consistently privileging 'male' interests (physical, financial) and downgrading harms to which women are more vulnerable (emotional, relational, reproductive), is real. Yet this structural discrimination is hard to challenge, or even recognise. The traditional, doctrinal approach shields value-choices implicit in the status quo. The 'immanent' values latent within the law's inherited categories are seen as the main source for proper legal reasoning. But these conventional, formal approaches blind us to the categories' discriminatory effects (and should we be surprised that tort retains a biased structure when female claimants suffered numerous legal disabilities, well into the twentieth century).[142] Chamallas agrees. Tort's 'architecture of bias' is not the result of 'bigotry' but rather 'cognitive processes that influence everyone's thinking'.[143] It is therefore essential not to accept 'the basic tort categories as neutral, static, and essential'.[144]

For example, it has recently been argued that negligence law should encompass situations where someone culpably fails to realise that a sexual partner is not consenting, or carelessly undermines their consent. Assuming that the defendant's carelessness in these respects could be proved, liability should not be obstructed by doubts whether non-consensual penetration would of itself be 'personal injury'. Cardi and Camallas think it is 'astonishing' that this should be in doubt. Such sexual invasion is 'prototypical physical harm' and should clearly be actionable in negligence – contrary to 'long-standing, misogynist cultural assumption that there is no physical harm from (mere) non-consensual intercourse unless the aggressor also inflicts extrinsic physical injuries, such as bruises or broken bones'.[145] Again this shows the moral and political choices lurking within the concept of 'actionable damage'.

'Loss of Autonomy' as Actionable Damage?

Rees v Darlington reaffirmed *McFarlane* with a 'gloss': a 'conventional' sum of £15,000 for invasion of the involuntary parents' autonomy. (This took up Lord Millett's suggestion in *McFarlane*, although additional to, not instead of, damages for pregnancy and childbirth.) The precise theoretical basis for this

---

[142] See P Mitchell, *A History of Tort Law 1900–1950* (Cambridge, Cambridge University Press, 2015) ch 4 ('Women') (judicial reasoning 'abrasively political beneath their camouflage of merely doing history's bidding'); ch 12 ('Husbands') (vicarious liability *for wives' torts*).

[143] Chamallas (n 2) 522.

[144] ibid 530.

[145] WJ Cardi and M Chamallas, 'A Negligence Claim for Rape' (2022) 101 *Texas LR* (forthcoming). (As they accept, all sexual touching would prima facie constitute battery – but with its defence of 'honest belief' (in consent), that tort does not reach non-consensual sex that is culpable but non-intentional.)

award is not entirely clear.¹⁴⁶ Lords Steyn and Hope, dissenting, complained about this (preferring to leave the question to Parliament).

Nolan argues that the *Rees* award recognises invasion of autonomy as actionable damage in negligence.¹⁴⁷ Autonomy is unquantifiable: hence the 'conventional sum', resembling the fixed statutory bereavement award.¹⁴⁸ But Nolan rejects the view that *Rees* removed the requirement of damage entirely, in favour of pure rights-vindication within a negligence claim. Such a function should be confined to the trespassory torts, which are actionable per se. There is good reason for the historical distinction. Trespass offers strong protection of rights but only within a carefully limited sphere: requiring intentional invasion in a particular form (eg direct physical contact in battery). The contrasting requirement of 'actionable gist damage' is central to negligence because the negligence tort lacks trespass's inherent limits on tortious conduct. Negligence 'applies paradigmatically to unintentional conduct, incorporates no requirement of directness, and encompasses a limitless variety of actions or omissions'. The damage requirement 'is therefore essential if negligence law is not unduly to restrict people's freedom of action'.¹⁴⁹

Nolan persuasively argues that *Rees* has not collapsed the distinction between trespass and negligence. Recognising 'invasion of autonomy' as actionable damage in negligence is nevertheless radical. Autonomy underlies many routine negligence claims – for example protection against personal injuries indirectly protects autonomy (which physical injuries can undoubtedly curtail). But, Nolan argues, treating 'autonomy in the round' as a freestanding cause of action would be far-reaching: to keep it 'within acceptable limits' negligence should respond only to *particular* invasions of autonomy (like wrongful birth – and perhaps also freedom of movement).¹⁵⁰ Craig Purshouse agrees.¹⁵¹ Since virtually *any* claim could be repackaged as 'invasion of autonomy' (even 'interference' that makes the claimant *better off*), it would collapse any boundaries on negligence liability. Autonomy is a vague and contested concept that would be incoherent with the core of actionable damage, which involves a significant objective deterioration in the claimant's position.

Rees is on any view a radical decision. It transcends the physical injury paradigm altogether. In Fordham's view, *Rees* shifts negligence towards the vindication of rights, taking advantage of the absence of a precise definition of 'actionable damage'. But she accepts the trend towards vindicating personal

---

¹⁴⁶ In *ACB v Thomson Medical* (n 113) 'loss of genetic affinity' was quantified as 30 per cent of the costs of raising the child, a 'conventional sum' having been rejected by the Singapore Court of Appeal.
¹⁴⁷ Nolan (n 52) 79–80.
¹⁴⁸ Fatal Accidents Act 1976, s 1A.
¹⁴⁹ Nolan (n 52) 79.
¹⁵⁰ ibid 87.
¹⁵¹ C Purshouse, 'Autonomy, Affinity, and the Assessment of Damages' (2018) 26 *Med LR* 675 (commending *ACB v Thomson Medical* n 113).

autonomy in the abstract is not uniform. *Chester v Afshar* vindicated the right to informed patient consent by the 'artificial' and 'contrived' invention of a causal link with the injurious physical side effects of non-negligent surgery.¹⁵² (In notable contrast to *Rees*, Lord Hoffmann's obiter suggestion of a 'modest solatium' to mark the wrong, in his dissenting speech was not taken up.)¹⁵³ Even in *Rees*, the court 'glossed over the details' of the conventional sum, leaving an 'ambiguous' basis. Fordham thinks it 'difficult to discern from the various circumstances any distinct philosophy or consistent pattern' of liability. Vindication of autonomy in negligence remains at a developmental stage, with the courts' reasoning correspondingly 'often somewhat oblique'.¹⁵⁴

Conclusion

This chapter has reviewed marginal 'personal injuries' cases. Beneath the surface we find fundamental shifts in ideas of 'actionable damage'. These have the potential to transform the nature of negligence and the interests it protects. That such an important transformation could take place partially concealed flows from the difficult concept of actionable damage itself. As Nolan suggests, it cannot be defined save by circularity: damage is 'actionable' simply when it is recognised as the 'gist' of a negligence claim. Even the 'easily identifiable' core of negligence – physical damage – is (as we have seen) 'difficult to define with any degree of precision'.¹⁵⁵

Questions such as 'wrongful life', 'preventive' damages, or anxiety-based claims are bound to be controversial. But tort lawyers' typical neglect of the basic question 'what kinds of damage are actionable' should cease. By bringing such questions to the surface, we reduce the chance that they can be determined by intuitive assumptions – even by social or masculine prejudice – rather than receiving open debate.

---

¹⁵² [2005] AC 134; see ch 2, 'Debate 4: "Informed Medical Consent" – Which Tort?'.
¹⁵³ *Chester v Afshar* ibid [33]–[34]. See further *Shaw v Kovac* [2017] 1 WLR 4773.
¹⁵⁴ Fordham (n 126) 663–64.
¹⁵⁵ D Nolan, 'Damage in the English Law of Negligence' [2013] *JETL* 259.

9

Psychiatric Illness, Emotional Harm and 'Shock'

No area of English tort law has been more fiercely criticised than the law on psychiatric injury (in older terminology, 'nervous shock'). To 'debate' it might seem like an exercise in defending the indefensible. Moreover liability has entered a dormant state – the common law consciously frozen,[1] pending legislative reform that remains absent from the government's agenda. Yet it raises fundamental questions about what interests tort law values, and how problematic categories of liability should be controlled – and by whom. How did we get here? Why is the law so disfigured by arbitrary rules? Are the 'policy reasons' behind them convincing, or even defensible? How should the law be reformed?

Debate 1
Physical Injuries, Shock, Distress and 'Recognisable Psychiatric Illness' – What Interest Should Tort Law Protect?

A Preference for the Physical?

The previous chapter discussed tort's historical preoccupation with 'physical injury'. Nowhere is it more apparent than in claims for mental and emotional disturbance. Tort is notoriously reluctant to compensate victims of psychiatric illness. 'Mere distress' cannot be the gist of a negligence claim, nor even in the intentional '*Wilkinson v Downton* tort'.[2] By contrast when associated with *physical* injury, such harms are generously treated. Both distress and mental illness are freely recoverable as 'consequential loss' in personal injuries claims.[3] (Declining to distinguish physical and psychiatric consequential injuries has

---

[1] Cf *Paul v Royal Wolverhampton NHS Trust* [2022] 2 WLR 917 (granting permission to appeal to Supreme Court).

[2] *Rhodes v OPO* [2016] AC 219.

[3] *Malcolm v Broadhurst* [1970] 3 All ER 508.

significant implications in practice: 'Whereas eggshell skulls are fortunately rare in medicine, the same is not true for eggshell personalities'.)[4] The courts' generosity extends to claimants in the 'zone of danger' but physically unharmed, who can recover damages for *unforeseeable* mental illness (eg recurrence of previous condition): *Page v Smith*.[5]

This reasoning has been cogently criticised.[6] It misunderstands the 'thin skull rule' (which compensates unforeseeable *consequential* injuries once the claimant shows they were negligently harmed by the defendant).[7] *Page v Smith* imposes liability on a defendant who was not even *negligent* in the relevant sense. The claimant had been unusually susceptible to a relapse. But if it was not foreseeable that an average road-user would suffer any psychiatric illness, how can the defendant possibly take care to avoid it? It is only careless to risk injuries foreseeable to persons of ordinary susceptibility. The holds for *physical* injury too: there would be 'no wrong' in 'merely brush[ing] against' somebody who had an unknown 'terrible tendency to bleed on slight contact'.[8] (In practice however, unusual susceptibility to *psychiatric* harm is far more common.)[9]

Aside from the 'eggshell skull' exception for *consequential* loss following from a proven (ie foreseeable) injury: 'The law expects reasonable fortitude and robustness of its citizens and will not impose liability for the exceptional frailty of certain individuals'.[10] This is out of fairness to defendants.[11] *Page v Smith* has therefore been rejected for violating basic negligence principles in other jurisdictions.[12] It may survive in England for pragmatic reasons: it simplifies ordinary road-accident litigation (like *Page v Smith*) since the court does not need to consider separately the foreseeability of physical and psychiatric injury.[13] The rule also exemplifies tort's preoccupation with physical injury, pressed to its logical extreme (or beyond it).

'Psychiatric Illness' or 'Nervous Shock'?

It isn't usually worth quibbling about labels. Arguably however, the old-fashioned 'nervous shock' and modern equivalent 'psychiatric illness' refer to

---

[4] S Wessely, 'Liability for Psychiatric Illness' (1995) 39 *J Psychosom Res* 659.
[5] [1996] AC 155.
[6] S Bailey and D Nolan, 'The *Page v Smith* Saga: A Tale of Inauspicious Origins and Unintended Consequences' [2010] *CLJ* 495.
[7] *White v Chief Constable* [1999] 2 AC 455, 470, 476 (Lord Goff, dissenting) (*White*).
[8] *Bourhill v Young* [1943] AC 92, 110 (Lord Wright).
[9] *Mustapha v Culligan of Canada Ltd* [2008] 2 SCR 114, [14] (McLachlin CJ): 'This ["ordinary fortitude"] question may be acute in claims for mental injury, since there is a wide variation in how particular people respond to particular stressors'.
[10] *White* (n 7) 463 (Lord Griffiths, dissenting).
[11] *Mustapha* (n 9) [15]–[16].
[12] *Tame v NSW* (2002) 211 CLR 317 (Australia); *Mustapha* (n 9) (Canada).
[13] See Law Com 5.11–5.16 (recommending retention of *Page v Smith*).

slightly different problems (as well as reflecting changing medical theories). One problematic situation is an injury that results through *perception* rather than physical impact (or other physical means). For example, an unexpected terrifying sound that triggers a heart attack. The 'problem' here is the absence of spatial limitations on those who might be affected in this way. A second quite distinct problem is how to define 'injury' in cases involving seriously upsetting experiences – but no physical harm. For example, a group exposed to toxic chemicals who have not (yet) developed any physical illness but who are understandably anxious about deteriorating health.[14] The 'problem' here is whether tort should treat *all* significant distress as 'actionable damage' or, if not, what the definition should be.

As discussed in the next section, English law uses 'recognisable psychiatric illness' as the definition of 'actionable damage'. While criticised, this is a relatively stable feature of the law. By contrast, defining the scope of claims for harmful 'perception' rather than 'impacts' is the core problem discussed in the remainder of the chapter. Of course *both* problems can arise in the same case and frequently do, as in the standard claim of someone traumatised by learning about a close relative's accidental death. But it is important to realise that they can arise separately. A fatal heart attack is clearly an actionable personal injury (death) – that is unproblematic, indeed undeniable. How could a heart attack, let alone death, be anything other than a physical injury to the person. The *means* of infliction, rather than the ultimate *injury*, is problematic here.[15]

This clarifies an unfortunate tendency in historical accounts. Today the usual label is 'psychiatric' damage. 'Nervous shock' is seen as an outmoded 'misleading and inaccurate expression'.[16] Yet the early leading cases invariably involved traumatised women suffering miscarriages, stillbirth or even death.[17] 'Psychiatric illness' utterly misdescribes those injuries. The label matters. In their leading account of tort's gendered approach to trauma, Martha Chamallas and Linda Kerber argue that the law's classification has disadvantaged women. Treating such cases as complaints about 'emotional disturbance' placed them at tort's margin rather than (as physical injury) at its centre. Tort doctrine 'transformed a recurring *physical* injury to women – fright-based miscarriages and other birth-related trauma – into a special type of *nonphysical* harm that the law

---

[14] *Rothwell v Chemical & Insulating Co* [2008] 1 AC 281.

[15] *Page v Smith* (n 5) at 181 (Lord Browne-Wilkinson) ('the end product [heart attack] is a physical condition although it has been brought about by a process [shock] which is not demonstrably a physical one but lies in the mental or nervous system').

[16] *Attia v British Gas* [1988] QB 304, 317 (Bingham LJ), on which compare *Page v Smith* [1994] RTR 293, 318 (Hoffmann LJ) ('mental or physical illness resulting from the effect of an event upon the mind ... used to be called "nervous shock" but the term has gone out of fashion ... It is sometimes called "psychiatric damage" but its distinguishing feature is its causation rather than its symptoms. It will include, for example, a miscarriage caused by severe fright').

[17] Eg *Dulieu v White* [1901] 2 KB 669, *Hambrook v Stokes Bros* [1925] 1 KB 141.

would not recognize'.[18] This is but one aspect of the systematic devaluation of women's interests:

> The law of torts values physical security and property more highly than emotional security and human relationships. This apparently gender-neutral hierarchy of values has privileged men, as the traditional owners and managers of property, and has burdened women, to whom the emotional work of maintaining human relationships has commonly been assigned.[19]

Many obstacles confront claims for psychiatric illness and shock-induced physical injuries. This is consistent with tort law's universally hesitant and sceptical protection against 'ethereal' (as opposed to physical) injuries.[20] But the early law's emphasis on physical injury was understandable. First, as noted, the cases in practice invariably involved physical injuries, albeit sustained by perception rather than physical impact. Indeed, second, this reflected contemporary medical understanding. Doctors believed that shock had a physical impact on the nervous system, producing physical symptoms (like miscarriage). Imogen Goold and Catherine Kelly have recently argued that it is inaccurate and unfair to claim that 'earlier generations of judges have regarded psychiatry and psychiatrists with suspicion, if not hostility'.[21] The early twentieth-century cases actually 'demonstrate a scientifically informed view of nervous shock congruent with the widely held medical view at the time'.[22] Judges did not display unwarranted scepticism, but on the contrary developed the early law in line with medical understanding. A solitary dictum dismissing 'imaginary' illnesses has been given undue prominence in historical accounts.[23] In fact that dictum had been 'uniformly discredited and disapproved ever since'.[24] That for many lawyers today, an alleged mistrust of psychiatry has become 'the accepted origin story' reflects merely our 'cultural enthusiasm for identifying and redressing prejudice'.[25]

That said, modern medicine's understanding has now changed. As discussed in the third Debate, strong objections to the '*Alcock* tests' emphasise their *medical irrelevance*. In particular the requirement of physical proximity in time and space (and perception through 'unaided senses').[26] Psychiatrists object that

---

[18] M Chamallas and LK Kerber, 'Women, Mothers, and the Law of Fright: A History' (1990) 88 *Michigan LR* 814, 833 (emphasis added).
[19] ibid 814.
[20] Nancy Levit, 'Ethereal Torts' (1992) 61 *Geo Wash LR* 136.
[21] *McLoughlin v O'Brian* [1983] 1 AC 410, 433 (Lord Bridge).
[22] I Goold and C Kelly, 'Who's Afraid of Imaginary Claims? Common Misunderstandings of the Origin of the Action for Pure Psychiatric Injury in Negligence 1888–1943' (2022) 138 *LQR* 58, 66.
[23] *Victorian Railway Commissioners v Coultas* (1888) 13 App Cas 222, 226.
[24] *Owens v Liverpool Corpn* [1939] 1 KB 394, 398–99.
[25] Goold and Kelly (n 22) 69.
[26] Another artificial requirement, the 'sudden shocking event' is blamed on the traditional 'nervous shock' label: see 'Abolition: "Sudden Shocking Event"' below.

there is no correlation between such physical phenomena and the likelihood of mental illness resulting. The courts probably realise this. They have feared an 'overwhelming influx' or 'cascade' of *genuine* mental trauma following major disasters (rather than imaginary or fraudulent claims).[27] To limit liability they have characteristically reached for 'awkward geographic indicators', physical 'mechanistic' tests which maximise predictability.[28] The tradition is longstanding. As early as 1902 'logic' favoured compensation for all 'nervous' injuries. But Massachusetts law retained the rule that the jar to the nervous system must be accompanied by a physical impact. Holmes CJ frankly accepted this was 'an arbitrary exception, based upon a notion of what is practicable'.[29] Policy, rather than scientific illiteracy, has driven the common law. Indeed when it comes to 'actionable damage', the professional psychiatric view is definitive.

'Recognisable Psychiatric Illness'

For 50 years actionable damage has been defined as a 'recognisable psychiatric illness'.[30] This rule is widely accepted.[31] The law's definition of 'psychiatric illness' deliberately piggy-backs on the medical definition here,. Perhaps inevitably so. Mental illness is not visible to the naked eye. The expert evidence of a psychiatrist (ie a doctor specialising in mental health) is needed to identify it. What evidence can the psychiatrist offer save their diagnosis of the claimant's illness (or not), using the agreed medical definition?

Nevertheless Jyoti Ahuja, herself a clinical psychologist, argues this is inappropriate. The law fails to understand that 'psychiatry's categories and classifications are designed for a different purpose entirely'.[32] In professional practice, psychiatrists diagnose illnesses to *treat* their patients. The key question for a doctor is whether medicine can/should treat the supposed 'mental illness'. Psychiatrists are wary of expanding diagnosis (expanding the categories of 'mental illness') which risks powerful psychoactive drugs being given to patients who will not benefit. Another reason for caution in diagnosis is the social stigma, even today, of being labelled mentally ill. For good reason, 'psychiatrists aspire to keep false-positive diagnoses of mental illness to a minimum'.[33]

Also, severity of distress and impact on the patient's life are not per se the psychiatrist's concern. Painful and debilitating psychological reactions commonly follow life events such as bereavements. Psychiatrists, however, focus on

---

[27] Goold and Kelly (n 22).
[28] Levit (n 20) 171.
[29] *Homans v Boston Elevated Railway* 62 NE 737 (1902).
[30] *Hinz v Berry* [1970] 2 QB 40 (Lord Denning MR) (contrasting with grief, sorrow and worry).
[31] Law Com No 249 (1998).
[32] J Ahuja, 'Liability for Psychological and Psychiatric Harm: The Road to Recovery' (2014) *Medical LR* 23.
[33] ibid 36.

abnormal reactions. For example, psychiatry's distinction between 'pathological grief disorder' and 'ordinary' grief is 'crucial for therapeutic purposes': the former responds to antidepressant drug treatment whereas the latter does not. Yet the distinction is *irrelevant* for assessing the severity of the damage done to the grieving person's life. And surely, Ahuja argues, that severity of impact is what *law* should be concerned with.

Nor are the boundaries of 'mental illness' drawn in a purely scientific way, as lawyers might assume. Ahuja cites the notorious example of homosexuality, once classified as a mental illness, then in 1973 removed from the definitive Diagnostic and Statistical Manual of Psychiatric Disorder ('DSM') by the psychiatry profession's vote (after campaigns by gay rights activists). This dramatic 'depathologizing' of non-hetero sexuality was evidently influenced by social *mores*. Another example is PTSD, 'consciously and deliberately' recognised to deal with Vietnam War veterans' trauma in 1970s America.[34] Lawyers may be surprised that medicine, like law, may be influenced directly by social concerns.

Perhaps tort law should be pleased that psychiatric medicine, like law, reflects the views of society at large. Yet, Rachael Mulheron asks, should psychiatric diagnosis be viewed as a purely medical question, on which the courts must always defer to the psychiatrist's professional opinion?[35] 'It often seems to be assumed that whether someone is suffering from a mental illness is a purely medical question. However, the concept of illness is, to some extent, a social construction'.[36] But would it not complicate litigation if courts could define 'mental illness' differently from the expert medical witnesses? The 'recognisable psychiatric illness' requirement has been justified as a 'powerful control mechanism' for trauma-based claims.[37] There is a sound legal basis for a clear exclusionary rule.[38]

Yet commentators note the uncertainties involved in diagnosing mental illness. The courts have 'canonised' the taxonomy of diseases in the DSM. Yet such manuals were simply not designed to provide clear legal rules. As Mulheron emphasises, the DSM is deliberately full of caveats and qualifications which assist its proper *medical* function (diagnosing illness correctly) while reducing its usefulness as a source of bright-line legal classifications. (The DSM itself notes the likelihood of its diagnostic information being 'misused or misunderstood' in the legal context.) Considerable disagreement between expert psychiatric witnesses is common (in a way that doctors would never disagree whether a claimant had broken their leg). This does not of itself discredit the medical concept of 'mental illness'. Trial courts constantly have to resolve

---

[34] Wessely (n 4).

[35] R Mulheron, 'Rewriting the Requirement for a "Recognized Psychiatric Injury" in Negligence Claims' (2012) 32 *OJLS* 77.

[36] D Ipp et al, *Review of the Law of Negligence: Final Report* (Canberra, Australian Government, 2002) 9.6.

[37] *CJD Litigation; Group B Plaintiffs v UK MRC* [2000] Lloyd's Rep Med 161, 163 (Morland J).

[38] MH Matthews, 'Negligent Infliction of Emotional Distress' (2009) 44 *Wake Forest LR* 1177.

factual disputes between experts. But if the main virtue of 'recognisable psychiatric illness' is thought to be its hard-edged certainty (by contrast with 'severe distress'), this seems questionable.

Simon Wessely (a future president of the Royal College of Psychiatrists) warned about the difficulty of tracing the *causes* of mental illness. First, causation is largely outside the concern of psychiatric clinical medicine, which focuses on symptoms and their treatment. How they were caused is immaterial. The sole exception is PTSD – uniquely defined as an abnormal response to a trauma (with particular relevance for tort claims, therefore). Yet PTSD illustrates Wessley's second main point. Causation in psychiatry is 'multifactoral'. While PTSD can by definition only arise in response to trauma, most people who suffer trauma still do *not* develop PTSD. PTSD's likelihood depends more on pre-existing personality. Mulheron quotes the psychiatrist who successfully campaigned for PTSD's recognition: 'pre-incident vulnerability factors (eg, psychiatric history) and post-incident social support contribute more to post-trauma morbidity than does the magnitude of the ... trauma'.[39]

It is usually hard to be sure what causes mental illness. Even with the illness most commonly associated with accidents and catastrophes (PTSD), the decisive factors lie beyond the trauma (although that might be the immediate trigger). As Wessely perceives, tort liability requires a clear, binary answer to whether the defendant's negligent conduct was a cause or not. But that requirement risks injustice in the present context, given psychiatry's nature as 'a dimensional, not a categorical discipline'. These are important points (which we will consider again in the discussion of employment claims, below).

'Mere Distress'

Negligently causing emotional distress short of a 'recognised psychiatric injury' is not actionable damage in English law (ie cannot generate a freestanding claim).[40] Why not? Should the law draw this sharp distinction between 'recognisable psychiatric illness' (personal injury) and other, 'lesser' emotional anguish? (Even the label seems problematic, given that 'emotional' reactions have a connotation of impulsiveness or excitability.)[41]

The accepted explanation is that liability for 'mere distress' would be too extensive. Gregory Keating analyses concerns in US law, which cautiously accepts such emotional distress claims.[42] When emotional distress is 'endemic' in human existence, our lives would become impossible if tort censured

---

[39] R Spitzer et al, 'Problems with the Post-traumatic Stress Disorder Diagnosis' (2008) 192 *Brit J Psychiatry* 3.
[40] *Hicks v Chief Constable of South Yorkshire* [1992] 2 All ER 65.
[41] H Teff, *Causing Psychiatric and Emotional Harm: Reshaping the Boundaries of Legal Liability* (Oxford, Hart, 2009) 5.
[42] Gregory C Keating, 'When is Emotional Distress Harm?' in SGA Pitel et al (eds), *Tort Law: Challenging Orthodoxy* (Oxford, Hart, 2013).

everything that foreseeably upsets another person. Keating notes that in all kinds of social settings people reasonably do things that will *unavoidably* distress others: managing a business; carrying on intimate relations (eg seeking a divorce); robust assertion of political opinions; criticism and shunning within religious communities; litigation (which is inevitably distressing for the other party) .... To extend liability from intentional/inevitable distress to its *careless* infliction would be 'even more stifling'. The modern world would need to be remade as a 'pastoral idyll'. The recognition of a general right to emotional tranquillity would, in short, have socially unacceptable consequences. Even if confined to *serious* distress such liability would 'modify every aspect of private social intercourse'.[43]

Lawyers seem to assume the subordinate position of emotional harms – axiomatically less serious than physical injuries. Yet they can be just as debilitating, potentially much more so. Given 'modern analgesics', physical pain may be easier to bear than emotional suffering.[44] Keating accepts this. On the other hand, we are often expected to face down unpleasant experiences by 'mastering our emotions'.[45] People frequently meet the most exasperating situations with 'relative calm' – and moreover we *should*. Tort law expects us to cope, not claim. For example, somebody distressed by aesthetic failings of their next-door neighbour's house rightly has no claim: 'We can be asked and expected to toughen up and live with each other's bad taste'.[46] By contrast *physical* injuries cannot be prevented or resolved by the victim's will. The requirement of phlegmatic 'coping' is again linked to concerns about crushing liability. We all have to deal with some harsh, hurtful and unpleasant behaviour because the alternative, litigation over distress caused by 'every case of fancied insult', would 'make life intolerable'.[47]

Yet Keating does not argue against *all* emotional distress claims. Mental anguish can be so severe and debilitating as to limit the claimant's 'agency' – that is, compromise their lives as much as a physical injury. In such situations we should *not* simply ask the victim to 'suck up' the distress. We rightly build up tight emotional bonds with our close family – especially parents' ties to their children. Such relationships are invested with such significance that there is clear vulnerability to life-shattering distress, should the other party (eg one's children) suffer significant injuries or death. Keating accepts this requires a value-judgement. One especially sensitive to their neighbour's luridly painted house is not praised for their developed aesthetic sensibilities, but told to 'toughen up'. That kind of sensitivity is not legally indulged. By contrast, one who renders themselves highly vulnerable to distress by emotionally investing in close loving relationships deserves tort's protection. Theirs is a worthy vulnerability cultivated by deep emotional attachment. It would be quite

---

[43] D Kennedy, 'The Structure of Blackstone's Commentaries' (1979) 28 *Buffalo LR* 205, 356.
[44] Teff (n 41) 1.
[45] Keating (n 42) 300.
[46] ibid 301.
[47] *Wallace v Shoreham Hotel* 49 A.2d 81, 83 (DC 1946).

undesirable to promote stoicism in the form of parental *detachment*. (In the earliest English case on 'secondary victims', Atkin LJ reasoned that compensation was at least as appropriate for a mother frightened about her *children's* safety as for one frightened for her *own* safety.)[48]

Keating's core example of actionable distress is the bereaved parent's suffering. Permanent, life-damaging grief is to be expected in *every* such bereavement. That does not mean it is 'psychiatric illness' – on the contrary, proposals to recognise grief as mental illness are intensely controversial within psychiatry. The concern is precisely to avoid medicalising ordinary everyday reactions which, however painful, should not be treated by strong mind-altering drugs. But why should such serious distress be excluded from *tort's* concern? The law aims to redress harm. Should tort law not respond to significant emotional harm beyond the psychiatric definition of 'mental illness'? Such cases need not be trivial. Mulheron notes the case of a new-born baby, wrongfully separated from her parents, who displayed behavioural and 'attachment' difficulties when they were reunited. Since this behaviour did not amount to a 'psychiatric illness' (but only 'Emotional responses to unpleasant experiences of even the most serious type') the child's damages claim failed.[49]

Serious, life-blighting distress is a plausible alternative to the current rule of 'recognisable illness'.[50] The present law 'fails to appreciate that there may be genuine cases of very serious all-consuming emotional upheaval which leave a person in a compromised state falling short of psychiatric illness'.[51] Such 'upheaval' is clearly harmful to the claimant (potentially much more damaging than a minor physical injury). As Lord Hoffmann noted, discussing the 'somewhat arbitrary' distinction between psychiatric illness and 'ordinary' reactions to trauma, 'feelings of terror and grief may have as devastating an effect upon people's lives as the "pain and suffering" consequent upon physical injury, for which damages are regularly awarded'.[52] Recovery could be limited to distress that exceeds the trivial or everyday upsets that we can be expected to deal with stoically. A sufficiently robust and narrow definition would address the concern that omnipresent liability would blight social life.

There is little prospect of such change in the English law of negligence.[53] Lord Hoffmann's remarks should not be taken out of context: the notorious decision in *White* was opposed to *any* extension of liability for psychiatric illness. Liberalisation on 'recognisable psychiatric illness' might only entrench the other restrictive rules in this area.[54] Nevertheless, there is a

---

[48] *Hambrook v Stokes Bros* [1925] 1 KB 141, 157.
[49] *MK v Oldham NHS Trust* [2003] Lloyd's Rep Med 1.
[50] Teff (n 41) 7–9.
[51] NJ Mullany and PR Handford, 'Moving the Boundary Stone by Statute – The Law Commission on Psychiatric Illness' (1999) 22 *UNSWLJ* 350, 369.
[52] *White* (n 7) 501.
[53] cf Scots Law Com (n 161).
[54] Mulheron (n 35). Cf Teff (n 41) ch 6 (discussed below in 'Another Compromise: Quid Pro Quo?').

strong intellectual case for a freestanding legal definition of extreme distress, instead of tort's co-option of a medical definition which is designed for other purposes.

Debate 2
Justifying the Restrictive Rules on Psychiatric Illness

This debate considers the complex rules on psychiatric illness. These are centred around the restrictive tests laid down in *Alcock v Chief Constable of South Yorkshire*. We explore those rules' development and basis. The many criticisms can be divided into two families. Some critics argue that policy-based reasoning is never legitimate (including in this area). Others, while accepting the basic legitimacy of policy concerns, question whether they can justify the law as developed in *Alcock* and cemented into place in *White v Chief Constable of South Yorkshire*. Can such arbitrary lines be successfully or justifiably drawn at common law? The boundaries of *Alcock* are also considered, including the important but overlooked law governing stress-at-work claims. This area shows how controls more nuanced than denial of duty of care might be used. We also consider the exception for 'primary victims': is it based on outmoded ideas of the importance of physical impact (or risking it in the 'zone of danger')? Or is this a way of cases that do not risk indeterminate liability, to which the rationale of *Alcock* is inapplicable?

The Alcock *Rules on 'Secondary Victims'*

Alcock is the 'controlling decision'[55] on claims by those who witness injury to another – bystanders or 'secondary victims'.[56] But rarely has a leading case faced such criticism. This section traces the development of the law.

Liability to bystanders expanded steadily throughout the twentieth century before serious judicial disagreement emerged in *McLoughlin v O'Brian* (1982),[57] *Alcock*'s precursor. The law first permitted 'near miss' claims brought by those terrified for their own safety.[58] But by the mid-twentieth century bystanders witnessing accidents could in principle recover damages, provided shock was reasonably foreseeable to a person of reasonable firmness.[59] Lord Hoffmann's account of this era is illuminating.[60] Liability turned on 'what was in theory a simple foreseeability test' (with no special 'control devices'). It was nevertheless '[kept] within narrow bounds by taking a highly restrictive view

---

[55] *White* (n 7) 496 (Lord Steyn).
[56] [1992] 1 AC 310 (*Alcock*).
[57] [1983] 1 AC 410.
[58] *Dulieu v White & Sons* [1901] 2 KB 669.
[59] Eg *King v Phillips* [1953] 1 QB 429.
[60] *White* (n 7) 501–02.

of the circumstances in which it was foreseeable that psychiatric injury might be caused'. For example a 'robust wartime view of the ability of the ordinary person to suffer horror and bereavement without ill effect' led to the denial of liability in *Bourhill v Young* (1942).[61]

The 1980s and 1990s saw significant retrenchment in psychiatric injury liability (as with pure economic loss). Referring to the former's 'ebb and flow' Lord Hoffmann warned:

> the earlier decisions ... cannot simply be laid out flat and pieced together to form a timeless mosaic of legal rules. Some contained the embryonic forms of later developments; others are based on theories of liability which had respectable support at the time but have since been left stranded by the shifting tides.[62]

In particular, the earlier courts' reliance on highly restrictive foreseeability had fallen 'out of touch with reality'. It was increasingly acknowledged that people suffer psychiatric illness from witnessing accidents to close relatives. In other words, the increasing medical and societal acceptance of the reality of such injuries affected law too.

Even in *McLoughlin v O'Brian* Lord Wilberforce remained concerned about the 'proliferation' of 'possibly fraudulent' claims (generated by 'an industry of lawyers and psychiatrists'), if the law on 'shock' were relaxed.[63] By the turn of the twenty-first century such scepticism was rejected. In *Frost v Chief Constable* Henry LJ thought objective psychological tests limited the potential for fraud, which was no greater than for back injuries.[64] The claimants in *Frost* (known on appeal to the House of Lords as *White*) were police officers who tried to rescue and assist those crushed in the Hillsborough football stadium disaster. Police work involves regular exposure to accidental death and injuries, and officers in 'everyday' accidents are expected to cope with this without becoming unwell. However, the psychiatric evidence established that the scenes at Hillsborough were uniquely horrifying, outside ordinary police experience. It was therefore foreseeable that even experienced police officers might suffer: 'disasters capable of being PTSD stressors against which "customary phlegm" is not necessarily protective are rare, but when they happen do not spare the robust'.[65] (Although the claims in *White* ultimately failed, no judge suggested that PTSD had been *unforeseeable*. Lord Steyn dismissed fears about 'fraudulent or bogus claims'.)[66]

A liberal approach would simply ask whether psychiatric injury was reasonably foreseeable. But *Alcock* halted the expansion of liability. Additional 'control' tests had to be satisfied too. The question of controls had divided the House of

---

[61] [1943] AC 92.
[62] *White* (n 7) 503.
[63] [1983] 1 AC 410, 421.
[64] [1998] QB 254, 280.
[65] ibid.
[66] *White* (n 7) 494.

Lords in *McLoughlin v O'Brian* (although all agreed the claim should succeed on the facts). Lord Scarman and Lord Bridge held reasonable foreseeability sufficient for liability. Lord Wilberforce argued for additional policy-based controls. In retrospect (Lord Hoffmann said), tort law had come 'within a hair's breadth' of confirming the simple foreseeability approach ('a slight change in the composition of the Appellate Committee [in *McLoughlin*] would have set the law on a different course').[67] By *Alcock* in 1992 however, 'the moment [had] passed' and the prevailing judicial attitude to tort liability had become 'a cautious pragmatism'.

The *Alcock* rules themselves are well-known. A secondary victim must (i) have close ties of love and affection with the person injured; must (ii) be proximate in time and space to the accident; must (iii) perceive it with their own unaided senses rather than learning about it second-hand; and must (iv) suffer a 'sudden shock' rather than a gradual appreciation or prolonged horror (eg at the bedside of a dying relative).[68]

The rules' express purpose was to limit claims which would otherwise succeed (involving psychiatric injury foreseeable to a 'reasonably robust' claimant). What justifies these limits? In principle such claims ought to succeed if (to quote Lord Hoffmann again) tort law were 'an Aristotelian system of corrective justice, [under which] there is obviously no valid distinction to be drawn between physical and psychiatric injury'.[69] Yet according to *Alcock* tort imposes artificial limits on corrective justice for reasons of 'policy'.

The 'policy' reasoning was rather muted in *Alcock* itself. In three of the four reasoned speeches policy was not even discussed. There were simply references to the width of liability, if it were based on foreseeability alone. Despite this hesitancy, *Alcock* was hailed as the landmark case in *White v Chief Constable*. It settled the law, and development or reform was for Parliament.[70] It was too late to go back on the *Alcock* rules.[71] Oddly, this deference to *Alcock* was accompanied by harsh criticism. According to Lord Goff (who dissented in *White*), the 'artificial' *Alcock* rules, 'being arbitrary in nature, are widely perceived to create unjust and unacceptable distinctions'.[72] For Lord Steyn the law on psychiatric injury was 'a patchwork quilt of distinctions which are difficult to justify'.[73] Lord Hoffmann stated 'the *Alcock* control mechanisms stand obstinately in the way of rationalisation and the effect is to produce striking anomalies'.[74] Remarkably, Lord Hoffmann thought *Alcock* had called off 'the search for principle'.[75] Little wonder that commentators have been so critical of the rules.

---

[67] ibid 502.
[68] *Sion v Hampstead HA* (1994) 5 Med LR 170.
[69] *White* (n 7) 503–04.
[70] ibid 500 (Lord Steyn).
[71] ibid 504 (Lord Hoffmann).
[72] ibid 487.
[73] ibid 500.
[74] ibid 506.
[75] ibid 507, 511.

Alcock *Rules: Rights-Based Critique*

Two kinds of critique are possible. The first prioritises rights and denies the legitimacy of 'policy reasoning' altogether. From the 'corrective justice' perspective, 'the [*Alcock*] control mechanisms merely reflect a vulgar scepticism about the reality of psychiatric injury or a belief that it is less worthy of compensation than physical injury'.[76] The rejection of policy reasoning is the unifying thread of the critique. It featured in Lords Scarman and Bridge's ultimately unsuccessful advocacy of a foreseeability-based approach in *McLoughlin v O'Brian*. Two leading academic rights-based approaches unite in condemning *Alcock*'s 'policy' reasoning (for Allan Beever indeed, judges reasoning from a 'raw intuition' that liability would go too far deserves 'contempt').[77] But on the identification of the relevant rights, Beever's and Robert Stevens' accounts diverge.

Stevens declares that tort law correctly recognises a right to mental health (although no right not to be distressed).[78] Liability for invading the right would be more appropriately controlled by 'robust' trial judges than by 'crude' and 'arbitrary' rules like *Alcock*'s (which are essentially 'legislative'). By contrast Beever, complaining about the lack of attention to the 'primary right that the cause of action protects', states there is 'no clear right to psychological integrity' before failing to reach a final conclusion about its existence.[79] These authors scarcely speak with one voice on how to replace the 'contemptible' policy approach. The crucial step of the argument is identifying the relevant rights.[80] At that stage we find either a merely restatement of what the law currently recognises (Stevens) or the suggestion that the law is probably wrong but a 'disappointing' failure to explore the question (Beever).

The court in *McLoughlin v O'Brian* was divided about policy reasoning. Two law lords rejected it – although they did not reason expressly about rights but assumed that if 'nervous shock' was reasonably foreseeable, liability followed (what Stevens condemns as the 'loss model' of tort law).[81] Lord Scarman's approach was founded on 'the balance ... between the functions of judge and legislature'.[82] Lord Scarman held that common law principle 'inexorably' required 'judges to follow the logic of the "reasonably foreseeable test" ... untrammelled by spatial, physical, or temporal limits'. It would 'obstruct the law's pursuit of justice' to limit liability to some arbitrary category. Interestingly, Lord Scarman confessed that he was 'by no means sure that the result is socially desirable'. Foreseeability-based liability could indeed

---

[76] ibid 504 (Lord Hoffmann).
[77] A Beever, *Rediscovering the Law of Negligence* (Oxford, Hart, 2007) 408.
[78] R Stevens, *Torts and Rights* (Oxford, Oxford University Press, 2007) 52–56.
[79] Beever (n 77) 410–11.
[80] ibid 411 ('The appropriate scope of liability is determined entirely by the right').
[81] Stevens (n 7) 1–2.
[82] *McLoughlin* (n 21) 429–31 (relied on in R Dworkin, *Law's Empire* (Cambridge, Mass, Harvard University Press, 1986)).

open the floodgates, causing 'social and financial problems'. Yet he reasoned it was for *Parliament* to limit 'socially unacceptable' liability. Questions of 'social, economic, and financial policy' were unsuitable for resolution through the litigation process. Where to draw the line of recovery was therefore 'not justiciable'.[83]

This stance was rejected by (eg) Lord Edmund-Davies.[84] Courts should give policy 'the closest scrutiny' and examine its 'clarity and cogency'. But policy was not *inadmissible* (no 'sleeveless errand'). Lord Edmund-Davies approved Winfield's view that although it was often wise to leave policy reasoning to the legislature, courts were nonetheless bound to take notice of public policy despite the difficulty of determining such 'ethical' questions.[85] The 'policy' approach ultimately prevailed in the key 1990s authorities of *Alcock* and *White*.

Alcock *Rules: Policy Critique*

Even accepting the propriety of (appropriately rigorous) policy reasoning, *Alcock* seems questionable. No single 'policy' justifies the special restrictions. Several have been suggested – but each powerfully criticised. It is unclear that taken together, the policies can justify depriving claimants 'of just compensation for reasonably foreseeable damage'.[86] Lord Wilberforce identified several heads of policy in *McLoughlin*. First, the fear of imaginary and fraudulent claims. This has long been dismissed: abolishing an entire cause of action because it might be abused is 'like employing a cannon to kill a flea'.[87] A related concern was 'evidentiary difficulties' when deciding whether psychiatric illness existed and what caused it. While the concept of 'recognisable psychiatric illness' can be difficult to apply, evidential problems arise in many areas of tort (eg physical diseases) without anyone suggesting this justifies outright abolition of the relevant liability.

Lord Wilberforce's third point was the converse of Lord Scarman's position: that it was open to Parliament to *extend* liability for psychiatric injury beyond the limited common law categories. It appears the judges assumed quite different starting points (cautious, or expansive), justifying them with the observation that the legislature could always change the law if it found it unsatisfactory. But this suggests the 'institutional competence' argument has little force because it can be used to justify *any* position on liability. Stapleton inclines towards Lord Wilberforce's view.[88] Because in practice Parliament has little time or appetite to legislate about tort liability, courts ought to take

---

[83] *McLoughlin* (n 21) 429–31.
[84] ibid 427–28.
[85] PH Winfield, 'Public Policy in the English Common Law' (1928) 42 *Harvard LR* 76, 97.
[86] *McLoughlin* (n 21) 429 (Lord Russell).
[87] Peter Mullany, *Mullany & Hanford's Tort Liability for Psychiatric Damage*, 2nd edn (Sydney, Law Book Co, 2006) 735.
[88] J Stapleton, *Three Essays on Torts* (Oxford, Oxford University Press, 2021) 29–31.

public concerns into account – doing so 'contributes a critical effectiveness to our constitutional arrangements'.

The *Alcock* controls have however been criticised for their *legislative* nature. They simply aim to draw the line of liability *somewhere*. Even if that 'somewhere' cannot be logically defended, it has to be done because liability for all foreseeable harm would be too wide. This is a plausible view of the *Alcock* 'strategy'. Yet the common law process is ill-suited to arbitrary line-drawing.[89] As Lord Wilberforce put it in a different tort context (deduction of collateral benefits from damages), while Parliament can enact a split-the-difference compromise that 'type of solution is not open to the courts'.[90] Indeed several of the *Alcock* judges thought it would be more satisfactory for limits on liability to be imposed by legislation and not the common law.[91] Although this resembles Lord Scarman's position in the *McLoughlin* debate, it did not ultimately dissuade the House of Lords from imposing 'control mechanisms' themselves.

Perhaps they should have left it to the legislature. For the *Alcock* rules do not have the clear-cut quality of statute. Compare the statutory bereavement claim available for spouses (and partners), for parents of minors, and nobody else.[92] According to Lord Steyn in *White*, 'The spectre of a wide a class of claimants in respect of bereavement led to an arbitrary but not necessarily irrational rule'.[93] The bereavement claim is at least clearly defined. The *Alcock* rules are by contrast uncertain (eg 'immediate aftermath'). 'What constitutes the immediate aftermath of an accident must necessarily depend upon the surrounding circumstances. To essay any comprehensive definition would be a fruitless exercise'.[94] There will be room for argument in marginal cases – even, perhaps, for expansion in sympathetic cases.

Equally, the *Alcock* judges explicitly declined to categorise the 'family relationships' qualifying for psychiatric injury claims. The analogy of the statutory bereavement list was rejected. Lord Oliver saw 'no logic and no virtue in seeking to lay down as a matter of "policy" categories of relationship within which claims may succeed … So rigid an approach would, I think, work great injustice and cannot be rationally justified'.[95] The question was whether the relationship was sufficiently close that the claimant's psychiatric illness from witnessing the other's injury was reasonably foreseeable. That was a question of fact. It could not be ruled out that friends, distant relations or (in horrific cases) complete strangers might be foreseeably injured.

Although this flexibility sounds sensible, it undermines the 'logic' of *Alcock* as a whole. The *Alcock* decision above all *rejected* reasonable foreseeability as

---

[89] See discussion in '*Fairchild* Enclave: A Special Rule for Mesothelioma?'.
[90] *Parry v Cleaver* [1970] AC 1, 39 (comparing Law Reform (Personal Injuries) Act 1948, section 2).
[91] See especially *Alcock* (n 56) 419 (Lord Oliver).
[92] Fatal Accidents Act 1976 s 1A.
[93] *White* (n 7) 492.
[94] *Alcock* (n 56) 423 (Lord Jauncey).
[95] ibid 415.

the sufficient test for psychiatric injury. The principle of foreseeability was over-ridden in other specific areas. Lord Oliver doubted whether distress was any less foreseeable in cases involving 'gradual realisation' not a sudden shocking event.[96] But he still denied compensation to those whose shock occurred after 'a dawning consciousness over an extended period'.[97] It is, to say the least, unclear why on ties of love and affection, the House of Lords reverted to a non-arbitrary foreseeability-based approach. *Alcock* here approaches self-contradiction. Also, the need for evidence on this point risks distasteful attempts to prove (and by defendants, disprove) the closeness of loving ties between siblings, cousins, friends etc.

White v Chief Constable held that *Alcock* must be applied strictly, as if it were a statute. That transformed *Alcock* into a set of rigid rules that cannot be extended by analogical development, implicitly acknowledging its status as judicial legislation. The court in *White* simultaneously hoped for reforming legislation to replace these common law rules because 'there are no refined analytical tools which will enable the courts to draw lines by way of compromise solution in a way which is coherent and morally defensible'.[98]

What can justify this extraordinary approach, with the notorious announcement that the search for principle had been 'called off'? Lord Steyn accepted it was important 'to explain what the policy considerations are so that the validity of my assumptions can be critically examined by others'.[99] He thought some policies were unconvincing. Lingering perceptions that psychiatric illness was somehow less serious were not socially acceptable. There was no special danger of fraudulent claims and 'diagnostic uncertainty' did not 'outweigh the considerations of justice supporting genuine claims'. However, two other factors were found more persuasive.

First, the concern about indeterminate liability examined in the next section. Second, Lord Steyn feared that the proliferation of tort claims could harm the victims themselves. The concern was not invented symptoms, but the *unconscious* effect of claiming for damages: 'litigation is sometimes an unconscious disincentive to rehabilitation'.[100] Jyoti Ahuja criticises this as paternalism, barring claims for the claimants' own good.[101] Would tort lawyers accept such an argument against *physical* injury claims, if recovery were slowed by the claimant's knowledge that compensation depended on their injuries' severity and duration? Ahuja states there is no empirical evidence that litigation worsens psychiatric illness. Indeed there are therapeutic benefits, when someone is injured by another, in a public finding of responsibility and/or apology. Yet not all psychiatrists agree. Wessely argues that there is a real effect

---

[96] ibid 416.
[97] ibid 417.
[98] *White* (n 7) 500.
[99] ibid 493.
[100] ibid 494.
[101] Ahuja (n 32).

of 'social reinforcement' – that is, the prospect of public recognition and compensation – on chronic psychiatric illness.[102] Litigation does not make people mentally ill; but it can worsen the prognosis for recovery of those already ill. Wessely concludes that there is a 'public health argument for restricting the spread of [psychiatric injury] litigation'.[103] Compare Lord Steyn's careful conclusion that 'this factor cannot be dismissed'.

'Floodgates'

What critics call 'the floodgates obsession' is the foundation of the *Alcock* rules.[104] Is the foundation secure? No convincing empirical evidence shows that foreseeability-based harm would be unmanageably wide. Probably it would be wider, but ordinarily we expect those who cause more harm to face greater liability: 'it is no objection to say that [recognising a claim] will occasion multiplicity of actions; for if men will multiply injuries, actions must be multiplied too; for every man that is injured ought to have his recompense'.[105] The 'floodgates' concern is therefore questionable. Its application depends more on judicial intuition than hard evidence. Can this justify rules as arbitrary and unjust as *Alcock*?

Lord Steyn in *White* was particularly concerned about the extent of liability. The width, unpredictability or indeterminacy of 'bystander' liability had been a constant theme in the case-law: the most prominent and durable reason for the special 'controls'. Lord Steyn noted the inherent boundaries to liability for *physical* injuries ('an element of immediacy'). The absence of such 'in built restrictions' in pure psychiatric injury claims (ie unrelated to physical harm to the claimant, or its apprehension) allowed much wider liability. This argument is central for the *Alcock* rules. The insistence on 'proximity in time and space', and 'perception by the claimant's own unaided senses', are medically unjustified. Instead, the rules artificially re-impose the obstacles to bystander 'shock' claims that are inherent in claims for *physical* injury.

Lord Steyn was also concerned that the burden of psychiatric injury liability could be 'disproportionate' for defendants. Negligence might be nothing more than a driver's 'momentary lapses of concentration'.[106] But this argument is weak, and its weakness is revealing. Lord Steyn's concern is unconvincing because it is a truism of tort law that although a defendant's negligence might be 'momentary' or slight, it could cause catastrophic harm. On the roads. Or a 'momentary lapse' during surgery. It seems 'disproportionate' that doctors doing their 'incompetent best' might be liable for millions of pounds in damages. But once liability is established, compensation is assessed according

---

[102] Wessely (n 4).
[103] ibid 666.
[104] Mullany and Handford (n 51) 374–81.
[105] *Ashby v White* (1703) 2 Ld Raym 938 (Holt CJ).
[106] *White* (n 7) 494.

to the extent of the claimant's injuries – liability is neither increased by gross negligence nor reduced by its slightness. This is simply the logic of tort law (the compensation fits the harm – *not* 'the punishment fits the tort'). Few question it for *physical* harm.[107] Questioning the proportionality of liability for psychiatric illness alone reflects its long-term relegation to second-class status, a less deserving form of injury.

It is plausible that psychiatric injury cases pose a greater threat of indeterminate liability, generally speaking. But the categorical distinction is crude. We cannot say that indeterminate liability is *never* a risk in physical illness cases (imagine toxic groundwater pollution or release of a highly infectious disease). Nor, conversely, is indeterminate liability *always* inherent in claims for psychiatric illness. As examined in the next sections of the debate, there are sub-categories of psychiatric harm to which the *Alcock* tests are accordingly inapplicable.

'Primary Victims': Zone of Danger or 'Involvement'?

The dichotomy between 'primary' and 'secondary' victims governs psychiatric illness claims. Yet the distinction is not entirely clear. A narrow reading, adopted in *White*, suggests that primary victims are *exclusively* those inside the zone of physical danger. Endangered persons can claim for psychiatric illness without satisfying the *Alcock* control mechanisms. On this strict view, all other claimants are deemed 'secondary victims' – traumatised by *another* person's injury – and must satisfy *Alcock*.

But it is controversial to define 'primary victim' using the hallmark of physical danger, entrenching the discredited view that 'real' injuries involve actual physical impact. The rule is at least relatively certain, categorising 'primary victims' as those within a defined physical space. This addresses the indeterminate liability or 'floodgates' concern. Hence there is no need to apply the artificial *Alcock* controls to those in physical danger. However, this rejoinder suggests a somewhat wider definition of 'primary victims', including all those actively participating in an accident (whether physically endangered or not). Notably, Lord Oliver originally defined 'primary victims' in this way.[108] On this view, *White* is regrettable.

The police claimants in *White* were held not to be primary victims notwithstanding their involvement in rescuing fans crushed in the Hillsborough disaster, unless themselves physically endangered. Ahuja argues that the law's historical emphasis on physical harm (or its narrow avoidance) should be rejected. By imposing liability for physical peril more readily than for a close

---

[107] cf J Waldron, 'Moments of Carelessness and Massive Loss' in DG Owen (ed), *Philosophical Foundations of Tort Law* (Oxford, Clarendon, 1995) (see ch 4, 'Questioning Moral Justice: Moral and Doctrinal Critique').

[108] *Alcock* (n 56) 407 (claimant 'directly involved in the accident ... can be properly said to be the primary victim').

relative's death, tort clings to utterly outmoded medical theories. 'This idea that the most serious emotional trauma arises from being in danger of some physical harm is astonishing in its emotional naivete'.[109] In lists of severe stressors in life (ie risk factors for causing psychiatric illness), bereavements are more potent causes than physical injury to the patient themselves. Sudden and unexpected bereavements (as in many tort cases) are an even greater risk factor. Ahuja's point is that if the law were to use the likelihood of psychiatric illness to organise its categories, it would treat those traumatised by injury to others *more* generously than those fearing for their own safety. The law's current priorities are back to front.

This critique is unanswerable given its premise. But it assumes that liability is here ordered according to susceptibility to psychiatric illness. Quite consciously, the law is not. *Alcock* was a turning point, rejecting an approach based on foreseeability of illness. The psychological evidence of stress and susceptibility would have been directly relevant for a foreseeability approach, but the law has intentionally chosen an artificially restrictive approach to 'secondary victims'. The main reason seems to be concern about the indeterminate class of traumatised claimants. The definition of 'primary victim' can be understood consistently with that. However *medically* irrelevant, the 'zone of injury' draws a tight circle around the physical accident, removing the risk of indeterminate liability. What appears inexplicable to psychologists might have a pragmatic, albeit artificial, legal function. The artificiality is confirmed by decisions holding that somebody *in danger* when traumatised by viewing injuries to another person can recover as a *primary victim*.[110] This appears irrational: the danger to the claimant being causally irrelevant.[111] But if 'primary victimhood' is nothing more than another 'control mechanism', liability would be consistent with its rationale.

Not everyone accepts this view. Dissenting in *White*, Lord Goff opposed the requirement of physical danger as a 'new artificial barrier against recovery' precisely because it would create 'unjust and unacceptable' distinctions, as *Alcock* had.[112] Even if we accept the majority view that the 'zone of injury' is a pragmatic expedient, does it do its job? It has been criticised both for being too restrictive and not restrictive enough:

> What is so magical about being within the range of foreseeable physical injury, except perhaps the mistaken view that the number of potential claimants will be limited by the nature of the case? ... [The number], depending on the circumstances, might in many cases be quite high and made even higher by the efforts of creative counsel.[113]

---

[109] Ahuja (n 32) 41.

[110] *Young v Charles Church (Southern) Ltd* (1997) 39 BMLR 146.

[111] cf *White* (n 7) 487–88 (Lord Goff, dissenting) (two hypothetical rescuers, one in danger the other not, both traumatised by witnessing train wreck casualties).

[112] ibid.

[113] FA Trindade, 'Nervous Shock and Negligent Conduct' (1996) 112 *LQR* 22, 24–25.

Trindade questioned whether everyone near the path of an out-of-control vehicle, or every resident of a city flown over by a stricken aircraft, would be a 'primary victim' and exempt from the *Alcock* controls. Note also legal difficulties about the 'worried well' in US product liability cases – consumers (perhaps in their millions) concerned that they may have been harmed a contaminated product. This seems like a classic broad class. Yet all users of the product would come within the 'zone of danger', facing a threat to their health. Rabin thinks the risk of crushing liability much worse in such cases than in 'bystander' cases (where, he suggests, *mass* observation of injuries to others is the exception not the rule).[114] English law would apparently let the 'anxious consumers' recover as primary victims, reserving the *Alcock* rules for the *less* expansive 'bystander' claims.

Such comments suggest the 'zone of danger' could be wide and uncertain. The converse criticism is that 'primary victimhood' should not be defined exhaustively by physical danger, if the aim is to identify which claims do not risk indeterminate liability. On this view, *White* was wrongly decided because all the police claimants, rescuing those injured in the crush, had *actively participated* in the incident. Since there is a finite number of active 'participants', distinguished from mere bystanders/chance witnesses, the *Alcock* controls appear unnecessary. Moreover, strong reasons favour liability to rescuers. The law usually views rescuer claims with notable sympathy, for example, taking a narrow view to causal and other defences.[115] English law, rejecting the 'fireman's rule' of some US states, also places no special restrictions on claims by *professional* rescuers injured in the line of duty.[116] The dissenting judges in *White* noted it had never previously been suggested that rescuers should be *in danger* before they could recover damages for psychiatric trauma.[117]

Surprisingly, these strong reasons failed to persuade the majority. The court felt public opinion would be outraged if the Hillsborough police succeeded in *White* when the Hillsborough relatives' claims had been dismissed in *Alcock*.[118] Lord Steyn declared: 'Thus far and no further'. *Alcock* marked the outer limits of liability which only Parliament could now extend (even though 'The law has long recognised the moral imperative of encouraging citizens to rescue persons in peril').[119] Lord Hoffmann agreed that it was just too late to go back on the

---

[114] Robert L Rabin, 'Emotional Distress in Tort Law: Themes of Constraint' (2009) 44 *Wake Forest LR* 1197, 1202.
[115] *Baker v TE Hopkins & Son Ltd* [1959] 1 WLR 966.
[116] *Ogwo v Taylor* [1988] AC 431.
[117] Cf *Chadwick v British Railways Board* [1967] 1 WLR 912.
[118] Eg *White* (n 7) 495: the 'imbalance ... might perplex the man on the Underground' (Lord Steyn).
[119] *White* (n 7) 498.

control mechanisms (which 'stand obstinately in the way of rationalisation' of the law).[120] To extend liability to the (police) rescuers

> would be unacceptable to the ordinary person because ... it would offend against his notions of distributive justice. He would think it unfair between one class of claimants and another ... He would think it wrong that policemen, even as part of a general class of persons who rendered assistance, should have the right to compensation for psychiatric injury out of public funds while the bereaved relatives are sent away with nothing.[121]

Lord Hoffmann held that, exceptionally, the law had to heed concerns about 'distributive justice'. It was impossible to 'pretend' that *Alcock* was 'founded on principle'. The court was not engaged (as it usually is?) 'in the bold development of principle' but merely the 'practical attempt ... to preserve the general perception of the law as system of rules which is fair between one citizen and another'.[122]

This is one of the most remarkable judgments in tort law. The usual principled approach to legal development was cast aside, fearful of public condemnation. Never mind that in future, altruistic traumatised rescuers would be excluded from recovery. Distorted law arose from the coincidence of *White* and *Alcock* both concerning the same scandalous tragedy.[123] Should *White* not be confined to this unique set of circumstances? The 'primary victim' category could be extended to rescuers who were *not* in physical danger and other active participants (eg those feeling responsible after innocently causing another's physical injuries).[124] Lord Hoffmann thought this an 'ingenious explanation which owes nothing to the actual reasoning' in cases such as *Dooley v Cammell Laird*, decided in 1951 using the then-current test of reasonable foreseeability. But he acknowledged 'grounds for treating such a rare category of case as exceptional and exempt from the *Alcock* control mechanisms'.[125] The House of Lords has subsequently held it arguable that traumatised parents who took an abusive foster child into their home were 'primary victims', even though they had been at no physical risk when he abused their other children.[126] Lord Slynn commented that the categories of primary victims were not finally closed, but still developing. This suggests that the wider notion of 'participatory' primary victimhood could be arguable, at least in the highest courts. Generally speaking however, the courts have been

---

[120] ibid 504, 506.
[121] ibid 510.
[122] ibid 511.
[123] In 2016, a coroner's inquest finally concluded that 97 Hillsborough fans had been unlawfully killed by gross police negligence.
[124] Eg *Dooley v Cammell Laird & Co* [1951] 1 Lloyd's Rep 271.
[125] *White* (n 7) 508.
[126] *W v Essex CC* [2001] 2 AC 592.

most unwilling to extend liability for psychiatric injury given the insistence on 'strict control mechanisms' in *White*.[127]

Stress at Work

The law takes a completely different approach to workplace stress claims. The distinction between primary and secondary victims does not readily fit the situation (or any situations where *nobody* is at risk of physical injury). It appears that so long as an employee's psychiatric injury results from stress, not from witnessing another being injured as a result of their employer's negligence (as in *White*), they are classified as 'primary victims'.[128] Employers owe well-established duties of care for the safety of their workers. It was held in *Walker v Northumberland CC* that the duty extends to protecting employees' *mental* health.[129] This has not been doubted since.

Liability for stress at work has therefore achieved 'independent existence', freed from the psychiatric injury 'control mechanisms'.[130] Why are the controls inapplicable when the *Alcock-White* caselaw 'Taken to its logical conclusion' suggests they should be?[131] First, the law has long required employers to safeguard workers and it would be odd if this meant exclusively their bodily and not mental wellbeing. With occupational stress a major social problem,[132] tort law would seriously disadvantage employees if it insisted on such a distinction. Since stress can be the cause of physical problems (eg ulcers or heart disease) as well as psychiatric disorders, how could the law sensibly compensate only the physical symptoms?[133]

Second, a pre-existing relationship between the claimant and defendant arguably removes the need for further control mechanisms. The employer-employee relationship is a prominent example, but there are various others.[134] In the leading Australian case *Annetts v Australian Stations*, the defendant employer gave reassurances to the plaintiffs about the safety of its employee, their teenaged son.[135] The defendants therefore owed a duty not to cause psychiatric injury to the plaintiffs. They breached it when their son died of dehydration in the desert. This could be viewed as an assumption of responsibility upon which the plaintiffs relied (by entrusting their son to the defendants). However Teff, while highly critical of *Alcock* and noting 'atypical' cases' potential to circumvent it, cautions against over-enthusiastic use

---

[127] *Taylor v A Novo (UK) Ltd* [2014] QB 150 [31] (Lord Dyson MR).
[128] *Hatton v Sutherland* [2002] EWCA Civ 76; [2002] I.C.R. 613, [21] (*Hatton*).
[129] [1995] ICR 702.
[130] Mullany & Handford (n 87) 540.
[131] *Hatton* (n 128) [19], [22].
[132] Anxiety and stress cause 55 per cent of working days lost to work-related illness: HSE Statistics, 2019–20.
[133] *Hatton* (n 128) [10].
[134] Mullany & Handford (n 87) ch 23.
[135] [2002] HCA 35; (2002) 211 CLR 317.

of assumption of responsibility, a 'haphazard' and 'malleable' concept.[136] Whatever the precise doctrinal basis for these 'antecedent relationship' cases, the key point is that 'the recognition of a duty of care does not raise the prospect of an intolerably large or indeterminate class of potential plaintiffs'.[137]

The English Law Commission (1998) approved *Walker v Northumberland* (applying the ordinary negligence approach to workplace stress claims) as 'logical and just'.[138] Yet one leading psychiatrist, although welcoming the Law Commission's other proposed reforms to the *Alcock* rules, was cautious about stress at work. Extending liability so freely to stressful jobs would create even more problems than 'accident-bystander' cases:

> Clinical practice suggests that few neurotic disorders are solely due to pressure of work, but work is a factor in many. Given the Law Commission's concern with not 'opening the floodgates' of litigation they are surprisingly relaxed about the implications of extending liability for psychiatric disorder beyond nervous shock and into the very murky world of 'stress'.[139]

Several factors indicated a potential flood of claims. First, the prevalence of 'eggshell personalities' – people with predispositions to mental illness for which occupational stress might be the trigger, though hardly the sole cause. Second and related, the clinical experience that much mental illness is the result of numerous factors ('Multifactorial aetiologies are the rule'). Wessely also feared that liability might not be in the interest of those with mental illness: the employability of 'the vast numbers of people with a previous episode of psychiatric disorder' would be compromised.[140] (Given that being unemployed is itself a major risk factor in mental illness, this would be positively counterproductive.)

The courts have 'controlled' stress-at-work claims by a robust approach to breach, causation, and assessment of damages – rather than denying a duty of care altogether. This is clear in the discussion and guidance laid down in the leading case, *Hatton v Sutherland*. Hale LJ cautioned against an over-exacting approach to the standard of care. The employer will often be unaware of an employee's inability to cope (since people understandably conceal this).[141] Even where psychiatric illness was reasonably foreseeable, the court should carefully consider what a reasonable employer could and should have done. Factors included the size of the organisation, the resources available to it, and the interests of other employees (who should not be prejudiced by assignment of extra duties to relieve another employee's stress).[142] Nor should tort law oblige an

---

[136] Teff (n 41) 127–28.
[137] *Annetts* (n 135) [239] (Gummow and Kirby JJ).
[138] Law Com No 249 (1998), 7.20–7.22.
[139] Wessely (n 4) 663.
[140] ibid 664.
[141] For criticism of this focus on 'individual susceptibility' (when psychological research suggests poor workplace practices have a more significant role): ACL Davies, 'Stress at Work: Individuals or Structures?' (2022) 51 *Industrial LJ* 403. Cf *Kozarov v Victoria* (n 192).
[142] *Hatton* (n 128) [33].

employer to dismiss or demote an employee, even if that appeared to be the only way to safeguard them.[143] Like Wessely, the court feared that setting the standard of care too high could have 'unforeseen and unwelcome effects'. In particular, 'employers may be even more reluctant than they already are to take on people with a significant psychiatric history', and readier to demote or dismiss those struggling to cope with stress.[144]

The *Hatton* guidelines also address stress-related illness's multi-causal nature. First, where the employee has a pre-existing vulnerability, this should be reflected in the assessment of damages. Specifically the principle that damages are reduced in proportion to the chance that the claimant might have suffered the psychiatric injury at some point in future, even had it not been for the defendant's negligence. For a demonstrably vulnerable claimant, this exceeds the standard discount for 'the vicissitudes of life'. (For example in *Page v Smith* there was ultimately a significant reduction in quantum of damages to reflect the probability that the claimant, who was at high risk of a recurrence of chronic psychiatric illness, would not have had a long and unbroken career even had the defendant not crashed their car into him.)[145] Thus, although a breakdown suffered by a claimant with an 'eggshell personality' will not be held too remote,[146] their vulnerability may well reduce damages.[147]

More controversially, the courts seek to identify which particular aspects of the psychiatric illness have been caused by the employer's negligence, and which by extraneous factors. This is important since, as seen, psychiatric illness is usually produced by the combination of many factors acting together (work being a common contributory factor, but rarely the sole cause). The legal difficulty is that where a tort contributes to an *indivisible* injury, the defendant is liable in full. The law never requires that the tort must be the sole cause – for does anything that happens have only one cause? In *Hatton v Sutherland* Hale LJ sought to circumvent the imposition of full liability by querying whether stress-related psychiatric illness is an 'indivisible injury'. Relying on a case where different aspects of a mental illness were causally apportioned between the separate impact of successive torts,[148] she stated:

> if it is established that the constellation of symptoms suffered by the claimant [also] stems from a number of different extrinsic causes then in our view a sensible attempt should be made to apportion liability accordingly.[149]

That would ensure the defendant 'pay[s] only for that proportion of the harm suffered for which he by his wrongdoing is responsible'.[150]

---

[143] ibid [34].
[144] ibid [14].
[145] ibid [42]; *Page v Smith* [1993] PIQR Q55.
[146] *Malcolm v Broadhurst* [1970] 3 All ER 508.
[147] See ch 5, 'The "No Better Off" Principle' ('no worse off' principle).
[148] *Rahman v Arearose Ltd* [2001] QB 351.
[149] *Hatton* (n 128) [41].
[150] ibid [36].

It is debateable whether mental illness can be 'divided' into separate aspects like this. Criticising the *Rahman* case (*Hatton's* forerunner), Weir argued the court should have rejected the 'absurd ... confected' report of the expert witnesses. In truth

> there is no scientific basis for any such attribution of causality: the claimant is not half-mad because of what the first defendant did and half-mad because of what the second defendant did, he is as mad as he is because of what both of them did. His mania is aetiologically indiscerptible, as when grief and shock combine to wreck the life of a parent who witnesses the death of her children.[151]

On this view, psychiatric illness is a binary, all-or-nothing matter. Just as in the classic examples: one is either dead or alive,[152] pregnant or not. Weir argued that this was quite different from steadily worsening physical conditions, the classic case for 'divisible' injury.[153] But subsequently in *Hatton*, Hale LJ saw 'no reason to distinguish [psychiatric] conditions from the chronological development of industrial diseases'.[154]

Since *Hatton*, the appropriateness of such apportionment has again been questioned.[155] Extrajudicially, Smith LJ warned that if there was 'really no sensible basis for apportionment', the court must not resort to 'speculation and guesswork'.[156] In particular her Ladyship thought psychiatric injury was '*par excellence* ... indivisible': 'As a rule, the claimant will have cracked up quite suddenly; tipped over from being under stress into being ill. The claimant will almost always have a vulnerable personality. But a defendant must take the claimant as he finds him'.[157] Smith LJ argued that psychiatric medicine posed distinctive evidential problems: 'doctors are not able to quantify the contributions which different factors have made. Psychiatry does not lend itself to the kind of statistical analysis which orthopaedic surgeons and oncologists can provide'.[158] Notwithstanding Smith LJ's critique, *BAE Systems (Operations) Ltd v Konczak* has reiterated the *Hatton* approach.[159] Out of concern for defendant employers (ie not making them unfairly liable for the entire illness when they only *contributed* to it), courts were encouraged to find a rational basis for apportionment, even if 'rough and ready'.

Stress-at-work claims are illuminating. They show the courts striving to control liability using the fact-sensitive doctrines of breach, causation and

---

[151] T Weir, 'The Maddening Effect of Successive Torts' [2001] *CLJ* 237, 238.
[152] *Arneil v Paterson* [1931] AC 560, 565 (Viscount Dunedin).
[153] *Thompson v Smiths Shiprepairers (North Shields) Ltd* [1984] QB 405.
[154] *Hatton* (n 128) [41].
[155] *Dickins v O2 plc* [2008] EWCA Civ 1144, [2009] IRLR 58, [45]–[47] (Smith LJ) and [53] (Sedley LJ).
[156] Dame J Smith, 'Causation – The Search for Principle' [2009] *JPIL* 101.
[157] ibid 103.
[158] ibid 104.
[159] [2017] EWCA Civ 1188; [2018] ICR 1.

damages, rather than ruling claims out categorically by the denial of a duty of care. The judges' determination to spare employers from excessive liability emerges clearly in the apportionment jurisprudence. The courts have pressed the notion of 'divisible injury' to the limit. As often noted, finding such 'divisibility' is unfair to claimants, who no longer recover full compensation (or will find it harder to do so if they have to trace and sue a number of tortfeasors rather than just one defendant).[160] But claimants are better off under an (artificial?) apportionment regime than by denying that the employer's duty extends to psychiatric illness. Half a loaf is better than no bread at all.

Debate 3
How Should the Law on Psychiatric Illness be Reformed?

The complex patchwork of liability for psychiatric illness in English law is often said to need reform. Most commentators think that the artificial controls are literally indefensible. There is considerable agreement that they should be abolished, but less consensus about their replacement. Some argue that anyone foreseeably injured should be able to claim. (As seen, this approach currently applies to 'primary victims' and occupational stress claims, but not 'secondary victims'.) An alternative proposal would abolish liability for psychiatric injury altogether, in the absence of any satisfactory intermediate stopping place. These could be seen as the pure positions at opposite ends of a spectrum. A pragmatic reformer might accept some controls on liability, while recommending modification or abandonment of other *Alcock* rules. That was the Law Commission's approach in 1998.

Despite its recommendations there has been no legislative reform. Probably that reflects lawyers' disagreement on how to improve the status quo. Governments will not risk 'wasting' legislative time on 'technical' law reform measures that are likely to face stiff opposition. The Scottish Government found a division of legal opinion about the merits of the Scots Law Commission's recommendations.[161] It has therefore declined to implement them. The variety of views expressed in a similar English consultation seemingly fortified the Ministry of Justice's view that development in the 'complex and sensitive' field of psychiatric injury was best left to the courts, rather than enacting the Law Commission's Bill.[162] Against this unpromising background, we analyse the various reform proposals.

---

[160] See Lord Rodger (dissenting) in *Barker v Corus* [2006] 2 AC 572; Weir (n 151).
[161] Scottish Government, *Civil Law of Damages: Issues in Personal Injury – Analysis of Written Consultation Responses* (2013) Part 3 (regarding Scots Law Commission, *Report No 196 on Damages for Psychiatric Injury* (2004)).
[162] MoJ, Response to Consultation on the Law of Damages CP(R) 9/07 (London, 2009).

A Foreseeability-Based Approach?

The main rival to the present law would extend liability to anyone whom the defendant ought reasonably to foresee at risk of psychiatric injury. There is a strong presumption in favour of duties of care to avoid direct, foreseeable *physical* injury. How can the current distinction within personal injury law, protecting a claimant's *mental* health less readily than their *bodily* health, be justified? Special restrictions on psychiatric injury 'perpetuate myths that damage to the body is more debilitating than damage to the mind and more worthy of support in a climate of limited accident compensation resources'.[163]

The principled case for this reform is strong. The objection is familiar: that liability would extend far too wide. The law must also consider fairness to defendants, who ought not to be crushed beneath unlimited liability. But just how extensive would liability become under the foreseeability-based approach? Ultimately the question is empirical. Comparative doctrinal analysis can also suggest the likely impact.

In 2002, 'sudden shock', 'proximity in time and space' and 'unaided perception' were rejected as legal preconditions for recovery in Australia.[164] Those factors' relevance, if any, was simply as *evidence* of how foreseeable psychiatric injury had been, with the evidential weight varying from case to case. This Australian development was a victory for the 'principled' foreseeability approach, unifying the rules on physical and psychiatric injury. Yet some of the judgments revealed concerns about it. Was it really appropriate to read across the approach from physical injury cases where duties of care so readily arise? Because the 'paradigm' physical injury case results from direct physical contact (eg a road accident)

> scant attention need be, or ever has been, paid to 'proximity' or some other feature intended to limit the class to whom the duty is owed. The class is limited by the nature of the harm inflicted and the mechanics of its infliction. And any difficult case is resolved by giving controlling significance to the importance of preserving bodily integrity.[165]

McHugh J said the foreseeability requirement in negligence had become so 'undemanding' that 'an affirmative answer to the question whether damage was reasonably foreseeable is usually a near certainty'.[166] These comments imply that a duty to avoid psychiatric injury would arise in nearly every case.

The existence of a general duty does not automatically mean universal *liability* since (of course) the other elements of negligence need to be established too. As seen, the English stress-at-work cases take a demanding approach to breach, causation and quantification to control liability. Hayne J, rejecting

---

[163] Mullany and Handford (n 51) 351.
[164] *Tame v NSW* [2002] HCA 35; (2002) 211 CLR 317 (*Tame*).
[165] ibid [265] (Hayne J).
[166] ibid [99].

'illogical' control mechanisms but envisaging an exacting focus on other elements of negligence as a replacement,[167] acknowledged that a test of ordinary foresight alone could produce overbroad liability.

More radically, McHugh J rejected modern negligence law's 'attenuated test of foreseeability'.[168] He viewed reasonable foreseeability not as purely factual but 'a compound conception of fact and value', requiring 'value judgment' by the court.[169] Hence 'policy considerations ... arguably enter into the determination of [what] the defendant ought reasonably to have foreseen'.[170] Michael Jones also advocates a nuanced approach to foreseeability.[171] While rejecting the artificial *Alcock* control mechanisms and preferring a foreseeability-based test, Jones argues that the law should retain different approaches to physical and mental injuries. A more cautious approach to psychiatric harm necessitates more demanding judgments about the 'reasonable foreseeability' of such harm.

This envisages continuing judicial control over liability by using a 'foreseeability' approach. But it would have radical implications across negligence law. The *Caparo* framework for novel duty cases separates foreseeability and policy questions. By combining them, McHugh J's and Jones's approach might reduce the transparency of reasoning. Rather than openly articulating policy reasons against liability, the court could manipulate the finding of foreseeability.[172] As Nolan points out, courts concerned about the extent of liability for psychiatric injury could apply foreseeability very strictly, meaning the current 'overt restrictions could simply be replaced by covert ones'.[173] This troubled the Law Commission. It rejected a pure foreseeability approach, predicting this would significantly increase the numbers of claims which 'in turn might lead the courts to make use of *policy considerations, concealed beneath the foreseeability test*, in an attempt to restrict the number of successful claims'.[174]

The Scottish Law Commission approved the distinction between physical and mental injury. People can be expected to endure a degree of mental distress at the hands of others, which is not true of physical injury. The Scottish report thus proposed a novel 'control device': was the mental harm something that the pursuer could reasonably be expected to put up with, without reparation?[175] Nolan hails this 'original and imaginative' proposal (albeit fearing

---

[167] ibid [260] ('Should a defendant bear entire responsibility, then, for a psychiatric injury of which the defendant's negligent conduct may have been only one cause among many others encountered by the plaintiff in life?').

[168] ibid [104].

[169] ibid [105].

[170] ibid [108].

[171] MA Jones, 'Liability for Psychiatric Damage: Searching for a Path between Pragmatism and Principle' in JW Neyers et al (eds), *Emerging Issues in Tort Law* (Oxford, Hart, 2007).

[172] See generally ch 6, 'The Triviality of Foreseeability'.

[173] D Nolan, 'Psychiatric Injury at the Crossroads' [2004] *JPIL* 1, 17.

[174] Law Com No 249 (1998), 6.8 (emphasis added).

[175] Scots Law Com No 196 (2004) 3.21.

that its uncertainty 'seriously undermines the case for the legislative implementation of this Report').[176] It is surely preferable to bring a difficult question into the open, rather than conduct a supposedly factual inquiry into 'reasonable foreseeability'. The Scottish proposal's transparency is better than unarticulated judicial suppositions about what persons of 'ordinary firmness' can 'phlegmatically' bear.

We should also note the chequered history of California's foreseeability approach. Having previously limited liability to those in the zone of physical danger, in 1968 the Californian courts adopted foreseeability of emotional injury as the sole test. The law was deliberately freed from 'fixed categories' or 'immutable rules'.[177] The liberalisation was poetically described: 'artificial islands of exceptions, created from the fear that the legal process will not work, usually do not withstand the waves of reality and, in time, descend into oblivion'.[178] *Dillon v Legg* was thought 'highly instructive' by Lord Bridge, advocating the 'principled' approach in *McLoughlin v O'Brian*.[179] However, California subsequently reverted to more restrictive liability. 'Bystander' claimants now have to show close relational ties to the person harmed, and physical proximity to the accident. *Dillon v Legg's* improbably-named reversal of 1989 criticised the foreseeability test as 'amorphous' and productive of 'ever widening circles of liability'.[180]

The reversal of *Dillon v Legg*, a leading light of 'foreseeability principle', somewhat undermines the reasoning of Lord Bridge and Lord Scarman in *McLoughlin v O'Brian*. However *Dillon*'s overruling did not deter the Australian courts. US negligence law's wider liability for 'emotional distress' necessitated stricter control mechanisms.[181] By contrast, Australian law's requirement of a 'recognisable psychiatric illness' avoided the indeterminacy of liability for negligently causing distress. (Of course English law retains the *Alcock* rules *in addition to* the 'recognisable psychiatric illness' requirement.)

The impact of legal reforms is ultimately an empirical question. Yet reliable empirical data are always difficult to find. Handford, defending the foreseeability approach, argues that it is unlikely to lead to an explosion of claims. Apart from the difficulty of proving a 'recognised illness' by expert medical evidence, litigation is distressing (being forced to relive the trauma) and damages may often be low.[182] To back up these plausible but speculative claims,[183] Handford cites a study finding that *Dillon v Legg* did not significantly increase Californian

---

[176] D Nolan, 'Reforming Liability for Psychiatric Injury in Scotland: A Recipe for Uncertainty?' (2005) 68 *MLR* 983.
[177] *Dillon v Legg* 68 Cal.2d 728 (1968).
[178] ibid 747.
[179] [1983] 1 AC 410, 439–40 (and 431 (Lord Scarman)).
[180] *Thing v La Chusa* 48 Cal.3d 644 (1989).
[181] *Tame* (n 164) [219] (Gummow and Kirby JJ).
[182] *Mullany & Handford* (n 87) 738.
[183] See similarly Teff (n 41) ch 5.

liability insurance costs.¹⁸⁴ But against this, the Law Commission estimated its proposals (which were short of full *Dillon v Legg* liberalisation) would add in the order of 2–5 per cent to motor liability insurance premiums.¹⁸⁵ The later Ministry of Justice impact assessment predicted that motor and public liability premiums would increase by 2.7%–2.9 per cent if the Commission's reforms were implemented. The National Health Service was 'particularly susceptible to claims not induced by shock or proximity in space and time to the accident' and faced substantially increased liability.¹⁸⁶

In the grubby politics of law reform, governments are understandably reluctant to load significant costs onto every driver in the land (all of them electors) and the cash-strapped NHS. (Albeit the government's figures were derived from defendants' representatives – the Association of British Insurers and the NHS Litigation Authority – and their figures have been questioned.¹⁸⁷ An independent 2003 report thought the Law Commission's cost estimate had been 'remarkably high').¹⁸⁸ Yet it is a legitimate complaint about law reform *by the courts* that judges impose burdens without any consideration or estimation of the resulting expense to the public.¹⁸⁹ Indeed some judges openly reject such concerns. Doubting the policy reasons for restricting psychiatric liability, Ward LJ commented:

> If I had to make the choice between redressing a wrong to an injured claimant and protecting the pocket of negligent defendants for economic reasons, then I would unrepentantly prefer to do justice than to achieve fiscal expediency.¹⁹⁰

Shortly after the liberalising decision in *Tame v NSW*, Australian states enacted a variety of legislative restrictions and caps on negligence liability and damages – albeit in reaction to concerns about the liability and insurance costs *generally*, not specifically for psychiatric illness.¹⁹¹ Nonetheless, as Handford regretfully describes, Australia has since taken a more restrictive approach to

---

¹⁸⁴ Peter A Bell, 'The Bell Tolls: Toward Full Tort Recovery for Psychic Injury' (1984) 36 *U Fla L Rev* 333, 366–67.
¹⁸⁵ Law Com 249 (1998) 1.12–1.13.
¹⁸⁶ Dept for Constitutional Affairs, *The Law on Damages* Consultation Paper CP 9/07 (2007) Annex B.
¹⁸⁷ Teff (n 41) 189.
¹⁸⁸ ibid 165 citing C Parsons, *An Analysis of Current Problems in the UK Liability Insurance Market* (London, Office of Fair Trading, 2003) 37.
¹⁸⁹ See eg D Campbell, 'The *Heil v Rankin* Approach to Law-Making: Who Needs a Legislature?' (2016) 45 *Common Law World Rev* 340.
¹⁹⁰ *Walters v Glamorgan NHS Trust* [2002] EWCA Civ 1792, [46].
¹⁹¹ See the Ipp Report (n 36). NB the state legislation varies and it is therefore now somewhat inaccurate to refer (as this chapter does) to 'Australian tort law' in the singular. But a significant common theme is the reimposition of limits on recovery, by legislation, after the judicial liberalisation in *Tame v NSW*.

workplace stress claims than English law.¹⁹² Legislation to curb common law liability could be seen as a warning not to reject control mechanisms on psychiatric injury. But it could also bolster Lord Scarman's recommendation that the courts should follow principle, however wide the resulting liability, leaving it to Parliament to impose restrictions. However crude, or unfair, a cap on damages, it is at least a 'bright-line' rule. As seen, a major criticism of the current English approach is that it produces arbitrary outcomes through unclear rules whose application is frequently litigated. This pleases nobody.

Outright Abolition?

The *Alcock* rules' restrictions on psychiatric injury claims seem indefensible. Commentators and judges express a catalogue of 'dyslogistic epithets', including 'artificial', 'illogical', 'arbitrary', 'embarrassing', 'irrelevant' and 'disastrous'. In *Alcock* itself Lord Oliver accepted that logic could not show where to draw the line. Yet in *White*, the House of Lords doubled down on *Alcock*, declaring the rules quite beyond redemption while simultaneously criticising the unreformable 'patchwork quilt' of liability.

If the rules are to be discarded, what should replace them? In the previous section we have considered the 'principled' approach founded on reasonable foreseeability alone. An equal and opposite reaction would be to abolish claims for psychiatric injury altogether. This might seem the only viable option, by a process of elimination, for those who think *Alcock* indefensibly arbitrary, but fear that liability based on foresight alone would be too broad.

The abolitionist position is usually attributed to Jane Stapleton. She believed the 'nervous shock' rules harmed the image and dignity of the law. The common law faces 'intolerable embarrassment' when unable to limit liability in a principled fashion. Psychiatric injury was the prime example, with the 'silliest rules', drawing 'ludicrous' and 'patently unconvincing' distinctions (that appear 'manifestly unjust to the non-lawyer'). *Alcock*'s reasoning and outcome were 'guaranteed to produce outrage'. The law was brought 'into disrepute' by the spectacle of grieving relatives forced to make 'unseemly arguments over meaningless boundaries'.¹⁹³ Stapleton's critique was as biting as those of Mullany and Handford, or Teff. But she wondered whether the only satisfactory solution was to abolish such claims altogether.¹⁹⁴

---

¹⁹² *Koehler v Cerebos (Australia) Ltd* [2005] HCA 15; (2005) 222 CLR 44 (cf *Kozarov v Victoria* [2022] HCA 12 (certain jobs may pose inherent risk of psychiatric injury; claimant was prosecutor investigating child sex offences)).

¹⁹³ J Stapleton, 'In Restraint of Tort' in PBH Birks (ed), *The Frontiers of Liability, Volume 2* (Oxford, Oxford University Press, 1994) 95.

¹⁹⁴ At least in the most problematic situation of persons traumatised by another's death or injury: *Mullany & Handford* (n 87) 181–82.

In *White* Lord Steyn said abolition would be contrary to precedent (obviously) and 'highly controversial', and thus only Parliament could do so.[195] Considering academic commentators' 'contradictory but equally radical suggestions for reform' Lord Hoffmann seemed more attracted to abolition. At least for those who view tort as an imperfect system that compensates only a minority of victims of accidents

> a uniform refusal to provide compensation for psychiatric injury adds little to the existing stock of anomaly in the law of torts and at least provides a rule which is easy to understand and cheap to administer.[196]

We have noted *Thing v La Chusa*, the Californian case which reimposed controls akin to the *Alcock* rules after 20 years' experience with a pure foreseeability approach. One of the judges would have abolished recovery in 'secondary victim' cases altogether. Kaufman J thought both alternative approaches unsatisfactory. He complained that while the majority judges 'freely ... almost cheerfully' admitted that their *Alcock*-resembling position was 'arbitrary', they underestimated the damage done to the integrity of the judicial process by such 'institutionalized caprice'. But Kaufman J did not support the *Dillon v Legg* foreseeability approach either. That 'experimentation' had led to 'even greater confusion and inconsistency'. The assertion in *Dillon* that courts could 'fix just and sensible boundaries on bystander liability' had turned out to be 'wholly illusory – both in theory and in practice'. Being distressed by injury to a loved one is 'inherently unsuitable to legal protection' because of its 'very universality'. All attempts to *limit* liability degenerate into 'inexplicable distinctions' produced by expediency, not principle. For Kaufman J, the only way to restore principle and avoid 'the inherently corrosive effect of arbitrary rules' was to limit recovery for shock to claimants physically injured or afraid for their *own* safety.[197] (In English terms, this would return tort law to its state before *Stokes v Hambrook Bros.*)[198]

Few support such a radical reform.[199] Most commentators advocate *expanded* liability, criticising the law's entrenched distinction between physical and mental injuries. Abolishing secondary victims' claims (or even psychiatric injury altogether) would have the opposite effect: deepening the discrimination against psychiatric illness, formalising its second-class status. It would prioritise tidiness over justice.[200] Ahuja expresses disappointment at the 'bewildering ... lack of sympathy' in the abolition proposal.[201] Neither the English nor Scottish Law Commissions seriously considered the option of abolition.

---

[195] *White* (n 7) 500.
[196] ibid 503, 504.
[197] 48 Cal.3d 644, 669–77 (1989).
[198] [1925] 1 KB 141.
[199] But cf Beever (n 77) 410–11.
[200] Law Com No 249 (1998) 6.3.
[201] Ahuja (n 32) 38.

However, it is worth bearing in mind that in many areas, those who reject the impurity of compromise face a stark choice between purer extremes, and there is no inevitability that their preferred position will prevail.

The Law Commission and 'Muddling Through'?

In 1998 the Law Commission recommended that most, but not all, *Alcock* restrictions should be abolished by statute.[202] In particular the Commission objected to legal rules that medical science had shown to be irrelevant. If ever implemented, this report would significantly extend liability, but not as far as the 'foreseeability principle'.

Commentators favouring liberalisation offered a partial welcome. Mullany and Handford are prominent critics of the artificial *Alcock* restrictions. However they found the Commission's half-hearted 'progressiveness' disappointing.[203] In particular Mullany and Handford regretted the Commission's 'veneration' of judicial fear about the floodgates of liability.[204] The floodgates concern depends on 'conjecture' not evidence, little more than 'fear propaganda'. The much-anticipated flood of unmeritorious claims was 'mythical', a risk accepted only because of constant repetition. If reform led to an increase in *meritorious* claims surely it 'will have achieved its very purpose'.[205]

We have noted the limited empirical evidence available to resolve such debates. But which side should bear the burden of proof? Teff argues the onus rests on those like the courts and the Law Commission who defend the *Alcock* rules' 'largely arbitrary deviations from the general principles of negligence law ... by reference to an unsubstantiated fear of opening the floodgates'.[206] Or should it be for those who challenge 'the wisdom of the common law' to prove that liability would *not* run out of control if the controls were abandoned? Even as it is, the Law Commission's proposals have not been implemented (nor the analogous Scottish proposals). It is hard to believe that the prospect of legislation would have been higher had the Law Commission's proposals been even more radical. Not without some sort of further compromise.

Retention: 'Recognisable Psychiatric Illness'

The Law Commission did not question the distinction between psychiatric illness (actionable damage) and 'non-compensatable mere mental distress'.[207] It seems to have assumed it was axiomatic. Commentators have also referred to the rule being 'almost universally supported'.[208] However, as seen in the first

---

[202] Law Com No 249, *Liability for Psychiatric Illness* (1998).
[203] Mullany and Handford (n 51) 350.
[204] ibid 378.
[205] ibid 381.
[206] Teff (n 41) 159.
[207] Law Com 249 (1998) 5.1–5.5.
[208] Nolan (n 176) 986.

debate it has increasingly been questioned. Teff asks why tort law has so closely followed psychiatry on *this* point, when (as we will see) the *Alcock* rules defy all insights of medical science.[209] The tort lawyer's ultimate interest is whether the harm is serious enough to warrant legal protection. Teff suggests that instead of arguing about labels devised by psychiatry for reasons irrelevant to the law's concerns, courts should examine whether a non-physical injury has substantially impaired the claimant's well-being. It would free the law from diagnostic controversy to examine the severity of impact on the claimant, rather than adjudicating upon classifications controversial within psychiatric medicine itself.[210] Tort, in his view, should abandon the 'recognisable illness' test 'almost casually' introduced by Lord Denning in *Hinz v Berry*.[211]

Other commentators favour the current definition of actionable damage. Notably including some advocates of foresight-based liability. Retaining the 'recognisable psychiatric illness' requirement could be an acceptable, principled way to limit liability. It was reaffirmed in *Tame v NSW* – as an alternative to the arbitrary restrictions US law places upon its wider category of 'emotional harm'. While Mullany and Handford have questioned whether such a firm commitment to 'recognisable psychiatric illness' is justifiable, they accept that it forms 'a deceptively effective limitation of litigation for mental disturbance'.[212] To go beyond the Law Commission and abolish this restriction too might be a liberalisation too far (at least without a balancing 'quid pro quo' such as Teff proposes).

Abolition: 'Sudden Shocking Event'

The Law Commission recommended legislative abolition of the requirement that the psychiatric illness was induced by sudden shock.[213] This appears to be a very longstanding rule – inherent in the old name 'nervous shock'. It fits naturally with the facts of the archetypal claim. (It is therefore questionable whether shock was a legal prerequisite, or just contingent on the fact-pattern in the early cases).[214] 'Shock' was elevated to a formal legal requirement in *Alcock*. It became 'perhaps the most crippling limitation' on claims despite its tenuous basis.[215]

'Shock' rules out recovery in atypical cases, for example claimants worn down by grief at a dying primary victim's bedside.[216] The Law Commission agreed with many commentators that it was 'harsh and seemingly arbitrary' to

---

[209] Teff (n 41) 7–9.
[210] ibid 144.
[211] ibid 57.
[212] Mullany and Handford (n 51) 379.
[213] Law Com 249 (1998) 5.28–5.33.
[214] M Fordham, 'Psychiatric Injury, Secondary Victims and the "Sudden Shock" Requirement' [2014] *Singapore JLS* 41.
[215] Mullany and Handford (n 51) 392.
[216] *Sion v Hampstead HA* (1994) 5 Med LR 170.

deny such claims simply because there was no 'sudden shock'.²¹⁷ In the current law, liability arises more readily for mental illness associated with paradigm tort accidents (especially PTSD) than for illnesses like depression. Yet all those illnesses cause equal suffering. The Royal College of Psychiatrists influentially submitted that the law's requirement of 'shock-induced' illness had 'no psychiatric meaning' and 'no scientific or clinical merit'.²¹⁸

The Commission's report remains unimplemented and common law development has been mixed. Notably Australia, where 'sudden shock' was first proposed as a distinct requirement of liability,²¹⁹ has now rejected it. Citing the English Law Commission with approval, *Tame v NSW* condemned the shock rule as 'harsh and arbitrary' and 'inconsistent in application'.²²⁰ The law had been distorted by inapt terminology. 'Nervous shock' was not merely a 'quaint' old-fashioned phrase but misled courts to reject valid claims.²²¹ Words should not become 'tyrants': 'Terminology should not impede appreciation of the nature and scope of psychiatric harm'.

According to this critique, courts have foolishly assumed the scientific reality of a rhetorical device. Liability has been 'imprisoned' by 'an outmoded [nineteenth century] scientific view about the nature of [psychiatric illness's] origins'.²²² However, the courts might have appreciated what they were doing. The elevation of 'shock' to a legal requirement could again be rationalised as a conscious strategy, anchoring psychiatric injury claims close to (albeit just outside) the classic tort accident's zone of physical danger.²²³ That this was artificial and precluded some meritorious claims was, on this view, the very point.

Quite apart from its medical illogicality though, that strategy does not confine liability very clearly and effectively. The only Australian judge to uphold the 'shock' requirement interpreted the facts of *Annetts* to satisfy it.²²⁴ In Teff's view, this reasoning had to be 'exceptionally broad and convoluted', 'far removed from [sudden shock's] doctrinal and commonsense meaning'.²²⁵ That awkward reasoning confirms the Law Commission's view that fixing a cut-off point for the 'suddenness' of a shock was 'essentially arbitrary'.²²⁶ The artificial rule does not even function as a clear-cut 'bright line'.

Nevertheless, English courts have not followed the Australian outright rejection of 'shock'. It has been quietly ignored in stress-at-work cases. There have been notably sceptical analyses in secondary victim cases too.²²⁷ At one

---

²¹⁷ Law Com 249 (1998) 2.63.
²¹⁸ ibid 5.29(2).
²¹⁹ *Jaensch v Coffey* (1984) 155 CLR 549 (Brennan J).
²²⁰ *Tame* (n 164) [207] (Gummow and Kirby JJ).
²²¹ ibid [204].
²²² *Campbelltown CC v Mackay* (1989) 15 NSWLR 501, 503 (Kirby P).
²²³ Mullany and Handford (n 51) 292.
²²⁴ *Annetts* (n 135) [362]–[364] (Callinan J).
²²⁵ Teff (n 41) 134.
²²⁶ Law Com 249 (1998) 5.29(4).
²²⁷ *Frost v Chief Constable* [1998] QB 254, 271 (Henry LJ).

point 'shock' was interpreted in claimant-friendly fashion in medical negligence cases.²²⁸ It is potentially difficult to satisfy the 'shock' condition in that context. It is unlikely that claimants will witness the medical negligence itself. To mitigate this, *Walters v Glamorgan* took an extended view of an ongoing shocking 'event', even (notwithstanding *White*) envisaging an 'incremental step advancing the frontiers of liability'.²²⁹ However following renewed emphasis on the *White* injunction 'Thus far and no further',²³⁰ 'shock' has been applied strictly in medical negligence cases. *Ronayne v Liverpool Women's Hospital* emphasised the need for a sudden, horrifying event and (distinguishing *Walters*) suggested that this would rarely be satisfied by witnessing a loved one's hospital death.²³¹ Burrows and Burrows contrast the 'disappointing' *Ronayne* case with the *Walters* court's 'enlightened' reasoning. The medical profession may welcome the restriction on liability that *Ronayne* uncritically re-imposed, but doctors' professional expertise ought to make them uncomfortable with legal rules that make no medical sense.²³²

Abolition: Proximity in Time and Space; Own Unaided Senses

The Law Commission's 'central recommendation' was legislative abolition of these two *Alcock* rules.²³³ They produced the 'most arbitrary' outcomes of all. But they were not workable limits on liability. It is difficult to draw a line between the 'immediate' and subsequent 'aftermath'. Commentators had expressed disgust at these rules' patent injustice. Should liability depend on a 'race with the ambulance'?²³⁴ How can it be legally relevant whether a body is still warm, or blood still wet?²³⁵

Above all, as with 'sudden shock' the rules were *medically* indefensible. A requirement of physical closeness in time and space was illogical since psychiatrics find '*emotional* involvement' rather than '*physical* presence … [affects] the level and nature of the injury suffered'.²³⁶ Similarly with the 'own unaided senses' restriction. Scientific research falsifies the law's assumption that trauma is greater for one who actually sees a relative's dead body. On the contrary, that can aid the grieving process. Where bodies are never recovered relatives may suffer greater distress. Those who do not actually see an accident can suffer horrifying vivid, imagined representations of the death: 'Contrary to judicial

---

²²⁸ Teff (n 41) 113–21.
²²⁹ *Walters* (n 190) [35] (Ward LJ); [53] (Clarke LJ).
²³⁰ *Taylor* (n 127).
²³¹ [2015] EWCA Civ 588.
²³² AS Burrows and JH Burrows, 'A Shocking Requirement' (2016) 24 *Med LR* 278. See *Walters* (n 190) [41] 'the psychiatric profession … may, for good reason, not understand or accept the illogicality of the law' (Ward LJ).
²³³ Law Com 249 (1998) 6.10–6.16.
²³⁴ Jones (n 171) 123.
²³⁵ Stapleton (n 193) 84 ('patently unconvincing').
²³⁶ *Coates v Government Insurance Office* (1995) 36 NSWLR 1, 11 (Kirby P).

assumptions, it does not appear that those who hear about the death from another source are spared much of the emotional pain that those who see it themselves have to endure'.[237] The law not only seems callous but also increasingly ridiculous in insisting on 'unaided senses'. It is 'hopelessly out of contact with the modern world of communications'.[238]

Just as with 'sudden shock', these rules have been removed from the common law in Australia ('obviously arbitrary ... [lacking] apparent logic or legal merit').[239] At best such 'proximity' could merely provide evidence of the foreseeability of psychiatric harm. In England however, the Law Commission's report has no prospect of implementation and the courts have re-affirmed their inability (or unwillingness) to reform the law themselves. These components of *Alcock* remain part of the law.

Reform: Ties of Love and Affection

Finally, the Law Commission recommended *retention* of the 'ties of love' requirement.[240] Here, medical evidence established its relevance: 'closeness of ties is a strong predictor of the bereavement response'.[241] A 'close correlation' exists between the intimacy of the claimant's relationship with the person injured and the foreseeability of psychiatric injury.[242] Yet why not treat this as solely an *evidential* matter, relevant for the foreseeability inquiry without necessarily being determinative? The Law Commission rejected that for a number of reasons.

First, their much-criticised acceptance that some control mechanisms were necessary to prevent uncontrolled liability. Second, the Law Commission aimed to promote certainty while reducing 'distressing cross-examination' about ties of love and affection. To achieve these goals required a statutory list. The Commission proposed that 'close ties' be presumed for listed categories of spouses, parents, children, siblings and long-term cohabitants. The presumption was to be *irrebuttable* – precisely to avoid defendants attempting to cast doubt on the closeness of the ties. Of course this approach might be over-inclusive in unusual cases involving estranged siblings etc.[243] As seen, in *Alcock* the House of Lords therefore required loving ties to be determined on the facts of each case. But this has 'harrowing evidential consequences' – claimants needing to prove how much they loved the primary victim, set against 'the benefits of this modest flexibility'.[244] Nolan comments that the Scottish

---

[237] Ahuja (n 32) 46.
[238] *Coates* (n 236) 11 (Kirby P).
[239] *Tame* (n 164) [221]–[222] (Gummow and Kirby JJ).
[240] Law Com No 249 (1998) 6.24–6.35.
[241] Ahuja (n 32) 47.
[242] Law Com No 249 (1998) 6.25.
[243] Cf *Alcock* (n 56) 406 ('The quality of brotherly love is well known to differ widely – from Cain and Abel to David and Jonathan') (Lord Ackner).
[244] *van Soest v Residential Health Managements* [2000] 1 NZLR 179, 209 (Thomas J).

Law Commission's proposal (a longer but *rebuttable* statutory list of relationships) would perpetuate the current law's 'distressing factual inquiries'.[245] Moreover, using presumptions rather than bright lines inevitably creates uncertainty. Even the English Commission's proposals would not entirely avoid this, since it would remain possible for claimants outside the statutory list to prove that they in fact had ties of love and affection as close as those on it.[246] There is, however, a danger that closed statutory lists (as in some Australian jurisdictions) could ignore 'relationships [that] increasingly defy traditional categories' in today's society.[247]

Another Compromise: Quid Pro Quo?

Harvey Teff has suggested a way to shake English law from its seemingly unreformable stasis. He fiercely criticises the current law.[248] It devalues interests in mental health and emotional wellbeing. Teff would not only abolish the *Alcock* 'control mechanisms' but replace the 'recognisable psychiatric illness' requirement. Tort should treat every significant disturbance of mental harmony, or substantial emotional pain and dysfunction, as actionable damage.[249] Teff welcomes the Australian decision in *Tame v NSW* as an 'exemplar' of common law development. He accepts that given the 'defeatism' and 'fatalism' in *White*, judicial reform is unlikely in England. (Since Teff wrote in 2009, there has been no revival of interest in legislative reform, and the common law has if anything ossified further.)[250]

Realistically, Teff accepts, there will be no legislation widening recovery for mental harm without a counter-balancing reform. A political trade-off is needed: to restrict tort liability in some respects as the price of liberalising the law on psychiatric injury. Teff's proposal is a monetary threshold for damages for *non-pecuniary loss* (he suggested £2,000) in *all* personal injury claims, that is, including physical injuries.[251] This would significantly reduce the overall number of tort claims (most of which concern minor injuries which cause no *financial* loss). Reducing numbers of minor claims would significantly reduce the 'processing costs' of the tort system. The minimum threshold would also significantly reduce the overall cost of tort compensation (two-thirds of which,

---

[245] Nolan (n 176) 992.
[246] Law Com 249 (1998) 6.32.
[247] P Vines et al, 'Is "Nervous Shock" Still a Feminist Issue?' (2010) 18 *Tort LR* 9, 24 ('Furthermore, this categorical approach is at odds with the feminist valuing of "connection … as part of the human experience"'); cf *Smith v Lancashire Teaching Hospitals* [2018] QB 804 (discriminatory list of bereavement claimants in s1A Fatal Accidents Act 1976).
[248] Teff (n 41).
[249] ibid 172–75.
[250] *Taylor* (n 127); *Ronayne* (n 231). Cf *Paul* (n 1) (Court of Appeal urging reconsideration by the Supreme Court and granting leave to appeal).
[251] Teff (n 41) ch 6.

according to the Pearson Commission's survey, consists of damages for pain, suffering and loss of amenity – only one-third compensating financial loss like medical expenses and diminished earnings).[252]

A detailed assessment of Teff's proposal would require full analysis of the purpose of monetary compensation for intangible harms (pain and suffering): are they solace, symbol or otherwise?[253] Such awards are certainly more controversial than compensation for financial loss, universally accepted to be literal replacement of like for like. Moreover, as Teff notes, non-pecuniary losses are not compensated at all in other compensation systems. They are absent from both government social security (which provides *financial* support for the incapacitated and unemployed) and private accident/life insurance (people do not insure themselves against pain and suffering, only the financial consequences of injury and death). Thresholds exist, excluding 'pain and suffering' awards for minor injuries, in (for example) the Criminal Injuries Compensation Scheme. The proposed limits would therefore not be unprecedented. They could be a welcome restriction on an anomalous head of damages.

Yet Teff accepts the proposal has a degree of arbitrariness. A claimant just over the threshold would recover in full, someone with slightly less serious injuries getting nothing at all. Is there not an irony in proposing an arbitrary cut-off for minor claims to free psychiatric injury from a different set of arbitrary rules? Teff responds that his 'procedural' proposals would do less harm to legal integrity than tort's current *substantive* arbitrary rules. But Weir wrote dismissively of a somewhat similar proposal made by Mullany and Handford: the authors would 'rob physical Peter to pay psychiatric Paul' – that is, victims of *physical* injury would be made worse off to benefit psychiatric injury claimants.[254] Teff's view, however, is that the law should prioritise compensation of severe mental harm (ie those who would currently receive nothing under the *Alcock* and *White* rules) over those who suffer minor physical injuries. Is tort's preference for physical harm so deep-rooted that it ranks the modest pain of bruises sustained in a gentle collision above the catastrophic mental breakdowns suffered after the Hillsborough stadium disaster?

Conclusion

This chapter has considered one of tort's most notorious problems. The English law on psychiatric injury has attracted unparalleled flights of abuse. It is said to symbolise failure on many levels – failures of the common law process and policy reasoning. Even failures of humanity and impartiality.

---

[252] Cmnd 7054-II (Royal Commission on Civil Liability and Compensation for Personal Injury, *Report: Volume Two: Statistics and Costings* (London, HMSO, 1979)) [520]–[521] (only in the highest-value claims does compensation for financial loss exceed non-pecuniary loss).

[253] eg A Ogus, 'Damages for Lost Amenities: For a Foot, a Feeling or a Function?' (1972) 35 *MLR* 1.

[254] T Weir, 'Book Review' [1993] *CLJ* 520, 522.

The courts themselves confess that they are unable to draw satisfactory lines to limit liability for injuries caused without inherent physical limits. That they have anyway persisted in this doomed attempt arguably exceeds the judicial function and assumes the role of the legislature.[255] However, it is not clear that the situation would be much improved if (as the House of Lords urged)[256] the *Alcock* rules had been enacted in statute. Albeit 'bathed in legitimacy' by the legislature's democratic mandate,[257] the line-drawing would be just as artificial.

Alcock seems a grotesque failure of policy-making by the courts. Yet its rights-based rival speaks with a very uncertain voice.[258] It apparently recommends full foreseeability-based recovery or at the opposite extreme, outright abolition of liability, depending on which rights-theorist we consult. As seen, in *White* either of those approaches was thought so radical that only the legislature could properly adopt it – which seems ironic when the rights-based approach is championed as peculiarly suitable for *judicial* application. Judges simply enforce the claimant's rights. Courts can therefore, Beever asserts, 'determine liability without any appeal to policy whatsoever'.[259] Yet following either rights-based theory would have a major redistributive effect. Beever's tentatively suggests that 'as there is no clear right to psychological integrity, there cannot be recovery for psychology injury unless it flows from the violation of some right' – in sharp contrast to the clearly established 'right to bodily integrity' which grounds actions for *physical* injury.[260] That 'no right' approach would deprive all mental-illness claimants of compensation. Stevens' approach would to the contrary (if the Law Commission's and government's estimates are correct) cost drivers and the NHS billions of pounds in additional cumulative liabilities. Should such momentous decisions be taken by the judiciary, excluding public concerns as irrelevant to 'rights-based adjudication' despite the public impact of their decisions?[261]

The law here exemplifies tort's decided preference for physical injury over 'intangible' harm. Its 'devaluation, diminishment, and dismissal of injuries to the psyche' rejects 'injuries that harm people profoundly – injuries that matter the most'.[262] Chamallas and Kerber stress the 'gender significance of the basic legal hierarchy that places material property rights above relations and emotions'.[263] Women, being more vulnerable to such harms, have been

---

[255] Stevens (n 78).
[256] n 90.
[257] Stapleton (n 84) 14 (Civil Liability Act 1936 (South Australia)).
[258] Stevens (n 78); Beever (n 77).
[259] Beever (n 77) 514.
[260] ibid 410 (albeit at 411 stressing that 'we need to decide whether people have a right to their psychological integrity or not', to determine the scope of liability).
[261] Cf Stapleton (n 84) 32 (since common law precedents affect society in general, courts are obliged to consider social concerns beyond the interests of the immediate parties).
[262] Levit (n 20) 191.
[263] Chamallas and Kerber (n 18).

systematically disadvantaged.²⁶⁴ Miscarriages have been egregiously misclassified as 'psychiatric' or 'emotional' injury. The 'objective' requirement of reasonable stoicism or phlegm presupposes that 'only supersensitive or abnormally delicate persons could suffer physical harms from fright'. (In 1941 Prosser noted some judges' 'distinctly masculine astonishment that any woman should ever be so silly as to allow herself to be frightened or shocked into a miscarriage'.)²⁶⁵ Modern brain science suggests hard-wired differences in men's and women's perceptions of trauma and stress.²⁶⁶ As Betsy Grey suggests, this raises a dilemma: if women are held to a different standard of 'reasonable firmness' it risks reinforcing 'stereotypical perceptions of female fragility and inadequacies'. Perhaps the answer is to take a more humane approach to 'ordinary firmness' for claimants of all genders. The historic paradigm of the deserving claimant – 'mentally healthy, emotionally stoic, risk-defying, and perhaps immortal' – is quite unreal.²⁶⁷

Gendered bias provides yet a further reason to review the restrictive rules in this area. Can such differential treatment be justified by judicial conjectures about 'indeterminate liability'? Could 'control' through the doctrines of breach and causation – rather than denying a duty outright – offer a more nuanced solution (as seen in workplace stress claims)? This said, Gary Schwartz queried whether wider liabilities should be recognised purely to benefit women (or to remove obstacles disproportionately bearing on women).²⁶⁸ He suggested that naked redistribution on gender grounds would be inconsistent with corrective justice. He also raised the risk of self-defeating generosity. The strictness of US product liability in cases involving birth defects has arguably led to fewer contraceptive drugs/devices being developed (or those available in other countries being marketed in America), an outcome 'evidently harmful to the interests and welfare of American women'.

Levit argues for the therapeutic benefits of recognising 'psychic injuries': 'the refusal to compensate an injury is a direct message about the worth of the injury; compensation legitimizes the interests', denominating them as 'worthy injuries'.²⁶⁹ Liability is not only about compensation, but sends a message about which interests the law (and through it society) values and protects. But Schwartz also questioned tort's 'expressive' role,²⁷⁰ noting that claims for causing death often fail if the relevant doctrinal rules cannot be satisfied – 'despite the importance of expressing the value of life'. Schwartz finally questioned how 'gendered' is the impact of tort's preference for physical injuries;

---

²⁶⁴ Davies (n 141) 403–04 states women are 'significantly more likely to report work-related stress'.
²⁶⁵ W Prosser, *Handbook on the Law of Torts* (St. Paul, Minn, West Publishing Co, 1941) 55.
²⁶⁶ BJ Grey, 'Sex-Based Brain Differences and Emotional Harm' (2020) 70 *Duke LJ Online* 29.
²⁶⁷ Levit (n 20) 192.
²⁶⁸ GT Schwartz, 'Feminist Approaches to Tort Law' (2001) 2 *Theoretical Inq L* 175.
²⁶⁹ Levit (n 20) 188–89.
²⁷⁰ S Hershovitz, 'Treating Wrongs as Wrongs: An Expressive Argument for Tort Law' (2017) 10 *Jo Tort L* 405.

the other distinction drawn, between physical property and pure economic loss, disadvantages *corporations*. While that is of course true, tort law's claim to place personal injuries at the top of the hierarchy of protected interests will ring hollow so long as mental injuries are accorded such second-class status. Comprehensive review by the Supreme Court is long overdue.[271]

---

[271] Cf *Paul* (n 1).

PART III

Nuisance

10

Private Nuisance and Property Rights

Prosser famously described nuisance as an 'impenetrable jungle'.[1] Some have attempted to harness its 'protean' or shape-shifting qualities to fill gaps in tort law such as the (former) absence of a harassment tort,[2] or the lack of an overarching tort of invasion of privacy.[3] These attempts have failed. Private nuisance can *only* coherently be understood as an action for protection of property rights. That 'restatement' of nuisance is considered in the first debate. How should the courts go about protecting property through nuisance law? Should they prioritise the defendant's use of their land, or the claimant's peaceful enjoyment (with which the defendant's use interferes)? Allan Beever argues that they must identify the 'most fundamental' land-use, from a purely rights-based perspective. Others maintain that public interest considerations also need to be considered in nuisance. The public interest plays an important, irreplaceable role in defining the limits of 'rights to the use and enjoyment of land'. This is examined in the second debate. Finally, the chapter's third debate examines in detail the 'balancing' process at the heart of nuisance doctrine (and exceptions to it). Does an exclusive focus on protection of property rights best explain the tort's structure?

Debate 1
Is Nuisance a Tort for Protecting Property Rights?

Should private nuisance be understood exclusively as an action protecting right in property? That is arguably the best explanation for the tort's overall purpose and for the shape of many of its constituent doctrines. The modern dominance of the view can be traced to the House of Lords' restatement of nuisance in *Hunter v Canary Wharf Ltd*.[4] Solutions to various doctrinal puzzles lie, it is suggested, in a better appreciation of the property-rights conception of nuisance. We explore standing, remedies and the outer limits of nuisance (ie kinds

---

[1] *Prosser and Keeton on Torts* 5th edn (St Paul, MN, West, 1984) 616.
[2] *Khorasandjian v Bush* [1993] QB 727.
[3] *Fearn v Tate Gallery* [2020] Ch 621.
[4] [1997] AC 655.

of interference that *never* generate liability). We also examine the difference between the rights protected by nuisance and those in the ECHR.

Property Rights: Standing to Bring a Claim

Nuisance was reaffirmed as 'a tort to land' in the landmark decision in *Hunter v Canary Wharf*. The reaffirmation was part of the House of Lords' ratio. Those living in affected houses had no standing to sue in nuisance unless they had a proprietary interest in the land (rather than merely the owner's permission (licence) to occupy it). Restricted standing flowed from the very definition of the tort. Just as we uncontroversially accept that only the owner of the land has standing to claim in trespass against those who physically cross the boundary, the same was true in nuisance. It was impossible to expand the standing test using 'policy' reasoning, contrary to the dissenting view of Lord Cooke. It was not to the point (*pace* Pill LJ) that in 'present-day conditions' the law should avoid 'inconsistencies' between family members occupying the same property, by distinguishing those from ownership rights and those without.[5] Lord Lloyd stated 'it is one thing to modernise the law by ridding it of unnecessary technicalities; it is another thing to bring about a fundamental change in the nature and scope of a cause of action'.[6]

The plaintiffs had argued: 'The true concern of the law ought not to be to protect a strict proprietorial right; rather, it is to protect the use and enjoyment of land'.[7] This 'concern' is precisely what the House of Lords rejected. A fallacy had arisen that nuisance contained a sub-category of 'interference with comfortable occupation of land', separate from actual physical damage to property. On this erroneous view, it seemed unjustifiable to recognise a claim for the landowner alone for their 'discomfort', and not for others living in the same house who might suffer equal or greater. But the premise was 'quite mistaken'.[8] The law does not include a separate tort of 'amenity nuisance' which protects a different kind of interest ('enjoyment'). In *all* cases, nuisance involves damage *to land*. That is obviously true when there is *physical* damage to or encroachment upon the land; but no less true of 'nuisance by interference with a neighbour's quiet enjoyment'. The 'essence' of nuisance was the same in each situation: 'namely, interference with land or the enjoyment of land'.[9] A landowner cannot recover for their own personal discomfort if they happen to occupy land affected by noise, smell or other 'sensory' nuisance. Compensation assesses *only* the diminished value of the land. Once this was understood, the standing rule (confining nuisance claims to the landowner) was both logical and justified – indeed inevitable.

---

[5] ibid 675 (Pill LJ) (CA).
[6] ibid 696.
[7] ibid 679 (Daniel Brennan QC).
[8] ibid 706 (Lord Hoffmann).
[9] ibid 696 (Lord Lloyd).

Lord Goff also reasoned from the rules on injunctions, a standard remedy in nuisance. The right to request an injunction is 'ordinarily vested in the person who has exclusive possession of the land'.[10] This point might seem obvious – only the holder of a right can complain about its invasion. It is of general application. It shows why, at common law, there could be no cause of action based on *somebody else's* death.[11] Legislation was required to create 'dependency' claims following a fatality.[12] But the rule remains that only the person who has been injured may sue in respect of those injuries.[13] Although tort lawyers do not often invoke the notion of 'privity' familiar in the law of contract, tort necessarily contains the same notion.[14] Only the holder of a right can claim to enforce it. In nuisance, it follows, logically only landowners can seek injunctions.

Lord Goff bolstered this point with more pragmatic reasons. As he noted, many nuisance disputes between neighbours are resolved by agreement rather than by a court – for example agreements limiting the hours at which noise is made, possibly in exchange for payment:

> But the efficacy of arrangements such as these depends upon the existence of an identifiable person with whom the creator of the nuisance can deal for this purpose. If anybody who lived in the relevant property as a home had the right to sue, sensible arrangements such as these might in some cases no longer be practicable.[15]

For Donal Nolan, standing points 'ineluctably' (and more clearly than any other rule) to nuisance's fundamentally *proprietary* nature.[16] Nolan also notes the strong links between trespass and nuisance. He criticises the support for the looser policy-based standing test, not least because the suggested alterative (Pill LJ's 'sufficient link') would be 'so vague as to be almost useless'.[17] Lord Hope summed up the orthodox approach: 'we are concerned here essentially with the law of property' (which is also demonstrated by servitudes, such as rights of way, being protected by claims in nuisance in English law).[18]

The House of Lords overruled *Khorasandjian v Bush*.[19] The Court of Appeal had there wrongly held telephone harassment to be within the scope of nuisance. It was not. The harassment was essentially unconnected to the occupation of land. Were a *landowner* being harassed by 'nuisance calls' on their landline, this would not be actionable in nuisance either. (Indeed in our

---

[10] ibid 692–93.
[11] *Baker v Bolton* (1808) 1 Camp 493.
[12] Lord Campbell's Act 1846 (now Fatal Accidents Act 1976).
[13] eg *West Bromwich Albion Football Club Ltd v El-Safty* [2006] EWCA Civ 1299.
[14] R Stevens, *Torts and Rights* (Oxford, Oxford University Press, 2007) 188–89.
[15] [1997] AC 655, 693.
[16] D Nolan, '"A Tort Against Land": Private Nuisance as a Property Tort' in D Nolan and A Robertson (eds), *Rights and Private Law* (Oxford, Hart, 2012) 473–75.
[17] ibid 474.
[18] [1997] AC 655, 723.
[19] [1993] QB 727.

smartphone society, it seems quaint and implausible that such abuse could be geographically specific to the home: our phones follow us wherever we go.) The *Hunter* majority noted with relief that Parliament had since addressed the social problem in *Khorasandjian* by enacting the Protection from Harassment Act 1997. The statutory intervention made it easier to condemn *Khorasandjian* for 'distort[ing] [common law] principles and creat[ing] anomalies merely as an expedient to fill a gap'.[20] The emphasis on principle is welcome to those who fear that tort is too easily misused as the common law's 'swiss army knife', an endlessly flexible problem-solving tool.[21] Compare Lord Cooke of Thorndon's dissenting view. Having complimented the *Hunter* majority for 'a major advance in the symmetry of the law of nuisance' he pointedly remarked that it did not 'strengthen the utility or the justice' of nuisance law.[22] In Lord Cooke's opinion the law lords' 'choice [for the restrictive path] is in the end a policy one between competing principles'.

Property Rights: Compensation

Damages in nuisance compensation invasion of the owner's property interest. That is obvious when there is physical damage to the property. Compensation reflects the resulting loss in value or the reasonable cost of repairs. But it is equally true for 'amenity nuisance'. As Lord Hoffmann put it in *Hunter*:

> inconvenience, annoyance or even illness suffered by persons on land as a result of smells or dust are not damage consequential upon the injury to the land. It is rather the other way about: the injury to the amenity of the land consists in the fact that the persons upon it are liable to suffer inconvenience, annoyance or illness.[23]

This is perhaps a puzzling passage. Also counter-intuitive was Lord Lloyd's insistence that 'reduction in amenity value is the same whether the land is occupied by the family man or the bachelor'; and so 'the quantum of damages in private nuisance does not depend on the number of those enjoying the land in question'.[24] The Court of Appeal subsequently drew back from the logic of Lord Lloyd's approach. Waller LJ reasoned that an 'actual loss of amenity' must be shown before substantial damages are awarded, and thus if a house affected by serious nuisance were empty at the time the landowner's damages would be nominal only.[25] Which view is correct?

---

[20] [1997] AC 655, 707 (Lord Hoffmann).
[21] A Beever, *Rediscovering the Law of Negligence* (Oxford, Hart, 2007) 314.
[22] [1997] AC 655, 711.
[23] ibid 706.
[24] ibid 696.
[25] *Dobson v Thames Water* [2009] EWCA Civ 28; [2009] 3 All ER 319, [34].

Nolan supports the views of Lord Lloyd and Lord Hoffmann in *Hunter*.[26] He argues that the primary function of a damages award in nuisance (when injunctive relief is unavailable) is to 'substitute' the property right invaded. This core 'substitutive' award is assessed entirely objectively. It does not depend on the amount or existence of actual loss.[27] The question is the impact on the *land* (and its value), not the impact on the occupiers. Thus, argues Nolan, damages are affected 'by the objective qualities of the land', for example its size and value. But damages are *unaffected* by the number of occupants and the extent they are actually inconvenienced. It is immaterial whether an occupant is especially sensitive to loud noise, or untroubled because 'stone deaf'. As Lord Hoffmann reasoned, the court must assess the diminution in letting value of the property during the period of the nuisance, since 'the value of the right to occupy a house which smells of pigs must be less than the value of the occupation of an equivalent house which does not'. (Estate agents are experts at estimating such land-value effects, including the 'intangible' impact of a 'transitory' nuisance.)[28]

Nolan thinks it 'unfortunate' that in *Dobson* Waller LJ 'seemed to baulk at the full rigour of the objective approach to damages'.[29] The Court of Appeal confused the strictly objective 'substitutive' award with damages awarded for losses *consequent on* the interference with the land. Such consequential losses certainly do have to be proved as actually suffered in fact. Moreover, consequential loss is *not* limited to interference with land. For example, Lord Hoffmann suggested a business unable to occupy its premises could include consequential loss of trading income in a nuisance claim,[30] or a farmer could recover when flooding on his land drowns livestock.[31] (Nolan sees no reason why consequential personal injury should not be recoverable too.)

The rights perspective illuminates this difficult issue. Damages for the invasion itself are the monetary equivalent of an injunction. 'Substitutive' compensation redresses the reduced objective value of the property right. It is objective and impersonal (and one might note, and question, also abstract and notional). Consequential loss (of a reasonably foreseeable kind)[32] is also recoverable. But it must be proved by evidence – it is 'actual' loss rather than abstract or notional harm.

Although 'substitutive' and 'consequential loss' damages are sharply distinct in theory, they can overlap in practice. Courts must beware double counting.

---

[26] Nolan (n 16) 477–80.
[27] Stevens (n 14) 60.
[28] [1997] AC 655, 706 (Lord Hoffmann).
[29] Nolan (n 16) 478.
[30] eg *Andrae v Selfridge Ltd* [1938] Ch 1. See further P Gilliker, 'Economic Wrongs and Private Nuisance: A Common Law Perspective' in J Eldridge et al, *Economic Torts and Economic Wrongs* (Oxford, Hart, 2021) ('*sangfroid* of nuisance towards … economic loss').
[31] [1997] AC 655, 706 (Lord Hoffmann) (eg *Halsey v Esso Ltd* [1961] 1 WLR 683 (smuts fouling washing on line)).
[32] *Cambridge Water v Eastern Counties Leather* [1994] 2 AC 264.

As David Howarth states, when a hotel's guests leave because of noise nuisance, the loss of business can be claimed as damages but the court must not compensate this twice over by also compensating the hotel's diminished rental value.[33] A particular difficulty concerns 'amenity damage'. The courts have accepted that in the absence of specific direct evidence of the diminished 'rental value' of land, it could be appropriate to award 'general damages' for impairment a pleasurable amenity – that is, for general loss of enjoyment.[34] As Lord Lloyd put it in *Hunter*: 'The effect of smoke from a neighbouring factory is to reduce the value of the land. There may be no diminution in the market value. But there will certainly be loss of amenity value so long as the nuisance lasts'.[35] It seems that 'amenity value' is here being used as a proxy, an indirect way of quantifying the (perhaps temporary) diminution of the land itself. Of itself that is unobjectionable. As the Supreme Court explained recently in a different context, courts sometimes make assumptions in the claimant's favour (eg relaxing the standard of proof) when it is difficult to assess damages: since it is the defendant's wrong that has ultimately caused the difficulty.[36] However, where a direct award for the reduced value of land is made, there can be no room for an *additional* award for loss of amenity.[37] As it is 'simply an alternative method of calculating the diminution in value of the property in cases where the damage attributable to the nuisance is not likely to be permanent',[38] again there would be double counting – compensating the claimant twice over for the same loss.

Nuisance and Human Rights

Those who advocate understanding of tort law through rights do not necessarily advocate an infusion of ECHR rights via the Human Rights Act 1998.[39] Nuisance overlaps with two European Convention rights: the right to one's home (article 8 ECHR: right to private and family life) and the right to peaceful enjoyment of possessions (article 1 of First Protocol to the ECHR). Understandably, claimants have sought to expand nuisance to protect those ECHR rights – including 'horizontal' claims (against other private parties) outside the remedies that the HRA gives against public authorities (ie in 'vertical' claims). Scholars disagree whether this is a legitimate way to develop the tort.

The ECHR's expansionary effect is welcomed by those who think nuisance too limited by its historical focus on protecting property rights. Authors in the

---

[33] D Howarth, *Textbook on Tort* (London, Butterworths, 1995) 509.
[34] *Coventry v Lawrence (No 1)* [2014] UKSC 13; [2014] AC 822 [172] (Lord Clarke).
[35] [1997] AC 655, 696.
[36] *One Step Ltd v Morris-Garner* [2018] UKSC 20; [2019] AC 649 [37]–[38] (Lord Reed).
[37] *Raymond v Young* [2015] EWCA Civ 456; *Chalmers v Diageo Scotland Ltd* [2019] CSOH 63; 2019 SLT 1184.
[38] *Raymond v Young* [2015] EWCA Civ 456 [29] (Patten LJ).
[39] For Robert Stevens' contrast between ECHR rights and the 'true' rights protected by tort see ch 2, 'Debate 3: Trespass and Constitutional Rights'.

years immediately following the HRA 1998 hailed its potential. Jane Wright called for the protection of nuisance to extend to every person's home, going beyond *Hunter v Canary Wharf*'s reasserted link with property ownership. Wright argued (in 2001): 'it is time for English law to move beyond the straitjacket of the forms of action'.[40] Similarly, Paula Giliker argued (2003) that the HRA 'has the potential to strike at the very heart of liability for torts protecting real property and change their fundamental character and long-standing relationship with property law'.[41] Giliker regretted tort law's emphasis on 'historical accuracy, rather than social protection'.[42] *Hunter* symbolised this attitude. Compare Fleming's view that limiting tort's protection to those who *own* their homes is 'invidious discrimination'.[43] Giliker argued that property torts like nuisance should be able to 'alter their essential character to meet modern social and political needs'.[44] The HRA could be the catalyst for such changes.

In fact though, this has not in fact happened and there seems little prospect that it will. Donal Nolan argues that the basis of the common law tort is quite different from article 8 (as developed by the Strasbourg Court). Any attempt to infuse ECHR rights into private nuisance would therefore be unwise.[45] Nolan identifies numerous significant differences.

A person's home is protected by article 8 whether they *own* it or not. Inevitably therefore, the scope of protection under the ECHR is wider than in nuisance, with its narrow standing test (exclusively for landowners) and the exclusively proprietary remedies, reaffirmed in *Hunter v Canary Wharf*. These fundamental doctrinal features of nuisance are incompatible with article 8. *Pace* Lord Lloyd in *Hunter*, a family of five certainly would be awarded higher damages than a person living alone, given the cumulatively greater interference with their Convention rights. Article 8 does not protect the value of property as such. Failure to keep such claims separate therefore leads to confusion. The *Dobson* case (mentioned above) involved allegations of intolerable smell and mosquito infestation against a public utility company. Parallel claims were brought in common law nuisance and under the HRA. Nolan suggests that the influence of article 8 contributed to the Court of Appeal's 'somewhat muddied' approach to the objective assessment of damages in nuisance.[46]

---

[40] J Wright, *Tort Law and Human Rights* (Oxford, Hart, 2001) 194. (A variation on the metaphor that the forms of action 'rule us from their graves' (FW Maitland, *The Forms of Action at Common Law* (Cambridge, Cambridge University Press, 1909)) or stand as 'ghosts of the past ... in the path of justice clanking their mediæval chains' (*United Australia Ltd v Barclays Bank Ltd* [1941] AC 1, 29 (Lord Atkin).)

[41] P Giliker, 'The Relationship Between Property Law and Tort Law' in Alistair Hudson (ed), *New Perspectives on Property Law: Obligations and Restitution* (Abingdon, Taylor and Francis, 2003).

[42] ibid 75.

[43] JG Fleming, *The Law of Torts* 10th edn (Sydney, Lawbook Co, 1998) 475.

[44] Giliker (n 41) 74.

[45] D Nolan, 'Nuisance' in D Hoffman (ed), *The Impact of the UK Human Rights Act on Private Law* (Cambridge, Cambridge University Press, 2011).

[46] ibid 183–86.

The Court of Appeal noted the fundamental misalignment of nuisance and ECHR rights in *Fearn v Tate Gallery*.[47] The court declined to use article 8 to extend nuisance to include the right 'not to be overlooked'. Overlooking fell squarely within article 8's protection of privacy rights but fit poorly inside nuisance (where for centuries the right had consistently been denied). Etherton MR reasoned that 'overlaying ... nuisance with article 8 would significantly distort the tort in some important respects'. Since 'nuisance is a property tort' it uses a 'depersonalised' metric of 'interference' and does not permit the public interest to justify such an invasion. A particular individual's sensitivity to interference is ignored, consistent with nuisance law's objective protection of property rights. By contrast, such individual characteristics 'may be highly relevant for the purposes of article 8' (eg heightened concern about invading *children's* privacy). Another fundamental divergence is that whereas article 8(2) obliges courts to balance possible public-interest justifications against an invasion of the right to private and family life (a structure reproduced right across the ECHR), 'Such considerations have no place in the tort of nuisance'. Given Nolan's unenthusiasm about absorbing article 8 into nuisance, he naturally welcomes its rejection in *Fearn*.[48] It shows the HRA's impact on nuisance has been a 'damp squib'.

Nolan notes yet other respects in which the Convention rights may be wider. The ECHR doctrine of 'positive obligations' extend public authorities' liability for omissions.[49] The ECHR may not accept a 'statutory authority' defence unless accompanied by compensation. Potentially, even 'unavoidable' interference with an individual's home life by noise, smoke, etc can only be justified as 'necessary in a democratic society' if compensation is paid for the interference.[50] Hence Lord Phillips MR's obiter suggestion

> where an authority carries on an undertaking in the interest of the community as a whole it may have to pay compensation to individuals whose rights are infringed by that undertaking in order to achieve a fair balance between the interests of the individual and the community.[51]

Nolan, however, suggests that the Strasbourg authority for this is weak, the conditions for requiring such payments undefined, and the ramifications 'not thought through'.[52]

---

[47] [2020] EWCA Civ 104; [2020] Ch 621, [91]–[93] (source of quotations in this paragraph). (Note that the Supreme Court heard an appeal against this decision in December 2021; judgment still awaited in August 2022).

[48] D Nolan, 'Nuisance and Privacy' (2021) 137 *LQR* 1.

[49] Cf *Hussain v Lancaster CC* [2000] QB 1 (common law); J Morgan, 'Nuisance and the Unruly Tenant' [2001] *CLJ* 382.

[50] *S v France* (1990) 65 DR 250.

[51] *Marcic v Thames Water* [2002] EWCA Civ 64; [2002] QB 929 [117].

[52] Nolan (n 45) 177, 193.

Tort has expanded significantly in other areas to meet the challenge of the HRA. The most notable transformation has remedied the common law's historic failure to protect rights of privacy.[53] An action for misuse of private information has arisen, irrespective of distortions to the underlying notion of 'confidentiality'. This contrasts with the cautious approach to nuisance and the ECHR. Perhaps it takes a serious gap in protection of rights before the courts are willing to do serious violence to doctrinal coherence. As it was doubtful whether 'mere overlooking' would anyway be a violation of article 8,[54] the *Fearn* strategy of leaving the problem to the legislature was understandable.[55]

The Boundaries of Nuisance: The Absence of Rights

Thinking of nuisance as 'a tort to land' can help clarify the scope of the tort in other ways too. Nuisance does not offer unlimited protection. A claim may fail even when conduct unquestionably diminishes the value of land. There is a tendency to call examples 'pure economic loss' cases. That expression is best avoided in the context of nuisance. It is at best a question-begging term, expressing a conclusion rather than a reason. It is clearer to engage directly with the question 'what rights over land should the law protect?' than to conceal it with formulae such as 'pure economic loss'.

Long-established authority means that landowners cannot complain if neighbours block a pleasant view.[56] Nor, the mirror image situation, if their neighbours overlook their land.[57] Nor if a neighbour's activities divert the flow of air,[58] or percolating groundwater,[59] to land. The absence of liability cannot be explained away as 'trivial' interferences that do not significantly affect the value of land. In *Aldred's Case*, Wray CJ reasoned that the law does not prevent obstruction of a view ('prospect') 'which is a matter only of delight, and not of necessity'.[60] But whether or not 'delight' is necessary to life, it is certainly marketable. A room with a view is *for that reason* more valuable: houses having sea views were on average £86,000 more expensive in December 2020.[61] Indeed Wray CJ himself acknowledged the economic forces at work noting 'it is a great commendation of a house if it has a long and large prospect'. Serious and costly interference was manifest in the other leading cases where the claims failed. In *Chastey v Ackland* the defendant's wall obstructed the free flow of air so that the smell ('exhalations') from a public urinal 'stagnated' in the yard of the

---

[53] Compare *Wainwright v Home Office* [2004] 2 AC 406 with *McKennitt v Ash* [2008] QB 73 (cited (unsuccessfully) by counsel for the claimants in *Fearn v Tate Gallery* [2020] Ch 621, 626).
[54] *Fearn* [2020] EWCA Civ 104; [2020] Ch 621 [90].
[55] *Fearn* ibid [84]–[85].
[56] *William Aldred's Case* (1610) 9 Co Rep 57b.
[57] *Fearn v Tate Gallery* [2020] EWCA Civ 104; [2020] Ch 621.
[58] *Chastey v Ackland* [1895] 2 Ch 389.
[59] *Bradford Corporation v Pickles* [1895] AC 587.
[60] (1610) 9 Co Rep 57b, 58b.
[61] www.rightmove.co.uk/news/articles/property-news/sea-view-homes-price-premium.

plaintiff's house. Clearly this must have been unpleasant and cannot have done much for the value of the house (at first instance Cave J, who incorrectly held it a nuisance, ordered the wall to be demolished). In *Bradford Corporation v Pickles*, the defendant threatened to empty the main drinking-water reservoir for the population of Bradford. That the court dismissed the claim showed remarkable indifference to the consequences (such as converting all Bradford 'into a howling desert').[62]

Significant loss was undeniable in these cases. But it is not *loss* alone that the law compensates. It must arise from invasion of a protected right, or it will be unrecoverable, '*damnum absque injuria*'.[63] 'Damnum' means being factually worse off. But crucially there must also be 'injuria', harm to a legally protected interest. In nuisance, the loss must flow from the invasion of recognised rights in land. As Etherton MR stated in *Fearn*, 'even in modern times the law does not always provide a remedy for every annoyance to a neighbour, however considerable'.[64]

This fundamental point explains why certain losses must fall outside nuisance law – viz losses unrelated to the use and enjoyment of land. Consider the trial judge's error in the 'encroaching Japanese Knotweed' case.[65] It was not *sufficient* to establish nuisance that the knotweed's presence made it more difficult to obtain a mortgage over (and diminished the sale-value of) the claimant's land. The right to 'enjoy' land does not include the right to realise its economic value. By suggesting that it did, the trial judge had collapsed the difference between protecting the *use of land* (which nuisance does) and protecting land as 'an investment or a financial asset' (which nuisance does not). Victoria Ball identifies the influence of negligence law behind such mistakes.[66] In the tort of negligence, the focus is compensation of *loss*. By contrast in property torts the primary focus is on protecting *rights*. It is erroneous to presuppose that whenever there is loss there must be invasion of a relevant right. Ball therefore praises nuisance cases like *Williams* and *Hunter* for stopping the 'slide' towards negligence-thinking. Consistent with Ball's approach Sandy Steel states that the 'gist of nuisance' is interference with land's amenity value. That is not co-extensive with reducing its economic value: 'If well-known gangsters move in next door, the market value of one's property may be reduced, but it need have no effect on one's ability to use the land'.[67] The reason, Steel suggests, is that it would spread the net of liability very wide and unduly curb liberty if *any* conduct that triggered substantial reductions in the value of another's land were actionable.

---

[62] AWB Simpson, *Victorian Law and the Industrial Spirit* (London, Selden Society, 1995) 17.
[63] *Hunter v Canary Wharf* [1997] AC 655, 699 (Lord Lloyd).
[64] *Fearn v Tate Gallery* [2020] EWCA Civ 104; [2020] Ch 621 [79].
[65] *Network Rail v Williams* [2019] QB 601 [46]–[48].
[66] V Ball, 'The Influence of "Loss" in the Property Torts' (2020) 31 *King's LJ* 426.
[67] S Steel, 'The Gist of Private Nuisance' (2019) 135 *LQR* 192.

The Court of Appeal ultimately held that the spread of knotweed did interfere with the claimant's enjoyment of his land, and was actionable accordingly.[68] This will not always be the case. It was not nuisance for a health authority to house mentally ill people on a residential housing estate under a 'care in the community' policy, even though it reduced the value of neighbouring houses.[69] While nuisance protects property rights, and their value, it ignores 'reductions in property values unrelated to impairments to the usefulness of a property'.[70] Nolan according writes that the defining essence of nuisance is 'interference with (or impairment of) the *usability* of the claimant's land'.[71]

Nolan usefully distinguishes three categories of rights in land.[72] These are the implicit basis of all claims in nuisance. First are 'natural rights' which all landowners enjoy against the world, by virtue simply of their ownership. Second, 'acquired rights' (eg easements). Third are 'no rights'. This category encompasses the cases considered in this section. There is no right to a view, no right to percolating groundwater, or not to be overlooked.

Nolan's categories usefully clarify the basic structure of nuisance, understood as a tort against land. But how, in practice, are the abstract categories defined in concrete terms? Precisely what rights do, and should, all landowners 'naturally' enjoy, and nuisance law protect? Conversely, what should go into the 'no rights' category, placing infringements are outside the scope of nuisance?

These questions have no straightforward answers. While codified legal systems often include a list of property rights which the law protects, such a canonical list is absent from the common law. It answers the questions as they arise, from case to case. This is either its great strength or a grave weakness. On the positive side, the answers are concrete, emerging from the crucible of actual disputes. The common law does not proceed by abstract deduction from first principles. The downside is a distinct lack of system. The English law is at best untidy, at its worst incoherent. Why is it that blocking a view with an ugly building is axiomatically non-actionable, but the spectacle of local sex-workers or pornographers sufficiently offends the senses to trigger nuisance liability?[73] (Note Kidner's criticism that the latter cases succumb to the fallacy that nuisance protects 'preservation of property values': 'the character of the neighbourhood' cannot be a protectable interest in land since it is 'always subject to demographic change'.)[74]

---

[68] *Network Rail Infrastructure* [2019] QB 601 [55].
[69] *C & G Homes Ltd v Secretary of State for Health* [1991] Ch 365.
[70] D Howarth, 'Clearing the Ground – Nuisance, Damage and Japanese Knotweed' [2019] *CLJ* 21.
[71] D Nolan, 'The Essence of Private Nuisance' in B McFarlane and S Agnew (eds), *Modern Studies in Property Law, Volume 10* (Oxford, Hart, 2019).
[72] See further Nolan (n 16).
[73] *Thompson-Schwab v Costaki* [1956] 1 WLR 335; *Laws v Florinplace Ltd* [1981] 1 All ER 659.
[74] R Kidner, 'Nuisance and Rights of Property' [1998] *Conveyancer* 267.

In drawing the boundaries of the tort, judges have relied on a mixture of doctrinal history and pragmatism. The absence of authority recognising a given right is a sufficient reason to dismiss a claim. Precedent is often reinforced by practical concerns about admitting the new right into the catalogue protected by nuisance. In *Fearn v Tate Gallery* the court noted that while being overlooked is an extremely common situation, centuries of case law revealed no decision recognising a right not to be overlooked – but many judicial statements to the contrary.[75] There were also 'policy' reasons not to recognise an action for 'mere overlooking'. It would be difficult to decide what precise degree of overlooking affected the amenity of the land, and this would be handled better by the planning control system than by tort law.[76] Further, the real ground of complaint was invasion of privacy rather than interference with interests in land. But extensions of privacy rights were better addressed by detailed legislation (and not 'the broad brush of common law').[77]

Above all the Court of Appeal feared that if mere overlooking were tortious, it would unduly constrain building in urban areas.[78] The concern was not new. It had explained the absence of a right to a view since at least the eighteenth century. Etherton MR quoted Lord Hardwicke LC: were the right to a view enforceable, 'there could be no great towns' because a nuisance injunction would prevent every new building.[79] Lord Blackburn similarly explained why landowners can acquire rights to light for their windows by prescription, but not a right to a view. The limited right to window-light 'could only impose a burthen upon land very near the house', by contrast it was 'expedient' not to recognise rights to views 'which would impose a burthen on a very large and indefinite area'.[80] Etherton MR thought this was 'purely a matter of policy' which logically applied also to the problem of overlooking. This too was 'commonplace and indeed inevitable' in 'cheek-by-jowl' urban living, so that all building would become tortious if overlooking were actionable in nuisance.[81] As Nolan comments, the reasoning in *Fearn* was 'essentially pragmatic'.[82] The court echoed 'the wisdom of earlier generations of judges in holding that overlooking cases are one such "species of injury of which the law takes no cognizance"'.[83]

The 'property rights' approach best explains the boundaries of nuisance. Reference to 'enjoyment' and 'amenity' should not mislead. The focus is not on the landowner's personal enjoyment. The inquiry is the 'useability' of *land*.

---

[75] [2020] EWCA Civ 104; [2020] Ch 621 [53] (Etherton MR).
[76] ibid [81]–[82].
[77] ibid [84].
[78] ibid [75].
[79] *Attorney General v Doughty* (1752) 2 Ves Sen 453, 453–54.
[80] *Dalton v Angus* (1881) 6 App Cas 740, 824.
[81] *Fearn* [2020] Ch 621 [78].
[82] Nolan (n 48) 4.
[83] *Tampling v James* (1865) 11 HLC 290, 317 (Lord Chelmsford).

But this better-focused approach is not necessarily straightforward. In deciding the extent of 'useability' rights, there is (according to Nolan) no neat, clear-cut approach. The most we can say is that the court must strike a balance between the importance of the right for the claimant owner, and the burden that respecting that right would place upon others. Hence the longstanding refusal to hold actionable an interference with a view. This is a fairly minor aspect of land's 'useability' but its protection would severely restrict neighbouring landowners' freedom to build on their land. Indeed, as noted, the *reductio ad absurdum* is that nobody could ever put up any new view-impinging structures.

The concern about restriction of freedom weighed heavily with the House of Lords' unanimous decision in *Hunter* that the Canary Wharf tower's interruption of television signals was not actionable nuisance.[84] Lord Goff suggested that nuisance usually involves something 'emanating from the defendant's land' onto the claimant's land – so merely interrupting the flow of a valuable thing (like television signals) is not enough. Nolan criticises this, noting a contradictory body of authority finding nuisance by 'interruption': interference with easements, rights of support and rights of way; the (admittedly dubious) cases about 'offensive' activities;[85] and arguably, nuisance by interrupting the supply of utilities (where a submission that nuisance requires an 'emanation' onto the claimant's land was directly rejected).[86] In *Fearn v Tate Gallery* at first instance, Mann J also rejected the 'mechanistic' suggestion that the absence of emanation complete barred claims in nuisance.[87] Nolan argues that weighing a claimant landowner's interests against the correlative restriction on their neighbours' freedom resists neat rationalisation by concepts such as 'physical emanation'. At best the emanation concept is a rule of thumb, not a strict prerequisite of nuisance liability.

The same can be said about another well-known taxonomy of nuisance. Lord Lloyd identified: '(1) nuisance by encroachment on a neighbour's land, (2) nuisance by direct physical injury to a neighbour's land; and (3) nuisance by interference with a neighbour's quiet enjoyment of his land'.[88] Having cited Lord Lloyd's catalogue however, the Court of Appeal recently observed:

> The difficulty with any rigid categorisation is that it may not easily accommodate possible examples of nuisance in new social conditions or may undermine a proper analysis of factual situations which have aspects of more than one category but do not fall squarely within any one category, having regard to existing case law.[89]

---

[84] [1997] AC 655.

[85] *Thompson-Schwab* and *Laws* (both n 73).

[86] *Barratt Homes Ltd v DWR Cymru Cyfyngedig (No 2)* [2013] EWCA Civ 233, [2013] 1 WLR 3486 [60] (Lloyd Jones LJ), [81] (Arden LJ).

[87] [2019] EWHC 246 (Ch); [2019] Ch 369 [167]–[168].

[88] *Hunter* (n 84) 695.

[89] *Network Rail v Williams* [2019] QB 601, [41] (Etherton MR).

Lord Lloyd's categories were 'merely examples of a violation of property rights'.

This warning suggests that nuisance is indeed 'protean'. 'It is impossible to give any precise or universal formula'[90] – the tort is 'immersed in undefined uncertainty',[91] its boundaries 'uncertain (and perhaps shifting)'.[92] An exclusive focus on property rights, and the useability of land, restricts the intractability of nuisance. But the problem of defining precisely what those rights are cannot be resolved by abstract categorisation.

Debate 2
Justifying the Rights-Based Approach

The property-rights approach to nuisance provides a coherent account of its rules, structure and boundaries. It 'fits' the law. But does the rights-based account successfully '*justify*' private nuisance? There is an obvious and powerful reason in its favour. The legal system confers landowners with rights over their property – and needs remedies to enforce and protect those rights. English property law's structure uses *tort* to remedy invasions of the rights that property law confers. Nuisance plays an indispensable role in the protection of rights over land. This gives a simple answer to the question, 'why should the law recognise a tort protecting the use and enjoyment of land'? It is an integral part of *property* law.[93]

Property law defines ownership of land and interests in it, governing the creation and transfer of rights in land. But 'land law' is not usually thought of as the location of rules remedying physical invasion or damage. For those we turn to the tort textbooks. Two torts specifically. Trespass deals with direct intrusion: any incursion over the boundary of the claimant's land is actionable in trespass, irrespective of damage. Trespass therefore encompasses an unauthorised short-cut, the overhanging eaves of a building, or a fence mistakenly erected along the wrong boundary line, right up to complete dispossession of the claimant, demolition of their buildings, or felling their trees. Nuisance deals with interference with use and enjoyment short of direct physical invasion. Physical *damage* to land will also be actionable in other torts, notably negligence.

Yet does nuisance simply protect rights defined elsewhere, in another department of the law? (On one view that is what *all* torts do, and they should indeed be considered in books about the relevant *rights* (eg property) rather than grouped spuriously together as 'tort law'.)[94] There seems more to nuisance

---

[90] *Sedleigh-Denfield v O'Callaghan* [1940] AC 880, 903 (Lord Wright).
[91] *Brand v Hammersmith Railway Co* (1867) LR 2 QB 223, 247 (Erle CJ).
[92] *Transco v Stockport MBC* [2003] UKHL 61; [2004] 2 AC 1 [96] (Lord Walker).
[93] A more common view in Scotland: GDL Cameron, 'Making Sense of Nuisance in Scots Law' (2005) 56 *NILQ* 236, 237.
[94] OW Holmes, 'Addison's *The Law of Torts*' (1871) 5 *Am LR* 440, 441 ('Torts is not a proper subject for a law book'); cf Stevens (n 14) 288.

than mechanically enforcing a ready-made list of 'rights over land'. There is no such list. On the contrary, 'rights to the use and enjoyment of land' are *defined and constituted by nuisance law*. To find out what aspects of use and enjoyment are protected and to what degree, the landowner must consult the tort of nuisance. Their potential claims and liabilities *are* the law's rules on what land-use can be protected against a neighbour's interference, and what land-use is permissible although it interferes with others' enjoyment of land. Nuisance plays an active role. It is not merely about enforcing a catalogue of rights defined by property law. Nuisance law *is* the catalogue. Tort *constitutes* this aspect of property-ownership. Nuisance *defines* owners' rights to the use and enjoyment of land. (If this intermingling of tort and property seems messy, English law is not alone. As Ciara Kennefick explains, the analogous French concept (*'troubles de voisinage'*) equally seems to hover between the two, 'no trivial conflation in a civil law system where the coherent classification of rules within codes is at the heart of the rule of law').[95]

The intrinsic 'justification' for nuisance law may simply be the protection of property rights. But that defines its role at a very abstract, formal level. A more important and difficult question is the precise content of the property rights in question. Accepting that nuisance both defines and enforces rights to the use and enjoyment of land, what *are* those rights? How strongly are they protected? What is their scope and limits? What is the justification for the *particular* rights over land that nuisance protects?

A wide range of arguments could be used to answer these questions. Should we examine 'real world impact', whether positive or negative, when recognising, limiting, balancing and otherwise defining rights to use and enjoy land? Many would accept that questions about rights need not be answered solely by 'internal', doctrinal rights-focused reasoning.[96] When discussing and deciding what rights should be legally recognised, lawyers cannot confine themselves *solely* to 'deontic' reasoning about rights and duties. It would risk sheer circularity: there is a right when there is a right. Rights' initial recognition, their ongoing development and their reconciliation when they conflict, must look beyond rights.

Yet it is not easy to study the real-world effect of decisions about nuisance. Concerns surround the competence and legitimacy of judges as policy-makers; the inherent limits of the common-law process and common-law doctrines as policy solutions; and controversies about identifying 'desirable social goals'.[97]

---

[95] C Kennefick, 'Nuisance and Coming to the Nuisance: The Porous Boundary between Torts and Servitudes in England and France' in Jean-Sébastien Borghetti and Simon Whittaker (eds), *French Civil Liability in Comparative Perspective* (Oxford, Hart, 2019) 238.

[96] NB Gregory C Keating, 'Corrective Justice: Sovereign or Subordinate?' in Andrew S Gold et al (eds), *The Oxford Handbook of the New Private Law* (Oxford, Oxford University Press, 2020) 51 ('The question of what rights people have is not a question of corrective justice. If anything, the question of what rights people have is a question of distributive justice').

[97] See ch 7, 'Debate 2: Policy and the Duty of Care'.

Some think policy reasoning so dangerous that it should be purged from the law altogether. In nuisance law (as elsewhere) the most prominent advocate is Allan Beever. We examine Beever's account of nuisance law purified of engagement with public policy, before turning to commentators who defend the role of policy considerations.

Protecting the 'More Fundamental' Use of Land: Beever's Theory of Nuisance

Beever's monograph on private nuisance advances a strictly rights-based account.[98] The central question is whether the claimant's or the defendant's use of land is *more fundamental* (when one party's activity interferes with the other's 'quiet enjoyment'). The 'more fundamental' land-use is defined as the more *general* one. A 'general' land-use is one that is fundamental to our understanding of property; a 'particular' one peripheral to that understanding.[99]

Beever accepts that this inquiry will not be easy. No clear hierarchy of land-uses exists to allow the straightforward resolution of nuisance disputes. The court must exercise judgement in characterising the parties' activities to decide how 'fundamental' they are. (Beever is sceptical that 'intractable' philosophical debates about property rights can provide any useful guidance – which must instead be found in the common law itself.)[100]

Beever's clearest guidance is negative. The courts must *not* take public policy or the public interest into account. Nuisance disputes are private. The parties' rights as individual property-owners must be determined, evaluated and compared with each other. This is a 'bilateral' enterprise – not a multilateral one. Other people's rights, and the interests of the public as a whole, are simply irrelevant. Third parties are not involved in the dispute between the claimant and defendant. Therefore it would be 'incoherent and contradictory' to take the public interest into account.[101] Beever accepts that many well-known judgments rely on public interest factors.[102] But Beever condemns such reasoning. It is inconsistent with the very nature of a *property right*: individuals' rights are 'trumps' that always prevail over the public interest.[103] Beever argues it is erroneous to assume that because the application of rights and principles requires

---

[98] A Beever, *The Law of Private Nuisance* (Oxford, Hart, 2013).
[99] ibid 21.
[100] ibid 24.
[101] ibid 16.
[102] eg *St Helen's Smelting Co v Tipping* (1865) 11 HLC 642, 650 (Lord WestburyLC) ('If a man lives in a town, it is necessary that he should subject himself to the consequences of those operations of trade which may be carried on in his immediate locality, which are actually necessary for trade and commerce, and also for the enjoyment of property, and for the benefit of the inhabitants of the town and of the public at large').
[103] Beever (n 98) 30 citing R Dworkin, *Taking Rights Seriously* (Cambridge, MA, Harvard University Press, 1977) ch 7.

'judgement', the court must fall back on public policy to resolve the dispute. This overstates the subjectivity of the true principled approach (ie comparing the fundamentality of the respective land-uses). Resorting to policy reasoning is unnecessary. Moreover, it is actively harmful. It involves the court in turning away from principles of *law* to public policy arguments lying outside the law – literally a distraction from what the court should be doing.[104]

Beever offers numerous examples of how his approach would apply to well-known nuisance cases. Liability was correctly imposed in the *St Helen's* case because having one's property physical undamaged is a more fundamental interest than running any kind of business. Or in *Sturges v Bridgeman*, because occupying a quiet room is more fundamental than operating noisy machinery.[105] Or in *Miller v Jackson*, because undisturbed living is more important than playing cricket.[106] Conversely, liability was correctly denied in *Hunter v Canary Wharf* because putting up buildings on one's land is more fundamental than watching television.[107] In the American *Fontainebleau Hotel* case, the defendant's building shaded an area of the plaintiff's hotel used by its guests for sunbathing.[108] Beever argues that the court correctly denied liability: constructing a building is a more fundamental use of land than lying in the sun. The hotel had suffered financial loss, but had no *right* that guests would stay there. Equally, a court had been correct to hold it was not nuisance to interrupt electricity supply: the claimant has a right to electricity only against the supplier (not the defendant who interrupts it), so this cannot be the basis for a nuisance claim.[109]

The significance of characterisation of the parties' conduct and activity is shown in Beever's discussion of the 'malice' cases. He argues that *Christie v Davey* was not a mere case of rivalrous noise.[110] The plaintiff gave music lessons. The sound of these annoyed the defendant who thus interrupted the lessons by making loud noises in his house (eg banging on tin trays). According to Beever it would be 'silly' to describe the parties' activities as similar. Music-making is a more 'fundamental' land-use than disruptive noisiness. Equally, in the *Hollywood Silver Fox* case, the defendant's activity was 'shooting guns to annoy the plaintiff' (not as they unconvincingly claimed shooting at rabbits), clearly a less fundamental land-use than the plaintiff's fur-farming.[111]

---

[104] ibid 46–47.
[105] (1879) 11 Ch D 852.
[106] [1977] QB 966.
[107] [1997] AC 655.
[108] 114 So.2d 357 (1959).
[109] Consider *Spartan Steel v Martin* [1973] QB 27 (cited Beever (n 98) 50); cf *Barratt Homes* (n 86) [53] ('an essential adjunct of Barratt's use of land in the present case was its ability to connect ... to water and sewerage services').
[110] [1893] 1 Ch 316.
[111] [1936] 2 KB 468.

Beever's Theory: Appraisal and Criticism

Is Beever's restatement of nuisance superior to conventional accounts, in which courts weigh-up the 'reasonableness' of the parties' activity using an open-ended list of factors including their conduct, its social value, and the local geographical context? We can question the Beever account's fit with the law, and also its justification.[112]

Beever's central negative claim is that public policy has no role to play in nuisance. As seen, Beever accepts that there are numerous statements of its relevance in leading cases. Beever argues that these should be rejected – in other words, he accepts (to this extent) that his thesis does not fit the current law. But in his view, the justification for a policy-free nuisance law (indeed private law generally) is so strong that it requires such revisionism. Beever claims that his account is more coherent – that is, in its unified concentration on property rights (rather than the dis-unified weighing of multiple factors, in conventional accounts of nuisance). It is perhaps inevitable that any unified theory will require certain legal rules to be rejected or revised. The common law, whatever its strengths, never in practice develops with the perfect coherence of a unitary theory. Glanville Williams once remarked that vicarious liability was 'the creation of many judges who have had different ideas of its justification or social policy, or no idea at all'.[113] That withering remark could be applied to many common law doctrines, all the work of many hands over many years (or centuries) – not the single-minded working-out of one governing idea. For this reason, we should not reject a theory like Beever's simply because it cannot fit all the extant legal materials. Perhaps no theory worthy of the name could do so. (An account with *perfect* 'fit' would merely list all the legal rules and cases, which would not score highly for coherence.)

While Beever explicitly rejects judicial reliance on public policy, he claims that his theory otherwise explains the law of nuisance and fits the outcomes of many leading cases. Yet the cases were certainly not *reasoned* using Beever's approach. Courts do not explicitly compare how fundamental are the competing land-uses. Dan Priel, noting this problem, questions whether Beever's account faithfully engages with nuisance doctrine 'internally': that would be an 'improbable feat … despite not being based on what is actually found in legal materials'.[114] Priel criticises Beever's selective citation of cases – a mere 'garnish' for his argument, rather than the starting point. Beever might believe that the courts have implicitly been using his approach, while not acknowledging it in their reasoning. But that resembles 'external' explanations of the law – such as the notorious claim by Law and Economics scholars that the common law develops economically efficient rules irrespective of conscious 'economic'

---

[112] See ch 1, 'What Makes a Good Theory?'.
[113] G Williams, 'Vicarious Liability and the Master's Indemnity' (1957) 20 *MLR* 220, 231.
[114] D Priel, 'Land Use Priorities and the Law of Nuisance – *The Law of Private Nuisance* by Allan Beever' (2015) 39 *Melb Univ LR* 346, 352.

reasoning by the courts.[115] Priel argues that if the courts' reasoning resembled Beever's comparative process, it is surprising that they have not produced 'even a tentative list of land use priorities which we could use as a guide. (If they did, presumably Beever would have reproduced it for us)'.[116] Beever has not as he claims returned nuisance law to older orthodoxy, rehabilitating forgotten ways of thinking.[117] His theory is entirely novel. (Indeed, Beever proclaims 'a new beginning' for nuisance law.)[118]

These criticisms suggest Beever's account fits the law less tightly than he claims. Perhaps Beever ultimately thinks 'fit' a relatively minor aspect of a theory's appeal. He states that appealing to the past is not a sufficient justification for a rule – reliance on precedent cannot advance *understanding* of the law.[119] But in a common law system that seems questionable. An account which freely rejected past precedents would scarcely be an account *of the law* at all. It would be an idealised account with (at best) partial overlap with the law as it stands. As Priel suggests, this appears to be a thoroughly 'external' perspective on (nuisance) law. It certainly rejects important foundational assumptions: 'For if there is one central idea to much common law thinking it is precisely that history, not pure reason, *is* a form of justification'.[120]

These are serious objections to Beever's 'comparative' theory's 'fit' with the law. But could it be redeemed by its superior 'justification' of nuisance law? This too may be doubted. Even taken on its own terms Beever's approach is difficult to apply, and not evidently superior to the standard view of nuisance (which Beever rejects as 'incoherent').[121] The public interest legitimately plays a greater role in nuisance than he accepts – and it is arguably implicit within Beever's own account.

Beever claims his theory is a significant improvement on conventional accounts based around 'unreasonableness'. He argues 'unreasonableness' has no fixed meaning and no explanatory power. For Beever it is less a reason than a premature conclusion – '"reasonableness" is what the court mouths in order to pretend that its decision has a genuine rational basis'.[122] This is a powerful critique of the status quo. But Priel responds that Beever's own account is no better. In some ways it resembles the conventional account that Beever so sharply criticises. To the extent that it differs, the abstract quality of the Beever theory makes it difficult to apply and open to manipulation. Let us examine these claims.

---

[115] eg GL Priest, 'The Common Law Process and the Selection of Efficient Rules' (1977) 6 *JLS* 65.
[116] Priel (n 114) 365.
[117] As Beever claims throughout *Rediscovering the Law of Negligence* (Oxford, Hart, 2007).
[118] Beever (n 98) 5.
[119] ibid 2–3.
[120] Priel (n 114) 363.
[121] Beever (n 98) ch 2.
[122] ibid 12.

While Beever accepts that determining the more fundamental land-use requires 'judgement' from courts, Priel argues that this seriously understates the difficulty of the task. Beever provides little guidance to how the court should actually do this, save imploring soundness of judgement and giving some examples. Yet these seem questionable. Why (asks Priel) does Beever characterise the defendant's activity as 'less fundamental' in *Christie v Davey*? The plaintiff was in the business of giving music-lessons while the defendant lived in the neighbouring premises working as a wood-carver (a trade requiring peace for concentration). Why prefer the plaintiff's business activities to the defendant's? Or indeed, the plaintiff's business to the defendant's peaceful *residential* occupation? A different characterisation of the same facts implies the opposite answer. In choosing between competing descriptions of land-use Beever 'never ... hints as to how we are to identify a description as more or less accurate. The result is a thoroughly unstable and very easily manipulable test'.[123]

Moreover, to the extent that the defendant deliberately and inexcusably interferes with the claimant's land use (as in the *Silver Fox* case), Priel argues that liability is inevitably imposed because that behaviour has no social benefit (indeed causes considerable social harm). Implicitly then, Beever seems to rely on judgements about social costs and benefits in characterising the parties' activities. Beever certainly denies this, in presenting his unfamiliar approach. But the result is merely a 'cumbersome' restatement of what already happens – in particular, comparison of the relative *value* of the competing activities. Such values can and do change over time. Priel poses a couple of telling questions. Should the law remain as dismissive of a claimant's right to sunlight, or to wind-flow, when we increasingly rely on renewable energy sources (eg solar panels and wind turbines)? In Beever's terms, might our assessment of what is more 'fundamental' evolve with society's attitudes and requirements? By contrast with the hotel sunbathing case, Priel cites the later US approach holding *balancing* in nuisance 'better suited to resolve landowners' disputes about property development in the 1980s than is a rigid rule which does not recognize a landowner's interest in access to sunlight'.[124] Is a wind turbine's owner in the business of generating electricity or protecting the environment?

Priel defends the 'reasonableness' metric that Beever criticises as unhelpful. On the conventional account, individuals know that to avoid liability in nuisance, they must act 'reasonably'. It is true that there are no clear-cut rules demonstrating what this means. Nor can there be. Nuisance has to apply in an 'almost endless myriad' of circumstances. What the courts can and do encourage is a reasonable accommodation between neighbours with conflicting interests, the spirit of 'live and let live' that Baron Bramwell famously articulated.[125] They do this by identifying all relevant factors and weighing them in the circumstances of each case.

---

[123] Priel (n 114) 366.
[124] *Prah v Maretti* (1982) 321 NW 2d 182, 190 (Abrahamson J).
[125] *Bamford v Turnley* (1860) 3 Best & Smith 62.

Vague though it is, Priel prefers this open-ended weighing to Beever's account. Given the enormous factual variations of nuisance cases, it is extremely difficult 'to conclusively prioritise certain activities as more fundamental than others' as Beever's theory demands. Indeed it is, Priel complains,

> close to meaningless to speak in the abstract of one activity being more fundamental than another. What the law should seek to do is make sure that both can co-exist, attempting to minimise potential conflicts between them.[126]

Even if conventional nuisance cases do not follow clear pre-ordained rules, Beever's approach would be even worse. Landowners would be required

> to master a complex and rigid list of land use priorities; in addition, and far more seriously, [Beever's approach] will require them to be familiar with the land uses of all their neighbours and be ready to alter their land use if one of their neighbours shifts to a higher-ranked land use.[127]

Priel argues that courts would find Beever's unfamiliar theory impossible to apply. This is ironic since one of Beever's major objections to policy reasoning is that judges are unqualified to assess public policy arguments. It is fair to point out the courts' limitations here. But there is limited capacity to apply Beever's approach too:

> judges also lack training and expertise in deciding in the abstract about land use priorities. I, for one, cannot think of anything in my legal education (or the time spent in law schools ever since) to help me answer this question.[128]

Priel identifies a still greater irony. Beever's approach would increase the need for public intervention to resolve competing land use. If it were possible to purge nuisance law of any evaluation of social benefit and public interest, and subject entire neighbourhoods to the court's designation of the 'most fundamental' land-use by any landowner in the vicinity, the results would surely be unworkable and unliveable. Nuisance adjudication would need rapid correction by the planning system. Beever's strict, abstract system is simply unfit to resolve complex land-use disputes in modern conditions. It would be made tolerable only by public intervention to overrule the priorities set by a rights-based law of nuisance. Such an unworldly, absolutist nuisance law would face regular negation. It would be side-lined or even abolished altogether.

In sum, Priel suggests that Beever's theory implicitly compares the social value of competing uses of land. It merely restates this familiar approach in fancier theoretical garb. If Beever's theory is actually more radical, and does

---

[126] Priel (n 114) 373.
[127] ibid 376.
[128] ibid 382.

exclude public interest considerations from nuisance law altogether, it dooms the tort to obsolescence. The planning system would take over completely to uphold the centrality of the public interest, if the common law refused to take it into account.

Defining Property Rights: The Role of the Public Interest

Beever's theory is an outlier. Most commentators accept that while property rights are the basis of private nuisance, that does not exclude consideration of the public interest. It plays two distinct roles. First, in defining the relevant rights to use and enjoy land. Second, in resolving nuisance disputes. Typically nuisance involves clashing property rights: both parties claiming the entitlement to use their property in a way that interferes with the other's land-use. The court must weigh these to reach a compromise or accommodation. The public interest is taking into account in defining property rights, in their protection, and in their reconciliation (when they compete). We examine the definition of rights in this section, and questions of application in the following section.

Maria Lee emphasises the central role played by public interest considerations.[129] There is no settled and uncontroversial list of 'rights to enjoy land' that nuisance law simply enforces. The relevant property rights 'are not clearly pre-defined'. On the contrary, by deciding what kinds of interference are actionable nuisance law is actively defining the property rights' content and scope: it 'shapes, or "constitutes", those rights'. It would be a mistake to suggest that property rights stand 'aloof ... from public welfare'.[130] Indeed, political debates about private ownership are some of the most venerable in Western philosophy: Plato thought that *common* ownership was vital for collective action and would reduce social division; Aristotle responded that *private* property supported prudent stewardship and individual responsibility.[131] Criticising Beever's purist approach, Lee questions how private lawyers' concepts of property can sensibly avoid considering 'the physical and social complexity of "land"'.[132]

Lee fully accepts that framing debates about the nature of property (its enjoyment and its protection) in public-interest terms does not make them easier to resolve. If anything the reverse. It is impossible to formulate 'an all-purpose definition of the public interest'.[133] It is fiercely contested. Nuisance shows how even public policies that sound universally desirable can generate

---

[129] M Lee, 'The Public Interest in Private Nuisance: Collectives and Communities in Tort' [2015] *CLJ* 329.
[130] ibid 355–56.
[131] eg J Waldron, 'Property and Ownership' (Historical Overview), *Stanford Encyclopedia of Philosophy* (2020): https://plato.stanford.edu/entries/property/.
[132] Lee (n 129) 332.
[133] ibid 331.

costs – for groups who bear the burden of a socially desirable activity. People naturally welcome economic growth and development. But any new enterprise 'might create jobs and taxes [but also] air pollution and associated amenity, environmental and health burdens'.[134] Are we to prioritise the environment or employment? What when environmental protection itself interferes with quiet enjoyment? (Lee notes that *Barr v Biffa* involved sewage from London being treated in rural Ware, Hertfordshire:[135] the claimants suffered the cost of others' waste and moreover, especially noxious smells resulted from pre-treatments that were 'supposed to increase the possibility of recycling'.) The competing interests of different groups of people are often 'starkly apparent in a private nuisance dispute'.[136]

The difficulties inherent in public policy reasoning might make Beever's approach seem comparatively appealing. But the ostrich strategy (burying our heads in the sand) suppresses open debate about the public interest. It obstructs transparent legal development. Indeed Lee criticises the common law approach as insufficiently transparent. Vital questions about land-use are resolved solely by abstract doctrinal debate. The conservative doctrinal approach in *Hunter v Canary Wharf* receives particular criticism.[137] There was little discussion of public interest questions in the House of Lords, even though the entire Docklands development had been conceived as a matter of national economic policy, to regenerate a derelict post-industrial district of London. The redevelopment deliberately bypassed the ordinary local planning process. *Hunter* had a regressive social effect. The claims were brought overwhelmingly by 'Eastenders' from low socio-economic backgrounds. Even plaintiffs who owned their homes (and had standing to sue) would recover little in damages. Compensation was calculated by the diminished value of their property. But because their houses were (at that time) of modest value, the damages they stood to recover were so small that the Legal Aid Board refused to continue funding their claims. It was deemed 'futile' to pursue low-value claims at comparatively high cost. (The *Hunter* plaintiffs complained unsuccessfully to the European Commission on Human Rights that their rights to their homes and right of access to the court had been violated, and they had been discriminated against on the grounds of poverty by the House of Lords' ruling that compensation reflected property values and not the effect on individuals' amenity.)[138]

In Lee's view, nuisance (and the courts) failed the plaintiffs in *Hunter*. She criticises the judges' apparent indifference to the context and the effect of their doctrinal restatement in a case 'saturated' with the public interest. Nor is *Hunter* unique. In *Cambridge Water v Eastern Counties Leather* the court

---

[134] ibid 343.
[135] [2012] EWCA Civ 312; [2013] QB 455.
[136] Lee (n 129) 342–43.
[137] M Lee, '*Hunter v Canary Wharf*' in C Mitchell and P Mitchell (eds), *Landmark Cases in the Law of Tort* (Oxford, Hart, 2010).
[138] *Khatun and 180 others v United Kingdom* (1998) 26 EHRR CD212.

expressly refused to consider policy questions about strict liability for industrial pollution, declaring that this was solely for the legislature.[139] Joanne Conaghan and Wade Mansell point out that this refusal to enter the debate occurred in a case with 'momentous implications' for the very same debate![140] This shows the courts' unwillingness to confront openly the true issues: the conflict between environmental protection and business.[141]

This tendency (and complaints about it) are nothing new. In 1894, American jurist Oliver Wendell Holmes deemed judges 'shy' about public policy reasoning, so decisions 'which really can stand only upon such [policy] grounds, often are presented as hollow deductions from empty general propositions like *sic utere tuo ut alienum non laedas*'.[142] Maria Lee thinks 'shyness' persists in the twenty-first century: 'The social, political, and economic complexity of judgments on the public interest is behind much of the scholarly and judicial suspicion'.[143] In her view however, the correct reaction is not to retreat to an illusory purity, excluding the public interest altogether (*pace* Beever). There is no satisfactory alternative to the difficult task of reconciling 'the internal demands of tort, including ... the centrality of justice between the parties, with broader collective considerations'.[144] And only if this difficulty is openly confronted can the vital task be performed. Priel similar argues that while public policy questions are controversial and the evidence to prove or disprove them is frequently weak, the law would be better served if academics sought to collect such evidence. Policy can be made tractable with expertise brought to bear. Legal academics would perform a valuable service if they engaged with such questions, rather than (as Beever urges) ignoring them entirely.[145]

Courts have not always disguised the public interest dimension in nuisance. Conaghan and Mansell argue that the 'pastoral fiction' woven by Lord Denning MR, as he famously describes a village cricket ground in *Miller v Jackson*,[146] was merely a 'charming disguise' for value-judgements about class, gender and race.[147] As clear examples of courts using 'distributional preferences' to decide

---

[139] [1994] 2 AC 264.

[140] J Conaghan and W Mansell, *The Wrongs of Tort* 2nd edn (London, Pluto Press, 1999) 147.

[141] ibid 148 (which did not prevent the court 'enthusiastically reaching an accommodation which is undoubtedly informed by their own perceptions of how that (unacknowledged) conflict should be resolved').

[142] OW Holmes, 'Privilege, Malice, and Intent' (1894) 8 *Harvard LR* 1, 3 (a maxim still cited as the 'basis' for strict liability in nuisance, eg *Southwark LBC v Mills* [2001] 1 AC 1, 20 (Lord Millett)).

[143] Lee (n 129) 347.

[144] Ibid 333.

[145] Priel (n 114) 383 ('It is here, not in *a priori* speculations, that legal academics can prove particularly useful to courts and to society').

[146] [1977] QB 966.

[147] (n 140) 138–39 (Lord Denning characterized the plaintiff as 'a newcomer, the sort of person who lives on a housing estate, who does not appreciate the finer points of cricket, who might even be female and who brings in her wake the threat of social disintegration as the young men are forced to abandon cricket and go to work in factories'!)

what interests deserve protection, Ogus and Richardson compare *Vanderpant v Mayfair Hotel Co*[148] with *Bridlington Relay v Yorkshire Electricity Board*.[149] Whereas Luxmoore J in *Vanderpant* thought noise that required the dining-room window of a Mayfair house to be closed during mealtimes constituted a nuisance, in *Bridlington Relay* Buckley J held that interrupting television signals was not sufficiently 'important a part of an ordinary householder's enjoyment of his property' to be actionable.[150] David Campbell deems this a good example of the judiciary's over-confident approach to evaluation of social welfare and economic efficiency, performed by Buckley J with 'a naiveté or an arrogance which simply takes one's breath away'.[151]

On the television question, compared with *Bridlington Relay* (30 years earlier) the House of Lords in *Hunter* were much more sympathetic to its importance. (Lord Goff noted its value for 'the aged, the lonely and the bedridden' for whom television 'transcends the function of mere entertainment'.)[152] But as seen, liability was nonetheless denied on the formalistic ground that the signals had been *interrupted* by the Canary Wharf tower built on the defendant's land, rather than something emanating *from* there onto the claimant's land (like the electromagnetic interference in *Bridlington Relay*). In his minority opinion, Lord Cooke rejected such fine distinctions holding that the public interest in the London Docklands redevelopment outweighed the claimants' interest in watching television at home. For Campbell however, this is further evidence of judges' 'unsustainably ambitious claims' to determine the public interest.[153]

Campbell notes the particular difficulties posed by new technology. When scientific knowledge about side-effects is uncertain, it is very difficult for government and legislatures to formulate a single general policy as optimal for society – let alone for the courts to do so. Discussion about genetically-modified organisms (GMOs) exemplifies the difficulties. What if GM crops cross-pollinate neighbouring farmers' non-GM fields? What if this causes farms to lose organic accreditation? Christopher Rogers analyses how such questions test the boundaries of nuisance.[154] Rogers thinks that 'biodiversity damage' is unlikely to be accommodated within the tort's focus on private property interests: it involves harm, rather, to a *public* good, the biome as a whole. Rogers queries whether cross-pollination could constitute *physical damage* to the claimant's crops. He criticises the longstanding requirement that physical damage

---

[148] [1930] 1 Ch 138.
[149] [1965] Ch 436.
[150] AI Ogus and GM Richardson, 'Economics and the Environment: A Study of Private Nuisance' [1977] *CLJ* 284, 319–20.
[151] D Campbell, 'Of Coase and Corn: A (Sort of) Defence of Private Nuisance' (2000) 63 *MLR* 197, 205.
[152] (n 4) 684–85.
[153] Campbell (n 151) 204.
[154] CP Rodgers, 'Liability for the Release of GMOs into the Environment: Exploring the Boundaries of Nuisance' [2003] *CLJ* 371.

must be visible to the naked eye rather than microscopic investigation.¹⁵⁵ Would drifting pollen constitute a 'natural' or 'non-natural' nuisance? Would organic farming be 'hyper-sensitive' land use?¹⁵⁶ Such questions are necessary for to apply orthodox nuisance law to this novel problem. But Maria Lee and Robert Burrell are impatient with such inquiries.¹⁵⁷ It is entirely unclear how a court would apply 'these quite indeterminate common law notions' to disputes about GM crops.¹⁵⁸ *Hunter*'s reaffirmation of nuisance as a tort to land, 'tells us nothing about what rights in property are or should be'. The 'restatement' of nuisance was distinctly incomplete. *Hunter* leaves courts to confront 'deeply political' questions as largely a matter of discretion.¹⁵⁹

Purity and Transparency

Transparency is another desideratum of a successful legal theory.¹⁶⁰ It should take seriously and explain the *reasoning* that characterises nuisance law – not only the outcomes of the cases. As seen, Beever's theory scores poorly for transparency. It implies either that the courts do not really mean to use public interest considerations in nuisance decisions. Or if they do so deliberately, they are wrong. Clearly Beever's aim is a radical transformation of the law, to purify it from the taint of 'policy'. But is that a damaging delusion rather than a noble project? In the absence of any canonical hierarchy of land-use rights, nuisance disputes cannot simply appeal to some list supplied by property law. It must actively compare the parties' clashing interests. Their individual autonomy is an important factor, as Beever emphasises. But in a world of high-density urban living, can the broader public interest be ignored?

Even if nuisance were solely about enforcing property rights, that would not magically resolve all controversies. There is no universally accepted definition of 'property' that can be applied 'logically and mechanically' and only a blithe commitment to 'timeless conservative conceptualism' could suppose such a definition exists.¹⁶¹ Property law's commitment to 'conceptual purity' is 'unrivalled across the field of contemporary law'. It presents a 'closed system of logic' that consciously ignores 'the "fairness" of its outcomes'.¹⁶² One can therefore see the attraction of basing nuisance on property, if the aim is to exclude political 'distributional' questions. Yet property law's façade of neutrality has

---

¹⁵⁵ *Salvin v Brancepath Coal* (1874) 9 Ch App 705.
¹⁵⁶ Cf now *Marsh v Baxter* [2015] WASCA 169.
¹⁵⁷ M Lee and R Burrell, 'Liability for the Escape of GM Seeds: Pursuing the "Victim"?' (2002) 65 *MLR* 517.
¹⁵⁸ Ibid 531.
¹⁵⁹ Ibid 534.
¹⁶⁰ Again see 'WHAT MAKES A GOOD THEORY?' in Ch 1.
¹⁶¹ MJ Radin, 'The Consequences of Conceptualism' (1986) 41 *Univ Miami LR* 239.
¹⁶² KJ Gray and SF Gray, 'The Rhetoric of Realty' in J Getzler (ed), *Rationalising Property, Equity and Trusts: Essays in Honour of Edward Burn* (London, LexisNexis UK, 2003).

been torn off by Lorna Fox O'Mahony.¹⁶³ Property law systematically favours wealthier people in society (owners) over other more precarious groups. These distributional effects are not debated or even acknowledged: they are to the contrary 'prone to be concealed within purportedly apolitical doctrine'.

From this perspective, it is entirely wrong-headed for tort law to hope to purify itself by riding on the coat-tails of 'property rights'. These are every bit as debatable.¹⁶⁴ It therefore mistaken to criticise (for example) legislative reforms to French nuisance law for responding to farmers' concerns (urban incomers seeking to enjoin countryside sounds and smells).¹⁶⁵ Kennefick deplores such 'capricious … political fiat' as a departure from the approved 'legal logic' of property law.¹⁶⁶ But such a socially important area of law cannot depend on 'logic' alone. The contestability of property must be acknowledged or political choices affecting citizens' lives and livelihoods will be concealed under a mask of 'neutral' doctrine.

Debate 3
Balancing or Strict Liability? Property Damage, Nuisance and Trespass

In this debate we consider balancing of interests in the amenity 'heartland' of nuisance, compared with strict liability for physical damage (where liability in nuisance resembles that in trespass to land). Are these features best explained by the property-rights approach?

Balancing is necessary in 'sensory' nuisance which damages amenity value. Contrary to the Dworkinian metaphor used by Beever, property rights do not operate as 'trumps' here, automatically defeating any countervailing public interest. The need for balancing was emphasised long ago in *Bamford v Turnley*.¹⁶⁷ Numerous factors are considered, for example duration, intensity, time of day of the interference. Pollock CB explained why the inquiry is *necessarily* relative:

> it cannot be laid down as a legal proposition or doctrine, that anything which, under any circumstances, lessens the comfort or endangers the health or safety of a neighbour, must necessarily be an actionable nuisance. That may be a nuisance in Grosvenor Square which would be none in Smithfield Market, that may be a nuisance at midday which would not be so at midnight, that may be a nuisance which is permanent and continual which would be no nuisance if temporary or occasional only. A clock striking the hour, or a bell ringing for

---

¹⁶³ L Fox O'Mahony, 'Property Outsiders and the Hidden Politics of Doctrinalism' [2014] *CLP* 409.
¹⁶⁴ D Cowan, L Fox O'Mahony and N Cobb, *Great Debates in Land Law* 2nd edn (London, Palgrave, 2016).
¹⁶⁵ Cf Cour d'appel, Riom (n 209).
¹⁶⁶ Kennefick (n 95) 244.
¹⁶⁷ (1862) 3 Best & Smith 66.

some domestic purpose, may be a nuisance, if unreasonably loud and discordant ... but although not unreasonably loud, if the owner, from some whim or caprice, made the clock strike the hour every ten minutes, or the bell ring continually, I think a jury would be justified in considering it to be a very great nuisance. In general, a kitchen chimney, suitable to the establishment to which it belonged, could not be deemed a nuisance, but if built in an inconvenient place or manner, on purpose to annoy the neighbours, it might, I think, very properly be treated as one. The compromises that belong to social life, and upon which the peace and comfort of it mainly depend, furnish an indefinite number of examples ... [and] all that the law can do is to lay down some general and vague proposition which will be no guide [sic] to the jury in each particular case that may come before them.[168]

This inescapable 'vagueness' prompted contemporary laments about nuisance's 'undefined uncertainty'.[169] A modern label for the approach is 'multi-factoral'. The only difference today is that judges have taken over from juries as decision-makers – and must give reasons for their decision. 'The critical question' courts have to decide is whether the interference goes beyond what someone can reasonably be expected to put up with: 'whether what [the claimant] was exposed to was *plus quam tolerabile* [in] all the surrounding circumstances of the offensive conduct and its effects'.[170]

This is a conventional, if very general, description of the core of nuisance law. A fuller account must also include the 'live and let live' exception and the 'locality' principle. The former, classically explained by Bramwell B in *Bamford v Turnley*,[171] holds that everyday activities necessary for the 'common and ordinary use and occupation of land and houses' are not actionable in nuisance, provided they produce 'comparatively trifling' interference and are 'conveniently done' (ie the defendant's behaviour 'shows as much consideration for the neighbours as can reasonably be expected').[172] The 'locality' rule requires that to decide whether interference with the landowner's enjoyment is actionable, it must be assessed in its geographical context. Was it intolerable in the *particular* locality or neighbourhood?

The extent to which such balancing is explicable by the property rights theory is debateable. First, though, we consider the exceptional strict liability in physical damage cases.

Strict Liability for Property Damage and Trespass

Under *St Helen's Smelting Co v Tipping* (alkali fumes causing death of plaintiff's trees), strict liability characterises nuisance when there is physical damage

---

[168] ibid 79–80.
[169] *Brand v Hammersmith Railway Co* (1867) LR 2 QB 223, 247 (Erle CJ).
[170] *Watt v Jamieson* 1954 SC at 58 (Lord President Cooper).
[171] (1862) 3 Best & Smith 66.
[172] *Southwark LBC v Mills* [2001] 1 AC 1, 16 (Lord Hoffmann).

to the land or structures/plants affixed to it. The maxim *sic utere tuo* still applies here (by contrast with the balancing necessary in 'amenity' cases). But why? David Howarth thinks it 'a puzzle'.¹⁷³ He rejects the idea that physical damage is always 'inherently worse'. Instead Howarth suggests that whereas 'sensory' interference diminishes the value of land only when it is more severe than the background noise and smell etc prevailing in a particular neighbourhood, physical damage inevitably impairs its value in *any* neighbourhood.¹⁷⁴ This is an ingenious explanation. A more cynical theory is that the *Tipping* decision 'constructed a grand compromise':¹⁷⁵ confronted with two conflicting lines of authority, one favouring a public-interest balancing approach,¹⁷⁶ the other the old strict liability for nuisance,¹⁷⁷ the law lords approved *both* tests but for different situations.

That 'compromise' endures to this day. Its staying power suggests that the law lords' diplomatic balancing act (between landowners like Tipping and industrialists like the alkali factories) was skilful. But some criticise *St Helen's v Tipping* for upsetting the doctrinal coherence of nuisance. Conor Gearty argues that cases involving physical damage should be deleted from nuisance altogether and left to the tort of negligence (where such damage is unquestionably actionable).¹⁷⁸ The advantage of this 'strategic surrender', in Gearty's view, would be to refocus attention upon the real heartland, the sensory interference cases which are actionable in nuisance or not at all (there is clearly no liability in negligence for loud noises or disgusting smells that do not cause personal injury or property damage). Despite the attractions of Gearty's argument, the courts have rejected it. First, *Rylands v Fletcher* is now conceived as a branch of private nuisance.¹⁷⁹ *Rylands* cases by definition involve catastrophic physical damage. Second, *Hunter v Canary Wharf* specifically disapproved the heretical view that sensory nuisance was a separate tort based around personal discomfort. *Hunter* reaffirmed the whole of nuisance as a tort *to land*. Physical damage to property was not only reaffirmed as component of nuisance – it was its paradigm.

Some commentators draw a parallel between *trespass* to land and the physical-damage species of nuisance (contrasting them with the balancing process that characterises 'amenity' nuisance). They are obviously not identical: trespass to land involves direct physical intrusion and is actionable per se, whereas (non-trivial) physical *harm* by an 'indirect' process constitutes this

---

¹⁷³ Howarth (n 33) 506.
¹⁷⁴ Howarth cites *Stearn v Prentice Bros* [1919] 1 KB 394 (rats breeding on defendant's land ate plaintiff's growing crops: exceptionally no liability despite physical damage).
¹⁷⁵ JPS McLaren, 'Nuisance Law and the Industrial Revolution – Some Lessons from Social History' (1983) 3 *OJLS* 155, 158.
¹⁷⁶ *Hole v Barlow* (1858) 4 CBNS 334.
¹⁷⁷ *Bamford v Turnley* (1862) 3 B & S 66.
¹⁷⁸ C Gearty, 'The Place of Private Nuisance in a Modern Law of Tort' [1989] *CLJ* 214.
¹⁷⁹ *Cambridge Water* (n 32).

species of nuisance. But where either of these is made out, liability is automatic. Street described trespass liability as 'both exceptionally simple and exceptionally rigorous'.[180] There is no question of weighing a landowner's right not to have their land invaded, or not damaged, against the defendant's interest in coming onto the land, or carrying out an activity that physically damages it. There is no need for such balancing: the law gives landowners a clear and absolute right of control. Somebody who wishes to come onto land must request the owner's permission. The trespass regime delegates decisions about land-use to owners – the court does not attempt to decide whether an intrusion might be 'reasonable in the circumstances' or 'justifiable as a matter of public interest'. Henry Smith defends this rights-protecting approach – as a sensible regulatory strategy.[181] Tort law declares a clear owner by the crude means of holding every gross physical violation to be trespass. This is a convenient simplification, protecting ownership in a way that does not require evaluation from the court. Trespass is a simple keep-off rule. The physical-damage species of nuisance (which Smith gives the vivid if unfamiliar American label of 'nuisance per se') also uses the basic 'exclusion' strategy of trespass. 'Nuisance is itself more exclusionary than is conventionally thought, and this quality reflects the benefits of delegation to owners'.[182]

The strictness of such 'rigorous' liability is not unfair to potential trespassers. Liability is easy to avoid: we need only keep off land that does not belong to us. (It has been suggested that the 'implied licence' doctrine softens this strict liability in situations where the landowner has apparently consented to the defendant's presence, or where such permission would (according to prevailing social norms) usually be presumed and the landowner has not clearly revoked it.)[183] Whereas in nuisance, which does not involve direct physical intrusion, liability is not always so obvious to the defendant. The defendant's alkali works in *Tipping* was some miles away from the plaintiff's country estate. In other nuisance cases, for example vibrations damaging buildings, there is likely to be direct physical proximity between the parties' land – literal 'neighbourhood'.

In practice however, foreseeability is not usually a contested issue in nuisance cases. As Howarth puts it, the question is less who started the interference but whether it should now stop.[184] By the time the parties are litigating about it, the defendant can no longer be in doubt that its activity is harming the claimant. For this reason, there is rarely any discussion about whether foreseeability is an essential element of nuisance liability. It is not – and cannot be – a live issue in actions seeking an injunction against an ongoing interference.[185]

---

[180] TA Street, *The Foundations of Legal Liability, Vol 1* (Northport, NY, Edward Thompson, 1906) 19.

[181] HE Smith, 'Exclusion and Property Rules in the Law of Nuisance' (2004) 90 *Virginia LR* 965.

[182] ibid 984.

[183] A Dorfman and A Jacob, 'The Fault of Trespass' (2015) 65 *Univ Toronto LJ* 48.

[184] Howarth (n 33).

[185] *Cambridge Water* (n 32) 300 ('ex hypothesi the defendant must be aware, if and when an injunction is granted, that such interference may be caused by the act which he is restrained from committing').

Still, in theory the defendant's actions could have caused irreversible damage to the claimant's land before the defendant became aware of this, where the claimant seeks only compensation (not an injunction) and the litigation is thus purely retrospective (an inquiry into past conduct). Such claims are typified by *Rylands v Fletcher*. It has been confirmed that a defendant will be liable for damage done by an *unforeseeable* escape.[186] After all, in the eponymous leading case the reservoir flooding the plaintiff's underground mine had been unforeseeable to the defendant. To that extent, nuisance may impose more stringent liabilities. Nevertheless on Smith's view, this branch of nuisance shares with trespass to land a sensible rationale for strict liability. These are clear-cut rules prohibiting conduct which is easy to avoid, whether gross physical incursions over the boundaries of the claimant's land, or inflicting actual physical damage on it.

Balancing Rights: 'Live and Let Live'

Outside physical damage cases, courts balance the parties' competing interests in the particular social and geographical context of the dispute. It might seem inevitable that this involves the sacrifice of rights to the public interest. But commentators such as Keating and Epstein argue that balancing is consistent with the protection of individual rights.

Keating argues that nuisance reconciles inevitable clashes *between individual rights*.[187] To produce a system of equal rights to the enjoyment of land, balancing through a reasonableness calculus is indispensable: 'Nuisance law's preoccupation with the reconciliation of rights whose salient property is that they clash makes reasonableness fundamental'. Keating's point is that most things we do on our land could interfere to *some* degree with our neighbours' quiet enjoyment – and vice versa. Any noise, smoke, vibrations, smell etc that my activities create will likely be perceived on my neighbour's land, and be irritating, unpleasant etc. Given how ubiquitous the potential is for neighbour disturbance, it would be unworkable to impose the absolute liability of trespass to land (described in the previous section). Strict liability works in trespass because that 'conflict' is easy to avoid. All we need do is stay on our own side of the boundary and no trespass occurs. There is simply no need to devise 'objectively fair reconciliation' of rights in trespass. It functions very well as a 'domain of essentially self-regarding behavior'. By contrast: '*The* problem of nuisance is reconciling rights whose exercise tends to interfere with one another'.[188]

This need for 'reconciliation' explains all the main features of nuisance liability, in Keating's view. Unlike trespass, nuisance is not actionable per se. There must be actual harm (either damage to the land or some 'visceral assaults' on the senses). Keating (like Pollock CB) recommends a *substantial interference* threshold of. Were nuisance to hold *any* detectable interference actionable,

---

[186] *Transco* (n 92) [33] (Lord Hoffmann).
[187] GC Keating, 'Nuisance as a Strict Liability Wrong' (2012) 4 *Jo Tort Law* 1.
[188] ibid (original emphasis).

however slight, people would be able to do little on their land. Virtually every activity would generate liability. The same concern explains why offending 'aesthetic sensibilities' should not be actionable (as seen, cases of spoiled views are *damnum absque injuria*). It would cripple the freedom to use our land as we wish if we were constrained by our neighbours' tastes. (We should be free to put up 'pink flamingos in our front yards'.)[189] Maureen Brady agrees, citing a dictum that if courts policed how property should look, they would 'trespass through aesthetics on the human personality'.[190]

Keating also thinks the law is correct to hold that common domestic activities are not actionable (even if they interfere with a neighbour's peaceful enjoyment of land). It would be a major restriction on freedom to prohibit ordinary everyday land-use. 'To deny people the right to such uses is to thwart the exercise of their agency in a fundamental way'. Indeed: 'Forbidding these nuisances would prevent the ordinary use and occupation of land'.[191] The *Bamford v Turnley* doctrine avoids these problems.

Its rule of 'give and take, live and let live' is *mutually beneficial*, as Bramwell B argued in the leading case:

> It is as much for the advantage of one owner as of another; for the very nuisance the one complains of, as the result of the ordinary use of his neighbour's land, he himself will create in the ordinary use of his own, and the reciprocal nuisances are of a comparatively trifling character.[192]

Richard Epstein argues that each landowner receives 'implicit in-kind compensation'. Not money (ie damages), but the reciprocal right to cause such interference themselves without incurring liability.[193] And as Keating observes, the 'implicit compensation' is actual rather than notional, given that landowners do frequently engage in common everyday activities while enjoying their immunity from being sued in nuisance. (In Epstein's words, 'it is safe to assume that virtually all persons will be in separate individual instances both wrongdoers and victim'.)[194] Epstein argues that once we take into account the costs of adjudication and enforcement in nuisance disputes, this immunity (with the 'implicit in-kind compensation') is a superior solution. It avoids 'the expensive and pointless process of making explicit offsetting payments'.[195]

But Epstein cautions that the immunity should not be over-extended. For example, accepting that everyone benefits from freedom to develop and build

---

[189] ibid. Or consider *Wernke v Halas* 600 N.E.2d 117 (1992) (toilet seat atop post overlooking plaintiff's land) ('Given our myriad and disparate tastes, life styles, *mores*, and attitudes, the availability of a judicial remedy for [aesthetic discomfort] would cause inexorable confusion').
[190] ME Brady, 'Property and Projection' (2020) 133 *Harvard LR* 1143, 1177–78.
[191] Keating (n 187).
[192] (1862) 3 B & S 66, 84.
[193] RA Epstein, 'Nuisance Law: Corrective Justice and Its Utilitarian Constraints' (1979) 8 *JLS* 49.
[194] ibid 84.
[195] Ibid 78.

on their land, this should apply only to *ordinary* developments. Thus Epstein argues that the defendant in *Andreae v Selfridge* should not have benefited from immunity.[196] The Court of Appeal held that people have to put up with the inevitable, but temporary, disruption caused by demolition and building on neighbouring land. The trial judge had held that the disputed construction work (the Selfridge's department store in Oxford Street) fell outside Bramwell B's category of things 'commonly done in the ordinary use and occupation of land'. Bennett J reasoned that demolishing six houses, excavating the site to a depth of 60 feet and riveting together a steel-framed replacement was not 'common and ordinary'.[197] The Court of Appeal disagreed but Epstein argues that Bennett J was correct. Building a giant department store was no everyday repair or extension. There was 'no remote likelihood, let alone real prospect, that the plaintiff [in *Andreae*] would at some future time inflict an uncompensated harm of equal severity upon the defendant'.[198] Thus in Epstein's view, there was no *reciprocity*. The Court of Appeal 'worked a major and impermissible redistribution of wealth'.

Compare Greene MR's view that the 'give and take' doctrine had to move with the times:

> when the rule speaks of the common or ordinary use of land, it does not mean that the methods of using land and building on it are in some way to be stabilized for ever. As time goes on new inventions and new methods enable land to be more profitably used, either by digging down into the earth or by mounting up into the skies. ... [It] is part of the normal use of land, to make use, upon your land, in the matter of construction, of what particular type and what particular depth of foundations and particular height of building may be reasonable, in the circumstances, and in view of the developments of the day.[199]

(Epstein himself allows that what is 'common and ordinary' changes over time: for example the smell of horses in urban areas was less likely to be actionable pre-1900, when horses were the usual mode of transport.) Still, while deciding what is 'usual' or everyday may be difficult when new technology emerges, the principle of *Bamford v Turnley* enjoys wide approval.

Balancing Rights: Locality and 'Ordinary Human Existence'

Keating suggests that similar reasoning underlies the 'locality rule'. Under this principle, claimants cannot complain about interference which is no worse than that prevailing in the locality at large. So in a polluted industrial area, a claimant would be unlikely to succeed in a claim about smoke, fumes and noise – unless the defendant's activity demonstrably and significantly exacerbated the

---

[196] [1938] Ch 1.
[197] [1936] 2 All ER 1413, 1424.
[198] Epstein (n 193) 87.
[199] [1938] 1, 6.

prevailing smoke, fumes and noise.²⁰⁰ This rule applies even though the interference is serious rather than 'trifling' and includes industrial activities as much domestic ones. It therefore goes considerably further than *Bamford v Turnley*. Nevertheless Keating argues the same principle justifies both:

> Normal uses within a locality are compatible with one another in a special way as far as nuisance law is concerned: they inflict similar kinds of fallout on each other and they are presumably insensitive to similar kinds of fallout.

If a locality is full of smoke-emitting factories we have 'specialized communities of reciprocal harm and benefit'.²⁰¹

Epstein doubts this. In his view it is inconsistent with individual rights to deny protection purely because others are behaving in a particular way. The emphasis on prevailing neighbourhood land-use 'undercuts one of the essential functions of private property, that of specifying for each person a domain of action in which he is not accountable to the whims or demands of any other group of individuals'.²⁰² Nuisance law places an idiosyncratic use (and user) of land outside 'neighbourliness'. But this threatens to replace personal autonomy with the tyranny of the majority. (Epstein does accept that there could often be implicit in-kind compensation given uniform activity throughout an area, 'parallel uses by nearly all concerned' – which is Keating's central point.)

A connected problem, for Epstein, is the *objective* approach under which a particular claimant's susceptibility to interference or harm is left out of account. This rule is again well established. English lawyers all know the semi-comic 'brown paper case' *Robinson v Kilvert*,²⁰³ and Knight Bruce VC's dictum that nuisance protects 'inconvenience materially interfering with the ordinary comfort physically of human existence, not merely according to elegant or dainty modes and habits of living, but according to plain, sober, and simple notions among English people'.²⁰⁴ But in the US case *Rogers v Elliot*, the plaintiff suffered convulsions at the sound of the defendant church ringing its bell.²⁰⁵ This can hardly be dismissed as trivial harm or excessive 'daintiness'. But the *Rogers* claim still failed on the grounds of the plaintiff's hyper-sensitivity. Epstein finds this outcome hard to explain on grounds of individual rights (corrective justice). He contrasts the rule in negligent personal injury cases that tortfeasors take their victims as they find them ('thin skulls' and all). Why not in nuisance? The impact can be severe, as in *Rogers v Elliot*. There is no prospect of the interference being reciprocal (thus no 'mutual in-kind compensation'); by definition, these are cases involving *unusual* sensitivity.

---

²⁰⁰ *Polsue & Alfieri Ltd v Rushmer* [1907] AC 121.
²⁰¹ Keating (n 187).
²⁰² Epstein (n 193) 63.
²⁰³ (1889) 41 Ch D 88.
²⁰⁴ *Walter v Selfe* (1851) 4 De G & Sm 315.
²⁰⁵ 146 Mass 349 (1888).

Epstein argues that 'utilitarian constraints' on rights mean that the idiosyncratic owner ultimately has to give way to locally prevailing uses of land, or the general objective standard of ordinary robustness ('plain living'). That is, the overall interests of society may prevail in a sufficiently clear case. It seems evident that if one residential occupier could close down all the factories in a generally industrial locality, society as a whole would be seriously impoverished. (Epstein here has support from dicta in the leading case of *St Helen's v Tipping*.)[206] While rights deserve special protection and 'do not rise and fall with each new refinement in economic theory', Epstein accepts that the law does not (and should not) take seriously the idea that they must be upheld even though 'the heavens fall' (*Fiat justitia, ruat cælum*). For example in cases of deviation from prevailing patterns of land-use the law holds that 'utilitarian constraints are sufficiently powerful to dominate'.[207]

Keating, however, disagrees that the various rules of objective reasonableness are 'utilitarian'. They are not constraints on individual rights imposed when the social costs of protecting them become excessive. Again, Keating's view is that objective balancing derives from the law's concern with reconciling individuals' competing rights. The problem nuisance law confronts is not a bilateral one (concerning only the two litigating parties) but *omnilateral*. What one does on one's land interferes with everyone else's (and is also interfered with *by* everyone else). Interference can easily cover an entire neighbourhood. The law cannot require parties to refrain from all such wide-ranging activities, which would stultify many common and beneficial uses of land. The multilateral dimension also makes it implausible that those involved can all reach binding agreements about what levels of interference to allow. Tort law has to devise and impose a mutually acceptable compromise. In doing so, Keating emphasises that nuisance must use a metric of *ordinary* use and enjoyment of land, tolerance of interference, etc. 'It is only possible to construct a regime of equal right if we take as our touchstone the needs, interests, and sensibilities of "ordinary people".'[208] (This principle is not limited to common-law systems. A French court, refusing to hold that noise from chickens constituted nuisance in a rural hamlet, commented that neither does the ship bother the sailor, nor flour the baker.)[209]

The rights that nuisance protects are general rights – enjoyed by all landowners equally. Inevitably, these must be derived from 'Common and ordinary uses [which] are ordinary and common precisely because they serve the needs and interests of most people'.[210] Conversely, nuisance law cannot protect unusually sensitive or idiosyncratic users. To *generalise* these in a system of equal rights would require everyone else in society to bend to the unusual.

---

[206] Quotation (n 102).
[207] Epstein (n 193) 89.
[208] Keating (n 187).
[209] Cour d'appel, Riom, 7 September 1995.
[210] Keating (n 187).

That is simply inconsistent with the notion of *equal* rights. Thus nuisance necessarily enforces prevailing standards. (As the *Elliott* court also noted, an objective approach produces relatively clear law: whereas if nuisance varied with every sensitive claimant's 'peculiar temperament', 'the standard for measuring it would be so uncertain and fluctuating as to paralyze industrial enterprises'.)[211]

Sandy Steel rejects Keating's rights-based account of the locality principle.[212] It would *not* be impossible to set landowners' rights above the prevailing local level of pollution. First, Steel rejects the notion that by buying land in a polluted/industrial area claimants *consent* to the prevailing level of interference. Even if a claimant vociferously objected to the pollution, it would make no difference to the defendant's liability! Deeming 'consent' is fictitious, except when claimants tolerate an interference that they could easily prevent (or move away from). Second, Steel rejects the notion that the community as a whole agrees to tolerate a certain level of pollution. Again, what evidence exists of such a deliberate choice? (As Steel notes, the best and strongest evidence would be public authority decisions in the planning process – but those are firmly excluded from consideration in nuisance cases.)[213] Even if there were strong evidence to prove a 'societal agreement', would it be right to enforce it over the objections of a dissenting claimant? This would prioritise society's autonomy (choices) over individuals' autonomy. (A position resembling Epstein's argument that strong public interests should prevail over individual rights.)

Steel accepts that various *collective* interests can support the locality rule. First, group autonomy (allowing the public as a whole to decide what kind of activity can take place). Second, the predictability of nuisance tracking generally prevailing land-use (consider the problem of one individual holding all others to ransom, by departing from the accepted standard). Third, the possible cost advantages of concentrating similar activities in particular localities (factories interfere less with other factories on an industrial estate than they would with homes or leisure facilities in 'mixed use' areas). As an American judge famously said, 'A nuisance may be merely a right thing in the wrong place like a pig in the parlor instead of the barnyard'.[214]

In *Adams v Ursell*, granting the plaintiff an injunction against a fish and chip shop adjoining his house, Swinfen Eady J denied that this caused 'great hardship to the defendant and to the poor people who get food at his shop' since he could 'carry on his business in another more suitable place … It by no means follows that because a fried fish shop is a nuisance in one place it is a nuisance in another'.[215] The law can prevent 'pig in the parlour' nuisances by appropriately

---

[211] 146 Mass 349, 353.
[212] S Steel, 'The Locality Principle in Private Nuisance' [2017] *CLJ* 145.
[213] *Wheeler v JJ Saunders Ltd* [1996] Ch 19 (see further ch 12, 'Debate 2: The Interaction of Tort and Regulation: Nuisance and Planning Permission').
[214] *Euclid v Ambler Realty Co* 272 US 365 (1926) (Sutherland J).
[215] [1913] 1 Ch 269, 271–72.

'zoning' such activities. (To the extent that it may be more costly to require a defendant to avoid (say) noise nuisance in an already noisy area, Steel agrees that there is a reason of justice to avoid unusually onerous obligations. But this does not justify the locality rule in its current width.) The problem with public interest arguments like this, as Steel says, is that they indicate that planning permission should be centrally relevant to nuisance law, not ignored by it. He concludes that English law's commitment to *both* the locality rule *and* the irrelevance of planning permission is fundamentally incoherent.

The courts freely accept that the locality rule accommodates decisions about 'zoning' and the public interest. The leading case of *Sturges v Bridgman* establishes that 'coming to a nuisance' is no defence – the defendant cannot raise their activity's long duration before interfering with the claimant (unless they can establish an easement by prescription).[216] The Court of Appeal noted a possible objection to their decision. That if

> carried out to its logical consequences, it would result in the most serious practical inconveniences, for a man might go – say into the midst of the tanneries of Bermondsey, or into any other locality devoted to a particular trade or manufacture of a noisy or unsavoury character, and, by building a private residence upon a vacant piece of land, put a stop to such trade or manufacture altogether.[217]

This concern was dismissed. As Thesiger LJ famously observed:

> it may be answered that whether anything is a nuisance or not is a question to be determined, not merely by an abstract consideration of the thing itself, but in reference to its circumstances; what would be a nuisance in Belgrave Square would not necessarily be so in Bermondsey; and where a locality is devoted to a particular trade or manufacture carried on by the traders or manufacturers in a particular and established manner not constituting a public nuisance, Judges and juries ... may be trusted to find, that the trade or manufacture so carried on in that locality is not a private or actionable wrong.[218]

The locality principle was the key: used here to give effect to the public interest. The judges were keenly concerned with the 'economic consequences' of their decision.[219] It also reduced the difficulty for longstanding, widespread patterns of land-use that might otherwise arise from the absence of a 'coming to the nuisance' defence.[220]

Perhaps fairness, justice and economic development shade into each other. Howarth comments that a reasonable individual would not want to bring

---

[216] (1879) 11 Ch D 852.
[217] ibid 865 (Thesiger LJ).
[218] ibid.
[219] RH Coase, 'The Problem of Social Cost' (1960) 3 *Jo L&E* 1, 20–21.
[220] For discussion of that doctrine's proprietary nature in English and French law see Kennefick (n 95).

commerce to a halt 'merely for their own convenience'.[221] In *Coventry v Lawrence*, Lord Carnwath considers the many activities which society finds valuable and 'need to be accommodated within the urban fabric'.[222] (Not limited to manufacturing industry: Lord Carnwath discusses disturbance created by a large football stadium.) Every individual landowner is also a member of society, and may reasonably be taken to share the general interest in reaching such 'accommodations'.

Conclusion

There have been attempts to expand nuisance into a freestanding tort protecting 'personal sensibility'. *Hunter v Canary Wharf* showed that this was a serious doctrinal misunderstanding. Nuisance is a tort to *land* and protects owners' 'sensibility' only insofar as it damages the land's use-value. Nuisance is not a 'swiss army knife'. It cannot be used to confer special protection, wider than that enjoyed by 'the man in the street', on landowners (or those who happen to be at home when they are injured). This seems egalitarian[223] (although as the Strasbourg challenge to *Hunter v Canary Wharf* indicated, the clarified law of nuisance especially benefits wealthy landowners).[224]

Yet restating nuisance as a tort to land raises as many questions as it answers. What rights should landowners enjoy over? By what reasoning process should they be defined, limited and reconciled with neighbouring owners' rights? Commentators disagree about the role of the public interest in well-known doctrines such as strict liability for physical damage, the locality principle, and the 'live and let live' exception. The 'purest' rights-based account, Allan Beever's, has tendentious 'fit', poor 'transparency' and even questionable 'justification'. This suggest the necessity of an accommodation between property rights and the public interest. There is not really a binary, yes–no choice. The question is to what *extent* is protection of property rights shaped by public interest concerns.

Doctrinal history casts a long shadow over any area of the common law. Nuisance is a very old tort. We accept as first principle the unusually broad protection it gives to rights over land – as opposed to other kinds of property, intangible economic interests, and even perhaps bodily security. Sarah Green, for example, compares nuisance law's protection of widely conceived rights to the use and enjoyment of land with tort's protection of chattels.[225] Actions for conversion (and negligence) protect the chattel-owner's right to possession and not to suffer physical damage. But unlike nuisance, there are

---

[221] Howarth (n 30) 500.
[222] *Coventry v Lawrence (No 1)* [2014] AC 822, [181]–[185].
[223] T Weir, *A Casebook on Tort*, 10th edn (London, Sweet & Maxwell, 2004) 418 ('democratic').
[224] *Khatun v UK* (n 138).
[225] S Green, 'Rights and Wrongs: An Introduction to the Wrongful Interference Actions' in A Robertson and D Nolan (eds), *Rights and Private Law* (Oxford, Hart, 2012).

no comparable rights to *use and enjoy* chattels. For example, a driver stuck in a traffic jam caused by another's negligent driving epitomises non-actionable 'pure economic loss', even though their use of their car has been significantly curtailed. Green understandably questions the law's 'highly inconsistent treatment of comparable legal rights' (ownership of chattels, ownership of land).

Stating that nuisance protects landowners' rights is the most coherent explanation for the doctrines analysed in this chapter. It is little more than a truism. The real difficulty is how to define those 'rights'. It is unclear whether it can be divorced from consideration of the public interest – or if this were possible, whether it would be desirable.

11

Economic Analysis of Nuisance

Coase's Analysis

Ronald Coase (1910–2013) was the intellectual godfather of law and economics. Nuisance law was the subject of his most celebrated article,[1] 'The Problem of Social Cost'.[2] Or more precisely, the clash between incompatible uses of land that is the stuff of nuisance. At the core of Coase's article is a powerful economic theory of startling simplicity. His prescriptions for nuisance *law* are less clear. Coase at least insisted that such questions should be approached by considering real-world facts rather than abstract theories and assumptions. Coase's famous thesis will be outlined in this section. Subsequent sections consider criticisms.

Coase's most striking argument is that if the parties could always make contracts with each other, the most valuable use of land would always prevail. This needs explanation. Coase first argued that the traditional way of viewing land-use disputes is unhelpful. Thinking of one party inflicting harm on the other, and needing to be restrained from doing so, 'obscures' the problem. It is actually 'reciprocal' in nature. In the well-known case of *Sturges v Bridgeman*, the doctor (desiring peace) is just as surely a 'cause' of the dispute as is the confectioner (with his noisy machinery).[3] To avoid harm to the doctor requires the infliction of harm on the confectioner.

> The problem is to avoid the more serious harm. ... [eg] whether it was worth while, as a result of restricting the methods of production which could be used by the confectioner, to secure more doctoring at the cost of a reduced supply of confectionery products.

This requires us to know, and compare, the value of what is being secured with what is sacrificed to secure it.

---

[1] By an impressive margin the all-time most-cited: FR Shapiro and M Pearse, 'The Most-Cited Law Review Articles of All Time' (2012) 110 *Mich L Rev* 1483, 1489.

[2] RH Coase, 'The Problem of Social Cost' (1960) 3 *JL&E* 1 (hereafter 'Coase').

[3] (1879) 11 Ch D 852.

The 'reciprocal cause' idea strikes lawyers as odd. But Coase's overall comparison of costs and benefits was scarcely novel. The same method was employed in a leading nineteenth-century nuisance, *Bamford v Turnley*. Bramwell B said that 'properly understood'

> a thing is only for the public benefit when it is productive of good ... on the balance of loss and gain to all. So that if all the loss and all the gain were borne and received by one individual, he on the whole would be a gainer.[4]

As Atiyah noted, Bramwell B's judgment contains many of the ideas later developed by the Law and Economics school, 'for instance, the suggestion that one could test the efficiency of the outcome by asking what would happen if the land were in the ownership of a single individual, a point also to be found in Richard A Posner's *Economic Analysis of Law*'.[5]

A concrete example may help. Imagine that I operate both a campsite and a pig-farm on my land. Occupancy of the campsite is low, and the fees I can charge are lower still, because campers dislike the smell of the pigs (which website reviews emphasise). I will need to decide whether I could make increased profits, all things considered, if I curtailed or closed the pig-farm: would higher profits from an enhanced campsite business outweigh the profits forgone from pig-farming? Or might it be worthwhile to purchase odour-control technology to reduce the pigs' interference with the campers? Or conversely, to close the campsite altogether and expand the pig-farm (increasing the associated odours)? Since I own both conflicting businesses, I bear all the costs and reap all the profits of their expansion, curtailment or modification. I should therefore balance them so as to maximise their joint economic value (overall profits from both).

Coase argues that the same process would occur when rivalrous activities are in different ownership, if there were no obstructions to the owners reaching agreements with each other (ie given costless or 'frictionless' transactions). It is in both of their interests to maximise the overall value ('the balance of loss and gain to all') since that means a larger 'cake' to divide between them. Provided each party knows the value of their own activity (and the profit they would forego if it were to cease), their agreement will favour the highest value land use. And crucially, this happens irrespective of how the law allocates the entitlement – that is, whether the 'harm inflicter' (in conventional terminology) is legally liable for that harm or not. Coase uses a simple example of a cattle rancher whose wandering cows eat a neighbouring farmer's corn. Does the economic value of keeping the cows on unfenced land exceed the value of the crops? If so then *even if the rancher would be liable* to the crop-farmer

---

[4] (1862) 3 Best & Smith 66.
[5] PS Atiyah, 'Liability for Railway Nuisance in the English Common Law: A Historical Footnote' (1980) 23 *JL&E* 191, 194 (citing RA Posner, *Economic Analysis of Law*, 2nd edn (Boston, Little, Brown, 1977) 48). The point about a single owner of 'a large tract of land' balancing conflicting activities is also made by Coase (n 2) 16.

under the law of nuisance (or trespass), the parties will reach agreement that permits the cattle-trespass to continue. The rancher benefits from that position more than the crop-farmer loses, so the rancher will offer to pay a sum which exceeds the crop-farmer's losses to induce him to agree to tolerate the trespassing cattle. Conversely, if the crops are the more valuable use, the parties will agree that cattle should be fenced in (or not kept at all). Such agreement will be reached even if the rancher is *not liable* for the damage done by the cows: the sum the crop-farmer will pay the rancher to fence in his wandering cattle will exceed the rancher's loss from forgoing the activity.

If parties should always bargain to the 'efficient outcome' (prioritising the highest-value land use), does this make nuisance law irrelevant? No. First, the law's background system of liabilities and entitlements certainly affects the *distribution* of costs and benefits between the parties. There is clearly a difference between exercising a right conferred by law and paying the other party *not* to exercise their legal right. (What an economist calls 'distribution' a lawyer might call 'justice'.) But Coase expressly leaves this to one side, observing: 'if market transactions were costless, all that matters (*questions of equity apart*) is that the rights of the various parties should be well-defined and the results of legal actions easy to forecast'.[6] Yet law determines how the benefits of economically optimal outcomes are to be shared. Surely this is no small thing.

Second, as seen, Coase limits his theory to 'costless market transactions'. As he immediately goes on to accept, such conditions are impossible in practice. There are always costs to transactions. In the real world, it is costly to communicate and negotiate with rivalrous owners. Even ascertaining the identity and whereabouts of those responsible for an interference, or affected by it, may be difficult. Sterk therefore suggests that a hypothetical absolute 'no emissions' rule would be unworkable in nuisance. It would place an intolerable burden upon those emitting 'generally inoffensive particles'. For example

> a bakery whose operation causes the smell of fresh bread to waft through a neighborhood [would be required] to obtain consent from all of its neighbors in order to obtain protection against future injunctions. ... [The] cost of those negotiations might preclude largelyinoffensive bakeries from operating, because any neighbor could hold out for payment in excess of the costs imposed by the bakery's smell.[7]

We should not overstate the problem: transaction costs are *not always* prohibitively high. If they were, no contract would ever be agreed about anything. Still, there are situations (Sterk's picturesque and far-fetched bakery example) where agreement is very difficult in practice. Here, as Coase accepts, nuisance

---

[6] Coase (n 2) 19 (emphasis added).
[7] Stewart E Sterk, 'Strict Liability and Negligence in Property Theory' (2012) 160 *Univ Pennsylvania LR* 2129, 2137.

law will indeed 'directly influence economic activity'. Courts must themselves decide which is the highest value land use. (Coase encourages them to do so for another reason too: it saves the costs of transacting around the legal rules if courts initially assign liability in an economically optimal fashion.)

This sketches the celebrated 'Coase theorem': parties will transact to the efficient outcome. The most valuable land use will, *by mutual agreement*, prevail – *irrespective of the law of nuisance* (provided only that the parties' entitlements are defined clearly enough to form the subject for transactions). Yet is truly *theoretical*. It describes an unreal world without 'transaction costs'. Coase ultimately accepts that nuisance law certainly does matter in the actual world. Parties do not always contract around the background rights and obligations set down by law. Therefore, if efficient use is to be made of society's limited resources, it appears that tort law must determine the highest-value land use itself, when incompatible activities clash.

That is the 'positive' programme for the economic analysis of nuisance. Notably, Coase himself seemed rather equivocal about his recommendations for nuisance law in 'The problem of social cost'. Coase took trouble to identify and praise examples of judges taking the economic impact of their decisions into account, albeit implicitly.[8] Conversely, he ridiculed other aspects of nuisance doctrine. Contrasting the different outcomes of cases about interruption of airflow, Coase remarked that for the determinative difference to be whether the air flowed along defined channels (thus permitting the acquisition of a right by prescription) 'is about as relevant as the colour of the judge's eyes'.[9] Legal doctrine is frequently 'to an economist, irrelevant. Because of this, situations which are, from an economic point of view, identical will be treated quite differently by the courts'.[10] Coase thus appeared impatient with traditional rights-based nuisance doctrine, preferring overt reasoning about economic efficiency.

However, Coase then turned from nuisance to government regulation. He attacked economists' conventional view that pollution should be discouraged by taxation of polluting activities. In theory, such a tax can make a polluting activity bear or 'internalise' the social costs of its activities (the harm would otherwise fall on other individuals/society – that is, the cost of pollution would be 'externalised'). While certainly attractive in theory, Coase objected that it is impossible to tax the right activities at the right rates in practice. He imagines a factory polluting the neighbourhood at $100 of harm. The conventional view is to levy a tax of $100. If the factory can install emissions control systems at a cost of $90 it will do so, being $10 better off than if it polluted and paid the tax. Thus it appears that the tax induces 'efficient precautions'. But says Coase, there might be lower-cost ways to avoid the pollution damage. What if

---

[8] Coase (n 2) 22 (nuisance law concepts such as 'reasonable use' showed 'some recognition, perhaps largely unconscious ... of the economic aspects of the questions at issue').

[9] ibid 15 (discussing *Bryant v Lefever* (1878) 4 CPD 172 and *Bass v Gregory* (1890) 25 QBD 481).

[10] ibid.

the neighbouring landowner could relocate its activity (avoiding the pollution) at a cost of $50. This would be the socially optimal solution (recall that under Coase's 'reciprocal' view of nuisance, the activity suffering from the pollution is as much a cause of the dispute as the activity emitting it). Given this insight (and the specific example with notional figures), taxes should not only be considered for polluters but for others in the area too. In practice this would be impossible. To set such taxes 'would require a detailed knowledge of individual preferences and I am unable to imagine how the data needed for such a taxation system could be assembled'.[11] Even if the tax could somehow be exactly proportionate to the amount of smoke emitted by the polluting factory, it may not produce the optimal outcome (the result of the tax may be 'too little smoke and too many people in the vicinity of the factory'). There is no reason to suppose that taxing the factory is always the optimal solution. Deciding what *would* optimally reduce social costs 'bristles with difficulties'.[12]

For Coase, these mistaken assumptions arise because economists compare an unregulated ('laissez faire') approach with an ideal form of government regulation. But that is unrealistic since we do not know how to attain such perfection in the real world. A better approach is to ask whether a given policy change would be an improvement on the status quo. There is certainly potential for state intervention to improve the situation. But it is not costless (the costs of government regulation can be 'heavy'). Nor is such regulation inevitably superior:

> there is no reason to suppose that the restrictive and zoning [ie planning] regulations, made by a fallible administration subject to political pressures and operating without any competitive check, will necessarily always be those which increase [economic] efficiency.[13]

Coase's general view of government action is sceptical. Simply because there is 'market failure' (a problem that is not optimally resolved by private transactions) it does not follow that state intervention would necessarily be an improvement. There can be 'regulatory failure' too. Note that Coase is *not* arguing that the unregulated market is necessarily better. His whole point is that we do not know without 'detailed investigation of the actual results of handling the problem in different ways': 'Satisfactory views on policy can only come from a patient study of how, in practice, the market, firms and governments handle the problem of harmful effects'.[14] Thus, although Coase envisages a law of nuisance overtly concerned to favour the highest-value use of land, he accepts state regulation's limited capacity (tort law being one species of government regulation). Even though transactions are never costless in the

---

[11] Coase (n 2) 41.
[12] ibid 42.
[13] ibid 18.
[14] ibid 18–19.

real world, agreements between owners of competing activities could still be the best route to economically efficient outcomes. (Note that 'best option' here means 'least flawed option, all things considered' – we are always comparing imperfect alternatives and not pointlessly searching for perfection, in the real world. Whether or not we are convinced by Coase's account of nuisance law, we must compare realistic alternative arrangements – not fall into the 'nirvana fallacy' of assuming some *idealised* system of regulation to spuriously 'deduce that the real is inefficient'.)[15]

CRITIQUE OF COASE: MISDESCRIPTION OF NUISANCE DOCTRINE

There are serious objections to the Coasian approach. First, discussed in the present section, that its 'fit' with the law of nuisance is, at best, imperfect. (The next section below questions the desirability and feasibility of open judicial assessment of the 'highest value land-use'.)

Coase could be said to overestimate the extent to which courts are concerned with economic efficiency, because he downplays nuisance law's 'invasion of rights' structure. The law does *not* usually treat nuisance disputes as a 'reciprocal' problem. It is true that Coase identifies one example of such reasoning. In *Bryant v Lefever* the plaintiff's chimney was made less effective (so that his fireplaces smoked) when the defendant built a vertical extension to an adjacent building.[16] The plaintiff's nuisance action failed. Bramwell LJ reasoned that the cause of the smoking fireplaces was not the defendant's taller house ('harmless enough'). The cause was the *plaintiff's* lighting fires with a chimney inadequate to draw the smoke away. Yet that remark does not seem an especially clear recognition of Coase's insistence that the smoke nuisance was caused by both the plaintiff's fire and the defendant's building ('Eliminate the wall *or* the fires and the smoke nuisance would disappear. ... [Clearly] *both* were responsible and *both* should be forced to include the loss of amenity due to the smoke as a cost in deciding whether to continue the activity which gives rise to the smoke').[17] Bramwell LJ's dictum does not justify Coase's claim (in his 'cursory' study) that the courts 'are aware ... of the reciprocal nature of the problem'.[18]

While it is logically true (of course) that cessation of either activity 'solves' the nuisance problem, lawyers think of the defendant's activity interfering with the claimant's quiet enjoyment. Typically this involves something emanating from the defendant's land onto the claimant's land.[19] Emanation is the 'causal paradigm' of nuisance.[20] Apart from unusual cases like *Bryant v Lefever*, it is literally unthinkable to describe the claimant's *mere presence* as causally relevant.

---

[15] Harold Demsetz, 'Information and Efficiency: Another Viewpoint' (1969) 12 *JL&E* 1, 1.
[16] (1878) 4 CPD 172.
[17] Coase (n 2) 13.
[18] ibid 19.
[19] See ch 10, 'The Boundaries of Nuisance: The Absence of Rights'.
[20] Richard A Epstein, 'Nuisance Law: Corrective Justice and Its Utilitarian Constraints' (1979) 8 *JLS* 49, 56–57.

Epstein condemns the 'causal nihilism' of Coase's position, vastly extending the concept of joint causation to encompass *both* parties in *every* nuisance case. Coase was even wrong about *Bryant v Lefever*. Bramwell LJ went on to say that the defendants had a *right* to build on their land and the plaintiff did *not* have a right to any particular flow of air to his chimney. For Epstein this reasoning shows how rights come first: 'for legal purposes the question of causation can be resolved only after there is an acceptance of some initial distribution of rights'. A decision about what is 'causally relevant' is inseparable from the determination of who has a right to do what.[21] On this view, Coase's whole approach is incompatible with the basic structure of nuisance law, in which the defendant *causes* interference and its actionability is decided by comparing the parties' respective rights.

Coase's admission that he had not made a 'thorough' study of nuisance law applies equally to his claim that courts frequently (although implicitly) take the economic impact of their decisions into account. This too is questionable. A more modest interpretation than Coase's would meet wide acceptance. Namely that while courts do sometimes take costs and benefits into account (both of the parties' respective activities and their way of carrying them out), and sometimes in marginal cases this can affect the outcome of a case, for the most part nuisance follows a clear and simple structure. Intolerable levels of interference are actionable, irrespective of whether it could be any different or the cost of reducing the interference.

Unreasonable behaviour can aggravate the case for liability; but liability may arise even when the defendant's conduct was impeccable. The degree of evaluation of the social benefits of activities is limited accordingly. True, where a defendant can easily modify their activity to reduce the level of interference, that is a factor weighing powerfully in favour of liability (eg in *Andreae v Selfridge*, carrying on noisy demolition works day and night to expedite the project was unreasonable;[22] it has been suggested that although the sound of babies crying at a nursery is not a nuisance, it might be otherwise if neglectful nurses did nothing to soothe the children's cries).[23] This is one ready explanation for 'malice' cases too:[24] it is straightforward to refrain from *deliberate* interference, and there is no 'opportunity cost' in desisting from conduct with no social value. On the other hand, courts frequently impose liability even though there was nothing the defendant could do to avoid the problem. In *Rapier v London Tramways* it was not suggested that there was anything the defendants should, or even could, have done to mitigate the 'stink' of horses stabled near the plaintiff's house. But they were liable nevertheless. It was irrelevant that the nuisance was unavoidable. Lindley LJ was unsympathetic:

> If the Defendants are right in saying that they cannot concentrate their stables to such an extent as is desirable without committing a nuisance to the

---

[21] ibid 58–60.
[22] [1938] Ch 1.
[23] *Moy v Stoop* (1909) 25 TLR 262.
[24] Eg *Hollywood Silver Fox Farm Ltd v Emmett* [1936] 2 KB 468.

neighbourhood, then they must not concentrate their horses to such an extent … If they cannot have 200 horses together, even when they take proper precautions, without committing a nuisance, all I can say is, they cannot have so many horses together.[25]

David Howarth describes the law in similar terms.[26] It would be 'too extreme' to say that the public benefit of the defendant's activity is always irrelevant. But its relevance is limited:

[Where] it is not clear whether the interference is substantial enough to count as a nuisance, the purpose and benefits of the defendant's activity will count, but not otherwise; … the utility of the defendant's conduct is relevant, but only as long as the damage is not too great; … there comes a point at which, whatever the loss to society, the degree of interference is so great that the plaintiff ought to win.[27]

To support the last point, Howarth cites cases where a strong public interest was not a defence to causing serious interference, including famously (on the majority view) playing cricket,[28] and an Irish case in which the country's only cement factory was held to be a nuisance in the middle of a housing shortage crisis.[29] Similarly, it has been held irrelevant that the defendant provides a 'vital environmental benefit' of 'strategic importance' for the treatment of London's sewage.[30] Traditionally under the '*Shelfer* rules' courts usually grant injunctions when nuisance is established, irrespective of whether the defendant is 'in some sense a public benefactor (eg, a gas or water company or a sewer authority)'.[31] However after the Supreme Court's discussion in *Coventry v Lawrence (No 1)* it can no longer be stated so confidently that the public interest is irrelevant to the court's discretion to grant damages in lieu of injunction.[32]

CRITIQUE OF COASE: JUDICIAL CAPACITY TO IDENTIFY 'HIGHEST VALUE USE OF LAND'

Other serious objections can be made to the Coasian approach. Some would reject the entire premise that tort law should try to maximise social wealth. This is inconsistent with the basic form and structure of nuisance law, which exists to protect property rights and redress their violation, as a matter of

---

[25] [1893] 2 Ch 588, 600.
[26] D Howarth, *A Textbook on Tort* (London, Butterworths, 1995) 502–03.
[27] ibid.
[28] *Miller v Jackson* [1977] QB 966.
[29] *Bellew v Irish Cement* [1948] IR 61.
[30] *Barr v Biffa Waste* [2012] EWCA Civ 312; [2013] QB 455 [31] (Carnwath LJ).
[31] *Shelfer v City of London Electric Lighting Co* [1895] 1 Ch 287, 316 (Lindley LJ).
[32] [2014] AC 822. See also *Miller v Jackson* (n 28) and see ch 12, 'Remedies and Planning Permission'.

corrective justice. This has been the subject of the previous chapter and will not be considered again here. (Note that Epstein, although maintaining that rights-protection is the primary explanation of nuisance law, accepts the 'constraints' from 'utilitarian' reasoning. For example, idealised justice may be so expensive to apply that cruder, simpler rules that are cheaper to administer may be preferable. Epstein also accepts that 'exceptionally', rights must give way to a sufficiently strong and demonstrable public interest, on condition that the infringer compensates the right-holder 'because forced exchanges represent less of an affront to corrective justice principles than do outright takings'.)[33]

Many lawyers accept that at least among other goals, nuisance law should pay some regard to its economic effects. As Ogus and Richardson put it in their pioneering English economic analysis, 'In a world of limited resources, ... a solution which is compatible with efficiency demands is not to be dismissed lightly'.[34] It is legitimate for society to make the most of its scarce resources. There is no overwhelming reason for private law to ignore this goal. (Albeit the authors accept that it can conflict with both corrective justice (rights enforcement) and society's sense of fairness (distributive justice). They also identify many nuisance rules that fit poorly with efficiency analysis.)

Perhaps the most interesting – or damning – criticisms of Coase's approach come from commentators who accept the legitimacy of the economic efficiency goal. The central complaint is that Coase expects too much from the courts. To decide which is the 'most valuable land use' is at the very least formidably complex. Thomas Merrill summarises the problem:

> Under a purely economic cost-benefit approach, the relevant question would be what combination of inputs and activity levels would either maximize the joint profits of the parties or minimize their joint costs. Thus the court should not only inquire into the damages suffered by A [the claimant] and similarly situated persons, and the value of increased production to B [the defendant] and allied interests, but also should ask what abatement techniques are available to B at what cost, and what avoidance techniques (such as soundproofing) are available to A and similarly situated persons and at what cost. It can easily be seen that to do such an analysis correctly, even in a simple case ... would be extraordinarily expensive.[35]

(The economist's phrase 'extraordinarily expensive' means 'impossible in practice'.) Coase, as seen, recommends that courts should engage in a cost-benefit comparison of the conflicting land uses. Coase envisages the judge becoming 'a miniature central planner'.[36] Given the notorious economic failings of socialist

---

[33] Epstein (n 20) 77.

[34] AI Ogus and GM Richardson, 'Economics and the Environment: A Study of Private Nuisance' [1977] *CLJ* 284, 294.

[35] Thomas W Merrill, 'Trespass, Nuisance, and the Costs of Determining Property Rights' (1985) 14 *JLS* 13, 18 n 21.

[36] Henry E Smith, 'Exclusion and Property Rules in the Law of Nuisance' (2004) 90 *Virginia LR* 965, 1015.

'centrally-planned economies' (most dramatically the Soviet Union's collapse circa 1990), the phrase is damning. Coase of course discussed the problem of 'government failure'. He seems to have overlooked its equal applicability to *judicial* determinations of 'highest value use'.

There seem to be two possible routes around this problem of competence. One is to adopt an apparently simpler 'cost internalisation' model (placing liability on the 'polluter'). The second relies on the insight in Coase's own theory and attempts to improve the prospects for parties reaching their own decisions and accommodations, by agreement, about the use of land.

First the cost-internalisation model. This is deceptively simple. Its intuitive appeal is strong, reflecting society's widely held belief that as a matter of fairness, polluters should pay for the damage they cause.[37] Second, it has a superficial economic appeal also. If the polluting activity is made to internalise all of the resulting costs (eg a coal-fired power station paying for forests damaged by acid rain) there are desirable consequences. Elementary economics shows that if the cost of the 'product' (the electricity generated) reflects its actual costs of production, the level of generation is at a socially optimal level. (By contrast if the electricity is artificially cheap because generation receives a subsidy by 'externalising' its pollution costs onto uncompensated forest-owners, the lower prices mean more electricity will be consumed than is economically justifiable.) 150 years ago, Bramwell B declared that an activity is for the public benefit *only if it can be done profitably when absorbing all the costs and harms caused to others*; in his view this justified making polluters strictly liable for such harm.[38]

However, on analysis this proves less simple. The reason was central to Coase's theorem. It is tendentious to talk about 'polluter' and 'victim' at all since the problem is *inherently* reciprocal. Each party to the dispute is a 'cause' – or more helpfully, each of them could modify their activities to avoid the problem. In Bramwell B's example in *Bamford v Turnley* (a steam locomotive emitting sparks which burn down adjacent woodland), it is not the railway company alone which can take action (running fewer trains, or none; using spark arresters to make the locomotives safer, etc). The owner of the wood could also take precautions (insert fire-breaks, install alarms or sprinklers, clear undergrowth …), or cease growing trees so close to the railway altogether. It seems we should place liability on the party which can avoid the problem most effectively – the modern statement of Bramwell's idea is not strict liability for 'polluters', but rather upon the 'cheapest cost avoider'.

That terminology is taken from Calabresi's classic analysis of *The Costs of Accidents*.[39] Calabresi's focus was indeed *accidents* on the roads etc, but

---

[37] Ogus and Richardson (n 34) 318–19.
[38] *Bamford v Turnley* 3 B & S 84–85.
[39] G Calabresi, *The Costs of Accidents: A Legal and Economic Analysis* (New Haven CT, Yale University Press, 1970).

Michelman has critically considered how the arguments apply to nuisance.[40] Michelman notes that the Calabresi's approach seems to supports the 'polluter pays' principle. But that is an oversimplification:

> The most sweeping arguments for strict liability ... would apparently assume that polluters are nearly always the cheapest cost avoiders, and while that assumption may have a certain gross plausibility for the whole universe of pollution-nuisance cases, there is no *a priori* reason for believing it to be valid in any particular case. In a given situation, the cheapest cost-avoiders may be, say, the few residential neighbors who would have to relocate out of a predominantly industrialized area.[41]

Mitigation is possible, short of outright relocation (or cessation of activities). Michelman instances a simple air pollution case where fumes could equally be reduced by scrubbers in a factory chimney or air conditioners ventilating next-door houses. It is unclear which would be cheaper. To decide would require detailed information about comparative costs. (Filtration can create new or displaced problems: one unintended result of nineteenth-century air pollution legislation was factories discharging toxins condensed from their chimneys into streams, causing terrible river pollution.) Another complication, as Michelman notes, is when a number of activities contribute to (or combine to produce) the relevant interference. Which of these would be 'cheapest cost avoider'?

Ultimately the cost-internalisation model faces the same criticism as Coase's hunt for the highest-value use of land. We first need to decide which party ought to internalise the costs. That choice could be made on a number of grounds, such as asking which party can mostly cheaply minimise the problem. But just as with Coase's cost-benefit comparison, the court would need vast amounts of complex information to set the rule accurately. The 'polluter pays' principle is appealing justice, but unlikely to be economically efficient in every case.

Information Theory in Nuisance and Trespass: Clear Rules and 'Coasian Bargaining'

A different response to Coase avoids intractable cost-benefit analysis altogether. Several commentators attempt to promote the conditions for 'Coasian bargaining'. The more that land-use disputes can be left to 'the market' (ie private transactions), the less need for courts actively to assign liabilities by weighing up the economic costs and benefits. Arguably the traditional structure of the property torts serves this 'agreement facilitating' function well.

It is widely accepted that *clearly established* rights are a necessary first step if people are going to agree to trade them. This points towards a clear and strict

---

[40] Frank I Michelman, 'Pollution as a Tort: A Non-Accidental Perspective on Calabresi's Costs' (1971) 80 *Yale LJ* 647.
[41] ibid 667–68.

system of property rights, and their protection by tort. Trespass is the paradigm tort for this model. Liability simply requires physical invasion of the claimant's land. There is no inquiry into the value of the defendant's conduct, the reasonableness of his belief, etc. Given the clarity and simplicity of trespass it is a low-cost way to define a landowner's rights. In result these can be very simply stated. Landowners are entitled to exclude all others from coming onto their land without permission. They need not give any reasons for the exclusion. They do not need to justify it. It is quite irrelevant that the trespasser would have benefited more from the trespass than it would have harmed the owner.

Jacque v Steenberg Homes Inc provides a vivid example.[42] The defendant needed to deliver a mobile home. The only road to its customer was blocked with snow. Steenberg Homes therefore asked to short-cut over the plaintiffs' field, neighbouring their customer's house. The plaintiffs unambiguously refused permission for this on several occasions. Steenberg Homes took the short-cut anyway, ploughing over the snow-covered field. Because no damage was caused to the plaintiffs' land they recovered $1 nominal damages – but in addition $100,000 exemplary damages. They had an absolute right to exclude the defendants (the right of exclusion is 'one of the most essential sticks in the bundle of rights that are commonly characterized as property'.)[43] Clearly Steenberg Homes saved considerable money and expense by taking the short-cut. But far from justifying its conduct, this reinforced the case for a punitive award.[44] There was need to deter those in the delivery business (or builders or 'recreational adventurers'), who might be tempted to trespass to gain a benefit. The court condemned Steenberg Homes' 'brazen' and 'reprehensible' conduct; their 'reckless disregard for the law, and for the rights of others'.

We have extensively analysed the rights-vindication basis of trespass to the person.[45] A similar rights-protecting rationale may be put forward for trespass *to land*. But one vital difference is that land is typically *traded* whereas bodily rights are not. There is reason for the law to facilitate a market in land transactions, including agreements giving permission to enter or use land in exchange for payment. There is no equivalent market in people trading their bodies for payment (or one viewed with ambivalence if not outright prohibition – consider organ selling; sex work; commercial surrogacy).[46] The clear, simple and absolute protection trespass gives to a landowner's right to exclude others can however be welcomed on the additional ground of supporting such a market. It encourages 'Coasian bargaining'.

---

[42] 209 Wis. 2d 605 (1997).

[43] *Kaiser Aetna v United States*, 444 US 164, 176 (1979).

[44] G Parchomovsky and A Stein, 'Reconceptualizing Trespass' (2009) 103 *Nw U L Rev* 1823 (nominal damages or market based 'mesne profits' insufficiently compensate trespass by comparison with freely granted injunctions against threatened invasions).

[45] See ch 2, 'Debate 2: Remedies and Vindication of Rights'.

[46] eg NJ McBride, *Key Ideas in Contract Law* (Oxford, Hart, 2017) ch 5.

Trespass invests land with 'that sole and despotic dominion which one man claims and exercises over the external things of the world, in total exclusion of the right of any other individual in the universe' (in Blackstone's famous phrase).[47] Making each owner the sole ('despotic') judge of the best use of their land is a sensible strategy. It delegates to landowners absolute power to decide who to permit to enter their land, for what purposes, and on what terms (eg price). The value of that delegation is what it *avoids*. It removes the need for *courts* to decide whether a would-be trespasser would use land better than its owner. As seen, such decision-making by a court (or other public authority) is problematic and costly. Thus if it can be left to each individual owner, it avoids a major regulatory difficulty.

In trespass cases, private negotiations can take place readily enough. Its demand to 'keep off!' is a simple rule, easily understood by non-lawyers, that we must ask the owner's permission before entering land for any purpose. Any negotiations will take place between a small number of parties (usually just two). As seen, the right is very clearly defined (by the strong protection against trespass to land). Thus the conditions for 'Coasian bargaining' are amply satisfied.

One exception illuminates the different legal treatment of nuisance. Trespass does not literally protect landowners' rights upward 'to the heavens' (*ad coelum*). The leading case, *Lord Bernstein v Skyviews*, holds that overflying aircraft do not trespass at a height which does not interfere with the ordinary use of land.[48] The 'colourful phrase' *cuius est solum, eius est usque ad coelum* could not be applied uncritically, without 'the absurdity of a trespass at common law being committed by a satellite every time it passes over a suburban garden'.[49] Doctrinally, an unusual hybrid test for trespass-by-aircraft emerges. Liability does not result simply from crossing the claimant's boundary. Aerial intrusion must 'interfere with the ordinary user of the land'. Although characterised as trespass in *Skyviews*, note that 'the [usual] mechanical entitlement-determination rule of trespass has been replaced by a judgment standard that looks very much like the law of nuisance'.[50]

The principle has limited scope. First, by statute strict liability arises when overflying aircraft cause any 'material loss or damage'.[51] (The provision fortified Griffiths J's belief that there should not be liability for aircraft trespass per se, in the absence of material harm.) Second the *Bernstein v Skyviews* 'judgmental standard' has not been applied to *subterranean* trespass (eg drilling or tunnelling). The maxim of ownership '… *et ad inferos*' ('to the infinite depths') does remain good law.[52] Lord Hope rejected the submission that trespass below the

---

[47] *Commentaries on the Laws of England Vol II* (Oxford, 1766) 2.
[48] [1978] QB 479. See also Civil Aviation Act 1982, s 76(1).
[49] [1978] QB 479, 487 (Griffiths J).
[50] Merrill (n 35) 31 (discussing *Martin v Reynolds Metals Co* 221 Or 86 (1959), trespass at the molecular level by toxic gas).
[51] Civil Aviation Act 1982, s 76(2).
[52] *Bocardo SA v Star Energy UK Onshore Ltd* [2010] UKSC 35; [2011] 1 AC 380.

ground should also depend on actual damage or unreasonable interference. Such a test would lead to great uncertainty, undermining a cardinal feature of property rights.[53] The same 'uncertainty' criticism could be made about the 'overflying' cases. Yet Lord Hope approved *Bernstein v Skyviews*. He noted the argument that upper airspace has become like a public highway – a resource to which the public as a whole has a just claim.[54] (Griffiths J had reasoned that landowners' rights had to be reconciled with 'the rights of the general public to take advantage of all that science now offers in the use of air space'.) Yet while technological advances now permit subterranean exploitation of land at ever-greater *depths*, it was by contrast inappropriate to declare that sub-surface land is a common resource like the public highway. (Note that valuable minerals, oil etc frequently lie far below the surface). Lord Hope accepted that at extreme depths the literal '*ad inferos*' maxim becomes unworkable owing to the curvature of the earth (*all* plots of land must ultimately converge at the earth's core!) – but a pipeline tunnelled 2,000 feet below the surface did not begin to approach such absurdity.[55]

An explanation for the 'aircraft exception' is that private transactions are *not* a realistic way to resolve such conflicts. It is simply not feasible for airlines to negotiate agreements with the thousands (even millions) of individuals who own the land that their aircraft fly over. (Whereas there is nothing impracticable about seeking landowners' permission before tunnelling beneath their land). To apply the normal strict trespass rule would make flight impossible. Therefore instead of landowners having the usual absolute protection of trespass law, liability arises only when flight interferes with ordinary land use (or causes actual physical damage).

This brings us back to nuisance at last. What is an exceptional problem for trespass law arises generally in nuisance. Aircraft pose the problem of minimal invasions of a multitude of titles. Such situations are far more common in nuisance since it is not limited to direct physical incursions onto land. 'Boundary trespass' is nearly always confined to disputes between immediate neighbours, or a small number of them (aircraft cases are the exception that proves the rule). But nuisance deals with intangible pollution such as noise and smell that can and does travel long distances. The dispersal of pollution may be difficult to predict. For this reason, some suggest that the clear and simple approach to liability for trespass is unrealistic in nuisance cases.[56] 'Coasian bargaining' becomes less likely as the number of parties and the variety of disputes increases. Classic nuisance can affect large groups of people to varying degrees. Hence the necessity of a qualified liability. Courts have to balance competing land-uses because of the obstacles to multipartite private agreement.

---

[53] ibid [25]–[26].
[54] ibid [26].
[55] ibid [27].
[56] Sterk (n 7).

To sum up the argument so far, the clear-cut 'mechanical' rules in *trespass* protect property-owners' absolute control over the land. Trespass's simple 'keep off' rule is easily understood by non-lawyers. Trespass doctrine does not attempt cost-benefit analysis (eg to decide whether the trespasser would make more socially valuable use of the land). It delegates all those decisions (what uses to permit on what conditions) to landowners. This avoids the court needing to make difficult calculations about 'highest value use'. The delegation strategy is possible precisely because in this situation, Coasian bargaining between landowners and would-be users is feasible. There is usually no difficulty in the would-be user identifying a potential trespass and negotiating with the owner for permission. But *nuisance* is different. Given that much larger numbers of parties are involved, delegation of *absolute* control to landowners is less attractive. Coasian bargaining is much less likely to take place. Thus, the argument runs, in nuisance courts do need to undertake cost-benefit analysis of the higher-value use of land.

On this view however, nuisance remains vulnerable to the criticism that courts face 'immense technical difficulties in deciding how to package original rights to achieve or even approximate this end' (ie determining the higher-value use of land).[57] Other commentators therefore argue that as with trespass, nuisance should also be concerned with facilitating Coasian bargaining. Henry Smith emphasises the parallels between trespass and nuisance, with this end in mind.[58] But is it feasible to remove balancing from nuisance altogether?

David Campbell is a prominent critic of the current law of nuisance.[59] Balancing the parties' interests is at its heart. To strike the balance correctly, courts must determine the 'socially optimal extent' of each activity. But judges lack evidence, experience and training to perform this difficult function. It is a 'Herculean' pretence to assume that the courts are competent in such cost-benefit analysis (Campbell alludes to Dworkin's fictional super-judge).[60] Campbell therefore attacks the premise of nuisance law, the 'belief that the court can evaluate the joint welfare of the affected parties better than they can themselves'. For Campbell, the central lesson from Coase's work is that parties may well be better placed to strike that balance. It is true that real-world 'Coasian bargaining' faces obstacles. But it is insufficient as a defence of nuisance to observe that parties sometimes fail to reach optimal agreements. The courts are not perfect judges of the highest-value use of land either. 'In our study of comparative failure, the market may fail less badly than the state'.[61] Thus for Campbell, nuisance law should stop trying to weigh the parties' interests and

---

[57] Epstein (n 20) 77.
[58] HE Smith, 'Exclusion and Property Rules in the Law of Nuisance' (2004) 90 *Virginia LR* 965.
[59] D Campbell, 'Of Coase and Corn: A (Sort of) Defence of Private Nuisance' (2000) 63 *MLR* 197.
[60] RM Dworkin, *Taking Rights Seriously* (Cambridge MA, Harvard University Press, 1977) 105–30.
[61] Campbell (n 59) 210.

instead attempt to lay down rules that would assist Coasian bargaining (which is positively hindered by the great uncertainty of current nuisance doctrine). Campbell envisages nuisance becoming 'a structure of bright-line rights'. As he concludes, the result would not resemble current nuisance law at all. This then is a call for radical reform.

What would a 'bright-line' law of nuisance look like? Trespass provides the model. Both Merrill and Smith draw analogies with the structure of trespass. Merrill argues that private agreements about nuisance are often feasible (as they are with trespass). Not *every* nuisance complaint involves a large number of parties. In some classic cases (eg *Sturges v Bridgeman*) the dispute is between immediate neighbours, or a small limited class (eg owners of gardens immediately adjoining the cricket ground in *Miller v Jackson*). In such cases, nuisance law should adopt the clear, mechanical rules of trespass. This would facilitate private agreement. Merrill proposes the 'bifurcation' of nuisance to serve this end. In some situations, he admits, the interference may extend over such a wide area that Coasian bargaining is impracticable; the parties are unlikely to reach agreed solutions. (The parallel in trespass, as discussed above, is overflying aircraft). Here Merrill accepts that there would still need to be weighing up.[62] But in localised disputes, 'private nuisance would have to be recast in more mechanical terms – perhaps by adopting [a] substantial physical invasion test'.[63]

This argument should not be overplayed. Certainly, 'Coasian bargaining' is assisted by clear 'bright line' or 'mechanical' rules. But to 'recast' private nuisance using precisely the same rules as trespass would surely be unacceptable. The rule that these commentators seem to have in mind is that *any* sort of emanation onto the claimant's land would be actionable without more. But a strict 'emanation' standard misdescribes that law and would lead to undesirable results. It would in some senses be underinclusive, and others extend too far. First underinclusion: there are many nuisance cases that do not involve 'emanations' (eg withdrawal of rights of support; blocking a right of way; cases like *Laws v Florinplace*[64] involving 'immoral conduct' on neighbouring land).[65] These cases reflect an important truth: that to protect rights to peaceful occupation, claims sometimes need to extend beyond the strict physical boundaries of the claimant's land. Legitimate

---

[62] Merrill (n 35) would classify these residual situations as 'public nuisance' since they interfere with a sufficiently large class of the public. But it is confusing to suggest that public and private nuisance are sub-categories of the same tort. *Public* nuisance is about interference with public rights (not landowners' rights). It is primarily a crime and primarily enforced by the Attorney-General (as representative of the public interest). 'Public and private nuisances are not in reality two species of the same genus at all. There is no generic conception which includes the crime of making a bomb-hoax and the tort of allowing one's trees to overhang the land of a neighbour': *Re Corby Group Litigation* [2008] EWCA Civ 463; [2009] QB 335, [27] (Dyson LJ, quoting *Salmond & Heuston on Torts*).

[63] Merrill (n 35) 46.

[64] [1981] 1 All ER 659.

[65] See further D Nolan, 'The Essence of Private Nuisance' in Ben McFarlane and Sinéad Agnew (eds), *Modern Studies in Property Law, Volume 10* (Oxford, Hart, 2019).

use of land can be affected by activities that do not 'emanate' over the boundary. To require boundary-crossing in nuisance (by a mistaken parallel with trespass) would be unacceptably crude: 'property is not physics'.[66]

Worse, to impose nuisance liability for *each and every* emanation (again, by parallel with trespass) would also be unworkable. It is easy to avoid going on to neighbouring land (to avoid the direct physical intrusion that is 'trespass'). It is quite impossible to avoid all 'emanations'. In the course of dull suburban domesticity, who can avoid occasional loud noises (children play, dogs bark), smoke (from a fireplace, barbecue or bonfire), or smells (of new-mown grass or the barbecued food) ... Yet to apply the trespass rule would deem all these 'nuisance'. It would make all land uninhabitable (unless we invent hermetically sealed, soundproof bubbles). For of course, the claimant would be equally unable to do those ordinary and necessary activities, given their reciprocal liabilities. Nuisance law has long recognised the 'live and let live' exception for just this reason.[67]

With more serious levels of interference, nuisance uses a balancing process precisely because the claimant is simultaneously asserting a power to control their neighbours' land use and exposing themselves to reciprocal liabilities – equally *to be controlled by* others. Balancing is *necessary* in nuisance. Not so much to implement a programme of economic efficiency. But to secure to all landowners an acceptable degree both of control (*over* others) and of freedom (*from* others' control). No wonder Merrill accepts that if nuisance were 'recast' as physical intrusion, it would have to retain certain balancing features – notably the 'live and let live' exception, and assessment by prevailing standards in the locality.

Henry Smith's account shows the potential, and limits, of the simplified 'trespassory' approach to nuisance. On the one hand, Smith denies that nuisance is always (or even usually) about weighing up the costs and benefits of the rival activities. That is how Law and Economics might conceive nuisance, but it seriously misdescribes the law. Although it might not be determinative, the fact of interference emanating over the boundary of the claimant's land remains hugely important. Quite contrary to Coase's 'reciprocal' view of a nuisance dispute, the law retains its 'presumption ... that there is a violation by the more active party, especially one sending physical objects, sound waves, vibrations, and so on across the boundary'.[68] Contrary to Coase's claim, there is good economic sense behind that traditional approach:

> By resolving all but the most difficult and high-stakes cases in terms of who crossed a boundary – with objects or sound waves or odors or so forth – the law can rely on a basic and cheap package of rights with a high degree of salience and ease of processing.[69]

---

[66] Christopher Essert, 'Nuisance and the Normative Boundaries of Ownership' (2016) 52 *Tulsa LR* 85, 96.
[67] See ch 10, 'Balancing Rights: "Live and Let Live"'
[68] Henry E Smith, 'Exclusion and Property Rules in the Law of Nuisance' (2004) 90 *Virginia LR* 965, 1004.
[69] ibid 1007.

Thus nuisance remains much closer to trespass than is 'conventionally thought' (ie in economic analysis of law). However, Smith accepts that this is not the whole story. In the 'difficult cases' to which he refers, there is need for some balancing (examining locality, any 'hypersensitivity', the 'live and let live' exception, etc). Given that nuisance sometimes involves such issues it 'puts more of the direct evaluation of [land-] uses in judges' hands than does the law of trespass'.[70] For Smith, while we must not overlook the trespass-like dimension of nuisance law (which Coase arguably does), nor should we overstate it.

Smith suggests that nuisance is difficult ('slippery') because it shifts between these two different 'strategies'. Sometimes nuisance applies a clear and crude rule, readily attaching liability to 'emanations' and delegating the compromise between conflicting land use to agreements between private individuals. Smith argues that this is the 'core' of nuisance. But as he accepts, the law 'also finetunes this hard-edged regime' with a *balancing* test. That approach supplements but does not supplant the harder edged, trespass-like dimension of nuisance.[71]

There is clearly a tension between these approaches, and within Smith's account. Clear rules' great claimed virtue is the basis for negotiated permission. But the more they are 'supplemented' by a balancing approach, the less clear the landowner's entitlements and the harder it is to negotiate about them. Smith tries to square the circle with public regulation. Smith's descriptive claim is that the fine-tuning strain of law nuisance law, 'has largely given way to potentially more effective rules of proper [land-] use from other sources, such as pollution control and zoning [ie planning]'.[72] This frees the common law of nuisance to pursue the clear-cut 'exclusionary' strategy: 'the presumption for exclusion can be fairly strong as long as other institutions generally, and administrative agencies in particular, can be expected to furnish a better governance regime than unilateral court activity'.[73] The question then becomes – how effective is public regulation of pollution, planning and so forth? This will be examined in the next chapter. A common theme in discussion of nuisance, regulation and the public interest is the threefold institutional division between landowners, courts, and other public agencies. Each have their limitations. Coase identified the problem of 'government failure' but this can equally affect the courts developing and applying the common law of nuisance. Given the limited competence of any regulator (judicial or otherwise), it is attractive to return to Coase's emphasis on private ordering. The arguments examined in this section suggests how nuisance could encourage landowners to reconcile their competing uses of land by mutual agreement. But the clarity and simplicity of the entitlements protected by *trespass* law are not available in nuisance. The conflicts addressed by nuisance are too pervasive. The intangible and reciprocal character of nuisance requires a more balanced solution. Necessary though this is, it does hamper 'Coasian bargaining'.

---

[70] ibid 974.
[71] ibid 1046.
[72] ibid 1047.
[73] ibid 1025.

12

Nuisance and the Environment: Tort, Regulation and Pollution

Nuisance seems the common law's most promising instrument of environmental protection. Once we countenance the *instrumental* use of tort law – as a means to some desirable public goal – there is no reason to confine our attention to the narrowly economic goal of 'efficiency' (see Chapter 11). Pollution and environmental degradation are leading public policy challenges of our age. Can tort law address them?

The answer is (as you might expect) debateable. On the one hand nuisance can be used against environmental harm. The archetypal nuisance claim involves pollution. The tort's rules give powerful advantages to claimants – strict liability and strong remedies (eg injunctions). On the other hand, nuisance has certain limitations. It does not respond to 'environmental harm' per se, but only invasions of an individual's property rights. Even where pollution does interfere with the use and enjoyment of land, there must be a well-resourced claimant willing and able to bring an expensive nuisance claim against the polluter. The tort of nuisance is part of private law: its enforcement is solely in the hands of individuals. This brings both advantages and disadvantages from a regulatory perspective.

How well does nuisance protect the environment in practice? What are the alternatives, and how do they compare with nuisance? The standard historical narrative gives nuisance poor marks in this examination. It did nothing to prevent the horrifying pollution caused by the industrial revolution and urbanisation in eighteenth- and nineteenth-century England. Both the substantive rules, and procedural shortcomings, hampered nuisance's use in fighting pollution. Only when the legislature enacted direct regulation of polluting industries, and the state evolved regulatory agencies to enforce that legislation, was the problem of pollution addressed – towards the end of the nineteenth century. To this day, it is suggested, nuisance has only a marginal role in environmental protection.

As will be seen, not all historians accept this standard view of nuisance as at best peripheral and at worst powerless. Nevertheless, the rise of public regulation is an undeniable historical fact. Nuisance today is not the only tool to address pollution, but complements a raft of legislation and government agencies (for example pollution, planning control, regulation of public utilities, etc).

How should nuisance and the modern regulatory approach interrelate? Again, we must beware the 'nirvana fallacy' of comparing tort law with some (non-existent) idealised form of regulation. Regulatory failure is common in the real world. In deciding which approach is society's imperfect best (ie the least flawed), tort law cannot be written off. Some kind of mixed strategy might be optimal. On that view, the relationship between nuisance and environmental regulation is of great importance. As will be seen, the law on that subject is rather tangled. One important task is to straighten this relationship out.

Debate 1
Nuisance and Environmental Protection – Potential and Limits

Private Property and the Environment

Private nuisance, like the rest of tort law, gives claims to individuals whose protected interests have been invaded by the defendant. In nuisance, the right to use and enjoy land. In important respects the protection is *strict*. Invasions must cross the threshold of 'unreasonableness': but that looks at their impact. If the interference is serious enough to be actionable, the defendant's conduct is irrelevant. In particular, the fact that the defendant has taken all reasonable precautions (or indeed all scientifically known steps) to limit interference is no defence. Where the nuisance is ongoing, the court will (normally) issue an injunction to prevent it.

The combination of strict liability and strong remedial protection offers considerable environmental protection. If a polluter causes intolerable interference with the claimant's property, its activity is likely to be enjoined. Such court-ordered cessation should bring immediate environmental benefits. Defendants have a powerful incentive to clean up their operations, so that they may continue without causing their neighbours a nuisance. This includes incentives to discover and use new technology. The fact that no technology currently exists to prevent the nuisance is irrelevant (ie not a defence). But if it would be profitable to innovate, mitigate and continue the activity – rather than cease altogether – the defendant's own economic self-interest provides the incentive.

However, nuisance does not respond to environmental harm per se. Only interference with *the claimant's property* is actionable. Frequently these do overlap. The fumes that damaged Mr Tipping's trees and estate of course polluted the wider environment.[1] Thus many others, and the environment generally, benefited when the St Helen's Smelting Co was enjoined.[2] Yet private property and the environment are by no means co-extensive. The gravest kinds of harm affect the 'unowned environment'. Consider plastic pollution of the oceans; species extinctions; depletions of the ozone layer; and (above all) climate

---

[1] (1865) 11 HL Cas 642.
[2] (1865) LR 1 Ch App 66 (injunction).

change with associated impact on weather patterns and sea levels. It would be difficult, probably impossible, to force any of these into the framework of private nuisance. (Perhaps property damage from flooding could be the result of climate change, but it would be difficult to prove causation from the indirect links between a defendant's carbon emissions and claimant's flood damage.)

Half a century ago, Lord Scarman observed in his Hamlyn Lectures:

> For environment a traditional lawyer reads property: English law reduces environmental problems to questions of property. Establish ownership or possession and the armoury of the English legal cupboard is yours to command.[3]

Lord Scarman noted the 'effectual remedy' of nuisance injunctions, the judicial development of new actions (*Rylands v Fletcher*) and expanded torts (modern negligence) to address environmental problems. However:

> The judicial development of the law, vigorous and imaginative though it has been, has been found wanting. Tied to concepts of property, possession, and fault, the judges have been unable by their own strength to break out of the cabin of the common law and tackle the broad problems of land use in an industrial and urbanised society.[4]

Since then, the courts have reaffirmed the property basis of private nuisance – as it were reinforcing the 'cabin'. As seen, in *Hunter v Canary Wharf*, Lord Cooke's solitary dissent doubted 'the utility or the justice' of the majority's property-rights restatement (while acknowledging its 'symmetry').[5] Lord Cooke prioritised the social usefulness of nuisance over doctrinal coherence – but in vain. *Hunter* is now the leading modern case on nuisance. Commentators lament that this 'conservative' doctrinal approach gives a bleak prognosis for nuisance's potential to protect the environment.[6] Contemporaneous with *Hunter*, the House of Lords restated *Rylands v Fletcher* as a branch of nuisance and refused invitations to extend it:

> The protection and preservation of the environment is now perceived as being of crucial importance to the future of mankind; ... it does not follow ... that a common law principle, such as the rule in *Rylands v Fletcher*, should be developed or rendered more strict to provide for liability in respect of such pollution. On the contrary, given that so much well-informed and carefully structured legislation is now being put in place for this purpose, there is less need for the courts to develop a common law principle to achieve the same end, and indeed it may well be undesirable that they should do so.[7]

---

[3] L Scarman, *English Law – The New Dimension* (London, Stevens, 1974) 51.
[4] ibid 53.
[5] [1997] AC 655, 711.
[6] K Stanton and C Willmore, 'Tort and Environmental Pluralism' in J Lowry and R Edmunds (eds), *Environmental Protection and the Common Law* (Oxford, Hart, 2000).
[7] *Cambridge Water Co Ltd v Eastern Counties Leather plc* [1994] 2 AC 264, 305 (Lord Goff) (cf 276–77 (Mann LJ) (CA)).

It light of this anaemic commitment to environmental protection, nuisance was labelled 'The pale green tort'.[8] *Cambridge Water* had major implications for the liability of polluters. The evasive declaration that it was not *the common law's* problem showed only that the court was determined not to engage with the important social question of reconciling environmental protection and economic development.

The claim in *Cambridge Water* failed because the damage (contamination of the plaintiff company's borehole) was too remote, failing the reasonable foreseeability test. The court seemed to view its decision on remoteness as merely a doctrinal tidying-up exercise. Maria Lee argues, however, that foreseeability-based remoteness was an 'inroad into strict liability [that] puts the risk of uncertainty, or unknowability, of effects onto the victims of new technology, without any real debate as to whether that is the better policy solution'.[9] However Weir suggested this aspect of *Cambridge Water* may be less momentous than it seems (noting that the *Wagon Mound* test of remoteness in *negligence* has had little impact in practice).[10] Weir predicted that other, more claimant-friendly views in *Cambridge Water* would prove to be of greater importance. Especially Lord Goff's deeming the use of chemicals in an industrial process to be 'an almost classic case of non-natural use'.[11]

That was a significant departure from the trial judge's decision. Ian Kennedy J had held that Eastern Counties Leather's activity was *not* 'non-natural' because it was for the 'general benefit of the community'. The tannery generated employment. Ian Kennedy J was influenced by authorities that suggested that undoubtedly dangerous activities were deemed 'natural' (ie not covered by *Rylands v Fletcher*) purely because they were carried out in the public interest – most notoriously, suggestions that manufacturing high explosives in wartime was a 'natural' use of land.[12] This approach was disapproved by the House of Lords. The defendant cannot point to the public benefit of their activity; *Rylands v Fletcher* applies to any 'extraordinary and unusual' activity, irrespective of the public interest (in suppressing unemployment, protecting national security, or otherwise).[13]

Yet another difficulty in *Cambridge Water* was the nature of the damage suffered. The presence of minute quantities of chemicals in the water company's borehole meant they could no longer use it to supply drinking water. Was this 'damage' to their land? Or had it damaged the water? Did the company even *own* the groundwater beneath their land? As Jenny Steele notes, these complex and difficult questions were avoided; the court was able to borrow EU drinking-water law's 'slightly ambiguous standard of "wholesomeness":

---

[8] J Conaghan and W Mansell, *The Wrongs of Tort* 2nd edn (London, Pluto Press, 1999) ch 6.
[9] M Lee, 'What Is Private Nuisance?' (2003) 119 *LQR* 298, 324.
[10] T Weir, *A Casebook on Tort*, 10th edn (London, Sweet & Maxwell, 2004) 463. (See ch 5, 'Debate 2: Remoteness, Causation and "Common Sense"').
[11] [1994] 2 AC 264, 309.
[12] *Read v J Lyons & Co Ltd* [1947] AC 156, 169–70, 174, 176–77, 186–87.
[13] See also *Transco Plc v Stockport MBC* [2004] 2 AC 1 [11] (Lord Bingham).

[even though] it could not be conclusively said that the concentrations of [chemicals] in question were necessarily dangerous'.[14] Lee similarly comments that 'The impact of regulatory standards is probably crucial in turning the harm into undisputed "damage"' – it would be difficult to see that the land/water had been 'physically damaged' without the EU directives on drinking water.[15] Steele contrasts this liberal decision (viz that there *had been* actionable damage in *Cambridge Water*) with other decisions that take a more traditional approach: for example, that radioactive contamination of land had not 'physically damaged' the property.[16] Clearly there can be borderline difficulties with what counts as 'physical harm' to land.[17] But even if 'contamination' or 'pollution' are defined generously, there will evidently be many kinds of environmental damage that affect the public and the environment in general, but not any particular individual landowner.

The limits of nuisance emerge in comparison with other approaches to pollution. For example the EU once proposed a new environmental tort, under which individual claimants could launch actions against polluters. This 2000 proposal was subsequently withdrawn.[18] The proposed new action would have been radically different from the common law. It would have covered environmental damage as a *general* concept, not one linked to and limited by private property. Thus it would have extended to the collective interest in a healthy environment, for example biodiversity. This transcends the limits of traditional tort law, where (to quote Lee) 'the very privateness of private law limits its use for environmental benefit'. On remedies too, the EU's white paper took a radically different approach. Damages would have been awarded to fund environmental *restoration* (rather than compensate owners for the diminution in the value of their land). This would have supplemented limited public funds for environmental clean-ups from those who cause such damage. The focus on restoration also avoided the difficulties in *valuing* harm done to the environment in general (eg a species extinction).

Short of such transformative legislation, tort law has clear, rigid limits. Private nuisance is internally coherent as 'a tort against land'. But it has limitations as a public policy tool.

Private Enforcement

The choice whether to claim is purely that of individual landowners. This has certain advantages as a regulatory 'strategy'. Even in an era of extensive public regulation (eg of pollution), it may be under-enforced by the relevant agencies

---

[14] J Steele, 'Private Law and the Environment: Nuisance in Context' (1995) 15 *Legal Stud* 236.
[15] Lee (n 9) 305 n 32.
[16] *Merlin v British Nuclear Fuels Plc* [1990] 2 QB 557. But contrast now: *Blue Circle Industries v Ministry of Defence* [1999] Ch. 289. (Both decisions about Nuclear Installations Act 1965 s 12.)
[17] See also M Lee and R Burrell, 'Liability for the Escape of GM Seeds: Pursuing the "Victim"?' (2002) 65 *MLR* 517 (see ch 10, 'Defining Property Rights: The Role of the Public Interest').
[18] See M Lee, 'Tort, Regulation and Environmental Liability' (2002) 22 *Legal Stud* 33.

for a number of reasons. These might be prosaic matters of lack of information or resources. The abstention may even be deliberate. Weir notes that under the procedure for statutory nuisance,[19] local authorities ('Those barons of the modern age ... the vigilantes of the environment') deal with nearly all situations of neighbour nuisance today.[20] But that has not made the tort entirely redundant. It remains useful, if 'only in the rare case where the noisome activity is agreeable to the local politicians'.[21]

Other commentators enlarge upon this point.[22] Steele notes that whereas there is little public involvement in the enforcement of regulations, tort claims enable 'participation' – even dissent from centrally set government policy. As Stanton and Willmore note, tort is an un-official system. An individual (or pressure group), by bringing a tort claim, can challenge received scientific wisdom or orthodox attitudes to levels of acceptable risk. Concerned individuals can therefore question the government's data and air alternative approaches to regulation (eg in calling for a strict 'precautionary principle' to deal with risks of unknown magnitude). Even if such claims fail, they bring matters to public attention and indeed the failure may assist a campaign for legislative reform.[23]

There are downsides. Stanton and Willmore accept that since liability does not typically attach to *normal* land-use in a particular locality, nuisance may not always be suitable for challenging consensus. More fundamentally, tort depends on well-resourced individuals being able and willing to fund expensive litigation. Some well-heeled 'vigilantes of the environment' are known to us from the law reports.[24] But how many individuals without extensive landed estates could afford a nuisance claim? As discussed, the *Hunter* decision was directly regressive in this respect. The plaintiffs would have recovered such low compensation that the Legal Aid Board discontinued funding for their claims.[25] Victims of pollution would today need to convince solicitors to take on their claims under conditional fee arrangements. John Murphy suggests that such a route could be made more attractive (to litigation lawyers) if exemplary damages were available against polluters.[26] Class actions, by aggregating a number of small claims, may also make such litigation economically viable.[27]

---

[19] Environmental Protection Act 1990, Part III (NB that while this basically uses the common law definition of nuisance, it is a defence 'that the best practicable means were used to prevent ... the nuisance': s 80(7)).

[20] Weir (n 10) 419.

[21] ibid citing *Halsey v Esso* [1961] 2 All ER 145 (oil refinery); *Tetley v Chitty* [1986] 1 All ER 663 (go-kart racing).

[22] Lee (n 9) 317.

[23] Stanton and Willmore (n 6).

[24] *AG v Birmingham* (1858) 4 K & J 528 (relator of action was Charles Adderley Esq, later Lord Norton).

[25] *Khatun and 180 others v United Kingdom* (1998) 26 EHRR CD212 (see ch 10, 'Defining Property Rights The Role of the Public Interest').

[26] J Murphy, 'Noxious Emissions and Common Law Liability: Tort in the Shadow of Regulation' in J Lowry and R Edmunds (eds), *Environmental Protection and the Common Law* (Oxford, Hart, 2000).

[27] Eg *Anslow v Norton Aluminium* [2012] EWHC 2610 (QB) (claim by 132 local residents).

There is also a growing possibility of commercial third-party litigation funding,[28] or claims by campaign groups. Nevertheless, nuisance claims may be unlikely when pollution 'inevitably' affects 'unco-ordinated, inarticulate and financially disadvantaged' sectors of society.[29]

The financial obstacles are formidable. But even if claimants always had sufficient means, private enforcement would be a mixed blessing. Maria Lee considers arguments for individual enforcement of *environmental law* (as tentatively but unsuccessfully proposed by the EU). It would obviously provide a larger pool of enforcers. To the extent that the law is currently under-enforced, this seems attractive. (We can also note, consistent with Murphy's proposal, that one common justification for exemplary damages is as a 'bounty' to encourage enforcement – thereby increasing the number of claims as well as their cost to tortfeasors, and so the overall deterrent effect.)[30] Yet Lee accepts that diffused, decentralised enforcement would be 'an unpredictable regulatory tool, and could shift the determination of environmental priorities away from the state'.[31]

At best, commentators agree, tort may *supplement* public enforcement of environmental law. Nuisance is a useful safeguard against governmental oversight – or deliberate inaction (eg apprehending economic harm from closure of polluting companies).[32] But it cannot replace it entirely. Historically, nuisance was the law's only weapon against pollution. That has long been untrue. (As Lord Scarman said, given tort's limits, 'the guarding of our environment has been found to require an activist, intrusive role to be played by the executive arm of government'.)[33] Environmental damage may trigger a *combination* of regulatory responses, criminal prosecution and tort liability. Since modern nuisance law can only be understood in the context of this extensive public regulation, how do and how should the two spheres interrelate? The following sections consider the effect of public regulation on nuisance liability. That effect is limited. Tort basically functions independently of regulations such as planning permission. But the law is by no means consistent.

Debate 2
The Interaction of Tort and Regulation – Nuisance and Planning Permission

With one major exception, nuisance liability is *not* displaced by regulation in a similar field. The 'major exception' is direct statutory authorisation of

---

[28] See generally https://associationoflitigationfunders.com.

[29] AI Ogus and GM Richardson, 'Economics and the Environment: A Study of Private Nuisance' [1977] *CLJ* 284, 314.

[30] eg AM Polinsky and S Shavell, 'Punitive Damages: An Economic Analysis' (1998) 111 *Harvard LR* 869.

[31] Lee (n 18) 49.

[32] Note that Norton Aluminium Ltd went into administration after losing the claim against it (n 27) (see M Lee, 'Private Nuisance in the Supreme Court' [2014] *JPEL* 705, 709 n 32).

[33] Scarman (n 3) 53.

an activity, which immunises it from liability in nuisance. But the defence is kept narrow. Notably, the grant of planning permission does not engage the 'statutory authority' defence. The doctrinal picture is reasonably clear. But some scholars, most prominently Maria Lee, argue that tort should not isolate itself from regulation so comprehensively. Decisions in (for example) the planning process could provide important evidence for resolution of public interest questions that are, Lee argues, at the heart of nuisance law.

The Defence of Statutory Authority

This defence ultimately depends on the construction of the relevant legislation. Clear words are required to displace claims in nuisance; the immunity, when it arises, is not absolute but requires the defendant to show they have taken all reasonable care not to interfere with others' interests.[34] In Penner's view, these rules 'attempt to fulfil the intentions of Parliament while at the same time derogating least from private rights'.[35] When the conditions are satisfied, Lord Roskill explained the defence:

> The underlying philosophy plainly is that the greater public interest arising from the construction and use of undertakings such as railways, must take precedence over the private rights of owners and occupiers of neighbouring lands not to have their common law rights infringed by what would otherwise be actionable nuisance. In short, the lesser private right must yield to the greater public interest.[36]

This 'philosophy' sounds far-reaching. But the courts have insisted that only specific authorisation by Parliament can make private rights 'yield' like this. Mere *regulatory* approval does not attract similar immunity. *Barr v Biffa Waste Services* is a good illustration of when statutory authority does *not* provide a defence.[37] The defendant ran a household waste tip. It operated under (legally required) permission from the Environment Agency, which imposed detailed conditions for mitigating smells. The defendants had persuaded the trial judge that nuisance law had to 'march in step' with the waste treatment legislation. The judge therefore dismissed the nuisance claims, despite finding significant interference with the claimant's land by foul smells. He deemed the tip 'reasonable user' provided the defendants complied with the terms of the Environment Agency's permit.[38] However, the Court of Appeal overruled this decision and held Biffa liable in nuisance.

Carnwath LJ disagreed emphatically with the trial judge's approach. There was no basis for making the common law 'march' with statutory schemes,

---

[34] See generally *Allen v Gulf Oil Refining Ltd* [1981] AC 1001.
[35] JE Penner, 'Nuisance and the Character of the Neighbourhood' (1993) 5 *J Env Law* 1, 24.
[36] *Allen* (n 34) 1023.
[37] [2012] EWCA Civ 312; [2013] QB 455.
[38] [2011] EWHC 1003 (TCC) | [2011] 4 All ER 1065, [304], [350], [376].

thereby cutting down private property rights. The fact that modern regulation is more complex and more extensive did not affect clearly established nuisance principles. There was no defence of statutory authority. It was therefore 'misconceived' for the judge 'to find an alternative route to the same effective end' by deeming compliance with the Environment Agency's permit to be 'reasonable user'.[39] The approach at trial had overcomplicated a simple case of bad-smell nuisance. Principles laid down in the nineteenth century remained 'resilient and effective': in particular, 'Parliament may also enact parallel systems of regulatory control; but, unless it is says otherwise, the common law rights and duties remain unaffected'.[40] There was a 'clash between … irreconcilable principles'. But the court had to dismiss Biffa's submission that

> it would be unfair and unrealistic if the cascade of legislation and the terms of their permit were ignored, so that they could comply with all their numerous obligations and the detailed provisions of their permit, and still find themselves liable to the claimants in nuisance, as if the legislation and the permit did not exist.[41]

In other words, from the perspective of nuisance law *Barr v Biffa* held that it was indeed 'as if the cascade of regulatory legislation did not exist'.

Planning Permission: No Defence

Barr v Biffa concerned an important but specialised area of environmental regulation. More commonly encountered is 'town and country planning' law. Since 1947, the UK has had a comprehensive scheme of planning control, whereby government permission is required for new building developments (extensions, changes of use, etc). This is strikingly different from the nineteenth century. When leading cases such as *St Helens v Tipping* or *Sturges v Bridgman* were decided, nuisance law was essentially the *only* legal limit on what owners could build or do on their land. To the extent that nuisance law's 'locality principle' effectively designates (or 'zones') neighbourhoods as appropriate for particular activities (eg residential, industrial, agricultural), should nuisance now take these planning decisions into account? The courts have held not. Compliance with planning permission is no defence in nuisance. This was reaffirmed by the Supreme Court in *Coventry v Lawrence*. We will first examine the reasons for nuisance law's decision effectively to ignore the planning system. We then consider when planning permission exceptionally might have relevance to nuisance liability.

Planning law and private nuisance differ on a number of levels. They are different in substance, in effect (ie remedies) and in procedure. Judges have relied

---

[39] *Barr* (n 37) [94].
[40] ibid [146].
[41] [2011] EWHC 1003 (TCC) | [2011] 4 All ER 1065, [3].

on all these differences in approach to justify nuisance law ignoring planning permission. Perhaps the most 'fundamental difference' concerns the role of the public interest. The planning system 'exists to protect and promote the public interest'. In deciding whether to grant permission, a planning authority should 'consciously … balance the likely benefits of a proposed development against any potential adverse consequences'.[42] Whereas nuisance protects individual property rights with no public interest defence. Lord Carnwath summed it up in *Coventry v Lawrence*:

> Planning decisions may require individuals to bear burdens for the benefit of others, the local community or the public as a whole. But, as the law stands, it is generally no defence to a claim of nuisance that the activity in question is of benefit to the public.[43]

Lord Neuberger observed that the 'political and economic considerations which properly may play a part in the thinking of the members of a planning authority' are quite irrelevant in nuisance – 'unless the law of nuisance is to be changed fairly radically'.[44] Conversely, planning authorities do not make decisions about common law rights and their protection. They leave this to the courts, through nuisance litigation. The aims and principles are quite different, notwithstanding a degree of overlap.

A second fundamental difference concerns remedies. Courts decline to allow planning permission to displace nuisance law because planners cannot award compensation or any other remedy to those adversely affected by a permitted development. The linkage between property and compensation is an ancient one: Blackstone, having defined private property as 'absolute … sacred and inviolable', accepted that the legislature could limit property rights while providing owners with 'full indemnification … [at] a reasonable price'.[45] When considering the statutory authority defence, the absence of compensation clauses is an 'important indication' that Parliament cannot have intended to protect the activity from nuisance liability.[46] On planning permission, Peter Gibson LJ influentially stated that the courts should be 'slow to acquiesce in the extinction of private [property] rights *without compensation*'.[47] The Supreme Court strongly agrees.[48]

Lord Neuberger contrasted the special procedure for 'nationally significant infrastructure projects' like airports or power stations.[49] The Planning Act 2008 expressly excludes a nuisance claim when such an infrastructure project is

---

[42] *Coventry v Lawrence (No 1)* [2014] AC 822 [192]–[193] Lord Carnwath.
[43] ibid [193].
[44] ibid [95].
[45] W Blackstone, *Commentaries on the Laws of England: Volume I* (Oxford, 1765) 135.
[46] *Allen v Gulf Oil Refining Ltd* [1981] AC 1001, 1016 (Lord Edmund-Davies).
[47] *Wheeler v JJ Saunders Ltd* [1996] Ch 19, 35 (emphasis added).
[48] *Coventry* (n 42) [165] (Lord Mance) [222] (Lord Carnwath).
[49] ibid [90] (see also [196] Lord Carnwath).

approved by ministerial order – but the statute expressly grants compensation to landowners 'injuriously affected'. By contrast the *absence* of statutory compensation in *ordinary* planning procedures (which are also *not* explicitly made a defence in nuisance) indicates that they should not affect landowners' rights to claim in tort.

Third come significant procedural differences. Individuals are entitled to bring nuisance actions to seek protection of their property rights. That sounds like a statement of the obvious – but planning permission is quite different. In the leading case Peter Gibson LJ described a system of 'administrative decisions which cannot be appealed and are difficult to challenge'.[50] Staughton LJ enlarged the point: 'The process by which planning permission is obtained allows for objections [to be made] by those who might be adversely affected, but they have no right of appeal if their objections are overruled'.[51] Planning decisions can be challenged through judicial review if *ultra vires* on public law grounds – but not appealed against on their merits. Not is it possible for those aggrieved by a planning decision to sue the authority in negligence – no duty of care arises since 'it would be wholly detrimental to the proper process of considering planning applications if the [planning authority] had to have regard to the private law interests of any persons who might be affected by the grant of permission'.[52] The court noted that although individuals could not sue the planning authority, they would have a nuisance claim against the activity. Indeed then, the preservation of nuisance liability (notwithstanding planning permission) makes it more palatable to protect planning decisions against challenge. The difficulty of challenge in turn justifies the preservation of nuisance. The systems' separate functions complement each other.

Therefore reasons of substance, remedies and procedure deny the 'statutory authority' defence to planning permission. That does not mean planning permission is always irrelevant. In *Coventry v Lawrence* it was accepted that if a planning authority has, using its expertise, laid down detailed mitigating conditions (eg how loud a noise may be made at what times of day), this could be relevant in a nuisance claim.[53] As Lord Carnwath said, 'a major problem when dealing with nuisance by noise is to establish any objective and verifiable criteria', and there was something to be said for using an authority's 'view of a fair balance' as the starting point in nuisance.[54] But as he accepted, such a 'benchmark' was ('of course') not binding on the court. Its usefulness would vary from case to case. In *Coventry* itself the undetailed planning permission offered 'little help'.

The evidential 'benchmarking' effect is not symmetrical: although it is no defence to comply with the permission, *failure* to comply points towards

---

[50] *Wheeler v JJ Saunders Ltd* [1996] Ch 19, 35.
[51] ibid 28.
[52] *Lam v Torbay BC* [1998] PLCR 30, 49.
[53] *Coventry* (n 42) [96] (Lord Neuberger).
[54] ibid [224], [226].

liability: since 'contravention of planning or environmental controls is unlikely to be reasonable'.[55] Similarly Lord Cooke suggested that erecting a building which exceeds permitted height or location restrictions would not be a 'reasonable use' of land: the planning permission would be taken to set 'what is acceptable in the community'.[56] Sandy Steel notes a problem with this: to the extent that defendants' freedom to use their land is being curbed by the terms of the planning permission, why should those *defendants'* private law rights be overridden by an administrative process without compensation (ie do the arguments above not cut both ways)?[57]

More significantly however, the Supreme Court in *Coventry v Lawrence* overruled the '*Gillingham*' line of cases. This had suggested that 'strategic' planning permission for 'major developments' could 'alter the character of a neighbourhood [with] the effect of rendering innocent activities which prior to the change would have been an actionable nuisance'.[58] Speaking for the majority, Lord Neuberger held it had been wrong to treat such grants of planning permission any differently.[59] All the same objections (substance, procedure, absence of compensation) applied. Also, the precise meaning of 'major developments' was obscure and drawing the distinction 'a recipe for uncertainty'. Indeed it would be 'paradoxical' if the larger the development (and so the greater the nuisance), the harder it would be to bring a claim.

Lord Carnwath dissented on this point, arguing that 'exceptionally' planning permission might bring about a 'fundamental change in the pattern of uses, which cannot sensibly be ignored in assessing the character of the area against which the acceptability of the defendant's activity is to be judged'.[60] Although this was not accepted by the majority, we have seen that there is now a special statutory category of national infrastructure projects expressly immunised from nuisance liability. While the majority do not put it this way, it could be that this clearly-defined statutory exception has taken over the function of the considerably less certain *Gillingham* doctrine at common law.[61] (Lee argues, however, that the 'safeguard' is not comprehensive – since there may be significant public activities which fall outside the 2008 Act.)[62] There is very little scope for relying on planning permission as a defence following *Coventry v Lawrence*.

---

[55] *Barr* (n 37) [76].
[56] *Hunter v Canary Wharf* [1997] AC 655, 721.
[57] S Steel, 'The Locality Principle in Private Nuisance' [2017] *CLJ* 145, 166.
[58] *Gillingham Borough Council v Medway (Chatham) Dock Co Ltd* [1993] QB 343, 359.
[59] *Coventry* (n 42) [86]–[91].
[60] ibid [223].
[61] M Lee, 'Tort Law and Regulation: Planning and Nuisance' [2011] *JPL* 986, 990 (Planning Act 2008 'has itself identified "strategic" [planning] decisions').
[62] M Lee, 'Private Nuisance in the Supreme Court' [2014] *JPEL* 705, 708.

Regulation and the Scope of Nuisance

We have seen that in *Barr v Biffa*, the court refused to change longstanding principles of nuisance to 'march in step' with the increasing volume of modern regulation. In straightforward nuisance cases, regulation will not displace well-established liabilities. It may be different when courts are considering future development of nuisance law.[63] In *Hunter v Canary Wharf* Lord Hoffmann declined to extend nuisance to interference with television signals. He thought it 'far more appropriate' to consider such developments, affecting 'many people over a large area', through the planning process: 'It enables the issues to be debated before an expert forum at a planning inquiry and gives the developer the advantage of certainty as to what he is entitled to build'.[64] This was more cost-effective than the unpredictable prospect of nuisance claims by an 'indeterminate number of plaintiffs, each claiming compensation in a relatively modest amount'. (On the other hand, as Lord Goff noted, the problem may not be appreciated until after the building has received approval and been built – when only a tort claim would provide protection.)[65] Although Lord Hoffmann did not view planning permission as a defence, the planning system was an important reason against expanding the scope of nuisance. In *Fearn v Tate Gallery*, Etherton MR similarly held that although not a defence

> planning laws and regulations would be a better medium for controlling inappropriate overlooking than the uncertainty and lack of sophistication of an extension of the common law cause of action for nuisance.[66]

As seen, Lord Goff also thought (considering *Rylands v Fletcher*) that extensions of strict liability for dangerous activities should be left to Parliament.[67] In the leading case of *Transco*, Lord Hoffmann expanded the point. Statute could impose absolute liability 'far stricter than under the rule in *Rylands v Fletcher*'. Conversely the legislation could exempt certain activities from liability altogether. The result was to 'avoid all argument over which insurers should bear the loss'.[68] Lord Hoffmann is undoubtedly correct that legislation can create absolute clarity. Parliament can lay down clear, certain and even arbitrary rules in a way that the common law cannot. The common law is based on principles which lack a canonical exhaustive statement (a point notoriously true of *Rylands v Fletcher* liability).

The courts compare government regulation and common law when deciding whether to expand nuisance to new situations – and the growing importance

---

[63] See *Coventry* (n 42) [198] (Lord Carnwath commenting on his own judgment in *Barr v Biffa*).
[64] [1997] AC 655, 710.
[65] ibid 687.
[66] [2020] EWCA Civ 104; [2020] Ch 621, [83].
[67] *Cambridge Water Co Ltd v Eastern Counties Leather plc* [1994] 2 AC 264, 305.
[68] *Transco* (n 13) [42].

of regulation in the modern state seems only to encourage 'doctrinal conservatism' in the common law of torts. Is this judicial faith in the regulatory process justified?

Remedies and Planning Permission

English law has embarked on an important debate about nuisance remedies. Its strong, century-long presumption in favour of injunctions was questioned by all five judges in *Coventry v Lawrence*.[69] There is now considerably greater scope to award damages in lieu of an injunction. The role of the public interest is the central question, and in particular grants of planning permission.

Prior to *Coventry v Lawrence* the law was extremely clear. The test laid down in *Shelfer*'s case authoritatively governed the question.[70] Once liability in nuisance was established the court would invariably grant an injunction as a matter of course, in all but exceptional cases.[71] (The approach was less strict in 'rights to light' cases,[72] which typically involve mandatory injunctions with the 'drastic' effect of ordering demolition of buildings put up in good faith.)[73] Lord Denning MR characteristically challenged this orthodoxy in *Miller v Jackson*.[74] The reaction was swift and decisive. *Shelfer*'s case was reasserted as the determinative authority.[75] Indeed it was arguably *over*-extended to lights cases.[76]

Although remedy was not a live issue before the Supreme Court in *Coventry*,[77] all the judges expressed consciously obiter views on 'the most important aspect of this case'.[78] In particular note Lord Neuberger (with whom the others agreed, subject to 'differences in emphasis')[79] and Lord Sumption. There were two main criticisms of the prevailing approach. First, it was *too* clear and settled: by adhering so 'slavishly' to *Shelfer*, the courts had fettered what should be 'a classic exercise of discretion'.[80] Second, it was wrong to exclude the public interest when this could 'obviously' be a relevant factor.[81] We now examine these points.[82]

An obvious criticism is that *Coventry* unsettles the law. Lord Neuberger indeed accepted that 'a degree of uncertainty is inevitable' when developing new

---

[69] *Coventry* (n 42).
[70] *Shelfer v City of London Electric Lighting Co* [1895] 1 Ch 287.
[71] *Dennis v MOD* [2003] EWHC 793 (QB) (no injunction against RAF aircraft).
[72] *Colls v Home & Colonial Store Ltd* [1904] AC 179.
[73] *Coventry* (n 42) [247] (Lord Carnwath).
[74] [1977] QB 966.
[75] *Kennaway v Thompson* [1981] QB 88, *Watson v Croft Promo-Sport* [2009] 3 All ER 249.
[76] *Regan v Paul Properties* [2007] Ch 135.
[77] *Coventry* (n 42) [238].
[78] ibid [171] (Lord Clarke).
[79] ibid [132] (Lord Neuberger).
[80] ibid [120] (Lord Neuberger), [159], [161] (Lord Sumption).
[81] ibid [124].
[82] See further D Nolan, 'Injunctions' in W Day and S Worthington (eds), *Challenging Private Law: Lord Sumption on the Supreme Court* (Oxford, Hart, 2020).

principles case-by-case.⁸³ This uncertainty could be mitigated, but not entirely removed, by seeking to give clear guidance 'to ensure that, while the discretion is not fettered, its manner of exercise is as predictable as possible'.⁸⁴ Certainty is a matter of degree. While equitable remedies are always a matter of discretion, they are governed by very well-established rules in other areas of private law. The rules governing specific performance in contract law are a good example (albeit the converse of the *Shelfer* approach: specific performance is the exceptional remedy in contract, damages normally providing an adequate response).⁸⁵

Jason Varuhas identifies a general trend away from strict protection of rights in private law, as courts increasingly favour a general balancing of all relevant interests (public and third party interests in addition to the rights of the litigating parties).⁸⁶ *Coventry v Lawrence* exemplifies the shift: 'Rights, quintessentially moral precepts, are sacrificed to broader societal concerns, especially wealth maximisation'.⁸⁷ Indeed writing as an 'unrepentant property lawyer' Martin Dixon criticises the Supreme Court for undermining 'the whole point of proprietary rights', the owner's absolute control over how their land is used.⁸⁸ But Lord Sumption had dismissed views of this kind as 'unduly moralistic', noting that 'if taken at face value would justify the grant of an injunction in *all* cases, which is plainly not the law'.⁸⁹ The criticism might be overstated given Lord Neuberger's concession that injunction should still be the 'prima facie' remedy, with the onus on the defendant to show why an injunction should *not* be granted.⁹⁰

Planning permission divided opinion. Most of the court favoured Lord Neuberger's view.⁹¹ Courts must take the public interest into account. It would clearly support an injunction if third parties in addition to the claimant were badly affected by the nuisance; conversely an injunction might be refused if it would close a business involving waste of resources, or job losses. If planning permission had been granted, and the planning authority had fairly taken public benefit into account in granting authorisation, that too would clearly be relevant. But Lord Neuberger deliberately went no further – planning permission was merely one factor to be weighed up. Lord Carnwath, agreeing, approved Maria Lee's view that 'The continued strength of private nuisance in a regulatory state probably depends on a more flexible approach to remedies'.⁹²

---

⁸³ *Coventry* (n 42) [132].
⁸⁴ ibid [121].
⁸⁵ ibid [159] (Lord Sumption).
⁸⁶ JNE Varuhas, 'The Socialisation of Private Law: Balancing Private Right and Public Good' (2021) 137 *LQR* 141.
⁸⁷ ibid 159.
⁸⁸ M Dixon, 'The Sound of Silence' [2014] *Conv* 79, 84.
⁸⁹ *Coventry* (n 42) [160] (emphasis added).
⁹⁰ ibid [121]. See Nolan (n 82) 172 (the *strength* of this presumption will have 'critical importance').
⁹¹ *Coventry* (n 42) [124]–[127].
⁹² ibid [239]–[240]; M Lee, 'Tort Law and Regulation: Planning and Nuisance' (2011) 8 *JPL* 986.

Lord Sumption alone went considerably further.[93] While he agreed with Lord Neuberger that planning permission is irrelevant to *liability* in nuisance,[94] he queried whether tort could without stultifying the planning system grant injunctions against activities that a planning authority had authorised. Lord Sumption tentatively concluded that to save nuisance from 'incoherence', 'it may well be that an injunction should as a matter of principle not be granted in a case where a use of land to which objection is taken requires and has received planning permission'.[95]

This suggestion is particularly controversial. It raises again a question debated about the leading false imprisonment case, *Lumba*.[96] Can a strict separation between liability and remedy be maintained, or does the award of a weaker remedy undermine the prior finding of liability? Regarding *Lumba*, the fear is that nominal damages undermine false imprisonment's strict protection against unlawful detention. In nuisance, that refusing an injunction because planning permission exists would apparently conflict with the orthodoxy (accepted even by Lord Sumption) that planning is *not a defence*. As Nolan says, the well-founded concerns about allowing administrative procedures to override property rights retain their force even if the focus shifts from liability to remedy.[97] At least in nuisance, damages will clearly be substantial and not merely nominal. Indeed Lord Neuberger indicated that damages in lieu of injunction should arguably compensate the claimant's inability to enforce their rights, 'assessed by reference to the *benefit to the defendant* of not suffering an injunction'.[98] Again, this was obiter and Lord Neuberger's suggestion of a gain-based element was pointedly not endorsed by other members of the court.[99]

Lord Sumption's approach can be criticised for overstating both the suitability of damages and the problems of injunctions. On damages, Lord Mance pointed out that financial remedies may be inadequate for nuisances suffered by home-owners, since peaceful living is valued 'for reasons largely if not entirely independent of money'.[100] On injunctions, Lord Sumption's charge of 'incoherence' assumes that an injunction inevitably leads to cessation of the activity (and thus 'will operate in practice in exactly the same way as a refusal of planning permission, but without regard to the factors which a planning authority would be bound to take into account').[101] But this too can be questioned. As historians such as Pontin have shown, the injunctions obtained in several

---

[93] *Coventry* (n 42) [155]–[158].
[94] See 'Planning Permission: No Defence' above.
[95] *Coventry* (n 42) [157], [161]. See also *Wheeler v Saunders* [1996] Ch 19, 35 (Peter Gibson LJ).
[96] *Lumba v Home Secretary* [2012] 1 AC 245. (See ch 2, 'Debate 2: Remedies and Vindication of Rights'.)
[97] Nolan (n 82) 170.
[98] *Coventry* (n 42) [128] (emphasis added).
[99] Cf *Coventry* ibid [173] (Lord Clarke), [248] (Lord Carnwath).
[100] ibid [168].
[101] ibid [157].

leading cases never shut down the defendant's activities entirely. They might have relocated, bought the claimant's land or otherwise compromised with them, or adapted their processes to continue without creating a nuisance.[102] Judges were aware that an injunction could encourage new methods of cleaning up industrial activities.[103] It is a standard matter for the court to facilitate such working-around by suspending the injunction for a period (ignored by the Supreme Court in *Coventry*).[104] Indeed Nolan argues that courts should weigh as a positive factor in favour of inunctions 'the possibility of beneficial ameliorative measures', the injunction being an incentive for 'innovative ways of reducing or eliminating the interference'.[105] Conversely if all possible mitigating measures have already been taken,[106] only complete elimination of the activity can avoid the nuisance.

Stepping back from *Coventry v Lawrence* we finally consider Stephen Tromans' classic critique of nuisance injunctions.[107] Tromans argued that the (then) stringency of the pro-injunction law could backfire and damage *claimants*' interests. He alleged that *substantive* nuisance doctrine recognises narrower liability, or wider defences, in situations where injunctions would be inappropriate. Some examples cited (eg 'one off' nuisances; landlords' restricted liability for tenants' nuisances) seem debatable. But Tromans is surely correct that the dominance of injunctions entails the narrow statutory authority defence.[108]

In cases like *Allen v Gulf Oil* courts have no choice but to uphold the defence because if they found nuisance they would be obliged to restrain, by an injunction, the activity authorised by Parliament. As Lord Roskill said, that would be 'illogical', defeating the statute's very purpose.[109] But Lord Denning MR had suggested a 'new principle' for construing statutes in nuisance cases.[110] Although the court should not grant injunctions to 'render useless' what Parliament had authorised, it did not follow that there should be no *damages*. On the contrary, Lord Denning said 'in principle property should not be damaged compulsorily except on proper compensation [for nuisance] being made ... as part of the legitimate expenses of [the defendant's] operation'.[111]

Lord Denning's suggestion has not been taken up. Jolowicz's contemporary criticism of *Allen* noted that the House of Lords failed to take seriously its power to award damages in lieu of an injunction. Yet it was 'almost perverse' for the court's 'reluctance to downgrade the plaintiff's remedy from an

---

[102] See 'Nuisance and Pollution Control: Underrated' below.
[103] *Imperial Gas Light & Coke Co v Broadbent* (1859) 7 HLC 600, 611 (Lord Campbell LC).
[104] Nolan (n 82) 170.
[105] ibid.
[106] Nolan (n 82) cites *Miller v Jackson* (n 74 above).
[107] S Tromans, 'Nuisance – Prevention or Payment?' [1982] *CLJ* 87.
[108] See 'The Defence of Statutory Authority' above.
[109] [1981] AC 1001, 1024.
[110] *Allen v Gulf Oil Refining* [1980] QB 156, 168–69 (CA).
[111] ibid.

injunction to mere damages [to be the reason] for denying the plaintiff redress in any form whatever'.[112] Tromans too criticised

> the absurd situation of one remedy which the courts will not give because it is too drastic, one which they will not give because it is not drastic enough ... The Allens of this world pay dearly for the judicial insistence that the plaintiff get nothing but the best by getting nothing at all.[113]

The court's historic devotion to injunctions is an example of the best being the enemy of the good, that is, preventing lesser protection through damages.

This issue could now be reconsidered following *Coventry v Lawrence*. Despite Lord Denning's claimed novelty there is ancient authority that property rights can be sacrificed to the public interest *only if compensation is paid*.[114] In the course of the nineteenth century, such views lost out to an *absolute* statutory defence (rather than one predicated on payment of compensation).[115] Crucially however, it was a debate between 'the opinions of individual judges on questions of economic and social policy'.[116] It would surely be appropriate to revisit the question posed by Lord Denning in *Allen v Gulf Oil*, rather than let the policy preferences of the majority in the leading nineteenth-century case settle the debate for all time.[117]

Tort and Regulation: Analysis

Maria Lee champions a closer engagement between tort law and public regulation. In her view, tort would condemn itself to social irrelevance if it attempted to ignore the regulatory context. Yet nuisance law currently lacks a proper appreciation of the nature of regulation. The rules examined above establish the irrelevance of planning permission. Lee insists, however, that there is no clear and simple hierarchy between tort and regulation. It is situation-specific, turning on the quality of the regulation in question. The law should take a more nuanced approach.

Other commentators too are critical of the relationship between nuisance and planning permission. Sandy Steel questions *Coventry v Lawrence*.[118] The Supreme Court reaffirmed the 'locality principle' – assessing nuisance in the particular geographical context. (If anything the decision has increased the importance of neighbourhood.) But Steel argues that assessing nuisance by the pattern of land use in a particular area inevitably incorporates a *collective* element. Other landowners' choices (or collective choices by the 'community')

---

[112] JA Jolowicz, 'Should Courts Answer Questions?' [1981] *CLJ* 226, 228–29.
[113] [1982] CLJ 87, 108.
[114] See Blackstone (text to n 45).
[115] See *Wildtree Hotels v Harrow LBC* [2001] 2 AC 1, 8–9 (Lord Hoffmann).
[116] ibid.
[117] *Hammersmith & City Railway v Brand* (1869) LR 4 HL 171.
[118] Steel (n 57).

directly affect whether nuisance protects the claimant's land use. Nuisance is not strictly bilateral (examining *solely* the parties to the litigation) but examines the wider pattern of land use in the locality.

Steel does not necessarily welcome this. He certainly does not argue for an instrumental law of nuisance designed (say) to reduce interference by 'zoning' similar activities together, or to maximise society's wealth. Steel's point is simply that the 'locality principle' *inherently* involves some notion of the public interest. According to *St Helen's v Tipping*,[119] on 'sensory' nuisance at least,[120] the court considers 'the place [and] the circumstances' of the alleged nuisance. The law lords expressly referred to the need to accommodate industry in the great manufacturing towns of Victorian England. Simpson deems this a fudge:a refusal to choose too clearly between strict liability and an overt public interest defence.[121]

If this 'collective interest' analysis of the 'locality' rule is correct, it sits uneasily with *Coventry v Lawrence*'s dismissal of planning permission. Planning decisions might be the best – or only – direct evidence of collective choices about patterns of land use. Thus as Steel says, the logic of the majority's decision to reject planning permission means that the locality principle is itself problematic.[122] By contrast, Lord Carnwath accepted the relationship between the two.[123] Nuisance often depends on 'locality'. In today's society the mixture of land uses constituting a 'locality' results primarily from planning authority decisions. Lord Carnwath noted that football stadiums often cause serious local disturbance on match days. But nuisance liability would be unlikely; society holds such activities important ones in urban areas by authorising their operation, subject to mitigating planning conditions.

James Penner argues that the locality principle does not involve weighing property rights against the public interest.[124] Its simple common-sense meaning is that people are entitled to expect greater peace and quiet in the countryside, much less in a busy town. Penner fears that crude cost-benefit analysis would seriously weaken environmental protection: it is difficult to quantify diffuse harm to the environment, but easy to appreciate the economic hardship when a polluting factory is shut down with a loss of jobs. 'Taking planning permission to indicate the neighbourhood [locality] standard simply adorns this weakening of protection with a spurious democratic legitimacy'.[125]

Is this dismissive attitude justified? Could planning permission at least provide some evidence of community decisions about what sorts of interference are

---

[119] (1865) 11 HL Cas 642.
[120] Cf ch 10, 'Debate 3: Balancing or Strict Liability? Property Damage, Nuisance and Trespass' (physical damage).
[121] AWB Simpson, 'Victorian Judges and the Problem of Social Cost' in *Leading Cases in the Common Law* (Oxford, Oxford University Press, 1995).
[122] Steel (n 57) 166.
[123] *Coventry* (n 42) [180]–[185].
[124] JE Penner, 'Nuisance and the Character of the Neighbourhood' (1993) 5 Jo Env Law 1.
[125] ibid 14.

tolerable in given neighbourhoods, as Lord Carnwath suggests? In Lee's view, no categorical answer can be given. The quality of regulatory decision-making varies. It depends on the kind of administrative process laid down by law, and how it operated in practice in a given case. Lee recommends that courts pay closer attention to these questions of process. As seen, in the *Hunter* case Lord Hoffmann thought the planning system a superior mechanism to resolve the problem of tall buildings. As Lee stresses however, the Canary Wharf tower was built under a special statutory system for the economic regeneration of the derelict London docks.[126] The area's ministerial designation for general redevelopment was *designed* to bypass the usual constraints of local authority planning control. Lord Hoffmann indeed noted that 'the normal protection offered to the community ... was largely removed' and local residents could feel aggrieved that their convenience had been sacrificed to Parliament's view of the national economic interest.[127] But he concluded, this particular local 'problem' could not justify a change in nationally applicable nuisance law; 'ordinarily' the planning system allows residents to object, and thereby to seek administrative resolution to signal-interference problems.

Lee thinks nuisance law failed the claimants in *Hunter*. They were left to suffer serious inconvenience without compensation. She is particularly critical of Lord Hoffmann's reliance on the planning process when Docklands' 'enterprise zone' designation intentionally removed the usual planning protection. Courts must pay much closer attention to the actual quality of the decision-making, in Lee's view. (Consider, for example, a defendant's unsuccessful submission that the nature of a locality may be altered by a 'planning process which involved a *fair and conclusive adjudication* on matters of public interest'.)[128] Lee accepts this would require a potentially difficult inquiry into the particular grant of planning permission (was all relevant information taken into account? Were objections properly considered?). She also accepts that it is difficult to say whether the actual permission for the Canary Wharf tower was a 'regulatory failure'. Parliament consciously by-passed local planning processes to expedite the Dockland redevelopment, precisely because 'parochial' local councils might prioritise existing land use (and existing residents) over new development.

An obvious objection to Lee's approach is that it would involve courts in political and factual controversy. However, Lord Carnwath cited Lee's worth with approval in *Coventry v Lawrence*, to justify assessment of the quality of the regulatory process when determining its effect on tort liability.[129] His Lordship

---

[126] M Lee, '*Hunter v Canary Wharf Ltd* (1997)' in C Mitchell and P Mitchell (eds), *Landmark Cases in the Law of Tort* (Oxford, Hart, 2010).

[127] [1997] AC 655, 710.

[128] *Watson v Croft Promo-Sport* [2009] EWCA Civ 15; [2009] 3 All ER 249, [29] (emphasis added).

[129] *Coventry* (n 42) [198] citing M Lee, 'Nuisance and Regulation in the Court of Appeal' [2013] JPL 277.

noted that such an exercise has frequently been carried out to justify courts rejecting the relevance of planning permission.[130] For example in *Wheeler v Saunders*, the grant had serious procedural flaws. The defendants' application for planning permission had given the 'misleading' impression that it would not intensify their pig-farming operations. The planners had also failed to consult the council's own environmental health department. Peter Gibson LJ described the grant of permission as 'incomprehensible'.[131] Faced with such a procedurally questionable planning process, little wonder that the court was unenthusiastic about allowing it to override the claimant's property rights. Other examples of procedural flaws include public inquiries allowing applicants to dictate their own acceptable levels of noise,[132] or a local authority granting permission to its own tenant.[133]

Controversy is inherent in balancing the public interest against private rights, as Lee fully accepts.[134] Even apparently neutral, obviously just principles can prove controversial. For example, it popular to call for 'polluters to pay' so that goods and services reflect their true (environmental and social) cost. But this is 'likely to involve regressive redistribution' – a more severe impact on lower-income groups, who spend a proportionately greater amount of their income on goods and services.[135] One reaction is, of course, to exclude all public interest considerations from nuisance. But Lee thinks such 'pure' approaches unattractive and unrealistic. Their 'purity' is an overreaction to a position that few people hold – the suggestion that nuisance liability should be determined *solely and directly* by weighing up the public interest. That is an Aunt Sally. Lee stresses that this is *not* how nuisance law is structured, nor should it be. The real task involves a balance: 'to reconcile the internal demands of tort, including its correlative structure and the centrality of justice between the parties, with broader collective considerations'.[136] Pure approaches at either end of the spectrum (eg rights-based accounts; Law and Economics) distract us from that task.

One problem, if we accept that that is the proper 'task' of nuisance law, is 'to discipline the unruliness of public interests' (as Lee puts it).[137] Its definition is obviously contestable. We cannot designate even 'environmental protection' as an uncontroversial public good. Its pursuit may close socially

---

[130] *Coventry* (n 42) [205], [212] (compare discussion in M Lee, 'Tort Law and Regulation: Planning and Nuisance' [2011] *JPL* 986).

[131] [1996] Ch 19, 36.

[132] *Watson* [2008] EWHC 759 (QB) | [2008] 3 All ER 1171, [54]–[56].

[133] *Tetley v Chitty* [1986] 1 All ER 663.

[134] Lee, 'The Public Interest in Private Nuisance: Collectives and Communities in Tort' [2015] *CLJ* 329.

[135] AI Ogus and GM Richardson, 'Economics and the Environment: A Study of Private Nuisance' [1977] *CLJ* 284, 319. (On the wider economic question cf A Thomas, 'Reassessing the Regressivity of the VAT' (OECD, 2000).)

[136] Lee (n 134) 333.

[137] ibid.

valuable industries, creating unemployment; and/or increase the cost of necessary public utilities (energy, water etc). Noise nuisance cases have often led to the loss of valuable public recreation. That there is such 'scholarly and judicial suspicion of the public interest' surely flows from the complex 'social, political, and economic' judgments that need to be made about it. Its definition is elusive in the abstract and controversial in concrete cases. No wonder that courts (and private law scholars) push these questions onto regulatory bodies, deferring to their superior information, expertise and legitimacy. Lee nevertheless suggests caution. Blanket deference in every case may overrate how well a given regulator works in practice. She questions the 'haste' with which courts sometimes defer to regulators (eg Lord Hoffmann's comments on the planning system in *Hunter*). There should instead be 'closer examination of the *limitations* of regulation'. Courts should investigate 'the empirical reality of a regulatory scheme' where used as a defence (or the claim is that tort would disrupt it).

Lee stresses that her approach should *not* be mischaracterised as requiring tort law's complete displacement by public regulation. On the contrary she is critical of *Marcic v Thames Water* where the court exceptionally held that the Water Industry Act 1991 'occupied the field', 'pre-empting' the common law altogether.[138] Such questions are inevitably difficult when Parliament has neither expressly preserved nor expressly curtailed the common law. (A glance at the tort of breach of statutory duty shows similar problems – and the futility of imploring the legislature to give a clearer answer.)[139] The *Marcic* dispute involved different groups' clashing interests (victims of flooding; customers facing higher water bills; Thames Water shareholders fearing lower dividends), not a true general 'public interest' question. The sums of money involved were large (about £1 billion to remedy all comparable flooding problems in the company's area).[140] However, Lee argues the judges deferred too readily to the regulatory scheme. They had an unjustifiably 'rosy' view of the industry regulator's performance of its tasks, given the dispute's history. Lord Nicholls held that the legislation struck a reasonable balance despite the fact that 'In Mr Marcic's case matters plainly went awry' because it had taken so long to alleviate the flooding of his property. Given that demonstrable flaw, Lee thinks Lord Nicholls wrong to conclude that 'the malfunctioning of the statutory scheme on this occasion does not cast doubt on its overall fairness as a scheme'.[141] Thames Water had (by the time of the House of Lords' decision) finally done the remedial work. That was surely influenced by Mr Marcic's nuisance claim,

---

[138] [2004] 2 AC 42. See M Lee, 'Occupying the Field: Tort and the Pre-emptive Statute' in TT Arvind and J Steele (eds), *Tort Law and the Legislature: Common Law, Statute and the Dynamics of Legal Change* (Oxford, Hart, 2013).

[139] *Cutler v Wandsworth Stadium* [1949] AC 398, 410 (Lord du Parcq).

[140] *Marcic v Thames Water* [2001] 3 All ER 698, [89] (evidence 'imprecise to the point of vagueness') (QBD).

[141] *Marcic* [2004] 2 AC 42 [43].

which focused the water company's attention on his situation. In future, after that the Water Industry Act was held to occupy the field, tort's 'publicity' function will be unavailable. Lee also points to the distinctive values that tort protects. In particular, courts are better able to protect property rights, especially when it will be costly and therefore unpopular.

Marcic seems an unusual case. Nolan argues that it turned on the specific situation of the privatised water industry. *Marcic* should not be seen as the 'harbinger of a trend in English law towards immunity from tort liability for activities conducted under regulatory oversight'.[142] In the light of Lee's criticisms, a narrow interpretation of *Marcic* should be encouraged.

Conclusion

The interrelation of tort and regulation is complex. The statutory authority defence is a special case. It depends ultimately on the constitutional imperative of Parliament's sovereignty, which the law of nuisance cannot contradict.[143] Other forms of regulation, lacking Parliament's direct authority, do not compel similar deference. The courts are accordingly sceptical about the relevance of government regulation, above all planning permission.

Yet Maria Lee's analysis of tort and regulation avoids easy answers or a clear hierarchy. Much depends on the details of particular regulatory processes ('regulation' is not all the same) and how well it has actually performed. We have noted Lord Carnwath's examination of such questions in *Coventry v Lawrence*. This surely informed his more nuanced approach to the planning permission question. As seen, he would 'exceptionally' allow strategic planning decisions to alter the character of the locality – but only where the authority demonstrated a 'considered assessment ... of the appropriate balance between public and private interests'.[144] Fascinatingly, whereas Carnwath LJ eloquently defended nuisance law's traditional autonomy from regulation in *Barr v Biffa*,[145] in *Coventry* he now questioned his earlier judgment. *Barr v Biffa* had been 'an accurate reflection of the historical position' yet could be criticised as 'overly simplistic' if taken as 'blueprint for the future development of [nuisance] law'.[146] Whereas Lord Neuberger's broad-brush remark that 'No doubt all planning applications take into account the public interest' fits with the majority's blanket dismissal of planning permission's relevance.[147] As Lee puts it, 'this reluctance to discriminate between administrative decisions goes a long way to explaining

---

[142] D Nolan, 'Tort and Regulation' in J Goudkamp et al (eds), *Taking Law Seriously: Essays in Honour of Peter Cane* (Oxford, Hart, 2021) 193.

[143] D Nolan, 'Nuisance, Planning and Regulation: The Limits of Statutory Authority' in A Dyson et al, *Defences in Tort* (Oxford, Hart, 2015).

[144] *Coventry* (n 42) [223].

[145] See ibid [92] (Lord Neuberger) on *Barr v Biffa* [2013] QB 455.

[146] *Coventry* [198] (Lord Carnwath).

[147] ibid [91].

Lord Neuberger's approach'.[148] But an obvious drawback of Lee's examination of the quality of regulation in each case is that 'the likely complexity of such enquiries threatens to undercut any advantage deference [to regulation] might otherwise offer in terms of simplification of the adjudicative task'.[149]

A more differentiated approach to regulation may yet rehabilitate the relevance of planning permission, where the public authority has given proper consideration to public interest issues that courts inevitably find difficult to resolve. When so much of nuisance law (balancing interests, the 'locality' principle) implicitly takes the public interest into account, it would be odd sweepingly to dismiss direct and reliable evidence when available. While maintaining that tort is independent from regulation, with separate aims and structures, Nolan accepts that where relevant (as with the nuisance 'balance'), standards laid down in regulation can usefully guide courts in tort cases.[150] (This is seen right across the law – as when driving in excess of statutory speed limits is highly relevant to, without being necessarily conclusive of, the question of 'negligence' at common law.) Nolan concludes that tort and regulation can be 'mutually complementary'. Tort correctly does not pay 'absolute deference' to regulations formulated for purposes other than the protection of individual rights. Outside the special situation of statutory authority (obedience to Parliament's will) or exceptional cases like *Marcic*, regulation should not be conclusive. There should not be a general 'regulatory compliance' defence.[151] But regulation can certainly inform tort adjudication, and should where appropriate be 'incorporated into [tort's] analytical frameworks'.[152]

Debate 3

Pollution and the Industrial Revolution – Nuisance in the Nineteenth (and the Twenty-First) Century

Should tort law be revived as a weapon against pollution? To decide whether tort or public regulation is the better solution to a social problem, they must be compared *empirically* using the facts of experience. Curiously, the fact-based literature is mostly historical. A body of research considers the role and the failures of both nuisance and statutory regulation in the nineteenth century. It was a time of unprecedented pollution from the new factories of the industrial revolution. Also, with rapidly expanded urban living, water pollution from sanitation (ie the invention of flushing toilets and modern sewerage) created terrible environmental problems downstream. It was a time of technical and legal

---

[148] M Lee, 'Private Nuisance in the Supreme Court: *Coventry v Lawrence*' [2014] *JPEL* 705.
[149] Nolan (n 82) 208.
[150] ibid.
[151] Compare Consumer Protection Act 1987 s.4(1)(a); *Wilkes v Depuy International* [2018] QB 627 [97]–[101] (compliance with product standards and regulations may have 'considerable weight' without being conclusive).
[152] ibid 181.

innovation. The standard view is that common law nuisance proved utterly inadequate to address these problems, for which statutory regulation enforced by governmental agencies was the only solution. However, Ben Pontin has challenged the consensus in his revisionist legal history.

The Received Historical Account

Classic articles by Brenner and McLaren established the conventional view of Victorian nuisance law.[153] They broadly agree that nuisance did very little to address the urgent social problems created by pollution, and that legislation had to come to the rescue. The reason for tort's inadequacy was more debatable. Brenner argues that the courts deliberately modified nuisance's historical strictness to protect industrial defendants. It was a clear policy choice: 'the legislature, the courts, and substantial segments of the public did favor industrialization, and they were anxious not to burden industry with damage actions'.[154] The stakes had become much higher. While in early modern England courts had willingly obliged noisome activities (soap-boiling or brick-building) to relocate from crowded urban areas in nuisance litigation, it was quite another thing to close a factory employing thousands of people. Although an overt 'public interest' defence was rejected, the 'locality principle' approved in *St Helen's v Tipping* led to much the same effect. It weighed 'comfort' against economic interests, and preferred the latter. In heavily polluted manufacturing towns the law of nuisance 'hardly existed'. Given *prevalent* filthy air and water, it was 'virtually impossible' to claim for anything short of physical damage ('To win a nuisance action against an industrial firm one practically had to prove trespass to land').[155] Nuisance demonstrably did nothing to prevent horrifying pollution.[156] Brenner remarks that given technical limitations at the time, and the presence of more urgent problems (eg cholera from undrained towns), it is hard to say that the low priority given to pollution was the wrong public policy choice. He also suggests a stricter law of nuisance might have made little difference. Still, Brenner concludes, the courts did not 'need to empty the nuisance standard of nearly all its contents of minimum decency'.[157]

McLaren disagrees that there was such a clear and conscious transformation of nuisance doctrine. The common law had long been committed to strict protection of property. As Bramwell B's judgments suggested, the tradition could

---

[153] JF Brenner, 'Nuisance Law and the Industrial Revolutions' (1974) 3 *JLS* 403; JPS McLaren, 'Nuisance Law and the Industrial Revolution – Some Lessons from Social History' (1983) 3 *OJLS* 155.

[154] Brenner, ibid 408.

[155] ibid 431.

[156] The Lords Select Committee on Noxious Vapours (1863) focused on St Helen's in the year of Tipping's famous case, finding desolation and serious respiratory diseases (in Brenner's words 'a wasteland').

[157] Brenner (n 153) 432.

be bolstered by contemporary economic theories of cost-internalisation.[158] While Bramwell's theoretical approach was unusual, the judiciary as a whole were conservative and committed to the 'tenacious notion of the sanctity of residential property or the landed estate'.[159] The doctrinal picture was equivocal. For every judge arguing that some pollution had to be tolerated in the cause of economic development, another reasoned that a stricter approach would encourage new technology to improve public health. Nuisance cases were surprisingly uncommon given the scale of the problem. When disputes reached court, the judges hesitated before siding with the industrialist rather than the polluted plaintiff. There were, in truth, deep divisions in legal opinion. The common law was not 'monolithic' and it 'could well have encouraged the victim of industrial pollution, as it may have done the perpetrator'.[160]

Yet McLaren thinks that the doctrinal continuity of nuisance was ultimately irrelevant. Even in the eighteenth century when '*sic utere tuo*' was unquestionably still the governing principle, nuisance law had not prevented serious pollution. For McLaren, the restrictions on nuisance were not so much doctrinal as *social* factors. These explain why there was strikingly little litigation until the 1850s, when the industrial revolution (which 'shatter[ed] the peace and tranquillity of every community which it touched') was very well advanced. Some of the barriers to claiming applied universally: for example litigation's great cost and the evidential difficulties of proving *which* factory chimney caused pollution (since joint and several liability for concurrent 'contributions' was not then recognised).[161] But the problems affected different social classes very differently:

> the urban working class were the prime victims of industrialization [but] the least well placed politically and economically to do anything to remedy or temper it. The availability of legal action to those who were not only in the employ of the polluters, but also whose domestic existence was ordered and living conditions dictated by them was entirely academic.[162]

Whereas middle-class Victorians had resources to avoid polluting factories, by moving to the expanding suburbs. (As McLaren shows, these suburbs were carefully protected from industrialisation by restrictive covenants and developed on well-drained land West (upwind) of industrial areas.) In short, those who could afford to sue usually didn't need to. The main victims of pollution could not afford litigation – and given economic realites and social hierarchy, workers suing their polluting *employer* would have been unthinkable.

Brenner and McLaren agree that tort failed to prevent extensive environmental damage. Brenner notes that *public* nuisance also proved a dead letter.

---

[158] See ch 11, 'Coase's Analysis'.
[159] McLaren (n 153) 193.
[160] ibid 190.
[161] Compare Alkali Act 1881, s 28.
[162] McLaren (n 153) 211.

Notwithstanding the extent of pollution, local authorities seemed unconcerned about it and certainly unwilling to bring prosecutions. (McLaren notes that industrial town councils were dominated by factory owners who would oppose any attempts to enforce the law.) Many polluters benefited from statutory authority which would protect them against indictments for nuisance.[163] Notwithstanding this, public health campaigners turned to the legislature. There were advantages in statutory solutions: 'explicit standards of allowable emission levels of smoke and other effluvia ... [being] best left to legislative control'.[164] But legislation was neither quick to emerge nor particularly effective. Parliament was well aware of the economic danger of closing down entire polluting industries. Thus according to McLaren, government initially showed 'sublime indifference [towards] environmental abuse'.[165] Only when technology allowed pollution to be reduced was legislation politically feasible. For example Simpson notes that the landmark Alkali Act 1863 was passed with basic acceptance by that industry. By contrast, Parliament declined to impose similar pollution limits on copper smelters because no technical means were available to condense copper fumes consistent with this important industry's continuation. Parliament's abstention seems to have triggered Tipping's famous nuisance action against the copper smelters of St Helen's: evidently, restrictions would have to come from common law, not legislation.[166]

Even when such legislation was passed it was not a panacea. As Brenner notes, it could simply replace one kind of pollution with another. Legislation like the Alkali Acts that required removal of pollutants from factory smoke actually increased *river* pollution: instead of sulphuric acid (say) being discharged as gas, its condensed form was simply dumped into any convenient watercourse. It was alarming but not unusual that canals in Bradford were so polluted they could be set alight. Improved drainage and sewerage greatly improved town sanitation, but largely by displacing the problem onto others. Raw sewage was again simply directed into rivers (or the sea), with inevitable harm to water quality and 'amenity' for landowners downstream.

Both technology and legislation improved as the nineteenth century wore on. If the legislation had mixed results then (as Brenner reminds us) that remains true today. Statutory regulation of pollution began in the 1840s when the problem was basically new and 'no legislature anywhere had previously faced a regulatory problem of comparable scope and complexity'.[167] The succession of inquiries and commissions, and resulting legislation, shows that the problem was taken seriously. Eventually that extended to enforcement too. Who would inspect factories and enforce the legislation? This needed the

---

[163] eg *Vaughan v Taff Vale Railway* (1860) 5 Hurl & N 679.
[164] Brenner (n 153) 424.
[165] McLaren (n 153) 220.
[166] Simpson (n 121).
[167] Brenner (n 153) 432.

creation of new agencies, or central government control, in a way that seems obvious today but was absolutely unprecedented two centuries ago. Such state agencies simply did not exist, nor had ever existed in Britain or anywhere else. Eventually, public health concerns drove the necessary governmental reforms:

> resolute action had to wait until progressive forces in local government began to press for and implement substantial urban improvements, and the central government finally accepted the need for radical reform of the institution of local government and the adoption of strong, uniform measures to protect public health.[168]

(On the 'strength' of the measures, note that even under the landmark Public Health Act 1875 it was a defence to show 'that the best available means have been taken for preventing injury thereby to the public health' (section 91) – a defence preserved in statutory nuisance today.)[169]

The conventional historical account therefore holds that despite its slow development, public regulation of pollution eventually fulfilled its potential – taking over from nuisance, which had woefully failed. Tort law then assumed the subsidiary role in environmental protection that it retains to this day.

Nuisance and Pollution Control: Underrated?

Ben Pontin acknowledges Brenner and McLaren's pioneering research. But he disagrees with their extremely negative conclusions about tort law.[170] Pontin rejects Brenner's claim that nuisance doctrine was adjusted to accommodate industrial polluters. The courts consistently favoured *plaintiffs* (typically, upper-class country landowners), consistently dismissed any public interest defence, and consistently issued injunctions to protect property rights. Pontin's distinctive contribution is to analyse what happened *after* a number of leading cases.[171] He argues that nuisance litigation had more positive effects than the critics allow.

Pontin studies various cases where the victorious claimant obtained an injunction against a polluter. Contrary to the concern that underlies much discussion of nuisance and injunctions, Pontin finds that the defendant's activity was *never* closed down altogether, with the consequent economic harm. Sometimes the defendant relocated to an area where it was less likely to face nuisance claims (after *Tipping*, the defendant smelter moved away from the plaintiff's

---

[168] McLaren (n 153) 218.
[169] Environmental Protection Act 1990, s 80(7).
[170] See eg B Pontin, 'Nuisance Law and the Industrial Revolution: A Reinterpretation of Doctrine and Institutional Competence' (2012) 75 *MLR* 1010; B Pontin, 'The Common Law Clean up of the Workshop of the World: More Realism about Nuisance Law's Historic Environmental Achievements' (2013) 40 *JL & Soc* 173.
[171] B Pontin, *Nuisance Law and Environmental Protection: A Study of Nuisance Injunctions in Practice* (Witney, Lawtext Publishing, 2013).

landed estate to the polluted centre of St Helen's – presumably (Pontin notes) further damaging the respiratory health of its working-class inhabitants). On one occasion the successful plaintiff sold his land to the defendant as a 'pollution sink'.[172] But mostly, Pontin finds, the defendant continued their activity but with *improved technical means to reduce pollution*.

Pontin argues that the copper industry, in particular, was cleaned up not by public regulation but by nuisance litigation. The threat of an injunction encouraged copper smelters to innovate. The great chemist Michael Faraday, no less, was engaged to address the problem of flue gas emissions. Ultimately an effective process to condense polluting copper fumes was invented. Pontin comments that nuisance liability was 'pivotal to a multi-million-pound market in pollution abatement technology which made Britain arguably the first broadly green industrial society and economy the world has known'.[173]

The copper industry was not unique. When it came to water treatment, nuisance was again a necessary spur. Pontin considers the protracted litigation by Warwickshire aristocrat Charles Adderley against Birmingham council for discharging untreated sewage, polluting the river on Adderley's country estate.[174] For 40 years until the end of the nineteenth century, Pontin finds, Birmingham was induced to invest in sewage treatment techniques by the threat of Adderley reactivating his litigation, triggering the enforcement of nuisance injunctions by sequestration of the council's assets and powers. In an earlier study, Leslie Rosenthal argued that the courts encouraged 'mutually acceptable compromises through negotiation'.[175] Adderley's initial landmark victory is famous for Page Wood VC's declaration that he would protect the plaintiff's 'clear right' to unpolluted water and it was 'matter of almost absolute indifference' that it would adversely affect the entire population of Birmingham: 'I am not sitting here as a committee for public safety'.[176] When it came to the crunch though, Rosenthal argues, subsequent judges were clearly unwilling to *enforce* the injunctions obtained against Birmingham. They cannot have ignored the calamitous effect of enjoining the city's entire drainage and sewerage system. The courts' pragmatic *deeds* (over remedies) speak louder than Page Wood VC's emotive *words*. Ultimately, social welfare certainly was taken into account.

Nor was the Birmingham case. A contemporary government survey found that 19 out of 20 local councils had invested in sewage treatment under pressure from threatened nuisance suits. Landed estates, owned by rich and powerful men, were being destroyed by untreated sewage. They had the means to bring nuisance claims, with the law on their side. Again Pontin claims that nuisance was one important factor in the 'greening' of the industrial revolution. He is

---

[172] *Farnworth v Manchester Corpn* [1930] AC 171.
[173] (2013) 40 JL & Soc 173, 197.
[174] Commencing with *AG v Birmingham* (1858) 4 Kay & Johnson 528 (Adderley's first great victory).
[175] L Rosenthal, 'Economic Efficiency, Nuisance, and Sewage: New Lessons from *Attorney-General v Birmingham*, 1858–95' (2007) 36 *JLS* 27.
[176] (1858) 4 K & J 528, 539.

dismissive of contemporary public regulation of river pollution, by contrast.[177] Pontin notes that persistently, urban pollution was (literally) dumped on rural areas. As well as sewage, there was greater reliance on electric heating when clean air legislation restricted open fires in town-houses. The power stations to generate the electricity were usually located far away, so that country-dwellers again suffered pollution for the benefit of urban residents.[178] (Mischievously, Pontin suggests that twenty-first-century onshore wind farms display the same tendency.)

Tort litigation could bring wider attention to neglected social problems. In particular, the plaintiff's victory in *Manchester Corporation v Farnworth* (1929) triggered public alarm about Battersea power station, then under construction in London. (Even King George V expressed his concerns.) The result was that very expensive 'scrubbers' were installed at Battersea to prevent sulphur pollution in the capital. (Pontin notes that for many decades afterwards, *rural* power stations still lacked this technology). Mostly however, Pontin dismisses the idea of tort as an early warning 'antenna', flagging up emergent social problems. Nuisance was more often a 'last resort' than an 'early warning', a remedy when public authorities lacked sufficient powers to control pollution or proved reluctant to use them.[179] Nuisance did become slightly more egalitarian in the twentieth Century, with the National Farmers' Union funding the aggrieved farmer's claim against the power station in *Farnworth*, and (government) Legal Aid the leading urban pollution case of *Halsey v Esso*.

Pontin does not claim that public regulation is redundant or ineffective in all cases. Nor does he claim that nuisance is a magic bullet. Pollution's persistence over centuries alongside the tort's existence makes such a thesis untenable. Pontin's approach has (as he accepts) limitations: by focusing on a handful of famous cases we gain a deep understanding of those particular disputes, but it is always dangerous to generalise from a small sample. Nevertheless, Pontin makes a strong case for the retention of nuisance as part of the law's arsenal in the fight against environmental damage. Nuisance is complementary to regulation, not subsidiary. It is 'co-equal, not interstitial' (gap-filling).[180]

Conclusion: Climate Change and Nuisance in the Twenty-First Century

Climate change is humanity's most pressing concern. It already provokes widespread civil disobedience. There is vigorous political debate about how, and how fast, to decarbonise the economy. Does nuisance have any role to play?[181]

---

[177] Cf M Lobban, 'Tort Law, Regulation and River Pollution: The Rivers Pollution Prevention Act and its Implementation, 1876–1951' in Arvind and Steele (n 138).
[178] *Manchester Corporation v Farnworth* [1930] AC 171.
[179] Cf *Halsey v Esso Ltd* [1961] 1 WLR 683.
[180] Pontin (n 171) 192.
[181] See Wendy Boythorn, 'Tort Law and Climate Change' (2021) 40 *Univ Queensland LJ* 421.

On an orthodox view, it does not. The reasons are an interrelation of doctrinal limitations and constitutional concerns. Doctrinally, climate change seems to engage no *private* right to use and enjoy land. It is unlikely to cause physical damage; it would be impossible to show the causal connection with any particular carbon-emitting activity. Some agricultural activity will become impossible, or less profitable, as temperatures rise. But if warmer-climate crops can still be grown successfully in the UK, a landowner persisting with traditional cold-climate farming would be barred as an 'ultra-sensitive' nuisance claimant. Climate change does not merely threaten *particular* landowners' use of their land. It threatens the way of life of everybody on earth. It affects the rights of the public as a whole. This pre-eminently seems a public interest problem that demands legislative solutions and government action. Parliament has enacted the Climate Change Act 2008. The courts regularly enforce this (and numerous other environmental duties) through judicial review.[182] Surely, however, it would exceed the judicial function to create new common-law rights to a safe climate/healthy environment, through the law of nuisance?

Environmental campaigners believe current legislative and government action wholly inadequate given the climate change emergency. Should the common law declare it is 'not our business'? Tort offers real advantages. It is enforceable by individuals, who can obtain powerful mandatory orders from the court. As seen, Pontin argues that nuisance's role in curbing pollution during the industrial revolution is underrated in conventional historical accounts. Although state regulation is much more extensive in the twenty-first than in the eighteenth and nineteenth Centuries, is nuisance irrelevant even today? Campaigners in America see tort law's potential.[183] Judge Goodwin (extrajudicially) castigates US law's 'wholesale failure ... to protect humanity from the collapse of finite natural resources by the uncontrolled pursuit of short-term profits'. The political branches have not acted – becoming 'captives of the industries they were formed to regulate'. In Judge Goodwin's view, 'only the judges are equal to the task of protecting the people's rights to clean air and safe drinking water'.[184] Such arguments became even more attractive during the Trump Administration, whose deregulatory policies unravelled longstanding environmental protection.[185]

US environmentalists have focused on *public* nuisance – to circumvent the 'landowner's rights' limitation.[186] To these campaigners' disappointment

---

[182] eg *Regina (Friends of the Earth) v Heathrow Airport Ltd* [2020] UKSC 52.

[183] D Rendleman, 'Rehabilitating the Nuisance Injunction to Protect the Environment' (2018) 75 *Wash & Lee LR* 1859.

[184] AT Goodwin, 'A Wake-Up Call for Judges' [2015] *Wisconsin LR* 785. See further Mary Christina Wood, '"On the Eve of Destruction": Courts Confronting the Climate Emergency' (2021) 97 *Indiana LJ* 239.

[185] Rendleman (n 183) 1861–62.

[186] For other social problems too: eg A Purcell, 'Using the Public Nuisance Doctrine to Combat Antibiotic Resistance' (2018) 68 *Am Univ LR* 339; J McCool, 'Convenience Gambling as a Public Nuisance: An Ancient Tort Solution to a Modern Problem' (2018) 9 *Wake Forest JL & Policy* 135; BP Billauer, 'The Sperminator as a Public Nuisance: Redressing Wrongful Life and Birth Claims in New Ways (A.K.A. New Tricks for Old Torts)' (2019) 42 *UALR LR* 1.

however, few US courts have innovated under the public nuisance rubric.[187] Indeed judges have been criticised for reliance on 'doctrines of avoidance' and not even ruling on the substantive merits.[188] US courts apparently think it impossible for them to eliminate pollution 'as a by-product of private litigation'. No matter how great a threat to the public, the problem lies 'beyond the circumference of one private lawsuit. It is a direct responsibility for government and should not thus be undertaken as an incident to solving a dispute between property owners'.[189] Huffman commends this abstentionism. Appealing to public nuisance invites judicial intervention on a highly uncertain basis – the 'alleged public right to be free from environmental harms'. The *political* process should decide between competing visions of the public interest. Courts lack institutional competence to make such choices. Judges should not usurp the constitutional function of the legislature, even if it is slow to act. In a democracy we are, for better or worse, governed by those elected to represent us. It is improper to use litigation to circumvent 'compromises inherent to the political branches'.[190] Other scholars argue for a wider role, criticising both political arguments like Huffman's and the formal-doctrinal limits on public nuisance that feature more prominently in English debates.[191] It remains to be seen whether such arguments convince US courts to expand the tort.

In English law the prospects for expansion are weaker still. Scholars have dismissed *public* nuisance as an anomaly that should be expelled from tort law.[192] Neyers explains its incoherence from the rights-based perspective.[193] On the orthodox account, individuals can claim in tort if they suffer 'special damage' from conduct committing the *crime* of public nuisance. But the only 'right' violated here is the *public* right to prevent such conduct. It makes no sense to allow an individual who (by definition) does *not* hold that public right to bring a claim based upon it. This violates the privity principle – rights can be enforced only by their holders.[194] The claimant might have suffered loss – but unrecoverable loss, not caused by violation of the *claimant's* rights: *damnum absque injuria*. It is insufficient that loss results from conduct in some general sense 'unlawful' (eg criminal).[195] Neyers suggests that the core of public nuisance could be rehabilitated by recognising *private* rights for individuals to use the public highway. But the exception proves the rule. The residuum of public nuisance does not involve private rights, only a catalogue of social interests like health, morality and public safety.

---

[187] JL Huffman, 'Public Nuisance: Public Rights, Private Rights, and the Common Good' (2022) 17 *JL Ecs & Policy* 314.

[188] AC Lin, 'Dodging Public Nuisance' (2020) 11 *UC Irvine LR* 489.

[189] *Boomer v Atlantic Cement Co*, 26 NY 2d 219 (1970) (private nuisance).

[190] Huffman (n 187) 345.

[191] L Kendrick, 'The Perils and Promise of Public Nuisance' (2023) *Yale LJ* (forthcoming).

[192] JR Spencer, 'Public Nuisance: A Re-Examination' [1989] *CLJ* 55, 56 ('an archaic monster'), 81–83 (abolition of the tort).

[193] JW Neyers, 'Reconceptualising the Tort of Public Nuisance' [2017] *CLJ* 87.

[194] R Stevens, *Torts and Rights* (Oxford, Oxford University Press, 2007) 173.

[195] *OBG Ltd v Allan* [2008] 1 AC 1.

Torts involve breach of private rights. Logically then, no tort claim can properly be derived from common law regulatory offences.

On this view, even if the courts recognised *public* environmental rights, *tort law* logically could not enforce them. In theory the courts might recognise *private* rights encompassing climate change. As an aspect of land ownership these would be actionable in nuisance. Or, as one Australian judge recently held,[196] before being overruled,[197] actionable in negligence through a freestanding duty of care (specifically to protect children against personal injury resulting from climate change).[198] Private nuisance has been powerfully, symmetrically and narrowly restated as a tort *against land*. Public nuisance is not even a proper tort. Perhaps *negligence*, whose categories are 'never closed', might be expansive enough to recognise new environmental rights, even if nuisance cannot.

The full-blooded policy reasoning in the Australian *Sharma* judgments indicates the likely future.[199] Were tort strictly limited to the enforcement of long-recognised rights, courts could avoid policy quick-sands for the firmer ground of doctrine and precedent.[200] But such an approach is inevitably conservative. It renders tort law incapable of responding to new problems like climate change. In *Smith v Attorney-General* (2022) the New Zealand High Court struck out a claim that the government had breached a duty to prevent climate change. Among other objections Grice J held that the novel duty had not been formulated by analogy with existing precedents, citing Lord Bingham's view that the Rule of Law 'precludes excessive innovation and adventurism by the judges. It is one thing to alter the law's direction of travel by a few degrees, quite another to set it off in a different direction'.[201] Alongside its in-built conservatism, development from existing liabilities also seems logically flawed. The first precedents which initially established categories of liability, and indeed development throughout the common law's long history, have all been based on the policy views of generations of judges.[202] Why must judges today defer to their ancestors' policy choices, disclaiming their competence to reason as earlier courts did? A pure, abstract rights approach inhibits new development. Are the dangers of policy reasoning so great that stultification of the judicial process is required? This is the central divide in tort theory today. The debate will continue with increasing urgency, as tort law confronts novel claims for environmental and social justice in our rapidly-changing technological society.

---

[196] *Sharma v Minister for the Environment* [2021] FCA 560 (Bromberg J). (See also eg *Milieudefensie v Royal Dutch Shell plc* (unreported 2021) (Netherlands), noted A Sanger [2021] CLJ 425.)

[197] *Sharma v Minister for the Environment* [2022] FCAFC 35.

[198] *Sharma* [2022] FCAFC 35 [482] (liability for personal injuries 'at the heart of the common law').

[199] Compare also *Smith v Fonterra Co-opertive Group Ltd* [2021] NZCA 552 (appeal to New Zealand Supreme Court heard August 2022) and *Smith v Attorney-General* [2022] NZHC 1693.

[200] *Robinson v Chief Constable of West Yorkshire* [2018] AC 736 (Lord Reed).

[201] [2022] NZHC 1693 [155]–[157] citing T Bingham, 'The Rule of Law' [2007] *CLJ* 67, 71.

[202] cf *Robinson* (n 200) [84] (Lord Mance).

INDEX

A
actionable damage, *see* physical injury
actions after death, *see* fatal accidents
aggravated damages, *see* damages
apportionment, *see* damages
asbestos, 58–60, 65, 72, 75, 197–199
  see also but-for causation; causation; *Fairchild;* mesothelioma
assault, 9, 15, 22, 26, 28, 34, 37, 138, 141, 205, *see also* **battery**
assumption of responsibility, *see* negligence

B
battery, 9, 11, 13–18, 28–29, 32–33, 36–40, 138, 216–217, *see also* assault
Beever's theory, *see* private nuisance
breach of duty, *see* negligence
burden of proof, 15, 61–62, 72–74, 76, 93, 96–97, 124, 251
but-for causation
  better off principle, 98–99, 107–109, 242
  involvement, 103, 105, 107–115, 124, 127, 131, 158
  multiple causes, 102–103
  multiple sufficient factors, 103–107
  necessity, 102, 108, 110, 112
  see also causation; *Fairchild*; loss of a chance

C
'*Caparo* test', 46, 141, 153–160, 169, 179–182, 186, 188–189, 246
  defence of, 157–159

causation, 54–127
  burden of proof, 72–75
  common sense causation, 127
  deterrence, 66–76
  economic analysis, 69–72
  empty duty argument, 72–75
  exceptional cases, 75–76
  foreseeable harm, 115–120
  interventions, 120–123
  'matching' problem, 82–84
  scope of duty, 126
  'two hunters' problem, 77–82
  see also but-for causation; compensation; foreseeability; remoteness
Coase's analysis, *see* private nuisance
compensation, 1–2, 11, 18, 20, 25, 27–31, 34, 38, 47–48, 53–58, 62–68, 76–77, 82, 84, 86, 88, 90–97, 107–108, 114, 117–118, 125, 128, 136, 138, 151, 194–195, 197, 203, 206, 209, 212–214, 223, 232–236, 239, 245, 250, 256–272, 285, 293–296, 326, 330–333, 337–340
  accident compensation schemes, 1, 55–57
  property rights, 266–268
  relationship with tort, 55–57
  see also Fairchild; private nuisance
consent, *see* negligence, private nuisance, trespass
consequential loss, *see* physical injury
consumer protection, 51, 83, 207, 344
  see also product liability
contributory negligence, 49, 51, 99–100, 114, 204–206
  see also defences

356 INDEX

corrective justice, 1, 5, 47–48, 53–69, 71, 77–94, 107, 110, 124, 161, 163–168, 173–177, 230–231, 259, 277, 294, 296, 308, 311
 aggregation, 84–88
 moral critique, 88–92
 policy, 173–175
 see also causation; policy; rights

D
damages
 aggravated, 19, 27–28, 67
 apportionment, 51, 99, 243–244
 exemplary, 19, 24–25, 27, 33, 67–69, 136, 138, 314, 327
 nominal, 18–28, 41, 266, 314, 336
 non-pecuniary losses, 256–257
 pain and suffering, 96, 213, 227, 257
 see also joint and several liability; physical injury, preventive damages; rights, vindication of
defamation, 11, 13, 29–30, 45
defective products, 207
 see also product liability
defences
 contributory negligence, 49, 51, 99–100, 114, 204–206
 illegality (*ex turpi causa*), 24, 49, 142
 public interest defence, 330, 348
 volenti non fit injuria, 49
deterrence, 27–28, 47–48, 66, 69–72, 88, 92–93, 100, 123, 125, 161
 see also causation
distress, *see* psychiatric illness
duty of care, 133–187
 abolishing the, 148–151
 defining the, 153–187
 foreseeability, 139–145
 'neighbour principle', 139, 147, 152, 161, 178, 187
 omissions, 16, 52, 59, 139, 150, 186, 206, 217
 policy, 160–177
 then and now, 146–148
 see also '*Caparo* test'; incrementalism; public authority, liability of; pure economic loss

E
economic loss, *see* **pure economic loss**
emotional harm, *see* **psychiatric illness**
exemplary damages, *see* **damages**

F
factual causation, *see* **but-for causation**
Fairchild, 54–66, 72, 74–77, 84, 87, 93, 95–96, 128, 233
 see also asbestos; but-for causation; mesothelioma
false imprisonment, 9, 11, 13–14, 31, 32, 336
fatal accidents, 4, 217, 233, 256, 265
foreseeability, *see* **duty of care, foreseeable harm, psychiatric illness**
floodgates, 232, 235–236, 241, 251
 see also psychiatric illness

G
gendered reasoning, *see* **physical injury**

H
'**hunters problem**', *see* **causation**

I
illegality, *see* **defences**
incrementalism, 177–187
 critique, 182–187
 fashions and, 177–182
 see also duty of care; negligence; neighbour principle
information theory, *see* **private nuisance**
interventions, 49, 117, 120–123, 129–130, 150
 see also causation

J
joint and several liability, 63, 100, 346
judicial capacity
 policy, 169–173
 private nuisance, 310–313

L
Law Commission, 33, 52, 67, 100, 171–172, 176, 185, 227, 241, 244, 246, 248, 251–258
 causation, 67
 duty of care, 171–172, 176, 185
 psychiatric illness, 241–256
 trespass, 33
loss of a chance, 46, 96
 see also but-for causation; causation

M
mesothelioma, 58, 60–65, 87, 96, 98, 233
 see also asbestos; but-for causation; causation; *Fairchild*
misfeasance, *see* **duty of care, liability of public authorities**

INDEX

N

negligence, 45–263
- assumption of responsibility, 52, 122, 127, 149, 156, 181, 186, 240–241
- breach of duty, 51, 58, 60, 73–74, 78–79, 96, 117, 122, 138, 141, 212
- comparison to strict liability, 51
- consent, 72, 95, 125, 216, 218
- introduction to, 45–52
- structure of, 49–51
- *see also* but-for causation; causation; defences; duty of care; incrementalism; physical injury; psychiatric illness; public authority liability; pure economic loss; remoteness; rights; social policy

nervous shock, *see* **psychiatric illness**
nominal damages, *see* **damages**
non-pecuniary losses, *see* **damages**
novus actus interveniens, *see* **interventions**
nuisance, *see* **private nuisance**

O

omissions, *see* **duty of care**

P

pain and suffering, *see* **damages**
pecuniary losses, *see* **damages**
personal injury, *see* **physical injury**
physical injury, 191–218
- actionable damage, 18, 38–39, 46, 49, 86, 95–96, 99, 100, 133, 149–150, 192, 199–200, 202–203, 207, 209, 211, 215–218, 221, 223, 225, 251–252, 325
- consequential loss, 197–199
- gendered reasoning, 213–216
- loss of autonomy, 216–218
- minor injuries, 197–199
- outer limits of, 200–202
- personal injury, 191–202
- preventive damages, 202–207
- wrongful birth, 207–218
- wrongful life, 208–209
- wrongful race, 211–212

policy, 6, 19–20, 32, 47, 49, 51–52, 64, 68, 81, 100–101, 106, 115, 119, 130, 140, 144, 150–177, 181–197, 204, 206, 212, 219, 223, 228, 230–234, 246, 248, 257–258, 264–266, 273–274, 277–288, 307, 321, 324–326, 338, 345, 351–353
- common law rights, 164–166
- evidence, 169–173
- legal certainty, 166–169
- *see also* corrective justice; judicial capacity; social policy; rights

psychiatric illness, 219–263
- abolition, 249–251, 252, 254
- *Alcock* tests, 64, 165, 222, 228–258
- comparison with nervous shock, 220–223
- comparison with physical injuries, 219–220
- foreseeability, 245–249
- floodgates, 235–236
- 'mere distress', 9, 195–196, 219, 225–228
- policy critique, 232–235
- primary victims, 150, 236–240, 252, 255
- recognisable, 223–225
- reform, 244–257
- restrictive rules, 228–240
- retention of, 251–252
- rights-based critique, 231–232
- secondary victims, 230, 250, 253
- stress at work, 98, 240–244
- ties of love and affection, 230, 234, 255–256
- zone of danger, 220, 228, 236–240
- *see also* Law Commission; trespass

primary victims, *see* **psychiatric illness**
private nuisance, 263–355
- balancing rights, 293–300
- Beever's theory, 278–284
- boundaries of, 271–276
- climate change, 350–355
- Coase's analysis, 303–313
- compensation, 266–268
- consent, 298, 305
- defining property rights, 284–288
- economic analysis, 303–323
- enforcement, 352–327
- environment, 321–327
- human rights, 268–271
- information theory, 313–323
- planning permission, 329–333
- pollution, 344–355
- property damage, 289–303
- property rights, 263–276
- regulation, 327–344
- rights-based approach, 276–289
- standing, 264–266
- statutory authority, 328–329
- strict liability, 290–293
- trespass, 289–303
- *see also* judicial capacity; scope; social policy; remedies; rights

product liability, 207, 238, 259
- *see also* consumer protection; defective products

public authority, liability of
  negligence, 52, 56, 100, 147–151, 169–177, 181, 185–189
  trespass, 4, 31–39
public interest
  negligence, 47, 65–67, 138, 155, 159–161, 163-
  private nuisance, 263, 270, 278, 281, 283–289, 291–293, 298–301, 310–311, 320, 324, 328, 330, 334–335, 341–345, 351–352
pure economic loss, 51–52, 78, 96, 149, 174, 177–189, 193, 195, 197, 202, 206–207, 212, 215, 229, 260, 271, 301

R
remedies
  negligence, 45, 66–69, 138–139, 195
  private nuisance, 263, 268–269, 276, 310, 314, 321, 325, 329–331, 334–336, 349
  trespass, 19–31, 34–35
remoteness of damage, 49, 95–133, 141–150, 158, 324
rights, 1–5, 9–41, 45–47, 51–52, 64, 68, 71, 77, 86–87, 96, 99, 109, 133, 160–166, 170, 174–177, 183, 188, 193–196, 205–208, 217, 224, 231, 258, 264–301, 305–353
  constitutional, 31–36
  property, 264–301
  rights-based approach, 161, 175, 193, 195, 206, 231–232, 258, 263, 276–289, 300, 341, 352
  vindication of rights, 19–31
rights-based approach, *see* rights

S
scope
  of duty, 50, 126–127, 143, 179
  of nuisance, 333–334
  of responsibility, 127–133

secondary victims, *see* psychiatric illness
shock, *see* psychiatric illness
social policy, 47–49, 161, 280, 338
  negligence, 47–49, 161
  private nuisance, 280, 338
  see also policy
stress, *see* psychiatric illness
strict liability, 10, 12–18, 31, 40–41, 51, 89–90, 106, 116, 286, 289–301, 305, 312–315, 321–324, 333, 339
  see also private nuisance; trespass

T
theory, 1–9, 24, 26, 49, 53–54, 64–66, 78, 81, 84–85, 87, 90–91, 104, 107, 167, 184, 198, 228, 250, 258, 267, 278, 280–293, 297, 303–305, 312–313, 353
  see also nuisance (Beever's theory, Coase's theory, information theory)
trespass, 7, 9–46, 116, 138, 205, 217, 264–268, 276, 289–294, 305, 311, 313–320, 339, 345
  actionability per se, 17–19
  consent, 36–45
  distinguished from negligence, 39–45
  strict liability, 12–17, 31–41
  see also defences; private nuisance; remedies; rights
trespass to the person, *see* assault, battery, false imprisonment
third parties
  acts of, 106, 122, 149–150
  private nuisance and, 278, 335
  see also interventions

V
vicarious liability, 55–56, 280
volenti non fit injuria, *see* defences

W
wrongful birth, *see* physical injury